Your UNIX

The Ultimate Guide

Your UNIX

The Ultimate Guide

Second Edition

Sumitabha Das

Higher Education

Boston   Burr Ridge, IL   Dubuque, IA   Madison, WI   New York   San Francisco   St. Louis
Bangkok   Bogotá   Caracas   Kuala Lumpur   Lisbon   London   Madrid   Mexico City
Milan   Montreal   New Delhi   Santiago   Seoul   Singapore   Sydney   Taipei   Toronto

The McGraw·Hill Companies

Higher Education

YOUR UNIX: THE ULTIMATE GUIDE, SECOND EDITION

Published by McGraw-Hill, a business unit of The McGraw-Hill Companies, Inc., 1221 Avenue of the Americas, New York, NY 10020. Copyright © 2006, 2001 by The McGraw-Hill Companies, Inc. All rights reserved. No part of this publication may be reproduced or distributed in any form or by any means, or stored in a database or retrieval system, without the prior written consent of The McGraw-Hill Companies, Inc., including, but not limited to, in any network or other electronic storage or transmission, or broadcast for distance learning.

Some ancillaries, including electronic and print components, may not be available to customers outside the United States.

This book is printed on acid-free paper.

1 2 3 4 5 6 7 8 9 0 QPF/QPF 0 9 8 7 6 5 4

ISBN 0–07–252042–6

Sponsoring Editor: *Kelly H. Lowery*
Developmental Editor: *Melinda D. Bilecki*
Marketing Manager: *Dawn R. Bercier*
Project Manager: *Peggy S. Lucas*
Senior Production Supervisor: *Sherry L. Kane*
Media Technology Producer: *Eric A. Weber*
Designer: *Laurie B. Janssen*
Cover Designer: *Studio Montage*
Cover photo credits: *Getty Images, Royalty-free*
Compositor: *International Typesetting and Composition*
Typeface: *10/12 Times Roman*
Printer: *Quebecor World Fairfield, PA*

Library of Congress Cataloging-in-Publication Data

Das, Sumitabha.
 Your UNIX : the ultimate guide / Sumitabha Das. — 2nd ed.
  p. cm.
 Includes bibliographical references and index.
 ISBN 0–07–252042–6 (hard copy : alk. paper)
 1. UNIX (Computer file). 2. Operating systems (Computers). I. Title.

QA76.76.O63D3495   2006
005.4'32—dc22   2004017054
                                                   CIP

www.mhhe.com

To my two uncles, D.L.D. and N.L.D.,
who couldn't wait to see this.

Contents in Brief

Appendixes

Contents

ix

List of Tables

Preface

A language is not worth knowing unless it teaches you to think differently.
> —Larry Wall (the creator of Perl) and Randal Schwartz

UNIX and C changed the way people used and learned about computers. Even though technology changes fast—sometimes, every month—certain approaches to technology remain unchanged. UNIX is one of them; it has survived the test of time. It's no wonder that theoretical courses on operating systems often use the UNIX system to illustrate key features. Thanks partly to Linux, things should remain this way in the foreseeable future too.

Yet, UNIX is still described by many as "unfriendly" and "unforgiving." Beginners feel overwhelmed by its sheer weight, and even experienced computer professionals feel lost in this mysterious universe. What bothers them is the UNIX "command line" associated with its myriad options and complex syntaxes. On other systems, the mouse does most of the work, so what's wrong with the UNIX way of doing things?

Nothing, absolutely nothing, it's just that perceptions differ. What is unfriendly and unforgiving to one can be quite friendly and smart to another. In fact, UNIX was deliberately designed to appear "unfriendly." It supports a repository of standalone *commands* that can also be used in combination to solve complex text manipulation problems. Add the shell's programming features, and you can at once develop both interactive and noninteractive applications—and even schedule them to run at specific times. This is what this book attempts to explain and advise: *There is a method to this madness.*

The excitement that UNIX generates lies in the fact that many of its powers are hidden. It doesn't offer everything on a platter; it encourages you to create and innovate. Figuring out a command combination or designing a script that does a complex job is a real challenge to the UNIX enthusiast. This is what UNIX is, and it had better remain that way. If you appreciate this, then you are on the right track, and this book is for you.

How This Book Is Different

I made no conscious decision to make this book different from others. Facing a UNIX box was my first encounter with computers, and prolonged periods of struggle with the system have led me to believe that the stumbling blocks to understanding UNIX are often different from what they are perceived to be. I couldn't wholeheartedly embrace the way people wrote on the subject, and instead conceived my own idea of the "true" UNIX book—a book that people would like to have with them all the time.

Real—life Examples UNIX concepts are simple but they are also abstract, and it's not often obvious why a certain feature is handled in a particular way. The mastery of this operating system requires a clear understanding of these concepts. I have made sure that the key features are explained clearly to reveal both their design considerations and their relevance in the real world. You'll find that most examples of this text refer to real-life situations.

Both a User's and Programmer's Guide There are mainly two categories of UNIX users: those who *use* its native tools and write shell scripts, and others who *develop* tools using the UNIX system call library. The "user" category is served by the first 13 chapters, which is more than adequate for an introductory UNIX course.

The "developer" is a systems programmer who also needs to know how things work, say, how a directory is affected when a file is created or linked. For their benefit, the initial chapters contain special boxes that probe key concepts. This arrangement shouldn't affect the beginner who may quietly ignore these portions. Systems programmers will find a wealth of material in Chapters 17 and 18 (new in this edition) that will help them in designing new tools using the system call library. I haven't seen any book that adequately addresses both user segments, but this book does.

Strong Learning Aids The pedagogical aids are a strong feature of this book, and you'll find nearly 250 instances of such aids in this text. They take on various names, for example, Note, Caution, and Tip. I consider Linux to be an important member of the UNIX family, so I have separately highlighted Linux features using the penguin as identifier.

I don't agree with the approach adopted by many authors of treating each shell in a separate chapter. Instead, I have discussed key concepts using mainly the Bourne shell, which I still think (even in 2004!) clearly reveals how the system interacts with the user. Deviations have been taken care of by separate asides for the C shell, Korn and Bash shells. Because the Bourne shell lacks sophisticated environment-related features, only a single chapter (Chapter 9) doesn't use Bourne as the main shell. I believe this approach is effective and it also saves time and space.

Numerous Questions and Exercises This book features an enormous number of questions that test the reader's knowledge—over 800 of them. More than a third of them are Self-Test questions, and their answers are provided in Appendix H. These questions are all targeted toward beginners who will do well to answer them before moving on to the next chapter.

More rigorous and extensive questioning is reserved for the Exercises section. Some of them pose real challenges, and it may take you some time to solve them. These exercises reinforce and often add to your knowledge of UNIX, so don't ignore them. The answers to these questions are available to adopters of the book at the book's Web site *http://www.mhhe.com/das*. You'll find a lot of additional material on this site that you can use to supplement this book.

What Has Changed In This Edition

While the fundamental UNIX story remains intact, my perceptions of the operating system have changed with time. This second edition provided me with an opportunity to completely overhaul the structure and content of the previous edition. The result is a concise and yet comprehensive book that has these features:

- Increased emphasis on concepts and their application. Implementation details that don't materially contribute to the understanding of concepts have been trimmed or deleted.
- Shell programming is covered with increased depth and with better examples. Advanced programming features of the Korn and Bash shells have been moved to an appendix.
- Updated coverage of security-related features. The Berkeley-based r-utilities have been removed, and coverage of **telnet** and **ftp** have been pruned. This edition features the Secure Shell and the basics of Public Key Cryptography.
- The pedagogical features—the Note, Tip and Caution asides and the end-of-chapter questions—have been given a major face-lift. The key chapters now have a larger number of questions, and many of them are quite challenging.
- There are special asides occurring in the beginning chapters that explain how a concept works in UNIX. Skip them if you don't intend to program in UNIX.
- C programmers who intend to use the system call library will be benefited by the inclusion of three new chapters:
    - Chapter 16: Program Development Tools
    - Chapter 17: Systems Programming I—Files
    - Chapter 18: Systems Programming II—Process Control
- It's widely felt that system and network administration deserves a separate book of its own. There's a single chapter this time that examines only the general issues.

These changes have resulted in fewer chapters (19 instead of 24) and fewer pages. However, the generic character of the book has been retained; it doesn't focus on any particular flavor of UNIX, but variations found in Solaris and Linux have been highlighted.

Understanding The Organization

This book is *logically* divided into essential and advanced sections. Essential UNIX is confined to the first 13 chapters that culminate with shell programming. Advanced material that includes TCP/IP tools, **perl** and systems programming, are covered in the remaining six chapters.

Introducing UNIX Chapter 1 reveals the key UNIX concepts through a simple hands-on session. This is followed by a brief history and presentation of the features of UNIX. Get introduced to the *kernel* and *shell,* who between them, handle the system's workload. Also understand the role played by standards bodies like POSIX and The Open Group in laying the framework for developing portable applications.

Chapter 2 presents the structure of the UNIX command line. It also discusses the techniques of using the **man** command to look up the online documentation. Also learn to use an email program, change your password and see what's going on in the system. Things can and will go wrong so you also need to know how to use the keyboard for corrective action.

Files The *file* is one of the two pillars that support UNIX, and the next four chapters discuss files. Chapter 3 discusses the various types of files you'll find on your system and the commands that handle them. You'll learn to create directories, navigate a directory structure and copy and delete files in a directory. UNIX also offers a host of compression utilities that you need to use to conserve disk space.

Files have attributes (properties) and Chapter 4 presents the major attributes, especially the ones displayed by the **ls -l** command. Be aware that your files and directories are open to attack, so learn to protect them by manipulating their permissions. Use *links* to access a file by multiple names. You'll also forget where you have kept your files, so you need to be familiar with the **find** command.

How productive you eventually are also depends on how well you exploit the features of your editor. Chapters 5 and 6 presents two of the most powerful text editors found in any operating environment: **vi** and **emacs**. You probably will need to know only one of them. A programmer probably uses the editor more than anyone else, so most examples in these two chapters use snippets of program code. Appendix C presents a summary of their features.

The Shell and Process You now need to understand a very important program that is constantly interacting with you—the shell. Chapter 7 presents the interpretive features of the shell including many of its *metacharacters*. Learn to use *wild cards* to match a group of similar filenames with a single pattern. Manipulate the input and output of commands using *redirection* and *pipes*. The shell is also a programming language, so you have to wait until Chapter 13 to understand it completely.

Chapter 8 introduces the *process* as the other pillar of the UNIX system. Processes are similar to files, and processes also have attributes. Understand how the *fork-exec* mechanism is used to create a process. Learn to control processes, move them between foreground and background and also kill them by sending them *signals*.

The UNIX shell provides excellent opportunities to customize your environment (Chapter 9). Understand and manipulate shell variables, create command *aliases* and use the *history* mechanism to recall, edit and re-execute previous commands. Choose a suitable shell that offers all these features and learn to use the initialization scripts to save the changes you've made to the environment.

Filters and Shell Programming The next three chapters deal with *filters*—those special commands in the UNIX tool kit that handle all text manipulation tasks. Chapter 10 presents the simple ones and shows how they are most effective when they are connected to one another. A special examples section features three real-life applications that are handled by these filters working in pipelines.

Chapter 11 discusses two powerful filters—**grep** and **sed**—that, between them, handle all pattern search, edit and replace operations. At this stage, you'll be introduced to *regular expressions,* an elaborate pattern matching mechanism that often make searching and replacement a lot easier.

When you can't handle a text manipulation problem with the other filters, you need to use **awk**. The command makes its appearance as a filter and a programming language in Chapter 12. Knowing **awk** and its standard programming constructs (like the **if, for**, and **while** constructs) should prepare you well for shell programming (and **perl**).

Eventually, you'll place all your commands and pipelines in *shell scripts.* Use the programming features of the shell discussed in Chapter 13 to develop both interactive and noninteractive scripts. Learn to design a script whose behavior depends on the *name* by which it is invoked. The three sample scripts featured in the chapter are compulsory reading for a shell programmer.

These thirteen chapters are all that the beginner needs to know initially. The next six chapters present some of the advanced features of UNIX that also include a chapter on system administration.

Advanced Topics Though networking wasn't part of the UNIX scheme of things, TCP/IP was first ported to UNIX. Chapter 14 covers the networking tools. Get introduced to *hostnames, IP addresses*, and *domain names* and how they are used by the Internet protocols (like HTTP). The chapter also introduces you to Public Key Cryptography and the Secure Shell.

We encounter **perl** in Chapter 15 as the most powerful filter and scripting language in the UNIX world. Most UNIX concepts are embedded in the design of **perl**, the reason why many UNIX users can't do without it. Even though we can't do justice to **perl** in a single chapter, Chapter 15 represents a useful beginning.

The next three chapters are directly or indirectly related to C programming. Chapter 16 presents the program development tools. Use the **make** utility and a powerful debugger for managing and debugging programs. Also, learn to maintain multiple versions of a program using SCCS and RCS.

Chapter 17 is the first of two chapters that feature the use of *system calls* in the C programming environment. This chapter discusses the system calls related to files and I/O. Write programs that perform directory-oriented functions like listing files. Also learn to fetch and manipulate file attributes stored in the inode.

Chapter 18 discusses the system calls related to processes. Learn to create processes using the **fork** and *exec* family of system calls. Once you've understood how the kernel maintains the metadata of an open file in memory, you'll be able to implement both redirection and pipelines, and handle signals in your programs.

Finally, every user must know the routine tasks related to system administration, and Chapter 19 addresses the basic issues in this domain. Understand the important security features provided by the system. Be familiar with the activities associated with system startup and shutdown, and how file systems are *mounted* and checked for consistency. Also learn to do some elementary backups.

Acknowledgments

I have been ably supported in this endeavor by Kelly Lowery and the team at McGraw-Hill. Many thanks go to the agile Melinda Bilecki who has been actively involved ever since the project was conceived. Apart from organizing and analyzing the reviews, she was almost everywhere, offering suggestions wherever possible. If this book appears both concise and comprehensive, credit must also go to the reviewers who were quick to point out what is relevant and what is not.

Laurie Janssen deserves praise for the way she handled the art work in general, and the cover design in particular. I must also thank Dawn Bercier for the marketing arrangements that she was responsible for. You should see a more informative and useful website with this edition, and full marks for this go to Eric Weber. Finally, I can't but admire Peggy Lucas who managed the production process with confidence and patience. There have been many others who couldn't be mentioned by name, but have contributed just the same.

Final Words of "Wisdom"

Most examples have been tested on Solaris and Linux, but I can't guarantee that they will run error-free on every system. UNIX fragmentation makes sweeping generalizations virtually impossible. If some commands don't work in the way specified in this text, don't conclude that the system has bugs. Nevertheless, bugs in these examples are still possible, and I welcome ones (along with your suggestions at *sumitabha@vsnl.com*) that you may hit upon.

Before I take leave, a note of caution would be in order. Many people missed the UNIX bus through confused and misguided thinking and are now regretting it. Let this not happen to you. Once you have decided to exploit UNIX, you'll learn to build on what's already provided without reinventing the wheel. Sooner rather than later, you'll find a world of opportunity and excitement opening up. Approach the subject with zeal and confidence; I am with you.

Sumitabha Das

Conventions Used in This Book

The key terms used in the book (like **regular expression**) are shown in a bold font. Apart from this, the following conventions have been used in this book:

- Commands, internal commands and user input in examples are shown in bold constant width font:

    Many commands in **more** including **f** and **b** use a repeat factor.
    The shell features three types of loops—**while**, **until**, and **for**.
    Enter your name: **henry**

- Apart from command output, filenames, strings, symbols, expressions, options, and keywords are shown in constant width font. For example:

    Most commands are located in /bin and /usr/bin.
    Try doing that with the name gordon lightfoot.
    Use the expression wilco[cx]k*s* with the -l option.
    The shell looks for the characters >, < and << in the command line.
    The -mtime keyword looks for the modification time of a file.

- Machine and domain names, email addresses, newsgroups, and URLs are displayed in italics:

    When henry logs on to the machine *uranus* ......
    User henry on this host can be addressed as *henry@calcs.planets.com*.
    The newsgroup *comp.lang.perl* discusses problems related to **perl**.
    Executables for all UNIX flavors are available at *http://www.perl.com*.

- Place-holders for filenames, terms, and explanatory comments within examples are displayed in italics:
    Use the -f *filename* option if this doesn't work.
    This process has a *controlling terminal*.
    $ **cd ../..**   *Moves two levels up*

The following abbreviations, shortcuts and symbols have been used:

- SVR4—System V Release 4
- sh—Bourne shell
- csh—C shell
- ksh—Korn shell
- $HOME/*flname*—The file *flname* in the home directory
- ~/*flname*—The file *flname* in the home directory
- foo, bar, and foobar—Generic file and directory names as used on Usenet
- .... for lines that are not shown
- This box ☐ indicates the space character.
- This pair of arrows ↹ indicates the tab character.

Your UNIX

The Ultimate Guide

## CHAPTER 1

Introducing UNIX

In this opening chapter, we commence our journey into the world of UNIX. We'll discover why a computer needs an operating system and how UNIX more than fulfills that requirement. Through a hands-on session, we'll learn to play with the UNIX system. We'll use the tools UNIX provides to perform the basic file and directory handling operations. We'll also have a glimpse of the *process* that makes a program run on UNIX.

As we absorb this knowledge, we'll place it against the rather turbulent background that UNIX had to grow through. We'll learn how contributions from different sources led to both the enrichment and fragmentation of UNIX. Knowledge of the design considerations will also help us understand why UNIX sometimes behaves in a seemingly awkward manner. We'll examine the UNIX architecture and understand how two agencies (the *kernel* and *shell*) between themselves handle all the work of the system.

Objectives

* Learn what an operating system is and how UNIX is different from other systems.
* Understand the role of the *system administrator*.
* Log in and out of a UNIX system.
* Run a few commands that report on the system.
* Use more commands to view processes and handle files and directories.
* Find out how UNIX got steadily fragmented by the emergence of other flavors.
* Understand the merging of POSIX and the Single UNIX Specification into a single UNIX standard.
* Learn about the emergence of Linux as a strong, viable and free alternative.
* Discover the UNIX architecture that includes the *kernel* and *shell*.
* Discover the two key features—the *file* and *process*—that UNIX rests on.
* Know the role of *system calls* in making programs work.
* Learn the "do-one-thing-well" philosophy that UNIX uses to solve complex problems.

1.1 The Operating System

Computers are designed to run programs. But a program can run only if the computer it is running on has some basic intelligence to begin with. This intelligence allocates memory for the program, runs each program instruction on the CPU, and accesses the hardware on behalf of the program. A special piece of preinstalled software performs this job. This software is known as the computer's *operating system.*

An **operating system** is the software that manages the computer's hardware and provides a convenient and safe environment for running programs. It acts as an interface between programs and the hardware resources that these programs access (like memory, hard disk, and printer). It is loaded into memory when a computer is booted and remains active as long as the machine is up.

To grasp the key features of an operating system, let's consider the management tasks it has to perform when we run a program. These operations also depend on the operating system we are using, but the following actions are common to most systems:

- The operating system allocates memory for the program and loads the program to the allocated memory.
- It also loads the CPU registers with control information related to the program. The registers maintain the memory locations where each segment of a program is stored.
- The instructions provided in the program are executed by the CPU. The operating system keeps track of the instruction that was last executed. This enables it to resume a program if it had to be taken out of the CPU before it completed execution.
- If the program needs to access the hardware, it makes a call to the operating system rather than attempt to do the job itself. For instance, if the program needs to read a file on disk, the operating system directs the disk controller to open the file and make the data available to the program.
- After the program has completed execution, the operating system cleans up the memory and registers and makes them available for the next program.

Modern operating systems are **multiprogramming**, i.e., they allow multiple programs to reside in memory. However, on computers with a single CPU, only one program can run at one time. Rather than allow a single program to run to completion without interruption, an operating system generally allows a program to run for an instant, saves its current state, and then loads the next program in the queue. The operating system creates a *process* for each program and then controls the switching of these processes.

Most programs often access the disk or the terminal to read or write data. These I/O operations keep the CPU idle, so the operating system takes the program out of the CPU while the I/O operation is in progress. It then schedules another program to run. The previous program can resume execution only after the I/O operation completes. This ensures maximum utilization of the CPU.

In addition to these basic services, operating systems provide a wide range of services—from creating files and directories to copying files across a network and performing backups. These tools are often standalone programs that don't form the core of the operating system, but they may be considered as additional services that benefit both users, programmers, and system administrators.

Knowing the functions performed by an operating system and the way they are implemented on your computer often helps you to write better programs. True, a lot can be done without knowing the operating system, but a UNIX professional needs to look beyond the big picture to discover how things actually work.

Note

In a multiprogramming environment, the operating system has to ensure that a process performing an I/O operation doesn't hold up the CPU. It must schedule another process while the I/O operation is in progress. The previous process is said to *block*, i.e., wait for the event to complete. We'll often use this term in this text to refer to this state of a process.

1.2 The UNIX Operating System

There have been many operating systems in the past, one at least from each hardware vendor. They were written in a near-machine language known as *assembler*. The operating systems were proprietary because assembler code developed on one machine wouldn't run on another. Vendors required consumers to purchase expensive proprietary hardware and software if two dissimilar machines needed to talk to each other. Ken Thompson and Dennis Ritchie changed all that forever. They created UNIX.

The UNIX operating system marks a strong departure from tradition. It has practically everything an operating system should have, but also introduces a number of concepts previously unknown to the computing community. Beginners with some experience in Windows think of UNIX in terms of it, quite oblivious to the fact that the similarities are only superficial. UNIX is way ahead of other systems in sheer power.

UNIX is not written in assembler but in C. C is a high-level language that was designed with portability considerations in mind, which explains why UNIX systems are available on practically every hardware platform. Apart from handling the basic operating system functions, UNIX offers a host of applications that benefit users, programmers, and system administrators. It encourages users to combine multiple programs to solve a complex problem. For programmers, UNIX offers a rich set of programming tools that aid in developing, debugging, and maintaining programs. UNIX is also more easily maintained than most systems.

One of these programs is the system's *command interpreter,* called the **shell**. You interact with a UNIX system through the shell. Key in a word, and the shell interprets it as a *command* to be executed. A command may already exist on the system as one of several hundred native tools, or it could be one written by you. However, as mentioned, the power of UNIX lies in combining these commands in the same way the English language lets you combine words to generate a meaningful idea. As you walk through the chapters of the text, you'll soon discover that this is a major strength of the system.

UNIX was written by programmers for their own use, so things that appear obvious to them don't always appear obvious to us. However, that doesn't imply that UNIX is unconquerable; in fact, it's great fun. If you are willing to put in some guided effort, you'll gradually see the UNIX story unfold with clarity and simplicity. Focus your attention on the essentials, and try to understand the designers' minds and objectives. Even though UNIX sometimes appears unfriendly, it in fact challenges you to unravel its mysteries. In this book, we take up the challenge.

Note

The UNIX system doesn't offer a fixed set of services. In fact, you have to use your imagination in devising improvised tools from the existing ones. This is what makes UNIX so challenging and exciting.

1.3   Knowing Your Machine

Unlike Windows, UNIX can be used by several users concurrently. In other words, a single copy of the operating system software installed on just one machine can serve the needs of hundreds of users. These users could use dumb terminals or their own desktop PCs to access a central UNIX computer. This computer will probably be located in a separate room with restricted access. If you are using a PC, then it must be configured properly before it can be used to connect to a UNIX system.

Things are quite different, however, when you are using a *workstation*. This is a computer capable of producing high-quality graphics but meant to be used by a single user. Unlike the dumb terminal, a workstation has its own CPU, memory (the RAM—random access memory), hard disk, CD-ROM, mouse as a pointing device, and printer. Since it has all the things that UNIX needs, a workstation can run its own UNIX. Desktop PCs are also often referred to as workstations because there are versions of UNIX (like Linux) that can run on them.

Even though workstations and PCs run UNIX and can be used in standalone mode, they are often connected to a larger, more powerful computer in the same way terminals are. There are a number of reasons you might want such an arrangement:

- The central computer is administered properly, and you might want to keep all your valuable files there so they are backed up regularly.
- You might want to use a powerful program that your workstation doesn't have but the central computer does.
- All your incoming and outgoing mail is handled by the central machine, which may be your only link with the outside world, i.e., the Internet.

Every workstation and PC provides a **terminal emulation** facility that makes it abandon its normal mode and behave like a simple dumb terminal instead. The workstation then doesn't use its own hard disk, CPU, or memory for doing any work except providing the minimal resources required by the terminal emulation software. The terminal emulation facility enables you to run a program on a remote machine using the remote machine's memory and CPU, and not your own. Create a file in this mode, and the file is saved on the remote machine's hard disk.

When you press a key, the computer generates a **character** which represents the smallest piece of information that you can deal with. It could be a letter, number, symbol, or control sequence (like *[Ctrl-f]*). The string 10:20 pm contains eight characters (one for the space). Every character is associated with a unique **ASCII value** (ASCII—American Standard Code for Information Interchange). The letter A has the ASCII value of 65, the bang (!) has the value of 33. Both take up one byte (eight bits) each on your computer. Many UNIX programs make use of these ASCII values.

Even though you may be completely familiar with the keyboard of your Windows PC, note that the functions of many of the keys change when the same PC doubles as a UNIX or Linux box. The *[F1]* key doesn't invoke help, and the *[Delete]* key may not always delete characters. Moreover, every key has some use in UNIX. When you see a symbol like `(backquote) used in this book, you must be able to locate it easily on your keyboard (on the top-left), and not confuse it with the ' (single quote), because they have totally different functions.

Using a combination of *[Alt]* and a function key, you can have multiple *virtual console* or terminal sessions on a single PC. You can log in several times to the same computer, with a separate "terminal" for each session. A single screen is shared by all sessions, which are accessed by using *[Alt][F1]*, *[Alt][F2]*, and so on.

1.4 The System Administrator

On a large system serving hundreds of users, someone has to be in charge of administration of the system. This person is known as the **system administrator**. The administrator is responsible for the management of the entire setup. She allocates user accounts, maintains file systems, takes backups, manages disk space, and performs several other important functions. She is the person to be contacted in case of a genuine problem.

If you own a workstation or PC that runs some flavor of UNIX, then you are probably its administrator. You are then directly responsible for its startup, shutdown, and maintenance. If you lose a file, it's your job to get it from a backup. If things don't work properly, you have to try all possible means to set them right before you decide to call a maintenance person.

If you are not the administrator, you can use a UNIX machine only after she has opened an account with a *user-id* and *password* for your use. These authentication parameters are maintained in two separate files on your system. You can't simply sit down at any terminal and start banging away unless you first log on to the system using a valid user-id–password combination.

The administrator uses a special user-id to log on to the system: it is called **root**. The root user has near-absolute powers; some programs can only be run from this account—for instance, the program that creates the user account itself.

1.5 Logging In and Out

Without further ado, let's get down to business and see for ourselves what a UNIX session is really like. A personal interaction with the system often drives home a point better than the preaching of textbooks (including this one). In this section, we'll quickly walk through the procedure of logging in and out of a UNIX box, but first let's consider the possible options we have today to connect to a UNIX machine.

The good old dumb terminal connected to the computer's serial port was once the only means of connecting to a UNIX system. Later, the TELNET program became popular for connecting in a network. For security reasons (explained in Chapter 13), the Telnet facility could be disabled on your system, and the *secure shell* (SSH) could be the only means of connecting to a remote UNIX box. In that case, UNIX and Linux users can use the **ssh** command, if available. Windows users may use Putty or any of the free SSH programs available on the Net.

1.5.1 Logging In

We'll ignore the password-free access that is permitted by the secure shell programs and consider the situation where the system authenticates you by your response to the login and password prompts. Each response should be followed by the *[Enter]* key. This is how user romeo gains access to the system:

```
SunOS 5.8
```
A Sun machine running Solaris 8

```
login: romeo[Enter]
Password: ********[Enter]
```
Password not shown

Note that the password is not shown on the screen for security reasons. The appearance of the login prompt signifies that the system is available for someone to log in and the previous user has logged out (i.e., finished her work and disconnected). The prompt here is preceded by SunOS 5.8, the version of the operating system in Solaris 8, the flavor of UNIX offered by Sun. Your system could show a different string here (if at all). If you make a mistake, this is what you could be seeing:

```
Login incorrect
login:
```

This simply tells us that either the user-id or password (or both) is incorrect. When you get both these parameters correct, the system lets you in:

```
Last login: Thu May  8 06:48:39 from saturn.heavens.com
$ _
```
The cursor shown by the _ character

The system here displays a message showing the last time you logged in. This is followed by the prompt string which here is a $. Your prompt string could be a % which is quite popular in the academic world. The system administrator, who uses the root account to log in, uses # as the prompt. Prompt strings can also be customized. Here's one that shows the current directory:

```
[/home/romeo]
```

Before we move on, be aware that a program known as the **shell** is now running at this terminal, waiting to take your input. Whatever we key in now goes as input to this program. UNIX offers a variety of such programs for you to choose from. The shell is the command interpreter that interacts both with the user and the operating system. When the administrator opens a user account, she also sets a specific shell for the user.

Linux systems come preconfigured with informative prompts like this one which shows the machine (saturn), username (romeo) and the current directory (/home/romeo):

```
romeo@saturn:/home/romeo >
```

We'll learn to customize our prompt string in a later chapter.

1.5.2 Logging Out

Before you try out some of the programs available on the system, you must first know how to log out. That also depends on the shell you use, so first try:

[Ctrl-d]
Keep [Ctrl] pressed and then press d

If this key sequence doesn't work but instead shows you the message Use "logout" to logout, then do as directed:

```
logout
```

If this doesn't work either, then use **exit** which works in most cases:

```
$ exit
login:                                          System now available for next user
```

The appearance of the login prompt makes the system available for the next user. Now log in again so that you can try out all the commands featured in the hands-on session that follows.

Note

Henceforth, we'll use the terms *privileged user, superuser,* and *system administrator* to refer to the root user account that is used by the administrator for logging in, and we'll use *nonprivileged user* to mean all other users. It's often important to make this distinction because the root user enjoys certain privileges that are denied others.

1.6 A Hands-On Session

After you have successfully made your entry by providing the user-id and password at the two prompts, you have free access to the UNIX command set reserved for general use. When you key in a word, the system interprets it as a *command* to do something. In most cases, the command signifies the execution of a program on disk that has the name you keyed in.

UNIX is sensitive to case, and UNIX commands are generally in lowercase. Try using the **date** command, but use **DATE** instead of **date**:

```
$ DATE
ksh: DATE: not found
```

Unlike in DOS, where both **date** and **DATE** display the same output, there's no command named **DATE** (no file named DATE) on the UNIX system. As mentioned before, in UNIX, lowercase is typically used more than uppercase.

We'll now acquaint ourselves with a few of these commands, which we categorize into three groups—system information, processes, and files. In this session, we'll use them only to get a feel of the system. The commands will be examined in more detail later in separate chapters.

Caution

Make sure the *[CapsLock]* key is not permanently set on your machine. When inserting a block of text in uppercase in editors like **vi** and **emacs**, we often set this key. When working at the prompt, however, nothing will work if the terminal is not set to lowercase.

1.6.1 System Information with date and who

Using date Every UNIX system maintains an internal clock that you can access to print the current system date and time. UNIX does it with a single command named **date**:

```
$ date
Wed Aug  6 19:31:56 GMT 2003
$ _
```
                                                    Prompt returns; you can now enter next command

DATE didn't work, but **date** did and returned the prompt. This format is seen in email messages except that the time zone (here, GMT) could differ on your system. It's worth noting that a nonprivileged user runs **date** with a limited scope; she can't change the system date which the privileged user (i.e., root) can.

Using who to View the List of Current Users   UNIX can be used concurrently by multiple users, and you might be interested in knowing who is using the system when you are. Use the **who** command:

```
$ who
romeo      console    May  9 09:31    (:0)
henry      pts/4      May  9 09:31    (:0.0)
steve      pts/5      May  9 09:32    (saturn.heavens.com)
$ _
```

There are currently three users—romeo, henry, and steve—sharing the CPU. These names are actually the user-ids they used to log in. The output also includes your own user-id, romeo, which you entered at the login prompt to gain entry to the system. The date and time of login are shown in three columns.

 Observe that when a command has completed its run, the prompt is returned. The return of the prompt indicates that all work relating to the previous command has been completed and the system is ready to accept the next command. Henceforth, we'll not indicate this return except in those situations where the return is significant.

 You logged in with the name romeo, so the system addresses you by this name and associates romeo with whatever work you do. Create a file, and the system will make romeo the owner of the file. Execute a program, and romeo will be owner of the process associated with your program. Send mail to another user, and the system will inform the recipient that mail has arrived from romeo.

Note

UNIX isn't just a repository of commands producing informative output. You can extract useful information from command output to use with other commands. For instance, you can extract the day of the week (here, Wed.) from the **date** output and then devise a program that does different things depending on the day the program is invoked. You can also "cut" the user-ids from the **who** output and use the list with the **mailx** command to send mail to all users currently logged in. The facility to perform these useful tasks with one or two lines of code makes UNIX truly different from other operating systems.

1.6.2   Viewing Processes with ps

The *process* is a key component of any operating system, so let's run a command that displays the processes running at our terminal. The **ps** command does this job, and the following command shows that currently only one is running:

```
$ ps
PID TTY      TIME CMD
1045 pts/2   0:00 ksh                                    Shell running all the time!
```

We observed that the shell program is always running at your terminal, and the **ps** output bears testimony to the fact. When you run several programs, there will be multiple lines in the **ps** output. The last column shows a process named **ksh**, which represents the Korn shell (an advanced shell from AT&T). This process has a unique number (1045, called the *PID,* the process-id) and is *killed* when you log out. In fact, the three commands and key sequences recommended for use in logging out in Section 1.5.2 kill this process.

Even though we are using the Korn shell here, you could be using another shell. Instead of **ksh**, you could see **sh** (the primitive Bourne shell), **csh** (C shell—still popular today), or **bash** (Bash shell—a very powerful shell and recommended for use). To know the one that is running for you, use the **echo** command like this:

```
$ echo $SHELL
/usr/bin/ksh                                                        The Korn shell
```

$SHELL is one of the several *shell variables* available on your system. Throughout this book, we'll compare the features of these shells and discover features available in one shell but not in another. If a command doesn't produce output as explained in this text, the problem can often be attributed to the shell.

1.6.3 Handling Files

UNIX maintains all data in containers called *files.* These files are assigned names, and a group of filenames are held together in another separate file known as a *directory.* In this section and in Section 1.6.4, we take a look at some of the basic commands offered by UNIX to handle files and directories.

Creating a File with echo There are several ways to create a file. Here we use the **echo** command with a special symbol (the >):

```
$ echo date > foo
$ _                                                      No display; prompt returns
```

The **echo** command is meant to display a message on the terminal, but here the message (date) goes to the file foo instead. We'll not concern ourselves with the role played by the shell here but simply note that the > is a convenient mechanism of *redirecting* command output.

Displaying a File with cat The **cat** command displays the contents of files, so let's use it to view the file that we just created:

```
$ cat foo
date
```

Observe that we used both the **echo** and **cat** commands with an additional word (date and foo). They are known as *arguments*. UNIX commands are often used with arguments, and the variety of these arguments make these commands behave in numerous ways.

Copying a File with cp We now use the **cp** command to copy the file foo that we just created:

```
$ cp foo foo.sh
$ _                                    No message; prompt returns
```

Note that **cp** needs two arguments and operates silently. If you run **cat foo.sh** now, **cat** will also display the string date.

Displaying List of Filenames with ls Now that we have two identical files, we can produce a list of their names with the **ls** command:

```
$ ls
foo     foo.sh
```

In Chapters 3 and 4, we'll use the **ls** command to display the attributes of files and directories.

Renaming a File with mv The **mv** command renames a file, and the following sequence renames foo.sh to foo.shell. We also confirm the action by running **ls**:

```
$ mv foo.sh foo.shell
$ ls
foo     foo.shell
```

Removing a File with rm The **rm** command deletes files, and this one removes the file foo.shell:

```
$ rm foo.shell
$ ls
foo                                          Only foo is left
```

ls confirms our action yet again. Observe that **cp**, **rm**, and **mv** behave silently and return the prompt; they don't clutter the screen with verbose output. Silence here implies success; the commands worked in the way they were expected to.

1.6.4   Handling Directories

The files foo and foo.sh are *ordinary files*. Every file has an association with a *directory*, and we often describe this association (somewhat loosely) by saying that a file *resides* in a directory. A user too is associated with a directory, and this is conveniently expressed by saying that a user is *placed* in a directory called the *current directory*. UNIX considers a directory as a file, and some commands work with both ordinary files and directories.

The file `foo` can be considered to reside in the current directory. This directory was not created by us but by the system administrator when opening an account for user romeo. But we can also create a directory, copy a file to it, navigate to that directory, and also remove it.

Creating a Directory with `mkdir` The `mkdir` command creates a directory. Here the command creates one named `scripts`:

```
$ mkdir scripts
$ _
```

We now have one file and one directory, both in the current directory. `ls` will now display both filenames, but if you follow it with -F, then you can identify a directory easily:

```
$ ls -F
foo      scripts/                                        -F marks directory with a /
```

`ls` here uses an argument that begins with a hyphen, but this argument is appropriately called an *option*. Options change the default behavior of a command, and the -F option modifies the `ls` output by using the / to mark a directory name.

Copying a File to a Directory The same command in UNIX often works with both a file and directory. For instance, the **cp** command can be used to copy a file to a directory. Here, **cp** copies `foo` to the `scripts` directory:

```
$ cp foo scripts                                          scripts here is a directory
$ _
```

Directory Navigation with `pwd` and `cd` We can know what the current directory is by using the **pwd** command and change it by using **cd**. Before we change our location, however, let's use **pwd** to find out how the command describes the current directory:

```
$ pwd
/home/romeo
```

This description is called a *pathname,* and it represents a hierarchy of three directory names. We are currently stationed in romeo which in turn is below home. The first / indicates the top-most directory called root, so home is below the root directory. Don't confuse this directory with the root user account.

Since our current directory contains a directory named `scripts`, we can now use the **cd** command to change our location to that directory:

```
$ cd scripts
$ pwd
/home/romeo/scripts
```

We have descended one level in this file system hierarchy. This directory should now contain the file foo that we copied earlier. List this directory with **ls**, and then remove foo with **rm**:

```
$ ls
foo
$ rm foo
$ _
```

The file is gone, and the directory is now empty. The directory can now be removed with **rmdir** but only when we move away from this directory. Let's return to the directory we came from before we use **rmdir**:

```
$ cd /home/romeo
$ pwd
/home/romeo
$ rmdir scripts
$ ls
foo
```

We now have a single file left in the current directory. We can remove it with **rm**, but why not run it like this?

```
$ sh foo
Wed Aug  6 21:31:36 GMT 2003
```

foo is a *shell script* that runs the **date** command! If we place some more command strings in this file, they will all be executed in a batch. (Chapter 13 discusses shell scripting in detail.)

All of these commands will be examined in some detail in the forthcoming chapters, so let's log out of the system. You know the technique of doing this by now. Generally, **exit** terminates most sessions:

```
$ exit
login:
```

Caution

Make sure that you log out after your work is complete. If you don't, anybody can get a hold of your terminal and continue working using your user-id. She may even remove your files! The login prompt signifies a terminated session, so don't leave your place of work till you see this prompt.

1.7 How It All Clicked

Until UNIX came on the scene, operating systems were designed with a particular machine in mind. They were invariably written in a low-level language (like assembler, which uses humanly unreadable code). The systems were fast but were restricted to the hardware they were designed for. Programs designed for one system simply wouldn't run on another. That was the status of the computer industry when Ken Thompson and Dennis Ritchie, of AT&T fame, authored the UNIX system for their own use.

In 1969, AT&T withdrew its team from the MULTICS project, which was engaged in the development of a flexible operating system that would run continuously and be used remotely. Thompson and Ritchie then designed and built a small system with an elegant file system, a command interpreter (the shell), and a set of utilities. To make UNIX portable, they rewrote the entire system in the C language that was invented by Ritchie himself. C is a high-level language, and programs coded in C run on all hardware. Portability became one of the strong features of UNIX.

1.7.1   Berkeley: The Second School

An U.S. government law (subsequently revoked) prevented AT&T from selling computer software. The company had no option but to distribute the product to academic and research institutions at a nominal fee, but it came without any support. From the AT&T product, the University of California, Berkeley (UCB), created a UNIX of its own. They called it *BSD UNIX* (BSD—Berkeley Software Distribution). Both of these versions became quite popular worldwide, especially in universities and engineering circles. Later, UCB gave up all development work on UNIX.

Berkeley filled in the gaps left behind by AT&T, and then later decided to rewrite the whole operating system in the way they wanted. They created the standard editor of the UNIX system (**vi**) and a popular shell (C shell). Berkeley also created a better file system, a more versatile mail feature, and a better method of linking files (symbolic links). Later, they also offered with their standard distribution a networking protocol software (TCP/IP) that made the Internet possible. Like AT&T, they also offered it practically free to many companies.

1.7.2   UNIX Gets Fragmented

Even though UNIX was written by programmers for programmers, its inherent strengths found favor within business circles. Sun used the BSD System as a foundation for developing their own brand of UNIX (then SunOS). Today, their version of UNIX is known as *Solaris*. Others developed their own brands: IBM had *AIX,* HP offered *HP-UX,* while DEC produced *Digital UNIX*—and now *Tru64 UNIX*. Then the Linux wave arrived, and most of these vendors began to offer Linux too. Today, most supercomputers run UNIX, and handheld devices increasingly use Linux.

As each vendor modified and enhanced UNIX to create its own version, the original UNIX lost its identity as a separate product. The BSD releases were much different from the AT&T System V releases, and the incompatibilities steadily mounted. Finally, AT&T took it upon themselves to unify many of these flavors into its last release— *System V Release 4* (SVR4). Shortly thereafter, AT&T sold its UNIX business to Novell, who later turned over the UNIX trademark to a standards body called X/OPEN, now merged with The Open Group.

Note   The UNIX trademark is currently owned by The Open Group.

1.7.3 The Internet

Even before the advent of SVR4, big things were happening in the U.S. Defense Department. DARPA, a wing of the department, engaged several vendors to develop a reliable communication system using computer technology. Through some brilliant work done by Vinton Cerf and Robert Kahn, DARPA's ARPANET network was made to work using packet-switching technology. In this technology, data is split into packets, which can take different routes and yet be reassembled in the right order. This was the birth of *TCP/IP*—a set of protocols (rules) used by the Internet for communication.

DARPA commissioned UCB to implement TCP/IP on BSD UNIX. ARPANET converted to TCP/IP in 1983, and in the same year, Berkeley released the first version of UNIX which had TCP/IP built-in. The computer science research community were all using BSD UNIX, and the network expanded like wild fire. The incorporation of TCP/IP into UNIX and its use as the basis of development were two key factors in the rapid growth of the Internet (and UNIX).

1.7.4 The Windows Threat

In the meantime, Microsoft was doing great things with Windows—a *graphical user interface* (GUI) that uses the mouse rather than arcane and complex command options to execute a job. Options could be selected from drop-down menu boxes and radio buttons, which made handling some of the basic operating system functions easier. Windows first swept the desktop market (with Windows 3.1/95/98) and then made significant inroads into the server market (with Windows NT/2000) which had been long dominated by UNIX.

When UNIX badly needed a Windows-type interface for its survival, the Massachusetts Institute of Technology (MIT) introduced *X Window*—the first windowing system for UNIX. X Window has many of the important features of Microsoft Windows plus a lot more. Every flavor of UNIX now has X along with a host of other tools that can not only handle files and directories but also update the system's configuration files.

Note   All said and done, the power of UNIX derives from its commands and their multiple options. No GUI tool can ever replace the **find** command that uses elaborate file-attribute matching schemes to locate files.

1.8 POSIX and the Single UNIX Specification

Dennis Ritchie's decision to rewrite UNIX in C didn't make UNIX very portable. In addition, UNIX fragmentation and the absence of a single conforming standard adversely affected the development of portable applications. To address the issue, AT&T created the *System V Interface Definition* (SVID). Later, X/Open (now The Open Group), a consortium of vendors and users, created the *X/Open Portability Guide* (XPG). Products conforming to this specification were branded UNIX95, UNIX98, or UNIX03, depending on the version of the specification.

Still another group of standards, the *Portable Operating System Interface for Computer Environments* (POSIX), was developed at the behest of the Institution of Electrical and Electronics Engineers (IEEE). POSIX refers to operating systems in general, but was based on UNIX. Two of the most-cited standards from the POSIX family are known as *POSIX.1* and *POSIX.2*. POSIX.1 specifies the C application program interface—the system calls. POSIX.2 deals with the shell and utilities.

In 2001, a joint initiative of X/Open and IEEE resulted in the unification of the two standards. This is the *Single UNIX Specification, Version 3* (SUSV3) that is also known as *IEEE 1003.1:2001* (POSIX.1). The "write once, adopt everywhere" approach to this development means that once software has been developed on any POSIX-compliant UNIX system, it can be easily ported to another POSIX-compliant UNIX machine with minimum modifications. We make references to POSIX throughout this text, but these references should be interpreted to mean the SUSV3 as well.

Tip

The Single UNIX Specification, Version 3 is available at *http://www.unix.org/version3/pr.html*. You must frequently consult this document when you use a command, an option, or a system call to confirm whether the usage is mandated by the specification.

1.9 Linux and GNU

Although UNIX finally turned commercial, Richard Stallman and Linus Torvalds had different ideas. Torvalds is the father of Linux, the free UNIX that has taken the computer world by storm. Stallman runs the Free Software Foundation (formerly known as GNU— a recursive acronym that stands for "GNU's Not Unix!"). Many of the important Linux tools were written and supplied free by GNU.

Linux is distributed under the GNU General Public License which makes it mandatory for developers and sellers to make the source code public. Linux is particularly strong in networking and Internet features, and is an extremely cost-effective solution in setting up an Internet server or a local internet. Today, development on Linux is carried out at several locations across the globe at the behest of the Free Software Foundation.

The most popular GNU/Linux flavors include Red Hat, Caldera, SuSE, Debian, and Mandrake. These distributions, which are shipped on multiple CD-ROMs, include a plethora of software—from C and C++ compilers to Java; interpreters like **perl**, **python**, and **tcl**; browsers like Netscape; Internet servers; and multimedia software. Much of the software can also be downloaded free from the Internet. All the major computer vendors (barring Microsoft) have committed to support Linux, and many of them have ported their software to this platform. This book also discusses Linux.

1.10 The UNIX Architecture

The entire UNIX system is supported by a handful of essentially simple, though somewhat abstract concepts. The success of UNIX, according to Thompson and Ritchie, "lies not so much in new inventions but rather in the full exploitation of a carefully selected set of fertile ideas, and especially in showing that they can be keys to the implementation of a small and yet powerful operating system." UNIX is no longer a small system, but it certainly is a powerful one. Before we examine the features of UNIX, we need to understand its architecture—its foundation.

1.10.1   Division of Labor: Kernel and Shell

Foremost among these "fertile ideas" is the division of labor between two agencies—the *kernel* and the *shell*. The kernel interacts with the machine's hardware, and the shell with the user. You have seen both of them in action in the hands-on session though the kernel wasn't mentioned by name. Their relationship is depicted in Fig. 1.1.

The **kernel** is the core of the operating system. The system's bootstrap program (a small piece of program code) loads the kernel into memory at startup. The kernel comprises a set of routines, mostly written in C, that communicate with the hardware directly. User programs (the applications) that need to access the hardware (like the hard disk or the terminal) communicate with the kernel using a set of functions called *system calls,* which we discuss shortly.

Apart from providing support to user programs, the kernel has a great deal of housekeeping to do. It manages the system's memory, schedules processes, decides their priorities, and performs other tasks which you wouldn't want to bother about. The kernel has work to do even if no user program is running. It is often called *the* operating system—a program's gateway to the computer's resources.

Computers don't have any inherent capability of translating user commands into action. That requires an interpreter, and that job in UNIX is handled by the "outer part"

FIGURE 1.1   *The Kernel-Shell Relationship*

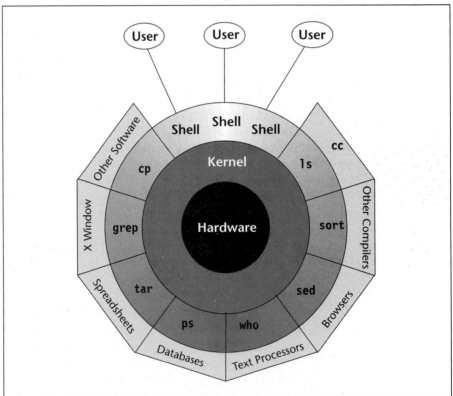

of the operating system—the **shell**. It is actually the interface between the user and the kernel. Even though there's only one kernel running on the system, there could be several shells in action—one for each user who is logged in.

When you enter a command through the keyboard, the shell thoroughly examines the keyboard input for special characters. If it finds any, it rebuilds a simplified command line, and finally communicates with the kernel to see that the command is executed. This interpretive action of the shell is examined in detail in Chapter 7.

Note

UNIX fragmentation becomes quite evident when you attempt to locate the kernel on your system. It is often named unix (genunix on Solaris) and could be located in directories /unix or /kernel. The shells are all available in /bin or /usr/bin.

Linux

The kernel is represented by the file /boot/vmlinuz. The shells are in /bin and /usr/bin.

1.10.2 The File and Process

Two simple entities support the UNIX system—the *file* and *process*—and Kaare Christian (*The UNIX Operating System,* John Wiley) makes two powerful abstractions about them: "Files have places and processes have life." **Files** are containers for storing static information. Even directories and devices are considered files. A file is related to another file by being part of a single hierarchical structure called the *file system*. Further, using the **cd** and **pwd** *(1.6.4)* commands, you can "place" yourself at a specific location in this hierarchy. Chapters 3 and 4 discuss file and directory handling.

The second entity is the **process** which represents a program in execution. Like files, processes also form a hierarchy, and are best understood when we consider one process as the child of another. Unlike files, which are static entities, processes resemble living organisms which are born and which die. UNIX provides the tools that allow us to control processes, move them between foreground and background, and even kill them. The basics of the process management system are discussed in Chapter 8.

1.10.3 The System Calls

The UNIX system—comprising the kernel, shell, and applications—is written in C. Though there are over a thousand different commands in the system, they often need to carry out certain common tasks—like reading from or writing to disk. The code for performing disk I/O operations is not built into the programs but is available in the kernel. Programs access these kernel services by invoking special functions called **system calls.** Often the same system call can access both a file and a device; the **open** system call opens both.

C programmers on a Windows system use the *standard library functions* for everything. You can't use the **write** system call on a Windows system; you need to use a library function like **fprintf** for that purpose. In contrast, the C programmer in the UNIX environment has complete access to the entire system call library as well as the standard library functions. You can use both **write** and **fprintf** in a C program meant for running on a UNIX system.

POSIX specifies the system calls that all UNIX systems must implement. Once software has been developed on one UNIX system using the calls mandated by POSIX, it can be easily moved to another UNIX machine. Chapters 17 and 18 deal with the basic system calls that you need to know to program in the UNIX environment.

1.11   Features of UNIX

UNIX is an operating system, so it has all the features an operating system is expected to have. However, UNIX also looks at a few things differently and possesses features unique to itself. The following sections present the major features of this operating system.

1.11.1   A Multiuser System

From a fundamental point of view, UNIX is a **multiprogramming** system. It permits multiple programs to remain in memory and compete for the attention of the CPU. These programs can be run by different users; UNIX is also a **multiuser** system. This feature often baffles Windows users as Windows is essentially a single-user system where the CPU, memory, and hard disk are all dedicated to a single user. The **who** output *(1.6.1)* showed three users working on the system.

For cycling through multiple jobs, the kernel uses the principle of **time-sharing**. It breaks up a unit of time into several slices, and a user's job runs for the duration of a slice. The moment the allocated time expires, the previous job is kept in abeyance and the next job is taken up. This process goes on till the clock has turned full-circle, and the first job is taken up once again. This switching happens several times in one second, so every user has the feeling that the machine is completely dedicated to her.

Note

A program can leave the CPU before its time quantum expires if it performs an operation that keeps the CPU idle. This has already been discussed in Section 1.1.

1.11.2   A Multitasking System Too

A single user can also run multiple tasks concurrently; UNIX is a **multitasking** system. It is common for a user to edit a file, print another one on the printer, send email to a friend, and browse the World Wide Web—all without leaving any of the applications. The X Window system exploits the multitasking feature by allowing you to open multiple windows on your desktop.

In a multitasking environment, a user sees one job running in the *foreground;* the rest run in the *background.* You can switch jobs between background and foreground, suspend, or even terminate them. As a programmer you can use this feature in a very productive way. You can edit a C program with the **vi** editor and then suspend the **vi** process to run the **cc** compiler. You don't need to quit **vi** to do that. This feature is provided by most shells.

Note

Today, we have machines with multiple CPUs that make it possible to actually earmark an entire processor for a single program (in a single-user and single-tasking situation).

1.11.3   A Repository of Applications

By one definition, UNIX represents the kernel, but the kernel by itself can't do anything that can benefit the user. To exploit the power of UNIX, you need to use the host of applications that are shipped with every UNIX system. These applications are quite diverse in scope. There are general-purpose tools, text manipulation utilities (called *filters*), compilers and interpreters, networked applications, and system administration tools. You'll also have a choice of shells.

This is one area that's constantly changing with every UNIX release. New tools are being added, and the older ones are being removed or modified. The shell and an essential subset of these applications form part of the POSIX specification. There are open-source versions for most of these utilities, and after you have read Chapter 16, you should be able to download these tools and configure them to run on your machine.

1.11.4   The Building-Block Approach

One of the strengths of UNIX emerges from the designers' belief that "small is beautiful." A complex task can be broken into a finite number of simple ones. The shell offers a mechanism called the *pipe* that allows the output of one command to serve as input to another. To take advantage of this feature a special set of commands (called *filters*) were designed where each command did "one thing well." By interconnecting these tools using the piping mechanism, you can solve very complex text manipulation problems.

You can now understand why the **who** output *(1.6.1)* doesn't display a header. If we wanted to count the number of users by connecting the **who** output to a word-counting program (like **wc**), a header line would have resulted in an erroneous count. This approach also explains why most commands are not interactive. If a command had to pause to take user input, then it can't be scheduled to run at a certain time of the day. Its output can't be used by another program without user intervention.

1.11.5   Pattern Matching

UNIX features very sophisticated pattern matching features. Many commands use filenames as arguments, and these filenames often have a common string. For instance, all C programs have the `.c` extension, and to back them up to tape with the **tar** command, we need not specify all of their filenames to **tar**. Instead, we can simply use a pattern `*.c`. The `*` is a special character (known as a *metacharacter*) that is used by the shell to match a number of characters. If you choose your filenames carefully, you can use a simple expression to access a whole lot of them.

Pattern matching isn't confined to filenames only. Some advanced tools (like **grep**, **sed**, and **awk**) also use a different metacharacter set for matching strings contained in files. In this scheme, a single pattern `printf.*name` matches all lines that contain both `printf` and `name`. This pattern is called a *regular expression*. This book heavily emphasizes the importance of regular expressions and shows how you can perform complex pattern matching tasks using them.

1.11.6   Programming Facility

The UNIX shell is also a programming language; it was designed for a programmer, not a casual end user. It has all the necessary ingredients, like control structures, loops, and variables, that establish it as a powerful programming language in its own right. These features are used to design **shell scripts**—programs that run UNIX commands in a batch.

Many of the system's functions can be controlled and automated by using these shell scripts. If you intend taking up system administration as a career, then you'll have to know the shell's programming features very well. Proficient UNIX programmers seldom refer to any other language (except **perl**) for text manipulation problems. Shell programming is taken up in Chapter 13.

1.11.7 Documentation

UNIX documentation is no longer the sore point it once was. Even though it's sometimes uneven, usually the treatment is quite lucid. The principal online help facility available is the **man** command, which remains the most important reference for commands and their configuration files. Today there's no feature of UNIX on which a separate textbook is not available. UNIX documentation and the man facility are discussed in Chapter 2.

Apart from the online documentation, there's a vast ocean of UNIX resources available on the Internet. There are several newsgroups on UNIX where you can post your queries in case you are stranded with a problem. The FAQ (Frequently Asked Questions)—a document that addresses common problems—is also widely available on the Net. Then there are numerous articles published in magazines and journals and lecture notes made available by universities on their Web sites.

With the goal of building a comfortable relationship with the machine, Thomson and Ritchie designed a system for their own use rather than for others. They could afford to do this because UNIX wasn't initially developed as a commercial product, and the project didn't have any predefined objective. They acknowledge this fact too: "We have not been faced with the need to satisfy someone else's requirements, and for this freedom we are grateful."

SUMMARY

A computer needs an *operating system* (OS) to allocate memory, schedule programs, and control devices. The UNIX system also provides a host of applications for the use of programmers and users.

Multiprogramming systems like UNIX allow multiple programs to reside in memory. Even though a program may run for the duration of the time slice allocated for it, it may prematurely leave the CPU during a *blocking* operation (like reading a file) that keeps the CPU idle.

You enter a UNIX system by entering a user-id and a password. You can terminate a session by using the **exit** or **logout** command or pressing *[Ctrl-d]*.

UNIX commands are generally in lowercase. **date** displays the system date and time. **who** displays the list of users logged on to the system. **ps** lists all processes running at a terminal. It always shows the shell process running.

You can display a file with **cat**, copy it with **cp**, rename it with **mv**, and remove it with **rm**.

mkdir creates a directory, **pwd** displays the pathname of the current directory, and **cd** changes the current directory. **rmdir** removes an empty directory.

UNIX was developed at AT&T Bell Laboratories by Ken Thompson and Dennis Ritchie. It was finally written in C. Notable work was also done at Berkeley. AT&T introduced System V Release 4 (SVR4) to merge their own version, Berkeley, and other variants.

Linux is a UNIX implementation that is constantly growing with contributions from the Free Software Foundation (formerly, GNU).

Modifications to the system made by vendors led to both enhancement and fragmentation of UNIX. Two merged standards, *POSIX* and the *Single UNIX Specification,* are today used as guidance for development work on UNIX.

All work is shared by the *kernel* and *shell*. The kernel manages the hardware, and the shell interacts with the user. The shell and applications communicate with the kernel using *system calls,* which are special routines built into the kernel.

The *file* and *process* are the two basic entities that support the UNIX system. UNIX considers everything as a file. A process represents a program (a file) in execution.

UNIX is a *multiuser* and *multitasking* system. Several users can use the system together, and a single user can also run multiple jobs concurrently.

UNIX uses a building-block approach in the design of some of its tools and lets you develop complex command routines by connecting these tools.

The UNIX **man** command is the primary online help facility available.

SELF-TEST

1.1   The _____ interacts with the hardware, and the _____ interacts with the user.

1.2   A *program* is synonymous with a *process*. True or false?

1.3   Every character has a number associated with it. What is it called?

1.4   If you see a prompt like mailhost login:, what do you think mailhost represents?

1.5   If the system echoes Login incorrect, does it mean that your user-id is incorrect?

1.6   Name the commands you used in this chapter to display (i) filenames, (ii) processes, (iii) users.

1.7   Run **ps** and note the PID of your shell. Log out and log in again, and run **ps** again. What do you observe?

1.8   Create two files, foo1 and foo2, with the **echo** command, and then use **cat foo1 foo2**. What do you observe?

1.9   Now run the command **cat foo[12]**, and note your observations.

1.10   Enter the command **echo SHELL**. What mistake did you make?

1.11   Create a file foo containing the words hello dolly. Now create a directory bar, and then run **mv foo bar**. What do you observe when you run both **ls** and **ls bar**?

1.12   Who are the principal architects of the UNIX operating system?

1.13   Why did AT&T virtually give away UNIX to the world?

1.14   Where did BSD UNIX originate? Name some features of UNIX that were first found in BSD UNIX.

1.15   Which flavor of UNIX is available for free and runs on the PC?

1.16   Identify the companies associated with the following brands: (i) Solaris, (ii) AIX, (iii) Tru64 UNIX.

1.17   What does X/OPEN represent? Who owns the UNIX trademark today?

1.18   Who are the two brains behind Linux?

1.19   What is the distinctive characteristic about the GNU General Public License?

1.20   Why is UNIX more portable than other operating systems?

1.21   Can you divide UNIX into two major schools? To which school does Sun's UNIX belong?

1.22   Why do UNIX tools perform simple jobs rather than complex ones?

1.23   What is the windowing system of UNIX known as?

1.24   Name some interpretive languages available on UNIX systems.

1.25   Name three notable Linux flavors.

EXERCISES

1.1   Operating systems like UNIX provide services both for programs and users. Explain.

1.2   What does a program do when it needs to read a file?

1.3   Does a program always complete its time quantum before it makes way for another program?

1.4   Explain the significance of the terms *multiprogramming, multiuser,* and *multitasking*.

1.5   Why are UNIX commands noninteractive, and why is their output not usually preceded by header information?

1.6   What are *system calls,* and what role do they play in the system? How is C programming so different and powerful in the UNIX environment compared to Windows?

1.7   Two UNIX systems may use the same system calls. True or false?

1.8   Name the three commands that you would try in sequence to log yourself out of the system. Which one of them will always work?

1.9   Run the following commands, and then invoke **ls.** What do you conclude?

```
echo > README[Enter]
echo > readme[Enter]
```

1.10   Enter the following commands, and note your observations: (i) **who** and **tty**, (ii) **tput clear**, (iii) **id**, (iv) **ps** and **echo $$**.

1.11   When you log in, a program starts executing at your terminal. What is this program known as? Name four types of this program that are available on a system.

1.12   What is the significance of your user-id? Where in the system is the name used?

1.13   What are the two schools of UNIX that initially guided its development? Mention the outcome of the standardization efforts that are currently in force today.

1.14   Create a directory, and change to that directory. Next, create another directory in the new directory, and then change to that directory too. Now, run **cd** without any arguments followed by **pwd**. What do you conclude?

1.15   Why is the shell called a *command interpreter*?

1.16   What is the one thing that is common to directories, devices, terminals, and printers?

Becoming Familiar with UNIX Commands

A major part of the job of learning UNIX is to master the essential command set. UNIX has a vast repertoire of commands that can solve many tasks either by working singly or in combination. In this chapter, we'll examine the generalized UNIX command syntax and come to understand the significance of its options and arguments. The complete picture of command usage is available in the man pages, and we'll learn to look up this documentation with the **man** command.

We'll next try out some of the general-purpose utilities of the system. We'll change the password and get comfortable with email using a command-line tool. We'll learn about other tools that tell us the date, the users of the system, and some specifics of the operating system. At times we need to consider situations where the output of these commands can be processed further. Finally, we take a look at the common traps that befall the user and how the **stty** command can change many keyboard settings.

Objectives

- Understand the breakup of the *command line* into *arguments* and *options*.
- Learn how the shell uses the PATH variable to locate commands.
- Learn how commands can be used singly or in combination.
- Use the **man** command to browse the UNIX documentation.
- Understand the organization of the documentation.
- Display messages with **echo**, and understand why **printf** is superior.
- Save all keystrokes and command output in a file with **script**.
- Understand email basics and why you need a command-line email program like **mailx**.
- Use **passwd** to change your own password.
- Know your machine's name and operating system with **uname**.
- Find out the users of the system with **who**.
- Display the system date in various formats with **date**.
- Know what can go wrong, and use **stty** to change keyboard settings.
- Get introduced to the X Window system.

2.1 Command Basics

UNIX commands are generally implemented as disk files representing executable programs. They are mainly written in C, but UNIX supports programs written in any language. When you run a command, the program is loaded into memory, and the CPU starts executing the instructions contained in the program.

UNIX is sensitive to the case of filenames though command names are generally in lowercase. These names are seldom more than four characters long. You can sometimes deduce the function from the name (like **cp** for copy) but sometimes not (like **grep** for searching for a pattern).

Unlike in Windows, UNIX doesn't require command names to have an extension (like .exe, .com, etc.). Extensions are used either for convenience or for conforming to a requirement imposed by the application. For instance, C and Java programs need to have the .c and .java extensions, respectively, because their respective compilers won't work otherwise. However, shell and **perl** scripts don't need the .sh or .pl extensions, though we often provide them for easier identification.

There's one command that's special—the shell. Unlike other commands, the shell is invoked the moment you log in and continues to run until you log out. We'll be constantly making references to the shell's behavior in these initial chapters before we embark on a detailed examination in Chapter 7.

Note

In case you begin to feel that all commands are loaded from disk, we need to make the distinction between *external* and *internal* commands. External commands exist on disk as separate files. But there's also a separate set of commands that are built into the shell executable. You have used one of them already—the **cd** command *(1.6.4)*. There's no file in the system named cd.

2.1.1 The PATH: Locating Commands

How does the shell know whether a command can be executed or not? The shell maintains a variable named PATH in its own environment (thus also known as an *environment variable*). PATH is set to a list of colon-delimited directories. You can display this list by simply evaluating the $-prefixed variable with the **echo** command:

```
$ echo $PATH
/bin:/usr/bin:/usr/ucb:/usr/xpg4/bin:.
```
Output in the C shell is a little different

There are five directories in this list. The fifth directory is signified by a dot that represents the current directory. When you enter a command, the shell looks in each of these directories to locate the file with that name. The following message shows that the **netscape** command is not available in any of these directories:

```
$ netscape
ksh: netscape:  not found
```

The Korn shell is running here and prints the message after failing to locate the file. This doesn't in any way confirm that **netscape** doesn't exist on this system; it could reside in a different directory. In that case we can still run it

- by changing the value of PATH to include that directory.
- by using a *pathname* (like /usr/local/bin/netscape if the command is located in /usr/local/bin).
- by switching to the directory where the executable is located and executing it from there.

Windows users also use the same PATH variable to specify the search path, except that Windows uses the ; as the delimiter instead of the colon. We have more to say about pathnames in Chapter 3, and we'll learn to change PATH in Chapter 9.

Note

The essential UNIX commands for general use are located in the directories /bin and /usr/bin. The commands showing graphical output are usually found in /usr/X11R6/bin or /usr/dt/bin. The commands used by the system administrator are found in /sbin and /usr/sbin.

2.1.2 Where Is the Command?

There are three commands that provide clues to the location of another command— **which**, **whereis**, and **type**. Sometimes you'll want to know whether a command is available in PATH before you decide to execute it. The **which** command tells you the directory that contains the command:

```
$ which grep
/usr/bin/grep
```

After searching the directories of PATH in sequence, **which** abandons its search the moment it locates a file named grep. You may not have **which** on your system, and POSIX doesn't require UNIX systems to offer this utility. If you are using a BSD-based UNIX system, then you can try the **whereis** command. This time let's try to locate **ls**:

```
$ whereis ls
ls: /usr/bin/ls /usr/ucb/ls                          Berkeley version also shown
```

Unlike **which**, which confines its search to the directories in PATH, **whereis** looks up a larger list. It finds two versions of **ls** on this Solaris system. Note that **whereis** is not also supported by POSIX.

As noted in a previous aside, all UNIX commands are not files; some are built into the shell. **which** and **whereis** don't consider this possibility, so if you look for the **echo** command, **which** says that it is in /usr/bin:

```
$ which echo
/usr/bin/echo
```

This is not the file that is executed when we run **echo**; modern shells have **echo** built in. The information output by **which** is only half true; a more authentic picture is presented by the **type** command:

```
$ type echo
echo is a shell builtin
```

So even if **which** shows the pathname of **echo**, **type** makes it clear that the shell will always run its own built-in command. DOS users are reminded that **type** doesn't display files but only points to the version that will be executed.

Note

which locates a command's disk file, but ambiguity arises when the command is also a shell builtin. As a general rule, the shell will ignore the disk version in preference to its own builtin. (However, we can override this preferential behavior.) The **type** command provides a more reliable picture of the command that is actually executed when it exists in different forms. **type** itself is a shell builtin and is not available in some versions of the C shell.

2.2 Command Structure

In Chapter 1, we used commands that had multiple words (like **mkdir scripts**) and one that had an embedded minus sign (**ls -F**). It's time we subjected a typical UNIX command to a dissective study. The structure of such a command is shown in Fig. 2.1.

This command sequence has five words. The first word is the command itself, and the remaining ones are its **arguments**. The **ls** command is specified here with four arguments. Two of the arguments begin with a hyphen (**-l** and **-t**) and are appropriately called **options**. The entire line is referred to as the **command line**. A command line is executed only after you hit *[Enter]*.

Every command has a fixed set of options. An option changes a command's default behavior, so if **ls** shows only the filenames, the **-l** and **-t** options show their attributes as well. Some commands use files (**note1** and **note2** here) and some don't. If used at all, the filename will generally be a command's last argument—after all options. (This is not always true; some options use filenames as their own "arguments.")

Caution

Beginners often forget to provide spaces between the command and the argument. You can get away with **DIR/P** instead of **DIR /P** in the DOS environment of Windows, but in UNIX you need to be careful:

```
$ ls-F
ksh: ls-F:  not found
```

The shell fails to recognize -F as an argument and treats ls-F as a single command. Obviously, this command doesn't exist in PATH.

A command is separated from its options and arguments by **whitespace**. This is a collective term that comprises a contiguous string of spaces and tabs (and newlines). You can liberally provide a lot of whitespace in the command line, but the shell ensures that arguments are separated by a single space *before* the command is run.

FIGURE 2.1   *Structure of a UNIX Command*

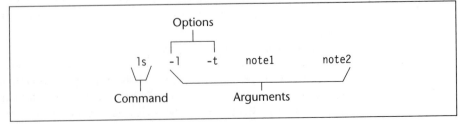

All error messages are not generated by the shell. When you use a command with an incorrect option, the shell locates the command all right, but the *command* this time finds the option to be wrong:

```
$ ls -z note
ls: illegal option -- z                          Error message from ls
usage: ls -1RaAdCxmnlogrtucpFbqisfL [files]
```

ls does have a large number of options (over 20), but it seems that **-z** is not one of them. Many commands also display the right syntax and options when you use them incorrectly.

Caution

Never create a filename that begins with a hyphen; many commands just won't work! It's common for a command to treat a filename beginning with a hyphen as one of its options. This often results in erroneous output. The previous **ls** command would have reacted no differently even if there was a file named -z.

Linux

Linux offers all of the UNIX-type options, but it also offers options using two hyphens and a meaningful word. For instance, it offers the synonym **ls --classify** in addition to **ls -F**. The expanded options are easy to remember; for example, it's easier to remember **--classify** than **-F**.

Options can often be combined with only one - sign. Take for instance this command line containing three options:

```
ls -l -a -t
```

ls is taken up in detail in Chapter 4, so don't bother about the significance of these three options. These are simple options, and UNIX lets you combine them in any order:

```
ls -lat                          Sequence of combination not always
ls -tal                          important, but sometimes is
```

Don't interpret the preceding discussions as a general prescription. Some commands won't let you combine options, as shown above, and some have options that begin with a +. Moreover, **awk** and **perl** use a programming script as an argument. But don't let this deter you; you would have already built up a lot of muscle before you take on these commands.

Note

C programmers and shell scripters need to count the number of arguments in their programs. It helps to be aware at this stage that there are some characters in the command line that are not really arguments—the |, >, and <, for instance. In Chapter 7, we'll make an amazing discovery that in the command line **who > foo**, foo is not an argument to **who!**

2.3 Flexibility of Command Usage

So far we executed commands in sequence—by waiting for the prompt to return before keying in the next command. UNIX provides a certain degree of flexibility in the usage of commands. We can enter multiple commands in one line, and their output need not always come to the terminal. The following discussions actually belong to the domain of the shell, but we need to be aware of them even if we don't understand fully how they work.

You don't have to wait for a command to complete before you type your next command. UNIX provides a full-duplex terminal which provides separate channels for input and output. Just go on typing even if the output of the previous command clutters the display. All commands are stored in a keyboard *buffer* (a temporary form of storage) and will eventually be passed on to the shell.

You can specify multiple commands in one line. Using a **;** as the delimiter of commands, you can specify more than one command before you hit *[Enter]*:

```
who ; ls note
```
ls executed after who

Here we have two command lines on a single line. The **;** is gobbled up by the shell and is not seen by the **who** command. The **;** is a *metacharacter,* and the UNIX shell understands a large number of metacharacters. You'll encounter many of them in Chapter 7.

A command line can be split into multiple physical lines. Sometimes you'll find it either convenient or necessary to spread out the command line into multiple lines. This is how the **echo** command works with most shells:

```
$ echo "This is[Enter]
> a three-line[Enter]
> text message"[Enter]
This is
a three-line
text message
```
A second prompt (>) appears . . .

. . . and disappears after quote is closed

Here we hit *[Enter]* twice to see the secondary prompt (>) appear, which disappeared after we closed the quote. The appearance of the > (or ?) indicates that the command line isn't complete.

C Shell

The above **echo** command won't work with the C shell. You'll have to enter a \ (backslash) before you press *[Enter]*. Moreover, the C shell often throws out a different secondary prompt (?). Its primary prompt is also different (%):

```
% echo "This is\[Enter]
? a three-line\[Enter]
? text message"
```
Some C shells don't show the ? at all.

Tip

Whenever you find the > or ? appearing after you have pressed *[Enter]*, it will often be due to the absence of a matching quote or parenthesis. In case you find that the problem persists even after providing it, just interrupt the command line with *[Ctrl-c]* or *[Ctrl-u]*. The significance of these keys is taken up in Section 2.14.

Command output need not always be seen on the terminal. We often save output in files like this:

```
who > userlist.txt
```
Output saved in userlist.txt

As discussed in Section 1.11.4, UNIX uses a modular approach to solving problems. The output of one command can be useful input for another:

```
who | wc -l
```
who piped to wc -l

This sequence counts the number of users logged in. Chapter 7 discusses how the > and | direct the shell to make the necessary I/O connections that could be used by programs.

2.4 man: **On-Line Help**

UNIX is ultimately mastered by looking up its documentation, which is available today in a number of forms of varying complexity. The earliest and most important is the one that is viewed with the **man** command—often called the *man documentation*. **man** remains the most complete and authoritative guide to the UNIX system. The documentation is also available in print and on the Internet.

To view the manual page of the **wc** command, use **man** with wc as argument:

```
man wc
```

The entire man page is dumped on the screen (Fig. 2.2). **man** presents the first page and pauses. It does this by sending its output to a *pager* program, which displays the contents of a file one page (screen) at a time. The pager is actually a UNIX command, and **man** is always preconfigured to be used with a specific pager. UNIX systems currently use these pager programs:

- **more**, Berkeley's pager, that's now available universally as a superior alternative to the original AT&T **pg** command (now obsolete). We'll be considering **more** in this text.
- **less**, the standard pager used on Linux systems, but also available for all UNIX platforms. **less** is modeled on the **vi** editor and is more powerful than **more** because it replicates many of **vi**'s navigational and search functions. The features of **less** are described briefly in Section 3.16.

On a man page that uses **more** as the pager, you'll see a prompt at the bottom-left of the screen which looks something like this:

```
--More--(26%)
```
less shows a : as the prompt

At this prompt you can press a key to perform navigation or search for a string. The key you press can be considered one of **man**'s (rather, the pager's) **internal commands**, and the character represented by the key often doesn't show up on the screen. Many UNIX utilities like **vi** and **mailx** also have their own internal commands. A set of internal commands used by **more** is listed in Table 3.3. We'll discuss only a few of them related to navigation and string search.

To quit the pager, and ultimately **man**, press **q**. You'll be returned to the shell's prompt.

FIGURE 2.2   *The man Page for* **wc** *(Solaris)*

```
User Commands                                                    wc(1)
NAME
     wc - display a count of lines, words and characters in a file
SYNOPSIS
     wc [ -c | -m  | -C ] [ -lw ] [ file ... ]
DESCRIPTION
     The wc utility  reads  one   or  more  input  files and, by default,
     writes the number of newline characters, words and bytes contained
     in  each input file to the standard output.


     The utility also writes a total count for all named  files, if more
     than one input file is specified.


     wc considers a word to be a non-zero-length string  of  characters
     delimited by white space (for example, SPACE, TAB ). See
     iswspace(3C) or isspace(3C).
OPTIONS
     The following options are supported:
     -c       Count bytes.
     -m       Count characters.
     -C       Same as -m.
     -l       Count lines.
     -w       Count words delimited by white space characters or new line
              characters. Delimiting  characters are Extended Unix Code (EUC)
              characters from any code  set  defined by iswspace().
     If  no option is specified the default is -lwc (count  lines, words,
     and  bytes.)
OPERANDS
     The following operand is supported:
     file  A path name of an input file. If no file operands  are
           specified, the standard input will be used.
USAGE
     See largefile(5) for the description of the behavior of wc when
     encountering files greater than or equal to 2 Gbyte (2 **31 bytes).
EXIT STATUS
     The following exit values are returned:
     0    Successful completion.
     >0   An error occurred.
SEE ALSO
     cksum(1),          isspace(3C),       iswalpha(3C),     iswspace(3C),
     setlocale(3C),     attributes(5),     environ(5),       largefile(5)
```

2.4.1   Navigation and Search

The navigation commands are numerous and often vary across UNIX implementations. For the time being, you should know these two commands which should work on all systems:

f or spacebar—Advances by one screen.
b—Moves back one screen.

The man documentation is sometimes quite extensive, and the search facility lets you locate a page containing a keyword quite easily. For example, you can call up the page containing the word clobber by following the / (frontslash) with the term:

/clobber*[Enter]*

The / and search string show up on the screen this time, and when you press *[Enter],* you are taken to the page containing clobber. If that's not the page you are looking for, you can repeat the search by pressing **n.** Some pager versions even highlight the search term in reverse video.

2.4.2   Further Help with man -k and man -f

POSIX requires **man** to support only one option (-k). Most UNIX systems also offer the **apropos** command that emulates **man -k**. When used with this option, **man** searches the NAME section of all man pages that contain the keyword. To know more about the cron facility, use

```
$ man -k cron
cron          cron (1m)       - clock daemon
crontab       crontab (1)     - user crontab file
queuedefs     queuedefs (4)   - queue description file for at, batch, and cron
```

cron is the UNIX scheduler that takes instructions from a crontab file, and to know more about it (Chapter 8), you need to look up the man pages of **cron** and **crontab**. Note that **cron** and **crontab** are documented in Sections 1m and 1 respectively on this Solaris system.

The -f option simply displays a one-line header from the NAME section. The **whatis** command emulates **man -f**. This is what **grep** does:

```
$ man -f grep
grep              grep (1)                   - search a file for a pattern
```

We use **grep** throughout this book for handling most pattern search issues. If this is the command you need, you can use **man grep** to learn that a pattern can match multiple strings.

2.5   The man **Documentation**

Vendors organize the man documentation differently, but in general you could see eight sections of the UNIX manual (Table 2.1). Later enhancements have added subsections (like 1C, 1M, 3N, etc.), but we'll ignore them in this text. You can see from the table that

TABLE 2.1   *Organization of the man Documentation*

Section	Subject (Solaris)	Subject (Linux)
1	User programs	User programs
2	Kernel's system calls	Kernel's system calls
3	Library functions	Library functions
4	Administrative file formats	Special files (in /dev)
5	Miscellaneous	Administrative file formats
6	Games	Games
7	Special files (in /dev)	Macro packages and conventions
8	Administration commands	Administration commands

the documentation is not restricted to commands; important system files used by these commands and system calls also have separate man pages.

Most of the commands discussed in this text are available in Section 1, and **man** searches the manuals starting from Section 1. If it locates a command in one section, it won't continue the search even if the command also occurs in another section. When a keyword is found in multiple sections, you should use the section number additionally as an argument. Depending on the UNIX flavor you are using, you may also need to prefix the -s option to the section number:

```
man 4 passwd                                    passwd also occurs in Section 4
man -s4 passwd                                     Solaris uses the -s option
```

This displays the documentation for a configuration file named /etc/passwd from Section 4. There's also an entry for **passwd** in Section 1, but if we had used **man passwd** (without the section number), **man** would have looked up Section 1 only and wouldn't have looked at Section 4 at all.

If you are using the X Window system, then you can use the **xman** graphic client to view man pages. Simply execute the command in any terminal window.

Note

There are two chapters in this text that feature the important system calls and some standard library functions. Sections 2 and 3 of the man documentation provide detailed documentation on their usage. To look up the **read** system call, you'll have to use **man 2 read** or **man -s2 read**.

2.5.1   Understanding a man Page

A man page is divided into a number of compulsory and optional sections. Every command doesn't have all sections, but the first three (NAME, SYNOPSIS, and DESCRIPTION) are generally seen in all man pages. NAME presents a one-line introduction to the command. SYNOPSIS shows the syntax used by the command, and DESCRIPTION (often the largest section) provides a detailed description.

The SYNOPSIS Section is the one that we need to examine closely, and we'll do that with reference to the man page of the **wc** command shown in Fig. 2.2. Here you'll find the syntax—the options and arguments used with the command. The SYNOPSIS follows certain conventions and rules which every user must understand:

- If a command argument is enclosed in rectangular brackets, then it is optional; otherwise, the argument is required. The **wc** man page shows all its arguments enclosed in three such groups. This means that **wc** can be used without arguments.
- The ellipsis (a set of three dots) implies that there can be more instances of the preceding word. The expression [file ...] signifies that **wc** can be used with more than one filename as argument.
- If you find a | (pipe) character in any of these areas, it means that only one of the options shown on either side of the pipe can be used. Here, only one of the options, -c, -m, and -C, can be used.

All options used by the command are listed in the OPTIONS section. Often, difficult options are supported by suitable examples. There's a separate section named EXIT STATUS which lists possible error conditions and their numeric representation. You need to understand the significance of these numbers when writing shell scripts and C programs in order to determine the actual cause of termination of a program.

2.5.2 Using man to Understand man

Since **man** is also a UNIX command like **ls** or **cat**, you'll probably first like to know how **man** itself is used. Use the same command to view its own documentation:

```
man man
```
Viewing man pages with man

From this man page you'll know that you can choose your pager too. The variable, PAGER, controls the pager **man** uses, and if you set it to less, then **man** will use **less** as its pager. This is how you set PAGER at the command prompt before you invoke **man**:

```
PAGER=less ; export PAGER
man wc
```
Set this shell variable and export it
before you run man

To evaluate the value of PAGER, use the command **echo $PAGER**. This setting is valid only for the current session. In later chapters, you'll understand the significance of the **export** statement and also learn to make this setting permanent so that its assigned value remains valid for all sessions.

Note

On some systems, **echo $PAGER** may not show you any value at all, in which case **man** is using a default pager. Some systems set this variable in the file /etc/default/man instead.

There can be more headers but we have covered the major ones. All said and done, commands having one or two man pages are generally easy to use, but not the ones that have tens of pages. **man** is more of a reference than a tutorial, and the manuals are good reading material only after you have sufficiently mastered the system.

Linux

info **and** --help**: Two Important Help Resources**

man pages are read in a linear manner (from beginning to end) and have obvious limitations. Linux offers two additional help facilities—the **info** command and the --help option. Most commands support the --help option though not all commands have info pages.

info info is GNU's info reader for browsing Texinfo documentation. Invoke it with a command (say, **info grep**) to see the documentation organized in *nodes* (Fig. 2.3). Each node is marked with an asterisk at the beginning of the line. As in Web pages, there are multiple levels here, and the deeper you descend a level the more detailed the treatment becomes.

Use the *[Tab]* key to move to a node and hit *[Enter]*. You'll see the current page replaced with another. **info** is a little difficult to use at first, but if you remember these four navigation commands initially, you should feel fairly comfortable:

n   Visits the next node
p   Visits the previous node
u   Returns to the previous level where *[Enter]* was pressed
l   Moves to the previously visited node

Within a page, you can use the *[PageUp]* and *[PageDown]* (or spacebar) keys in the normal way for paging. You should be careful about using other keys because you may get stuck in the middle. In case that happens and these keys don't take you to the desired point, just quit with **q** and reenter **info**. When in doubt, press **h** to see the complete list of key sequences.

--help   Some commands have just too many options, and sometimes a quick lookup facility is what you need. The --help option displays a compact listing of all options. Here's an extract from the **find** --help output that shows its options in a compact manner:

```
tests    (N can be +N or -N or N): -amin N -anewer FILE -atime N -cmin N
         -cnewer FILE -ctime N -empty -false -fstype TYPE -gid N -group NAME
         -ilname PATTERN -iname PATTERN -inum N -ipath PATTERN -iregex PATTERN
         -links N -lname PATTERN -mmin N -mtime N -name PATTERN -newer FILE
         -nouser -nogroup -path PATTERN -perm [+-]MODE -regex PATTERN
         -size N[bckw] -true -type [bcdpfls] -uid N -used N -user NAME
actions: -exec COMMAND ; -fprint FILE -fprint0 FILE -fprintf FILE FORMAT
         -ok COMMAND ; -print -print0 -printf FORMAT -prune -ls
```

A Linux command invariably offers far more options than its UNIX counterpart. You'll find this lookup facility quite useful when you know the usage of the options, but can't recollect the one you require.

FIGURE 2.3   *The info Page of* **grep**

```
File: grep.info,  Node: Top,  Next: Introduction,  Up: (dir)

Grep
****

    `grep' searches for lines matching a pattern.

    This document was produced for version 2.5.1 of GNU `grep'.

* Menu:

* Introduction::        Introduction.
* Invoking::            Invoking `grep'; description of options.
* Diagnostics::         Exit status returned by 'grep'.
* Grep Programs::       `grep' programs.
* Regular Expressions:: Regular Expressions.
* Usage::               Examples.
* Reporting Bugs::      Reporting Bugs.
* Copying::             License terms.
* Concept Index::       A menu with all the topics in this manual.
* Index::               A menu with all `grep' commands
                            and command-line options.
--zz-Info: (grep.info.gz)Top, 23 lines --Top-- Subfile: grep.info-1.gz----------
Welcome to Info version 4.2. Type C-h for help, m for menu item.
```

In the remainder of this chapter, we'll examine a few general-purpose utilities that you need to be familiar with. Many of these utilities report on the state of the system and form important ingredients in shell programming.

2.6   echo: **Displaying Messages**

We used the **echo** command in Section 1.6.3 to save some data in a file. The command is often used in shell scripts to display diagnostic messages on your terminal or to issue prompts for taking user input:

```
$ echo "Filename not entered"                          Shell version of echo used here
Filename not entered
```

echo is often used to evaluate shell variables. This is how you find out the shell you are using:

```
$ echo $SHELL                                          Variables are evaluated with $
/usr/bin/ksh                                                         The Korn shell
```

UNIX fragmentation comes to light when you attempt to use **echo** with **escape sequences**. The AT&T version of **echo** supports escape sequences, but not BSD. An escape sequence begins with a \ and is followed by a single character or a zero-prefixed number. For instance, \c is an escape sequence. When it is placed at the end of a string that's used with **echo,** the cursor is placed at the end of the output string rather than on the next line:

```
$ echo "Enter filename: \c"
Enter filename: $ _                                   Prompt and cursor in same line
```

This is how we use **echo** in a shell script to accept input from the terminal. Like \c, there are other escape sequences (Table 2.2). Here are two commonly used ones:

\t—A tab which pushes text to the right by eight character positions.
\n—A newline which creates the effect of pressing *[Enter]*.

There's another type of escape sequence that uses ASCII octal values (numbers that use the base 8 contrasted with the standard decimal system, which uses 10). **echo** interprets a number as octal when it is preceded by \0. For instance, *[Ctrl-g]* (the BELL character) has the octal value 07. This is how you can use **echo** to sound a beep:

```
$ echo "\07"                                                    \007 will also do
..... beep heard .....
```

This is our first encounter with octal values as command arguments. Later, we'll see that the **tr**, **awk**, and **perl** commands also use octal values. For reasons that are covered later, it helps to enclose the arguments within quotes.

⚠️
Caution

echo escape sequences are a feature of System V. BSD doesn't recognize them, but it supports the -n option as an alternative to the \c sequence:

```
echo "Enter filename: \c"                                          System V
echo -n "Enter filename: "                                              BSD
```

Even though we don't use the disk version of **echo** nowadays, the bad news is that the shells also respond in different ways to these escape sequences. Rather than go into these details, a word of caution from POSIX would be appropriate: use **printf**.

T A B L E 2.2 *Escape Sequences Used by* **echo** *and* **printf**

Escape Sequence	Significance
\a	Bell
\c	No newline (cursor in same line)
\f	Formfeed
\n	Newline
\r	Carriage return
\t	Tab
\\	Backslash
\0n	ASCII character represented by the octal value n, where n can't exceed 377 (decimal value 255)

BASH

Bash, the standard shell used in Linux, interprets the escape sequences properly only when **echo** is used with the -e option:

```
echo -e "Enter filename: \c"
```

We'll be using these escape sequences extensively in this text, so if you are a Bash user (which most Linux users are), you must commit this option to memory.

2.7   printf: **Alternative to** echo

Unless you have to maintain a lot of legacy code that uses **echo**, choose **printf**. Like **echo**, it exists as an external command, but it's only Bash that has **printf** built-in. **printf** also recognizes escape sequences, except that unlike **echo**, you must use \n to explicitly specify a newline:

```
$ printf "No filename entered\n"                          \n not required in echo
No filename entered
```

Like its namesake in the C language, **printf** also uses *format specifiers*. This is how you display the shell you are using:

```
$ printf "My current shell is %s\n" $SHELL
My current shell is /usr/bin/ksh
```

The %s format used for printing strings acts as a placeholder for the value of $SHELL. **printf** here replaces %s with the value of $SHELL. C language users should note the absence of the parentheses and the comma between the format specifier and its matching arguments.

2.8   script: **Recording Your Session**

This command, virtually unknown to many UNIX users, lets you "record" your login session in a file. **script** is not included in POSIX, but you'll find it useful to store in a file all commands that you invoke, their output and error messages. You can later view the file. If you are doing some important work and wish to keep a log of all your activities, then you should invoke **script** immediately after you log in:

```
$ script
Script started, file is typescript
$ _                                                          Another shell!
```

The prompt returns, and all of your keystrokes (including the one used to backspace) that you now enter here get recorded in the file typescript. After your recording is over, you can terminate the session with **exit**:

```
$ exit                                                       Or use [Ctrl-d]
Script done, file is typescript
$ _                                                          Back to login shell
```

You can now view this file with the **cat** command. **script** overwrites any previous typescript that may exist. If you want to append to it, look up the man page to locate the -a option.

The file created by **script** contains the control character, *[Ctrl-m]*, at the end of every line. The **cat** command won't show this character, but on your **vi** editor this character appears as ^M. Later, you should be able to view it (with **cat -v**) and remove it both interactively (with **vi**) and noninteractively (with **sed**).

2.9 Using Email with mailx

You are probably well-versed in email semantics already. Even if you are totally comfortable using a GUI program like Netscape, Mozilla, or Outlook Express, it's necessary to know one command-line tool that can be used noninteractively in shell scripts: **mailx**, the only mail utility that POSIX requires all UNIX systems to support. Using the shell's redirection features (like the < and |) and **mailx** options, we should be able to generate mail headers and message body on the fly.

An email message is identified by a sender and a recipient both of which appear as headers in the message. We'll save the discussions on these headers for Chapter 14. Sender and recipient can be on the same or different machines or *hosts*. Accordingly, an email address can take the following forms:

henry   *User henry on same host*
henry@saturn   *On a different host*
henry@heavens.com   *On the Internet*

Received mail is deposited in a **mailbox**. This is simply a text file *that may contain binary attachments in encoded form*. When a message has been viewed, it moves from the mailbox to the **mbox**. In mail jargon, these files are often referred to as *folders*.

Note

GUI programs don't make use of the default mailbox but instead maintain it, along with other folders that store sent and unsent mail, in a separate directory. Only command-line tools make use of the mail handling features offered by the UNIX system.

2.9.1 Sending Mail

mailx works in the sending or receiving mode. When you invoke it with the email address of the recipient as argument, the command works in the interactive sending mode. Key in the subject, and then the message body. Finally press *[Ctrl-d]* (or a solitary .) to terminate your input. This is how henry sends mail to charlie:

```
$ mailx charlie                                    charlie is on same host
Subject: New System
The new system will start functioning next month.
Convert your files by next week - henry
[Ctrl-d]                                    Some systems require a dot here
EOT                                         System indicates end of text
```

The sent message lands in charlie's mailbox. If this interactive mode were the only means of using **mailx** for sending mail, you'd be better off using Netscape or Outlook Express. What makes **mailx** a "true" UNIX program is that it can be used noninteractively as well:

```
mailx -s "New System" charlie < message.txt
```

The -s option takes care of the subject, and the message body is obtained from the file message.txt using a shell feature called *redirection*. No GUI mail program can be used in this way.

Though POSIX doesn't require **mailx** to copy messages to other people, most versions support the -c (carbon copy) and -b (blind carbon copy) options. Multiple recipients should be enclosed in quotes:

```
mailx -s "New System" -c "jpm,sumit" -b andrew charlie < message.txt
```

This command sends a message to charlie with carbon copies to jpm and sumit, and a blind carbon copy to andrew.

Note

What makes this method of invocation remarkable is that the subject and recipients need not be known in advance, but can be obtained from shell variables. The message body could even come from the output of another program. You can use this feature to design automated mailing lists.

2.9.2 Receiving Mail

Incoming mail is appended to the mailbox, a text file named after the user-id of the recipient. The mailbox is located in the directory /var/mail (/var/spool/mail in Linux). charlie's mail is appended to /var/mail/charlie. We are often prompted to read the mailbox by this message from the shell:

```
You have new mail in /var/mail/charlie
```

charlie now has to invoke the **mailx** command in the receiving mode (without using an argument) to see the mailbox. The system first displays the headers and some credentials of all incoming mail *that's still held in the mailbox*:

```
$ mailx
mailx version 5.0 Wed Jan  5 16:00:40 PST 2000  Type ? for help.
"/var/mail/charlie": 5 messages 2 new 5 unread
 U 1 andrew@heavens.com   Fri Apr  3 16:38   19/567  "sweet dreams"
 U 2 MAILER-DAEMON@heaven  Sat Apr  4 16:33   69/2350  "Warning: could not se"
 U 3 MAILER-DAEMON@heaven  Thu Apr  9 08:31   63/2066  "Returned mail: Cannot"
 N 4 henry@heavens.com    Thu Apr 30 10:02   17/515  "Away from work"
>N 5 henry@heavens.com    Thu Apr 30 10:39   69/1872  "New System"
?                                                       The ? prompt
```

The pointer (>) is positioned on the fifth message; we call this the *current message*. charlie can either press *[Enter]* or the number of the message showed in the second column to view the message body. The following message is typically seen on charlie's screen:

```
Message 5:
>From henry@heavens.com  Thu Apr 30 10:39:14 2000
Date: Tue, 13 Jan 2003 10:06:13 +0530
From: "henry blofeld" <henry@heavens.com>
To: charlie@saturn.heavens.com
Subject: New System

The new system will start functioning next month.
Convert your files by next week - henry
```

? **q**   *Quitting* mailx *with* q
```
Saved 1 message in /home/charlie/mbox
$ _
```

As mentioned before, after a message has been seen by the recipient, it moves from the mailbox to the mbox. This is generally the file named mbox in the user's home directory (the directory where the user is placed upon logging in).

2.9.3 mailx Internal Commands

Internal commands are not the sole preserve of the shell. **mailx** also has its own internal commands (Table 2.3) that you can enter at the ? prompt. You can see the next message (if there is one) using the concept of *relative addressing*. Enter a + to see the next message or a - to display the previous one. A message can also be accessed by its number:

3   *Shows message number 3*

T A B L E 2.3   *Internal Commands used by* **mailx**

Command	Action
+	Prints next message
-	Prints previous message
N	Prints message numbered N
h	Prints headers of all messages
d N	Deletes message N (The current message if N is not specified)
u N	Undeletes message N (The current message if N is not specified)
s flname	Saves current message with headers in flname (mbox if flname is not specified)
w flname	Saves current message without headers in flname (mbox if flname is not specified)
m user	Forwards mail to user
r N	Replies to sender of message N (The current message if N is not specified)
q	Quits mailx
! cmd	Runs UNIX command cmd

Replying to mail   charlie can reply to a message by using the **r** (reply) command, which switches **mailx** to the sending mode. Every mail program has a mechanism of deducing the sender's details, and, consequently, the **r** command is usually not used with an address:

```
? r
To: henry@heavens.com                          Sender's address automatically inserted
Subject: Re: File Conversion
I am already through.
[Ctrl-d]
EOT
```

Saving Messages   Generally all mail commands act on the current message by default. With the **w** command, you can save one or more messages in separate files rather than the default mbox:

```
w note3                                  Appends current message to note3
w 1 2 3 note3                            Appends first three messages to note3
```

You can later view these messages with their headers using **mailx -f note3**.

Deleting Mail   To delete a file from the mailbox, use the **d** (delete) command. It actually *marks* mail for deletion; the mail actually gets deleted only after quitting **mailx**.

2.10   passwd: **Changing Your Password**

The remaining commands in this chapter relate to our UNIX system, and we'll first take up the **passwd** command that changes the user's password. If your account has a password that is already known to others, you should change it immediately:

```
$ passwd
passwd: Changing password for romeo
Enter login password: *******                        Asks for old password
New password: ********                              New password to be
Re-enter new password: ********                            entered twice
passwd (SYSTEM): passwd successfully changed for romeo
```

passwd changes the password of the user running the command. If everything goes smoothly, the new password is *encrypted* (scrambled) by the system and stored in the file /etc/shadow (/etc/passwd on older systems). This file is used by the system for authentication every time you log in.

Many systems conduct certain checks on the password string to ensure that you don't choose easy-to-remember passwords. Systems often insist on a minimum length or a mix of letters and numerals. Contrary to popular belief, it is safer to note the password down rather than try to remember it—and then forget it. The author employs the technique of choosing the name of one of his childhood heroes and then inserting the digits of the year of birth using a predetermined algorithm. If you adopt this approach, you need to note down only the algorithm and the name of the hero. It's not difficult to obtain the year of birth of our heroes.

Today, many users in a network connect to a UNIX machine using an SSH program where the password is not used for authentication. Rather, it's Public Key-based cryptography that authenticates users (and is discussed in Section 14.8). The `/etc/passwd` file is used only when users connect through the console, a dumb terminal, or the **telnet** command.

Note

A nonprivileged user like you can change only your own password, but the system administrator (the privileged user) uses the same command to change any user's password. This is discussed in Chapter 19.

2.11   uname: **Your Machine's Name and Operating System**

The **uname** command displays certain features of the operating system running on your machine. By default, it simply displays the name of the operating system:

```
$ uname
SunOS                                                    Linux shows Linux
```

This is the operating system used by Sun Solaris. Using suitable options, you can display certain key features of the operating system and also the name of the machine. The output depends on the system you are using.

The Current Release (-r)   A UNIX command often varies across versions so much so that you'll need to use the -r option to find out the version of your operating system:

```
$ uname -r
5.8                                                        This is SunOS 5.8
```

This is a machine running SunOS 5.8, the operating system used by the Solaris 8 environment. If a command doesn't work properly, it could either belong to a different "implementation" (could be BSD) or a different "release" (may be 4.0, i.e., System V Release 4 of AT&T).

The Machine Name (-n)   Every machine has a name (the hostname), and if your network is connected to the Internet, this hostname is a component of your machine's *domain name*. The -n option tells you the hostname:

```
$ uname -n
mercury.heavens.com                                   The complete domain name
```

Here, *mercury* is the hostname and *heavens.com* is the domain name. Many UNIX networking utilities use the hostname as an argument. To copy files from a remote machine named *mercury,* you have to run **ftp mercury**.

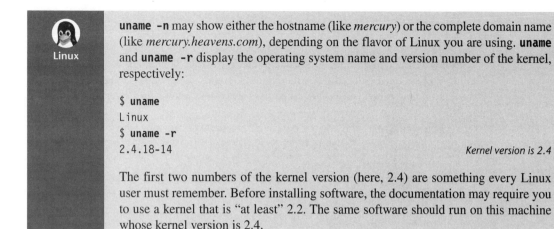

uname -n may show either the hostname (like *mercury*) or the complete domain name (like *mercury.heavens.com*), depending on the flavor of Linux you are using. **uname** and **uname -r** display the operating system name and version number of the kernel, respectively:

```
$ uname
Linux
$ uname -r
2.4.18-14
```
Kernel version is 2.4

The first two numbers of the kernel version (here, 2.4) are something every Linux user must remember. Before installing software, the documentation may require you to use a kernel that is "at least" 2.2. The same software should run on this machine whose kernel version is 2.4.

2.12 who: **Know the Users**

Let's take a look at two commands that we introduced in the hands-on session of Chapter 1. We saw the users logged in with the **who** command. Let's now examine the other columns of the command's output:

```
$ who
root       console    Aug  1  07:51   (:0)
romeo      pts/10     Aug  1  07:56   (pc123.heavens.com)
juliet     pts/6      Aug  1  02:10   (pc125.heavens.com)
project    pts/8      Aug  1  02:16   (pc125.heavens.com)
andrew     pts/14     Aug  1  08:36   (mercury.heavens.com)
```

The first column shows the user-ids of the five users currently working on the system. The second column shows the filenames of the devices associated with the respective terminals. romeo's terminal has the name pts/10 (a file named 10 in the pts directory). The third, fourth, and fifth columns show the date and time of logging in. The last column shows the hostname from where the user logged in. Users can log in remotely to a UNIX system, and all users here except root have logged in remotely from four different hosts.

One of the users shown in the first column is obviously the user who invoked the **who** command. To know that specifically, use the arguments am and i with **who**:

```
$ who am i
romeo      pts/10     Aug  1 07:56   (pc123.heavens.com)
```

UNIX provides a number of tools (called *filters*) to extract data from command output for further processing. For instance, you can use the **cut** command to take out the first column from the **who** output and then use this list with **mailx** to send a message to these users. The ability to combine commands to perform tasks that are not possible to achieve using a single command is what makes UNIX so different from other operating systems. We'll be often combining commands in this text.

2.13   date: **Displaying the System Date**

The UNIX system maintains an internal clock meant to run perpetually. When the system is shut down, a battery backup keeps the clock ticking. This clock actually stores the number of seconds elapsed since the **Epoch**: January 1, 1970. A 32-bit counter stores these seconds (except on 64-bit machines), and the counter will overflow sometime in 2038.

You can display the current date with the **date** command, which shows the date and time to the nearest second:

```
$ date
Mon Aug 11 17:04:30 GMT 2003
```

The command can also be used with suitable +-prefixed format specifiers as arguments. For instance, you can print only the month, using the format +%m:

```
$ date +%m
08
```

or the month name:

```
$ date +%h
Aug
```

or you can combine them in one command:

```
$ date +"%h %m"
Aug 08
```

When you use multiple format specifiers, you must enclose them within quotes (single or double) and use a single + symbol as a prefix. Here's a useful list of the other format specifiers:

d—The day of the month (1 to 31).
y—The last two digits of the year.
H, M, and S—The hour, minute, and second, respectively.
D—The date in the format *mm/dd/yy*.
T—The time in the format *hh:mm:ss*.

Note

You can't change the date as an ordinary user, but the system administrator uses the same command with a different syntax to set the system date! This is discussed in Chapter 19.

2.14   stty: **When Things Go Wrong**

Different terminals have different characteristics, and your terminal may not behave in the way you expect it to. Sometimes you may want to change the settings before you run a program. The **stty** command changes terminal settings but also displays them when used with the -a option:

```
$ stty -a
speed 38400 baud; rows = 24; columns = 80; ypixels = 0; xpixels = 0;
intr = ^c; quit = ^\; erase = ^?; kill = ^u;
eof = ^d; eol = <undef>; eol2 = <undef>; swtch = <undef>;
start = ^q; stop = ^s; susp = ^z; dsusp = ^y;
isig icanon -xcase echo echoe echok -echonl -noflsh
-tostop echoctl -echoprt echoke -defecho -flusho -pendin iexten
```

stty shows the settings of several *keywords* in this trimmed output. The first line shows 38,400 as the baud rate (the speed) of the terminal. The other keywords take two forms:

- *keyword* = *value*
- *keyword* or *-keyword*. The - prefix implies that the option is turned off.

Let's now understand the significance of some of these keywords and then use **stty** to change the settings.

2.14.1 Changing the Settings

Interrupting a Command (intr)   Sometimes you might want to interrupt a program before it completes. The **stty** output shows intr as the **interrupt** key, which here is set to ^c (a caret and c signifying *[Ctrl-c]*). Pressing this key on this machine should terminate a program. You can define a different key for this function:

```
stty intr DEL                                          The [Delete] key
```

To revert to the original setting, use **stty \^c**. The \ is often used in UNIX to emphasize that the character following it needs to be interpreted differently. Here, it suggests that ^ needs to be understood as the control character.

Changing the End-of-File Key (eof)   When using **mailx**, you used *[Ctrl-d]* to terminate input. Many commands like **cat** and **wc** also use the **eof** or **end-of-file** character which **stty** understands as the keyword eof. The **stty** output shows eof set to ^d (*[Ctrl-d]*). You can change this setting also in the manner described previously.

Backspacing (erase)   Backspacing is controlled by the **erase** character, which is set to ^?, the key labeled *[Backspace]*. Sometimes backspacing may not work at all and instead produce a series of ^H characters every time you press the key:

```
$ password^H^H^H                                 [Backspace] pressed three times
```

This often happens when you log on to a remote machine whose terminal settings are different from your local one. Try using *[Ctrl-h]* or *[Delete]* or explicitly assign the *[Backspace]* key in this way:

```
stty erase [Backspace]                      Press the [Backspace] key after erase
```

Suspending a Job (susp)   Modern shells allow you to suspend a job and then resume it later. **stty** shows *[Ctrl-z]* as the **stop** character. When a command is running you can press this key, but do so only after you have read Section 8.11.

TABLE 2.4   **stty** *Settings and Keyboard Commands to Try When Things Go Wrong*

stty *Keyword*	*Typical Setting*	*Function*
erase	[Ctrl-h]	Erases text
interrupt	[Ctrl-c] or [Delete]	Interrupts a command
eof	[Ctrl-d]	Terminates input to a program that expects input from the keyboard
stop	[Ctrl-s]	Stops scrolling of display and locks keyboard
start	[Ctrl-q]	Resumes scrolling of display and unlocks keyboard
kill	[Ctrl-u]	Kills command line without executing it
quit	[Ctrl-\]	Kills running command but creates a core file containing the memory image of the program
susp	[Ctrl-z]	Suspends process and returns shell prompt; use **fg** to resume job
echo	-	Enables display to echo keyboard input (-echo to disable)
sane	-	Restores terminal to normal status

Entering a Password through a Shell Script (echo)   Shell programmers often manipulate echo to let shell programs accept passwords without displaying them on screen. Here it is on, but we can turn it off with **stty -echo**. You should turn it off after the entry is complete by using **stty echo**.

When Everything Else Fails (sane)   **stty** is also used to set the terminal characteristics to values that will work on most terminals. Use **stty sane** to restore sanity to the terminal.

These key functions are summarized in Table 2.4. Note that the default key sequences (like eof and interrupt) could be different on your system. In any case, you are advised against tampering with too many settings.

Tip   Keep these two keys in mind: [Ctrl-c], the interrupt key, used to interrupt a running program and [Ctrl-d], the eof key, used to signify the end of terminal input to a program that's expecting input from the terminal.

2.15   The X Window System

Finally, let's briefly examine an alternative to the command line interface. Every UNIX system supports a Graphic User Interface (GUI), which generically is known as the *X Window* system. Like the ubiquitous Microsoft Windows, X (i.e., X Window) displays every application in a separate window. It uses the mouse to invoke programs, display menus, select options, and handle cut-copy-paste operations. Because X uses a bit-mapped display (where every pixel on the screen is handled individually), Web browsers like Netscape, Mozilla, and Konqueror *must* run under X.

X was originally developed to work in a network, and Section 14.12 examines the networking features of X. But X also supports a host of applications that can be used in standalone mode. However, the use of X is strongly discouraged for handling tasks that are better handled by the command line. Alternatively, you can use this command line from a window running under X. This application is called the *terminal emulator,* which along with a file management program, is discussed next.

Unlike Windows, the look-and-feel of the X Window system has until recently varied widely across UNIX and Linux systems. Today, vendors have standardized on the *Common Desktop Environment* (CDE), and you could be using one. Linux doesn't offer the CDE; you may either be using GNOME or KDE there.

2.15.1 The Terminal Emulator

X supports a program called the **terminal emulator** which runs a shell in a window (Fig. 2.4). You can enter any UNIX command from the shell prompt of this window. UNIX commands use a character-based display, but you can also invoke any graphical X program from the emulator window. This is how you run Netscape:

```
netscape &                                    Run all X programs in the background with &
```

The earliest emulator program is **xterm**, but every UNIX system features a variety of them including **dtterm** that is offered by CDE. Every emulator features a menu and a scrollbar that allows you to recall previous commands and their output. The **exit** command that kills your login session on a character terminal kills the window and its associated shell here.

Almost every X application allows cut-copy-paste operations. To copy text from one window to another, first highlight the text with the left mouse button; *the text automatically gets copied to a buffer.* Now select the other window, click on the desired location, and then the middle button (or both buttons simultaneously when using a two-button mouse). The copied text is pasted on this window. Using this technique, you can re-execute a long command line on a different window or copy text from a Web page to your **vi** editor. Usually cut-copy-paste operations are also available as menu options.

FIGURE 2.4   *The* **dtterm** *Terminal Emulator Program*

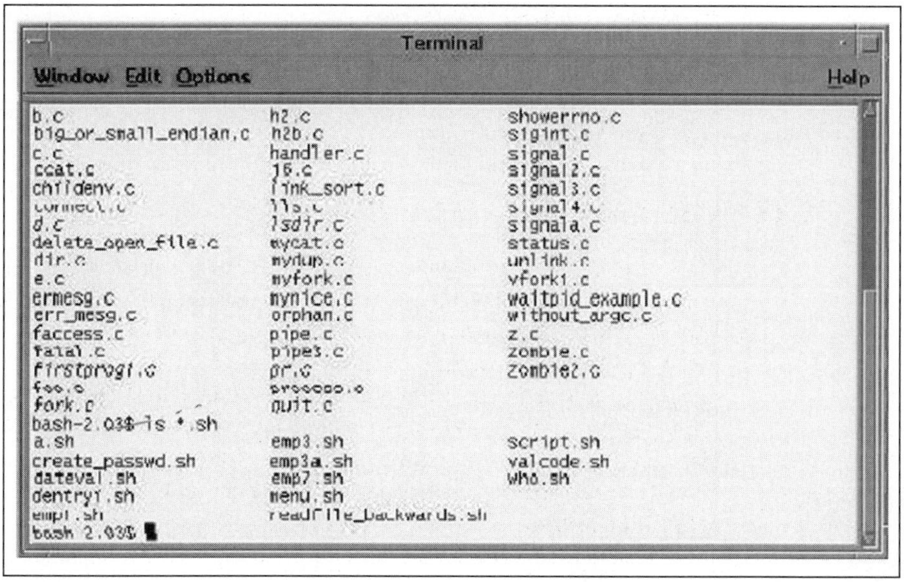

You can have several terminal emulators (apart from several programs) on your desktop, and you can invoke a separate application in each one of them. You can also switch from one application to another without quitting any of them.

Tip

If you have difficulty in copy-paste operations using the technique described above, you can use the window menu which also offers options to do the same work. Often, the keys are the same ones used in Microsoft Windows—*[Ctrl-c]* for copying and *[Ctrl-v]* for pasting.

2.15.2 The File Manager

We use files all the time, copying, moving, and deleting them several times a day. Every X implementation offers a file management program that can perform these tasks. A file manager can also be used to view file contents and execute programs. Windows offers a similar application—Windows Explorer. The file manager on the CDE is **dtfile**, which is shown in Fig. 2.5. Linux users may use Konqueror instead. However, your system may contain other file managers.

Using menu options, you can create and remove directories. Try creating some. To copy or move files from one directory to another, you need to work with two windows of the same program. Look up the menu option that splits a window. Every file is represented by an icon, and you select it by clicking it with the mouse. You can also select multiple files by pressing *[Ctrl]* and then clicking on each icon. To select all files, use the option offered by the menu; it often is *[Ctrl-a]*. You can now drag the files by keeping the left mouse button pressed and drop them to their new location by releasing the button. Files can thus be copied and moved in this way.

In Chapter 3, you'll use the **mkdir**, **rmdir**, **cp**, and **mv** commands for file and directory handling. You'll see how effortlessly you can work with groups of files and

FIGURE 2.5 *Two Views of the* **dtfile** *File Manager*

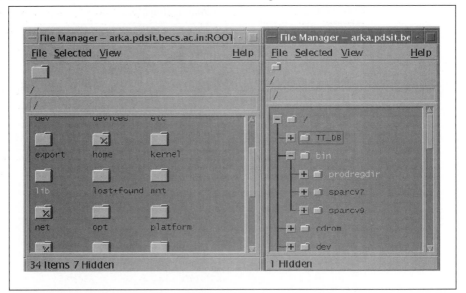

directories using these commands. However, it's good to know the X techniques now because that will help you appreciate the power of the UNIX command line interface later. The limitations of the X method of doing things will soon become apparent.

SUMMARY

UNIX commands are case-sensitive but are generally in lowercase. They need not have any specific extensions. Commands for general use are located in the directories /bin and /usr/bin. The shell variable, PATH, specifies the search list of directories for locating commands.

The shell treats a command either as *external* when it exists on disk or *internal* when it is built into the shell. Commands like **man** and **mailx** also have their own internal commands.

The *command line* comprises the command, and its *options* and *arguments*. Commands and arguments are separated by *whitespace*. Multiple commands can be delimited with a ;, and a command sequence can be split into multiple lines.

Use the **man** command to look up the documentation for a command, a configuration file, or a system call. Most commands are found in Section 1. You'll find system calls and library functions in Sections 2 and 3.

echo displays a message on the screen. It supports *escape sequences* (like \c and \007). The command has portability problems, the reason why **printf** should be used. **printf** also supports format specifiers (like %d).

script logs all user activities in a separate file named typescript.

A mail message is saved in a text file called *mailbox*. Mail is moved to the *mbox* after it is viewed. **mailx**, a command-line mail program, can be used interactively and also noninteractively from shell scripts.

date displays any component of the system date and time in a number of formats. **passwd** changes a user's password. The system administrator can change the system date and the password of any user.

uname reveals details of your machine's operating system (-r and -s). It also displays the hostname (-n) that is used by networking commands.

who displays the users working on the system.

stty displays and sets various terminal attributes. It defines the key that interrupts a program (intr), suspends a job (susp), and marks the end-of-file (eof). **stty sane** sets the terminal to some standard values.

The X Window System provides a Graphical User Interface (GUI) for users to run programs that involve graphics. X also provides several applications including a *terminal emulator* and a file management program.

SELF-TEST

2.1   Enter a : and press *[Enter]*. Next run **type** :. What do you conclude?

2.2   UNIX commands must be in lowercase and must not have extensions. True or false?

2.3   Name three UNIX commands whose names are more than five characters long.

2.4   Find out whether these commands are internal or external: echo, date, pwd, and ls.

2.5   If two commands with the same filename exist in two directories in PATH, how can they be executed?

2.6   How is the current directory indicated in PATH?

2.7   How many options are there in this command? ls -lut chap01 note3

2.8   If you find yourself using options preceded by two hyphens (like --all), which flavor of UNIX could you be using?

2.9   What is the name given to the command, and its options and arguments?

2.10   How do you find out the version number of your operating system?

2.11   Why are the directories /bin and /usr/bin usually found first in PATH?

2.12   What is *whitespace*? Explain the treatment the shell metes out to a command that contains a lot of whitespace.

2.13   Do you need to wait for a command to finish before entering the next one?

2.14   Why doesn't this command run in the way it is meant to?
       printf "Filename: %s\n", fname

2.15   What is a *pager*? Name the two standard pagers used by **man**.

2.16   You located the string crontab in a man page by searching with **/crontab***[Enter]*. How do you find out the other occurrences of this string in the page?

2.17   You don't know the name of the command that could do a job. What do you do?

2.18   How do you find out the users who are idling from the man documentation of **who**?

2.19   What is the difference between the *mailbox* and *mbox*?

2.20   The **passwd** command didn't prompt for the old password. When do you think that can happen? Where is the password stored?

2.21   Can you change the system date with the **date** command?

2.22   Enter the **uname** command without any arguments. What do you think the output represents?

2.23   How will you record your login session in the file foo?

2.24   Interpret the following output of **who am i:**

       romeo   pts/10   Aug 1 07:56   (pc123.heavens.com)

2.25   How do you determine the erase, kill, and eof characters on your system?

2.26   You suddenly find your keyboard is displaying uppercase letters even though your *[CapsLock]* key is set properly. What should you try?

EXERCISES

2.1   Enter a # before a command and press *[Enter]*. What do you see, and how do you think you can take advantage of the behavior?

2.2   Name three major differences between UNIX commands and Windows programs.

2.3   A program file named foo exists in the current directory, but when we try to execute it by entering foo, we see the message foo: command not found. Explain how that can happen.

2.4   If a command resides in a directory which is not in PATH, there are at least two ways you can still execute it. Explain.

2.5   Where are the commands used by the system administrator located?

2.6   You won't find the **cd** command either in /bin or /usr/bin. How is it executed then?

2.7   If you find the **echo** command in /bin, would you still call it an external command?

2.8   Is an option also an argument? How many arguments are there in this command? cat < foo > bar

2.9   Why shouldn't you have a filename beginning with a -?

2.10   Reduce the number of keystrokes to execute this command: tar -t -v -f /dev/fd0.

2.11   Look up the **tar** man page to find out whether the command **tar -cvfb 20 foo.tar *.c** is legitimate or not. Will the command work without the - symbol?

2.12   Both commands below try to open the file foo, but the error messages are a little different. What could be the reason?

```
$ cat foo
cat: foo: No such file or directory
$ cat < foo
bash: foo: No such file or directory
```

2.13   Invoke the commands **echo hello   dolly** and **echo "hello   dolly"** (three spaces between hello and dolly). Explain the difference in command behavior.

2.14   What does the secondary prompt look like, and when does it appear?

2.15   What do the | and the three dots in the SYNOPSIS section of these man pages indicate as shown below?

```
/usr/xpg4/bin/tail [ -f | -r ]
/usr/bin/ls [ -aAbcCdfFgilLmnopqrRstux1 ] [ file ... ]
```

2.16   If a command, filename, and a system call have the same name and are available in Sections 1, 5, and 2 respectively, how will you display the man pages of each one of them?

2.17   Your system doesn't have the **apropos** command. What will you do?

2.18   The command **echo "Filename: \c"** didn't place the cursor at the end of the line. How will you modify the command to behave correctly if your shell is (i) Bash, (ii) any other shell?

2.19   What is an *escape sequence*? Name three escape sequences used by the **echo** command, and explain the significance of each.

2.20   Use **printf** to find out the hex and octal values of 255.

2.21   Run **ps**, then the **script** command, and then run **ps** again. What do you notice?

2.22   In what way is the **mailx** command superior to a GUI program like Netscape or Mozilla?

2.23   Can you have the same user-id more than once in the **who** output?

2.24   Both your local and remote machines use identical versions of UNIX. How do you confirm whether you are logged in to a remote machine or not?

2.25   Which command does the nonprivileged user use to change the system date and time?

2.26   Display the current date in the form *dd*/*mm*/*yyyy*.

2.27   You need to accept a secret code through a shell script. What command will you run in the script to make sure that your keyboard input is not displayed? How do you then revert to the normal setting?

2.28   Explain why it is possible to key in the next command before the previous command has completed execution.

2.29   What will you do to ensure that *[Ctrl-c]* interrupts a program? Will it work the next time you log in?

## CHAPTER 3

The File System

U NIX looks at everything as a file, and any UNIX system has thousands of
files. For convenience, we make a distinction between ordinary files and
directories that house groups of files. In this chapter, we'll create directories, navigate the
file system, and list files in a directory. We'll also examine the structure of the standard
UNIX file system.

In addition, we'll copy, move, and delete files, and understand how these actions
affect the directory. Some commands exhibit *recursive* behavior by descending a directory
structure to perform some action. Because we frequently encounter Windows systems,
we need to be able to move files between UNIX and Windows systems. As Internet
users, we also need to handle compressed files that we download. However, we don't
tamper with the major file attributes in this chapter.

Objectives

- Understand the initial categorization of files into *ordinary, directory,* and *device.*
- Learn the hierarchical structure of the file system, and how UNIX organizes its own data.
- Understand the significance of the *home directory* and *current directory.*
- Create and remove directories with **mkdir** and **rmdir**.
- Navigate the file system with **cd** and **pwd**.
- Become aware of the significance of *absolute* and *relative* pathnames.
- List files with **ls**.
- Copy, rename, and delete files with **cp**, **mv**, and **rm**.
- View text files with **cat** and **more**.
- Count the number of lines, words, and characters with **wc**.
- Learn how UNIX handles printing and using **lp** and **lpr**.
- Display the nonprintable characters in a file with **od**.
- Convert between UNIX and DOS formats with **unix2dos** and **dos2unix**.
- Compress files with **gzip** and create *archives* comprising multiple files with **tar**.
- Perform both compressing and archiving with **zip**.

3.1 The File

The *file* is a container for storing information. As a first approximation, we can treat it
simply as a sequence of characters. UNIX doesn't impose any structure for the data held

in a file. It's for you to do that to suit your programs. A file doesn't contain an end-of-file (eof) mark, but that doesn't prevent the kernel from knowing when to stop reading the file. Neither the file's name nor its size is stored in the file. File attributes are kept in a separate area of the hard disk, not directly accessible to users, but only to the kernel.

The shell is a file and so is the kernel. UNIX treats directories and devices like the hard disk, CD-ROM, and printer as files as well. As an initial exercise, let's understand a file as being of three types:

- **Ordinary file**—Also known as a *regular file*. It contains only data as a stream of characters.
- **Directory file**—A folder containing the names of other files and subdirectories as well as a number associated with each name.
- **Device file**—This represents a device or peripheral. To read or write a device, you have to perform these operations on its associated file.

There are other types of files, but we'll stick to these three for the time being. We need to make this distinction between file types because the significance of a file's attributes often depends on its type. Execute permission for an ordinary file means something quite different from that for a directory. You can't directly put something into a directory file, and a device file isn't really a stream of characters. Some commands work with all file types, but some don't.

3.1.1   Ordinary (Regular) File

An **ordinary file** is the most common file type containing a stream of data. This type of file can be further divided into two types:

- Text file
- Binary file

A **text file** contains only printable characters. All C and Java program sources and shell and Perl scripts are text files. A text file contains *lines* where each line is terminated with the *linefeed* (LF) character, also known as *newline*. When you press *[Enter]* while inserting text in a text editor like **vi** or **emacs**, the LF character is appended to every line. You won't see this character normally, but there is a command (**od**) which can make it visible.

A **binary file**, on the other hand, contains both printable and nonprintable characters that cover the entire ASCII range (0 to 255). Most UNIX commands are binary files, and the object code and executables that you produce by compiling C programs are also binary files. Picture, sound, and video files are binary files as well (with few exceptions). Displaying such files with a simple **cat** command produces unreadable output and may even disturb your terminal's settings.

3.1.2   Directory File

A **directory** contains no data as such, but maintains some details of the files and subdirectories that it contains. The UNIX file system is organized with a number of directories and subdirectories. You can also create them when you need to group a set of files pertaining to a specific application.

A directory file contains an entry for every file and subdirectory that it houses. If you have 20 files in a directory, there will be 20 entries in the directory. Each entry has two components:

- The filename.
- A unique identification number for the file or directory (called the *inode number*).

If a directory bar contains an entry for a file foo, we commonly (and loosely) say that the directory bar contains the file foo. Though we'll often be using the phrase "contains the file" rather than "contains the filename," you must not interpret the statement literally. A directory contains the filename and not the file's contents.

You can't, however, write a directory file, but you can perform some action that makes the kernel write a directory. For instance, when you create or remove a file, the kernel automatically updates its corresponding directory by adding or removing the entry (inode number and filename) associated with the file.

Note

The name of a file can only be found in its directory. The file itself doesn't contain its own name or any of its attributes like its size or time of last modification.

3.1.3   Device File

You'll also be printing files, installing software from CD-ROMs, or backing up files to tape. All of these activities are performed by reading or writing the file representing the device. For instance, when you restore files from tape, you read the file associated with the tape drive.

A **device file** is indeed special; it's not really a stream of characters. *In fact, it doesn't contain anything at all.* You'll soon learn that every file has some attributes that are not stored in the file but elsewhere on disk. The attributes of a device file entirely govern the operation of the device. The kernel identifies a device from its attributes and then uses them to operate the device.

Now that you understand the three types of files, you shouldn't feel baffled by subsequent use of the word in the book. The term *file* will often be used in this book to refer to any of these types, though it will mostly be used to mean an ordinary file. The real meaning of the term should be evident from its context.

3.2   What's in a (File)name?

On most UNIX systems today, a filename can consist of up to 255 characters. Files may or may not have extensions, and can consist of practically any ASCII character except the / and the NULL character (ASCII value 0). As a general rule you should avoid using unprintable characters in filenames. Further, since the shell has a special treatment for characters like $, `, ?, *, & among others, it is recommended that only the following characters be used in filenames:

- Alphabetic characters and numerals.
- The period (.), hyphen (-), and underscore (_).

UNIX imposes no restrictions on the extension, if any, that a file should have. A shell script doesn't need to have the `.sh` extension even though it helps in identification. But the C compiler expects `.c` program files and Java expects `.java`. DOS/Windows users must also keep these two points in mind:

- A filename can comprise multiple embedded dots; `a.b.c.d.e` is a perfectly valid filename. Moreover, a filename can also begin with a dot or end with one.
- UNIX is sensitive to case; `chap01`, `Chap01`, and `CHAP01` are three different filenames, and it's possible for them to coexist in the same directory.

Caution

Never use a `-` at the beginning of a filename. You'll have a tough time getting rid of it! A command that uses a filename as an argument often treats it as an option and reports errors. For instance, if you have a file named `-z`, **cat -z** won't display the file but interpret it as an invalid option.

3.3 The File System Hierarchy

All files in UNIX are organized in a hierarchical (an inverted tree) structure (Fig. 3.1). This hierarchy has a top called **root**, which serves as the reference point for all files. root is actually a directory that is represented by a / (frontslash). Don't mix up the root directory with the user-id root which is used by the system administrator to log in. In this text, we'll be using both the name "root" and the symbol / to represent the root directory.

FIGURE 3.1 *The UNIX File System Tree*

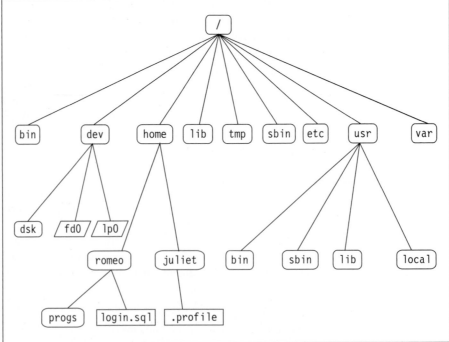

The root directory (/) has a number of subdirectories under it. These subdirectories have more subdirectories and other files under them. For instance, home is a directory under root, and romeo is yet another directory under home. login.sql is presumably an ordinary file under romeo. Every hierarchy contains parent-child relationships, and we can conveniently say that romeo is the parent of login.sql, home is the parent of romeo, and / (root) is the parent of home.

We can specify the relation login.sql has with root by a pathname: /home/romeo/login.sql. The first / represents the root directory and the remaining /s act as delimiters of the pathname components. This pathname is appropriately referred to as an **absolute pathname** because by using root as the ultimate reference point we can specify a file's location in an absolute manner. To view this file, we need to use **cat /home/romeo/login.sql**.

When you specify a file using absolute pathnames, you have a mechanism of identifying a file uniquely. No two files in a UNIX system can have identical absolute pathnames. You can have two files with the same name, but in different directories; their pathnames will also be different. Thus, the file /home/romeo/progs/fork.c can coexist with the file /home/romeo/safe/fork.c.

It's obvious that the parent is always a directory. home and romeo are both directories as they are both parents of at least one file or directory. An ordinary or device file like login.sql can't be the parent of another file.

Caution

We don't always use absolute pathnames in our command lines. When you access a file in the current directory or in its subdirectories, the first / should be dropped. The command **cat /progs/foo.c** is different from **cat progs/foo.c**.

3.4   The UNIX File System

Now let's take a cursory look at the structure of the UNIX file system. This structure had changed constantly over the years until AT&T proposed one in its SVR4 release. Though vendor implementations vary in detail, broadly the SVR4 structure has been adopted by most vendors. Fig. 3.1 shows a heavily trimmed structure.

For our initial comprehension, we'll stick to the directories presented below. It helps, from the administrative point of view at least, to view the entire file system as comprising two groups. The first group contains the files that are made available during system installation:

- /bin and /usr/bin   These are the directories where all the commonly used UNIX commands (binaries, hence the name bin) are found. Note that the PATH variable always shows these directories in its list.
- /sbin and /usr/sbin   If there's a command that you can't execute but the system administrator can, then it would probably be in one of these directories. You won't be able to execute most (some, you can) commands in these directories. Only the system administrator's PATH shows these directories.
- /etc   This directory contains the configuration files of the system. You can change a very important aspect of system functioning by editing a text file in this directory. Your login name and password are stored in files /etc/passwd and /etc/shadow.

- /dev   This directory contains all device files. These files don't occupy space on disk. There could be more subdirectories like pts, dsk, and rdsk in this directory.
- /lib and /usr/lib   These directories contain all library files in binary form. You need to link your C programs with files in these directories.
- /usr/include   This directory contains the standard header files used by C programs. The statement #include <stdio.h> used in most C programs refers to the file stdio.h in this directory.
- /usr/share/man   This is where the man pages are stored. There are separate subdirectories here (like man1, man2, etc.) that contain the pages for each section. For instance, the man page of **ls** can be found in /usr/share/man/man1, where the 1 in man1 represents Section 1 of the UNIX manual. These subdirectories may have different names on your system (like sman1, sman2, etc., in Solaris).

Users also work with their own files; they write programs, send and receive mail, and create temporary files. These files are available in the second group shown below:

- /tmp   The directories where users are allowed to create temporary files. These files are wiped away regularly by the system.
- /var   The variable part of the file system. Contains all your print jobs and your outgoing and incoming mail.
- /home   On many systems, users are housed here. romeo would have his home directory in /home/romeo. However, your system may use a different location for home directories.

On a busy system, it's in directories belonging to the second group that you could experience rapid depletion of available disk space. You'll learn later to house some of these directory structures on separate *file systems* so that depletion of space (and corruption) in one file system doesn't affect other file systems.

3.5   Using Absolute Pathnames with Commands

Absolute pathnames have universal application. They can be used both with the command name or its argument if it represents a filename. To illustrate the latter, we often use the command

cat /etc/passwd

to look up the passwd file in the directory /etc. The command will also work if we use the absolute pathname for **cat** as well:

/bin/cat /etc/passwd   *Assuming that* cat *exists in* /bin

We don't need to use the absolute pathname with **cat** because it is found in /bin or /usr/bin, both of which are standard components of PATH. But there are two possible situations when a command *must* be used with an absolute pathname:

- If **netscape** is available in /usr/local/bin, and this directory is not included in PATH, then we need to use **/usr/local/bin/netscape**.
- A command sometimes occurs in two directories both of whom could be in PATH. For instance, on Solaris systems two versions of **grep** are found in /usr/bin and /usr/xpg4/bin, and if /usr/bin occurs prior to /usr/xpg4/bin on our system:

  PATH=/bin:/usr/bin:/usr/xpg4/bin:.

  then we need to use **/usr/xpg4/bin/grep** to take advantage of the features of **grep** that conforms to the X/Open Portability Guide.

However, if you are frequently accessing programs in a certain directory, it often makes sense to include the directory itself in PATH. The technique of doing that is shown in Section 9.3.

3.6 The HOME Variable and ~: The Home Directory

When you log on to the system, say using romeo as the user-id, you are placed in your **home directory.** The shell variable HOME maintains the absolute pathname of this directory:

```
$ echo $HOME
/home/romeo
```

The system administrator sets the home directory for a user in /etc/passwd at the time of opening a user account. On many UNIX systems, home directories are maintained in /home, but your home directory could be located differently (say, in /export/home). It's often convenient to refer to a file foo located in the home directory as $HOME/foo.

Most shells (except Bourne) also use the ~ symbol to refer to the home directory. It is a little tricky to use because it can refer to any user's home directory and not just your own. For instance, you can also access $HOME/foo as ~/foo. If user juliet has the same file in her home directory, then romeo can access it as ~juliet/foo. The principle is this: A tilde followed by / (like ~/foo) refers to one's own home directory, but when followed by a string (~juliet) refers to the home directory of that user represented by the string.

Tip

In your shell scripts, never refer to files in your home directory or in its subdirectories by their absolute pathnames. Use $HOME/progs rather than /home/romeo/progs. This lets you move the scripts to a different system where the home directory is different, say, /u2/romeo, because $HOME evaluates differently. Since shell scripts are often written in the Bourne shell don't use the ~.

3.7 pwd and cd: Navigating the File System

Just as a file has a location, UNIX makes users believe that they too are placed in a specific directory. It also allows you to move around in the file system. At any instant of time, you are located in a directory known as the **current directory**. The **pwd** (**p**rint **w**orking **d**irectory) command displays the absolute pathname of this directory:

```
$ pwd
/home/romeo
```

Navigation is performed with the **cd** (**c**hange **d**irectory) command. This command can be used both with or without an argument. When used with one, it switches to the directory:

```
$ pwd
/home/romeo
$ cd progs                              Switches to the progs directory
$ pwd
/home/romeo/progs
```

The command **cd progs** means: "Change your subdirectory to progs under the current directory." We didn't use an absolute pathname here (cd /home/romeo/progs) because that would require more keystrokes.

　　　cd can also be used without an argument; it simply returns you to your home directory:

```
$ pwd
/home/romeo/progs
$ cd                                    cd used without arguments
$ pwd                                   reverts to the home directory
/home/romeo
```

Attention, DOS users! **cd** invoked without an argument doesn't display the current directory. We often use this form when we have moved away (to say, /home/juliet) and now want to make an immediate return:

```
$ cd /home/juliet
$ pwd
/home/juliet
$ cd                                    Returns to home directory
$ pwd
/home/romeo
```

The **cd** command can sometimes fail if you don't have proper permissions to access the directory. This doesn't normally happen unless you deliberately tamper with the directory's permissions. Navigation with the **cd** command using mostly absolute pathnames is illustrated in Fig. 3.2. Directory permissions are examined in Section 4.4.

Note

Unlike in DOS, when **cd** is invoked without arguments, it simply reverts to its home directory. It doesn't show you the current directory!

FIGURE 3.2 *Navigation with the* **cd** *Command*

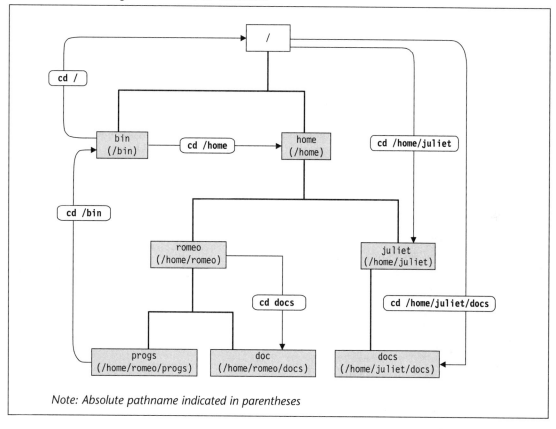

Note: Absolute pathname indicated in parentheses

3.8   Relative Pathnames (. and ..)

The command **cd progs** worked because progs resides in the current directory. This command will also work if progs contains a directory scripts under it:

```
cd progs/scripts
```
                                                              progs is in current directory

A file is looked for in the current directory if its pathname doesn't begin with a /. progs/scripts is not an absolute pathname because it doesn't begin with a /. UNIX allows the use of two symbols in pathnames that use the current and parent directory as the reference point:

- **.** (a single dot)   This represents the current directory.
- **..** (two dots)   This represents the parent directory.

Pathnames that begin with either of these symbols are known as **relative pathnames**. The command **cd progs** is really a synonym for **cd ./progs**, so progs/scripts is also a relative pathname. The usefulness of the . becomes obvious when we execute our own **cat** program that exists in the current directory. Since **cat** also exists in /bin, we need to use **./cat foo** to run our version of **cat** rather than the standard one.

Tip

Make sure that the name of a shell script or C program written by you doesn't conflict with one in the UNIX system by using either **type**, **which**, or **whereis** with the program name you have developed. If you find that a program of the same name exists in another directory in PATH, then you must run your own program with **./foo.**

Now let's turn our attention to the .. for framing relative pathnames. In a previous example we used **cd /home/juliet** when our current directory was /home/romeo. We could easily have used a relative pathname here:

```
$ pwd
/home/romeo
$ cd ../juliet                              Moves one level up and then down
$ pwd
/home/juliet
$ cd ..                                      Moves one level up
$ pwd
/home
```

Note the second invocation of **cd** uses .. as a single argument. We often use this compact method to ascend the hierarchy. You can also combine any number of such sets of .. separated by /s:

```
$ pwd
/home/romeo/pis
$ cd ../..                                    Moves two levels up
$ pwd
/home
```

The significance of the pathname components changes here; the .. on the right of the / is the parent of the .. on the left. Contrast this with **cd bar1/bar2** where bar1 is the parent of bar2. The use of relative pathnames using .. is depicted in Fig. 3.3.

The . and .. can also be gainfully used with commands that use a directory name as argument. Consider these sequences that use the **cp** command for copying a file:

```
cp /home/juliet/addressbook.sam .
cp addressbook.sam ..
```

In the first case, the file is copied to the current directory. The second command copies the same file from the current directory to the parent directory.

Note

Absolute pathnames can get very long if you are located a number of "generations" away from root. Whether you should use one depends solely on the relative number of keystrokes required. Even though the relative pathname required fewer key depressions in all these examples, that may not always be true.

FIGURE 3.3 *Navigation with Relative Pathnames*

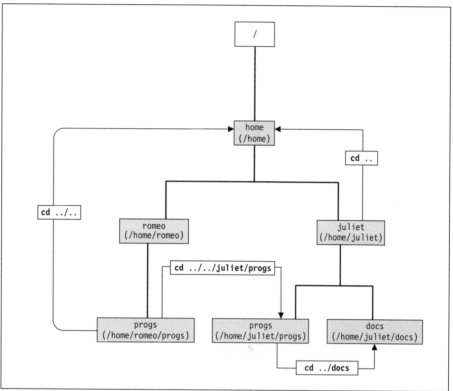

<hr>

3.9 mkdir: **Making Directories**

The **mkdir** (**make dir**ectory) command creates one or more directories. Let's use this command to create one or more directories in our home directory:

```
mkdir patch
mkdir patch dbs doc
```
Three directories created

The second example provides the first justification for using commands rather than GUI programs. Can you use a Windows Explorer-type program to create three directories as effortlessly as you do with **mkdir**? That's not all: a single invocation of **mkdir** can even create a directory tree. Here's how you create both a directory progs and two subdirectories, include and lib:

```
mkdir progs progs/include progs/lib
```
Creates the directory tree

Note that the sequence of arguments is important; first progs has to be created and then its subdirectories. Sometimes the system refuses to create a directory:

```
$ mkdir test
mkdir: Failed to make directory "test"; Permission denied
```

This can happen due to these reasons:

- The directory `test` may already exist.
- There may be an ordinary file by that name in the current directory.
- The permissions set for the current directory don't permit the creation of files and directories by the user. You'll most certainly get this message if you try to create a directory in `/bin`, `/etc`, or any other directory that houses the UNIX system's files.
- There may be no space left on the file system to permit creation of files and directories.

We'll take up file and directory permissions in Chapter 4.

3.10   `rmdir`: **Removing Directories**

`rmdir` (**rem**ove **dir**ectory) removes empty directories. We can reverse the previous actions of **mkdir** like this:

```
rmdir patch
rmdir patch dbs doc                                    Directories must be empty
```

We can also delete the directory tree that we created with **mkdir**. This time we must delete the subdirectories before the parent directory:

```
rmdir progs/lib progs/include progs               Removes the directory tree
```

A directory can also be removed with the **rm** command. If you are using **rmdir**, the following conditions need to be fulfilled:

- The directory is empty. However, the **rm** command can remove a nonempty directory.
- The user's current directory is above the directory.

Let's test these rules by trying to delete the directory tree `progs` that was created with **mkdir:**

```
$ rmdir progs
rmdir: `progs': Directory not empty              Contains include and lib
$ cd progs ; pwd
/home/romeo/progs
$ rmdir include lib                                        progs is now empty
$ rmdir .                                          but you can't delete it ...
rmdir: `.': Invalid argument
$ cd .. ; pwd                                      unless you move up and ...
/home/romeo
$ rmdir progs                                        run rmdir from here
$ _
```

The **mkdir** and **rmdir** commands work only in directories *owned* by the user. A user is the owner of her home directory, so she can use these commands in her home directory tree.

Unless other users are negligent, one user can't remove directories belonging to other users. The concept of ownership is discussed in Chapter 4.

How Files and Directories Are Created and Removed

A file (ordinary or directory) is associated with a name and a number, called the *inode number*. When a file or directory is created, an entry comprising these two parameters is made in the file's parent directory. The entry is removed when the file is deleted. Fig. 3.4 highlights the effect of **mkdir** and **rmdir** when creating and removing the subdirectory progs in /home/romeo.

FIGURE 3.4   *Directory Entry after* **mkdir** *and* **rmdir**

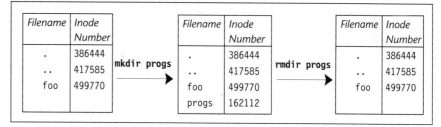

We'll discuss the significance of the entries **.** and **..** that you'll find in every directory. In this chapter and the next, we'll be monitoring this directory for changes that are caused by some of the file-handling commands.

3.11   ls: Listing Files

The **ls** (**list**) command lists files—rather their names. By default (i.e., when used without arguments), it reads the current directory for the list. The default output could show the filenames in multiple columns:

```
$ ls
08_packets.html      helpdir
TOC.sh               progs
calendar             usdsk06x
cptodos.sh           usdsk07x
dept.lst             usdsk08x
emp.lst
```

Viewed from top to bottom and then from left to right, the default output is ordered in **ASCII collating sequence** (numbers first, uppercase, and then lowercase). However, using certain options, the ordering sequence can be altered.

ls can also be used with one or more filenames to check whether a file is available:

```
$ ls calendar /bin/perl
calendar                                              calendar available
/bin/perl: No such file or directory                  but not /bin/perl
```

When the Argument Is a Directory The behavior of **ls** changes when its argument is a directory. Rather than simply display the name of the directory (like it did for calendar above), **ls** displays its contents:

```
$ ls helpdir
forms.hlp       graphics.hlp        reports.hlp
```

There are three files in the directory helpdir. But you can also make **ls** display simply the name of the directory without listing its contents. Use the -d option: **ls -d helpdir**.

ls can be configured to display filenames in different colors. Generally, executables and directories are shown in separate colors. Run the **alias** command, and make sure that **ls** is redefined on your system like this:

```
alias ls='ls --color=tty'
```

If you don't see this output, then simply run the **alias** command as shown above. **alias** is an internal command of the Bash shell, and it's likely that you would be using this shell if you are using Linux.

3.11.1 ls Options

In this chapter, we discuss a few **ls** options from Table 3.1. The other options are taken up in later chapters. We have already used one (-d) for suppressing listing of the contents of a directory. On many systems, **ls** displays filenames in multiple columns by default, but if that doesn't happen on your system, use the -x option.

TABLE 3.1 *Options to* ls

Option	Description
-x	Multicolumnar output
-F	Marks executables with *, directories with /, and symbolic links with @
-a	Shows all filenames beginning with a dot including . and ..
-R	Recursive list
-r	Sorts filenames in reverse order (ASCII collating sequence by default)
-l	Long listing in ASCII collating sequence showing seven attributes of a file *(4.1)*
-d *dirname*	Lists only *dirname* if *dirname* is a directory *(4.1.1)*
-t	Sorts filenames by last modification time *(4.10)*
-lt	Sorts listing by last modification time *(4.10)*
-u	Sorts filenames by last access time *(4.10)*
-lu	Sorts by ASCII collating sequence but listing shows last access time *(4.10)*
-lut	As above but sorted by last access time *(4.10)*
-i	Displays inode number *(4.6)*

Identifying Directories and Executables (-F) The default output of **ls** doesn't identify directories or binary executables, but the -F option does. Combining it with -x produces a multicolumnar output as well:

```
$ ls -Fx                                          Combining the -F and -x options
08_packets.html        TOC.sh*        calendar*         cptodos.sh*
dept.lst               emp.lst        helpdir/          progs/
usdsk06x               usdsk07x       usdsk08x          ux2nd06
```

Note the use of the * and / as type indicators. The * indicates that the file contains executable code and the / refers to a directory. There are two subdirectories here: helpdir and progs.

Showing Hidden Files Also (-a) Filenames beginning with a dot have a special place in the UNIX system. They are usually found in the home directory, but **ls** doesn't show them by default. Use the -a (all) option:

```
$ ls -axF
./                 ../             .cshrc            .emacs
.exrc              .kshrc          .netscape/        .profile
.sh_history        .shosts         .xinitrc          08_packets.html*
TOC.sh*            calendar*
  .....
```

There are several filenames here beginning with a dot. The file .profile contains a set of instructions that are performed when a user logs in. It is discussed later. Another file, .exrc, contains a sequence of startup instructions for the **vi** editor. We'll also examine the significance of .shosts when we discuss the secure shell.

　　The first two files (. and ..) are special directories. Recall that we used the same symbols in relative pathnames to represent the current and parent directories *(3.8)*. Whenever you create a subdirectory, these "invisible" directories are created automatically by the kernel. You can't remove them nor can you write into them. They help in holding the file system together.

Recursive Listing (-R) The -R (recursive) option lists all files and subdirectories in a directory tree. This traversal of the directory tree is done recursively till there are no subdirectories left:

```
$ ls -xR
08_packets.html  TOC.sh       calendar     cptodos.sh
dept.lst         emp.lst      helpdir      progs
usdsk06x         usdsk07x     usdsk08x     ux2nd06

./helpdir:                                        Three files in helpdir
forms.hlp        graphics.hlp reports.hlp

./progs:                                          Four files in progs
array.pl         cent2fah.pl  n2words.pl   name.pl
```

The list shows the filenames in three sections—the ones under the home directory and those under the subdirectories `helpdir` and `progs`. Note the subdirectory naming conventions followed; `./helpdir` indicates that `helpdir` is a subdirectory under `.` (the current directory).

Note

If `ls` displays a list of files when used with a single filename as argument, you can conclude that the file is actually a directory. `ls` then shows the contents of the directory. The -d option suppresses this behavior.

3.12   cp: **Copying Files**

We now take up the three essential commands that you can't do without—**cp** (**c**opy), **rm** (**rem**ove), and **mv** (**m**ove or rename). Even though UNIX commands are generally noninteractive, all three commands can also be made to run interactively.

Copies serve as good backups. The **cp** command copies one or more files or directory structures. The syntax requires at least two filenames to be specified:

```
cp fork.c fork.c.bak
```

If the destination file (`fork.c.bak`) doesn't exist, **cp** first creates it. Otherwise, it simply overwrites the file without any warning. So check with `ls` whether the destination file exists before you use **cp**.

The destination can also be a directory. The following example shows two ways of copying a file to the `progs` directory:

```
cp fork.c progs/fork.c.bak              fork.c copied to fork.c.bak under progs
cp fork.c progs                         fork.c retains its name under progs
```

cp is often used with the shorthand notation, `.` (dot), to signify the current directory as the destination. The two commands below do the same thing:

```
cp /home/juliet/.profile .profile            Destination is a file
cp /home/juliet/.profile .              Destination is the current directory
```

When **cp** is used to copy multiple files, the last filename *must* be a directory and must already exist because **cp** won't create it:

```
cp chap01 chap02 chap03 progs                 progs must exist as a directory
```

If these files are already resident in `progs`, then they will be overwritten. The shell can help in abbreviating this command line. You can use the metacharacter `*` as a suffix to `chap` to match all these filenames:

```
cp chap* progs                          Copies all files beginning with chap
```

We'll continue to use the `*` as a shorthand for multiple filenames. The metacharacters related to filenames are discussed in Section 7.3. Can you do this job with ease using a GUI program like the file manager?

Note

In the previous example, **cp** doesn't look for a file named chap*. Before it runs, the shell expands chap* to regenerate the command line arguments for **cp** to use.

Caution

cp will fail if the source is read-protected or the destination is write-protected. File permissions are discussed in Section 4.2.

3.12.1   cp Options

Interactive Copying (-i) **cp** turns interactive when the -i (interactive) option is used and the destination file also exists:

```
$ cp -i chap01 unit01
cp: overwrite unit01 (yes/no)? y
```

A y at this prompt overwrites the file; any other response leaves it uncopied. In Section 9.4 we consider a technique by which **cp** can be made to behave in this manner by default.

Copying Directory Structures (-R) The -R (recursive) option can be used to copy an entire directory tree. This command copies all files and subdirectories in progs to newprogs:

```
cp -R progs newprogs                                        newprogs must not exist
```

Attention! For this program to run in the way it is meant to, make sure that newprogs doesn't exist. **cp -R** will then create it as well as its associated subdirectories. Run the command twice, and you'll see different results!

3.13   mv: **Renaming Files**

Once you have used **cp**, you'll feel comfortable with **mv**. This command renames a file or directory. It can also move a group of files to a directory. This is how you rename fork.txt to fork.c:

```
mv fork.txt fork.c                                        Creates or overwrites destination
```

You can move multiple files, but only to a directory. **mv** can also rename a directory:

```
mv fork1.c fork2.c fork3.c progs                            Or mv fork*.c progs
mv progs c_progs                                            Directory renamed
```

As in **cp -R**, there's a difference in behavior depending on whether c_progs exists or not (see Self-Test). **mv** also supports a -i option which makes it behave interactively (See Tip in Section 3.14.1).

3.14 rm: **Deleting Files**

Files tend to build up on disk and should be removed regularly to free disk space. The **rm** command deletes files *as well as directories*. Here it deletes three files:

rm chap01 chap02 chap03   *rm chap* could be dangerous to use!*

rm is often used with a * to delete all files in a directory. Here it empties the directory progs:

rm progs/*

rm can also clean up the current directory:

$ **rm** *   *All files gone!*
$ _

DOS users, beware! You won't encounter the message All files in directory will be deleted! You need to be extremely careful when using the * with **rm** because a deleted file can't be recovered. The * used here is equivalent to *.* used in DOS.

Note

The * doesn't match filenames beginning with a dot. So **rm** * leaves hidden files undeleted. The technique of deleting such files is discussed in Section 7.3.3.

3.14.1 rm Options

Like **cp** and **mv**, **rm** -**i** also behaves interactively, so we'll not discuss this option. Instead, we examine two extremely risky options: -R and -f.

Recursive and Dangerous Deletion (-r or -R) The command **rm** * doesn't remove directories, but **rm** supports a -R (or -r) option to recursively delete an entire directory tree. This command

rm -R *   *Leaves out hidden files*

deletes all files and subdirectories in the current directory. Note that the directories don't need to be empty for **rm** to remove them.

Forcing Removal (-f) **rm** doesn't delete files that have the write permission removed. Instead, it prompts for user confirmation as evident from this behavior on a Solaris and Linux system:

rm: foo: override protection 444 (yes/no)?   *Solaris*
rm: remove write-protected regular file `foo'?   *Linux*

We'll take up permissions and examine the significance of 444 in Chapter 4. **rm** will still delete this file if you respond with a y. But the -f option overrides this minor protection also.

TABLE 3.2   *Usage of* **cp**, **rm**, *and* **mv** *Commands*

Command Line	Action
cp note ..	Copies file note to the parent directory
cp ../note .	Copies file note from the parent directory to the current directory
rm ../bar/index	Deletes file index in the bar directory placed at the same hierarchical location as the current directory
mv foo1 foo2 /foo1/foo2	Moves files foo1 and foo2 to the directory /foo1/foo2
rm -r bar	Deletes complete directory structure of bar. Will delete only bar if it is an ordinary file
cp -r . ../bar	Copies current directory tree to the directory bar under the parent directory (bar must exist)
mv ../* .	Moves all files from the parent directory to the current directory

And when you combine the -r option with it, it could be the most dangerous thing that you've ever done:

rm -rf *   *Deletes everything in the current directory and below*

If you don't have a backup, then these files will be lost forever. Note that this command will delete hidden files in all directories except the current directory.

Even though the **cp**, **rm**, and **mv** commands use simple syntaxes, you'll often be using them with pathnames—both absolute and relative. Table 3.2 shows how these commands can handle a wide variety of arguments.

Caution

Make sure you are doing the right thing before you use **rm** *. Be doubly sure before you use **rm -rf** *. The first command removes only ordinary files in the current directory. The second one removes everything—files and directories alike. If the root user (the super user) invokes **rm -rf** * in the / directory, the entire UNIX system will be wiped out from the hard disk!

Tip

To protect your files from accidental overwriting or deletion you can redefine the three commands so that they always execute with the -i option. Aliases are taken up in Chapter 8, but you can use one here. The syntax of the definition depends on the shell you use:

Korn and Bash	*C Shell*
alias cp="cp -i"	alias cp "cp -i"
alias mv="mv -i"	alias mv "mv -i"
alias rm="rm -i"	alias rm "rm -i"

The Bourne shell doesn't support aliases, where shell functions would be the choice. Shell functions are discussed in Chapter 13.

How a Directory Is Affected by cp, mv, *and* rm

cp, **mv**, and **rm** work by modifying the directory entry of the file they work on. As shown in Fig. 3.5, **cp** adds an entry to the directory with the name of the file and the inode number that is allotted by the kernel. **mv** replaces the name of an existing directory entry without disturbing its inode number. **rm** removes an entry from the directory.

F I G U R E 3.5   *Directory Status after* **cp**, **mv**, *and* **rm**

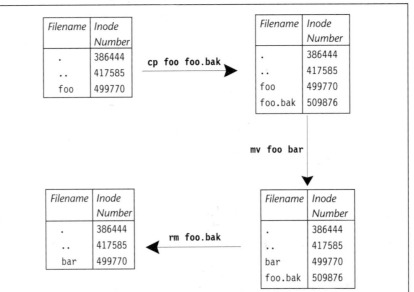

This is a rather simplistic view, and is true only when source and destination are in the same directory. When you "mv" a file to a directory that resides on a separate hard disk, the file is *actually* moved. You'll appreciate this better after you have understood how multiple file systems create the illusion of a single file system on your UNIX machine.

The action of **rm** also needs to be studied further. A file is not actually removed by deleting its directory entry. There could be "similar" entries (ones having the same inode number) for this file in this or another directory. We'll examine this directory table again when we take up file attributes in Chapter 4.

3.15   cat: **Displaying and Concatenating Files**

Most of the remaining commands in this chapter are concerned with content handling. We begin with **cat**, the command that displays the contents of one or more files. It's suitable for displaying small files:

```
$ cat /etc/passwd
root:x:0:1:Super-User:/:/usr/bin/bash
daemon:x:1:1::/:
bin:x:2:2::/usr/bin:
sys:x:3:3::/:
adm:x:4:4:Admin:/var/adm:
lp:x:71:8:Line Printer Admin:/usr/spool/lp:
.......Remaining lines suppressed .......
```

This is how user information is structured. We'll discuss the significance of each of the seven fields in Chapter 19, but just note that the root user uses Bash as the shell on this Solaris system. **cat** simply prints each byte in the file without any header and trailer information.

The name "cat" expands to "concatenation," which means it can concatenate multiple files. **cat**'s output by default comes to the terminal, but we often save it in a file using the shell's > symbol:

```
cat foo.c foo1.c foo2.c > foo4.c
```

We don't use **cat** to view executables because it produces junk. In Chapter 7, we'll use **cat** to even create a file to highlight an important feature of the shell.

3.16 more: **The UNIX Pager**

The **man** command internally uses **more** to display its output a page at a time. **more** today has replaced **pg**, the original pager of UNIX. Linux offers both **more** and **less** (discussed in an aside at the end of this section). You need to use **more** rather than **cat** to view large files:

```
more /etc/inetd.conf
```
Press q to exit

Apart from the first page, you also see at the bottom the filename and percentage of the file that has been viewed:

```
--More--(17%)
```

Like **mailx**, **more** is used with its internal commands that don't show up when you invoke them. **q**, the exit command, is an internal command. The AT&T and BSD versions of this command differ widely in both usage and capabilities. The POSIX specification is based on the BSD version. You have to try out the commands shown in Table 3.3 to know whether they apply to your system. **more** has a fairly useful help screen too; hitting **h** invokes this screen.

Navigation You must have viewed a number of man pages by now, so you should be familiar with these two navigation keys:

f or the spacebar   One page forward
b   One page back

TABLE 3.3   *Internal Commands of* **more** *and* **less**

more	less	Action
Spacebar or f	Spacebar or f or z	One page forward
20f	-	20 pages forward
b	b	One page back
15b	-	15 pages back
[Enter]	j or [Enter]	One line forward
-	k	One line back
-	p or 1G	Beginning of file
-	G	End of file
/pat	/pat	Searches forward for expression *pat*
n	n	Repeats search forward
-	?pat	Searches back for expression *pat*
. (a dot)	-	Repeats last command
v	v	Starts up **vi** editor
!cmd	!cmd	Executes UNIX command *cmd*
q	q	Quit
h	h	Help

Remember that the letters are not displayed on the screen. These navigation commands and many others can be prefixed by a number called the **repeat factor**. This simply repeats the command that many times. This means you can use **10f** for scrolling forward by 10 pages and **30b** for scrolling back 30 pages. (**vi** also uses this feature; both **more** and **vi** were developed at Berkeley.)

Repeating the Last Command (.) **more** has a repeat command, the dot (the same command used by **vi**), that repeats the last command you used. If you scroll forward with **10f**, you can scroll another 10 pages by simply pressing a dot. This is a great convenience!

Searching for a Pattern You have seen the pattern search feature when using **man**. Press a **/** and then the pattern:

/ftp[*Enter*]   *Looks for* ftp

You can repeat this search by pressing **n** as many times until you have scanned the entire file. Move back with **b** (using a repeat factor, if necessary) to arrive at the first page.

Using more in a Pipeline We often use **more** to page the output of another command. The **ls** output won't fit on the screen if there are too many files, so the command has to be used like this:

ls | more   *No filename with* more!

We have a *pipeline* here of two commands where the output of one is used as the input of the other. Pipes are a feature of the shell, and the topic is taken up in Chapter 7.

Linux

less—The Standard Pager

Even though every Linux system offers **more**, its standard pager is ironically named **less**. In many respects it is a superset of **more**. You'll find **vi** features in **less** as well, like the commands that permit one-line movement:

j   One line up
k   One line down

Unlike **more**, **less** can search for a pattern in the reverse direction also. The sequence **?ftp** searches backwards for **ftp**. But **less** does have one serious limitation: unlike **more** (which uses the **.**), it can't repeat the last command.

3.17   wc: **Counting Lines, Words and Characters**

The **wc** (word count) command counts lines, words, and characters. It takes one or more filenames as its arguments and displays a four-columnar output. Let's first "cat" a file:

```
$ cat infile
I am the wc command
I count characters, words and lines
With options I can also make a selective count
```

Now run **wc** without options to verify its own claim made above:

```
$ wc infile
     3    20    103 infile
```

wc counts 3 lines, 20 words, and 103 characters. The filename has also been shown in the fourth column. The meanings of these terms should be clear to you as they are used throughout the book:

- A **line** is any group of characters not containing a newline.
- A **word** is a group of characters not containing a space, tab, or newline.
- A **character** is the smallest unit of information, and includes a space, tab, and newline.

wc offers three options to make a specific count. The -l option makes a line count:

```
$ wc -l infile
     3 infile                                                    Number of lines
```

The -w and -c options count words and characters, respectively. Like **cat**, **wc** doesn't work with only files; it also acts on a data stream. You'll learn all about these streams in Chapter 7.

3.18   lp: **Printing a File**

The printing system in UNIX requires a user to *spool* (line up) a job along with others in a print queue. A separate program monitors this print queue and then picks up each job in turn for printing. The spooling facility in System V is provided by the **lp** (**l**ine **p**rinting) and **cancel** commands. Linux uses the BSD system.

You must have your printer configured properly before you can use **lp**. The following **lp** command prints a single copy of the file rfc822.ps (a document containing an Internet specification in the form of a Request For Comment):

```
$ lp rfc822.ps                                             A Postscript file
request id is pr1-320 (1 file)
$ _                                                    Prompt returns immediately
```

lp notifies the request-id, a unique string that can later be accessed with other commands. The job will be picked up from the queue and printed on the default printer. If the default is not defined or if there is more than one printer in the system, use the -d option:

```
lp -dlaser chap01.ps                                  Printer name is laser
```

You can notify the user with the -m (mail) option after the file has been printed. You can also print multiple copies (-n):

```
lp -n3 -m chap01.ps                           Prints three copies and mails user a message
```

Even though we used **lp** with filenames, this will not always be the case. You are aware that the shell's | symbol allows us to use **ls | more**. The same symbol also lets us use **ls | lp**.

3.18.1   Other Commands in the lp Subsystem

The print queue is viewed with the **lpstat** (**l**ine **p**rinter **stat**us) command. By viewing this list, you can use the **cancel** command to cancel any jobs submitted by you. **cancel** uses the request-id or printer name as argument:

```
cancel laser                                  Cancels current job on printer laser
cancel pr1-320                                Cancels job with request-id pr1-320
```

You can cancel only those jobs that you own (i.e., you have submitted yourself), but the system administrator can cancel any job. **cancel** is effective only when a job remains in the print queue. If it is already being printed, **cancel** can't do a thing.

How UNIX Printers Work

Most UNIX printers are of the *Postscript* variety; i.e., they can properly print files formatted in Postscript, like the files rfc822.ps and chap01.ps used in the examples. (Postscript files are easily identified by the extension .ps.) When you select *Print* from the *File* menu of any GUI program, the program converts the data to Postscript which then serves as input to the printer.

No such conversion, however, takes place when you use **lp** to print a text file like /etc/passwd. If you have a text file to print, use a Postscript conversion utility before you use **lp**. On Solaris, you can use the program **/usr/lib/lp/postscript/postprint** before running **lp**.

Linux has a rich set of tools that convert text files to Postscript. Check whether you have the programs **a2ps** or **enscript** on your system. Both eventually call up **lpr**, the BSD printing program used by Linux.

Printing with **lpr**, **lpq**, and **lprm**

Berkeley devised its own system for printing which has been subsequently adopted by many UNIX systems as well as Linux. This system uses the **lpr** command for printing. The command normally doesn't throw out the job number:

```
lpr /etc/group
```

As in System V, you can mail job completion, print a specific number of copies, and direct output to a specific printer:

```
lpr -P hp4500 foo.ps                              Prints on printer hp4500
lpr -#3 foo.ps                                           Prints 3 copies
lpr -m foo.ps                                  Mails message after completion
```

lpq displays the print queue showing the job numbers. Using one or more job numbers as arguments to **lprm**, you can remove from the print queue only those jobs that are owned by you:

```
lprm 31                                            Removes job number 31
lprm -                                      Removes all jobs owned by the user
```

3.19   od: **Viewing Nonprintable Characters**

Binary files contain nonprinting characters, and most UNIX commands don't display them properly. You can easily identify an executable file written in C by examining its first few bytes which is known as the *magic number*. These bytes are often characters in the extended ASCII range and can't be viewed with **cat** or **more**. We need to use **od**.

The **od** (octal dump) command displays the octal value of each character in its input. When used with the -bc options, the output is quite readable. We'll use **od -bc** to look at the executable **/bin/cat** and **/bin/ls**. Since the output won't fit on the screen, we need to pipe it to **more**. We show below the first 16 characters of **cat** and 32 characters (2 lines) of **ls**:

```
$ od -bc /bin/cat | more
0000000 177 105 114 106 001 002 001 000 000 000 000 000 000 000 000 000
        177   E   L   F 001 002 001  \0  \0  \0  \0  \0  \0  \0  \0  \0
$ od -bc /bin/ls | more
0000000 177 105 114 106 001 001 001 000 000 000 000 000 000 000 000 000
        177   E   L   F 001 001 001  \0  \0  \0  \0  \0  \0  \0  \0  \0
0000020 002 000 003 000 001 000 000 000 060 221 004 010 064 000 000 000
        002  \0 003  \0 001  \0  \0  \0   0 221 004  \b   4  \0  \0  \0
```

Each line displays 16 bytes of data in octal, preceded by the offset (position) in the file of the first byte in the line. The first character has the ASCII octal value 177, and the next three comprise the string ELF. All C executables have the same first four characters. The second line shows the text representation of each character wherever possible.

You can try a similar exercise with **tar** archives and "gzipped" files after you have completed this chapter. **od** also displays escape sequences like \r and \n, and we'll see them when we use the command again for examining DOS files.

3.20   dos2unix **and** unix2dos: **Converting Between DOS and UNIX**

You'll sometimes need to move files between Windows and UNIX systems. Windows files use the same format as DOS, where the end of line is signified by two characters—CR (\r) and LF (\n). UNIX files, on the other hand, use only LF. Here are two lines from a DOS file, foo, viewed on a UNIX system with the **vi** editor:

```
Line 1^M                                  The [Ctrl-m] character at end
Line 2^M
```

There's a ^M (*[Ctrl-m]*) representing the CR sequence at the end of each line. An octal dump confirms this:

```
$ od -bc foo
0000000 114 151 156 145 040 061 015 012 114 151 156 145 040 062 015 012
          L   i   n   e       1  \r  \n   L   i   n   e       2  \r  \n
```

Conversion of this file to UNIX is just a simple matter of removing the \r. Some UNIX systems feature two utilities—**dos2unix** and **unix2dos**—for converting files between DOS and UNIX. The behavior of these commands varies across systems, so you need the help of **man** to determine which of the following actually works on your system:

```
dos2unix foo foo.unix                 Output written to foo.unix—Solaris
dos2unix foo > foo.unix                            Taking shell's help
dos2unix foo                          Output written back to foo—Linux
dos2unix foo foo                              Same as above—Solaris
```

When you use **od** again, you'll find that the CR character is gone:

```
$ od -bc foo.unix
0000000 114 151 156 145 040 061 012 114 151 156 145 040 062 012
          L   i   n   e       1  \n   L   i   n   e       2  \n
```

unix2dos inserts CR before every LF, and thus increases the file size by the number of lines in the file. The syntactical form that works for **dos2unix** also works for **unix2dos**.

Note

If you view the UNIX file foo.unix on Windows using Notepad but without performing the conversion, you'll see a single line, Line 1Line2. In fact, whenever you see a single line on a Windows machine that should have been multiple lines, satisfy yourself that you are viewing an unconverted UNIX file.

Caution

Never perform this conversion on a binary file. If you have downloaded a Windows program (say, a .EXE file) on a UNIX machine, the file must be transferred to the Windows machine without conversion. Otherwise, the program simply won't execute.

3.21 tar: **The Archival Program**

For sending a group of files to someone either by FTP (the file transfer protocol) or email, it helps to combine them into a single file called an **archive**. The **tar** (tape archiver) command is an archiver which we consider briefly here and in detail in Chapter 19. It supports these *key* options; only one option can be used at a time:

-c   Creates an archive
-x   Extracts files from archive
-t   Displays files in archive

In addition, we'll frequently use two options: -f for specifying the name of the archive and -v to display the progress. This is how we create a file archive, archive.tar, from two uncompressed files:

```
$ tar -cvf archive.tar libc.html User_Guide.ps
a libc.html 3785K                                          -v (verbose) displays list
a User_Guide.ps 364K                                            a indicates append
```

By convention, we use the .tar extension, so you'll remember to use the same **tar** command for extraction. Move this .tar file to another directory and then use the -x option for extracting the two files:

```
$ tar -xvf archive.tar                                              Extracts files
x libc.html, 3875302 bytes, 7569 tape blocks                   x indicates extract
x User_Guide.ps, 372267 bytes, 728 tape blocks
```

You'll now find the two files in the current directory. **tar** is most useful for archiving one or more directory trees.

To view the contents of the archive, use the -t (table of contents) option. It doesn't extract files, but simply shows their attributes in a form that you'll see more often later:

```
$ tar -tvf archive.tar
-rw-r--r-- 102/10  3875302 Aug 24 19:49 2002 libc.html
-rw-r--r-- 102/10   372267 Aug 24 19:48 2002 User_Guide.ps
```

You'll understand the significance of these columns after you have learned to interpret the ls -l output. But you can at least see the individual file size (third column) and the filename (last column) in this output.

3.22 gzip: **The Compression Program**

Eventually you'll encounter compressed files on the Internet or need to compress one yourself before sending it as an email attachment. Your UNIX system may have one or more of these compression programs: **gzip**, **bzip2**, and **zip**. The degree of compression depends on the type of file, its size, and the compression program used. In this section we take up **gzip** and its decompression sibling, **gunzip**.

gzip provides the extension .gz to the compressed filename and removes the original file. This command compresses an HTML file:

```
gzip libc.html                                         Replaces with libc.html.gz
```

To see the amount of compression achieved, use the -l option:

```
$ gzip -l libc.html.gz                                          .gz not necessary
compressed  uncompr. ratio uncompressed_name
   788096   3875302 79.6% libc.html
```

Uncompressing a "gzipped" File (-d) To restore the original and uncompressed file, you have two options: use either **gzip -d** or **gunzip:**

```
gunzip libc.html.gz                                        Retrieves libc.html
gzip -d libc.html.gz                                                      Same
```

You'll have to understand why two commands have been offered to do the same job when one of them would have sufficed. Are **gzip** and **gunzip** one and the same file? This question is related to file attributes, and we discuss file attributes in the next chapter.

To view compressed plain text files, you really don't need to "gunzip" (decompress) them. Use the **gzcat** and **gzmore** (or **zcat** and **zmore**) commands if they are available on your system.

Using with tar An additional layer of compression helps bring down the file size, the reason why **gzip** is often used with **tar** for creating a compressed archive. Here we "gzip" the file archive.tar that was created in Section 3.21 with **tar**:

```
gzip archive.tar                                        Archived and compressed
```

This creates a "tar-gzipped" file, archive.tar.gz. This file can now be sent out by FTP or as an email attachment to someone. To extract the files from this compressed archive, we simply have to reverse the procedure: use **gunzip** to decompress the archive and then run **tar**:

```
gunzip archive.tar.gz                                    Retrieves archive.tar
tar -xvf archive.tar                         Extracts libc.html and User_Guide.ps
```

A great deal of open-source UNIX and Linux software are available as ".tar.gz" files on the Internet. To be able to extract files from this archive, the recipient needs to have both **tar** and **gunzip** (or **gzip**) at her end.

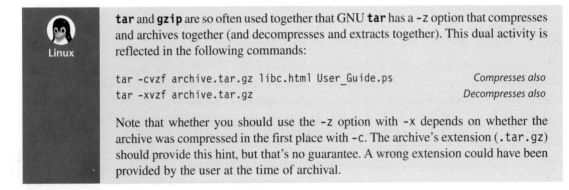

tar and **gzip** are so often used together that GNU **tar** has a -z option that compresses and archives together (and decompresses and extracts together). This dual activity is reflected in the following commands:

```
tar -cvzf archive.tar.gz libc.html User_Guide.ps              Compresses also
tar -xvzf archive.tar.gz                                    Decompresses also
```

Note that whether you should use the -z option with -x depends on whether the archive was compressed in the first place with -c. The archive's extension (.tar.gz) should provide this hint, but that's no guarantee. A wrong extension could have been provided by the user at the time of archival.

Note

For some years, **gzip** reigned as the most favored compression agent. Today we have a better agent in **bzip2** (and **bunzip2**). **bzip2** is slower than **gzip** and creates .bz2 files. **bzip2** options are modeled on **gzip**, so if you know **gzip** you also know **bzip2**. GNU **tar** also supports compression with **bzip2** in the --bzip option. Provide the extension .tar.bz2 to the compressed archive so that the person at the other end knows how to handle it.

3.23   zip: **The Compression and Archival Program**

The popular PKZIP and PKUNZIP programs are now available as **zip** and **unzip** on UNIX. **zip** combines the compressing function of **gzip** with the archival function of **tar**. So instead of using two commands to compress an archive (say, a directory structure), you can use only one—**zip**.

zip requires the first argument to be the compressed filename; the remaining arguments are interpreted as files and directories to be compressed. A previous archival and subsequent compression in two previous examples could have been achieved with **zip** in the following way:

```
$ zip archive.zip libc.html User_Guide.ps
  adding: libc.html (deflated 80%)
  adding: User_Guide.ps (deflated 66%)
```

The unusual feature of this command is that it *doesn't* overwrite an existing compressed file. If archive.zip exists, files will either be updated or appended to the archive depending on whether they already exist in the archive.

Recursive Compression (-r) For recursive behavior, **zip** uses the -r option. It descends the tree structure in the same way **tar** does except that it also compresses files. You can easily compress your home directory in this way:

```
cd ; zip -r sumit_home.zip .                          cd is same as cd $HOME
```

Using unzip **zip** files are decompressed with **unzip**. **unzip** does a noninteractive restoration if it doesn't find the same files on disk:

```
$ unzip archive.zip
Archive:  archive.zip
  inflating: libc.html
  inflating: User_Guide.ps
```

But if the uncompressed file exists on disk, then **unzip** makes sure that it's doing the right thing by seeking user confirmation:

```
replace libc.html? [y]es, [n]o, [A]ll, [N]one, [r]ename: y
```

You can respond with y or n. You can also rename the file (r) to prevent overwriting or direct **unzip** to perform the decompression on the remaining files noninteractively (A).

Viewing the Archive (-v) You can view the compressed archive with the -v option. The list shows both the compressed and uncompressed size of each file in the archive along with the percentage of compression achieved:

```
$ unzip -v archive.zip
Archive:  archive.zip
 Length   Method   Size   Ratio   Date     Time    CRC-32    Name
 ------   ------   ----   -----   ----     ----    ------    ----
3875302   Defl:N  788068   80%   08-24-02  19:49  fae93ded  libc.html
 372267   Defl:N  128309   66%   08-24-02  19:48  7839e6b3  User_Guide.ps
 ------           ------   ---                              -------
4247569          916377    78%                             2 files
```

3.24 Other Ways of Using These Commands

The commands discussed in this chapter don't always take input from files. Some commands (like **more** and **lp**) use, as alternate sources of input, the keyboard or the output of another command. Most of the other commands (like **wc**, **cat**, **od**, **gzip**, and **tar**) can also send output to a file or serve as input to another command. Some examples in this chapter (and previous ones) have shown this to be possible with the > and | symbols. The discussion of these techniques is taken up in Chapter 7.

SUMMARY

We considered three types of files—*ordinary, directory,* and *device.* A directory maintains the inode number and name for each file. The kernel uses the attributes of a device file to operate the device. File attributes are maintained in the inode.

A filename is restricted to 255 characters and can use practically any character. Executable files don't need any specific extensions.

UNIX supports a hierarchical file system where the top-most directory is called *root.* An *absolute* pathname begins with a / and denotes the file's location with respect to root. A *relative* pathname uses the symbols . and .. to represent the file's location relative to the current and parent directory, respectively.

pwd tells you the current directory, and **cd** is used to change it or to switch to the *home* directory. This directory is set in /etc/passwd and is available in the shell variable HOME. A file foo in the home directory is often referred to as $HOME/foo or ~/foo.

mkdir and **rmdir** are used to create or remove directories. To remove a directory bar with **rmdir**, bar must be empty and you must be positioned above bar.

By default, **ls** displays filenames in *ASCII collating sequence* (numbers, uppercase, lowercase). It can also display hidden filenames beginning with a dot (-a). When used with a directory name as argument, **ls** displays the *filenames* in the directory.

You can copy files with **cp**, remove them with **rm**, and rename them with **mv**. All of them can be used interactively (-i), and the first two can be used to work on a complete directory tree (-r or -R) i.e., recursively. **rm -r** can remove a directory tree even if is not empty.

cat and **more** are used to display the contents of a file. **more** supports a number of internal commands that enable paging and searching for a pattern. Linux offers **less** as a superior pager.

lp submits a job for printing which is actually carried out by a separate program. Linux and many UNIX systems use the **lpr** command for printing. Both can be *directly* used to print Postscript documents.

wc counts the number of lines, words, and characters. **od** displays the octal value of each character and is used to display invisible characters.

The **dos2unix** and **unix2dos** commands convert files between DOS and UNIX. DOS files use CR-LF as the line terminator, while UNIX uses only LF.

gzip and **gunzip** compresses and decompresses individual files (extension: .gz). **tar** can archive a directory tree and is often used with **gzip** to create compressed archives (extension: .tar.gz). **zip** and **unzip** use .zip files. **zip** alone can create a compressed archive from directory structures (-r). **bzip2** is better than them (extension: .bz2).

SELF-TEST

3.1   How long can a UNIX filename be? What characters can't be used in a filename?

3.2   State two reasons for not having a filename beginning with a hyphen.

3.3   Name the two types of ordinary files, and explain the difference between them. Provide three examples of each type of file.

3.4   Can the files note and Note coexist in the same directory?

3.5   Frame **cd** commands to change from (i) /var/spool/lp/admins to /var/spool/mail, (ii) /usr/include/sys to /usr.

3.6   Switch to the root directory with **cd,** and then run **cd** .. followed by **pwd.** What do you notice?

3.7   Explain the significance of these two commands: ls .. ; ls -d ..

3.8   Can you execute any command in /sbin and /usr/sbin by using the absolute pathname?

3.9   If the file /bin/echo exists on your system, are the commands **echo** and **/bin/echo** equivalent?

3.10 Look up the man pages of **mkdir** to find out the easiest way of creating this directory structure: share/man/cat1.

3.11 If **mkdir test** fails, what could be the possible reasons?

3.12 How do you run **ls** to (i) mark directories and executables separately, (ii) also display hidden files?

3.13 What will **cat foo foo foo** display?

3.14 A file contains nonprintable characters. How do you view them?

3.15 How will you copy a directory structure bar1 to bar2? Does it make any difference if bar2 exists?

3.16 Assuming that bar is a directory, explain what the command **rm -rf bar** does. How is the command different from **rmdir bar**?

3.17 How do you print the file /etc/passwd on the printer named laser on System V (i) to generate three copies, (ii) and know that the file has been printed?

3.18   How will you find out the ASCII octal values of the numerals and alphabets?

3.19   Run the **wc** command with two or more filenames as arguments. What do you see?

EXERCISES

3.1   Describe the contents of a directory, explaining the mechanism by which its entries
       are updated by **cp**, **mv**, and **rm**. Why is the size of a directory usually small?

3.2   How does the device file help in accessing the device?

3.3   Which of these commands will work? Explain with reasons: (i) mkdir a/b/c,
       (ii) mkdir a a/b, (iii) rmdir a/b/c, (iv) rmdir a a/b, (v) mkdir /bin/foo.

3.4   The command **rmdir c_progs** failed. State three possible reasons.

3.5   Using **echo**, try creating a file containing (i) one, (ii) two, and (iii) three dots.
       What do you conclude?

3.6   The command **rmdir bar** fails with the message that the directory is not empty.
       On running **ls bar**, no files are displayed. Why did the **rmdir** command fail?

3.7   How does the command **mv bar1 bar2** behave, where both bar1 and bar2 are
       directories, when (i) bar2 exists and (ii) bar2 doesn't exist?

3.8   Explain the difference between the commands **cd ~charlie** and **cd ~/charlie**.
       Is it possible for both commands to work?

3.9   charlie uses /usr/charlie as his home directory and many of his scripts refer
       to the pathname /usr/charlie/html. Later, the home directory is changed to
       /home/charlie, thus breaking all his scripts. How could charlie have avoided
       this problem?

3.10   Why do we sometimes run a command like this—./update.sh instead of
       update.sh?

3.11   What is the sort order prescribed by the ASCII collating sequence?

3.12   The commands **ls bar** and **ls -d bar** display the same output—the string bar.
       This can happen in two ways. Explain.

3.13   Assuming that you are positioned in the directory /home/romeo, what are
       these commands presumed to do, and explain whether they will work at all:
       (i) cd ../.., (ii) mkdir ../bin, (iii) rmdir .., (iv) ls ...

3.14   Explain what the following commands do: (i) cd, (ii) cd $HOME, (iii) cd ~.

3.15   The command **cp hosts backup/hosts.bak** didn't work even though all files
       exist. Name three possible reasons.

3.16   You have a directory structure $HOME/a/a/b/c where the first a is empty. How
       do you remove it and move the lower directories up?

3.17   Explain what the following commands do: (i) rm *, (ii) rm -i *, (iii) rm -rf *.

3.18   What is the significance of these commands? (i) mv $HOME/include .,
       (ii) cp -r bar1 bar2, (iii) mv * ../bin.

3.19   Will the command **cp foo bar** work if (i) foo is an ordinary file and bar is a
       directory, (ii) both foo and bar are directories?

3.20   Explain the significance of the repeat factor used in **more**. How do you search
       for the pattern include in a file and repeat the search? What is the difference
       between this repeat command and the dot command?

3.21   Look up the man page for the **file** command, and then use it on all files in the /dev directory. Can you group these files into two categories?

3.22   How do DOS and UNIX text files differ? Name the utilities that convert files between these two formats?

3.23   Run the **script** command, and then issue a few commands before you run **exit**. What do you see when you run **cat -v typescript**?

3.24   Run the **tty** command, and note the device name of your terminal. Now use this device name (say, /dev/pts/6) in the command **cp /etc/passwd /dev/pts/6**. What do you observe?

3.25   How do you use **tar** to add two files, foo.html and bar.html, to an archive, archive.tar, and then compress the archive? How will you reverse the entire process and extract the files in their original uncompressed form?

3.26   Name three advantages **zip** has over **gzip**.

3.27   How do you send a complete directory structure to someone by email using (i) **tar**, (ii) **zip**? How does the recipient handle it? Which method is superior and why? Does **gzip** help in any way?

3.28   What is meant by *recursive* behavior of a command? Name four commands, along with a suitable example of each, that can operate recursively.

File Attributes

In Chapter 3, you created directories, navigated the file system, and copied, moved, and removed files without any problem. In real life, however, matters may not be so rosy. You may have problems when handling a file or directory. Your file may be modified or even deleted by others. A restoration from a backup may be unable to write to your directory. You must know why these problems occur and how to prevent and rectify them.

The UNIX file system lets users access files that don't belong to them—without infringing on security. A file also has a number of attributes that are changeable by certain well-defined rules. In this chapter, we'll use the **ls** command in all possible ways to display these attributes. We'll also use other commands to change these attributes. Finally, we'll discuss **find**—one of the most versatile attribute handling tools of the UNIX system.

Objectives

- Learn the significance of the seven fields of the **ls -l** output (*listing*).
- Use **chmod** to change file permissions in a relative and absolute manner.
- Understand the significance of directory permissions and how they ultimately impact a file's access rights.
- Understand the concept of the *user mask* and how **umask** changes the default file and directory permissions.
- Become familiar with *file systems* and the *inode* as a file identifier.
- Create hard links to a file with **ln**.
- Learn the limitations of hard links and how they are overcome by *symbolic links*.
- Know the importance of *ownership* and *group ownership* of a file and how they affect security.
- Use **chown** and **chgrp** to change the owner and group owner of files on BSD and AT&T systems.
- Locate files by matching one or more file attributes with **find**.

4.1 ls Revisited (-l): Listing File Attributes

File attributes are stored in the **inode**, a structure that is maintained in a separate area of the hard disk. Before we examine the contents of the inode, let's first have a look at some of the

FIGURE 4.1   *Listing of Files with* `ls -l`

```
$ ls -l
total 24
-r--r--r--  1 256    105      13921 Jul 26  2001 987
-rw-rw-rw-  1 romeo  metal      473 Jul 13 21:36 CallByRef.java
-rwxr-xr-x  1 root   root      6496 Aug 10 10:20 a.out
-rwxr-xr--  2 romeo  metal      163 Jul 13 21:36 backup.sh
drwxr-xr-x  2 romeo  metal      512 Aug 10 10:42 c_progs
lrwxrwxrwx  1 romeo  metal       17 Aug 11 00:49 hex.c -> c_progs/hexdump.c
-r--r--r--  1 romeo  metal      268 Jul 13 21:36 prime.c
-rwxr-xr--  2 romeo  metal      163 Jul 13 21:36 restore.sh
drwxrwxr-x  2 romeo  metal      512 Aug 10 10:45 shell_scripts
```

major attributes which are listed by the `ls -l` command. The output in UNIX lingo is often referred to as the **listing**, and a typical listing is shown in Fig. 4.1.

The list shows seven labeled fields in nine columns with the filenames ordered in ASCII collating sequence. Each field here represents a file attribute, and all these attributes (except the filename) are stored in the inode. We'll discuss most of these attributes in detail in this chapter, but let's understand their significance first:

Type and Permissions   The first column of the first field shows the file type. Here we see three possible values—a - (ordinary file), d (directory), or l (symbolic link). Most files here are ordinary files, but `c_progs` and `shell_scripts` are directories. We'll discuss the symbolic link later. The remaining nine characters form a string of permissions which can take the values r, w, x, and -.

Links   The second field indicates the number of links associated with the file. UNIX lets a file have multiple names, and each name is interpreted as a link. Directories have a link count of at least two, but here two ordinary files (`backup.sh` and `restore.sh`) also have two links each. Are they the same file?

Ownership and Group Ownership   Every file has an owner. The third field shows romeo as the owner of most of the files. A user also belongs to a group, and the fourth field shows metal as the group owner of most of the files. The owner can tamper with a file in every possible way—a privilege that is also available to the root user. We'll discuss how two files having different ownership and group ownership (987 and `a.out`) have crept into this directory.

Size   The fifth field shows the file size in bytes. This actually reflects the character count and not disk space consumption of the file. The kernel allocates space in blocks of 1024 bytes or more, so even though `backup.sh` contains 163 bytes, it could occupy

1024 bytes on this system. The two directories show smaller file sizes, but that is to be expected because the size of a directory depends on the number of filenames it contains—whatever the size of the files themselves.

Last Modification Time The sixth field displays the last modification time in three columns—a time stamp that is stored to the nearest second. The file named 987 shows the year; the year is displayed if more than a year has elapsed since it was last modified (six months in Linux). You'll often need to run automated tools that make decisions based on a file's modification time. This column shows two other time stamps when **ls** is used with certain options.

Filename The last field displays the filename which can be up to 255 characters long. If you would like to see an important file at the top of the listing, then choose its name in uppercase—at least, its first letter.

The entire list is preceded by the words total 24; a total of 24 blocks are occupied by these files in the disk. There are other file attributes (like the inode number), and sometimes we combine the -l option with other options for displaying other attributes or ordering the list in a different sequence. We'll now examine each of these attributes and learn to change it.

4.1.1 Listing Directory Attributes (-ld)

We can use **ls -l** with filenames as arguments for a selective listing. But since **ls bar** lists the contents of bar if it is a directory, we need to combine the -l and -d options to force the listing:

```
$ ls -ld c_progs shell_scripts
drwxr-xr-x   2 romeo    metal        512 Aug 10 10:42 c_progs
drwxrwxr-x   2 romeo    metal        512 Aug 10 10:45 shell_scripts
```

While we maintain that a directory is also a file, the significance of its permissions, link count, and size differ with ordinary files.

Note

To see the attributes of a directory bar rather than the filenames it contains, use **ls -ld bar**. Note that simply using **ls -ld** won't show the listing of all subdirectories in the current directory. Strange though it may seem, **ls** has no option to list only directories!

4.2 File Permissions

UNIX has a simple and well-defined system of assigning permissions to files. Observe from the listing in Fig. 4.1 that permissions can vary a great deal between files. Let's examine the permissions of backup.sh:

```
-rwxr-xr--   2 romeo    metal        163 Jul 13 21:36 backup.sh
```

UNIX follows a three-tiered file protection system that determines a file's access rights. To understand how this system works, let's break up the permissions string of this file

FIGURE 4.2   *Structure of a File's Permissions String*

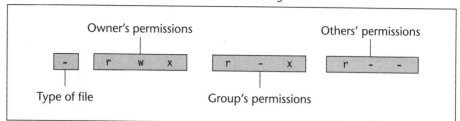

into three groups as shown in Fig. 4.2. The initial - (in the first column) signifies an ordinary file and is left out of the permissions string.

Each group here represents a *category*. There are three categories representing the user (owner), group owner, and others. Each category contains three slots representing the read, write, and execute permissions of the file. r indicates read permission, which means **cat** can display the file. w indicates write permission; you can edit such a file with an editor. x indicates execute permission; the file can be executed as a program. The - shows the absence of the corresponding permission.

The first category (rwx) shows the presence of all permissions. The file is readable, writable, and executable by the owner of the file. Identifying the owner is easy; the third field shows romeo as the owner. You have to log in with the username romeo for these privileges to apply to you.

In a similar manner, the second category (r-x) indicates the absence of write permission for the group owner of the file. This group owner is metal as shown in the fourth field. The third category (r--) applies to others (neither owner nor group owner). This category is often referred to as the *world*. This file is world-readable, but others can't write or execute it.

A file or directory is created with a default set of permissions that is determined by a simple setting (called *umask*), which we'll discuss later. Different systems have different umask settings, but to make sure that you also obtain the same initial permissions, use **umask** in this manner before creating a file, date.sh (a shell script), containing the string date:

```
$ umask 022
$ echo date > date.sh ; ls -l date.sh
-rw-r--r--  1 romeo    metal          5 Aug 16 16:05 date.sh
```

All users have read permission, only the owner has write permission, but the file is not executable by anyone:

```
$ ./date.sh                                    Preferred way to run shell scripts
ksh: ./date.sh: cannot execute
```

How does one then execute such a file? Just change its permissions with the **chmod** (**ch**ange **mod**e) command. With this command, you can set different permissions for the three categories of users—owner, group, and others. It's important that you understand them because a little learning here can be a dangerous thing. A faulty file permission is a sure recipe for disaster.

Note

The group permissions here don't apply to romeo (the owner) even if romeo belongs to the metal group. The owner has its own set of permissions that override the group owner's permissions. However, when romeo renounces the ownership of the file, the group permissions then apply to him.

4.3   chmod: **Changing File Permissions**

Before we take up **chmod**, let's decide to change a habit. Henceforth, we'll refer to the owner as *user* because that's how the **chmod** command (which changes file permissions) refers to the owner. In this section, whenever we use the term *user,* we'll actually mean *owner*.

We'll now use **chmod** to change a file's permissions. The command uses the following syntax:

chmod [-R] *mode file* ...

POSIX specifies only a single option (-R). The *mode* can be represented in two ways:

- In a relative manner by specifying the changes to the current permissions.
- In an absolute manner by specifying the final permissions.

We'll consider both ways of using **chmod**, but just remember that only the owner of this file (romeo) can change these permissions.

4.3.1   Relative Permissions

When changing permissions in a relative manner, **chmod** only changes the permissions specified in *mode* and leaves the other permissions unchanged. The structure of a **chmod** command is shown in Fig. 4.3. The *mode* as used in the syntax contains three components:

- User *category* (user, group, others)
- The *operation* to be performed (assign or remove a permission)
- The type of *permission* (read, write, execute)

F I G U R E 4.3   *Structure of a* **chmod** *Command*

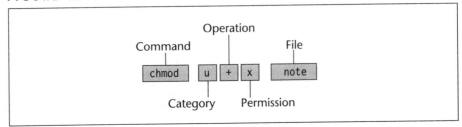

TABLE 4.1 *Abbreviations Used by* **chmod**

Category	Operation	Permission
u—User	+—Assigns permission	r—Read permission
g—Group	-—Removes permission	w—Write permission
o—Others	=—Assigns absolute permission	x—Execute permission
a—All (ugo)		

To make the file date.sh executable, frame a suitable expression by using appropriate characters from each of the three columns of Table 4.1. We need to assign (+) execute permission (x) to the user (u). The expression required is u+x:

```
$ chmod u+x date.sh                                          Execute permission for user
$ ls -l date.sh
-rwxr--r--   1 romeo    metal          5 Aug 16 16:05 date.sh
$ ./date.sh                                             Now execute the shell script
Sat Aug 16 16:16:12 GMT 2003
```

Permissions are removed with the - operator. This is how we revert to the original permissions:

```
$ chmod u-x date.sh ; ls -l date.sh
-rw-r--r--   1 romeo    metal          5 Aug 16 16:05 date.sh
```

The expression can comprise multiple categories. This is how we assign execute permission to all:

```
$ chmod ugo+x date.sh ; ls -l date.sh
-rwxr-xr-x   1 romeo    metal          5 Aug 16 16:05 date.sh
```

The synonym a is available for ugo, so ugo+x is the same as a+x (or even +x). We can also assign multiple permissions:

```
$ chmod go-rx date.sh ; ls -l date.sh
-rwx------   1 romeo    metal          5 Aug 16 16:05 date.sh
```

How do we revert now to the original permissions? We need to remove the execute permission from user and assign read permission to the other two categories. This requires two expressions, and using a comma as a delimiter between them, we can use a single invocation of **chmod:**

```
$ chmod u-x,go+r date.sh ; ls -l date.sh
-rw-r--r--   1 romeo    metal          5 Aug 16 16:05 date.sh
```

However, this isn't convenient; we had to use a complex expression to revert to the default permissions. Whatever the current permissions are, we should be able to assign permissions in an absolute manner. **chmod** can do that too.

4.3.2 Absolute Assignment

The = operator can perform a limited form of absolute assignment. It assigns only the specified permissions and removes other permissions. Thus, if a file is to be made read-only to all, we can simply use one of these three forms:

```
chmod ugo=r date.sh
chmod a=r date.sh
chmod =r date.sh
```

This technique has its limitations; you just can't set all nine permission bits explicitly. Absolute assignment is actually done with octal numbers. You may or may not be familiar with this numbering system, so a discussion would be in order.

Octal numbers use the base 8, and octal digits have the values 0 to 7. This means that a set of three bits can represent one octal digit. If we represent the permissions of each category by one octal digit, then this is how the permissions can be represented:

- Read permission—4 (Octal 100)
- Write permission—2 (Octal 010)
- Execute permission—1 (Octal 001)

For each category we add up the numbers. For instance, 6 represents read and write permissions, and 7 represents all permissions as can easily be understood from the following table:

Binary	Octal	Permissions	Significance
000	0	---	No permissions
001	1	--x	Executable only
010	2	-w-	Writable only
011	3	-wx	Writable and executable
100	4	r--	Readable only
101	5	r-x	Readable and executable
110	6	rw-	Readable and writable
111	7	rwx	Readable, writable, and executable

We have three categories and three permissions for each category, so three octal digits can describe a file's permissions completely. The most significant digit represents user, and the least significant one represents others. **chmod** can use this three-digit string as the expression.

The default file permissions on our system are rw-r--r--. This is octal 644, so let's use it with **chmod:**

```
$ chmod 644 date.sh ; ls -l date.sh
-rw-r--r--  1 romeo    metal        5 Aug 16 16:05 date.sh
```

Some network applications store the password in a configuration file in the home directory. This file must be made unreadable to group and others. For this you need the expression 600:

```
$ cd ; chmod 600 .netrc ; ls -l .netrc
-rw------- 1 romeo    metal        50 Aug 16 16:50 .netrc
```

It's obvious that 000 indicates the absence of all permissions and 777 signifies all permissions for all categories. But can we delete a file with permissions 000? Yes, we can. Can we prevent a file with permissions 777 from being deleted? We can do that, too. We'll soon learn that it's the directory that determines whether a file can be deleted, not the file itself. Table 4.2 shows the use of **chmod** both with and without using octal notation.

Note   A file's permissions can only be changed by the owner (understood by **chmod** as user) of the file. One user can't change the protection modes of files belonging to another user. However, this restriction doesn't apply to the privileged user, root.

4.3.3   Recursive Operation (-R)

chmod -R descends a directory hierarchy and applies the expression to every file and subdirectory it finds in the tree-walk:

```
chmod -R a+x shell_scripts
```

So, to use **chmod** on your home directory tree, "cd" to it and use it in one of these ways:

```
chmod -R 755 .                                          Works on hidden files also
chmod -R a+x *                                          Leaves out hidden files
```

When you know the shell metacharacters well, you'll appreciate the difference between the two invocations. The dot is generally a safer bet, but note that both commands change

T A B L E 4.2   chmod *Usage*

Initial Permissions	Symbolic Expression	Octal Expression	Final Permissions
rw-r-----	o+rw	646	rw-r--rw-
rw-r--r--	u-w,go-r	400	r--------
rwx------	go+rwx	777	rwxrwxrwx
rwxrw--wx	u-rwx,g-rw,o-wx	000	---------
---------	+r	444	r--r--r--
r--r--r--	+w	644	rw-r--r-- *(Note this)*
rw-rw-rw-	-w	466	r--rw-rw- *(Note this)*
rw-rw-rw-	a-w	444	r--r--r--
---------	u+w,g+rx,o+x	251	-w-r-x--x
rwxrwxrwx	a=r	444	r--r--r--

the permissions of directories also. What do permissions mean when they are applied to a directory? Just read on.

4.4   The Directory

A directory stores the filename and inode number. So the size of a directory is determined by the *number* of files housed by it and not by the size of the files. A directory also has its own set of permissions whose significance differs a great deal from ordinary files. Let's use the same umask setting and then create a directory:

```
$ umask 022 ; mkdir progs ; ls -ld progs
drwxr-xr-x   2 romeo    metal        512 Aug 16 09:24 progs
```

All categories have read and execute permissions and only the user has write permission. A directory's permissions also affect the access rights of its files. This area is the source of a great deal of confusion, so let's examine these permissions carefully.

4.4.1   Read Permission

Read permission for a directory means that the *list* of filenames stored in that directory is accessible. Since **ls** reads the directory to display filenames, if a directory's read permission is removed, **ls** won't work. Consider removing the read permission first from the directory progs:

```
$ chmod u-r progs
$ ls progs
progs: Permission denied
```

However, this doesn't prevent you from reading the files separately if you know their names.

4.4.2   Write Permission

Write permission for a directory implies that you are permitted to create or remove files in it (that would make the kernel modify the directory entries). Security issues are usually related to a directory's write permission, so let's try out a couple of tests with the directory that we just created.

First, we'll restore the read permission and then copy a file with permissions 644 to this directory:

```
chmod u+r progs ; cp date.sh progs
```

Now let's "cd" to this directory and display the listing both of the directory and the filename in it:

```
$ cd progs ; ls -ld . date.sh
drwxr-xr-x   2 romeo    metal        512 Aug 16 09:39 .
-rw-r--r--   1 romeo    metal          5 Aug 16 09:39 date.sh
```

Both file and directory have write permission for the user. date.sh can now be both edited and deleted. We can also create a new file in this directory.

Directory's Write Permission Off; File's Write Permission On Let's remove the directory's write permission and then check whether we can delete the file:

```
$ chmod u-w . ; ls -ld . ; rm date.sh
dr-xr-xr-x  2 romeo    metal        512 Aug 16 09:59 .
rm: date.sh not removed: Permission denied
```

Removing a file implies deletion of its entry from the directory. It's obvious that date.sh can't be deleted. But can it be edited? Yes, of course; the file has write permission which means you can edit it with your **vi** editor. *Modifying a file doesn't affect its directory entry in any way.*

Directory's Write Permission On; File's Write Permission Off We now reverse the previous setting by restoring the directory's write permission and removing it from the file:

```
$ chmod u+w . ; chmod u-w date.sh ; ls -ld . date.sh
drwxr-xr-x  2 romeo    metal        512 Aug 16 09:59 .
-r--r--r--  1 romeo    metal          5 Aug 16 09:39 date.sh
```

We can create a file in this directory, that's obvious, but can we delete date.sh?

```
$ rm date.sh
rm: date.sh: override protection 444 (yes/no)? yes
```

rm turns interactive when it encounters a file without write permission. Note that the absence of write permission in date.sh only implies that it can't be modified. But whether it can be deleted or not depends entirely on the directory's permissions.

Directory's Write Permission Off; File's Write Permission Off Now that date.sh is gone, let's get it again from the parent directory and then switch off the write permission for both file and directory:

```
$ cp ../date.sh .
$ chmod u-w date.sh . ; ls -ld . date.sh
dr-xr-xr-x  2 romeo    metal        512 Aug 16 10:11 .
-r--r--r--  1 romeo    metal          5 Aug 16 10:11 date.sh
```

This is the safest arrangement you can have. You can neither edit the file nor create or remove files in this directory.

We can now summarize our observations in this manner:

- The write permission for a directory determines whether you can create or remove files in it because these actions modify the directory.
- Whether you can modify a file depends solely on whether the file itself has write permission. Changing a file doesn't modify its directory entry in any way.

Note

The term "write-protected" has a limited meaning in the UNIX file system. A write-protected file can't be written, but it can be removed if the directory has write permission.

Caution

Danger arises when you mistakenly assign the permissions 775 or 777 to a directory. In the present scenario, 775 allows any user of the metal group to create or remove files in the directory. 777 extends this facility to the world. As a rule, you must never make directories group- or world-writable unless you have definite reasons to do so. Sometimes, you'll have a good reason *(19.4.3)*.

4.4.3 Execute Permission

Executing a directory just doesn't make any sense, so what does its execute privilege mean? It only means that a user can "pass through" the directory in searching for subdirectories. When you use a pathname with any command:

```
cat /home/romeo/progs/date.sh
```

you need to have execute permission for each of the directories in the pathname. The directory home contains the entry for romeo, and the directory romeo contains the entry for progs, and so forth. If a single directory in this pathname doesn't have execute permission, then it can't be searched for the name of the next directory. That's why the execute privilege of a directory is often referred to as the *search* permission.

A directory has to be searched for the next directory, so the **cd** command won't work if the search permission for the directory is turned off:

```
$ chmod 666 progs ; ls -ld progs
drw-rw-rw-  2 romeo    metal        512 Aug 16 10:11 progs
$ cd progs
ksh: progs: permission denied
```

As for regular files, directory permissions are extremely important because system security is heavily dependent upon them. If you tamper with the permissions of your directories, then make sure you set them correctly. If you don't, then be assured that an intelligent user could make life miserable for you!

4.5   umask: **Default File and Directory Permissions**

When you create files and directories, the permissions assigned to them depend on the system's default setting. The UNIX system has the following default permissions for all files and directories:

- rw-rw-rw- (octal 666) for regular files.
- rwxrwxrwx (octal 777) for directories.

However, you don't see these permissions when you create a file or a directory. Actually, this default is transformed by subtracting the **user mask** from it to remove one or more

TABLE 4.3   *Effect of* **umask** *Settings on Default Permissions*

umask *Value*	*Default File Permissions*	*Default Directory Permissions*
000	rw-rw-rw-	rwxrwxrwx
002	rw-rw-r--	rwxrwxr-x
022	rw-r--r--	rwxr-xr-x
026	rw-r-----	rwxr-x--x
046	rw--w----	rwx-wx--x
062	rw----r--	rwx--xr-x
066	rw-------	rwx--x--x
222	r--r--r--	r-xr-xr-x
600	---rw-rw-	--xrwxrwx
666	---------	--x--x--x
777	---------	---------

permissions. To understand what this means, let's evaluate the current value of the mask by using **umask** without arguments:

```
$ umask
022
```

This is an octal number which has to be subtracted from the system default to obtain the *actual* default. This becomes 644 (666-022) for ordinary files and 755 (777-022) for directories. When you create a file on this system, it will have the permissions rw-r--r--. A directory will have the permissions rwxr-xr-x.

    umask is a shell built-in command. A user can also use this command to set a new default. Here's an extreme setting:

umask 000   *All read-write permissions on*

A umask value of 000 means that you haven't subtracted anything, and this could be dangerous. The system's default then applies (666 for files and 777 for directories). All files and directories are then writable by all; nothing could be worse than that! However, a mask value of 666 or 777 doesn't make much sense either; you'll then be creating files and directories with no permissions.

    The important thing to remember is that no one—not even the administrator—can use **umask** to turn on permissions not specified in the systemwide default settings. However, you can always use **chmod** as and when required. The systemwide umask setting is placed in one of the machine's startup scripts, and is automatically made available to all users. The effect of some of these settings on file and directory permissions is shown in Table 4.3

4.6 File Systems and Inodes

Before we take up links, we need some idea of the way files are organized in a UNIX system. So far, we have been referring to the UNIX file hierarchy as a "file system" as if all files and directories are held together in one big superstructure. That is seldom the case, and never so in large systems. The hard disk is split up into distinct **partitions** (or *slices*), with a separate **file system** in each partition (or slice).

Every file system has a directory structure headed by root. If you have three file systems, then you are dealing with three separate root directories. One of these file systems is called the **root file system** which is more equal than others in at least one respect: its root directory is also the root directory of the combined UNIX system. The root file system contains most of the essential files of the UNIX system. At the time of booting, the other file systems *mount* (attach) themselves to the root file system, creating the illusion of a single file system to the user.

Every file is associated with a table called the **inode** (shortened from index node). The inode is accessed by the **inode number** and contains the following attributes of a file:

- File type (regular, directory, device, etc.).
- File permissions (the nine permissions and three more).
- Number of links (the number of aliases the file has).
- The UID of the owner.
- The GID of the group owner.
- File size in bytes.
- Date and time of last modification.
- Date and time of last access.
- Date and time of last change of the inode.
- An array of pointers that keep track of all disk blocks used by the file.

Observe that the inode doesn't store either the name of the file or the inode number. Both attributes are stored in the directory. `ls` displays the inode number with the `-i` option:

```
$ ls -i date.sh
   254414 date.sh
```

Every file system has its own set of inodes stored in a separate area of the disk. Since a UNIX machine usually comprises multiple file systems, you can conclude that the inode number for a file is unique in a *single* file system.

How cat and ls Work

When you run **cat foo**, the kernel first locates the inode number of foo from the current directory. Next, it reads the inode for foo to fetch the file size and the addresses of the disk blocks that contain the file's data. It then goes to each block and reads the data till the the number of characters displayed is equal to the file size.

When you execute `ls -l progs` where progs is a directory, the kernel looks up the directory progs and reads all entries. For every entry, the kernel looks up the inode to fetch the file's attributes.

Three More Permission Bits

So far, we restricted our discussions to nine permission bits. But the inode stores 12 permission bits. We'll be discussing the remaining three bits at different points in the text, but a brief discussion is presented here for completeness.

After completing Chapter 8, you'll appreciate that file permissions actually apply to the *process* run by the user. When you run **cat foo**, a process named **cat** is created from the **cat** program. Even though the **cat** executable is owned by root, the UID of the **cat** process is that of the user running the program.

This scheme works in most instances except for certain critical events. A process must sometimes take on the powers of the *owner* of the program, especially in situations where the owner is root. The **passwd** command (which changes your own password) modifies the file /etc/shadow even though the file is unreadable to nonprivileged users. Thus, **passwd** must run as if it's executed by the superuser.

Two permission bits determine whether a process will run with the UID and GID of the owner and group owner. These two bits, *set-user-id* (SUID) and *set-group-id* (SGID), can be set with **chmod**, and we'll reexamine them in Chapter 19.

The third bit, the *sticky bit,* also applies to a file, but today it is more useful when set on a directory. Such directories can be shared by a group of users in a safe manner so that they can create, modify, and remove their own files and not those of others. The sticky bit is also taken up in Chapter 19.

4.7 ln: **Creating Hard Links**

Why is the filename not stored in the node? So that a file can have multiple filenames. When that happens, we say the file has more than one **link**. We can then access the file by any of its links. A file's link count is normally one, but observe from Fig. 4.1 that backup.sh has two links:

```
-rwxr-xr--  2 romeo    metal       163 Jul 13 21:36 backup.sh
```

The **ln** command links a file, thus providing it with an alias and increasing the link count by one. This count is maintained in the inode. **ln** can create both a *hard* and a *soft* link (discussed later) and has a syntax similar to the one used by **cp**. Before we use it to create a hard link, let's recall the listing of date.sh which we used in Section 4.2, and then link it with who.sh:

```
$ ls -li date.sh                                              -i displays inode number
   254414 -rw-r--r--  1 romeo    metal     5 Aug 16 09:38 date.sh
$ ln date.sh who.sh                                          Link count increases to 2
$ ls -il date.sh who.sh
   254414 -rw-r--r--  2 romeo    metal     5 Aug 16 09:38 date.sh
   254414 -rw-r--r--  2 romeo    metal     5 Aug 16 09:38 who.sh
```

Prior to the invocation of **ln**, the current directory had an entry containing date.sh and its inode number, 254414. After the invocation, the kernel performed two tasks:

- It added an entry to the directory for the filename who.sh, but having the same inode number.
- It also updated the link count in the inode from one to two.

Note that there's actually one file and that we can't refer to them as two "files," but only as two "filenames." Changes made in one alias (link) are automatically available in the others. If you create one more link (using, for example, **ln who.sh ps.sh**), another directory entry will be created and the link count would be incremented to three.

ln won't work if the destination filename exists, but you can force linking with the -f option. You can also use **ln** with multiple files (i.e., create a link for each), but then the destination filename must be a directory. Here's how you create links for all shell scripts in the directory shell_scripts:

```
ln *.sh shell_scripts
```

If *.sh matches 27 filenames, then there will be 27 linked filenames in shell_scripts; i.e., there will be 27 entries in that directory.

We use **rm** to remove files. Technically speaking, **rm** simply reverses the action of **ln;** the kernel removes the directory entry for the link and brings down the link count in the inode. The following command removes one link:

```
$ rm who.sh ; ls -l date.sh
   254414 -rw-r--r--   1 romeo     metal      5 Aug 16 09:38 date.sh
```

The link count has come down to one. Another **rm** will further bring it down to zero. A file is considered to be completely removed from the system when its link count drops to zero.

rm and **ln** are complementary, which is evident from the names of the system calls they use—**unlink** and **link**. The effect they have on the inode and directory is depicted in Fig. 4.4.

FIGURE 4.4   *Effect of* **ln** *and* **rm** *on Inode and Directory*

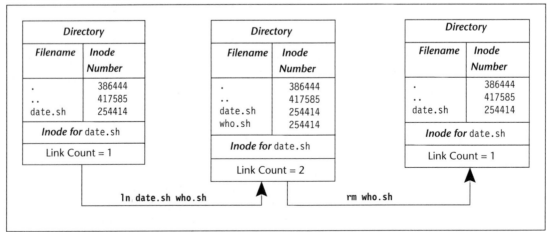

4.7.1   Where to Use Hard Links

Links are an interesting feature of the file system, but where does one use them? We can think of three situations straightaway:

1. Let's consider that you have written a number of programs that read a file `foo.txt` in `$HOME/input_files`. Later, you reorganized your directory structure and moved `foo.txt` to `$HOME/data` instead. What happens to all the programs that look for `foo.txt` at its original location? Simple, just link `foo.txt` to the directory `input_files`:

   ln data/foo.txt input_files   *Creates link in directory* input_files

   With this link available, your existing programs will continue to find `foo.txt` in the `input_files` directory. It's more convenient to do this than modify all programs to point to the new path.

2. Links provide some protection against accidental deletion, especially when they exist in different directories. Referring to the previous application, even though there's only a single file `foo.txt` on disk, you have effectively made a backup of this file. If you inadvertently delete `input_files/foo.txt`, one link will still be available in `data/foo.txt`; your file is not gone yet.

3. Because of links, we don't need to maintain two programs as two separate disk files if there is very little difference between them. A file's name is available to a C program (as `argv[0]`) and to a shell script (as $0). A single file with two links can have its program logic make it behave in two different ways depending on the name by which it is called. There's a shell script using this feature in Section 13.8.2.

Many UNIX commands are linked. Refer to Section 3.22, where we posed the question whether **gzip** and **gunzip** were two separate files. This question can now easily be answered by looking at their inode numbers:

```
$ cd /usr/bin ; ls -li gzip gunzip
    13975 -r-xr-xr-x   3 root      bin        60916 Jan  5  2000 gunzip
    13975 -r-xr-xr-x   3 root      bin        60916 Jan  5  2000 gzip
```

They are, in fact, one and the same file. The listing shows the existence of a third link as well, but how does one locate it? Doing an **ls -li** and then looking for entries with the same inode number may not always work; a link could be available in another directory. The **find** command which can do this job is discussed in Section 4.11.

4.8   ln Again: Creating Symbolic Links

To understand why we need symbolic links, let's extend the example that we considered as the first point in Section 4.7.1. Imagine that a hundred files in the directory `input_files` have been moved to the directory `data` as part of the reorganization process. To ensure that all programs still "see" the files in their original location, we could hard-link these files to the new data directory, but that would mean adding a hundred entries to this directory. It's here that one encounters two serious limitations of hard links:

- You can't link a file across two file systems. In other words, if input_files and data are on two separate file systems, you can't connect a file in one file system with a link to the other.
- You can't link a directory even within the same file system.

A **symbolic link** overcomes both problems. Until now, we have divided files into three categories (ordinary, directory, and device); the symbolic link is the fourth file type. Observe the listing in Fig. 4.1 yet again to locate the file hex.c:

```
lrwxrwxrwx  1 romeo  metal    17 Aug 11 00:49 hex.c -> c_progs/hexdump.c
```

A symbolic link is identified by the l (el) as the file type and the pointer notation, ->, that follows the filename. The **ln** command creates symbolic links also, but needs the -s option. We can create a symbolic link to date.sh, but this time the listing tells you a different story:

```
$ ln -s date.sh date.sym
$ ls -li date.sh date.sym
  254414 -rw-r--r--    1 romeo    metal       5 Aug 16 09:38 date.sh
  254411 lrwxrwxrwx    1 romeo    metal       7 Aug 18 06:52 date.sym -> date.sh
```

Here, date.sym is a symbolic link to date.sh. Unlike a hard link, a symbolic link is a separate file with its own inode number. date.sym simply contains the pathname date.sh as is evident from the file size (date.sh contains 7 characters). The two files are not identical; it's date.sh that actually has the contents. A command like **cat date.sym** *follows* the symbolic link and displays the file the link points to.

A symbolic link can also point to an absolute pathname, but to ensure portability, we often make it point to a relative pathname:

```
$ ln -s ../jscript/search.htm search.htm
$ ls -l search.htm
lrwxrwxrwx  1 romeo  metal 21  Mar 2 00:17 search.htm -> ../jscript/search.htm
```

To return to the problem of linking a hundred files in the directory data, you can use **ln** to connect data to a symbolic link named input_files:

```
ln -s data input_files
```
                                                                    First argument is a directory

Being more flexible, a symbolic link is also known as a **soft link** or **symlink**. As for a hard link, the **rm** command removes a symbolic link even if it points to a directory.

Symbolic links are used extensively in the UNIX system. System files constantly change locations with version enhancements. Yet it must be ensured that all programs still find the files where they originally were. Windows shortcuts are more like symbolic links.

A symbolic link has an inode number separate from the file that it points to. In most cases, the pathname is stored in the symbolic link and occupies space on disk. However, Linux uses a *fast symbolic link* which stores the pathname in the inode itself provided it doesn't exceed 60 characters.

Caution

Think twice before you delete the file or directory that a symlink points to. For instance, removing `date.sym` (considered in a previous example) won't affect us much because we can easily recreate the link. But if we remove `date.sh`, we would lose the file containing the data:

```
$ rm date.sh ; cat date.sym
cat: cannot open date.sym
```

A disaster of greater magnitude could occur if we remove `data` instead of `input_files`. We would then lose all hundred files! In either case, `date.sym` and `input_files` would point to a nonexistent file. These links are known as *dangling* symbolic links.

Note

The **pwd** command is built into most shells (except the C shell). When you use **cd** with a symbolic link in one of these shells, **pwd** shows you the path you used to get to the directory. This is not necessarily the same as the actual directory you are in. To know the "real" location, you should use the external command **/bin/pwd**.

4.9 File Ownership

The **chmod** and **ln** commands will fail if you don't have the *authority* to use them, i.e., if you don't own the file. Observe the listing of this file:

```
rw-r--r--  1 romeo    metal       5 Aug 16 09:38 date.sh
```

romeo can change all attributes of `date.sh` but not juliet—even if she belongs to the metal group. But if juliet copies this file to her home directory, then she'll be the owner of the copy and can then change all attributes of the copy at will.

Several users may belong to a single group. People working on a project are generally assigned a common group, and all files created by group members (who have separate user-ids) have the same group owner. However, make no mistake: The privileges of the group are set by the owner of the file and not by the group members.

When the system administrator creates a user account, she has to assign these parameters to the user:

- The **user-id (UID)**—both its name and numeric representation.
- The **group-id (GID)**—both its name and numeric representation. The administrator has to assign the group name also if the GID represents a new group.

The file `/etc/passwd` maintains three out of the four parameters. They are shown in Fig. 4.5 for a sample entry for the user romeo. The UID is shown in the first field (the name) and the third (the number). The fourth field signifies the GID (number only). The

FIGURE 4.5   *The UID and GID Components in* /etc/passwd

group database is maintained in /etc/group and contains the GID (both number and name). The inode however stores only the numbers, and commands like **ls** use these files as translation tables to display the names rather than the numbers. We'll discuss these two files when we add a user account in Chapter 19.

To know your own UID and GID without viewing /etc/passwd and /etc/group, use the **id** command:

Tip

```
$ id
uid=1003(romeo) gid=101(metal)
```

Whatever files this user creates will have romeo as the owner and metal as the group owner.

4.9.1   chown: Changing File Ownership

There are two commands meant to change the ownership of a file or directory—**chown** and **chgrp**. UNIX systems differ in the way they restrict the usage of these two commands. On BSD-based systems, only the system administrator can change a file's owner with **chown**. On the same systems, the restrictions are less severe when it comes to changing groups with **chgrp**. On other systems, only the owner can change both.

We'll first consider the behavior of BSD-based **chown** (**ch**ange **own**er) that has been adopted by many systems including Solaris and Linux. The command is used in this way:

chown *options owner* [:*group*] *file(s)*

chown transfers ownership of a file to a user, and the syntax shows that it can change the group as well. The command requires the (UID) of the recipient, followed by one or more filenames. Changing ownership requires superuser permission, so let's first change our status to that of superuser with the **su** command:

```
$ su
Password: ********                                      This is the root password!
# _                                                      This is another shell
```

su lets us acquire superuser status if we know the root password and returns a # prompt, the same prompt used by root. To now renounce the ownership of the file date.sh to juliet, use **chown** in the following way:

```
# ls -l date.sh
-rw-r--r--   1 romeo    metal                  5 Aug 18 09:23 date.sh
# chown juliet date.sh ; ls -l date.sh
-rw-r--r--   1 juliet   metal                  5 Aug 18 09:23 date.sh
# exit                                          Switches from superuser's shell
$ _                                                    to user's login shell
```

Once ownership of the file has been given away to juliet, the user file permissions that previously applied to romeo now apply to juliet. Thus, romeo can no longer edit date.sh since there's no write privilege for group and others. He can't get back the ownership either. But he can copy this file in which case he becomes the owner of the copy.

4.9.2 chgrp: Changing Group Owner

By default, the group owner of a file is the group to which the owner belongs. The **chgrp** (**ch**ange **group**) command changes a file's group owner. On systems that implement the BSD version of **chgrp** (like Solaris and Linux), a user can change the group owner of a file, but only to a group to which she also belongs. Yes, a user can belong to more than one group, and the one shown in /etc/passwd is the user's main group. We'll discuss *supplementary groups* in Chapter 19 featuring system administration.

    chgrp shares a similar syntax with **chown**. In the following example, romeo changes the group ownership of a file to dba (no superuser permission required):

```
$ ls -l prime.c
-r--r--r--   1 romeo    metal          268 Jul 13 21:36 prime.c
$ chgrp dba prime.c ; ls -l prime.c
-r--r--r--   1 romeo    dba            268 Jul 13 21:36 prime.c
```

This command will work on a BSD-based system if romeo is also a member of the dba group. If he is not, then only the superuser can make the command work. Note that romeo can reverse this action and restore the previous group ownership (to metal) because he is still owner of the file and consequently retains all rights related to it.

Using chown to Do Both As an added benefit, UNIX allows the administrator to use only **chown** to change both owner and group. The syntax requires the two arguments to be separated by a **:**

```
chown juliet:dba prime.c                        Ownership to juliet, group to dba
```

Like **chmod,** both **chown** and **chgrp** use the -R option to perform their operations in a recursive manner.

Tip

If you want members of a project to be able to read and write a set of files, ask the system administrator to have a common group for them and then set the permissions of the group to rwx. There's a better way of doing this (with the sticky bit), and it is discussed in Section 19.4.3.

4.9.3 How to Handle Intruders

View the original listing in Fig. 4.1 to detect two intruders in romeo's directory. Neither file is owned by romeo nor group-owned by metal:

```
-r--r--r--  1 256     105      13921 Jul 26  2001 987
-rwxr-xr-x  1 root    root      6496 Aug 10 10:20 a.out
```

To explain why numbers rather than names appear in the first line, recall that `ls -l` does a number-name translation. It prints the owner's name by looking up `/etc/passwd` and the group name by looking up `/etc/group`. These numbers are obviously not there in these files, so `ls` printed them as they are. Problems of this sort are often encountered when files are transferred from another system.

For the second file, romeo could have acquired root status to change the ownership of a file and then forgotten to revert to the normal user before compiling a C program. To remedy this situation, romeo needs to use the superuser account to run **chown** and **chgrp** on this file or ask the system administrator to do that job for him.

4.10 Modification and Access Times

The inode stores three time stamps. In this section, we'll be discussing just two of them (the first two of the following list):

- Time of last file modification   *Shown by* `ls -l`
- Time of last access   *Shown by* `ls -lu`
- Time of last inode modification   *Shown by* `ls -lc`

Whenever you write to a file, the time of last modification is updated in the inode. A file also has an access time, i.e., the last time someone read, wrote, or executed the file. This time is distinctly different from the modification time that gets set only when the contents of the file are changed. `ls -l` displays the last modification time, and `ls -lu` displays the last access time.

A directory can be modified by changing its entries—by creating, removing, and renaming files in the directory. Note that changing a file's contents only changes its last modification time but not that of its directory. For a directory, the access time is changed by a read operation only; creating or removing a file or doing a "cd" to a directory doesn't change its access time.

Even though `ls -l` and `ls -lu` show the time of last modification and access, respectively, the sort order remains standard, i.e., ASCII. However, when you add the -t option to -l or -lu, the files are actually displayed in *order* of the respective time stamps:

```
ls -lt     Displays listing in order of their modification time
ls -lut    Displays listing in order of their access time
```

Many tools used by the system administrator look at these time stamps to decide whether a particular file will participate in a backup or not. A file is often incorrectly stamped when extracting it from a backup with **tar** or **cpio**. Section 19.3.1 discusses how the **touch** command is used to rectify such situations.

Note

It's possible to change the access time of a file without changing its modification time. In an inverse manner, when you modify a file, you generally change its access time as well. However, on some systems, when you redirect output (with the > and >> symbols), you change the contents but not the last access time.

Tip

What happens when you copy a file with **cp?** By default, the copy has the modification and access time stamps set to the time of copying. Sometimes, you may not like this to happen. In that case, use **cp -p** (preserve) to retain both time stamps.

4.11   find: **Locating Files**

find is one of the power tools of the UNIX system. It *recursively* examines a directory tree to look for files matching some criteria and then takes some action on the selected files. It has a difficult command line, and if you have ever wondered why UNIX is hated by many, then you should look up the cryptic **find** documentation. However, **find** is easily tamed if you break up its arguments into three components:

find *path_list selection_criteria action*

Fig. 4.6 shows the structure of a typical **find** command. The command completely examines a directory tree in this way:

- First, it recursively examines all files in the directories specified in *path_list*. Here, it begins the search from /home.
- It then matches each file for one or more *selection_criteria*. This always consists of an expression in the form *-operator argument* (-name index.html). Here, **find** selects the file if it has the name index.html.
- Finally, it takes some action on those selected files. The action -print simply displays the **find** output on the terminal.

All **find** operators (also referred to as *options* in this text) begin with a hyphen. You can provide one or more subdirectories as the *path_list* and multiple *selection_criteria* to match one or more files. This makes the command difficult to use initially, but it is a program that every user must master since it lets her make file selection under practically any condition.

As our first example, let's use **find** to locate all files named a.out (the executable file generated by the C compiler):

```
$ find / -name a.out -print
/home/romeo/scripts/a.out
/home/andrew/scripts/reports/a.out
/home/juliet/a.out
```

F I G U R E 4.6 *Structure of a **find** command*

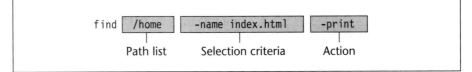

Since the search starts from the root directory, **find** displays absolute pathnames. You can also use relative names in the path list, and **find** will then output a list of relative pathnames. Moreover, when **find** is used to match a group of filenames with a wildcard pattern, the pattern should be quoted to prevent the shell from looking at it:

```
find . -name "*.c" -print                          All files with extension .c
find . -name '[A-Z]*' -print                       Single quotes will also do
```

The first command looks for all C program source files in the current directory tree. The second one searches for all files whose names begin with an uppercase letter. You must not forget to use the -print option because without it, **find** on UNIX systems will look for files all right but won't print the list.

find in UNIX displays the file list only if the -print operator is used. However, Linux doesn't need this option; it prints by default. Linux also doesn't need the path list; it uses the current directory by default. Linux even prints the entire file list when used without any options whatsoever! This behavior is not required by POSIX.

4.11.1   Selection Criteria

The -name operator is not the only operator used in framing the selection criteria; there are many others (Table 4.4). We'll consider the selection criteria first, and then the possible actions we can take on the selected files.

Locating a File by Inode Number (-inum) Refer to Section 4.7.1, where we found that **gzip** has three links and **gunzip** was one of them. **find** allows us to locate files by their inode number. Use the -inum option to find all filenames that have the same inode number:

```
$ find / -inum 13975 -print                  Inode number obtained from Section 4.7.1
find: cannot read dir /usr/lost+found: Permission denied
/usr/bin/gzip
/usr/bin/gunzip
/usr/bin/gzcat                                          "Cats" a compressed file
```

Now we know what the three links are. Note that **find** throws an error message when it can't change to a directory. Read the Tip below.

If you use **find** from a nonprivileged account to start its search from root, the command will generate a lot of error messages on being unable to "cd" to a directory. Since you might miss the selected file in an error-dominated list, the error messages should be directed by using the command in this way: find / -name typescript -print 2>/dev/null. Note that you can't do this in the C shell. Section 7.7 explains the significance of 2>/dev/null.

File Type and Permissions (-type and -perm) The -type option followed by the letter f, d, or l selects files of the ordinary, directory, and symbolic link type. Here's how you locate all directories of your home directory tree:

TABLE 4.4 *Major Expressions Used by* **find** *(Meaning gets reversed when – is replaced by +, and vice versa)*

Selection Criteria	Selects File
-inum *n*	Having inode number *n*
-type *x*	If of type *x*; *x* can be f (ordinary file), d (directory), or 1 (symbolic link)
-perm *nnn*	If octal permissions match *nnn* completely
-links *n*	If having *n* links
-user *usname*	If owned by *usname*
-group *gname*	If owned by group *gname*
-size +*x*[c]	If size greater than *x* blocks (characters if c is also specified) (*Chapter 19*)
-mtime -*x*	If modified in less than *x* days
-newer *flname*	If modified after *flname* (*Chapter 19*)
-mmin -*x*	If modified in less than *x* minutes (*Linux only*)
-atime +*x*	If accessed in more than *x* days
-amin +*x*	If accessed in more than *x* minutes (*Linux only*)
-name *flname*	*flname*
-iname *flname*	As above, but match is case-insensitive (*Linux only*)
-follow	After following a symbolic link
-prune	But don't descend directory if matched
-mount	But don't look in other file systems
Action	*Significance*
-print	Prints selected file on standard output
-ls	Executes **ls -lids** command on selected files
-exec *cmd*	Executes UNIX command *cmd* followed by {} \;
-ok *cmd*	Like -exec, except that command is executed after user confirmation

```
$ cd ; find . -type d -print 2>/dev/null
```
.   Shows the . also
./.netscape   *Displays hidden directories also*
./java_progs
./c_progs
./c_progs/include
./.ssh

Note that the relative pathname **find** displays, but that's because the pathname itself was relative (.). **find** also doesn't necessarily display an ASCII sorted list. The sequence in which files are displayed depends on the internal organization of the file system.

The -perm option specifies the permissions to match. For instance, -perm 666 selects files having read and write permission for all user categories. Such files are security hazards. You'll often want to use two options in combination to restrict the search to only directories:

```
find $HOME -perm 777 -type d -print
```

find uses an AND condition (an implied -a operator between -perm and -type) to select directories that provide all access rights to everyone. It selects files only if both selection criteria (-perm and -type) are fulfilled.

Finding Unused Files (-mtime and -atime) Files tend to build up incessantly on disk. Some of them remain unaccessed or unmodified for months—even years. **find**'s options can easily match a file's modification (-mtime) and access (-atime) times to select them. The -mtime option helps in backup operations by providing a list of those files that have been modified, say, in less than 2 days:

```
find . -mtime -2 -print
```

Here, -2 means *less* than 2 days. To select from the /home directory all files that have not been accessed for more than a year, a positive value has to be used with -atime:

```
find /home -atime +365 -print
```

Note

+365 means greater than 365 days; -365 means less than 365 days. For specifying exactly 365, use 365.

4.11.2 The find Operators (!, -o, and -a)

There are three operators that are commonly used with **find**. The ! operator is used before an option to negate its meaning. So,

```
find . ! -name "*.c" -print
```

selects all but the C program files. To look for both shell and **perl** scripts, use the -o operator which represents an OR condition. We need to use an escaped pair of parentheses here:

```
find /home \( -name "*.sh" -o -name "*.pl" \) -print
```

The (and) are special characters that are interpreted by the shell to run commands in a group *(7.6.2)*. The same characters are used by **find** to group expressions using the -o and -a operators, the reason why they need to be escaped.

The -a operator represents an AND condition, and is implied by default whenever two selection criteria are placed together.

4.11.3 Operators of the Action Component

Displaying the Listing (-ls) The -print option belongs to the *action* component of the **find** syntax. In real life, you'll often want to take some action on the selected files and not just display the filenames. For instance, you may want to view the listing with the -ls option:

```
$ find . -type f -mtime +2 -mtime -5 -ls                    -a option implied
475336 1 -rw-r--r-- 1 romeo users 716 Aug 17 10:31 ./c_progs/fileinout.c
```

find here runs the **ls -lids** command to display a special listing of those regular files that are modified in more than two days and less than five days. In this example, we see two options in the selection criteria (both -mtime) simulating an AND condition. It's the same as using \(-mtime +2 -a -mtime -5 \).

Taking Action on Selected Files (-exec and -ok) The -exec option allows you to run any UNIX command on the selected files. -exec takes the command to execute as its own argument, followed by {} and finally the rather cryptic symbols \; (backslash and semicolon). This is how you can reuse a previous **find** command quite meaningfully:

find $HOME -type f -atime +365 -exec rm {} \;   *Note the usage*

This will use **rm** to remove all ordinary files unaccessed for more than a year. This can be a risky thing to do, so you can consider using **rm**'s -i option. But all commands don't have interactive options, in which case, you should use **find**'s -ok option:

```
$ find $HOME -type f -atime +365 -ok mv {} $HOME/safe \;
< mv ... ./archive.tar.gz > ? y
< mv ... ./yourunix02.txt > ? n
< mv ... ./yourunix04.txt > ? y
    .......
```

mv turns interactive with -i but only if the destination file exists. Here, -ok seeks confirmation for every selected file to be moved to the $HOME/safe directory irrespective of whether the files exist at the destination or not. A y deletes the file.

find is the system administrator's tool, and in Chapter 19, you'll see it used for a number of tasks. It is specially suitable for backing up files and for use in tandem with the **xargs** command (See Going Further of Chapter 7).

Note

The pair of {} is a placeholder for a filename. So, -exec cp {} {}.bak provides a .bak extension to all selected files. Don't forget to use the \; symbols at the end of every -exec or -ok option.

SUMMARY

The **ls -l** command displays the *listing* containing seven file attributes. **ls -ld** used with a directory name lists directory attributes.

A file can have read, write, or execute permission, and there are three sets of such permissions for the *user, group,* and *others*. A file's owner uses **chmod** to alter file permissions. The permissions can be *relative* or *absolute*. The octal digit 7 includes read (4), write (2), and execute permissions (1).

Permissions have different significance for directories. Read permission means that the filenames stored in the directory are readable. Write permission implies that you are permitted to create or remove files in the directory. Execute (or *search*) permission means that you can change to that directory with the **cd** command.

The *umask* setting determines the default permissions that will be used when creating a file or a directory.

Multiple *file systems,* each with its own root directory are *mounted* at boot time to appear as a single file system. A file's attributes are stored in the *inode* which is identified by the *inode number*. The inode number is unique in a single file system.

A file can have more than one name or *link,* and is linked with **ln**. Two linked filenames have the same inode number. A *symbolic link* contains the pathname of another file or directory and is created with **ln -s**. The file pointed to can reside on another file system. **rm** removes both types of links.

Hard links provide protection against accidental deletion but removing the file pointed to by a symlink can be dangerous. Both links enable you to write program code that does different things depending on the name by which the file is invoked.

chown and **chgrp** are used to transfer ownership and group ownership, respectively. They can be used by the owner of the file on AT&T systems. On BSD systems, **chown** can be used only by the superuser, and a user can use **chgrp** to change her group to another to which she also belongs.

A file has three time stamps including the time of last modification and access.

find looks for files by matching one or more file attributes. A file can be specified by type (-type), name (-name), permissions (-perm), or by its time stamps (-mtime and -atime). The -print option is commonly used, but any UNIX command can be run on the selected files with or without user confirmation (-ls, -exec, and -ok).

SELF-TEST

4.1   What do you understand by the *listing* of a file? How will you save the complete listing of all files and directories (including the hidden ones) in the system?

4.2   Show the octal representation of these permissions: (i) rwxr-xrw-, (ii) rw-r-----, (iii) --x-w-r--.

4.3   What will the permissions string look like for these octal values? (i) 567, (ii) 623, (iii) 421

4.4   What does a group member require to be able to remove a file?

4.5   If a file's permissions are 000, can the superuser still read and write it?

4.6   You removed the write permission of a file from group and others, and yet they could delete your file. How could that happen?

4.7   Try creating a directory in the system directories /bin and /tmp and explain your observations.

4.8   Copy a file with permissions 444. Copy it again and explain your observations.

4.9   How do you ensure that all ordinary files created by you have rw-rw---- as the default permissions?

4.10   How do you display the inode number of a file?

4.11   What does the inode store? Which important file attribute is not maintained in the inode? Where is it stored then?

4.12   What do you mean by saying that a file has three *links*?

4.13   How do you remove (i) a hard link, (ii) a symbolic link pointing to a directory?

4.14   How do you link all C source files in the current directory and place the links in another directory, bar?

4.15   A symbolic link has the same inode number as the file it is linked to. True or false?

4.16   How do you link foo1 to foo2 using (i) a hard link, (ii) a symbolic link? If you delete foo2, does it make any difference?

4.17   Copy the file /etc/passwd to your current directory and then observe the listing of the copy. Which attributes have changed?

4.18   Where are the UID and GID of a file stored?

4.19   How is **chown** different from **chgrp** on a BSD-based system when it comes to renouncing ownership?

4.20   Explain with reference to the dot and * what the following commands do: (i) chown -R project ., (ii) chgrp -R project *.

4.21   When you invoke ls -l foo the access time of foo changes. True or false?

4.22   View the access time of a file with ls -lu foo before appending the **date** command output to it using **date >> foo**. Observe the access time again. What do you see?

4.23   Devise a **find** command to locate in /docs and /usr/docs all filenames that (i) begin with z, (ii) have the extension .html or .java..

EXERCISES

4.1   A file contains 1026 bytes. How many bytes of disk space does it occupy?

4.2   Does the owner always belong to the same group as the group owner of a file?

4.3   Explain the significance of the following commands: (i) ls -ld ., (ii) ls -l ...

4.4   Create a file foo. How do you assign all permissions to the owner and remove all permissions from others using (i) relative assignment and (ii) absolute assignment? Do you need to make any assumptions about foo's default permissions?

4.5   From the security viewpoint, explain the consequences of creating a file with permissions (i) 000, (ii) 777.

4.6   Examine the output of the two commands below on a BSD-based system. Explain whether romeo can (i) edit, (ii) delete, (iii) change permissions, (iv) change ownership of foo:

```
$ who am i ; ls -l foo
romeo
-r--rw----    1 sumit    romeo         78 Jan 27 16:57 foo
```

4.7   Assuming that a file's current permissions are rw-r-xr--, specify the **chmod** expression required to change them to (i) rwxrwxrwx, (ii) r--r-----, (iii) ---r--r--, (iv) ---------, using both relative and absolute methods of assigning permissions.

4.8   Use **chmod -w .** and then try to create and remove a file in the current directory. Can you do that? Is the command the same as **chmod a-w foo**?

4.9   You tried to copy a file foo from another user's directory, but you got the error message cannot create file foo. You have write permission in your own directory. What could be the reason, and how do you copy the file?

4.10   What do you do to ensure that no one is able to see the names of the files you have?

4.11   The command **cd bar** failed where bar is a directory. How can that happen?

4.12   If a file has the permissions 000, you may or may not be able to delete the file. Explain how both situations can happen. Does the execute permission have any role to play here?

4.13   If the owner doesn't have write permission on a file but her group has, can she (i) edit it, (ii) delete it?

4.14   If **umask** shows the value (i) 000, (ii) 002, what implications do they have from the security viewpoint?

4.15   The UNIX file system has many root directories even though it actually shows one. True or false?

4.16   What change takes place in the inode and directory when a filename is connected by a hard link?

4.17   If **ls -li** shows two filenames with the same inode number, what does that indicate?

4.18   What happens when you invoke the command **ln foo bar** if (i) bar doesn't exist, (ii) bar exists as an ordinary file, (iii) bar exists as a directory?

4.19   How can you make out whether two files are copies or links?

4.20   Explain two application areas of hard links. What are the two main disadvantages of the hard link?

4.21   You have a number of programs in $HOME/progs which are called by other programs. You have now decided to move these programs to $HOME/internet/progs. How can you ensure that users don't notice this change?

4.22   Explain the significance of *fast symbolic links* and *dangling symbolic links*.

4.23   Explain how **ls** obtains the (i) filename, (ii) name of owner, (iii) name of group owner when displaying the listing.

4.24   How will you determine whether your system uses the BSD or AT&T version of **chown** and **chgrp**?

4.25   The owner can change all attributes of a file on a BSD-based system. Explain whether the statement is true or false. Is there any attribute that can be changed *only* by the superuser?

4.26   What are the three time stamps maintained in the inode, and how do you display two of them for the file foo?

4.27   How can you find out whether a program has been executed today?

4.28   Explain the difference between (i) ls -l and ls -lt, (ii) ls -lu and ls -lut.

4.29   Use **find** to locate from your home directory tree all (i) files with the extension .html or .HTML, (ii) files having the inode number 9076, (iii) directories having permissions 666, (iv) files modified yesterday. Will any of these commands fail?

4.30   Use **find** to (i) move all files modified within the last 24 hours to the posix directory under your parent directory, (ii) locate all files named a.out or core in your home directory tree and remove them interactively, (iii) locate the file login.sql in the /oracle directory tree, and then copy it to your own directory, (iv) change all directory permissions to 755 and all file permissions to 644 in your home directory tree.

## CHAPTER 5

The vi/vim Editor

N o matter what work you do with the UNIX system, you'll eventually write some C programs or shell (or **perl**) scripts. You may have to edit some of the system files at times. For all of this you must learn to use an editor, and UNIX provides a very old and versatile one—**vi**. Bill Joy created this editor for the BSD system. The program is now standard on all UNIX systems. Bram Moolenaar improved it and called it **vim** (**vi im**proved). In this text, we discuss **vi** and also note the features of **vim**, available in Linux.

Like any editor, **vi** supports a number of internal commands for navigation and text editing. It also permits copying and moving text both within a file and from one file to another. The commands are cryptic but often mnemonic. **vi** makes complete use of the keyboard where practically every key has a function. There are numerous features available in this editor, but a working knowledge of it is all that you are required to have initially. The advanced features of **vi** are taken up in Appendix C.

Objectives

- Know the three modes in which **vi** operates for sharing the workload.
- Repeat a command multiple times using a *repeat factor*.
- Insert, append, and replace text in the *Input Mode*.
- Save the buffer and quit the editor using the *ex Mode*.
- Perform navigation in a relative and absolute manner in the *Command Mode*.
- The concept of a *word* as a navigation unit for movement along a line.
- Learn simple editing functions like deleting characters and changing the case of text.
- Understand the use of *operator–command* combinations to delete, yank (copy) and move text.
- Copy and move text from one file to another.
- Undo the last editing action and repeat the last command.
- Search for a pattern, and repeat the search both forward and back.
- Replace one string with another.
- Master the three-function sequence to (i) search for a pattern, (ii) take some action, and (iii) repeat the search and action.
- Customize **vi** using the **:set** command and the file ~/.exrc.
- Become familiar with two powerful features available in **vim**—word completion and multiple undoing.
- Map your keys and define abbreviations *(Going Further)*

5.1   vi **Basics**

vi is unlike other editors. It operates in three modes, and specific functions are assigned to each mode. We can see these modes at work when we add some text to a file. Invoke **vi** with the name of a nonexistent file, say `sometext`:

```
vi sometext
```

vi presents you a full screen with the filename shown at the bottom with the qualifier, [New File]. The cursor is positioned at the top, and all remaining lines of the screen (except the last) show a ~. You can't take your cursor there yet; they are nonexistent lines. The last line is used for running some commands and displaying system-generated messages.

You are now in the *Command Mode*. In this mode you pass commands to act on text. Pressing a key doesn't show it on screen but could perform a function like moving the cursor to the next line or deleting a line. You can't use the Command Mode to enter or replace text.

Now press the key marked **i**, and you are in the *Input Mode,* ready to input text. Subsequent key depressions will now show up on the screen as text input. Insert a few lines of text, each line followed by *[Enter],* as shown in Fig. 5.1. If you see something that shouldn't be there, backspace to wipe it out. If a word has been misspelled, use *[Ctrl-w]* to erase the entire word.

The **current line** is the one on which the cursor is now located (like the current directory). At this moment, the last line is the current line. Now press the *[Esc]* key to revert to *Command Mode.* Press it again, and you'll hear a beep; a beep in **vi** indicates that a key has been pressed unnecessarily.

Now that you are in Command Mode, you can move horizontally along the current line using the keys **h** and **l** (el). Press **h** to take the cursor left and **l** to take it right. Use a *repeat factor* and try **5h** and **3l** to see whether the cursor moves five spaces left and three spaces right. The repeat factor is explained in Section 5.2. Simple navigation in the four directions is discussed in Section 5.6.1.

FIGURE 5.1   *Inserting Some Text*

```
    You started text insertion by pressing i.[Enter]
    Don't forget to press [Esc] after keying in text.[Enter]
    Then use the h and l keys to move the cursor horizontally.[Enter]
    Also try using j and k for moving up and down.[Enter]
    Note that your text is still in the buffer and not on disk.[Enter]
    Finally, use :x[Enter] to save the buffer to disk and quit vi.[Enter]
    ~
    ~
    ~
    ~
    ~

    :x[Enter]                              Saves work and quits editor
```

The entered text hasn't been saved on disk yet but exists in some temporary storage called a *buffer*. To save this buffer, you must switch to the *ex Mode* or *Last Line Mode* (the third mode) by entering a : (colon), which shows up in the last line. Next enter an x and press *[Enter]:*

:**x***[Enter]*	*Must be in Command Mode first*
"sometext" 6 lines, 232 characters	
$ _	*Quits editor—back to shell prompt*

The file is saved on disk, and **vi** returns the shell prompt. To modify this file, you'll have to invoke **vi sometext** again. But before moving ahead, let's summarize the modes used by **vi**:

- **Command Mode**—The default mode where every key pressed is interpreted as a command to run on text. Navigation, copying, and deleting text are performed in this mode. You used **h** and **l** in this mode to move the cursor along a line.
- **Input Mode**— This mode is invoked by pressing one of the keys shown in Table 5.1. Every key pressed subsequently shows up as text. Pressing *[Esc]* in this mode takes **vi** to Command Mode. We used **i** as an Input Mode command.
- **ex Mode** or **Last Line Mode**—This mode is used for file handling and performing substitution. **vi** was originally hard-linked to a line editor named **ex**; that's where this mode got its name from. A : in the Command Mode invokes this mode, and is then followed by an ex Mode command. **vi** normally switches to the Command Mode after the ex Mode command is run, though we used :**x** to save the buffer and quit **vi**.

Much of the chapter deals with Command Mode commands where most of the action is. Some of these commands also have ex Mode equivalents which are sometimes easier to use. But all three modes also have their own exclusive features, and an editing session in **vi** involves constant switching between modes as depicted in Fig. 5.2.

5.1.1 The File .exrc

The default behavior of **vi** is adequate for novices, but as you get comfortable with it, you'll feel the need to customize it. **vi** reads the file $HOME/.exrc (same as ~/.exrc in some

TABLE 5.1 *Input Mode Commands*

Command	Function
i	Inserts text to left of cursor (Existing text shifted right)
a	Appends text to right of cursor (Existing text shifted right)
I	Inserts text at beginning of line (Existing text shifted right)
A	Appends text at end of line
o	Opens line below
O	Opens line above
r*ch*	Replaces single character under cursor with *ch* (No *[Esc]* required)
R	Replaces text from cursor to right (Existing text overwritten)
s	Replaces single character under cursor with any number of characters
S	Replaces entire line

FIGURE 5.2 *The Three Modes*

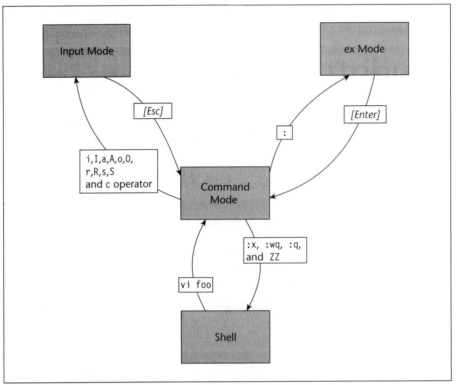

shells) on startup. If **ls -a** doesn't show this file in your home directory, then you can create or copy one. Linux users must note that **vim** generally doesn't use .exrc, but only .vimrc.

Many ex Mode commands can be placed in this file so they are available in every session. You can create abbreviations, redefine your keys to behave differently, and make variable settings. Your .exrc will progressively develop into an exclusive "library" containing all shortcuts and settings that you use regularly. It could be your most prized possession, so always keep a backup of this file.

5.2 A Few Tips First

We are about to take off, but before we do, a few tips at this stage will stand you in good stead. You must keep them in mind at all times when you are doing work with **vi**:

- *Make use of the repeat factor.* Like **more** *(3.16)*, **vi** also supports the use of a **repeat factor** as a command prefix to repeat the command as many times as the prefix. So if the Command Mode command **k** moves the cursor up one line, then **10k** moves it up 10 lines. Use the repeat factor wherever you can to speed up operations.

- *Undo whenever you make a mistake.*   If you have made a mistake in editing, either by wrongly deleting text or inserting it at an incorrect location, then as a first measure, just press *[Esc]* and then **u** to undo the last action. If that makes matters worse, use **u** again. Linux users should instead use *[Ctrl-r]*.
- *Use [Ctrl-l] to clear the screen.*   If the screen gets garbled, enter this control sequence in the Command Mode to redraw the screen. If you hit *[Ctrl-l]* in the Input Mode, you'll see the symbol ^L on the screen. Use the backspace key to wipe it out, press *[Esc]*, and then hit *[Ctrl-l]*.
- *Don't use [CapsLock] on most occasions.*   **vi** commands are case-sensitive; **a** and **A** are different Input Mode commands. Even if you have to activate *[CapsLock]* to enter a block of text in uppercase, make sure you deactivate it after text entry is complete.
- *Don't use the PC navigation keys*   Avoid using the keys marked Up, Down, Left, and Right, *[PageUp]* and *[PageDown]*. Many of them could fail when you use **vi** over a network connection. **vi** provides an elaborate set of keys for navigation purposes.
- **vi** reads the TERM variable to determine the file that contains the terminal's characteristics. As discussed later *(9.3)*, **vi** actually reads a file in a specific directory to know the control sequences that apply to the terminal name assigned to TERM. You should always check TERM whenever **vi** behaves in an awkward manner.

Note

Only the keys g, K, q, v, V, and Z have no function in the standard **vi** implementation. Some of them are defined, however, in **vim**.

5.3 Input Mode—Entering and Replacing Text

In this section, we take up all the commands that let you enter the Input Mode from the Command Mode. When a key of the Input Mode is pressed, it doesn't appear on the screen, but subsequent key depressions do. We'll consider the following commands:

- Insert and append (**i**, **a**, **I**, and **A**)
- Replace (**r**, **R**, **s**, and **S**)
- Open a line (**o** and **0**)

Always keep in mind that after you have completed text entry using any of these commands (except **r**), you must return to the Command Mode by pressing *[Esc]*. Most of these commands can also be used with a repeat factor, though you'll need to use it with only some of them.

Before you start using the Input Mode commands, enter this ex Mode command:

`:set showmode`*[Enter]*

Tip

Enter a : (the ex Mode prompt), and you'll see it appearing in the last line. Follow it with the two words and press *[Enter]*. showmode sets one of the parameters of the **vi** environment. Messages like INSERT MODE, REPLACE MODE or CHANGE MODE, etc. will now appear in the last line when you run an Input Mode command. We'll learn later to make the setting permanent by placing it in `$HOME/.exrc`.

5.3.1   Inserting and Appending Text (i and a)

The simplest type of input is the insertion of text. Just press

i   *Existing text will be shifted right*

Pressing this key changes the mode from Command to Input. Since the showmode setting was made at the beginning (with `:set showmode`), you'll see the words INSERT MODE at the bottom-right corner of the screen. You can now input as much text as you like.

   If the **i** command is invoked with the cursor positioned on existing text, text on its right will be shifted further without being overwritten. The insertion of text with **i** is shown in Fig. 5.3. All figures in this chapter use this shaded box ▋ to represent the cursor and the ☐ to signify a space (when its presence isn't all that obvious).

   There are other methods of inputting text. To append text to the right of the cursor, use

a   *Existing text will also be shifted right*

followed by the text you wish to key in (Fig. 5.4). After you have finished editing, press *[Esc]*. With **i** and **a**, you can input several lines of text.

5.3.2   Inserting and Appending Text at Line Extremes (I and A)

I and **A** behave somewhat like **i** and **a** except that they work at line extremes by also performing the necessary navigation to move there:

I   Inserts text at beginning of line.
A   Appends text at end of line.

FIGURE 5.3   *Inserting Text with* **i**

Original Text	vi Commands	Transformed Text
printf(▋No entry);	**i**"*[Esc]*	printf(▋"No entry);
printf("No entr▋);	**i**\n"*[Esc]*	printf("No entry\n▋);
if (x < 5) { ▋break;	**i***[Tab][Esc]*	if (x < 5) { ▋break;

FIGURE 5.4   *Appending Text with* **a**

Original Text	vi Commands	Transformed Text
echo "Filename:▋"	**a**\c*[Esc]*	echo "Filename:\▋"
if [▋$x -gt 5]	**a**☐*[Esc]*	if [▋$x -gt 5]
cas▋	**a** $# in*[Esc]*	case $# i▋
echo "▋"	**10a****[Esc]*	echo "*********▋"

These two commands are suitable for converting code to comment lines in a C program (Fig. 5.5). A comment line in C is of the form /* *comment* */. Use **I** on an existing line that you now wish to convert to a comment, and then enter the symbols /*. After pressing *[Esc]*, use **A** to append */ at the end of the line and press *[Esc]* again. A document author often needs to use **A** to add a sentence to a paragraph.

C language programmers sometimes precede a block of comment lines with a pattern like this:

/**

It seems that there are 70 asterisks here, and to draw them you should use a repeat factor. After you have entered / in the Input Mode, press *[Esc]*, and then enter **70a***/*[Esc]*. You'll see 70 asterisks appended to the /.

Tip

5.3.3   Opening a New Line (o and 0)

Often it has been observed that people migrating from a word-processing environment use a convoluted sequence to open a new line below the current line. They move the cursor past the end of the current line and then press *[Enter]*. In **vi**, you are better off using **o** and **0** instead. To open a line below *from anywhere in a line,* simply press

o   *Opens a new line below the current line*

This inserts an empty line below the current line (Fig. 5.6). **0** also opens a line but above the current line. Note that to insert a line before the first line, you need **0** and not **o**. Press *[Esc]* after completing text input.

FIGURE 5.5   *Using* **I** *and* **A**

Original Text	vi Commands	Transformed Text
Set up an infinite loop	**I**/*▓*[Esc]	/*Set up an infinite loop
/*Set up an infinite loop	**A**▓*/*[Esc]	/* Set up an infinite loop */▓
exit(0)	**A**;[Enter]}[Esc]	exit(0); }

FIGURE 5.6   *Opening a New Line with* **o** *and* **0**

Original Text	vi Commands	Transformed Text
#count.sh: Counts patterns	**o**#[Esc]	#count.sh: Counts patterns #▓
#count.sh: Counts patterns #	**0**#!/bin/sh[Esc]	#!/bin/sh▓ #count.sh: Counts patterns #

5.3.4   Replacing Text (r, s, R, and S)

To change existing text, **vi** provides mainly four commands (actually, more) as shown in the heading. To replace a single character with another, you should use

r   *No [Esc] required*

followed by the character that replaces the one under the cursor (Fig. 5.7). You can replace a single character only in this way. **vi** momentarily switches from Command Mode to Input Mode when **r** is pressed. It returns to the Command Mode as soon as the new character is entered. There's no need to press *[Esc]* when using **r** and the replacement character, since **vi** expects a single character anyway.

When you want to replace the letter d with 10f in a **printf** statement in C, you need to replace one character with three. In that case, press

s   *Replaces one character with many*

vi deletes the character under the cursor and switches to Input Mode (Fig. 5.8). It may also show a $ at that location to indicate that replacement will not affect text on its right. Now enter 10f and press *[Esc]*. To replace multiple characters, use a repeat factor. **3s** replaces three characters with new text.

R and **S** act in a similar manner compared to their lowercase versions except that they act on a larger group of characters:

R   Replaces all text on the right of the cursor position.
S   Replaces the entire line irrespective of the cursor position. (Existing line disappears)

Using **R** in **vi** is like using *[Insert]* to activate the overwrite mode in Windows. Try using the repeat factor with **R** and **S**, and see whether you can take advantage of this feature. Use of **R** and **S** is shown in Fig. 5.9.

FIGURE 5.7   *Replacing a Single Character with* **r**

Original Text	vi Commands	Transformed Text
`printf("Enter filename/c");`	**r**	`printf("Enter filename\c");`
`printf("Filename: %d\n", fname);`	**rs**	`printf("Filename: %s\n", fname)`

FIGURE 5.8   *Replacing Text with* **s** *and* **S**

Original Text	vi Commands	Transformed Text
`printf("CPU Time: %d\n", ct);`	**s10f**	`printf("CPU Time: %10f\n", ct);`
`while (x -gt 5)`	**3s>***[Esc]*	`while (x > 5)`
`while(1)`	**3s true***[Esc]*	`while true`

FIGURE 5.9   *Replacing Text with* **R** *and* **S**

Original Text	vi Commands	Transformed Text
while (1)	**R**true*[Esc]*	while true
echo "Error"	**S**printf **"Command failed\n"***[Esc]*	printf "Command failed\n"

You have now been able to enter the Input Mode in 10 ways. The functions of these 10 keys are summarized in Table 5.1.

Caution

Remember to switch to the Command Mode from Input Mode by pressing *[Esc]*. If you forget to do that, all Command Mode commands will show up as text input in which case you have to backspace to erase the text. Repeated pressing of *[Esc]* won't make any difference to **vi** except that it has a built-in capability to indicate with a beep if a key has been pressed unnecessarily. Try this by pressing *[Esc]* several times. You are now in the Command Mode.

Linux

A superb text completion feature is available in **vim**. If the string printf is available in the file, you don't need to enter the entire string ever. Just key in as much as is necessary to make the string unique (say, up to pr), and then press

[Ctrl-p]   *vim attempts to complete string*

vim expands pr to printf if this is the *only* word beginning with pr. In case there are other words, repeated pressing of the key shows all matching words in turn. In case you have to view the list backwards, use *[Ctrl-n]*.

5.3.5   Entering Control Characters (*[Ctrl-v]*)

If you write shell scripts to send some escape sequences to your printer or terminal, then you would need to enter control characters. In **vi**, some of these characters are directly enterable, but generally a control character has to be preceded by *[Ctrl-v]* to be interpreted properly.

For instance, to enter *[Ctrl-h]*, you have to first press *[Ctrl-v]* and then *[Ctrl-h]*. You'll then see this on the screen:

^H   *Just one character here*

Even though you feel you are seeing a ^ (caret) and an H, there's only a single character out there. You can position the cursor only on the ^ and not on the H; that's how you identify control characters anyway.

The same technique can be adopted for entering the *[Esc]* character. Press *[Ctrl-v][Esc]*, and you'll see the *[Esc]* character looking like this:

^[*Just one character here*

This too is a single character. Insertion of a control character is shown in Fig. 5.10. If *[Ctrl-v][Esc]* doesn't work, then use this: *[Ctrl-v][Ctrl-[]* (Control with [).

FIGURE 5.10   *Insertion of a Control Character*

Original Text	vi Commands	Transformed Text
:map #1 :w	**A***[Ctrl-v][Ctrl-m][Esc]*	:map #1 :w^M
echo "Time up"	**i***[Ctrl-v][Ctrl-g]*	echo "Time up^G"

5.4 Saving Text and Quitting—The ex Mode

When you edit a file using **vi**—or, for that matter, any editor—the original file isn't disturbed as such, but only a copy of it that is placed in a *buffer* (a temporary form of storage). These are the three operations that we commonly perform with the buffer:

- Save and continue editing (**:w**).
- Save and exit (**:x** and **:wq**).
- Abandon all changes and quit (**:q** and **:q!**).

The necessary ex Mode commands are shown in parentheses. From time to time, you should save your work by writing the buffer contents to disk to keep the disk file current (or, as we say, in *sync*). When we talk of saving a file, we actually mean saving this buffer. The essential save and exit commands are shown in Table 5.2.

5.4.1 Saving Your Work (:w)

You know how to save the buffer and exit the editor *(5.1)*. For extended sessions with **vi**, you must be able to save the buffer and *remain* in the editor. Enter a **:** and **w**:

```
:w[Enter]
"sometext", 8 lines, 275 characters
```

You can now continue your editing work normally; only make sure that you execute this command regularly. You may want to keep a backup of your work by using **:w** with a filename:

```
:w anotherfile                                             anotherfile must not exist
"anotherfile" [New File] 8 lines, 275 characters written
```

Attention! Even though you have just written to anotherfile, your current file continues to be sometext. Windows users should note that this alternate file saving facility is different from the *Save As . . .* option of the *File* menu, which saves to a different file but also makes the new file the current one.

Tip

It's common practice to ignore the readonly label when opening a file that doesn't have the write permission bit set. When you attempt to save the file with **:w**, **vi** retorts with the message File is read only. You should have been careful in the first place, but there's hope: Just save the file with a different name (say, **:w foo**) after making sure that foo doesn't exist. Look up Table 5.2 for the command to use when foo also exists.

TABLE 5.2 *Save and Exit Commands of the ex Mode*

Command	Action
:w	Saves file and remains in editing mode
:x	Saves file and quits editing mode
:wq	As above
:w n2w.pl	Like *Save As* ..... in Microsoft Windows
:w! n2w.pl	As above, but overwrites existing file
:q	Quits editing mode when no changes are made to file
:q!	Quits editing mode after abandoning changes
:n1,n2w build.sql	Writes lines *n1* to *n2* to file build.sql
:3,10w build.sql	Writes lines 3 to 10 to file build.sql
:.w build.sql	Writes current line to file build.sql
:$w build.sql	Writes last line to file build.sql
:!*cmd*	Runs *cmd* command and returns to Command Mode
:sh	Escapes to UNIX shell (use **exit** to return to **vi**)
[Ctrl-z]	Suspends current session and escapes to UNIX shell (only for shells supporting job control; use **fg** to return to **vi**)
:e note1	Stops editing current file and edits file note1
:e!	Loads last saved edition of current file (Like *Revert* in Microsoft Windows)
:e#	Returns to editing most recently edited file

5.4.2 Saving and Quitting (:x and :wq)

You know how to save and quit the editor (i.e., return to the shell); use **:x**:

:x*[Enter]*
"sometext", 8 lines, 303 characters
$ _

You can also use **:wq** as a synonym to **:x**. But that requires an additional keystroke, and this author doesn't use it.

Tip

The best way to save and quit the editor is to use **ZZ**, a Command Mode command, instead of :x or :wq. But there's a danger that you might hit *[Ctrl-z]* instead and suspend the process. If that happens, turn to Section 8.11 for remedial action.

5.4.3 Aborting Editing (:q)

It's also possible to abort the editing process and quit the editing mode without saving the buffer. The **q** (quit) command is used to do that:

:q*[Enter]*   *Won't work if buffer is unsaved*
$ _

vi also has a safety mechanism that prevents you from aborting accidentally if you have modified the file (buffer) in any way. The following message is typical when you try to do so:

```
No write since last change (:quit! overrides)
```

You haven't saved the changes and are trying to quit; that's what the message says. If you still want to abandon the changes, then use

:q!   *Ignores all changes made and quits*

to return you to the prompt irrespective of the status of the buffer—no questions asked. The ! makes its appearance in the editor's message every time **vi** feels that you could be doing something that is potentially unsafe.

Note

In general, any ex Mode command used with a ! signifies an abort of some type. It can be used to switch to another file without saving the current one, or reload the last saved version of a file. You can even use it to overwrite a separate file.

5.4.4   Writing Selected Lines

The **:w** command is an abbreviated way of executing the ex Mode instruction **:1,$w**. The **w** command can be prefixed by one or two *addresses* separated by a comma. The following two ex Mode commands write a single line and 41 lines respectively to a separate file:

```
:5w n2words.pl                                              Writes 5th line to another file
:10,50w n2words.pl                                         Writes 41 lines to another file
```

There are two symbols used with **w** that have special significance—the dot and $. The dot represents the current line while $ represents the last line of the file. You can use them singly or in combination:

```
:.w tempfile                            Saves current line (where cursor is positioned)
:$w tempfile                                                            Saves last line
:.,$w tempfile                                              Saves current line through end
```

If tempfile exists and is writable by you, **vi** issues yet another warning:

```
"tempfile" File exists - use "w! tempfile" to overwrite
```

You know what **vi** is saying: Use **:w! tempfile** to overwrite tempfile. The ! is the universal overriding operator in the ex Mode, and you'll be using it often.

Note

In the ex Mode, the current line number is represented by . (dot) and the last line is denoted by $. The command w is the same as 1,$w. Both commands address the entire file.

5.4.5   Escape to the Shell (:sh and *[Ctrl-z]*)

How do do you edit and compile your C program repeatedly? You need to make a temporary escape to the shell to run the **cc** command. There are two ways; the first method is to use the ex Mode command, **sh**:

```
:sh
$ _                                                          You haven't quit vi yet
```

This returns a shell prompt. Execute **cc** or any UNIX command here and then return to the editor using *[Ctrl-d]* or **exit**. Don't make the mistake of running **vi** once again, as you'll then have two instances of **vi**—an undesirable situation. Table 5.2 shows how you can run a single command using **:!** and remain in the editor.

Note

The shell that shows its presence by the $ or % prompt is determined by the setting of your SHELL variable. This is the last field in /etc/passwd and assigned when the account is opened *(19.3.2)*. Even though sh actually represents the Bourne shell, :sh is a generic shell escape command. Just run **echo $SHELL** to find out the shell you are using.

The second method will work if your shell supports job control (which most shells do). You can then *suspend* the current **vi** session. Just press *[Ctrl-z]* and you'll be returned a shell prompt. Run your commands and then use the **fg** command to return to the editor. Job control is discussed in Section 8.11.

5.5   Recovering from a Crash (:recover and -r)

Accidents can and will happen. The power will go off, leaving work unsaved. However, don't panic; **vi** stores most of its buffer information in a hidden swap file. Even though **vi** removes this file on successful exit, a power glitch or an improper shutdown procedure lets this swap file remain on disk. **vi** will then complain the next time you invoke it with the same filename.

   The complaint usually also contains some advice regarding the salvage operation. You'll be advised to use either the ex Mode command **:recover** or **vi -r foo** to recover as much of foo as possible. After you have done that, have a look at the buffer's contents and satisfy yourself of the success of the damage control exercise. If everything seems fine, save the buffer and remove the swap file if **vi** doesn't do that on its own.

Caution

You can't be assured of complete recovery every time. You may see junk when using **vi -r** (or **:recover**), in which case, don't save the file and simply quit (with **:q!**). Start **vi** again normally; recovery is not possible here. Linux users should note that in these situations, they may be required to delete the file .foo.swp if foo has recovery problems.

5.6   Navigation

We'll now consider the functions of the Command Mode. This is the mode you come to when you have finished entering or changing text. We begin with navigation whose

TABLE 5.3 *Navigation and Scrolling Commands*

Command	Function
Relative Motion	
h (or *[Backspace]*)	Moves cursor left
l (or spacebar)	Moves cursor right
5l	Moves 5 characters right
k	Moves cursor up
10k	Moves 10 lines up
j	Moves cursor down
Scrolling	
[Ctrl-f]	Scrolls full page forward
5[Ctrl-f]	Scrolls 5 full pages forward
[Ctrl-b]	Scrolls full page back
[Ctrl-d]	Scrolls half page forward
[Ctrl-u]	Scrolls half page back
[Ctrl-l]	Redraws the screen (no repeat factor)
Word Navigation	
b	Moves back to beginning of word
4b	Moves back 4 words to beginning of word
e	Moves forward to end of word
w	Moves forward to beginning of word
8w	Moves forward to beginning of 8th word
Line Navigation and Absolute Movement	
0 (zero) or |	Moves to beginning of line
30|	Moves to column 30
^	Moves to first word in line
$	Moves to end of line
1G	Moves to beginning of file
40G	Moves to line 40
G	Moves to end of file

commands are listed in Table 5.3. Don't forget to avoid the cursor control keys for navigation as advised in Section 5.2.

5.6.1 Relative Movement in the Four Directions (h, j, k, and 1)

vi provides the **h, j, k**, and **1** commands to move the cursor in the four directions. These keys are placed adjacent to one another in the middle row of the keyboard. Without a repeat factor, they move the cursor by one position. Use these commands for moving the cursor vertically:

k   Moves cursor up
j   Moves cursor down

To move the cursor along a line, you have already used these commands in the preliminary session:

h   Moves cursor left
l (el)   Moves cursor right

The repeat factor can be used as a command prefix with all these four commands. Thus, **4k** moves the cursor 4 lines up, and **20h** takes it 20 characters to the left. Note that this motion is *relative;* you can't move to a specific line number with these keys. Navigation with the four keys is shown in Fig. 5.11.

Tip

To remember the keys that move the cursor left or right, observe these four keys on your keyboard. The left-most key, **h**, moves the cursor to the left, and the right-most key, **l**, moves it right.

5.6.2 Scrolling *([Ctrl-f], [Ctrl-b], [Ctrl-d], and [Ctrl-u])*

Faster movement can be achieved by scrolling text in the window using the control keys. The two commands for scrolling a page at a time are

[Ctrl-f]   Scrolls forward
[Ctrl-b]   Scrolls back

You can use the repeat factor, as in **10***[Ctrl-f]*, to scroll 10 pages and navigate faster in the process. You can scroll by a half page as well:

[Ctrl-d]   Scrolls half page forward
[Ctrl-u]   Scrolls half page back

The repeat factor can also be used here.

5.6.3 Word Navigation (b, e, and w)

Moving by one character is not always enough, and you'll often need to move faster along a line. **vi** understands a *word* as a navigation unit which can be defined in two

FIGURE 5.11 *Relative Navigation with* **h**, **j**, **k**, *and* **l**

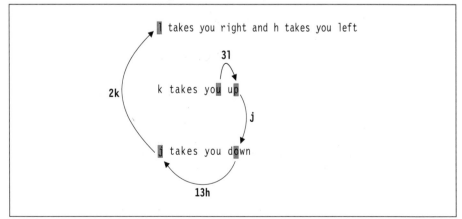

ways, depending on the key pressed. If your cursor is a number of words away from your desired position, you can use the word-navigation commands to go there directly. There are three basic commands:

b   Moves back to beginning of word
w   Moves forward to beginning of word
e   Moves forward to end of word

A repeat factor speeds up cursor movement along a line. For example, **5b** takes the cursor five words back, while **3w** takes the cursor three words forward. A word here is simply a string of alphanumeric characters and the _ (underscore). Bash is one word; so is sh_profile. tcp-ip is three words; the hyphen by definition becomes a word too.

The commands **B**, **E**, and **W** perform functions similar to those of their lowercase counterparts except that they skip punctuation. The word definition also gets changed here, but we'll ignore these minor details.

5.6.4   Moving to Line Extremes (0, |, and $)

Moving to the beginning or end of a line is a common requirement. This is handled by the keys **0**, **|**, and **$**. To move to the first character of a line, use

0 (zero) *or* | 30| *moves the cursor to column 30*

The | takes a repeat factor and by using it, you can position the cursor on a certain column. To position the cursor on column 30, use **30|**.

We used $ as the line address in the ex Mode to represent the last line of the file. The same symbol in the Command Mode represents the end of line. To move to the end of the current line, use

$ *Moves to end of line*

The use of these two commands along with those that use units of words (**b**, **e**, and **w**) is shown in Fig. 5.12.

5.6.5   Absolute Movement (G)

Upon startup, **vi** displays the total number of lines in the last line. At any time, you can press *[Ctrl-g]* to know the current line number:

"/etc/passwd" [Read only] line 89 of 179 --49%--

The cursor is on line 89 (49% of 179), and this write-protected file has 179 lines in all. Compilers also indicate line numbers in their error messages. You need to use the **G** command with the line number as repeat factor to locate the offending lines. To move to the 40th line, use

40G   *Goes to line number 40*

and to move to the beginning of the file, use

1G   *Goes to line number 1*

FIGURE 5.12   *Finer Navigation with* **b, e, w, 0,** *and* **$**

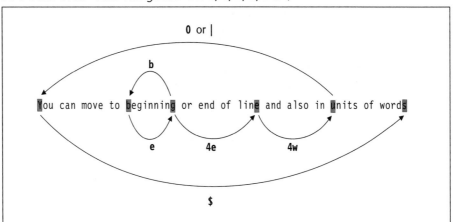

The end of the file is reached by simply using

G   *Goes to end of file*

   The ex Mode offers equivalent commands for moving between lines. The previous three commands can be replaced by **:40**, **:1** and **:$**, respectively (along with *[Enter]*).

Note

5.7   Editing Text without Operators

Editing operations change the contents of the buffer. These operations are performed with commands of both the Input and Command Modes. Having seen the Input Mode commands, let's turn our attention to the ones used in the Command Mode. The simple ones don't use *operators,* but the powerful ones do. Let's first use the simple ones before we take up operator-based editing.

5.7.1   Deleting Text (x, X, and dd)

The **x** and **X** commands are used to delete one or more contiguous characters. Move the cursor to any location and press

x   *Deletes a single character*

The character under the cursor gets deleted, and text on the right shifts left to fill up the space. A repeat factor also applies here, so **4x** deletes the current character as well as three characters from the *right* (Fig. 5.13).

   A Windows Notepad or Wordpad user would be surprised to note that when the cursor is at the end of a line, **x** doesn't pull up the following line. Instead, it deletes text on the *left* of the cursor.

   Text deletion to the left is otherwise handled by the **X** command. Keep it pressed, and you'll see that you have erased all text to the beginning of the line.

How about deleting a line? The command to use is a two-character string named **dd.** Move the cursor to any point on a line and then use

```
dd
```

to delete the current line. Even though we are not discussing operators in this section (**dd** is actually a special use of an operator), you need to know this special command because line deletion is a frequent editing operation. The topic actually belongs to Section 5.9.1.

5.7.2   Moving Text (p)

Text movement requires you to perform an additional task: Put the deleted text at the new location with **p** or **P**. **vi** uses these two commands for all "put" operations that follow delete or copy operations (even when using operators). The significance of **p** and **P** depends on whether they are used on parts of lines or complete lines.

For instance, to correct sdtio.h to stdio.h, you'll have to transpose the characters d and t, i.e., delete the d and put it after the t. Move your cursor to the d in sdtio.h and then use **x** and **p** as shown Fig. 5.14.

Since we worked on parts of lines, associate the word "right" with **p** and "left" with **P**. **P** places text on the left of the cursor.

5.7.3   Joining Lines (J)

In word processors, you join the current and next line by moving the cursor to the end of line and pressing *[Delete]*. This technique won't work in **vi**. To join the current line and the line following it, use

```
J
```
                                          4J *joins following 3 lines with current one*

J removes the newline character between the two lines to pull up the line below the current line (Fig. 5.15). Joining, however, is restricted to the maximum line size that your **vi** editor can support. It could be around 2000 (as in Solaris) or unlimited (in Linux).

FIGURE 5.13   *Deleting Text with* **x**

Original Text	vi Commands	Transformed Text
$x=5	x	x=5
#!/usr/bin/sh	x	#!/usr/bin/sh
#!/usr/bin/sh	4x	#!/bin/sh

FIGURE 5.14   *Transposing Characters with* **x** *and* **p**

Original Text	vi Commands	Transformed Text
sdtio.h	x	stio.h
stio.h	p	stdio.h

FIGURE 5.15 *Joining Lines with* **J**

Original Text	vi Commands	Transformed Text
int main(void) {	J	int main(void) {
while true do	A ;*[Esc]*J	while true ; do

FIGURE 5.16 *Changing Case with* **~**

Original Text	vi Commands	Transformed Text
if ["$answer" = "Y"]	~	if ["$answer" = "y"]
mail=/var/mail/romeo	4~	MAIL=/var/mail/romeo

5.7.4 Changing Case (~)

vi uses the **~** (tilde) command to toggle the case of text. To reverse the case of a section of text, move the cursor to the first character of the section and then press

~   *Upper becomes lower, lower becomes upper*

If you have to do this for a string of a hundred characters, use a repeat factor: **100~**. The ~ is not suitable for changing an entire line to uppercase if some characters in the line are already in uppercase; those characters then turn to lowercase. The changing of case is shown in Fig. 5.16.

5.8 Correcting a C Program

With so many commands at our disposal, let's go through an editing session that corrects some common mistakes found in C programs. Though the changes required seem to underestimate the programmer, it's a great way to learn **vi**. Fig. 5.17 shows the file foo.c both before and after correction.

Except for line 2, all of the other lines need to be corrected. Beginners of C programming tend to drop the < and > around the include filename. Single quotes are used when double quotes are required. It's common folly both to forget to include the \n in the **printf** statement and the **;** as the statement terminator. The **exit** function must be used with an argument, and the closing brace has to be inserted at the end. Table 5.4 lists the **vi** sequences that perform this transformation.

Try the commands in the specified sequence after downloading foo.c from the Web site. If you make a mistake, don't forget to press **u** (after *[Esc]*) to undo the last editing action. If there are multiple mistakes, simply reload the last saved version with **:e!** and then start all over again.

FIGURE 5.17 foo.c *with Errors (Left), after Correction (Right)*

`#include stdio.h`
`#include <errno.h>`
`int quit(char *message) {`
`   printf('Error number %10d', errno)`
`   exit;`
	`#include <stdio.h>`
	`#include <errno.h>`
	`void quit(char* message) {`
	`   printf("Error number %d\n ", errno);`
	`   exit(1);`
	`}`

TABLE 5.4 **vi** *Commands Required to Correct Program in Fig. 5.17*

Command	Action
`1G`	Moves to line 1
`2w`	Moves to s in `stdio.h`
`i<[Esc]`	Inserts <; shows `<stdio.h`
`A>[Esc]`	Appends >; shows `<stdio.h>`
`2j`	Move 2 lines below
`3svoid[Esc]`	Replaces `int` with `void`
`j2e`	Moves to first ' on next line
`r"`	Replaces ' with "
`4w`	Moves to 1 in 10
`2x`	Deletes 10 ; shows %d
`a\n☐[Esc]`	Appends \n and a space to %d
`l`	Moves to closing '
`r"`	Replaces ' with "
`A;[Esc]`	Appends ; at end of line
`j$`	Moves to end of next line; at ; in `exit`;
`i(1)[Esc]`	Inserts (1) after `t` in `exit`
`o}[Esc]`	Opens line below and inserts }
`:x`	Saves and quits **vi**

5.9   Editing Text with Operators

Arguably, **vi**'s strongest feature is its ability to combine an **operator** with a command to handle any type of deletion or copying task. This opens up a new domain of commands for you to work with. In this text, we consider the following operators:

d—Delete
y—Yank (copy)
c—Change

An operator alone can't perform any function unless it is combined with a command or itself. When used with itself (i.e., twice), it can handle a very specialized function.

TABLE 5.5 A Few Specimen Operator-Command Combinations

Command	Function
d$ or D	Deletes from cursor to end of line
5dd	Deletes 5 lines
d/}	Deletes from cursor up to first occurrence of }
d30G	Deletes from cursor up to line number 30
y$ or Y	Yanks from cursor to end of line
3yw or y3w	Yanks three words from cursor position
5yy	Yanks five lines
yG	Yanks from cursor to end of file
y?case	Yanks from cursor up to first occurrence of string case in reverse direction
c0	Changes from cursor to beginning of line
3cw or c3w	Changes three words
cc	Changes current line

These operators also take a repeat factor. Table 5.5 lists the various ways these operators are used in combination with other Command Mode commands.

Note

An operator, when doubled by itself (like **dd**, **yy**, and **cc**), acts only on the current line.

5.9.1 Deleting and Moving Text (d, p, and P)

We used **x** and **X** for deletion; now let's see how deletion is performed with operators. Consider that you have to delete text from the present cursor position to the end of the line. You can frame the command yourself if you recall that the **$** takes the cursor to end of a line. The answer is simple:

d$ *Deletes rest of line*

d$ is a combination of an operator and a navigation command. **w** moves forward one word, and **G** takes the cursor to the end of file, so we can confidently use these commands:

dw   Deletes one word
3dw   Deletes three words
dG   Deletes from current cursor position to end of file

Note how we could easily devise specialized functions by following a simple set of rules. The operator–command theory, however, takes a backseat when deleting lines. Entire lines are removed with the **dd** "command" (rather a doubled operator), which can also be used with a repeat factor. Move the cursor to any line and then press:

dd   Deletes a single line
6dd   Deletes current line and five lines below

FIGURE 5.18   *Deleting and Moving Text with the **d** Operator and **p***

Original Text	vi Commands	Transformed Text
case $# in #Check arguments	**d$**	case $# in
echo "Enter the filename\c"	**2dw**	echo "filename\c"
close(fd1); close(fd2);	**dd**	close(fd2);

if (access("foo", R_OK) == -1)
    printf("Not readable ");
if (access("foo", F_OK) == -1)
    quit("File not found", 1);
	2dd	if (access("foo", F_OK) == -1)
		    quit("File not found", 1);

Now put the two deleted lines here:
if (access("foo", F_OK) == -1)
    quit("File not found", 1);
	p	if (access("foo", F_OK) == -1)
		    quit("File not found", 1);
		if (access("foo", R_OK) == -1)
		    printf("Not readable ");

How do we move text? Use the **p** and **P** commands in the same way we used them with **x** and **X** *(5.7.1)* except that there are four possibilities this time:

- When we delete *entire* lines, we have to think in terms of "below" and "above" the current line. **p** places text below the current line, and **P** places text above.
- When we delete a partial line, say, a word with **dw**, we can put the deleted word only to the left (with **p**) or right (with **P**) of the cursor position, and not above or below the current line.

Fig. 5.18 illustrates the use of the **d** operator for line deletion and movement.

5.9.2   Yanking Text (y, p, and P)

The **y** operator yanks (or copies) text. It is used in the same way the **d** operator is combined with another command or used by itself. You can yank a word, a group of words, line segments or even entire lines with this operator. Moreover, the **p** and **P** commands act in the same way for putting the copied text at its destination.

For instance, to yank five lines of text, move the cursor to the first of these lines and press

5yy

Next, move the cursor to the new location, and press

p *or* P

to put the copied text below the current line. Adopting the same logic used for the **d** operator, one can say that **y$** yanks text from current position to end of line, and **y1G** (or **1yG**) copies text from current cursor position to the beginning of the file. See for

FIGURE 5.19 *Copying Lines with the* **y** *Operator and* **p**

Original Text	vi Commands	Transformed Text
close(fd1);	**yy**	close(fd1); *(No change)*
close(fd1);	**p**	close(fd1); close(fd1);

FIGURE 5.20 *Changing Text with the* **c** *Operator*

Original Text	vi Commands	Transformed Text
#!/bin/sh	**c$usr/bin/bash***[Esc]*	#!/usr/bin/bash
fprintf(STDOUT, "Error\n");	**cwstderr***[Esc]*	fprintf(stderr, "Error\n");
if grep stderr foo foo1 foo2	**3cwfoo****[Esc]*	if grep stderr foo*

yourself where **p** places the copied text—right or below. Copying lines is illustrated in Fig. 5.19.

5.9.3 Changing Text (c)

The **c** operator changes text, but in the Input Mode. **cw** changes a word, and **c$** changes text to the end of the line. This time, the boundary limiting your area of operation could be indicated by a $, but you may not see the $ on all systems.

If you change three words with **3cw**, a $ may appear at the end of the third word (**vim** excepted). The inserted text overwrites the characters delimited by the $ that temporarily appears on the screen. If the replaced text is larger, then once the cursor moves up to the $ marker, further insertion shifts existing text to the right. You must use *[Esc]* to terminate the change operation. Changing text is shown in Fig. 5.20.

5.10 Copying and Moving Text from One File to Another

You can perform cut-and-paste and copy-and-paste operations between two files using modified forms of the above techniques. You need to be familiar with these additional features:

- **vi** uses the **:e foo** command to switch to another file. But this operation will only work if the current file is saved.
- You can toggle between the current and the previous file using either **:e#** or *[Ctrl-^]*.
- To copy or move text between two files, the standard buffer that we restore from using **p** or **P** won't do. We have to use a special buffer that can have any letter as its name. The buffer a is accessed with **"**a. So, to copy a line to this buffer, we need to use **"ayy**.

Space constraints don't permit discussion of these features in this edition, but this knowledge is adequate to copy or move a block of text from one file to another. Just follow these steps for moving text:

1. Delete the text into a buffer a. If you are deleting four lines, then use **"a4dd**, where the normal delete command is preceded by the string **"a**.
2. Save the current file with **:w**.
3. Open a new file using the ex Mode command **:e foo**.
4. Navigate to the desired location, press ", the buffer name (a) and p to place the copied text below the current line: **"ap** (the normal put command preceded by **"a**).
5. You can now go back to the previous file using **:e#** or *[Ctrl-^]*.

To copy text, replace the delete command with the yank command. To copy four words from one file to another, just use **4yw** instead of **4dd**; everything else remains the same, except that you don't need to save the original file this time. The filling up of a buffer named a is a special case of a general **vi** feature—the ability to copy or move up to 26 sections of text.

Tip

The sequence **:e#** or *[Ctrl-^]* may not work if the current buffer is unsaved. For this to work at all times, make the ex Mode setting **:set autowrite** or **:set aw**. This ensures that the file is saved automatically before the switch occurs.

Linux

To copy or move a block of text, **vim** doesn't need to use the "a symbols at all. Just delete or copy the text, save the file with **:w** if necessary, switch to the next file with **:e foo**, and then paste the text with **p**. **vim** requires the buffer symbols only when multiple sections are copied or moved.

5.11 Undoing Last Editing Instructions (u and U)

vi's most notable weakness is its undo feature that uses the **u** and **U** commands. Unlike the Windows-based word processors as well as **emacs**, the **u** command permits only single-level undoing. You can only reverse your previous editing instruction by pressing

u   *Must use in Command Mode; press [Esc] if necessary*

Another **u** at this stage will undo this too, i.e., restore the original status. So, if you have used **10dd** at the wrong location, then before you do anything else, just press **u**. The command undoes changes made in the Input Mode also. If you have wrongly inserted a block of text, press *[Esc]* and then **u**.

When a number of editing changes have been made to a single line, **vi** allows you to discard all the changes *before you move away from the line.* The command

U   *Don't move away from current line*

reverses all changes made to the current line, i.e., all modifications that have been made since the cursor was moved to this line.

Caution

Make sure the cursor has not been moved to another line before invoking **U**, in which case it won't work.

Linux

Multiple Undoing and Redoing **vim** supports multilevel undoing. **u** behaves differently here; repeated use of this key progressively undoes your previous actions. You could even have the original file in front of you! Further, **10u** reverses your last 10 editing actions. The function of **U** remains the same.

You may overshoot the desired mark when you keep **u** pressed, in which case use *[Ctrl-r]* to redo your undone actions. Further, undoing with **10u** can be completely reversed with **10***[Ctrl-r]*. The undoing limit is set by the ex Mode command **:set undolevels**=*n,* where *n* is set to 1000 by default.

5.12 Searching for a Pattern (/ and ?)

vi is extremely strong in search and replacement activities. Searching can be made in both forward and reverse directions and can be repeated. It is initiated from the Command Mode by pressing a /, which shows up in the last line. For example, if you are looking for the string printf, enter this string after the /:

/printf*[Enter]*   *Searches forward*

The search begins forward to position the cursor on the first instance of the word. **vi** searches the entire file, so if the pattern can't be located until the end of file is reached, the search *wraps around* to resume from the beginning of the file. If the search still fails, **vi** responds with the message Pattern not found.

Likewise, the sequence

?*pattern[Enter]*

searches backward for the most previous instance of the pattern. The wraparound feature also applies here but in the reverse manner.

5.12.1 Repeating the Last Pattern Search (n and N)

The **n** and **N** commands repeat a search where **n** and **N** don't exactly play the roles you'd expect them to. For repeating a search in the direction the previous search was made with / or ?, use

n   *Repeats search in same direction of original search*

The cursor will be positioned at the beginning of the pattern. You can then carry out some editing function, say, change a word with **cw**. You can press **n** repeatedly to scan all instances of the string and then repeat the change wherever you want.

N reverses the direction pursued by **n**, which means you can use it to retrace your search path. The search and repeat actions are illustrated in Fig. 5.21, and the commands are summarized in Table 5.6.

FIGURE 5.21 *Search and Repeat with* **/** *and* **n**

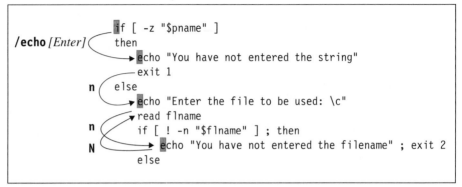

TABLE 5.6 Search and Replace Commands

Command	Function
/pat	Searches forward for pattern *pat*
?pat	Searches backward for pattern *pat*
n	Repeats search in same direction along which previous search was made (no repeat factor)
N	Repeats search in direction opposite to that along which previous search was made (no repeat factor)
:n1,n2s/s1/s2/	Replaces first occurrence of string or regular expression *s1* with string *s2* in lines *n1* to *n2*
:1,10s/find/look/g	Replaces all occurrences of find with look in lines 1 to 10
:.,$s/find/look/gc	Interactively replaces find with look from current line through end
:s	Repeats last substitution on current line (*Linux only*)

What makes searching in **vi** powerful is that the search pattern is not confined to a simple string. You can also use a *regular expression* that comprises some special characters similar to the way wild cards are used for matching filenames. There's a separate chapter devoted almost exclusively to regular expressions (Chapter 11), and most of what is discussed there applies to **vi** too.

Note

n doesn't necessarily repeat a search in the forward direction; the direction depends on the search command used. If you used **?printf** to search in the reverse direction in the first place, then n also follows the same direction. In that case, N will repeat the search in the forward direction, and not n.

5.13 Repeating the Last Command (.)

Most editors don't have the facility to repeat the last *editing* instruction, but **vi** has. The **.** (dot) command is used for repeating both Input and Command Mode commands. The principle is: Use the actual command only once, and then repeat it at other places with the dot command.

To take a simple example, if you have deleted two lines of text with **2dd**, then to repeat this operation elsewhere, all you have to do is to position the cursor at the desired location and press

.   *Use u to undo this repeat*

This will repeat the last editing instruction performed; i.e., it will also delete two lines of text.

  The . command is indeed a very handy tool. As another example, consider that you have to indent a group of lines by inserting a tab at the beginning of each line. You need to use **i***[Tab][Esc]* only once, say on the first line. You can then move to each line in turn by hitting *[Enter]* and simply pressing the dot. A group of lines can be indented in no time.

Tip

The three commands, / (search), **n** (repeat search), and . (repeat last editing command), form a wonderful trio of search–search-repeat–edit-repeat commands. You'll often be tempted to use this trio in many situations where you want the same change to be carried out at a number of places.

For instance, if you want to replace some occurrences of int with double, then first search for int with **/int**, change int to double with **cw**, repeat the search with **n**, and press the . wherever you want the replacement to take place. Yes, you wouldn't like printf to also show up (int is embedded there), which means you need to use *regular expressions* to throw printf out.

5.14 Substitution—Search and Replace (:s)

vi offers yet another powerful feature, that of substitution, which is achieved with the ex Mode's **s** (substitute) command. It lets you replace a pattern in the file with something else. The / serves as the delimiter of the syntax components:

:*address*/*source_pattern*/*target_pattern*/*flags*

The *source_pattern* here is replaced with *target_pattern* in all lines specified by *address*. The *address* can be one or a pair of numbers, separated by a comma. For instance, 1,$ addresses all lines in a file. The most commonly used flag is g, which carries out the substitution for all occurrences of the pattern in a line. The following example shows a typical substitution command:

:1,$s/double/float/g   *Can also use % instead of 1,$*

Here, double is replaced with float globally throughout the file. If you leave out the g, then the substitution will be carried out for the *first* occurrence in each addressed line.

  The target pattern is optional. If you leave it out, then you'll delete all instances of the source pattern in all lines matched by the address:

:1,50s/unsigned//g   *Deletes* unsigned *everywhere in lines 1 to 50*

FIGURE 5.22   *Interactive Substitution with* :s

```
message="has scheduled the $1 command"        msg="has scheduled the $1 command"
^^^^^^y                                        e_message="are not using the $1 command"
e_message="are not using the $1 command"       if grep "$1" $crondir/henry ; then
 ^^^^^^n                                          echo "henry $msg"
if grep "$1" $crondir/henry ; then             elif grep "$1" $crondir/julie ; then
   echo "henry $message"                          echo "julie $msg"
              ^^^^^^y                           else
elif grep "$1" $crondir/julie ; then              echo "The three users $e_message"
   echo "julie $message"                        fi
              ^^^^^^y
else
   echo "The three users $e_message"
                        ^^^^^^n
fi
              Before Substitution                            After Substitution
```

As shown above, you can choose the range of lines that are to be affected by the substitution. The following examples should make addressing clear:

`:3,10s/msg/message/g`	*All occurences in lines 3 through 10*
`:$s/msg/message/g`	*All occurences in last line*
`:.s/echo/printf/`	*Only first occurrence in current line*

Interactive Substitution   Sometimes you may want to selectively replace a string. In that case, add the c (confirmatory) parameter as the flag at the end:

`:1,$s/message/msg/gc`

Each line is selected in turn, followed by a sequence of carets in the next line, just below the pattern that requires substitution (Fig. 5.22). A y performs the substitution; any other response doesn't. This sequence is repeated for each of the matched lines in turn. In the present case, the substitution is performed for only three of the five lines.

> The interactive substitution feature in **vim** is both friendlier and more powerful than its UNIX counterpart. The string to be replaced is shown in reverse video, and a prompt appears in the last line of the screen:
>
> `replace with fprintf (y/n/a/q/^E/^Y)?`
>
> Apart from responding with y or n, you have the option of aborting (q) the substitution process or making it noninteractive (a). *[Ctrl-e]* and *[Ctrl-y]* are meant for scrolling.

Linux

5.15   set: **Customizing** vi

vi can be tailored by redefining keys or abbreviating frequently used strings, but in this section we examine some of the variable settings that benefit the programmer. These

TABLE 5.7 **set** *Options*

Option	*Abbreviation*	*Significance*
autoindent	ai	Next line starts at previous indented level
autowrite	aw	Writes current file automatically whenever switching files with :e
ignorecase	ic	Ignores case when searching for patterns
magic	–	Treats regular expression characters as special when searching for patterns
number	nu	Displays line numbers on screen
showmatch	sm	Shows momentarily match to a) and }
showmode	–	Displays a message when **vi** is in Input Mode
tabstop	ts	Sets tabs for display (default: 8 spaces)
wrapscan	ws	Continues pattern search by moving to other end of a file so that entire file is scanned

settings (Table 5.7) can be made at the ex Mode prompt, but they become permanent only when they are placed in ~/.exrc (or ~/.vimrc in Linux).

The **:set** command is used to set **vi** variables, and we have used some of them already (like **:set showmode**, **:set autowrite**, etc.). Many of these variables can have the string no prefixed to their name, in which case the setting is deactivated. For instance, noautowrite (or noaw) negates autowrite (or aw). Other variables are of the form *variable=value*. Let's take a look at some of these variables.

Automatic Indentation (autoindent) Programmers need to provide indentation to their code for easier readability. Nested **if** statements along with their corresponding **fi**s should appear at the right indentation. This aspect is taken care of when you use the following **set** statement:

:set autoindent   *Or* :set ai

When this option is set, an *[Enter]* in the Input Mode places the cursor in the next line at the current indentation.

Numbering Lines (number) The number setting shows all lines duly numbered. This makes it easier to debug programs. To reverse this setting (i.e., to switch back to the nonumber option), you simply have to prefix the string no to the option:

:set nonumber

Ignoring Case in Pattern Searches (ignorecase) The search commands (not the substitution ones) may or may not pursue a case-insensitive search. That depends on the ignorecase setting. By default, this is generally off, but you can turn it on with **:set ignorecase**.

See Matching } or) (`showmatch`) Another option, especially useful for C, Java, and **perl** programmers, enables the programmer to see momentarily the matching bracket to a) or }. The `showmatch` option helps you locate matching brackets:

```
:set showmatch
```

When text is entered in the Input Mode, the moment a) or } is entered, the cursor will jump to its matching counterpart and stay there for a fraction of a second before returning to its current location. If a match is not found, the system responds with a beep.

Setting Tab Stops (`tabstop=`*n*) Too many nested programming constructs often cause a line to wrap around. To some extent, this can be alleviated by changing the default tab setting (8 spaces). You can reduce this value, say, to 4, with `:set tabstop=4`.

All settings made with **set** are displayed with the `:set all` command. If you find these settings useful, then save them in ~/.exrc (~/.vimrc in **vim**). **vi** reads this file only once, upon startup, so you have to restart **vi** after you have modified .exrc.

➤ *GOING FURTHER*

5.16 map: **Mapping Keys of Keyboard**

The **map** command lets you assign a set of keystrokes to a key. Take, for instance, the key sequence **:w**[*Enter*] that saves your buffer. You can map the key g to this sequence by using **map** in the ex Mode:

```
:map g :w^M
```
^M signifies the [Enter] key

This mapping also includes the *[Enter]* key, which **vi** understands as *[Ctrl-m]* (shown as ^M). This character is entered by first pressing *[Ctrl-v]* and then *[Ctrl-m]* (5.3.5). You can now press **g** in the Command Mode to save your buffer. To map a function key, say *[F1]*, use #1 to signify the key. On some systems like Solaris, you'll have to first press *[Ctrl-v]* and then the actual function key itself.

You can also map keys in the Input Mode using the ! as suffix to **map**. This sequence maps the function key *[F2]* in the Input Mode:

```
:map! #2 ^[:w^M
```
Function key [F2] is #2

The string ^[is actually the *[Esc]* character which first switches **vi** to the Command Mode before saving the buffer.

The **:map** command displays the mapped environment. **:unmap** cancels a Command Mode map, and **:unmap!** cancels an Input Mode map.

Did you know that you can compile your C program or execute a shell or **perl** script from inside the editor with a single keystroke? **vi** understands the current file as %, so **cc** % compiles the current file. Let's map the function key *[F3]* to invoke this function:

Tip

```
:map #3 :!cc %^M
```
[F3] now compiles current C program

The ex Mode command :! invokes a temporary shell escape (Table 5.2) which is used to run **cc** (the C compiler). To invoke a shell or **perl** script, make this mapping of the function key *[F4]*:

```
:map #4 :!%^M
```
[F4] now executes current script

These are two important mappings used by this author. Note that scripts need to have execute permission, so you should first use :!chmod 755 % to assign this permission. You don't have to leave **vi** for this task either.

5.17 abbr: **Abbreviating Text Input**

The **abbreviate** command (itself abbreviated to **ab**) is used to expand short strings to long words. The syntax is similar to **map** except that the string that is mapped can consist of more than one character. Here are some important abbreviations that benefit C and Java programmers:

```
:ab pf printf
:ab incstd #include <stdio.h>
:ab sopl System.out.println
:ab psvm public static void main (String args[])
```

To consider the first example, when you enter the word pf, followed by a key which is neither alphanumeric nor _ (underscore), pf gets expanded to printf.

Store all sets, maps, and abbreviations in $HOME/.exrc ($HOME/.vimrc for **vim**). Carry this file with you wherever you go; it could be your most precious possession. The other features of **vi** are taken up in Appendix C.

SUMMARY

vi operates in three modes. The *Command Mode* is used to enter commands that operate on text or control cursor motion. The *Input Mode* is used to enter text. The *ex Mode* (or *Last Line Mode*) is used for file handling and substitution.

Most of the Input and Command Mode commands also work with a *repeat factor* which generally performs the command multiple times.

The Input Mode is used to insert (**i** and **I**), append (**a** and **A**), replace (**r** and **R**), and change (**s** or **S**) text and to open a line (**o** and **O**). The mode is terminated by pressing *[Esc]*.

You can enter control characters (using *[Ctrl-v]* first) and then the character. The *[Esc]* character is inserted using *[Ctrl-v][Ctrl-[]*.

The ex Mode is invoked by pressing a : in the Command Mode. You can save your work (:**w**), exit the editor after saving (:**x**), and quit without saving (:**q** and :**q!**). You can write selected lines to a separate file by using line addresses with :**w**. Sometimes you'll need to escape to a shell (:**sh**) without quitting the editor.

Navigation is performed in the Command Mode. You can move in the four directions (**h**, **j**, **k**, and **l**) or move along a line, using a *word* as a navigation unit. You can move back (**b**) and forward (**w**) to the beginning of a word. Beginning of a line is reached with **0** and end of line with **$**. You can know your current line number (*[Ctrl-g]*) and go to a specific line number (**G**). You can use the control keys to page forward and back.

You can delete characters (**x** and **X**) without using operators. Deleted text can be put at another location (**p** and **P**).

vi's editing power lies in its operators. By combining an operator with a Command Mode command, you can delete (**d**), yank (**y**), and change (**c**) text in practically any manner. When the operator is used doubly, the operation affects the current line only.

vi can repeat (**.**) and undo (**u**) the last editing instruction. You can undo all changes made to the current line (**U**). **vim** in Linux can perform multiple levels of undo and redo with **u** and *[Ctrl-r],* respectively.

You can search for a pattern (**/** and **?**) and repeat (**n** and **N**) the search in both directions. The **/**, **n** and **.** commands form a very useful trio for interactive replacement work.

The ex Mode is also used for substitution (**:s**). Substitution can be global (g flag) or confirmatory (c flag). Both search and replace operations also use *regular expressions* for matching multiple patterns.

With the **:set** command, lines can be numbered (number) and automatically indented (autoindent). You can ensure that a file is saved before switching (autowrite). Searches can be made case-insensitive (ignorecase). The no prefix reverses a setting.

All **:set** commands should be placed in $HOME/.exrc (or .vimrc for **vim**) so they are always available on startup.

SELF-TEST

5.1   How will you insert a line (i) above the current line, (ii) below the current line?

5.2   How will you (i) replace has with have in the current line, (ii) change the current line completely?

5.3   Your screen shows junk. How do you clear it?

5.4   Name three ways of exiting a **vi** session after saving your work. How do you abort an editing session?

5.5   You pressed **50k** to move the cursor 50 lines up, but you see 50k input as text. What mistake did you make, and how do you remove the three characters?

5.6   In the current line, how do you take your cursor to the (i) 40th character, (ii) beginning, (iii) end?

5.7   Name the commands required to move quickly to the fifth word of a line and replace its four characters with the string counter.

5.8   Find out the number of words in this string as interpreted by (i) **vi** and (ii) **wc**— 29.02.2000 is_last_day_of_February.

5.9   Explain which of the following commands can be repeated or undone: (i) 40k, (ii) *[Ctrl-f],* (iii) 5x, (iv) J.

5.10 You have incorrectly entered the word Comptuer. How will you correct it to Computer?

5.11 Five contiguous lines contain only lowercase letters. How do you combine them to a single line and then convert the entire line to uppercase?

5.12 How will you compile a C program without leaving the editor?

5.13   What is the significance of the **n** and **N** commands?

5.14   Every time you press a **.** (dot), you see a blank line inserted below your current line. Why does that happen?

5.15   How do you save the current line to a separate file? What do you do if the file exists?

5.16   How do you (i) delete text from the current line to the beginning of the file, (ii) copy 10 characters, (iii) copy 10 words?

5.17   How will you copy 5 lines of text from one file to another? How do you then toggle between the two files?

5.18   How do **u** and **U** differ? When will **U** fail to work?

5.19   Fundamentally, how are **d** and **y** different from Command Mode commands like **j** and **$**?

5.20   How do you noninteractively and globally replace Internet with Web in all lines of a file?

5.21   How will you revert to the last-saved version of a file?

5.22   How will you ensure that **vi** automatically saves a file when moving from one file to another?

EXERCISES

5.1   Name the three modes of **vi,** and explain how you can switch from one mode to another.

5.2   How will you add /* at the beginning of a line and */ at the end?

5.3   How do you remove the characters that you inserted in Exercise 5.2?

5.4   **vi** refuses to quit with **:q**. What does that indicate, and how do you exit anyway?

5.5   Explain what the following commands do: (i) `:.,10w foo`, (ii) `:$w! foo`. In which mode are the commands executed, and what difference does it make if foo already exists?

5.6   In the midst of your work, how can you see the list of users logged in? If you have a number of UNIX commands to execute, which course of action will you take?

5.7   Name the commands required to move to the line containing the string #include, delete four lines there, and then place the deleted lines at the beginning of the file.

5.8   Name the commands required to replace (i) echo 'Filename: \c' with echo -n "Filename: " (ii) printf("File not found\n"); with fprintf(stderr, "File not found\n"); (iii) echo "1234567890" with echo "12345678901234567890".

5.9   How do you copy text from the current cursor position to the following? (i) the character under the cursor, (ii) the beginning of line, (iii) 10 words, (iv) following text up to the string esac.

5.10   What commands will you use to delete (i) text from the current cursor position to end of file, (ii) entire contents of file?

5.11   How do you move to line number 100 and then write the remaining lines (including that line) to a separate file?

5.12   Name the commands required to interactively replace printf(with fprintf(stderr,. How will you repeat the action globally?

5.13   How will you search for a pattern printf and then repeat the search in the opposite direction the original search was made?

5.14   Name the commands required to noninteractively replace all occurrences of cnt with count in (i) the first 10 lines, (ii) the current line, (iii) all lines. How do you repeat the exercise in an interactive manner?

5.15   Name the commands required to delete text delimited by { and } where both characters occur after the current cursor position. HINT: Follow the pattern search with a terminating / and use a + after the /.

5.16   If the power to the machine is cut off while a **vi** session is active, how does it affect your work? What salvage operation will you try?

5.17   You copied 20 lines with **20yy**, then switched to another file with **:e foo**, but when you tried to paste these lines back with **p**, it didn't work. Why?

5.18   You made some changes to a read-only file and then found that you can't save the buffer. What course of action will you take without quitting the editor?

5.19   You created a shell script with **vi**. How will you make the file executable and then execute the script without leaving the editor?

5.20   Frame a command to change text from the current position to the first occurrence of the pattern Packet Switching.

5.21   You need to shift the first five lines to the right by two spaces. How do you do that (i) interactively, (ii) noninteractively?

5.22   How will you ensure that **vi** (i) automatically saves a file when moving from one file to another, (ii) expands each tab to three spaces?

5.23   Copy /etc/passwd to passwd. Name the **vi** commands required to save the first 10 lines in passwd1, the next 10 in passwd2, and the rest in passwd3.

5.24   List the editing and navigation commands required to convert the following text:

```
# include<errno.h>
void quit (char *message)
{
    printf("Error encountered\n");
    printf("error number %d, ", errno);
    printf("quitting program\n");
    exit(1);
}
```

to this:

```
#include <stdio.h>
#include <errno.h>
void quit (char *message, int exit_status) {
    /* printf("Error encountered\n"); */
    fprintf(stderr, "Error number %d, quitting program\n", errno);
    exit(exit_status);
}
```

The GNU emacs Editor

Apart from **vi**, many UNIX systems also offer the **emacs** full-screen editor. It was created by Richard Stallman (the founder of GNU, now the Free Software Foundation). As you might expect, **emacs** is offered by all Linux flavors. It owes its origin to a set of macros, but **emacs** today is more than an editor. It presents a complete operating environment from which you can handle mail and browse the Web using suitable addons. However, we'll confine ourselves to the editing functions only.

Even though **vi** often uses fewer keystrokes, **emacs** is arguably more powerful than **vi**. Its repertoire includes over a thousand commands that can perform seemingly impossible editing tasks. It's no wonder then that many users have a fanatical attachment to this editor. This chapter is presented in the same manner as Chapter 5 with a similar sequence of topics. If you have gleaned the essentials of **vi** from Chapter 5, then you'll know what to expect from **emacs** in this chapter.

Objectives

- Understand the use of the control and *meta* keys.
- Repeat a command multiple times using a *digit argument* and *universal argument*.
- Invoke **emacs** commands with **M-x** and exploit the command completion feature.
- Input text and control characters.
- Save the buffer and quit the editor.
- Perform navigation in a relative and absolute manner.
- Understand a *region* as a section of text for collective manipulation.
- Understand the role of the *kill ring* in delete and copy operations.
- Delete, copy, and move text using a region.
- Change case of text.
- Undo and redo previous commands.
- Make an *incremental* and *nonincremental* search for a string.
- Replace a string both noninteractively and interactively using the **query-replace** command.
- Handle multiple windows and buffers.
- Customize **emacs** by setting variables and using the file ~/.emacs.

- Use the help facilities available.
- Recover copied and killed text from the kill ring. *(Going Further)*
- Map keys, define abbreviations and macros. *(Going Further)*

6.1   emacs **Basics**

Unlike **vi**, **emacs** may not be automatically installed on your system. Make sure that you have **emacs** installed and then invoke it with a filename:

```
emacs emfile
```

In this full-screen mode (Fig. 6.1), the top line features a menu in reverse video. The **mode line** near the bottom also appears in reverse video. This line shows the filename (emfile) and the **current line** of the cursor; L7 is line number 7. Note the two asterisks to the left of F1; this signifies a modified buffer. Initially, you should see three hyphens at this position.

The last line, known as the **minibuffer**, shows an **emacs**-generated message. This line is used by users to enter **emacs** commands and by **emacs** to display system messages. With three lines taken away by **emacs** for its own use, just 22 lines are available for editing.

You can now enter text right away, using *[Enter]* to separate lines. To erase text, use the *[Backspace]* key instead of *[Ctrl-h]*. This is the key **emacs** uses to call up its help facility. You can also use *[Ctrl-d]* or *[Delete]* to delete the character under the cursor. In this chapter, we'll use this shaded box ▮ to represent the cursor.

After you have keyed in text shown in the figure, the cursor is positioned on the last line of text. You can now move horizontally along the current line. Press *[Ctrl-b]* to move the cursor back and *[Ctrl-f]* to move it forward. You can also move to the previous line using *[Ctrl-p]* and the next line using *[Ctrl-n]*. In addition, there are faster means of navigation available; they are discussed in Section 6.6.

The entered text hasn't been saved on disk yet but exists in some temporary storage called a *buffer*. To save this buffer, enter this sequence:

[Ctrl-x][Ctrl-c]   This is C-x C-c

FIGURE 6.1   *Inserting Some Text*

```
 File Edit Options Buffers Tools Help
 Any key pressed shows up as input.[Enter]
 Unless you use the control and meta keys.[Enter]
 These keys are used for navigation and text editing.[Enter]
 Also try using [Ctrl-n] and [Ctrl-p] for moving up and down.[Enter]
 We'll refer to them as C-n and C-p.[Enter]
 Note that your text is still in the buffer and not on disk.[Enter]
 Finally, use C-x C-c to save the buffer to disk and quit emacs.▮
 .....blank lines ......
--1-:**-F1  emfile        (Text Fill)--L7--C56--All--------------------
 Save file /home/sumit/personal/project7/emfile? (y, n, !, ., q, C-r or C-h)
```

emacs produces this message:

```
Save file /home/romeo/project7/emfile? (y, n, !, ., q, C-r or C-h)
```

A y saves the buffer to its disk file, and **emacs** returns the shell prompt. To modify this file, you'll have to invoke **emacs emfile** again.

Note

If your version of **emacs** shows the menu at the top, you can use it when invoking this editor from a terminal emulator window (like **xterm**) in the X Window system *(2.15)*. Many **emacs** commands can be invoked from this menu.

6.1.1 The Control and Meta Keys

Like most word processors and unlike **vi**, **emacs** is a "mode-less" editor; any key pressed is always entered as text. So to perform navigation and text editing, you need to use the control and *meta* keys. When you look up the **emacs** documentation, you'll find key sequences described like these:

C-e	This is *[Ctrl-e]*.
C-x C-b	This is *[Ctrl-x][Ctrl-b]*.
C-x b	*[Ctrl-x]* b; this is different from *[Ctrl-x][Ctrl-b]*.
M-e	This is *[Meta-e]*.

You need to understand the difference between the second and third sequence. **C-x C-b** is actually *[Ctrl-x][Ctrl-b]*, where you need to do this:

1. Keep *[Ctrl]* pressed.
2. Press x and b in sequence and release them.
3. Release *[Ctrl]*.

The previous command lists all buffers. However, **C-x b**, the command used to switch to a buffer, is represented by a different key sequence:

1. Enter *[Ctrl-x]* in the normal way.
2. Release both keys.
3. Singly press b.

Note

The generalized sequence C-x C-y is different from C-x y where x and y are two printable characters. You need to keep the *[Ctrl]* key pressed in the first while hitting y, but not in the second.

Let's now turn to the meta key. **M-e** represents *[Meta-e]* for those keyboards that support a key named meta. For other systems including PCs, the *[Alt]* key often behaves like meta. On the Sun workstation, you'll probably have to use the keys with the diamond symbol on them. Some sequences require the use of both the control and meta keys.

In this chapter, we'll be using the standard **emacs** notation to represent control and meta key sequences. For example, we'll represent *[Ctrl-x]* as **C-x** and *[Meta-y]* as **M-y**. There will be very few exceptions.

Tip

In case neither *[Meta]* nor *[Alt]* works, you have another choice—the *[Esc]* key. This key is never kept pressed. To invoke M-e, press *[Esc]*, release it, and then press e.

Note

If you press *[Ctrl-x]* and then take more than one second to press the next key, the string C-x- appears in the minibuffer. This is an indication that the command has not been completed. Press *[Ctrl-g]* to cancel your action.

6.1.2   Entering Commands Directly (M-x)

When you press a valid key, **emacs** executes a command associated with the key. For instance, there is a **key binding** available between **C-n** and the **next-line** command which is executed by **emacs** when *[Ctrl-n]* is pressed. This is more of an exception than a rule. **emacs** has over a thousand built-in commands, and obviously only a few of them have key bindings. If a command doesn't have a key binding, then you need to key in the command.

All **emacs** commands are invoked first by pressing **M-x** (which could be *[Alt-x]*) and then the command string. This is how you invoke the **next-line** command:

M-x **next-line***[Enter]*   *M-x could be [Alt-x]*

When you enter the key represented by **M-x**, you'll see the string M-x in the minibuffer. Key in the string next-line and hit *[Enter]*. The cursor moves down one line. If your *[Alt]* key doesn't work, then use *[Esc]* **x next-line.** Make sure you release *[Esc]* before you hit **x**.

These commands are generally hyphenated, meaningful strings which can often be very long (like **nonincremental-repeat-search-forward**). Keying in every letter of a command can be tedious and self-defeating. Fortunately, you don't need to enter the complete string ever because **emacs** supports a completion feature that does part of the work for you.

Tip

emacs also supports a history facility which lets you recall previous commands that were *explicitly* invoked using **M-x**. This history is maintained for the duration of the session. To display the last command in the minibuffer, press **M-x** and then the Up key. You can access the entire history list by repeated use of the Up and Down keys.

6.1.3   The File .emacs

As you get comfortable with **emacs**, you'll feel the need to customize it. **emacs** reads $HOME/.emacs (same as ~/.emacs in most shells) on startup. If **ls -a** doesn't show this file in your home directory, then you can create or copy one. The entries in .emacs are written in LISP—the language originally used to write **emacs**.

Many **emacs** commands can be placed in this file so they are available in every session. You can create abbreviations, redefine your keys to behave differently, and make variable settings. Your .emacs will progressively develop into an exclusive "library" containing all shortcuts and settings that you use regularly. It could be your most prized possession, so always keep a backup of this file.

Note

Your login directory may already have .emacs containing entries that change the defaults assumed in this chapter. This could make some of the commands either work differently or not at all. Until you learn how to use this file, just rename it (using **mv .emacs .emacs.bak**) or invoke **emacs** with the -q option. This option ignores .emacs at startup.

6.2 A Few Tips First

We are about to take off, but before we do, a few tips at this stage will stand you in good stead. You must keep them in mind at all times when you are doing work with **emacs**:

- *Make use of the digit argument.* Like **more** *(3.16)* and **vi**, **emacs** also supports the use of a **digit argument** as a command prefix to repeat the command as many times as the prefix. So if **C-p** moves the cursor up one line, then **M-5 C-p** moves it up 5 lines. Use it wherever you can to speed up operations. The Tip at the end of the section presents a similar feature that is invoked with **C-u**.

- *Use the command completion feature.* When invoking an **emacs** command directly with **M-x**, remember that you don't need to enter the entire command string. Enter as much to make the string unique and use *[Tab]* to let **emacs** complete it to the extent it can. For a taste of this feature, hit **M-x**, key in ov, and hit *[Tab]*. **emacs** expands ov to overwrite-mode, the command used to determine whether text input overwrites existing text or not.

- *Cancel a sequence with* **C-g**. **emacs** often takes input from you in the minibuffer. It may ask you for a filename or a search string. Pressing a wrong key, say, **C-x** when **M-x** is expected, can often leave you stranded. In situations like this, simply cancel the current command with **C-g**. If it doesn't do what you expect, use it twice.

- *Undo whenever you make a mistake.* If you have made a mistake in editing, say by incorrectly deleting text, then press **C-x u** or **C--** (Control and hyphen) to undo the last action. The key behaves in a circular manner, undoing as long as it can before it starts redoing all over again. This feature is discussed in Section 6.10.

- *Use the text completion feature.* If the string printf is available in the file, you don't need to enter the entire string ever. Just key in as much as is necessary to make the string unique (say, up to pr), and then press

  M-/   emacs *attempts to complete string*

  emacs expands pr to printf if this is the *only* word beginning with pr. In case there are other words, repeated pressing of the key shows all matching words in turn.

- *Use* **C-x 1** *to close a window.* **emacs** sometimes switches to the multiwindow mode, especially when you view its documentation. To remove the other window, use this key sequence. Window handling is discussed in Section 6.13.

- *Use* **C-1** *to clear the screen.* If the screen gets garbled, enter this control sequence.

Tip

Apart from the digit argument, you can sometimes find the **universal argument** more convenient to use. The key associated with this is **C-u**, which can be repeated multiple times. When you use **C-u C-f**, the cursor moves forward by 4 characters. Every additional **C-u** multiplies the number of repeats by a factor of 4. This means **C-u C-u C-f** moves the cursor 16 characters forward, and **C-u C-u C-u C-b** moves the cursor back by 64 characters. To move 70 characters from the current position, use a mix of the universal argument (for 64) and digit argument (for 6).

6.3   Inserting and Replacing Text

Most word processors and editors offer two modes of text input—the **insert mode** and **overwrite mode**. By default, **emacs** works in the insert mode where text input shifts existing text to the right. **emacs** can also work in the overwrite mode which replaces all characters the cursor moves over. You can switch to this mode in two ways:

- By pressing the *[Insert]* key which acts as a toggle switch. The first invocation takes you to overwrite mode; the next one returns you to insert mode.
- By issuing the **overwrite-mode** command with **M-x**. When the string M-x shows up in the minibuffer, enter overwrite-mode:

  M-x **overwrite-mode***[Enter]*

This also has a toggling effect, so let's repeat the command twice, each time using a different technique:

- Use the command completion feature. Enter **M-x**, the string ov and then *[Tab]*; you'll see the string overwrite-mode in the minibuffer.
- Use the history facility. Press **M-x** and then the Up key; the previous command shows up in the minibuffer.

Tip

Before you start editing, look at the mode line. If it shows the word Ovwrt, then you are in the overwrite mode. Switch to this mode only when you specifically need it; otherwise use the default insert mode.

6.3.1   Entering Control Characters (C-q)

If you write shell scripts to send some escape sequences to your printer or terminal, then you need to enter control characters. However, **emacs** uses the control keys for everything, which is the reason why it traps them as **emacs** commands when you try to enter them. To place a control character, say, **C-m**, in a file, you have to precede it with **C-q**:

C-q C-m   *Shows ^M*

This shows up on the screen as ^M (Fig. 6.2), but there's only a single character out there. You can position the cursor only on the ^ and not on the M.

The same technique can be adopted for entering the *[Esc]* character. Press **C-q** *[Esc]*, and you'll see the *[Esc]* character looking like this:

^[*Just one character here*

This too is a single character.

FIGURE 6.2   *Inserting a Control Character*

Original Text	emacs Commands	Transformed Text
sed 's/$//'	C-q C-m	sed 's/^M$//'
echo "Time up"	C-q C-g	echo "Time up^G"

6.4 Saving Text and Quitting

Whether you are using **vi** or **emacs**, it's only a **buffer** (a temporary storage containing a copy of the file) that you edit and not the file directly. Changes to the buffer are written to the disk file with a saving operation. When we talk of saving a file, we actually mean saving this buffer. These are the three operations that we commonly perform with the buffer:

- Save and continue editing.
- Save and exit.
- Abandon all changes and quit.

Unlike **vi**, **emacs** supports an *autosave* feature that periodically saves the buffer to a *different* disk file. However, you should regularly save the buffer yourself, but in the same file to keep it current (or, as we say, in *sync*). The essential save and exit commands are shown in Table 6.1.

6.4.1 Saving Your Work (C-x C-s and C-x C-w)

You know how to save the buffer and exit the editor *(6.1)*. For extended sessions with **emacs**, you must be able to save the buffer and *remain* in the editor. Run **emacs emfile**, make some changes, and enter this sequence:

```
C-x C-s
```
Saves in same file

This saves the buffer to emfile. Often, you might want to have a copy by providing a different filename. In that case, use **C-x C-w** and enter the filename at the prompt:

```
Write file: ~/project7/emfile.txt
```
Saves in different file

T A B L E 6.1 *Save and Exit Commands*

Command	Function
C-x C-s	Saves file and remains in editing mode
C-x C-w	Writes to a different file (Like *Save As . . .* in Microsoft Windows)
C-x C-c	Quits editing mode with or without saving
C-u C-x C-c	Saves and exits without prompting
C-x C-z	Suspends current session and escapes to UNIX shell (Use **fg** to return to **emacs**)
C-z	As above
M-x shell	Escapes to UNIX shell in current window (Use **C-x b**[*Enter*] to return to **emacs**)
M-! *cmd*	Runs *cmd* command and returns to editor (Requires [*Shift*])
M-x revert-buffer	Loads last saved edition of current file (Like *Revert* in Microsoft Windows)
M-x recover-file	Loads last autosaved version of current file

The new filename now appears on the mode line, *which means that this is the current file also.* In fact, the window is now associated with the buffer for emfile.txt. (The buffer for emfile still exists.) When writing to a different file, **emacs'** behavior stands in sharp contrast to **vi**'s; **vi** doesn't make the new file the current one *(5.4.1).*

Loading Last Saved Version (revert-buffer)   You may sometimes need to ignore all unsaved changes you made. You can reload the last saved version with the **revert-buffer** command:

M-x **revert-buffer**   *Use* revert*[Tab] to complete*

This updates the buffer with the disk file. You'll soon encounter a similar command—**recover-file**—which loads the autosaved version of the file.

6.4.2   Quitting the Editor (C-x C-c)

As mentioned earlier, you can save your buffer or abort the changes before you quit the editor. **emacs** offers a single command that handles these two issues:

C-x C-c

If no changes have been made to the buffer since it was last saved by you, you are immediately returned the prompt. But if you have made changes, then **emacs** needs to know whether you would like to save them:

Save file /home/romeo/project7/emfile? (y, n, !, ., q, C-r or C-h)

There are seven options here, but you only need to remember that a y saves the file and quits the editor. Sometimes, you won't want to answer these questions, but save and exit as quickly as possible. There's a special sequence for doing this:

C-u C-x C-c   *Keep [Ctrl] pressed and hit* u, x, *and* c

Aborting the Session   To abandon all changes made to the buffer, simply respond with an n at the prompt shown previously. **emacs** responds with yet another message:

Modified buffers exist; exit anyway? (yes or no)

The safety mechanism makes sure that you know what you are doing. This time, you have to enter either yes to abort the editing session or no to continue with editing (y or n won't do).

6.4.3   Escape to the Shell (C-x, C-z, and M-x shell)

How do you edit and compile your C program repeatedly? You need to make a temporary escape to the shell to run the **cc** command. There are two ways; the first method is to use the **shell** command with **M-x**:

M-x **shell**   *Use* she*[Tab] to complete*

This returns you a shell prompt *but in a new buffer named* shell. Execute **cc** or any UNIX command here, and all command output and keystrokes are stored in this buffer. You can even save this buffer in the usual manner (with **C-x C-s**) or return to the previous buffer with **C-x b**[*Enter*]. Note that **exit** at the prompt will kill the shell but not the window. Table 6.1 shows how you can run a single command using **M-!** and return to the current buffer.

The second method will work if your shell supports job control (which most shells do). You can then *suspend* the current **emacs** session. Just press **C-z** or **C-x C-z**, and you'll be returned a shell prompt. Run your commands and then use the **fg** command to return to the editor. Job control is discussed in Section 8.11.

6.5 Recovering from a Crash

Unlike **vi**, **emacs** has an **autosave** feature that automatically saves a copy of the buffer every 300 keystrokes (or 30 seconds if the user is idle). However, **emacs** doesn't autosave to the same file, but to one which uses a # on either side of the original filename. For instance, the file emfile is autosaved as #emfile# in the current directory.

Because of autosaving, you can lose at most 300 keystrokes of work in case of a system crash. You can then replace your current buffer with the last autosaved file using the **recover-file** command:

M-x **recover-file**   *Try completion*

After you have entered the filename (with a # on both sides), **emacs** displays the listing of both files (Fig. 6.3). Here, the autosaved version is eight minutes newer than the last saved version. If you need the newer version, enter yes at the prompt. **emacs** also makes sure of reminding you at startup whenever it finds the autosaved version to be of more recent origin.

Tip

Autosaved files tend to build up, especially when you edit files and finally decide not to save the changes. You must remove the autosaved versions—but only interactively—using the command **rm -i #*** or **rm -i \#***, depending on the shell you are using.

FIGURE 6.3   *Recovering a File with* **recover-file**

```
    -rw-r--r--   1 romeo    dialout   2658   Sep 19 09:14  /home/romeo/p5/#note1#
    -rw-r--r--   1 romeo    dialout   2677   Sep 19 09:06  /home/romeo/p5/note1
    ....
--1-:%%--F1   *Directory*            (Help View)--L1--All--------------------------
Recover auto save file /home/romeo/p5/#note1#? (yes or no) yes
```

6.6   Navigation

We'll now consider the various navigation functions that are listed in Table 6.2. Navigation can be both relative and absolute, and most navigation functions have key bindings.

6.6.1   Movement in the Four Directions (C-b, C-f, C-p, and C-n)

emacs uses the control keys to perform relative movement in the four directions. These keys are quite intuitive—b (back), f (forward), p (previous line), and n (next line). Keeping these in mind, the keys to move left and right become:

C-b   Moves cursor back
C-f   Moves cursor forward

TABLE 6.2   *Navigation and Scrolling Commands*

Command	Function
Relative Motion	
C-f	Moves forward
C-b	Moves back
C-n	Moves to next line
C-p	Moves to previous line
M-6 C-n	Moves 6 lines down
C-u C-f	Moves 4 characters forward
C-u C-u C-b	Moves 16 characters back
Scrolling	
C-v	Scrolls full page forward
M-v	Scrolls full page back
C-l	Redraws screen and positions cursor at center
Word Navigation	
M-f	Moves forward by one word
M-b	Moves back to beginning of word
M-5 M-b	Moves back by 5 words
C-u M-f	Moves forward by 4 words
Line and File Extremes	
C-a	Moves to beginning of line
C-e	Moves to end of line
M-<	Moves to beginning of file
M->	Moves to end of file
Absolute Movement	
M-x goto-line[*Enter*]40	Moves to line 40 (interactive)
C-u 40 M-x goto-line	Moves to line 40 (noninteractive)
M-x line-number-mode	Toggles line number display mode on mode line

and the keys to move up and down are:

C-p   Moves cursor to previous line
C-n   Moves cursor to next line

The digit argument applies here; **M-4 C-b** moves the cursor four places back. You can also use a universal argument; **C-u C-u C-p** moves the cursor up 16 lines. The relative navigation commands are shown in Fig. 6.4.

6.6.2 Scrolling (C-v and M-v)

For scrolling up and down, the key to remember is v. It's used with either the *[Ctrl]* or meta key depending on whether you are scrolling forward or back. To scroll forward, use

C-v

and to scroll back, use

M-v   *Meta this time*

The digit argument applies here too, so you can scroll several screens at a time.

6.6.3 Word Navigation (M-f and M-b)

Moving by one character is not always enough; you'll often need to move faster along a line. Like **vi**, **emacs** recognizes a *word* as a navigation unit. If your cursor is a number of words away from your desired position, you can use the word-navigation commands to go there directly. To move to the beginning of a word, use

M-f   C-f *would move one character forward*

and to move back by one word, use

M-b   C-b *would move one character back*

F I G U R E 6.4   *Relative Navigation*

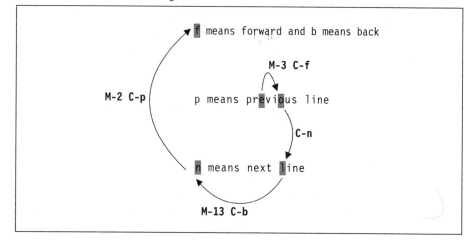

A digit argument speeds up cursor movement along a line. For example, **M-5 M-f** takes the cursor five words forward, while **M-3 M-b** moves three words back. However, to move four words forward, the universal argument would be better; simply use **C-u M-f**. The use of these two commands is shown in Fig. 6.5.

6.6.4   Moving to Line and File Extremes

Moving to Line Extremes (C-a and C-e)   You can move swiftly to the beginning or end of a line by using the keys **C-a** and **C-e**. To move to the beginning of a line, use

C-a

and to move to the end of the line, use

C-e

Do the digit arguments work here? Check that out for yourself. The use of these two commands is shown in Fig. 6.5.

Moving to File Extremes (M-< and M->)   **emacs** uses the symbols < and > to move to the beginning and end of a file. To go to line number 1, use

M-<   *Use [Shift]*

and to reach the end of the file, use

M->   *Use [Shift]*

Though we used the term *file* here, these commands actually navigate to the two ends of the buffer.

FIGURE 6.5   *Navigation Along a Line*

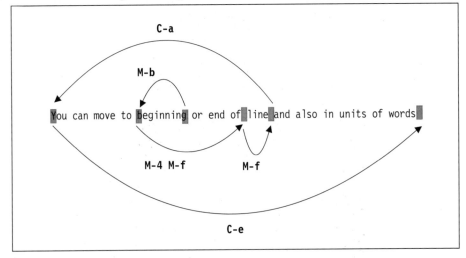

6.6.5 Absolute Movement

By default, **emacs** shows the current line number on the mode line with an L prefix. The **goto-line** command lets you navigate to a specific line number. When you use this command, **emacs** prompts for the line number:

```
Goto line: 40                                       Cursor moves to line 40
```

Unfortunately, **emacs** doesn't have a key binding for the **goto-line** command, but Section 6.19 shows how you can create one.

Tip

If **emacs** doesn't show you the line number on the mode line, use the **line-number-mode** command for the L to appear with the current line number. This command has no key binding and is also a toggle switch; run it again to reverse the current setting.

6.7 Working with Regions

emacs lets you mark the two ends of a block of text and define it as a **region**. Deletion, case changing, and copying functions work on a region. To define a region, take your cursor to the point where you want your region to begin and press either of these key sequences:

```
C-[Spacebar]                                              Sets invisible mark
C-@
```

Now use the navigation keys to move the cursor to the point that signifies the end of the region. This may or may not highlight the text (modern **emacs** versions do), but a region is defined automatically. To toggle between the two ends, use

```
C-x C-x
```

You'll see the cursor jumping back and forth, confirming that a region has been defined. You can now run some commands on this region.

The current position of the cursor (at the end of the region) is known to **emacs** as *point*. There's virtually no difference between cursor and point, except that the point is located just before the cursor. We'll ignore this subtle difference in this text.

Tip

To mark the entire buffer as a region, use the shortcut **C-x h** anywhere in the text. You then don't need to define the two ends of the region explicitly.

6.8 Deleting, Moving, and Copying Text

emacs has separate commands to delete characters, words and lines. It can also delete text defined as a region. On the other hand, you can copy text *only* as a region. We'll first discuss the commands that don't require regions and then the ones that do. Table 6.3 lists the editing commands that are discussed in the forthcoming sections.

TABLE 6.3   *The Editing Functions*

Command	Function
C-@	Defines beginning of region
C-[Spacebar]	As above
Deleting Text	
C-d or [Delete]	Deletes character
M-6 C-d	Deletes 6 characters
M-d	Deletes word
C-k C-k	Deletes (kills) current line
M-6 C-k	Deletes 6 lines
C-x C-o	Deletes all following blank lines
C-w	Deletes text in region
Copying and Moving Text	
M-w	Copies text in region
C-y	Puts deleted or copied text on right of cursor
Transposing and Joining Text	
C-t	Transposes (interchanges) character with previous one
C-x C-t	Transposes current line with previous one
M-^	Joins current line with previous line (requires [Shift])
Changing Case	
M-u	Converts word to uppercase
M-4 M-u	Converts 4 words to uppercase
M-1	Converts word to lowercase
M-c	Capitalizes word; converts first character to uppercase
M-5 M-c	Converts first character of 5 words to uppercase
C-x C-u	Converts entire text in region to upper
C-x C-1	Converts entire text in region to lower
Undoing and Redoing	
C-x u	Undoes last editing action
C--	As above (control and hyphen)
C-_	As above (control and underscore; requires [Shift])

6.8.1   Deleting Text

emacs uses three different key sequences for deleting characters, words, and lines:

C-d   Deletes characters
M-d   Deletes words
C-k   Deletes lines in part or full

A digit argument works with all of them. For instance, **M-5 C-d** deletes five characters and shifts text on the right of the cursor to the left to fill up the space (Fig. 6.6).

FIGURE 6.6   *Deleting Text with* **C-d**

Original Text	emacs Commands	Transformed Text
$x=5	**C-d**	x=5
#! /usr/bin/sh	**C-d**	#!/usr/bin/sh
#!/usr/bin/sh	**M-4 C-d**	#!/bin/sh

FIGURE 6.7   *Killing Words and Lines*

Original Text	emacs Commands	Transformed Text
echo "Enter the filename\c"	**M-d**	echo "Enter filename\c"
echo "Enter the filename\c"	**M-2 M-d**	echo " filename\c"
case $#in #Check arguments	**C-k**	case $# in
close(fd1); close(fd2);	**C-k C-k**	close(fd2);

if (access("foo", R_OK) == -1)
   printf("Not readable ");
if (access("foo", F_OK) == -1)
   quit("File not found", 1);
	M-2 C-k	if (access("foo", F_OK) == -1)
		      quit("File not found", 1);

Killing Words (M-d) **emacs** uses the meta key for deleting a larger group of characters—usually words. **M-d** deletes a word, but you need a digit argument to delete multiple words:

```
M-5 M-d
```
                                                                    Deletes five words

This *kills* five words and stores the deleted text in memory. A *word* is simply a string of alphanumeric characters. We'll soon understand what "killing" actually means.

Killing Lines (C-k) Partial or complete lines are removed with **C-k**. By default, the command deletes all text from the current position to the end of line. To kill text to the beginning of line, you need to use **M-0** as well:

```
M-0 C-k
```
                                                           Deletes text till line beginning

Strange as it may seem, there's no simple command to kill an entire line. **C-k** is the main key here, but you need to position the cursor at line beginning (with **C-a**) before using the command. The unusual feature of this command is that you need two **C-k** invocations to kill a single line but only one for multiple lines:

```
C-k C-k   Kills entire line
M-6 C-k   Kills 6 lines
```

In the first case, the initial **C-k** kills text till the last visible character in the line. The second **C-k** removes the newline character that remains after the first invocation. Killing of words and lines is shown in Fig. 6.7.

Tip

emacs can remove a group of blank lines with **C-x C-o**.

6.8.2   The Kill Ring

We used the words "delete" and "kill" freely as if the two are interchangeable, but, strictly speaking, they are not. **C-k** is termed a kill operation because the removed text is sent to a storage area called the **kill ring**. By default, this ring stores the last 30 deletions (kills, actually), and they can all be recovered.

Commands that delete a single character and whitespace fall into the "delete" category. The text erased by these commands is not saved in the kill ring. However, when you kill one or more words or lines of text, the deleted text is saved in the kill ring. Except for **C-d**, practically all delete operations are actually kill operations. Henceforth, we'll be using the word "delete" in kill situations too, so take care not to interpret this word in its strictest sense.

The kill ring doesn't just receive text from deleted text; even copied text is sent to the kill ring. We'll discover that when we learn to copy text.

Note

emacs stores a group of consecutive deletions up to the next nonkill operation as a *single* group in the kill ring. For instance, you can delete four words with M-4 M-d, eight lines with M-8 C-k, and then restore them together with C-y, the key you'll be using for moving and copying text. If you move the cursor a little between two kill operations, then the kill ring will store two groups which have to be restored separately.

6.8.3   Deleting Text in a Region (C-w)

For deleting arbitrary sections of text, create a region as described in Section 6.7. Just to make sure that mark and point are properly set, use **C-x C-x** a couple of times and then use

C-w   *Deletes text in a region*

The text in the region is deleted, and text after point moves up to fill the vacuum. Text deletion in a region is shown in Fig. 6.8.

Tip

To delete the contents of the entire buffer, define the region using C-x h and then use C-w.

6.8.4   Moving and Copying Text (C-y)

Text is moved by restoring it from the kill ring, and **C-y** is universally used in this process. For instance, if you kill a line with **C-k   C-k,** you can restore it at the new location by using

C-y   *Universal key for putting back text*

The deleted text is then put to the right of the cursor at the new location. You have just moved some text. You can delete three words with **M-3 M-d** and then use **C-y** to restore them too.

For copying text, you *must* work with a region. While **C-w** deletes text in a region, the command to copy text is

M-w   *Define a region first*

FIGURE 6.8 *Killing Text in a Region*

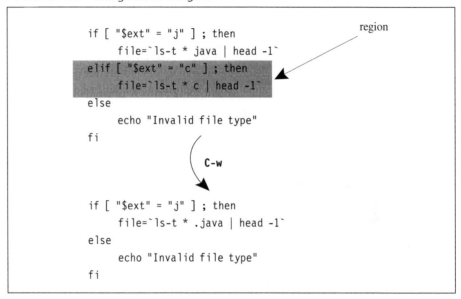

This copies the text to the kill ring. The copied text is also restored with **C-y** in the same way killed text is.

6.8.5 Copying and Moving Text from One File to Another

You can perform cut-and-paste and copy-and-paste operations between two files using a modified form of the above techniques. To do this, you need to be familiar with these additional features:

- **emacs** uses the command **C-x C-f foo** to switch to another file.
- You can toggle between the current and previous file using **C-x b**.

To move a block of text from one file to another, just follow these steps:

1. Define a region and kill the selected text using **C-w**.
2. Open a new file using **C-x C-f foo**.
3. Navigate to the desired location and then press **C-y** to paste the killed text.
4. You can go back to the previous file using **C-x b** and then press *[Enter]* at the default selection.

You can now copy and move text freely across a file, and even from one file to another. But remember that you must not leave the editor at any time.

6.8.6 Transposing Text (C-t)

You can interchange two adjacent characters or lines quite easily. The key sequence to remember is **C-t**. If you have made a mistake of spelling computer as compuetr, then move the cursor to the t and press

C-t   et *becomes* te

FIGURE 6.9   *Transposing Text*

Original Text	emacs Command	Transformed Text
sd▮io.h	**C-t**	std▮o.h
export PATH	**C-x C-t**	PATH=.
P▮TH=.		▮xport PATH

You can transpose two lines too. Just move the cursor to the lower line and use

C-x C-t

Transposing text is shown in Fig. 6.9.

6.9 Changing Case of Text

emacs has comprehensive features for changing case of text. They can be used on a single character, one or more words, or a region. To convert a single character to uppercase, use

M-c   *First character converted to uppercase*

This moves the cursor to the beginning of the next word, so if you keep the key pressed, it will capitalize the remaining words of the text. If you have 10 words to capitalize, then use a digit argument: M-10 M-c.

To convert an entire word to uppercase, move to the beginning of the word and then press

M-u   *Entire word converted to uppercase*

In a similar manner, you have to use **M-1** (el) for converting a word to lowercase. All three commands move the cursor to the next word and also use a digit argument. Changing case of characters and words is shown in Fig. 6.10.

For transforming case in large blocks of text, use a region. The commands to convert text in a region are:

C-x C-u   Converts entire text in region to upper
C-x C-1   Converts entire text in region to lower

Note

You may find the feature of case conversion of region disabled on your system. **emacs** then prompts you for enabling the feature permanently. This is controlled by the **upcase-region** and **downcase-region** commands. If you answer y at the final prompt when converting a region to uppercase, then **emacs** makes this setting in .emacs:

(put 'upcase-region 'disabled nil)

We'll learn to customize **emacs** at the end of this chapter.

FIGURE 6.10   *Changing Case*

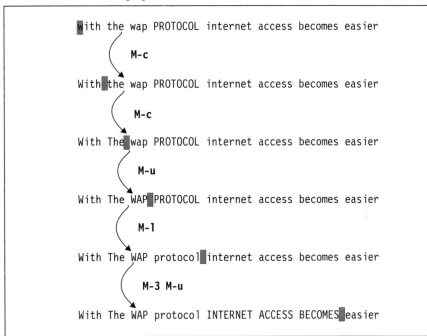

6.10   **Undoing and Redoing Editing**

emacs supports an undo-redo feature which can both reverse and restore previous editing actions. According to the **emacs** documentation, the feature is useful and "worthy enough" to have two key sequences assigned to it:

```
C-x u
C--                                                With hyphen—convenient to use
```

As advised in Section 6.2, if you inadvertently make a change to the buffer, just press either of these key combinations. Undoing and redoing are handled by the same key. Initially, every invocation of the undo key reverses the most recent change made to the buffer. If you continue to hit the key, you'll eventually undo every single change made to the buffer. The two asterisks on the mode line will disappear, and finally the system could tell you this:

```
No further undo information                                    All changes undone
```

This was the state of the buffer when you opened this file. What happens if you continue to press the undo key? Surprise, surprise: the round-robin feature starts redoing everything that you had undone, and in no time you could be back to square one.

Note

There's a limit to the number of editing instructions that can be undone (or redone). The number is controlled by the **emacs** variable undo-limit, which is set to 20,000 bytes by default. When the undo information exceeds this limit, *garbage collection* takes place in FIFO-style, and the oldest commands are discarded.

6.11   Searching for a Pattern

emacs supports a number of pattern matching schemes. The search can be made both for a simple string as well as a *regular expression*. In this section, we'll consider string searches and use two search techniques—*incremental* and *nonincremental* search.

6.11.1   Incremental Search (C-s and C-r)

When using **incremental search**, **emacs** begins the search the moment you start keying in the search string. For instance, as you key in the four letters of chop (the search string), **emacs** first checks for c, then ch, and so forth. Thus this search is faster than conventional searches.

Incremental search is invoked with **C-s** followed by the search string. To look for the string chop, press **C-s** and then initially enter c, the first character of the string:

I-search: **c**   *Search starts!*

The search starts immediately, and the cursor moves to the first instance of c (if there is one). As you key in the entire string, you'll find the cursor constantly moving across the text. Finally, if the string chop is there in the file, the cursor moves there. *You must press [Enter] now to mark the termination of your search string.*

To search backward, use **C-r** instead of **C-s**; everything else remains the same. But don't forget to press *[Enter]* after you have located the string. Incremental search is shown in Fig. 6.11.

6.11.2   Repeating the Last Incremental Search (C-s and C-r)

The same commands—**C-s** and **C-r**—repeat the search, but are used without the string. Note that you'll have to press this key twice for the first repeat. In case you are at the end or beginning of a file, **emacs** first issues this message:

Failing I-search: chop   *Searching for* chop

Like **vi**, **emacs** supports a **wraparound** feature that ensures that the entire file is scanned no matter where the search was launched from. Next time you press **C-s**, the search wraps around the end to resume from the beginning of the file.

Caution

To cancel a search, you must press *[Esc]* or *[Enter]*. Even if you backspace to completely erase the search string (which also makes the cursor retrace its path), you'll still be in search mode. Any text you key in now will be added to the search string and not to the file buffer. **emacs** will beep and continue to flash the error message shown above. Press *[Esc]* or *[Enter]* to return you to the normal mode.

FIGURE 6.11   *Incremental Search for String* chop

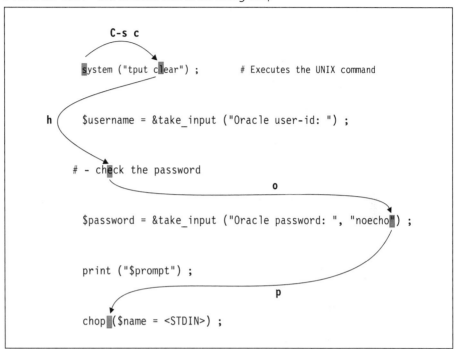

6.11.3   Nonincremental Search

You can also opt for a simple "vanilla" or **nonincremental search** in the way used in other editors. You require the same keys initially (**C-s** or **C-r**), but when the search pattern is asked for, simply press *[Enter]* and input the string at the next prompt:

```
I-search: [Enter]
Search: chop[Enter]
```

You can repeat this search in the same way you repeat an incremental search. The search and repeat commands are summarized in Table 6.4, and nonincremental search is illustrated in Fig. 6.12.

What makes searching in **emacs** powerful is that the search pattern is not confined to a simple string. You can also use a *regular expression* that comprises some special characters similar to the way wild cards (like the *) are used for matching filenames. There's a separate chapter devoted almost exclusively to regular expressions (Chapter 11), and most of what is discussed there applies to **emacs** too. The search commands for regular expressions are, however, different (Appendix C).

Tip

If you happen to be near a word which is also the string you want to search for, then there's no need to key in the string. Move your cursor to the space before the word, press **C-s** and then **C-w** to copy the word to the minibuffer. You can now use **C-s** to repeat the search. An extremely useful facility!

FIGURE 6.12   *Nonincremental Search for String* copies

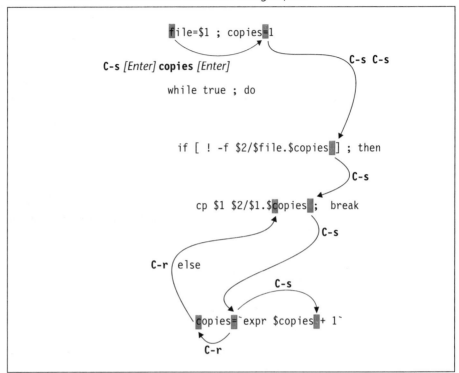

TABLE 6.4   *Search and Replace Commands*

Command	Function
C-s *pat*	Incremental search forward for pattern *pat*
C-r *pat*	Incremental search back for pattern *pat*
C-s *[Enter] pat*	Nonincremental search forward for pattern *pat*
C-r *[Enter] pat*	Nonincremental search back for pattern *pat*
C-s	Repeats search in forward direction (incremental and nonincremental)
C-r	Repeats search in reverse direction (incremental and nonincremental)
[Esc] or *[Enter]*	Cancels search
M-x replace-string	Replaces string noninteractively
M-%	Replaces string interactively (requires *[Shift]*)
M-x query-replace	As above

▨ 6.12   Substitution—Search and Replace

emacs offers yet another powerful feature, that of substitution, which lets you replace a pattern with something else. Replacement can be both interactive and noninteractive. We'll first examine noninteractive substitution.

Noninteractive Substitution There's no key binding available for noninteractive substitution, so you have to run the **replace-string** command (with **M-x**). emacs prompts twice for the two strings:

```
M-x replace-string[Enter]
Replace string: float[Enter]
Replace string float with: double[Enter]
```

The string float is replaced with double throughout the buffer. If you feel that this hasn't done quite what you expected, then undo the operation with **C-x u** or **C--**.

Interactive Substitution Interactive replacement is performed with the **query-replace** command, which fortunately is bound to **M-%** (requires *[Shift]*). **emacs** prompts for both strings:

```
Query replace: float[Enter]
Query replace float with: double[Enter]
```

The cursor moves to the first instance of float, and **emacs** poses this question:

```
Query replacing float with double: (? for help)
```

Pressing a ? will list 10 options, but in most cases, you'll need only these:

y or spacebar	Replaces current occurrence and moves to next
n	Doesn't replace and skips to next
q or *[Enter]*	Exits without replacing
.	Replaces this instance only and quits
!	Replaces all remaining occurrences without asking

emacs offers similar options when you try to quit without saving the buffer. They, however, have different meanings here. Use **q** to abort the replace operation when you have performed all replacements that you needed to make. On the other hand, you may have made a number of replacements already, and now feel that no further confirmation is needed for the rest. In that case, use **!** to let **emacs** complete the remaining replacements.

▨ 6.13   Using Multiple Windows and Buffers

emacs often switches to the multiwindow mode, and you can't revert to the original single-window state unless you know how to handle windows. As discussed previously, every file opened by **emacs** is associated with a buffer which you view in one or more windows. However, there's no relationship as such between the buffer and the window. When you close the window, the buffer remains open. You can also kill a buffer without closing the window. The following sections should help in making the subtle distinction between the two.

6.13.1 Handling Windows

emacs windows can contain anything; they may be either empty or contain the same or different files. We'll limit our discussions to two windows since most of us feel comfortable with just two.

To view the same file in two separate windows, use

C-x 2   *Splits into 2 windows*

You'll see the screen split in two, which in Fig. 6.13 shows slightly different segments of the same file. To move to the other window, use

C-x o   *To the other window*

The letter o is a mnemonic for "other"; it takes you to the other window. Every time you issue this command, the cursor alternates between the two windows. If you had three windows, you would be moving to each of these windows in turn.

You can now independently scroll text in both windows (with **C-v** and **M-v**). Editing changes made in one window are also reflected in the other window since both windows are associated with the same file and buffer.

FIGURE 6.13 *A Split Window*

```
Buffers Files Tools Edit Search Mule Insert Help
option=-e
while echo $option "Designation code: \c"
do
      read desig
              case "$desig" in
      [0-9][0-9]) if grep "^$desig" desig.lst >/dev/null # If code exists
              then echo "Code exists"
--1-:--F1  dentry1.sh          (Shell-script Abbrev)--L1--Top--------------------
              case "$desig" in
      [0-9][0-9]) if grep "^$desig" desig.lst >/dev/null # If code exists
              then echo "Code exists"
                    continue                # Go to loop beginning
                  fi ;;
              *) echo "Invalid code" ; continue ;;
              esac
--1-:--F1  dentry1.sh          (Shell-script Abbrev)--L1--Top--------------------
```

Tip

You can scroll forward in the other window without actually moving there by using **C-M-v**, but unfortunately you can't scroll back.

Closing Windows To make the current window the only window on the screen and close all other windows, use

C-x 1   *Kills all other windows*

In a converse manner, you can also kill the current window and move to the other window by using

C-x 0 *(zero)*   *Kills this window*

Once again, killing a window doesn't kill the buffer that was being viewed in that window; it remains in the buffer list.

Changing Window Size If one window requires a larger screen, you can increase its vertical size:

C-x ^   *Increases window's size*

Decreasing the size of a window is a bit awkward. It's easier to move to the other window with **C-x o** and then increase the size of that window.

Opening a File You may want to open a different file in one window. You probably know this command already:

C-x C-f   *Opens a new file*

After you have entered a different filename, you'll have two different files (and buffers) in two windows. Now, if **C-x C-f** opens a wrong file, will you use this command again? No, you must *kill* the current buffer and load another one using

C-x C-v   *Replaces current buffer*

Both commands, **C-x C-f** and **C-x C-v**, are used to open a second file even when you are working in a single window (the normal **emacs** mode).

Caution

Instead of using C-x C-v, if you had used C-x C-f yet again, you would have still held on to the buffer of the previous file that you wrongly called up. Unlike **vi**, **emacs** neither saves nor kills the current buffer before calling up another one, so it's easy to have a number of them in the buffer list if you don't use C-x C-v.

6.13.2   Handling Buffers

emacs offers a number of commands that show you the buffer list, select a buffer from the list, and open files. You can switch to any buffer with this command:

C-x b   *Calls up another buffer*

FIGURE 6.14 *Displaying the Buffer List with* **C-x b**

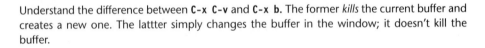

```
In this buffer, type RET to select the completion near point.


Possible completions are:
*Messages*                        *scratch*
convert.sh                        dentry1.sh



--1-:--F1  *Completions*      (Completion List Abbrev)--L1--All----------------
Switch to buffer: (default *scratch*)
```

emacs offers the previous buffer name that was edited in that window as the default. In case you want to return to the last edited file, simply press *[Enter]*. When you are editing two files alternately, you can toggle between the current file and the immediately preceding file in this way.

When the buffer you want to edit is not the default one shown by **C-x b**, you can enter the name yourself or view the list and select one from there. Enter **C-x b**, and when the prompt appears, hit *[Tab]* and then use the completion feature to select a filename from the list. A typical buffer list is shown in Fig. 6.14.

Note

Understand the difference between **C-x C-v** and **C-x b**. The former *kills* the current buffer and creates a new one. The lattter simply changes the buffer in the window; it doesn't kill the buffer.

The buffer list in the figure shows a *scratch* buffer that **emacs** always makes available to you for making notes. You can position yourself in the buffer list by using **C-x o**—twice, if required. You can then select any buffer by moving the cursor and pressing *[Enter]*. You can close this window by using **C-x 0** or cancel the entire action altogether with **C-g**.

There's a separate command for displaying the buffer list. It's a little different from the one that switches you to another buffer:

C-x C-b   *Displays buffer list*

You have two windows now, and the lower one shows the pathnames of all active buffers, their types and sizes (Fig. 6.15). You can move to this window using **C-x o** and then select a file to open in the lower window. The commands used to handle windows and buffers are shown in Table 6.5.

Tip

If you have to work with a number of files, invoke **emacs** with multiple filenames. The buffers for all files are created and held in the buffer list. Use **C-x C-b** to select a buffer for editing in a separate window and **C-x b** to display a different buffer in the current window.

FIGURE 6.15   *The Buffer List Displayed by* **C-x C-b**

```
    MR Buffer          Size  Mode           File
    -- ------          ----  ----           ----
    .   dentry1.sh      733  Shell-script  /home/romeo/project5/dentry1.sh
        convert.sh      520  Shell-script  /home/romeo/project5/convert.sh
        *Completions*   172  Completion List
        conv2pm6.sh     322  Shell-script  /home/romeo/project5/conv2pm6.sh
        *scratch*         0  Lisp Interaction
    *   *Messages*      240  Fundamental
    *% *Buffer List*    431  Buffer Menu


  --1-:%*-F1  *Buffer List*        (Buffer Menu Abbrev)--L3--All---------------------
```

TABLE 6.5   *Handling Windows and Buffers*

Command	Function
Window Handling	
C-x 2	Splits current window into 2 windows
C-x o	Moves to other window
C-x 1	Kills all other windows and makes this window the only window
C-x 0	Kills this window only
C-x ^	Increases vertical size of current window (Requires *[Shift]*)
C-M-v	Scrolls text forward in other window (no scrolling back facility available)
Buffer and File Handling	
C-x b	Edits another buffer in current window
C-x C-b	Displays buffer list; edits buffer in separate window
C-x k	Kills current buffer
C-x C-f	Stops editing current file and edits another file
C-x C-v	Replaces current buffer with another file

6.14   Using the Help Facility (C-h)

emacs has an elaborate help facility that provides you with detailed information about its commands, keys, modes, and variables. You can call up the tutorial or the multilevel info documentation as well. The help facility is organized in a number of modules, and they are all invoked with **C-h** (Table 6.6).

TABLE 6.6   *The Help Facility*

Command	Deals with
C-h k	Function performed by keystroke (detailed)
C-h c	Function performed by keystroke (one-line)
C-h f	Function performed by command
C-h w	Whereis; key binding available for command
C-h v	Function of variable and its current setting
C-h a	Commands that use a concept
C-h t	Runs tutorial
C-h i	Runs info reader

6.14.1   Accessing Help by Key (C-h k)

Beginners generally face two problems: they are unable to remember the function of a key sequence or what a command does. The first problem is handled by **C-h k** (key). On pressing it, **emacs** asks you to enter a key sequence:

```
Describe key: [Ctrl-y]                                    Seeking help for C-y
```

This is the command we use to paste copied or deleted text. **emacs** responds with a description of the key sequence in a separate window:

```
C-y runs the command yank
   which is an interactive compiled Lisp function.
(yank &optional ARG)
Reinsert the last stretch of killed text.
More precisely, reinsert the stretch of killed text most recently
killed OR yanked. Put point at end, and set mark at beginning.
    .......
```

This explanation is quite detailed and should be quite useful. Since your cursor is still in the previous window, you can close the help window with **C-x 1**.

6.14.2   Accessing Help by Function Name (C-h f and C-h w)

emacs supports over a thousand commands, and only a few of them have key bindings. **C-h f** and **C-h w** are two key sequences that you'll need to use to know more about these commands. To know what a command does, use **C-h f** (function) and enter the command name:

```
Describe function (default *): recover-file
```

As before, a separate window displays the description of the **recover-file** command:

```
recover-file is an interactive compiled Lisp function.
(recover-file FILE)
Visit file FILE, but get contents from its last auto-save file.
```

This description was short enough to fit in the window, but sometimes you'll need to scroll the other window (with **C-M-v**) to see the rest of the text. Note that you can't scroll back; to do that, you'll have to visit that window first (with **C-x o**).

Sometimes, you'll remember the command name, but not its key binding. For instance, you'll probably remember that interactive substitution is performed with **query-replace**, but can you recall its key binding? Use **C-h w** (where-is):

```
Where is command (default *): query-replace
```

emacs displays a single-line message in the minibuffer:

```
query-replace is on M-%, menu-bar search query-replace
```

This shows **M-%** as the shortcut, but it also guides you to the menu option *search>query-replace* that is available at the top of the screen. You'll be able to take advantage of this menu facility when you use **emacs** in the X Window system.

6.14.3   Viewing the Tutorial and info Documentation (C-h t and C-h i)

Finally, let's have a look at two other useful help features. You can invoke the **emacs** tutorial with **C-h t** (tutorial). This is an excellent introduction to the editor and serves as good reading material for beginners. Use **C-x b** to quit to the previous buffer.

More detailed than the tutorial is the info documentation that is invoked with **C-h i** (info). This takes you to the top of the "info tree." Linux systems offer a lot of info documentation for many commands, and this tree shows them all. Scroll down to position the cursor on the line showing Emacs: (emacs) and press *[Enter]* to view the **emacs** documentation menu.

You'll recall *(2.5.2—Linux)* that info documentation is organized in multiple nodes (levels). The nodes are indicated by asterisks at the beginning of the line. You can take your cursor to any of these nodes and press *[Enter]* to obtain detailed information on that topic. To return to the previous level, use **u**. To quit the info mode, use **q**. For refreshing your knowledge of the info commands, look up Section 2.5.2—Linux.

6.15   Customizing emacs: Setting Variables

emacs can be tailored by redefining keys or abbreviating frequently used strings, but in this section we examine its variables. **emacs** uses three commands to set its variables:

- **set-variable**   This command assigns values to variables from within the editor.
- **setq** and **setq-default**   These commands are used in ~/.emacs to make the settings permanent.

Variables may take on numeric, string, or boolean values. Boolean values may be t or nil. Let's now examine some of the variables.

auto-save-timeout   This is set to a numeric value signifying the number of seconds of inactivity that results in an automatic saving operation. To know its default value, use the **describe-variable** command or **C-h v**, and key in the variable name:

```
Describe variable: auto-save-timeout                              Use completion feature
```

emacs now shows you the current setting in a separate window along with a few lines of related documentation:

```
auto-save-timeout's value is 30
Documentation:
*Number of seconds idle time before auto-save.
Zero or nil means disable auto-saving due to idleness.

  .......
```

After you have finished viewing the documentation, kill this window with **C-x 1**. You can now change the value of this variable to, say, 60 seconds with the **set-variable** command (using **M-x**):

```
Set variable: auto-save-timeout
Set auto-save-timeout to value: 60
```

This setting remains valid for the rest of the session when using this buffer. To make it permanent, you have to use either **setq** or **setq-default** in .emacs:

```
(setq auto-save-timeout 60)
```
                                                                       Note the enclosing parentheses

auto-save-interval You can also set the number of keystrokes that result in an autosave operation. This is controlled by the variable auto-save-interval. By default, it is set to 300, but you can change it in .emacs:

```
(setq auto-save-interval 200)
```

Other Variables Let's discuss briefly the significance of some of the other important variables. Here are some settings that you may want to have in your .emacs file:

```
(setq-default case-fold-search nil)              Searches are case-sensitive
(setq tab-width 4)                               Number of spaces a tab expands to
(setq line-number-mode t)                        Shows line number on mode line
(setq blink-matching-paren t)                    Explained below
(setq kill-ring-max 50)                          Capacity of kill ring
(setq abbrev-mode t)                             Abbreviation mode on
```

The annotations provide adequate explanation except for blink-matching-paren. It enables the programmer to see momentarily the matching bracket to a) or }. Here, it is set to t, so when a) or } is entered, the cursor moves back to its matching counterpart and stays there for a fraction of a second before returning to its current location.

Local and Global Variables emacs makes a distinction between *local* and *global* variables. A local variable applies only to the buffer in which it is defined and overrides any global values that may be defined for the variable. **setq** sets a local variable, and **setq-default** sets a variable to its default (global) value. We'll not go into further details except to suggest that if the **setq** command doesn't work, use the **setq-default** command instead.

After you have used **emacs** to edit ~/.emacs, you don't need to quit and restart the editor for the changes to take effect. Just run the **load-file** command to make **emacs** reread .emacs. This facility is not available in **vi**.

➤ *G O I N G   F U R T H E R*

6.16 Recovering Multiple Deletions (M-y)

You can fetch the last 30 entries in the kill ring provided you follow certain rules. Recall that recovery is possible only for copied text and text that is deleted with a kill operation. When you have made multiple deletions or copies using the techniques described previously, move to the new location and restore the most recent deletion or copy with **C-y**. If that is not the right one, this time use

M-y   *Works only after an initial* C-y

This undoes the last entry fetched and restores the next entry. The command behaves in a circular manner, undoing and restoring the next entry every time it is pressed.

6.17 Abbreviating Text (abbrev-mode)

emacs lets you abbreviate long words. You have to first switch on the abbreviation mode (off by default) before you can use the feature. To turn it on, use

M-x **abbrev-mode**

The word Abbrev should appear in the mode line, which means that you can now define an abbreviation. Let's use this feature to abbreviate the Java method System.out.println to sopl. First enter sopl in any line, press **C-x**, and then input the string aig:

sopl C-x aig

emacs now prompts for the expansion. Type System.out.println in the minibuffer, and you'll see sopl expanded to this string. You have defined your abbreviation.

To make your abbreviations available in all sessions, you should save them. Use **M-x write-abbrev-file** and enter, say, ~/.emacs_abbrevs as the name of the file that will hold your abbreviations. You must now tell **emacs** to enable abbreviation and load this file at startup. Place these lines in .emacs:

```
(setq-default abbrev-mode t)                                     t indicates true value
(read-abbrev-file "~/.emacs_abbrevs")
```

As discussed earlier, the **setq-default** command is used to set global variables. If you want all future abbreviations to go to the file, then place an additional entry in .emacs:

```
(setq save-abbrevs t)
```

You can list (**list-abbrevs**), edit (**edit-abbrevs**), and disable your abbreviations (**kill-all-abbrevs**). Note that all these commands must be preceded by **M-x** when you run them from the keyboard.

6.18 Customizing the Keyboard

vi users, who use **30G** to move to line 30, are often horrified to note the absence of a key binding for the **goto-line** command in **emacs**. The **global-set-key** function creates a key binding, so let's bind **goto-line** to **C-x w**. But before that, let's check whether it already has one binding. Look up **C-h c** in Table 6.6 and then press this key sequence:

```
Describe key briefly: [Ctrl-x] w
C-x w is undefined
```

This key is undefined, so use the **global-set-key** command to bind the **goto-line** command with this key. **emacs** requires two inputs:

```
Set key globally: [Ctrl-x] w                          The key sequence
Set key C-x w to command: goto-line                   The mapped command
```

You can now press **C-x w** and then enter the line number to navigate to a line. To make this binding permanent, place this entry at the end of .emacs:

```
(global-set-key "\C-xw" 'goto-line)                   There's a ' here
```

Note the unusual LISP syntax which requires the key binding to be enclosed within double quotes. The command to run must be preceded by one single quote. Note the conventions used: \C-x is *[Ctrl-x]*. The other escape sequences that you can use here are: \e for *[Esc]* and \r for *[Enter]*.

6.19 Using Macros

We often need to map a set of keystrokes to a short sequence. This is handled in **emacs** by a **macro**, a user-defined command that executes a group of key sequences. Macro definitions start with the **C-x (** command. Once pressed, **emacs** goes into the "recording" mode and records all your keystrokes till you press **C-x**.

    emacs badly needs to have a short key sequence for copying the current line, so we'll create a macro for it:

```
C-x (                                            Definition starts
C-a                                     Moves to beginning of line
C-[Spacebar]                                          Sets mark
C-e                                          Goes to end of line
M-w                                             Copies region
C-x                                            Definition ends
```

This macro doesn't yet have a name, but you can still execute it to copy the current line in this way:

```
C-x e                                  Then place it anywhere with C-y
```

This sequence executes the **call-last-kbd-macro** command. To save it in .emacs, you first need to give it a name (say, cp1). Invoke the **name** command and then input cp1 as the macro name:

```
Name for last kbd macro: cp1
```

You can now copy a line by issuing the command **M-x cp1**. Open the file .emacs (with **C-x C-f**), move to the end of the file, and then type this:

M-x **insert-kbd-macro**   *Enter* cp1 *at prompt*

The LISP code that **emacs** inserts into this file looks like this:

```
(fset 'cp1
   "\C-a\C-@\C-e\C-[w")                                           C-[w is M-w
```

After you have saved .emacs, the macro named **cp1** is available for use. An **emacs** macro goes further and lets you define points where it will pause to take user input. However, we won't discuss this feature in this book.

SUMMARY

emacs is a full-screen "mode-less" editor. Commands are entered in the *minibuffer* and messages are displayed on the *mode line*. **emacs** reads ~/.emacs on startup.

Most commands also work with a *digit argument* or *universal argument,* which repeats the command multiple times. An **emacs** command is invoked with **M-x**. Some commands have *key bindings,* but most commands don't.

The **overwrite-mode** command determines whether existing text is preserved or overwritten. A control character or *[Esc]* is entered by preceding the command with **C-q**.

emacs autosaves a file every 300 keystrokes or 30 seconds. You can save a file using the same name (**C-x C-s**) or a different name (**C-x C-w**). You can quit with or without saving (**C-x C-c**). Sometimes you'll need to escape to a shell (**M-x shell**) without quitting the editor.

The keys b, f, p, and n used with Control move the cursor back, forward, to the previous and next lines. You can also move by units of *words* (**M-f** and **M-b**), and to the beginning (**C-a**), or end (**C-e**) of a line. Scrolling is done with **C-v** (forward) and **M-v** (back).

The **goto-line** command is used to move to a specific line number. You can also directly go to the beginning (**M-<**) or end (**M->**) of a file.

You can delete a character (**C-d**), kill a word (**M-d**) and a line (**C-k C-k**). Killed (and copied) text goes to the *kill ring* from where it can be recovered later.

A *region* is defined by first marking its beginning (**C-[Spacebar]**). You can kill (**C-w**) or copy text in a region (**M-w**). Killed or copied text is put at the new location with **C-y**.

Text can be capitalized (**M-c**). The case of complete words is changed with **M-u** (upper) and **M-l** (lower). An entire region can also be converted (**C-x C-u** and **C-x C-l**).

Editing can be undone and redone with the same key: **C-x u** or **C--**. **emacs** starts redoing when undoing is complete.

Search can be both *incremental* and *nonincremental* (**C-s** and **C-r**). Replacement can be both noninteractive (**replace-string**) and interactive (**query-replace** or M-%).

You can split the screen into two (**C-x 2**), navigate across windows (**C-x o**), and close the current window (**C-x 0**) or all other windows (**C-x 1**). You can open a new file (**C-x C-f**) or replace the current buffer with another file (**C-x C-v**). You can change the buffer associated with your window (**C-x b**) or list all buffers (**C-x C-b**).

emacs supports an extensive help facility (**C-h**). You can find out what a key does (**C-h k**), the function of a command (**C-h f**) or its key binding (**C-h w**). You can also view the tutorial (**C-h t**) and info documentation (**C-h i**).

emacs variables are set with **setq** and **setq-default**. You can make your searches case-sensitive (case-fold-search), set the period of inactivity for autosaving (auto-save-timeout and auto-save-interval), and alter the size of the kill ring (kill-ring-max).

SELF-TEST

6.1   If text input overwrites existing text what could the reason be? How do you reverse the current setting?

6.2   If you don't see the line number on the mode line, what setting will you make?

6.3   Which keys are associated with the *digit argument* and *universal argument?* To delete 16 words, which command will you use?

6.4   What is the difference between the commands **C-x C-s** and **C-x C-w**?

6.5   Describe the key sequences required to complete the following commands: (i) replace-string, (ii) recover-file, (iii) query-replace.

6.6   Name the command to use when (i) **emacs** asks you for more input after you have entered a wrong command, (ii) your screen shows junk.

6.7   Why doesn't **C-h** work as the backspacing character in **emacs**?

6.8   In the midst of your session you want to find out the time. How do you do that without escaping to a shell prompt?

6.9   In the current line, how do you move the cursor to the (i) 40th character, (ii) beginning, (iii) end?

6.10   How do you move the cursor to the (i) beginning, (ii) end of a file?

6.11   Explain which of the following actions can be undone: (i) M-f C-p, (ii) C-v, (iii) M-6 C-d, (iv) C-t.

6.12   How do you delete all text from the (i) current cursor position to end of line, (ii) current line without deleting the line?

6.13   Describe the steps needed to define a region. How do you toggle between the two ends of a region?

6.14   You have incorrectly entered the word System as Sytsem. How will you correct it?

6.15   What is the significance of the **C-s** and **C-r** commands?

6.16   How do you globally replace printf with fprintf (i) interactively, (ii) noninteractively?

6.17   How do you revert to the (i) last-saved version, (ii) autosaved version of a file?

6.18   You executed a command which split your current window in two. How do you now (i) move to the other window, (ii) close the window that you just moved to?

6.19   Repeated use of **C-x C-f** can lead to the creation of too many buffers. Explain how that can be handled by using a different command.

6.20   Enter these sequences and make your observations: (i) C-h k C-h k, (ii) C-h k C-h f.

EXERCISES

6.1   Invoke **emacs foo** and note the commands required to do the following: (i) Enter this statement: echo "Time to get up!^G". (ii) Save the buffer. (iii) Escape to the shell to make the file executable. (iv) Return to the editor. (v) Exit the editor. How did you enter the control character shown as ^G?

6.2   Which file does **emacs** normally read on startup? How can you ensure sure that it doesn't read the file?

6.3   Describe two ways of using a shortcut to repeat the **goto-line** command that was invoked once in the current session.

6.4   Name the commands required to add /* at the beginning of a line and */ at the end.

6.5   If you see the string ^[, what could it represent? In case you find that it is a single character, how do you (i) enter it, (ii) copy it?

6.6   Explain what the following commands do: (i) C-x C-c, (ii) C-u C-x C-c, (iii) C-x C-z. How do you revert to the normal mode in (iii)?

6.7   How will you set things up so that you can toggle between the beginning and end of a file using a simple key sequence?

6.8   In the midst of your work, you need to execute a number of UNIX commands. What course of action will you adopt?

6.9   How do you save the buffer of foo1 to (i) the same file, (ii) foo2?

6.10   What is the difference between the commands **recover-file** and **revert-buffer**?

6.11   Name the commands required to do the following: (i) move forward to the line containing the string #include, (ii) delete that line and three lines below, (iii) move to the beginning of file, (iv) place the deleted lines before the current line.

6.12   All delete operations are not kill operations. Explain.

6.13   Name the commands required to copy (i) the character under the cursor, (ii) text to the beginning of line, (iii) 10 words, (iv) following text up to the string esac?

6.14   Name the commands required to copy 5 lines of text from file foo1 to foo2. How do you toggle between the two files?

6.15   Name the most convenient way of deleting (i) 3 words, (ii) 16 words.

6.16   How do you delete the following? (i) text from the current cursor position to end of file, (ii) entire contents of file.

6.17   Find out the **emacs** commands that begin with write and then use one to save a region *directly* to a file.

6.18   You need to undo the last three changes. What key sequence will you use? How do you now redo the changes that you have just undone?

6.19   You need to simply know whether a string exists in the current file. Which search technique will you use?

6.20   How do you search for a pattern `printf` and then repeat the search in the opposite direction from which the original search was made? To make the search case-insensitive what setting do you need to make?

6.21   If the power to the machine is cut off while an **emacs** session is active, how does it affect your work? What salvage operation will you try?

6.22   How do you convert to uppercase (i) the character under the cursor, (ii) 5 words, (iii) entire file?

6.23   Open a file `foo` with **emacs**. Name the commands required to (i) split the current window, (ii) move to the lower window, (iii) open `foo2` in that window, (iv) save both buffers and exit.

6.24   Name the commands required to delete lines 11 to 30 and then restore lines 11 to 20 and 21 to 30 at two different locations. What precaution do you need to take?

6.25   Explain how to find out the significance of (i) M-y, (ii) `revert-buffer`.

6.26   How do you customize **emacs** so that it (i) autosaves the buffer after every 100 keystrokes, (ii) expands every tab to four spaces?

## CHAPTER 7

The Shell

This chapter introduces the agency that sits between the user and the UNIX system. It is called the *shell*. All of the wonderful things that we can do with UNIX are possible because the shell does a lot of work on our behalf that could be tedious for us to do on our own. The shell looks for special symbols in the command line, performs the tasks associated with them, and finally executes the command. For example, it opens a file to save command output whenever it sees the > symbol.

The shell is a unique and multifaceted program. It is a command interpreter and a programming language rolled into one. On the other hand, it is a process that creates an environment to work in. All of these features deserve separate chapters for discussion, and you'll find the shell discussed at a number of places in this book. In this chapter, we focus on the shell's basic interpretive activities. We have seen some of these activities in previous chapters (like **rm *** or **ls | more**), but it is here that we need to examine them closely.

Objectives

- Gain an overview of the shell's interpretive cycle.
- Learn the significance of *metacharacters* and their use in *wild cards* for matching multiple filenames.
- Know the use of *escaping* and *quoting* to remove the meaning of a metacharacter.
- Learn the difference between use of double and single quotes.
- Discover the significance of the three *standard files (streams)* that are available to every command.
- Learn how the shell manipulates the default source and destination of these streams to implement *redirection* and *pipelines*.
- Know the importance of making the command ignorant of the source of its input and destination of its output.
- Understand what *filters* are and why they are so important in UNIX.
- Learn the significance of the files /dev/null and /dev/tty.
- Know the use of *command substitution* to obtain the arguments of a command from the standard output of another.

- Understand shell variables and why they are so useful.
- Learn additional wild cards used by the Korn shell and Bash *(Going Further)*.
- Learn about passing a list of filenames down a pipeline for use by **xargs** *(Going Further)*.

7.1   The Shell as Command Processor

When you log on to a UNIX machine, you first see a prompt. Even though it may appear that nothing is happening, a UNIX command is in fact running at the terminal. But this command is special; it starts functioning the moment you log in and withers away when you log out. This command is the *shell*. If you run the **ps** command (that shows processes), you'll see it running:

```
$ ps
   PID TTY     TIME CMD
   526 pts/6   0:00 ksh                              Korn shell running
```

When you key in a command, it goes as input to the shell. The shell first scans the command line for **metacharacters**. These are special characters that mean nothing to the command, but mean something special to the shell. The previous example (**ps**) had none of these characters, but we did encounter these characters before (section numbers shown in parentheses):

```
echo date > date.sh                                                  (4.2)
rm *                                                                (3.14)
ls | more                                                           (3.16)
```

When the shell sees metacharacters like the >, |, *, etc. in its input, it translates these symbols to their respective actions *before* the command is executed. It replaces the * with all filenames in the current directory so that **rm** ultimately runs with these names as arguments. On seeing the >, the shell opens the file date.sh and connects **echo**'s output to it. The shell recreates the command line by removing all metacharacters and finally passes on the command to the kernel for execution.

Note that the shell has to interpret these metacharacters because they usually mean nothing to the command. To sum up, the following activities are typically performed by the shell in its interpretive cycle:

- It issues the prompt and waits for you to enter a command.
- After a command is entered, the shell scans the command line for metacharacters and expands abbreviations (like the * in **rm** *) to recreate a simplified command line.
- It then passes on the command line to the kernel for execution.
- The shell waits for the command to complete and normally can't do any work while the command is running.
- After command execution is complete, the prompt reappears and the shell returns to its waiting role to start the next cycle. You are now free to enter another command.

You can change this default behavior and instruct the shell not to wait so you can run multiple commands. We'll examine the technique of doing that in Chapter 8.

7.2   Shell Offerings

Your UNIX system offers a variety of shells for you to choose from. Over time, shells have become more powerful by the progressive addition of new features. The shells we consider in this text can be grouped into two categories:

- The Bourne family comprising the Bourne shell (**/bin/sh**) and its derivatives—the Korn shell (**/bin/ksh**) and Bash (**/bin/bash**).
- The C Shell (**/bin/csh**) and its derivative, Tcsh (**/bin/tcsh**).

To know the shell you are using, invoke the command **echo $SHELL**. The output could be one of the absolute pathnames of the shell's command file shown in parentheses above.

In this chapter, we discuss the common features of the Bourne family. Korn and Bash are supersets of Bourne, so anything that applies to Bourne also applies to them. A few of them don't apply to the C shell and are noted as and when they are encountered. You may not want to know all this now, but it does pay to know the shell you are using at this stage.

7.3   Pattern Matching—The Wild Cards

In previous chapters, you used commands with more than one filename as arguments (e.g., **cp chap01 chap02 chap03 progs**). Often, you'll need to use a command with similar filenames:

```
ls chap chap01 chap02 chap03 chap04 chapx chapy chapz
```

The common substring here is chap, and the shell offers a facility of representing these filenames by a single pattern. For instance, chap* represents all filenames beginning with chap. You can use this pattern as an argument to a command rather than supply a long list of filenames which the pattern represents. The shell will expand it suitably *before the command is executed.*

The metacharacters used to match filenames belong to a category called **wild cards** (something like the joker that can match any card). In the following sections, we'll discuss the significance of the various metacharacters in the wild-card set that are listed in Table 7.1.

7.3.1   The * and ?

The * Now let's get into the specifics. The * (a metacharacter) is one of the characters of the shell's special set, and we have used it before (**rm *** in Section 3.14). This character matches any number of characters including none. When it is appended to the string chap, the pattern chap* matches filenames beginning with the string chap—including the file chap. You can now use this pattern as an argument to **ls**:

```
$ ls -x chap*
chap chap01 chap02 chap03 chap04 chap15 chap16 chap17 chapx chapy
chapz
```

TABLE 7.1   *The Shell's Wild Cards and Application*

Wild Card	Matches
*	Any number of characters including none
?	A single character
[ijk]	A single character—either an *i, j* or *k*
[x-z]	A single character that is within the ASCII range of the characters x and z
[!ijk]	A single character that is not an i, j or k *(Not in C shell)*
[!x-z]	A single character that is not within the ASCII range of the characters x and z *(Not in C shell)*
{pat1,pat2...}	*pat1, pat2*, etc. *(Not in Bourne Shell; see Going Further)*
!(flname)	All except *flname (Korn and Bash; see Going Further)*
!(fname1|fname2)	All except *fname1* and *fname2 (Korn and Bash; see Going Further)*

Examples	
Command	**Significance**
ls *.lst	Lists all files with extension .lst
mv * ../bin	Moves all files to bin subdirectory of parent directory
gzip .?*.?*	Compresses all files beginning with a dot, followed by one or more characters, then a second dot followed by one or more characters
cp chap chap*	Copies file chap to file chap* (* loses meaning here)
cp ?????? progs	Copies to progs directory all six-character filenames
cmp rep[12]	Compares files rep1 and rep2
rm note[0-1][0-9]	Removes files note00, note01 . . . through note19
lp *.[!o]	Prints all files having extensions except C object files
cp ?*.*[!1238] ..	Copies to the parent directory files having extensions with at least one character before the dot, but not having 1, 2, 3 or 8 as the last character

When the shell encounters this command line, it immediately identifies the * as a metacharacter. It then creates a list of files from the current directory that match this pattern. It reconstructs the command line as below, and then hands it over to the kernel for execution:

```
ls -x chap chap01 chap02 chap03 chap04 chap15 chap16 chap17 chapx chapy chapz
```

What happens when you use **echo** with the * as argument?

```
$ echo *
array.pl back.sh calendar cent2fah.pl chap chap01 chap02 chap03 chap04 chap15 ch
ap16 chap17 chapx chapy chapz count.pl date_array.pl dept.lst desig.lst n2words.
pl name.pl name2.pl odfile operator.pl profile.sam rdbnew.lst rep1.pl
```

You simply see a list of files! All filenames in the current directory match a solitary *, so you see all of them in the output. If you use **rm *** in this directory, all these files will be deleted.

Note

Windows users may be surprised to know that the * may occur anywhere in the pattern and not merely at the end. Thus, *chap* matches all the following filenames—chap newchap chap03 chap03.txt.

Caution

Be careful when you use the * with **rm** to remove files. You could land yourself in a real mess if, instead of typing **rm *.o** which removes all the C object files, you inadvertently introduce a space between * and .o:

```
$ rm * .o                                                    Very dangerous!
rm: .o: No such file or directory
```

The error message here masks a disaster that has just occurred; **rm** has removed all files in this directory! Whenever you use a * with **rm**, you should pause and check the command line before you finally press *[Enter]*. A safer bet would be to use **rm -i**.

The ?   The ? matches a single character. When used with the same string chap (as chap?), the shell matches all five-character filenames beginning with chap. Place another ? at the end of this string, and you have the pattern chap??. Use both these expressions separately, and the meaning of the ? becomes obvious:

```
$ ls -x chap?
chapx  chapy  chapz
$ ls -x chap??
chap01  chap02  chap03  chap04  chap15  chap16  chap17
```

Both the * and ? operate with some restrictions that are examined in Section 7.3.4.

7.3.2 The Character Class

The patterns framed in the preceding examples are not very restrictive. With the knowledge we have, it's not easy to list only chapy and chapz. Nor is it easy to match only the first four chapters from the numbered list. You can frame more restrictive patterns with the **character class**.

The character class comprises a set of characters enclosed by the rectangular brackets [and], but it matches a *single* character in the class. The pattern [abcd] is a character class, and it matches a single character—an a, b, c, or d. This pattern can be combined with any string or another wild-card expression so that selecting chap01, chap02, and chap04 now becomes a simple matter:

```
$ ls chap0[124]
chap01  chap02  chap04
```

Range specification is also possible inside the class with a - (hyphen); the two characters on either side of it form the range of the characters to be matched. Here are two examples:

```
ls chap0[1-4]                                     Lists chap01, chap02, chap03 and chap04
ls chap[x-z]                                              Lists chapx, chapy and chapz
```

A valid range specification requires that the character on the left have a lower ASCII value than the one on the right.

Note

The expression [a-zA-Z]* matches all filenames beginning with a letter, irrespective of case. You can match a word character by including numerals and the underscore character as well: [a-zA-Z0-9_].

Negating the Character Class (!) The solution that we prescribe here unfortunately doesn't work with the C shell, but with the other shells, you can use the ! as the first character in the class to negate the class. The two examples below should make this point amply clear:

```
*.[!co]                                          Matches all filenames with a single-character
                                                      extension but not the .c or .o files.
[!a-zA-Z]*                                   Matches all filenames that don't begin with a letter.
```

Even though the character class is meant to be used with a group of characters, it's the only way you can negate a match for a single character. Thus, to match all files with single-character extensions except those ending with .o (i.e., C object files), you have to use a character class as a "dummy class":

```
*.[!o]                                                                 Not the .o files
```

C Shell

The ! can't be used to negate a character class at all. In fact, the C shell has no mechanism for doing so.

The Mystery of the find *Command*

It's true that a command doesn't perform wild-card expansion on its own and runs only after the shell has expanded the wild cards. The **find** command is an exception. It supports wild cards (probably the only UNIX command having this feature) in the filename that's used as a parameter to the -name option:

```
find / -name "*.[hH][tT][mM][lL]" -print          All .html and .HTML files
find . -name "note??" -print                        Two characters after note
```

Here, we are using the same wild-card characters, but this time they are a feature of **find** and not of the shell. **find** supports only the Bourne shell set. By providing quotes around the pattern, we ensured that the shell can't even interpret this pattern. In fact, allowing the shell to do that could be disastrous! You'll learn about this insulating feature shortly.

7.3.3 Matching the Dot

The behavior of the * and ? in relation to the dot isn't as straightforward as it may seem. The * and ? don't match

- all filenames *beginning* with a . (dot).
- the / of a pathname.

If you want to list all hidden filenames in your directory having at least three characters after the dot, then the dot must be matched explicitly:

```
$ ls .???*
.bash_profile   .exrc   .netscape  .profile
```

However, if the filename contains a dot anywhere but at the beginning, it need not be matched explicitly. For example, the expression *c also matches all C programs:

```
$ ls *c
access.c
check_permissions.c
runc
shell.c
toc
```

Note

There are two things that the * can't match. First, it doesn't match a filename beginning with a dot, but it can match any number of embedded dots. For instance, apache*gz matches apache_1.3.20.tar.gz. Second, the * doesn't match the / in a pathname. You can't use **cd /usr*local** to switch to /usr/local. The ? also operates with these two restrictions.

7.3.4 Rounding Up

Some of the wild-card characters have different meanings depending on where they are placed in the pattern. The * and ? lose their meaning when used inside the class, and are matched literally. Similarly, - and ! also lose their significance when placed at other locations. There are other restrictions, but we can ignore them for now.

What if the shell fails to match a single file with the expression chap*? There's a surprise element here; the shell also looks for a file named chap*. You should avoid using metacharacters when choosing filenames, but if you have to handle one, then you have to turn off the meaning of the * so that the shell treats it literally. This deactivation feature is taken up in the next section.

Note

The expression [!!] matches a single character filename that is not a !. This doesn't work in the C shell and Bash, which use the ! for a different purpose. Bash needs to use [!\!] here, but the C shell can't negate a character class at all.

Tip

When organizing information in files that need to be accessed as a group, choose the filenames with care so you don't need to use too many patterns to match them.

7.4 Escaping and Quoting

You might well think that since the shell transforms the wild-card characters, filenames musn't contain these characters. That's correct thinking, but the real world is far from perfect. One of the examples featured in Table 7.1 shows how easy it is to actually

create a file named chap* (**cp chap chap***). This creates problems as the pattern chap*
also matches the filename chap*:

```
$ ls chap*
chap   chap*  chap01  chap02  chap03  chap04  chap15  chap16  chap17  chapx
chapy  chapz
```

This file can be a great nuisance and should be removed immediately, but that won't be
easy. **rm chap*** removes all these files. We must be able to protect all special characters
(including wild cards), so the shell is not able to interpret them. The shell provides two
solutions to prevent its own interference:

- **Escaping**—Providing a \ (backslash) before the wild card to remove (escape) its
  special meaning.
- **Quoting**—Enclosing the wild card, or even the entire pattern, within quotes (like
  "chap*"). Anything within these quotes (barring few exceptions) are left alone by
  the shell and not interpreted.

In most cases you can use either mechanism, but some situations warrant the use of
quotes. Sometimes you also need to make a distinction between single and double quotes,
but more of that later.

7.4.1   Escaping

When the \ precedes a metacharacter, its special meaning is turned off. In the pattern
*, the \ tells the shell that the asterisk has to be treated and matched literally instead of
being interpreted as a metacharacter. Using this feature, we can now remove only the
file named chap*:

```
rm chap\*                                              Doesn't remove chap1, chap2
```

This feature is known as **escaping**. You have seen **stty** using this feature *(2.14),* and
you'll see other application areas also. Here's another example:

```
rm chap0\[1-3\]                                          Removes only chap0[1-3]
```

Escaping the Space   Apart from metacharacters, there are other characters that are
special—like the space. The shell uses it to delimit command-line arguments. So, to
remove the file My Document.doc which has a space embedded, a similar reasoning
should be followed:

```
rm My\ Document.doc                                   Without the \ rm would see two files
```

Escaping the \ Itself   Sometimes you may need to interpret the \ itself literally. You
need another \ before it, that's all:

```
$ echo \\
\
$ echo The newline character is \\n
The newline character is \n
```

Ignoring the Newline Character Command lines that use several arguments often overflow to the next line. To ensure better readability, split the wrapped line into two lines but make sure that you input a \ before you press *[Enter]*:

```
$ find /usr/local/bin /usr/bin -name "*.pl" -mtime +7 -size +1024 \[Enter]
> -size -2048 -atime +25 -print                            Note the >
```

The \ here ignores *[Enter]*. It also produces the second prompt (which could be a > or a ?), which indicates that the command line is incomplete. For better readability, you should split long pipelines *(7.8)* into multiple lines wherever possible.

Note

The space, \, and LF (the newline character generated by *[Enter]*) are also special and need to be escaped if the shell is to be prevented from interpreting them in the way it normally does.

7.4.2 Quoting

There's another way to turn off the meaning of a metacharacter. When a command argument is enclosed in quotes, the meanings of all enclosed special characters are turned off. Here's how we can run some of the previous commands, using a mix of single- and double-quoting this time:

```
echo '\'                                              Displays a \
rm 'chap*'                                       Removes file chap*
rm "My Document.doc"                    Removes file My Document.doc
```

Escaping also turns out to be a tedious affair when there are just too many characters to protect. Quoting is often a better solution. The following example shows the protection of four special characters using single quotes:

```
$ echo 'The characters |, <, > and $ are also special'
The characters |, <, > and $ are also special
```

We could have used escaping here, but then we would need to use a \ in front of each of these four metacharacters. We used single quotes because they protect all special characters (except the single quote). Double quotes are more permissive; they don't protect (apart from the double quote itself) the $ and the ` (backquote):

```
$ echo "Command substitution uses `` while TERM is evaluated using $TERM"
Command substitution uses  while TERM is evaluated using vt100
```

Observe that the pair of backquote characters (``) and the variable $TERM have been interpreted by the shell inside double quotes. The value of $TERM is vt100 for this terminal, and `` evaluated to a null command. Now try out the same example using single quotes:

```
$ echo 'Command substitution uses `` while TERM is evaluated using $TERM'
Command substitution uses `` while TERM is evaluated using $TERM
```

Note

It's often crucial to select the right type of quote, so bear in mind that single quotes protect all special characters except the single quote and \. Double quotes, however, allow a pair of backquotes (` `` `) to be interpreted as *command substitution* characters, and the $ as a variable prefix. There is also a reciprocal relationship between the two types of quotes; double quotes protect single quotes, and single quotes protect the double.

7.4.3 Escaping in echo

We used **echo** in Section 2.6 with escape sequences like \n and \t. The \ has a reverse meaning there; it treats the characters n and t as special rather than remove their special meaning because n and t don't have special meaning. These escape sequences are always used within quotes to keep the shell out. But what is **echo**?

```
$ type echo
echo is a shell builtin
```

We have a funny situation here. We quoted **echo**'s arguments to keep the shell out of the picture only to learn that **echo** is built into the shell! For this purpose, the shell treats **echo** as an external command (which it once was).

7.5 Redirection

Before we commence our discussions on redirection, let's first understand what the term *terminal* means since we'll be using it often. In the context of redirection, the terminal is a generic name that represents the screen, display, or keyboard (or even an X window that emulates a terminal). Just as we refer to a directory as a file, we'll also sometimes refer to the keyboard as a terminal.

We see command output and error messages on the terminal (display), and we sometimes provide command input through the terminal (keyboard). The shell associates three files with the terminal—two for the display and one for the keyboard. Even though our terminal is also represented by a specific device name, commands don't usually read from or write to this file. They perform all terminal-related activity with the three files that the shell makes available to every command.

These special files are actually **streams** of characters which many commands see as input and output. A stream is simply a sequence of bytes. When a user logs in, the shell makes available three files representing three streams. Each stream is associated with a default device, and—generically speaking—this device is the terminal:

- **Standard Input**—The file (or stream) representing input, which is connected to the keyboard.
- **Standard Output**—The file (or stream) representing output, which is connected to the display.
- **Standard Error**—The file (or stream) representing error messages that emanate from the command or shell. This is also connected to the display.

A group of UNIX commands reads from and writes to these files. A command is usually not designed to send output to the terminal but to this file. Likewise, it is not designed to accept input from the keyboard either, but only from a standard file which it sees as a stream. Every command that uses streams will always find these files open and available.

Even though the shell associates each of these files with a default physical device, this association is not permanent. The shell can easily unhook a stream from its default device and connect it to a disk file (or to any command) the moment it sees some special characters in the command line. You, as user, have to instruct the shell to do that by using symbols like > and < in the command line. This means that instead of input and output coming from and to the terminal, they can be redirected to come from or go to any disk file.

7.5.1 Standard Input

We have used the **cat** and **wc** commands to read disk files. These commands have an additional method of taking input. When they are used without arguments, they read the file representing the **standard input**. This file is indeed special; it can represent three input sources (Fig. 7.1):

- The keyboard, the default source.
- A file using redirection with the < symbol (a metacharacter).
- Another program using a pipeline (to be taken up later).

When you use **wc** without an argument and have no special symbols like the < and | in the command line, **wc** obtains its input from the default source. You have to provide this input from the keyboard and mark the end of input with *[Ctrl-d]:*

```
$ wc
Standard input can be redirected
It can come from a file
or a pipeline
[Ctrl-d]
        3      14      71
```

The **wc** command, which takes the stream from standard input, immediately counts 3 lines, 14 words, and 71 characters. Now run **wc** with a filename as argument:

```
$ wc /etc/passwd
     21      45    1083 /etc/passwd
```

There's a fourth column here; **wc** prints the filename because it opened the file itself. In the other example, no filename was specified, so no filename was output. **wc** simply read the standard input file that was opened by the shell when you logged in.

FIGURE 7.1 *Three Sources of Standard Input*

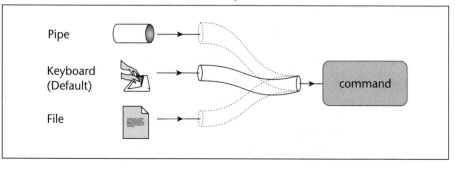

The shell's manipulative nature is useful here. It can reassign or **redirect** the standard input to originate from a file on disk. This redirection requires the < symbol:

```
$ wc < /etc/passwd
     21     45    1083
```

The filename is missing once again, which means that **wc** didn't open /etc/passwd. It read the standard input file as a stream but only after the shell made a reassignment of this stream to a disk file. The sequence works like this:

1. On seeing the <, the shell opens the disk file, /etc/passwd, for reading.
2. It unplugs the standard input file from its default source and assigns it to /etc/passwd.
3. **wc** reads from standard input which has earlier been reassigned by the shell to /etc/passwd.

The important thing here is that **wc** has no idea where the stream came from; it is not even aware that the shell had to open the file /etc/passwd on its behalf!

You may have already framed your next question. Why bother to redirect the standard input from a file if the command can read the file itself? After all, **wc** can also use a filename as argument! The answer is that there are times when you need to keep the command *ignorant* of the source of its input. This aspect, representing one of the most deep-seated features of the system, will gradually expose itself as you progress through these chapters.

Note

When the standard input is redirected to come from a file (with <), it's the shell that opens the file. The command here is totally ignorant of what the shell is doing to provide it with input. However, when you invoke a command with a filename as argument, it's the command that opens the file and not the shell.

Taking Input Both from File and Standard Input When a command takes input from multiple sources—say, a file and standard input, the - symbol must be used to indicate the sequence of taking input. The meaning of the following sequences should be quite obvious:

```
cat - foo                          First from standard input and then from foo
cat foo - bar                      First from foo, then standard input, and then bar
```

The third source of standard input is the pipe, which is discussed later *(7.8)*. There's a fourth form of standard input which we have not mentioned here. It's the *here document* that has application in shell programming and hence is discussed in Chapter 13.

7.5.2 Standard Output

All commands displaying output on the terminal actually write to the **standard output** file as a stream of characters, and not *directly* to the terminal as such. There are three possible destinations of this stream (Fig. 7.2):

- The terminal, the default destination.
- A file, using the redirection symbols > and >>.
- As input to another program using a pipeline (to be taken up later).

FIGURE 7.2 *The Three Destinations of Standard Output*

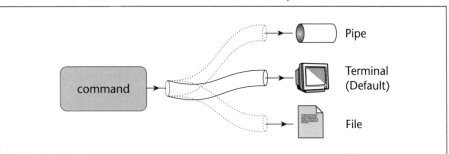

The shell can effect redirection of this stream when it sees the > or >> symbols in the command line. You can replace the default destination (the terminal) with any file by using the > (right chevron) operator, followed by the filename:

```
$ wc /etc/passwd > newfile
$ cat newfile
    21    45    1083 /etc/passwd
```

The first command sends the word count of /etc/passwd to newfile; nothing appears on the terminal screen. The sequence works like this:

1. On seeing the >, the shell opens the disk file, newfile, for writing.
2. It unplugs the standard output file from its default destination and assigns it to newfile.
3. **wc** (and not the shell) opens the file /etc/passwd for reading.
4. **wc** writes to standard output which has earlier been reassigned by the shell to newfile.

And all this happens without **wc** knowing that it is in fact writing to newfile! Any command that uses standard output is also ignorant about the destination of its output.

If the output file doesn't exist, the shell creates it before executing the command. If it exists, the shell overwrites it, so use this operator with caution. The shell also provides the >> symbol (the right chevron used twice) to append to a file:

```
wc sample.txt >>newfile                              Doesn't disturb existing contents
```

Redirection can also be used with multiple files. The following example saves all C programs:

```
cat *.c > c_progs_all.txt
```

The standard output of one command can also be used by another command as its standard input. This is the third destination of standard output and is taken up in the discussion on pipes *(7.8)*.

Note

When the output of a command is redirected to a file, the output file is created or truncated by the shell before the command is executed. Any idea what **cat foo > foo** does?

7.5.3 The File Descriptor

Before we proceed any further, you should know that each of the three standard files is represented by a number, called a **file descriptor**. A file is opened by referring to its pathname, but subsequent read and write operations identify the file by this file descriptor. The kernel maintains a table of file descriptors for every process running in the system. The first three slots are generally allocated to the three standard streams in this manner:

0—Standard input
1—Standard output
2—Standard error

These descriptors are *implicitly* prefixed to the redirection symbols. For instance, > and 1> mean the same thing to the shell, while < and 0< also are identical. We need to explicitly use one of these descriptors when handling the standard error stream. If your program opens a file, in all probability, the file will be allocated the descriptor 3.

How Redirection Works

The concepts related to redirection are pretty simple. A command like **ls** writes to file descriptor 1, and this remains true even when you use **ls > foo**. To save the **ls** output in **foo**, the shell has to manipulate this file descriptor before running **ls**. It closes the standard output and then opens **foo**. Since the kernel allocates the lowest unallocated integer in the file descriptor table, **foo** is assigned the value 1. The **ls** output is thus captured in **foo**.

Even though the concept appears simple, its implementation requires two processes. After all, if the shell closes its own standard output file, how does it display its own messages? In reality, the shell creates a copy of its own process, performs the descriptor manipulation in the copied process, and even runs the **ls** command in that process. The shell's own file descriptors are then left undisturbed. Chapter 18 discusses how the **dup**, **dup2**, and **fcntl** system calls are used to implement redirection.

7.5.4 Standard Error

When a command runs unsuccessfully, diagnostic messages often show up on the screen. This is the **standard error** stream whose default destination is the terminal. Trying to "cat" a nonexistent file produces the error stream:

```
$ cat foo
cat: cannot open foo
```

cat fails to open the file and writes to the standard error. If you are not using the C shell, you can redirect this stream to a file. Using the symbol for standard output obviously won't do; you need to use the 2> symbols:

```
$ cat foo > errorfile
cat: cannot open foo                          Error stream can't be captured with >
```

```
$ cat foo 2> errorfile
$ cat errorfile
cat: cannot open foo
```

Even though standard output and standard error use the terminal as the default destination, the shell possesses a mechanism for capturing them individually. You can also append standard error in the same way you append standard output:

```
cat foo 2>> errorfile
```

or redirect them separately:

```
foo.sh > bar1 2>bar2
```

What about saving both streams in the same file? The descriptor replicating mechanism, which does this job, is taken up shortly.

C Shell

The standard error is handled differently by the C shell, so the examples of this section won't work with it. In fact, the C shell merges the standard error with the standard output; it has no separate symbol for handling standard error only. The command **cat foo >& bar** saves both standard output and standard error in bar.

Tip

If you have a program that runs for a long time and is not error-free, you can direct the standard error to a separate file and then stay away from the terminal. On return, you can examine this file for errors.

7.5.5   Filters—Using Both Standard Input and Standard Output

We return to the input and output streams to ask ourselves this question: Do all commands use the features of standard input and standard output? No, certainly not. From this viewpoint, the UNIX commands can be grouped into four categories:

Commands	*Standard Input*	*Standard Output*
mkdir, rmdir, cp, rm	No	No
ls, pwd, who	No	Yes
lp, lpr	Yes	No
cat, wc, gzip	Yes	Yes

Commands in the fourth category are called **filters**, and the dual stream-handling feature makes filters powerful text manipulators. Note that most filters can also read *directly* from files whose names are provided as arguments. Four separate chapters are earmarked for filters in this text. Some of the commands discussed in previous chapters can also be made to behave as filters.

Since **wc** is a filter, you can redirect **wc**'s standard input to come from a file and save the output in yet another. This can be done in any of these ways:

```
wc < calc.txt > result.txt                    Using both standard input and output
wc > result.txt < calc.txt
```

```
wc>result.txt<calc.txt                                          No whitespace!
> result.txt < calc.txt wc                              As above, but command at end
```

The last example illustrates a departure from the statement made previously *(2.2)* that the first word in the command line is the command. In the last example, **wc** is the last word in the command line. Rather than use these combinations, you'll find it more convenient to stick to the first form.

The indifference of a command to the source of its input and destination of its output is one of the most profound features of the UNIX system. It raises the possibility of commands "talking" to one another so that the output of one command can be used as input to another. Very soon we'll discuss pipes, and you'll see how two or more commands communicate with one another.

7.6   Collective Manipulation

So far, we have used the > to handle a *single* stream of a *single* command. But the shell also supports collective stream handling. This can happen in these two ways:

- Handle two standard streams as a single one using the 2>&1 and 1>&2 symbols.
- Form a command group by enclosing multiple commands with the (and) symbols or { and } symbols. You can then use a single instruction to control all commands in the group.

Both concepts have important applications. We must understand them now because these features will be recalled when discussing processes, shell programming, and systems programming.

7.6.1   Replicating Descriptors

Though standard output and standard error are two separate streams, you can manipulate them collectively. It's like redirecting a single stream. The symbols required are a little cryptic to look at but quite intuitive:

1>&2   Send the standard output to the destination of the standard error.
2>&1   Send the standard error to the destination of the standard output.

In either case, both streams are associated with a single file. The first set is often used inside shell scripts in this way:

```
echo "Filename not entered" 1>&2                                     Same as >&2
```

Note that the **echo** statement has not been redirected here. If a script containing this statement is redirected, then the output of **echo** won't go to the file but would be sent to the standard error, the terminal. To save this message in a file, you have to provide redirection separately:

```
$ echo "Filename not entered" 2>error.txt 1>&2
$ cat errror.txt
Filename not entered
```

The 2> symbol reassigns standard error to error.txt and 1>&2 sends the standard output of **echo** to the standard error. Note the sequence: first we redirect and then specify the replication of the descriptor.

Tip

Some programs (like **perldoc**) are designed to write to the standard error. Piping the output to **more** doesn't help. To use the pager with these programs also, use 2>&1 to send standard error to the standard output. If you run **perldoc perlop 2>&1 | more**, you'll be able to separately view each page of the **perl** documentation.

7.6.2   Command Grouping

Sometimes, we need to manipulate a group of commands collectively: redirect them, run them in the background, and so on. The ( ) and { } handle a command group. We can use the first set to redirect the standard output of a command group using a single >:

```
( ls -x *.c ; echo ; cat *.c ) > c_progs_all.txt
```

This saves all C program sources in a file preceded by a multicolumn list of programs acting as a table of contents. The **echo** command serves to insert a blank line between them. The { } can also be used for this purpose:

```
{ ls -x *.c ; echo ; cat *.c ; } > c_progs_all.txt
```

Note the **;** at the end of the **cat** command that is required if the opening and closing curly braces are placed in the same line. You don't need it when the } is located in a separate line.

Though we could use the two sets of symbols interchangeably here, there are distinct differences between them. After we study processes, we'll be able to identify those situations where one group applies and not the other. We'll use the curly braces extensively when programming with the shell.

7.7   /dev/null **and** /dev/tty: **Two Special Files**

/dev/null Quite often, and especially in shell programming, you'll want to check whether a program runs successfully without seeing its output or saving it in a file. You have a special file that accepts any stream without growing in size—the file /dev/null:

```
$ cat /etc/passwd >/dev/null
$ cat /dev/null
$ _                                                    Size is always zero
```

Check the file size; it's always zero. /dev/null simply incinerates all output written to it. This facility is also useful in redirecting error messages. Consider the **find** command that was used in the Tip in Section 4.11.1:

```
find / -name typescript -print 2>/dev/null
```

The file /dev/null is actually a pseudo-device because, unlike all other device files, it's not associated with any physical device.

The file /dev/null can also be used as a "dummy" file when we need a command to work with two files but only one is available. Consider the **grep** command *(11.2)* which displays lines containing a pattern. The command also displays filenames when used with multiple filenames as arguments. But since the command used with the -exec operator of **find** *(4.11.3)* works with a single file at a time, we can use /dev/null to provide an additional argument to **grep**:

Tip

```
find . -name "*.c" -exec grep printf {} /dev/null \;
```

This command now shows the filename prepended to every line containing printf. Without /dev/null, **grep** would output only the line containing the pattern, and you wouldn't know which file the line comes from.

/dev/tty The second special file in the UNIX system is the one indicating one's terminal—/dev/tty. But make no mistake: *This is not the file that represents standard output or standard error.* Commands generally don't write to this file, but you'll be required to redirect some statements in shell scripts to this file.

Consider, for instance, that romeo is working on terminal /dev/pts/1 and juliet on /dev/pts/2. Both romeo and juliet, however can refer to their own terminals with the same filename—/dev/tty. Thus, if romeo issues the command

```
who >/dev/tty
```

the list of current users is sent to the terminal he is currently using—/dev/pts/1. Similarly, juliet can use an identical command to see the output on her terminal, /dev/pts/2. Like /dev/null, /dev/tty can be accessed independently by several users without conflict.

You may ask why one would need to specifically redirect output to one's own terminal since the default output goes to the terminal anyway. Sometimes, you need to specify that explicitly. Apart from its use in redirection, /dev/tty can also be used as an argument to some UNIX commands. Section 7.9 makes use of this feature, while some situations are presented in Chapter 13 (featuring shell programming).

Note

The size of /dev/null is always zero, and all terminals can be represented by /dev/tty.

7.8 Pipes

To understand pipes, we'll set ourselves the task of counting the number of users currently logged in. We'll first attempt the task using the knowledge we possess already. The **who** command produces a list of users—one user per line, and we'll save this output in a file:

```
$ who > user.txt
$ cat user.txt
root         console  Aug  1   07:51   (:0)
romeo        pts/10   Aug  1   07:56   (pc123.heavens.com)
juliet       pts/6    Aug  1   02:10   (pc125.heavens.com)
project      pts/8    Aug  1   02:16   (pc125.heavens.com)
```

If we now redirect the standard input of the **wc -l** command *(3.17)* to come from user.lst, we would have effectively counted the number of users:

```
$ wc -l < user.txt
    4                                          Counts the number of users
```

This method of running two commands separately has two obvious disadvantages:

- For long-running commands, this process can be slow. The second command can't act unless the first has completed its job.
- You require an intermediate file that has to be removed after completion of the job. When handling large files, temporary files can build up easily and eat up disk space in no time.

Here, **who**'s standard output was redirected, as was **wc**'s standard input, and both used the same disk file. The shell can connect these streams using a special operator—the | (pipe)—and avoid the creation of the disk file. You can make **who** and **wc** work in tandem so that one takes input from the other:

```
$ who | wc -l                                  No intermediate files created
    4
```

The output of **who** has been passed directly to the input of **wc**, and **who** is said to be **piped** to **wc**. When a sequence of commands is combined together in this way, a **pipeline** is formed. The shell sets up this interconnection; the commands have no knowledge of it.

The pipe is the third source and destination of standard input and standard output, respectively. You can now use one to count the number of files in the current directory:

```
$ ls | wc -l
    15
```

Note that no separate command was designed to tell you that, though the designers could easily have provided another option to **ls** to perform this operation. And because **wc** uses standard output, you can redirect this output to a file:

```
ls | wc -l > fkount
```

There's no restriction on the number of commands you can use in a pipeline. But you must know the behavioral properties of these commands to place them there. Consider this command sequence which prints the man page of **grep** on the printer:

```
man grep | col -b | lp                         Don't print these pages!
```

The online man pages of a command often show the keywords in boldface. These pages contain a number of control characters which are removed here by the **col -b** command. Like **col**, **lp** also reads its standard input from **col**'s output and prints the file. For a pipeline like this to be feasible, the leftmost command (here, **man**) must be able to write to standard output while the rightmost command (here, **lp**) must be able to read from standard input. Intermediate commands (here, **col**) must be able to do both, i.e., behave like a filter.

7.8.1   When a Command Needs to Be Ignorant of Its Source

We've made several references to a command being ignorant of its source and destination. When and why is this ignorance essential for us? To appreciate this point, let's use the **wc** command to display the *total* size of all C programs:

```
$ wc -c *.c
   2078 backtalk.c
    231 beyond_array.c
    .......                                                 Output trimmed here
   1944 dog.c
    884 hexdump.c
    214 swap.c
 940101 total
```

The display shows the total usage at 940,101 bytes, but it also shows the usage for each file. We are not interested in individual statistics this time; what we need is a single figure representing the total size. To do that, you must make **wc** ignorant of its input source. You can accomplish this by feeding the concatenated output stream of all these files to **wc -c** as its input:

```
$ cat *.c | wc -c
940101
```

When do we need a single figure? We can use this command sequence as a control command in a shell script to determine whether the files will fit on a diskette:

```
if [ `cat *.c | wc -c` -lt 1474560 ] ; then
   echo 'These files will fit in a single 3.5" diskette'
fi
```

Note how the single quotes protect the double quote in the **echo** statement. We'll learn to use the **if** construct in Chapter 13, which features shell programming. The two backquotes (``` `` ```) denote command substitution, which is discussed shortly.

Note

In a pipeline, the command on the left of the | must use standard output, and the one on the right must use standard input.

7.9   tee: **Creating a Tee**

tee is an external command and not a feature of the shell. It duplicates its input, saves one copy in a file, and sends the other to the standard output. Since it is also a filter, **tee** can be placed anywhere in a pipeline. The following command sequence uses **tee** to display the output of **who** and save the output in a file as well:

```
$ who | tee user.txt
romeo      pts/2      Sep   7     08:41    (pc123.heavens.com)
juliet     pts/3      Sep   7     17:58    (pc122.heavens.com)
sumit      pts/5      Sep   7     18:01    (mercury.heavens.com)
```

tee doesn't perform any filtering action on its input; it gives out exactly what it takes. You can crosscheck the display with the contents of the file user.txt:

```
$ cat user.txt
romeo      pts/2    Sep   7   08:41    (pc123.heavens.com)
juliet     pts/3    Sep   7   17:58    (pc122.heavens.com)
sumit      pts/5    Sep   7   18:01    (mercury.heavens.com)
```

You can pipe **tee**'s output to another command, say **wc**:

```
$ who | tee user.txt | wc -l
      3
```

How do you use **tee** to display both the list of users and its count on the terminal? Since the terminal is also a file, you can use the device name /dev/tty as an argument to **tee**:

```
$ who | tee /dev/tty | wc -l                              /dev/tty used as command argument
romeo      pts/2    Sep   7   08:41    (pc123.heavens.com)
juliet     pts/3    Sep   7   17:58    (pc122.heavens.com)
sumit      pts/5    Sep   7   18:01    (mercury.heavens.com)
      3
```

The advantage of treating the terminal as a file is apparent from the above example. You couldn't have done so if **tee** (or, for that matter, any UNIX command) had placed restrictions on the type of file it could handle. Here the terminal is treated in the same way as any disk file.

7.10 Command Substitution

The shell enables the connection of two commands in yet another way. While a pipe enables a command to obtain its standard input from the standard output of another command, the shell enables one or more command *arguments* to be obtained from the standard output of another command. This feature is called **command substitution**.

To consider a simple example, suppose you need to display today's date with a statement like this:

```
The date today is Sat Sep  7 19:01:16 GMT 2002
```

The last part of the statement (beginning from Sat) represents the output of the **date** command. How does one incorporate **date**'s output into the **echo** statement? With command substitution it's a simple matter. Use the expression `date` as an argument to **echo**:

```
$ echo The date today is `date`
The date today is Sat Sep  7 19:01:56 GMT 2002
```

When scanning the command line, the ` (backquote or backtick) is another metacharacter that the shell looks for. There's a special key on your keyboard (generally at the top-left) that generates this character, and it should not be confused with the single quote ('). The shell executes the enclosed command and replaces the enclosed command line with the output of the command. For command substitution to work, the command so "backquoted" must use standard output. **date** does; that's why command substitution worked.

Commands that use filenames as arguments can use command substitution to obtain their arguments from a list:

```
ls `cat filelist`
```

Here, `filelist` contains a list of filenames. You can also use this feature to generate useful messages. For example, you can use two commands in a pipeline and then use the output as the argument to a third:

```
$ echo "There are `ls | wc -l` files in the current directory"
There are 58 files in the current directory
```

The command worked properly even though the arguments were double-quoted. It's a different story altogether when single quotes are used:

```
$ echo 'There are `ls | wc -l` files in the current directory'
There are `ls | wc -l` files in the current directory
```

This was to be expected because we had already tried out a similar exercise earlier *(7.4.2)*. The ` is one of the few characters interpreted by the shell when placed within double quotes. If you want to echo a literal `, you have to use single quotes.

Command substitution has interesting application possibilities in shell scripts. It speeds up work by letting you combine a number of instructions in one. You'll see more of this feature in subsequent chapters.

Note

Command substitution is enabled when backquotes are used within double quotes. If you use single quotes, it's not.

KORN Shell

BASH Shell

POSIX recommends the use of the form $(*command*) rather than the archaic `*command*` for command substitution. The Korn and Bash shells offer both forms. The POSIX form requires you to place the command inside parentheses and have a $ before them:

```
$ echo The date today is $(date)
The date today is Sat Sep  7 19:15:33 GMT 2002
```

Whether or not you should use the POSIX notation is something you have to decide for yourself. Make sure that you don't have to run your shell scripts with the Bourne shell before you decide to adopt this form.

7.11 Shell Variables

The shell supports variables that are useful both in the command line and shell scripts. You have already encountered some of them like HOME and SHELL. Variable usage in the Bourne family differs from that in the C shell. In this section and elsewhere, we discuss

Bourne-type variables. The features of C shell variables are noted in the aside at the end of this section.

A variable assignment is of the form *variable=value* (no spaces around =), but its evaluation requires the $ as prefix to the variable name:

```
$ count=5                                       No $ required for assignment
$ echo $count                                   but needed for evaluation
5
```

A variable can also be assigned the value of another variable:

```
$ total=$count                                  Assigning a value to another variable
$ echo $total
5
```

Caution

Programmers should note that there must not be any whitespace on either side of the = symbol. The command line x =5 is interpreted by the shell as the x command running with the =5 argument!

Variable names begin with a letter but can contain numerals and the _ as the other characters. Names are case-sensitive; x and X are two different variables. Unlike in programming languages, shell variables are not typed; you don't need to use a char, int, or long prefix when you define them. In fact, you don't even have to declare them before you can use them. All shell variables are of the string type, which means that even a number like 123 is stored as a string rather than in binary. (This may not remain true in the future.)

All shell variables are initialized to null strings by default. While explicit assignment of null strings with x="" or x='' is possible, you can also use this as a shorthand:

```
x=                                              A null string
```

A variable can be removed with **unset** and protected from reassignment by **readonly**. Both are shell internal commands:

```
unset x                                         x  is now undefined
readonly x                                      x  can't be reassigned
```

Tip

By convention, variable names used by the UNIX system and software packages are in uppercase. You are advised to use lowercase variable names in your shell scripts simply to distinguish them from system variables.

C Shell

The C shell uses the **set** statement to set variables. There either has to be whitespace on both sides of the = or none at all:

```
set count = 1                                   Both statements are valid
set count=1                                     but set count= 1 won't work
```

The evaluation is done in the normal manner (**echo $count**). The C shell uses another statement, **setenv**, to set an *environment variable*. These variables are discussed in Chapter 9.

7.11.1 Effects of Quoting and Escaping

To assign a multiword string to a variable, you can escape each space character, but quoting (single or double) is the preferred solution:

```
message=You\ didn't\ enter\ the\ filename
message="You didn't enter the filename"
```

Now that you have another special character ($) that is gobbled up by the shell, you may still need to interpret it literally without it being evaluated. This time we have escaping and single-quoting as our options:

```
$ echo The average pay is \$1000
The average pay is $1000
$ echo 'The average pay is $1000'
The average pay is $1000
```

Like the backquote, the $ is also evaluated by the shell when it is double-quoted. Here are two examples:

```
$ echo "The PATH is $PATH and the current directory is `pwd`"
The PATH is /bin:/usr/bin:. and the current directory is /home/romeo/workc
$ echo "The average pay is $1000"
The average pay is 000
```

The first example shows both command substitution and variable evaluation at work; but have a look at the second example. Here, the shell evaluated a "variable" $1. It is not defined, so a null string was output. $1 belongs to a set of parameters that are called *positional parameters (13.3),* signifying the arguments that you pass to a script.

Note

Whether you use double or single quotes depends on whether you want command substitution and variable evaluation to be enabled or not. Double quotes permit their interpretation, but single quotes don't.

7.11.2 Where to Use Shell Variables

Setting Pathnames If a pathname is used several times in a script, you should assign it to a variable. You can then use it as an argument to any command. Let's use it with **cd** in this manner:

```
$ progs='/home/romeo/c_progs'
$ cd $progs ; pwd
/home/romeo/c_progs
```

A shell script would generally contain this definition at the beginning, and then it could be used everywhere—both in the script and in other scripts run from that script. It means less typing, but there's another advantage. In a later reorganization, if the location of c_progs changes to, say, /export/home/romeo/c_progs, then you simply need to change the variable definition, and everything will work in the same way as before.

Using Command Substitution You can also use the feature of command substitution to set variables:

```
$ mydir=`pwd` ; echo $mydir
/home/romeo/c_progs
```

You can store the size of a file in a variable too:

```
size=`wc -c < foo.txt`
```

We used the < symbol to leave out the filename in the value assigned to size. If we had used foo.txt as an argument instead, then size would have contained a two-word string.

The UNIX system also uses a number of variables to control its behavior. There are variables that tell you the type of terminal you are using, the prompt string that you use, or the directory where incoming mail is kept. These variables are often called **environment variables** because they are available in all processes owned by a user. (The variable mydir or size is not.) A detailed discussion on the significance of the major environment variables will be taken up in Chapter 9.

7.12 Shell Scripts

The shell offers the facility of storing a group of commands in a file and then executing the file. All such files are called **shell scripts**. You'll also find people referring to them as shell programs and shell procedures. The instructions stored in these files are executed in the interpretive mode—much like the batch (.BAT) files of Windows.

The following shell script has a sequence of three commands stored in a file script.sh. You can create the file with **vi** or **emacs**, but since this takes only three lines, you can use **cat** instead:

```
$ cat > script.sh
directory=`pwd`                                    Beginning of standard input
echo The date today is `date`
echo The current directory is $directory
[Ctrl-d]                                           End of standard input
$ _
```

The extension .sh is used only for the purpose of identification; it can have any extension or even none. Try executing the file containing these commands by simply invoking the filename:

```
$ script.sh
script.sh: execute permission denied
```

Executable permission is usually necessary for any shell procedure to run, and by default, a file doesn't have this permission on creation. Use **chmod** to first accord executable status to the file before executing it:

```
$ chmod u+x script.sh
$ script.sh
```

```
The date today is Thu Feb 17 11:30:53 EST 2000
The current directory is /home/romeo/project5
```

The script executes the three statements in sequence. Even though we used the shell as an interpreter, it is also a programming language. You can have all the standard constructs like **if**, **while**, and **for** in a shell script. The behavior of the UNIX system is controlled by many preinstalled shell scripts that are executed during system startup and those written by the system administrator. We explore shell programming in Chapter 13.

7.13   The Shell's Treatment of the Command Line

Now that you have seen the major interpretive features of the shell, it's time we made a summary of these activities. After the command line is terminated by hitting the *[Enter]* key, the shell goes ahead with processing the command line in one or more passes. The sequence varies with the shell you use, but broadly assumes the following order:

- *Parsing*   The shell first breaks up the command line into words using spaces and tabs as delimiters, unless quoted. All consecutive occurrences of a space or tab are replaced here with a single space.
- *Variable evaluation*   All words preceded by a $ are evaluated as variables, unless quoted or escaped.
- *Command substitution*   Any command surrounded by backquotes is executed by the shell, which then replaces the standard output of the command into the command line.
- *Redirection*   The shell then looks for the characters >, <, and >> to open the files they point to.
- *Wild-card interpretation*   The shell finally scans the command line for wild cards (the characters *, ?, [and]). Any word containing a wild card is replaced by a sorted list of filenames that match the pattern. The list of these filenames then forms the arguments to the command.
- PATH *evaluation*   The shell finally looks for the PATH variable to determine the sequence of directories it has to search in order to hunt for the command.

The preceding sequence can be considered as a simplistic treatment of the shell's behavioral pattern. There are many more characters that the shell looks for that have been ignored here. And the shell itself can be viewed from different perspectives. Chapter 8 examines the process of the shell. Later chapters describe the shell's environment (Chapter 9) and its programming features (Chapter 13).

➤ *GOING   FURTHER*

7.14   More Wild Cards

Matching Totally Dissimilar Patterns   This feature, not available in the Bourne shell, enables us to match totally dissimilar patterns. How does one copy all the C and Java source programs from another directory? Delimit the patterns with a comma, and then put curly braces around them (no spaces please!):

```
cp $HOME/prog_sources/*.{c,java} .
```
Won't work in Bourne shell

This works in the Korn, Bash, and C shells. The Bourne shell would require two separate invocations of **cp** to do this job. Using the curly brace form, you can also access multiple directories:

```
cp /home/romeo/{project,html,scripts}/* .
```
Won't work in Bourne shell

This copies all files from three directories (project, html, and scripts) to the current directory. Isn't this convenient?

The Invert Selection Feature If you have used Windows Explorer, you would no doubt have used the Invert Selection feature. This option reverses the selection you make with your mouse and highlights the rest. Bash and Korn also provide a similar feature of matching all filenames except those in the expression. For instance, this expression

```
!(*.exe)
```
All files without .exe extension

matches all except the .exe files. If you want to include multiple expressions in the exception list, then use the | as the delimiter:

```
cp !(*.jpg|*.jpeg|*.gif) ../text
```

This copies all except the graphic files in GIF or JPEG format to the text directory. Note that the parentheses and | can be used to group filenames only if the ! precedes the group.

BASH Shell

> The exclusion feature won't work in Bash unless you make the setting **shopt -s extglob**. Even if you don't understand what this means, simply place this statement in .bash_profile or .profile, whichever is your startup file *(9.9.1)*.

7.15   xargs: **Building a Dynamic Command Line**

Sometimes, the filenames used by commands can be determined only at runtime. UNIX provides a real dark horse—the **xargs** command—that can run any command, *but obtains the file list from standard input.* This feature is often used to handle the problem created by **find**'s -exec operator. If **find** produces a list of 200 files for removal with -exec rm {} \;, the **rm** command has to be executed 200 times.

   xargs comes to our rescue here as it lets **rm** (or, for that matter, any UNIX command) be used just once with 200 filenames as arguments. The following command lines do the same thing except that the second one does it much faster:

```
find /usr/preserve -mtime +30 -exec rm -f {} \;
find /usr/preserve -mtime +30 -print | xargs rm -f
```

xargs here obtains the file list from **find** and supplies a *single* set of arguments to **rm**. So even if **find** selects 30 files, **rm** is executed only once. You could say that command substitution can also do the same job, but **xargs** has other advantages.

Commands usually have limits on the number of arguments they can handle. **xargs** uses the -n option to provide the specified number of arguments for a single invocation of the command:

```
find / -name core -size +1024 -print | xargs -n20 rm -f
```

If **find** locates 100 files, **rm** will be invoked five times—each time with 20 filenames as arguments. A useful tool indeed!

SUMMARY

The shell is a program that runs when a user logs in and terminates when she logs out. It scans the command line for *metacharacters* and rebuilds it before turning it over to the kernel for execution. The shell may or may not wait for the command to terminate.

The shell matches filenames with *wild cards*. It can match any number of characters (*) or a single one (?). It can also match a *character class* ([ ]) and negate a match ([!]). The * doesn't match a filename beginning with a dot.

A wild card is *escaped* with a \ to be treated literally, and if there are a number of them, then they should be *quoted*. Single quotes protect all special characters, while double quotes enable command substitution and variable evaluation.

Files are accessed with small integers called *file descriptors*. The shell makes available three files representing *standard input, standard output,* and *standard error* to every command that it runs. It manipulates the default source and destination of these streams by assigning them to disk files.

The file /dev/null never grows in size, and every user can access her own terminal as /dev/tty.

Pipes connect the standard output of one command to the standard input of another. Commands using standard output and standard input are called *filters*. A combination of filters placed in pipelines can be used to perform complex tasks which the commands can't perform individually.

The external **tee** command duplicates its input. It saves one to a file and writes the other to the standard output.

Command substitution enables a command's standard output to become the arguments of another command.

The shell supports *variables* which are evaluated by prefixing a $ to the variable name. The variables that control the workings of the UNIX system are known as *environment variables*.

The shell is also a scripting language, and a group of commands can be placed in a *shell script* to be run in a batch.

SELF-TEST

7.1   Why does the shell need to expand wild cards? How does it treat the * when used as an argument to a command (like **echo** *)?

7.2   What is the significance of the command **ls** *.*? Does it match filenames that begin with a dot?

7.3   How do you remove only the hidden files of your directory? Does **rm** * remove these files as well?

7.4   Match the filenames chapa, chapb, chapc, chapx, chapy, and chapz with a wild-card expression.

7.5   Is the wild-card expression [3-h]* valid?

7.6   Devise a command that copies all files named chap01, chap02, chap03, and so forth through chap26 to the parent directory. Can a single wild-card pattern match them all?

7.7   Frame wild-card patterns (i) where the last character is not numeric, (ii) that have at least four characters.

7.8   When will **cd** * work?

7.9   Which UNIX command uses wild cards as part of its syntax?

7.10   How do you split a long command sequence into multiple lines?

7.11   Name the three sources and destinations of standard input and standard output.

7.12   Is the output of the command **cat foo1 foo2 >/dev/tty** directed to the standard output?

7.13   Is this a legitimate command, and what does it appear to do? >foo <bar bc

7.14   How do you save your entire home directory structure including the hidden files in a separate file?

7.15   What is the file /dev/null used for?

7.16   The commands **cat** and **wc**, when used without arguments, don't seem to do anything. What does that indicate, and how do you return the shell prompt?

7.17   How do you create a filename containing just one space character? How can you "see" the space in the **ls** output?

7.18   How do you find out the number of (i) users logged in, (ii) directories in your home directory tree?

7.19   Enter the commands **echo "$SHELL"** and **echo '$SHELL'**. What difference do you notice?

7.20   Command substitution requires the command to use (i) standard input, (ii) standard output, (iii) both, (iv) none of these.

7.21   Attempt the variable assignment x = 10 (space on both sides of the =). Does it work if you are not using the C shell?

7.22   To append .c to a variable x, you have to use the expression (i) $x.c, (ii) $x".c", (iii) ${x}.c, (iv) any of these, (v) only the first two.

EXERCISES

7.1   What happens when you use (i) **cat > foo** if foo contains data, (ii) **who >> foo** if foo doesn't exist, (iii) **cat foo > foo**, (iv) **echo 1> foo**?

7.2   What does the shell do with the metacharacters it finds in the command line? When is the command finally executed?

7.3   Devise wild-card patterns to match the following filenames: (i) foo1, foo2 and Foo5, (ii) quit.c, quit.o and quit.h, (iii) watch.htm, watch.HTML and Watch.html, (iv) all filenames that begin with a dot and end with .swp.

7.4   Explain what the commands **ls .*** and **ls *.** display. Does it make any difference if the -d option is added?

7.5 How do you remove from the current directory all ordinary files that (i) are hidden, (ii) begin and end with #, (iii) have numerals as the first three characters, (iv) have single-character extensions? Will the commands work in all shells?

7.6 Devise wild-card patterns to match all filenames comprising at least three characters (i) where the first character is numeric and the last character is not alphabetic, (ii) not beginning with a dot, (iii) containing 2004 as an embedded string except at the beginning or end.

7.7 Explain what these wild-card patterns match: (i) [A-z]????*, (ii) *[0-9]*, (iii) *[!0-9], (iv) *.[!s][!h].

7.8 A directory bar contains a number of files including one named -foo. How do you remove the file?

7.9 You have a file named * and a directory named My Documents in the current directory. How do you remove them with a single command using (i) escaping, (ii) quoting?

7.10 Explain the significance of single- and double-quoting including when one is preferred to the other. What are the two consequences of using double quotes?

7.11 When will **wc < chap0[1-5]** work? How can you remove chap0[1-5] if you have a file of that name?

7.12 Explain why the error message is seen at the terminal in spite of having used the 2> symbol:

```
$ cat < foo 2>bar
ksh: cannot open foo: No such file or directory
```

7.13 How do the commands **wc foo** and **wc < foo** differ? Who opens the file in each case?

7.14 You want to concatenate two files, foo1 and foo2, but also insert some text after foo1 and before foo2 from the terminal. How will you do this?

7.15 Execute the command **ls > newlist**. What interesting observation can you make from the contents of newlist?

7.16 How will you add the tags <html> and </html> to the beginning and end respectively of foo.html?

7.17 What are *file descriptors*? Why is 2> used as the redirection symbol for standard error?

7.18 Create a file foo with the statement **echo "File not found"** in it. Explain two ways of providing redirection to this statement so that the message comes to the terminal even if you run **foo > /dev/null**.

7.19 How do the programs prog1, prog2, and prog3 need to handle their standard files so they can work like this? prog1 | prog2 | prog3.

7.20 Use command substitution to print the (i) calendar of the current month, (ii) listing of a group of filenames stored in a file.

7.21 Explain the behavior of this command:
echo '`find $HOME -type d -print | wc -l`' > list. How do you modify it to work correctly?

7.22 When will the command **cd `find . -type l -name scripts -print`** work? If it does, what do **pwd** and **/bin/pwd** display?

7.23 What is a *filter*? For the statement `foo` to work, does **foo** have to be a filter?

7.24   Look up the **tar** and **gzip** documentation to find out how a group of files can be archived and compressed without creating an intermediate file.

7.25   How will you store in a variable count (i) the total size of all C source files (.c), (ii) the total number of lines in a file?

7.26   Interpret these statements and the message displayed (if any): (i) $x=5, (ii) directory='pwd'=`pwd`.

7.27   A file foo contains a list of filenames. Devise a single statement, with suitable explanation, that stores in a variable count the total character count of the *contents* of these files. (HINT: Both command substitution and **cat** have to be used twice.)

The Process

Everything, they say, in UNIX is a file. In this chapter, we look at some of these files as originators of processes. A process is a UNIX abstraction that enables us to look at files and programs in another way. A file is treated as a simple file when it lies in a dormant state on disk. It can also be understood as a process when it is executed. Like living organisms, processes are born; they give birth to other processes and also die. Processes make things "happen" in UNIX.

Since UNIX is multitasking, hundreds or even thousands of processes can run on a large system. Processes belong to the domain of the kernel, which is responsible for their management. In this chapter, we'll examine the process attributes and understand the process creation mechanism. We'll learn to control these processes by moving them between foreground and background and killing them when they get out of control. We'll also examine the process scheduling facilities offered by UNIX.

Objectives

- Learn the kernel's role in process management.
- Understand the similarities between files and processes.
- View process attributes with **ps**.
- Learn how a process is created using *fork, exec,* and *wait*.
- Understand the significance of the ( ) and { } operators in running a command group.
- Know how the **export** statement affects the inheritance mechanism.
- Run a job in the background with & and prevent its termination with **nohup**.
- Get introduced to *signals* and to using **kill** with specific signals.
- Use the *job control* commands to switch control from one job to another.
- Schedule jobs for one-time execution with **at** and **batch**.
- Use the **cron** scheduler and examine the *crontab* file to schedule jobs to run periodically.

8.1 Process Basics

A process is simply an instance of a running program. It is said to be *born* when the program starts execution and remains alive as long as the program is active. After execution is complete, the process is said to *die*. A process also has a name, usually the name of the program being executed. For example, when you execute the **grep** command, a process named **grep** is created. Most UNIX commands that we execute actually run as processes; very few don't.

Even though a process originates from a program, a process can't be considered synonymous with a program. There are a number of ways that the two can differ. First, when two users run the same program, there's one program on disk but two processes in memory. Second, when you execute a shell script (also a program) containing a pipeline of three commands, you have three processes. Finally, a program can itself split into two or more processes while it is running; that's how processes are created anyway, as you'll learn later.

The shell serves the user, but the kernel handles processes. It manages memory and schedules processes so that each process has a fair share of the CPU and other resources. It provides a mechanism by which a process is able to execute for a finite period of time and then relinquish control to another process. The kernel has to save the state of the current process (like the instruction it was currently executing) so that when its turn comes up again for execution, the kernel knows where to resume. All this happens more than once a second, making the user oblivious to the switching process.

Files and processes have a lot in common. A process is always created by another process, so except for the first process, every process has a *parent*. Processes also are arranged in a hierarchical structure with the first process occupying the top. It's like the root directory of the file system. Just as a directory can have multiple filenames in it, the multitasking nature of UNIX permits a process to have multiple children.

Files have attributes and so do processes. Most process attributes are stored in the **process table**, a separate structure maintained in memory by the kernel. You could say that the process table is the inode for processes. A process retains an entry in this table till it dies "properly." Because the table is of finite size, there is a limit to the maximum number of processes that can run on a system. We'll have to understand what "proper" death actually means.

Most process attributes are inherited by the child from its parent, and we discuss these attributes in Section 8.6. However, there are some attributes that are not inherited and are allocated by the kernel when a process is born:

- The **Process-id (PID)** Each process is identified by a unique integer called the Process-id (PID). We need the PID to control a process, for instance, to kill it. The first process has the PID 0.
- The **Parent PID (PPID)** The PID of the parent is also available in the process table. When several processes have the same PPID, it often makes sense to kill the parent rather than all its children separately.

Things do go wrong at times. A process may go berserk and multiply rapidly, bringing the system to a complete standstill. However, UNIX provides us with the tools to understand the process hierarchy and control processes.

8.2 The Shell and init

When you log in, the process representing the shell starts running at your terminal. This process may be **sh**, **ksh**, **csh**, or **bash**. The shell maintains a set of environment variables, and you have already encountered some of them like PATH and HOME. The shell's own pathname is stored in SHELL, but its PID is stored in a special "variable", $$. To know the PID of your current shell, type

```
$ echo $$                                          The PID of the current shell
1078
```

The PID of your login shell obviously can't change as long as you are logged in. When you log out and log in again, your login shell will be assigned a different PID. Knowledge of the PID is often necessary to control the activities at your terminal, especially when things go wrong.

The PPID of every login shell is always 1. This is the **init** process: the second process of the system. **init** is a very important process and, apart from being the parent of users' shells, it is also responsible for giving birth to every service that's running in the system—like printing, mail, Web, and so on. We'll examine **init** in Section 8.4 and also in Chapter 19.

Note

Commands like **cat** and **ls** run as separate processes. The shell executes a shell script by creating an extra shell process that runs each of the commands in the script. However, built-in commands of the shell like **echo**, **pwd**, and **cd** don't create a process at all. In an aside entitled "How **cd** Works" near Section 8.7, you'll learn why **cd** can't work in a separate process.

8.3   ps: **Displaying Process Attributes**

Let's now use the **ps** (process status) command to display some process attributes. **ps** fetches these attributes from the process table. Compare this to **ls** which looks up the inode to retrieve a file's attributes. By default, **ps** displays the processes owned by the user invoking the command:

```
$ ps
    PID TTY       TIME CMD
   1078 pts/4    0:00 bash                          The login shell of this user
```

Your login shell is **bash** (CMD) and has the PID 1078, the same number echoed by the special variable, $$. It is running at the terminal /dev/pts/4 (TTY). The cumulative processor time (TIME) that has been consumed since the process started is negligible. That is to be expected because the shell is mostly sleeping—waiting for a command to be entered and waiting for it to finish. This process has a *controlling terminal,* but you'll come across a group of processes that don't have one. You'll then know what a controlling terminal is.

ps presents a snapshot of the process table. This picture gets outdated by the time it is displayed. On some systems, you might see **ps** itself in the output. **ps** is a highly variant command; its actual output varies across different UNIX flavors. BSD and System V are at war here: there are hardly any options common to both systems (Table 8.1). Solaris uses the System V version while Linux accepts both options. The POSIX specification closely resembles the System V options.

TABLE 8.1   *Options to* **ps**

POSIX Option	BSD Option	Significance
-f	f	Full listing showing the PPID of each process
-e or -A	aux	All processes including user and system processes
-u *usr*	U *usr*	Processes of user *usr* only
-a	-	Processes of all users excluding processes not associated with terminal
-l	l	Long listing showing memory-related information
-t *term*	t *term*	Processes running on terminal *term* (say, /dev/console)
-j	j	Displays PGID also

Displaying the PPID (-f) Since knowing the parentage is often important, the -f option displays a fuller listing that includes the PPID:

```
$ ps -f
     UID      PID  PPID  C    STIME    TTY    TIME   CMD
   sumit     1081  1078  0  19:03:39   pts/4  0:00   vi create_user.sh
   sumit     1082  1081  0  19:03:41   pts/4  0:00   /usr/bin/bash -i
   sumit     1078     1  0  19:01:53   pts/4  0:00   -bash
```

Apart from the **vi** editor, there are two shells running here, and the -f option easily identifies a login shell by the hyphen preceding the command name. Note that **init** is the parent of the login shell (PID 1078, PPID 1). Here, we have an unusual hierarchy. The **vi** process is the child of the login shell, and the second shell is the child of **vi**. How did that happen? Remember that we can escape to the shell using **:sh** *(5.4.5)*?

We'll ignore the C header for the time being. STIME shows the time the process started. CMD this time displays the full command line, an advantage when you don't remember the exact options you have used. But others can easily know the name of the file you are working on, and sometimes you don't want that to happen.

Other Options **ps -u** followed by a user-id displays the processes owned by the user-id. The -a option displays processes run by all users, irrespective of their ownership. We'll discuss two important options (-e and -l) after we have studied the process creation mechanism.

8.4   **System Processes and** init

Even though no one may be using the system, a number of system processes keep running all the time. They are spawned during system startup by **init** (PID 1), the parent of the login shell. The **ps -e** command lists them all, and Fig. 8.1 shows a trimmed and annotated list.

System processes that have no **controlling terminal** are easily identified by the ? in the TTY column. A process that is disassociated from the terminal can neither write to the terminal nor read from it. You can't press *[Ctrl-c]* to interrupt the process either.

FIGURE 8.1   *The* **ps -e** *Output on Solaris*

```
$ ps -e
   PID TTY        TIME CMD
     0 ?          0:01 sched         Takes care of swapping
     1 ?          0:00 init          Parent of all shells
     2 ?          0:00 pageout       Part of the kernel—not exec'd
     3 ?          4:36 fsflush       Part of the kernel—not exec'd
   194 ?          0:00 syslogd       Logs all system messages
   170 ?          0:00 inetd         Server side of FTP and TELNET
   231 ?          0:00 lpsched       The printer daemon
   200 ?          0:00 cron          Schedules your jobs
   247 ?          0:00 sendmail      Handles your mail
  2931 ?          0:00 in.telne      Serves your TELNET requests
   292 ?          0:00 dtlogin
  1436 ?          0:00 in.rlogi      Serves your RLOGIN requests
  3054 pts/2      0:00 bash
  3006 ?          0:01 dtwm          Handles windows on X Window
  2908 pts/4      0:00 vi
  2993 pts/6      0:00 bash
```

Such processes are also known as **daemons**. Many of these daemons are actually sleeping (a process state) and wake up only when they receive input.

Daemons do important work for the system. The **lpsched** daemon controls all printing activity. **sendmail** handles both your incoming and outgoing mail. Your TCP/IP network won't run FTP and TELNET without the **inetd** daemon. **cron** looks at its control file once a minute to decide what **it** should do. You'll learn about some of these daemons and other system processes in subsequent chapters. We'll consider the **cron** daemon in this chapter.

Linux

Linux uses the BSD version of the **ps** command, which has notable differences with its System V counterpart. **ps** in Linux supports three types of options—the BSD options that don't use a dash, the POSIX options that use a single dash, and the GNU-style options which use -- (2 hyphens). We'll consider the Red Hat Linux implementation of the BSD options in this discussion.

Displaying Process Ancestry (ps f) Locating ancestry by matching PIDs and PPIDs can be a grueling affair; a visual representation of the process tree is what Linux **ps** offers with the f option. Here's a section of the output obtained by using the U option also:

```
$ ps f U sumit
   PID TTY    STAT TIME    COMMAND
   936 pts/0  S    0:00    \_ /bin/bash
 14833 pts/0  S    0:00    |  \_ vim yrunix07
```

```
  938 pts/2  S     0:00   \_ /bin/bash
14835 pts/2  R     0:00   |  \_ ps f -u sumit
  945 pts/4  S     0:00   \_ /bin/bash
14831 pts/4  S     0:00      \_ rlogin arka
 1047 ?      S    22:08   /usr/lib/mozilla-1.0.1/mozilla-bin
14579 ?      S     0:22   |  |  \_ /usr/lib/acroread/Reader/intellinux/bin/a
```

System Processes (ps ax) A typical Linux system shows a host of system processes, but Linux uses the ax option to display them. Here's a vastly censored display:

```
$ ps ax
PID TTY STAT TIME COMMAND
  1 ?   S    0:14 init                                          Parent of login shell
  2 ?   SW   0:00 (kflushd)
  3 ?   SW   0:00 (kpiod)
  4 ?   SW   0:02 (kswapd)
  5 ?   SW   0:00 (mdrecoveryd)
115 ?   S    0:00 inetd                                             Internet daemon
125 ?   S    0:00 sshd                                            Secure shell server
133 ?   SW   0:00 lpd                                               Printer daemon
146 ?   SW   0:00 squid -D                                            Proxy server
148 ?   S    0:00 sendmail: accepting connections on port 25      Mail server
160 6   SW   0:00 /sbin/mingetty tty6                      Process at the terminal
161 ?   S    0:00 crond                                       System's chronograph
162 ?   S    0:03 httpd                                               Web server
```

By default, Linux comes preconfigured with a number of network services, and the ax option should show them all. If users are unable to connect using the secure shell, the administrator has to check whether **sshd** is running. If they can't print their files, the status of **lpd** needs to be checked.

Full Listing (ps u) The **ps u** command approximates to **ps -l** (discussed in Section 8.8.1) of POSIX. The output, however, displays a number of new columns:

```
$ ps u
USER   PID  %CPU %MEM  SIZE   RSS TTY STAT START TIME COMMAND
sumit  192  0.0   3.5  1892  1088   1 S   20:55 0:00 -bash
sumit  216  0.0   1.9  1576   600   5 S   20:59 0:00 sh /usr/X11R6/bin/sta
sumit  237  0.0   2.9  1908   904   5 S   20:59 0:01 fvwm95
sumit  321  0.0   4.1  1904  1260   1 S   21:02 0:03 vi +12 /home/sumit/pr
sumit 3708  0.1  28.4 20732  8728   4 S   09:17 0:04 /opt/netscape/netscap
```

The percentage CPU and memory usage of each command are shown under %CPU and %MEM respectively. Here, the Web browser **netscape** has taken up more than a quarter of the memory space. If you find degradation in your system's performance, this option will help you locate the possible culprits. The amount of space the program occupies in memory (in kilobytes) is shown under SIZE and RSS.

The top Command Apart from **ps**, the **top** command also shows CPU usage in a more humanly readable form. This command also shows **ps**-like output, but its first five lines make most interesting reading:

```
11:14am  up  3:31,  6 users,  load average: 0.00, 0.00, 0.00
57 processes: 55 sleeping, 1 running, 1 zombie, 0 stopped
CPU states:  0.3% user,  0.9% system,  0.0% nice, 98.8% idle
Mem:   30628K av,  29092K used,   1536K free,  17144K shrd,   1376K buff
Swap: 40088K av,   9868K used,  30220K free                 10636K cached
```

There's a whole lot of information here: the free and used memory of the system and the state of the CPU. Most of the memory is used up (1536K out of 30,628K available), but the CPU is idling 98.8 percent of the time. This is a very useful command for the system administrator.

8.5 The Process Creation Mechanism

How is a process created? Knowledge of the process creation cycle will enable you to write and debug shell scripts and programs that create processes (Chapter 18). A process can only be created by another process, and the creation mechanism involves three phases. We call them *fork, exec,* and *wait,* mostly named after system calls of the same name. The three phases are discussed below:

- **Fork**   Forking creates a process by creating a copy of the existing process. The new process has a different PID, and the process that created it becomes its parent. Otherwise, parent and child have the same process image. If the child doesn't do an exec, both parent and child would continue to execute the same code from the point forking was invoked.
- **Exec**   Forking creates a process, but it is not enough to run a new program. To do that, the forked child needs to overwrite its own image with the code and data of the new program. This mechanism is called *exec,* and the child process is said to *exec* a new program. No new process is created here; the PID and PPID of the exec'd process remain unchanged.
- **Wait**   While the child is executing a new program, the parent *normally* waits for the child to die. It then picks up the *exit status* of the child (explained shortly) before it does something else.

To use an example, when you run **cat** from the shell, the shell first forks another shell process. The newly forked shell then overlays itself with the executable image of **cat**, which then starts to run. The parent (the original shell) waits for **cat** to terminate and then picks up the exit status of the child. This is a number returned by the child to the kernel, and has great significance in both shell programming and systems programming.

Note

The names *fork, exec,* and *wait* are derived from the system calls that perform these functions. There's no exec system call as such; we use the term to refer to a group of six functions which perform the exec operation. One of them is a system call; the other five are library functions.

8.6   Inherited Process Attributes

When a process is forked and exec'd, the new program has a different PID and PPID than its parent. However, it inherits most of the environment of its parent. The important attributes that are inherited are:

- The **real UID** and **real GID** of the process. These are attributes that we relate to a file, but here they represent the UID and GID of the user running the program (and not of the file that is executed). These parameters are stored in the entry for the user in /etc/passwd.
- The **effective UID** and **effective GID** of the process. These are generally the same as their "real" cousins but some processes behave differently. (See inset.)
- The current directory from where the process was run. You must remember this to understand why you can't create a process to change your current directory.
- The descriptors of all files opened by the parent process. Recall that these are small integers that are used to identify opened files *(7.5.3)*. Note that normally the kernel reserves the first three slots (0, 1, and 2) in the file descriptor table for the shell's standard streams.
- Environment variables (like HOME and PATH). Every process knows the user's home directory and the path used by the shell to look for commands.

Inheritance here implies that the child has its own *copy* of these parameters and can thus alter the operating environment it has inherited. This also means that the modified environment is not available to the parent process.

When Real UID Differs from Effective UID

Why does every process have two UIDs and two GIDs (real and effective) as shown in the list of inherited process attributes? Most programs we run have the real UID and GID the same as the effective UID and GID. Now consider the listing of these two programs:

```
$ ls -l /bin/cat /usr/bin/passwd
-rwxr-xr-x   1 root     root      14264 2002-09-10 18:43 /bin/cat
-rwsr-xr-x   1 root     shadow    68680 2002-09-11 00:43 /usr/bin/passwd
```

When romeo runs **cat**, the real and effective UID of the **cat** process are the same—romeo. As a nonprivileged user, romeo can't use **cat** to open a file that is readable only by root.

Now notice the bit marked s in the permissions field of **passwd**. This bit, called the *set-user-id* (SUID), changes the normal ownership scheme. When romeo runs **passwd**, the real UID is still romeo, *but the effective UID is root, the owner of the program*. Because it's the effective UID, not the real UID, that determines the access rights of the process, the **passwd** process run by romeo can open any file that is readable only by root. We have more to say about SUID in Chapters 18 and 19.

8.6.1   When Variables Are Inherited and When They Are Not

Environment variables like HOME and TERM are available to all processes. However, that may not be so with all user-defined variables. Let's define one at the current shell prompt and then spawn a second shell:

```
$ x=5
$ bash                                                       Bash child shell
$ echo $x

$ _                                                          x not visible here.
```

By default, a user-defined variable is not inherited by a child process. To make it visible to all child processes, we must use the shell's **export** statement. Let's return to the parent shell and then repeat the exercise, this time using **export**:

```
$ exit                                                              Exit child
$ x=5 ; export x                                      Make assignment and export it
$ bash                                                          Spawn a child
$ echo $x
5                                                            x visible in child
$ x=10 ; echo $x                                       Now change the value in child
10
$ exit                                                     Quit to the parent shell
$ echo $x                                              Is the change visible here?
5                                                                         No!
```

We can summarize our observations in this way:

- A variable defined in a process is only local to the process and is not available in a child process.
- When you export the variable, its value is available recursively to all child processes.
- However, when the child alters the value of the variable, the change is not seen in the parent. This should not surprise us since the child works with its own copy of the environment.

When writing shell scripts that call other scripts, we need to use **export** in the calling script so an exported variable is available in the called script. **export** is widely used in the system's startup files, and you'll meet it again in Chapter 9.

8.7   When You Can't Use a Separate Process

There are times when you just can't use a process to do a job. Consider this sequence which displays a message and then attempts to quit:

```
$ ( echo "You have not keyed in 3 arguments" ; exit )
You have not keyed in 3 arguments
$ _
```

The sequence meant to terminate the current shell, but it didn't happen. Commands grouped within ( ) are run in a sub-shell. An **exit** statement in a sub-shell terminates the sub-shell (which in any case will happen here) and thus doesn't affect the parent. Now, repeat the exercise using the curly braces:

```
$ { echo "You have not keyed in 3 arguments" ; sleep 2 ; exit ; }
You have not keyed in 3 arguments
... After two seconds ...
login:
```

The message is clear: Commands grouped within {} are executed in the current shell. Here, the sequence used **exit** to terminate the login shell. In a shell script, it will terminate the script. That's what we'll be doing often in Chapter 13. In Chapter 9, you'll learn the use of the dot command which executes a shell script but without using a separate process.

8.8 Process States and Zombies

At any instant of time, a process is in a particular *state*. A process after creation is in the *runnable* state before it actually runs (state *running*). While the process is running, it may invoke a disk I/O operation. The process then has nothing to do except wait for the I/O to complete. The process then moves to the *sleeping* state to be woken up when the I/O operation is over. A process can also be *suspended* by pressing a key (usually, *[Ctrl-z]*). Processes whose parents don't wait for their death move to the *zombie* state.

When a process dies, its parent picks up the child's exit status (the reason for waiting) from the process table and frees the process table entry. However, when the parent doesn't wait (but is still alive), the child turns into a **zombie**. A zombie is a harmless dead child that reserves the process table slot. You can't kill a zombie.

It's also possible for the parent itself to die before the child dies. The child then becomes an **orphan** and the kernel makes **init** the parent of all orphans. When this adopted child dies, **init** waits for its death.

How cd Works

How does the **cd** command work? Unlike **pwd** and **echo**, which exist both as external and internal commands of the shell, there's no disk file called **cd**. In fact, you can't create a program to change a directory. Why? Because the current directory is a process attribute that is inherited by the child *(8.6)*.

You can try changing a directory both using ( ) and {}, and you'll find that one form works but not the other:

```
$ pwd
/home/romeo
$ ( cd progs ; pwd )                          cd in ( ) changes directory
/home/romeo/progs                                       only in sub-shell
$ pwd
/home/romeo                                      but not in parent shell
$ { cd progs ; pwd ; }                  But cd in {} changes directory
/home/romeo/progs                                  in the current shell ...
```

```
$ pwd                                          and the directory change
/home/romeo/progs                                      is also permanent
```

If you had to create a child process and then change the directory in the child, the change would only be seen in the child and not in the parent. It would then be impossible to change directories. That's why a directory change must take place without creating a child.

8.8.1   ps -1: Detailed Process Listing

The **ps -1** command (**ps aux** in Linux) provides an informative listing of processes. Apart from the usual attributes that we are familiar with, it also displays their state, priority, and size of the process in memory:

```
$ ps -1 -u sumit
F  S  UID   PID  PPID C  PRI NI  ADDR   SZ  WCHAN   TTY    TIME CMD
8  S  102  1081  1078 0   51 20     ?  226      ?   pts/4  0:00 vi
8  S  102  1101  1099 0   41 20     ?  297      ?   pts/3  0:00 bash
8  T  102  1106  1101 0   49 20     ?  117          pts/3  0:03 find
8  T  102  1108  1106 0   48 20     ?  113          pts/3  0:00 rm
8  R  102  1082  1081 0   51 20     ?  297          pts/4  0:00 bash
8  S  102  1078  1076 0   51 20     ?  297      ?   pts/4  0:00 bash
```

Observe the second column which shows the process states as single-letter abbreviations. The list displays three process states (T, S, and R), but this Solaris system can display five possible states:

O   Running on the CPU.
S   Sleeping. Process is waiting for an event to take place.
R   Runnable. The process simply needs to be selected for running.
T   Suspended. User pressed *[Ctrl-z]*.
Z   Zombie. Parent didn't wait for the death of the child.

The **ps** output shows zombie processes as the string <defunct> in the last column. If too many zombie processes develop on a machine, a system reboot may be required to clear them.

UID indicates the owner of the process; this should be the user-id of the user running the **ps** command. Column PRI shows the process priority, a high value denoted low priority. SZ shows the size of the process in virtual memory. The unit of measure is a page, where a page is typically 8192 bytes.

8.9   Signal Handling

The UNIX system often needs to communicate the occurrence of an event to a process. This event could originate from the hardware (like a floating point exception), from the keyboard (like *[Ctrl-c]*), from a program, or from other sources. This communication is made by sending a **signal** to the process. The process can respond by doing one of these things:

- Let the default action take place. Every signal is associated with a default action, which in most cases, terminates the process. But there are signals whose default action is to suspend the process or even be ignored.
- Ignore the signal.
- Trap the signal. The process "catches" the signal by invoking a signal handling function. This is a user-defined function if the process is associated with a C program, and the **trap** statement if it is a shell script. Your own function might still specify termination but may remove some temporary files before it does so.

Each signal, identified by a number, is designed to perform a specific function. The commonly used ones are shown in Table 8.2. Because the same signal number may represent two different signals on two different machines, signals are better represented by their symbolic names having the SIG prefix.

When you press the interrupt key, the SIGINT signal (number 2) is sent to the current foreground process. This kills the process if it is not designed to catch or ignore that signal. SIGQUIT directs a process to produce a core dump (a file named core in the current directory). Chapter 18 discusses how we can develop user-defined code to catch a signal. In this chapter, we are concerned with a signal's default action only.

Irrespective of what you do, there are two signals that a process can't ignore or run user-defined code to handle: SIGKILL and SIGSTOP. The SIGKILL signal *must* terminate a process, and SIGSTOP *must* suspend one. We'll now learn to use the **kill** command to send specific signals to processes.

8.9.1 kill: Premature Termination of a Process

The **kill** command sends a signal *usually* with the intention of killing the process. **kill** is an internal command in most shells; the external **/bin/kill** is executed only

TABLE 8.2 *List of Commonly Used Signals*

Signal Number		Signal Name	Function
Solaris	*Linux*		
1	1	SIGHUP	Hangup—modem connection is broken; restarts a daemon
2	2	SIGINT	Terminal interrupt—user hits interrupt key
3	3	SIGQUIT	Quit from terminal—process produces a core dump file
9	9	SIGKILL	Surest kill—can't be trapped
15	15	SIGTERM	Default termination signal used by **kill** command
24	20	SIGTSTP	Suspends process—user hits *[Ctrl-z]*
18	17	SIGCHLD	Child terminates—kernel sends signal to parent
26	21	SIGTTIN	Suspends process—background process attempts to read from terminal
27	22	SIGTTOU	Suspends process—background process attempts to write to terminal (with **stty tostop**)

when the shell lacks the kill capability. The command uses one or more PIDs as its arguments, and by default uses the SIGTERM (15) signal. Thus,

```
kill 105
```
                                                It's like using `kill -s TERM 105`

terminates the job having PID 105. To facilitate premature termination, the & operator *(8.10.1)* displays the PID of the process that's run in the background. If you don't remember the PID, use the **ps** command to find out and then use **kill**.

     If you run more than one job—either in the background or in different windows in the X Window system—you can kill them all with a single **kill** statement. Just specify all their PIDs with **kill**:

```
kill 121 122 125 132 138 144
```

If all of these processes have the same parent, you may simply kill the parent to kill all its children. However, when you use **nohup** *(8.10.2)* with a set of commands and log out, you can't kill the parent as **init** acquires their parentage. You then have to kill the processes individually because you can't kill **init**.

Note

As with files, you own those processes spawned by commands you execute. It's natural that you can kill only those processes that you own and that you can't kill processes of other users. Moreover, certain system processes having the PIDs 0, 1, 2, 3, and 4 simply can't be killed in this manner.

Using kill with Other Signals By default, **kill** uses the SIGTERM signal to terminate the process. You may have noticed that some programs simply ignore it and continue execution normally. In that case, the process can be killed with the SIGKILL signal (9). This signal can't be generated at the press of a key, so you must use **kill** with the signal name (without the SIG):

```
kill -s KILL 121
kill -9 121
```
                                Recommended way of using `kill`
                        Same as above but not recommended

A simple **kill** command (with TERM) won't kill the login shell. You can kill your login shell by using any of these commands:

```
kill -9 $$
kill -s KILL 0
```
                                $$ stores PID of current shell
                        Kills all processes including the login shell

If your shell supports job control (as most shells do), you can use **kill** with a slightly different syntax to terminate a job. We'll be discussing job control in Section 8.11.

Tip

To view the list of all signal names and numbers that are available on your machine, use the command **kill -l** (list) or view the file /usr/include/sys/signal.h.

Note

At first, **kill** was used only to terminate a process. Today, with so many signals available, the name "kill" today has become a misnomer: all signals don't kill a process. In Chapter 18, we'll examine the **kill** system call to learn that **kill** can also suspend a job or even direct a suspended job to continue!

8.10   Running Jobs in Background

We now turn our attention to *jobs* and *job control*. All shells understand a **job** as a group of processes. The pipeline `ls | wc` is a job comprising two processes. We can manipulate a job in shell-independent and shell-dependent ways. This section dwells on the former, and Section 8.11 discusses the latter.

UNIX is a multitasking system that allows a user to run more than one job at a time. This feature works in all shells, allowing us to relegate time-consuming or low-priority jobs to the *background* and to run an important one in the *foreground*. There are two ways of running jobs in the background–with the shell's & operator and the **nohup** command.

8.10.1   &: No Logging Out

The & is the shell's operator used to run a process in the background. The parent in this case doesn't wait for the child's death. Just terminate the command line with an &; the command will run in the background:

```
$ sort -o emp.lst emp.lst &
550                                                    The job's PID
$ _                                     Shell doesn't wait; prompt returns
```

The shell immediately returns the PID of the invoked command (550) and then the prompt. This means that the shell doesn't wait for the death of **sort** (though it will eventually pick up its exit status). You can now enter your next command, and using an & with each, you can run as many jobs in the background as the system load permits.

Generally, the standard output and standard error of a background job are connected to the terminal. Unless you redirect them properly, they'll get mixed up with the output of other jobs. However, a background job can't read from the terminal. If it tries to do so in the Bourne shell, the job is terminated. In other shells, the job is suspended. We'll have more to say about handling the standard streams when we take up job control.

Because UNIX can't prevent users from running multiple jobs, you would do a disservice to your peers if you didn't exercise discipline when using the &. It's also important that you don't idle after using &; otherwise, it makes no sense to have run a job in the background in the first place.

Tip

For most shells, the system variable $! stores the PID of the last background job. So you can kill the last background process using `kill $!`.

8.10.2   nohup: Log Out Safely

When a command is run with **nohup** (**no h**ang**up**), the process continues to run even after the user has logged out. This feature is not required in the Bash and C shells because background processes in these shells continue to run even after the user has logged out, but is required for the Bourne and Korn shells. You must use the & with it as well:

```
$ nohup sort emp.lst &
586                                                   PID of this job
Sending output to nohup.out
```

Some shells display this message. In the absence of redirection, **nohup** sends the standard output of the job to nohup.out. You can now safely log out of the system without aborting the command. If you are running the command from a window, then close the window. Log in again or run **ps** from another window or terminal to notice something quite significant:

```
$ ps -f -u romeo
   UID   PID  PPID  C   STIME TTY  TIME COMMAND
  sumit  586     1 45 14:52:09  01  0:13 sort emp.lst
```

The shell died on logging out but its child (**sort**) didn't; it turned into an orphan. As discussed previously, all orphans are adopted by **init**, and this is what has happened here. When **sort** dies, **init** will perform the necessary "waiting" tasks that will eventually pick up the exit status from the process table.

Unlike the &, which needs to be affixed only to the end of the command line, **nohup** needs to be used with each command in a pipeline:

```
nohup grep 'director' emp.lst & | nohup sort &
```

Jobs are not aborted after the user has logged out even if they were run with & and without **nohup**. However, this is not the case with the Bourne and Korn shells. Moreover, the **nohup** command in the C shell doesn't send the standard output of the command to nohup.out. It has to be separately redirected to a file.

8.11 Job Control

Before we turn to job control, let's understand process groups. Every process belongs to a **process group** (a Berkeley feature that lets you control a group of processes working for a common cause). Each process in the group has the same **process group-id (PGID)**. The C shell, Korn shell, and Bash support job control, where every job has a separate PGID. This allows manipulation of process groups separately. A signal sent to a process group reaches out to all members of the group.

Job control enables you to move jobs between foreground and background, suspend, continue, and kill them. The commands used in job control are shown in Table 8.3.

TABLE 8.3 *Job Control Commands*

Command	Significance
fg	Brings job to foreground
bg	Moves job to background
suspend	Suspends a job
[Ctrl-z]	Suspends current foreground job
jobs	Lists active jobs
kill	Kills job

A job is identified by its *job-id* which is different from the PID, the process identifier. However, a job can also be identified by other means, and job control commands can be used both with job-ids and other job identifiers as arguments.

For a quick tour, let's run this **find** command and then use the job control commands for manipulating it. We'll initially run **find** in the background with standard output and standard error redirected suitably:

```
$ find / -name a.out -print > files_to_remove 2>/dev/null &
[1] 1287                                                          Shows both job-id and PID
```

Note that both job number and PID are displayed; this shell supports job control. Subsequent job control commands can now access this job as %1. You can now use the **fg** command to bring this job to the foreground:

```
$ fg %1
find / -name a.out -print > files_to_remove 2>/dev/null
```

Apart from the *%job_id* form, there are other ways of accessing a job. At this point, you can now suspend this foreground job by pressing *[Ctrl-z]:*

```
[Ctrl-z]
[1]+  Stopped        find / -name a.out -print >files_to_remove 2>/dev/null
```

Observe that the job has not been terminated yet; it's only suspended ("stopped"). *[Ctrl-z]* is **stty**'s suspend character *(2.14.1)* and should work if your default **stty** setting has not been disturbed. You can now use the **bg** command to push this suspended job to the background:

```
$ bg %1
[1]+ find / -name a.out -print >files_to_remove 2>/dev/null &
```

The job starts running once again. Before we run the **jobs** command, let's run a few more jobs in the background:

```
$ ls -lR / > system_list 2>/dev/list &
[2] 1288
$ du -s /users1/* > disk_usage &
[3] 1289
```

The **jobs** command lists all jobs that are either running or suspended. The output shows that none of the three commands has completed execution:

```
$ jobs
[1]   Running        find / -name a.out -print >files_to_remove 2>/dev/null &
[2]-  Running        ls -lR / >system_list 2>/dev/list &
[3]+  Running        du -s /users1/* >disk_usage &
```

When a job completes, the shell notifies the user but makes sure that the message doesn't get mixed up with the screen output associated with another job. The shell waits for the prompt to appear (after you hit *[Enter]*) and then issues a message:

```
[2]-  Exit 1         ls -lR / >system_list 2>/dev/list
```

Job 2 has completed execution. You should get a similar message from each of the other jobs after you hit *[Enter]*. If you decide to change your mind, you can kill a job with the shell's built-in **kill** command, which has a more flexible syntax compared to **/bin/kill**. You can also use a job number with **kill**:

```
$ kill %3
[3]+ Terminated    du -s /users1/* >disk_usage
```

Note

You can use the notify setting of your shell to ensure that job completion is intimated immediately and not at the next prompt. This is discussed in Section 9.8.

Apart from using job_ids, we can also access a job by a string that represents either the command name or an embedded string in the command line. These are the three ways you identify a job to the system:

%*n*   Job number *n*
%*stg*   Job name that begins with *stg*
%?*stg*   Job name that contains an embedded *stg*

So, **fg %find** brings to the foreground a job whose name begins with find, while **kill %?users1** kills the job that has the string users1 embedded in the command line (the **du** command line in the examples used previously).

Make sure that you don't terminate your session after you have suspended a job. When you try to do so, the shell alerts you:

```
You have stopped jobs.
```

Caution

A second press of the logout sequence will ignore this message and actually log you out of the system. This could be dangerous. You may have suspended a **vi** session with a lot of work unsaved. Whenever you get such a message, you should use the **jobs** command to see how many suspended jobs you have, use **fg** to move each one to the foreground, and then terminate it gracefully.

8.11.1 Handling Standard Input and Standard Output

In all of these examples, we redirected the standard output and standard error of the background jobs because they normally come to the terminal. However, in job control shells, you can use the **stty tostop** setting to ensure that a job is suspended the moment it tries to write to the terminal:

```
stty tostop
```

Now if you run a job that produces a single line of output, say the command **du -s /home &**, the command will do all the necessary processing before the kernel suspends the job when it tries to write the summary information:

```
[1]+ Stopped                du -s /home
```

This is a great convenience with those commands that perform a lot of processing but create only summary information. You can view this output any time using **fg %1**; the shell will save the output for you.

Background jobs, however, can't accept input from the terminal. Try this by running **vi** in the background:

```
$ vi &
[2]+  Stopped                 vi
```

Whenever a background job tries to read its standard input from the terminal, the kernel sends a signal (Table 8.2) and suspends the process. You have no option but to bring the job to the foreground to allow data to be input from the keyboard.

If you have access to the superuser account that uses a job control shell, and need to constantly switch between privileged and nonprivileged modes, then you can use the **suspend** command in the superuser mode to suspend the root shell and return you to the normal shell:

```
# suspend
[1]+  Stopped                 su
$ _
```

Tip

You can return to the superuser mode, by using any of the identifiers discussed previously (like %1, %su, etc.). Note that this won't work if the superuser is using the Bourne shell (which often is the case).

8.12 at **and** batch: **Execute Later**

UNIX provides sophisticated facilities to schedule a job to run at a specified time of day. If the system load varies greatly throughout the day, it makes sense to schedule less urgent jobs at a time when the system overheads are low. The **at** and **batch** commands make such scheduling possible.

8.12.1 at: One-Time Execution

at schedules jobs for one-time execution. The command runs with the scheduled date and time as arguments. The command to run is specified at the at> prompt:

```
$ at 14:08
at> empawk2.sh
[Ctrl-d]
commands will be executed using /usr/bin/bash
job 1041188880.a at Sun Dec 29 14:08:00 2002
```

The jobs are submitted to a queue. The job-id is derived from the number of seconds since the Epoch. It's the most meaningful method of making such numbers unique across several years. At 2:08 p.m. today, the program **empawk2.sh** will be executed. Though you know this now, unfortunately, there's no way you can find out the name of the scheduled program later.

Unless redirected, the standard output and error will be mailed to the user. Alternatively, you may provide redirection at the `at>` prompt itself:

```
at 15:08
empawk2.sh > rep.lst
```

at also offers keywords like now, noon, today, and tomorrow. It also offers the words hours, days, weeks, and so forth to be used with the + symbol. The following forms show the use of some of the key words and operators:

`at 15`	*24-hour format assumed*
`at 3:08pm`	
`at noon`	*At 12:00 hours today*
`at now + 1 year`	*At the current time after one year*
`at 3:08pm + 1 day`	*At 3:08 p.m. tomorrow*
`at 15:08 December 18, 2001`	
`at 9am tomorrow`	

You can also use the `-f` option to take commands from a file. To mail job completion to the user, use the `-m` option. Jobs are listed with **at -l** and removed with **at -r**.

8.12.2   batch: Execute in Batch Queue

batch also schedules jobs for later execution, but unlike with **at**, jobs are executed as soon as the system load permits. The command doesn't take any arguments but uses an internal algorithm to determine the execution time. This prevents too many CPU-hungry jobs from running at the same time. The response of **batch** is similar to **at** otherwise:

```
$ batch < empawk2.sh
commands will be executed using /usr/bin/bash
job 1041185673.b at Sun Dec 29 13:14:33 2002
```

Any job scheduled with **batch** goes to a special **at** queue, and can also be removed with **at -r**.

8.12.3   Restricting Use of at and batch

All users may not be able to use the **at** and **batch** commands. The access to these commands is restricted and controlled by the files `at.allow` and `at.deny`. The locations are system-dependent; look up the FILES section of the man page of **at** for location of the files. If they exist at all, they could be in /etc, /etc/cron.d or /usr/lib/cron. They can only be edited by the superuser.

`at.allow` controls the primary level of security. If it is present, only the users listed in the file are permitted to use **at** and **batch**. If it is not present, the system checks `at.deny` for a list of users who are barred from using these commands. If neither file is present, only the system administrator is permitted to invoke **at** and **batch**.

8.13 cron and crontab: **Running Jobs Periodically**

The **ps -e** command always shows the **cron** daemon running. This is the UNIX system's chronograph, ticking away every minute. **cron** is not a one-time scheduler like **at** but a periodic one. Every minute it wakes up from its sleeping state to look up a *crontab* file for instructions to be performed at that instant. After executing them, it goes back to sleep, only to wake up the next minute.

The crontab file is named after the user-id and is typically located in /var/spool/cron/crontabs. This location is, however, system-dependent. romeo has a file of the same name in this directory. Every scheduled job is specified as a single line in this file. The specification can get a little complex, but let's begin with a simple one shown in Fig. 8.2.

There are six fields in the line, and the first five completely determine how often the command will be executed. The list below shows the significance of the fields with their permissible values shown in parentheses:

1. The minute (00 to 59)
2. The hour (0 to 23)
3. The day (0 to maximum number of days in month)
4. The month (1 to 12)
5. The day of the week (0 to 6, 0 being a Sunday)
6. Command to run

This **find** command runs at 18:15 hours on June 30 every year. We didn't make use of the fifth field (which doesn't have much relevance here) and preferred to place a * there. As with **at**, in the absence of redirection, the standard output of the command is mailed to the user.

To create a crontab entry, first use your **vi** editor to create a file foo with an entry of your choice. Then use the **crontab** command

```
crontab foo
```

to place the entry in the directory /var/spool/cron/crontabs. You can see the contents of your crontab file with **crontab -l** and remove it with **crontab -r**.

FIGURE 8.2   *The Components of a crontab Entry*

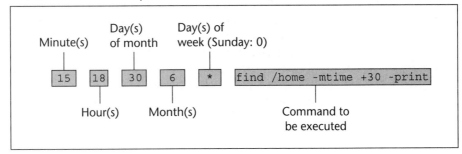

Caution

If you use `crontab -` to provide input through the standard input and then decide to abort it, you should terminate it with the interrupt key applicable to your terminal, rather than *[Ctrl-d]*. If you forget to do that, you'll remove all entries from your existing crontab file!

cron's strength lies in its unusual number matching system. You can match one or more numbers if you keep in mind these rules:

- A * used in any of the first five fields matches any valid value.
- A set of numbers is delimited by a comma. 3,6,9 is a valid field specification.
- Ranges are possible and need not be restricted to a single digit. 00-10 includes all integer values between 0 and 10.

Things don't appear so simple when crontab fields conflict with one another. Take, for instance, this entry:

```
00-10 17 * 3,6,9,12 5  find / -newer .last_time -print > backuplist
```

The first two fields indicate that the command is to run every minute from 17:00 hours to 17:10 hours. The third field (being a *) specifies that it should run every day. The fourth field (3,6,9,12), however, restricts the operation to four months of the year. The fifth field limits execution to every Friday.

So, who overrides whom? Here, "Friday" overrides "every day." The **find** command will thus be executed every minute in the first 10 minutes after 5 p.m., every Friday of the months March, June, September, and December (of every year).

So, what are the rules that determine which fields have the ultimate say? This question arises when a * occurs in the third, fourth, or fifth fields. The rules are clearly laid down by POSIX and Table 8.4 shows all possible combinations of these fields.

Caution

Unless you are sure, never use a * in the minute field. You'll receive a mail every minute, and this could completely use up your mail quota if the command produces high-volume output.

cron is mainly used by the system administrator to perform housekeeping chores, like removing outdated files or collecting data on system performance. It's also extremely useful to periodically dial up to an Internet mail server to send and retrieve mail.

Linux

The number matching system goes beyond POSIX requirements. It allows the use of step values which enable us to use compact expressions. You can use 3-12/3 instead of 3,6,9,12 that was used in our examples. Moreover, a * comes in handy here; */10 in the minutes field specifies execution every 10 minutes. The crontab file also supports a MAILTO variable which sends mail to the user whose name is assigned to the variable. The mail is suppressed if we set MAILTO="".

cron looks in a control file in /var/spool/cron in Red Hat. It additionally looks up /etc/crontab which specifies the user as an additional field (the sixth). This file generally specifies the execution of files in the directories cron.hourly, cron.daily, cron.weekly, and cron.monthly (in /etc).

TABLE 8.4 *Sample crontab Entries (First five fields only)*

Fields	Matches
*When a * occurs in any of the third, fourth, and fifth fields*	
00-10 17 * * *	Every day
00-10 17 * 3,6,9,12 *	Every day but restricted to four months
00-10 17 10,20,30 * *	Three days in a month
00-10 17 * * 1,3	Monday and Wednesday
00-10 17 * 3,6,9,12 1,3	Either every day of four months or Monday and Wednesday of every month
00-10 17 10,20,30 * 1,3	Either three days of every month or Monday and Wednesday of every month
Other Examples	
0,30 * * * *	Every 30 minutes on the half-hour.
0 0 * * *	Midnight every day.
55 17 * * 4	Every Thursday at 17:55 hours.
30 0 10,20 * *	00:30 hours on the tenth and twentieth of every month.
00,30 09-17 * * 1-5	On weekdays every half hour between 9 and 17 hours.

anacron cron assumes that the machine is run continuously, so if the machine is not up when a job is scheduled to run, **cron** makes no amends for the missed opportunity. The job will have to wait for its next scheduled run. The **anacron** command is often more suitable than **cron. anacron** periodically inspects its control file (/etc/anacrontab) to see if there's a job which has "missed the bus." If it finds one, it executes the job.

8.13.1 Controlling Access to cron

All users may not be able to use **cron**. As with **at** and **batch**, the authorization to use it is controlled by two files, cron.allow and cron.deny. If cron.allow is present, only users included in this file are allowed to use this facility. If this file is not present, cron.deny is checked to determine the users who are prohibited. In case neither of them is present, depending on the system configuration, either the system administrator only is authorized to use **cron** or all users are allowed access.

SUMMARY

A process is an instance of a running program. It is identified by the *process-id* (PID) and its *parent PID* (PPID). Process attributes are maintained in the *process table* in memory.

Because of multitasking, a process can *spawn* multiple processes. The login shell is a process (PID = $$) that keeps running as long as the user is logged in.

You can list your own processes with **ps**, view the process ancestry (-f), all users' processes (-a), and all system processes (-e). BSD uses a different set of options.

System processes, often called *daemons,* are generally not attached to a terminal and not invoked specifically by a user. **init** is the parent of most daemons and all users' shells.

A process is created by *forking,* which creates a copy (a child) of itself. The child then uses *exec* to overwrite itself with the image of the program to be run.

The child turns into a *zombie* on termination. The kernel doesn't remove its process table entry until the parent picks up the *exit status* of the child. Premature death of the parent turns the child into an *orphan,* and **init** takes over the parentage of all orphans.

The child's environment inherits some parameters from the parent, like the real and effective UID and GID, the file descriptors, the current directory, and environment variables. However, changes in the child are not made available in the parent.

Built-in shell commands like **pwd** and **cd** don't fork a separate process. Shell scripts use a sub-shell to run the commands in a script.

The UNIX kernel communicates with a process by sending it a *signal.* Signals can be generated from the keyboard or by the **kill** command. You can kill a process with **kill,** and use **kill -s KILL** if a simple **kill** doesn't do the job.

A job can be run in the background. **nohup** ensures that a background job remains alive even after the user has logged out.

The C shell, Korn and Bash shells enable job control. You can move jobs between foreground and background (**fg** and **bg**) and suspend (*[Ctrl-z]*) them. You can list jobs (**jobs**) and also kill them (**kill**).

You can schedule a job for one-time execution with **at**, or run it when the system load permits with **batch. cron** lets you schedule jobs so that they run repeatedly. It takes input from a user's *crontab* file where the schedule and frequency of execution is specified by five fields using a special number matching system.

SELF-TEST

8.1   What is the significance of the PID and PPID? Without using **ps**, how do you find out the PID of your login shell?

8.2   How do you display all processes running on your system?

8.3   Which programs are executed by spawning a shell? What does the second shell do?

8.4   Name some commands that don't require a separate process.

8.5   Name the two system calls required to run a program.

8.6   How will you find out the complete command lines of all processes run by user timothy?

8.7   Run **ps** with the appropriate option, and note some processes that have no controlling terminal.

8.8   How will you use **kill** to ensure that a process is killed?

8.9   How will you kill the last background job without knowing its PID?

8.10 How do you display the signal list on your system?

8.11 Should you run a command like this? `nohup compute.sh`

8.12 The **jobs** command displayed the message `jobs: not found`. When does that normally happen?

8.13 In the midst of an editing session with **vi** or **emacs**, how do you make a temporary exit to the shell and then revert to the editor?

8.14 How do you find out the name of the job scheduled to be executed with **at** and **batch**?

8.15 Frame an **at** command to run the script dial.sh tomorrow at 8 p.m.

8.16 Interpret the following crontab entry:

```
30 21 * * * find /tmp /usr/tmp -atime +30 -exec rm -f {} \;
```

8.17 You invoked the **crontab** command to make a crontab entry and then changed your mind. How do you terminate the standard input that **crontab** is now expecting?

8.18 How does the system administrator become the exclusive user of **at** and **cron**?

EXERCISES

8.1 Mention the significance of the two parameters, $$ and $!. Explain the differing behavior of the command **echo $$** when run from the shell prompt and inside a shell script.

8.2 Mention the similarities that you find between processes and files.

8.3 If two users execute the same program, are the memory requirements doubled?

8.4 What are the two options available to a parent after it has spawned a child? How can the shell be made to behave in both ways?

8.5 Explain the significance of this command: ps -e | wc -l.

8.6 Explain the attributes of *daemon* processes using three examples. How do you display and identify them?

8.7 Which process will you look for in the **ps** output if you are not able to (i) print, (ii) send out mail, (iii) log in using the secure shell?

8.8 Unlike the built-in commands, **pwd** and **echo**, which also exist as separate disk files, why is there no file named **cd** on any UNIX system?

8.9 Which process do you think may have the maximum number of children? What is its PID? Can you divide its children into two categories?

8.10 How is a process created? Mention briefly the role of the **fork** and *exec* system calls in process creation.

8.11 Name five important process attributes that are inherited by the child from its parent.

8.12 A shell script foo contains the statement **echo "$PATH $x"**. Now define **x=5** at the prompt, and then run the script. Explain your observations and how you can rectify the behavior.

8.13 What is a *zombie,* and how is it killed?

8.14 Explain whether the following are true or false: (i) A script can be made to ignore all signals. (ii) The parent process always picks up the exit status of its children. (iii) One program can give rise to multiple processes.

8.15 What is the difference between a process run with & and one run with **nohup**?

8.16 What are *signals*? Name two ways of generating signals from the keyboard. Why should we use **kill** with signal names rather than their numbers?

8.17 What is the difference between a *job* and a *process*? How do you (i) suspend the foreground job, (ii) move a suspended job to the background, (iii) bring back a suspended job to the foreground?

8.18   Interpret these crontab entries and explain if they will work:
       (i) `* * * * * dial.sh`, (ii) `00-60  22-24  30  2  *  find.sh`,
       (iii) `30  21  * * * find /tmp /usr/tmp -atime +30 -exec rm -f {} \;`.

8.19   Frame a crontab entry to execute the `connect.sh` script every 30 minutes on
       every Monday, Wednesday, and Friday between the times of 8 a.m. and 6 p.m.

8.20   Create a directory `foo`, and then run a shell script containing the two commands
       cd foo ; pwd. Explain the behavior of the script.

8.21   What does the **exit** command do? Why doesn't it log you out when run in your
       login shell like this? (`exit`)

8.22   The cron facility on your system is not working. How do you check whether the
       process is running at all and whether you are authorized to use **cron**?

8.23   The administrator has decided that most users will be allowed to use **at** and
       cron. What should she change that requires minimum effort?

The Shell—Customizing the Environment

The shell is different from other programs. Apart from interpreting metacharacters, it presents an environment that you can customize to suit your needs. These needs include devising shortcuts, manipulating shell variables, and setting up startup scripts. A properly setup shell makes working easier, but the degree of customization possible also depends on the shell you use.

This chapter presents the environment-related features of the Bash shell, but also examines the differences with three other shells—Bourne shell, C shell, and Korn shell. After reading this chapter, you may want to select your shell. To aid you in this task, let it be said right here that you'll have a headstart over others if you select either Korn or Bash as your login shell.

Objectives

- Learn the evolution of the four shells—Bourne shell, C shell, Korn shell, and Bash.
- Discover the difference between *local* and *environment* variables.
- Examine some environment variables like PATH, SHELL, MAIL, and so forth.
- Use *aliases* to invoke commands with short names.
- Use the *history* mechanism to recall, edit, and run previously executed commands.
- Edit any previous command line using the **vi**-like *in-line editing* feature.
- Use the *tilde substitution* feature to shorten pathnames that refer to the home directory.
- Prevent accidental overwriting of files and logging out using **set -o**.
- Make environment settings permanent using *profiles* and *rc* scripts.
- Manipulate the directory stack *(Going Further)*.

9.1 The Shells

The UNIX shell is both an interpreter and a scripting language. This is one way of saying that a shell can be interactive or noninteractive. When you log in, an **interactive shell** presents a prompt and waits for your requests. This type of shell supports job control, aliases, and history. An interactive shell runs a **noninteractive shell** when executing a shell script.

Every feature used in a shell script can also be used in an interactive shell, but the reverse is not true. Job control and history have no meaning in a shell script. In this chapter, we are mostly concerned with interactive shells.

Steve Bourne developed the first shell for UNIX. The Bourne shell was weak as an interpreter but had reasonably strong programming features. The C shell was created by Bill Joy at Berkeley to improve the interpretive features of Bourne. But Joy's shell wasn't suitable for programming. For some time, it was normal to use the C shell for interpretive work and the Bourne shell for programming. Had this trend continued until this day, this chapter would have focused almost entirely on the C shell.

Things changed when David Korn developed the Korn shell. It combined the best of both worlds—the interactive features of the C shell and the programming features of Bourne. Korn offered important features likes aliases and command history (which the Bourne shell lacked) and offered additional programming constructs not available in Bourne. While Korn was a complete superset of Bourne, it lacked some features of the C shell like directory stack manipulation. Korn's alias handling is also somewhat weak.

Bash was created by GNU as a Bourne-again shell. It was a grand superset in that in combined the features of the Korn and C shells. Bash was developed to ultimately conform to the POSIX shell specification. Bash is arguably the best shell to use. But habits often die hard. The C shell still has takers, but many of its devoted users have migrated to the Tcsh shell. Many of the C shell features discussed in this chapter will also work with Tcsh.

9.1.1 Setting Your Shell

Your login shell is set at the time of creation of your account. It is determined by the last field of your entry in /etc/passwd and is available in the SHELL variable. Before you begin, you need to know the shell you are using:

```
$ echo $SHELL
/usr/bin/bash
```

To try out all the examples of this chapter with each of the shells, you should be able to change your shell as and when required. Check which one of the following works best for you:

- Run the **chsh** command to change the entry in /etc/passwd. However, this command is not available on all non-Linux systems.
- Make a temporary switch by running the shell itself as a command. This is how you can run a C shell as a child of your login shell and then terminate it to move back to your login shell:

```
$ csh                                        C shell runs as child
% exit                                       Terminates C shell
$ _                                          Back to login shell
```

- Ask the system administrator to change the entry in /etc/passwd. If you own the machine, you can do that from the superuser account *(19.3.3)*.

In this chapter, we'll use Bash as the base shell. Differences with Korn and Bourne are pointed out in separate asides. The C shell is covered at the end of the chapter.

9.2 Environment Variables

Shell variables are of two types—local and environment. PATH, HOME, and SHELL are **environment variables**. They are so called because they are available in the user's total environment—the sub-shells that run shell scripts, and mail commands and editors. Local variables are more restricted in scope as shown by this example:

```
$ DOWNLOAD_DIR=/home/romeo/download
$ echo $DOWNLOAD_DIR
/home/romeo/download
```

DOWNLOAD_DIR is a local variable; its value is not available to child processes. Run a Bourne sub-shell with **sh**, and check whether you can see the variable there:

```
$ sh                                            Create a child shell
$ echo $DOWNLOAD_DIR                   Is DOWNLOAD_DIR visible in child?
                                                       It is not!
$ echo $PATH                                   But is PATH visible?
/bin:/usr/bin:.:/usr/ccs/bin                            It is!
$ exit                                          Terminate child
$ _                                    and come back to login shell
```

The **set** statement displays all variables available in the current shell, but the **env** command displays only environment variables. We show a concise list:

```
$ env
HOME=/home/romeo
IFS='                                       IFS includes newline
'                                    So closing quote is on next line
LOGNAME=romeo
MAIL=/var/mail/romeo
MAILCHECK=60
PATH=/bin:/usr/bin:.:/usr/ccs/bin
PS1='$ '
PS2='> '
SHELL=/usr/bin/bash
TERM=xterm
```

By convention, environment variable names are defined in uppercase though nothing prevents you from using a different scheme. **env** is an external command and runs in a child process. It thus lists only those variables that it has inherited from its parent, the shell. But **set** is a shell built-in and shows all variables visible in the current shell. **set** will display the value of DOWNLOAD_DIR but not **env**.

Applications often obtain information on the process environment through these environment variables. **vi** reads TERM and **mailx** looks up MAIL. Applications are not designed to run from a specific shell, so environment variables always present information in the *name=value* format. They may, however, be assigned differently in the different shells (like the C shell).

9.2.1   export: Creating Environment Variables

To make DOWNLOAD_DIR visible in all child processes, it needs to be *exported*. We have already used the shell's **export** statement in Chapter 8 to enforce variable inheritance. **export** simply converts a local variable to an environment variable:

```
export DOWNLOAD_DIR
```

The **export** statement can be used before or after the assignment. You can also perform both operations in a single statement:

```
export DOWNLOAD_DIR=/home/romeo/download                    Won't work in Bourne
```

The reason why we don't use **export** with variables displayed by **env** is that the job has already been done. Some variables were made available by the process creation mechanism when the shell was created. Others are made available by the shell itself when it executes some initialization scripts. You'll know more about these scripts in Section 9.9.

Note   You export a variable only once in a session. You don't need to export it again just because you have reassigned it. PATH is an exported variable, and you don't need to use **export** **PATH** after you have modified it.

BOURNE Shell   You can't export and assign in a single statement. Use separate statements: x=5 ; export x.

KORN Shell   Everything applies to this shell.

C Shell   Variables are assigned, exported, and displayed differently by **set** though not by **env**. There's no **export** statement here; this shell uses the **setenv** statement to both assign and export variables. See Section 9.10.1.

9.3   The Common Environment Variables

Environment variables control the behavior of the system (Table 9.1). If they are not set properly, you may not be able to use some commands without a pathname, use **vi** on a remote connection, or obtain notification on receipt of mail. As discussed before, many of these variables are exported and made available to the shell by its ancestors.

The Command Search Path (PATH)   PATH lists the directories searched by the shell to locate an executable command *(2.1.1)*. Its current value, as displayed by **env**, shows a list of four directories:

```
$ echo $PATH
/bin:/usr/bin:.:/usr/ccs/bin
```

TABLE 9.1 *Common Environment Variables*

Variable	Significance
HOME	Home directory—the directory a user is placed on logging in
PATH	List of directories searched by shell to locate a command
LOGNAME	Login name of user
USER	As above
MAIL	Absolute pathname of user's mailbox file
MAILCHECK	Mail checking interval for incoming mail
MAILPATH	List of mailboxes checked by shell for arrival of mail
TERM	Type of terminal
PWD	Absolute pathname of current directory *(Korn and Bash only)*
CDPATH	List of directories searched by **cd** when used with a nonabsolute pathname
PS1	Primary prompt string
PS2	Secondary prompt string
SHELL	User's login shell and one invoked by programs having shell escapes

We often reassign PATH to include one or more directories. To add /usr/xpg4/bin to the PATH list, reassign this variable by concatenating the old value with the new:

```
$ PATH=$PATH:/usr/xpg4/bin                          Colon to be added
$ echo $PATH
/bin:/usr/bin:.:/usr/ccs/bin:/usr/xpg4/bin
```

On this Solaris system, you'll find many commands (like **grep**) of the same name in both /usr/bin and /usr/xpg4/bin (directory for X/Open-compliant programs). Running **grep** will execute /usr/bin/grep (since /usr/bin appears earlier in PATH), so you need to use an absolute pathname here for running the X/Open version.

Your Home Directory (HOME) When you log in, UNIX places you in the home directory named after your user-id. Its pathname is available in the HOME variable:

```
$ echo $HOME
/home/romeo
```

The home directory is set by the administrator in /etc/passwd. The line for this user shows the home directory in the last but one field:

```
romeo:x:208:50::/home/romeo:/usr/bin/bash
```

You can reassign HOME, but it will *not* change the home directory as such, only the directory that **cd** switches to when used without arguments. This happens because a simple **cd** implies **cd $HOME**.

Mailbox Location and Checking (MAIL, MAILPATH, and MAILCHECK) It's not the mail software that informs the user that mail has arrived. That job is done by the shell.

Unless MAILPATH is defined, the shell knows the location of a user's mailbox from MAIL. This location is generally /var/mail or /var/spool/mail (Linux). romeo's mail is saved in /var/mail/romeo on an SVR4 system.

Users often use multiple mail handling programs which have different locations for their mailboxes. MAILPATH represents a colon-delimited list of these files. Here's one setting that shows **mailx** and Netscape as the mail handling programs for this user:

```
MAILPATH=/var/mail/romeo:$HOME/nsmail/Inbox
```

MAILCHECK determines how often the shell checks the file defined in MAIL or MAILPATH for the arrival of new mail (The **set** output shows 60). If the shell finds the file modified since the last check, it informs the user with the familiar message You have mail in /var/mail/romeo.

The Prompt Strings (PS1, PS2, and PWD) The shell uses two prompts. The primary prompt string PS1 is the one you normally see. Multiline commands are displayed by the shell with a > prefixing each subsequent line:

```
$ find / -name a.out -mtime +365 \
> -exec rm {} \;
```

The > is the secondary prompt string stored in PS2. Though PS2 is generally a >, your system may not use $ as PS1. To use a different primary prompt string, change PS1:

```
$ PS1="C> "
C> _                                                          Like DOS prompt
```

Bash can also display the current directory in the prompt by embedding the PWD variable in PS1. Whenever you change your directory, the prompt also changes:

```
$ PS1='[$PWD] '                                        Must use single quotes
[/home/romeo] cd /etc
[/etc] _                                    Prompt changes; current directory is /etc
```

PWD is a rather unusual variable; it is reevaluated every time the working directory changes. With a prompt set like this, you really don't need to use the **pwd** command at all.

Tip

Confusion often arises when you work concurrently on your local machine and a remote one (using, say, **ssh**). If the prompts are identical in both, then you may need to use the **uname -n** command to identify the machine you are logged into. Bash supports a number of escape sequences in PS1, and if you set PS1 like this, then you will always know where you are:

```
$ PS1="\h> "
saturn> _                                         saturn is the machine's name
```

The escape sequence \h displays a machine's hostname. You can also add PWD for added benefit. Look up the Bash documentation for the other escape sequences.

BOURNE Shell Neither PWD nor escape sequences are supported. Normally, PS1 and PS2 are set to $ and >, respectively.

KORN Shell Everything except the escape sequences apply.

C Shell Look up Section 9.10.1.

The Directory Search Path (CDPATH) CDPATH lets you avoid using pathnames when using **cd** to navigate to certain directories. Consider this setting, which includes both the current and parent directory:

```
CDPATH=.:..:/home/romeo
```

The shell searches three directories when using **cd**—this time to look for a directory. Now imagine that you have two directories, include and lib, under your current directory, and you are currently located in include. Since CDPATH includes the parent directory, you don't need to use **cd ../lib** to go to lib:

```
$ pwd
/home/romeo/include
$ cd lib ; pwd
/home/romeo/lib
```

When you use **cd lib**, the shell first looks up the current directory for lib, failing which it searches the parent directory (..) and then /home/romeo. Make sure that you always include the current directory in CDPATH because otherwise that would suppress **cd**'s normal behavior.

Shell Used by Commands with Shell Escapes (SHELL) SHELL displays your login shell (not necessarily the shell you are using). Programs like **more**, **vi**, and **emacs** provide a *shell escape* to let you run a UNIX command. SHELL determines the shell these programs use. Look at the sample line in the discussion on the HOME variable; the last field sets the value of SHELL.

The Terminal Type (TERM) TERM indicates the type of terminal you are using. Every terminal has certain characteristics that are defined in a control file in the terminfo directory (in /usr/lib or /usr/share/lib). This directory contains a number of subdirectories named after the letters of the alphabet. A terminal's control file is available in a directory having a one-letter name that is the same as the first letter of the terminal name. For instance, vt100 terminals use the file /usr/share/lib/terminfo/v/vt100.

Some utilities like the **vi** editor are terminal-dependent, and they need to know the type of terminal you are using. If TERM isn't set correctly, **vi** won't work and the display will be faulty. TERM is also important when you log on to a remote machine.

Your Username (LOGNAME and USER) System V and BSD use two different variables to indicate your user-id. One or both variables may be available on your system. You can use the one that applies to your system in a shell script to prevent certain users from running the script.

The other variables used by Bash will be discussed in later sections that feature the history facility and startup files. We'll examine the IFS variable when we take up shell programming.

9.4 Aliases

The shell supports **aliases** as a mechanism of assigning shorthand names for commands or for redefining commands to run with specific options. Aliasing is done with the **alias** statement, a built-in feature of the shell.

You often use the **ls -l** command, so if an alias named **ll** doesn't exist on your system, you can create one. The definition resembles an assignment of a shell variable:

```
alias ll='ls -l'
```
Quoting necessary for multiple words

Don't use whitespace around the =. Also, use quotes when the alias value has multiple words. You can now execute **ls -l** simply by using

```
ll
```
Executes ls -l

To consider another example, we often use the **cd** command with long pathnames. If there's a sequence that you use often, then it makes sense to convert the sequence into an alias:

```
alias cdsys="cd /usr/include/sys"
```

An alias is recursive, which means that if **a** is aliased to **b** and **b** is aliased to **c**, **a** should run **c**.

You can also use aliasing to redefine an existing command, so it is always invoked with certain options. Here are two useful aliases:

```
alias cp="cp -i"
alias rm="rm -i"
```

The **cp -i** command behaves interactively when the destination file exists. However, **rm -i** always behaves interactively. With aliases now defined for them, every time you invoke these commands, their aliased versions are executed. How can you now use the original external commands? Just precede the command with a \. This means that you have to use **\cp foo1 foo2** to override the alias.

alias by default displays all aliases. You can see a specific alias definition by using **alias** with the name. An alias is unset with **unalias**:

```
$ alias cp
alias cp='cp -i'
$ unalias cp ; alias cp
bash: alias: cp: not found
```

A set of useful aliases is displayed in Table 9.2. Three of them show section numbers where the command used in the alias has been explained. Too much aliasing can be confusing and difficult to remember, so exercise restraint when defining them. Aliases are good to begin with, but eventually you'll be using *shell functions,* which offer a superior form of aliasing.

Note

Just because the alias **cp** works with arguments, don't interpret that to mean that the alias accepts arguments. It's simply that the shell expands the alias before running the command line. Only C shell aliases use arguments.

KORN Shell

Everything applies to this shell.

BOURNE Shell

It doesn't support aliases. Using shell functions is the only option.

C Shell

Aliaising in this shell is very powerful. See Section 9.10.2.

TABLE 9.2 *Useful Aliases*

Alias Definition	Significance
alias ls='ls -F'	Marks directories, executables, and symlinks
alias l.='ls -d .*'	Lists all files beginning with a dot
alias ..="cd .."	Moves one directory up
alias ...="cd ../.."	Moves two directories up
alias cx="chmod a+x"	Assigns execute permission to all
alias h="history 20"	Lists last 20 commands *(9.5)*
alias cls="tput clear"	Clears the screen
alias path='echo PATH=$PATH'	Displays current PATH (Note use of single quotes)
alias lm="ls -t | head -n 1"	Displays last modified filename *(10.6)*
alias vil="vi `ls -t | head -n 1`"	Edits last modified file with **vi**
alias chp="ps -e | grep"	Checks if a specific process is running *(11.4.4)*
alias lsd='ls -la | grep "^d"'	Lists only directories

9.5 Command History

The **history** feature lets you recall previous commands (even those executed in previous sessions), edit them if required, and re-execute them. The shell assigns each command an **event number**. By default, the **history** command in Bash displays the complete event list that is saved in a history file. Using a numeric argument, we can display the last five commands:

```
$ history 5                                              Last five commands
36 vi hexdump.c
37 cc hexdump.c
38 tar cvf /dev/fd0 *.doc
39 cp *.c ../backup
40 history 5                                  Also includes command invoked to obtain list
```

You can use this list to re-execute previous commands, perhaps after performing some substitution. Table 9.3 summarizes these features which are discussed next with suitable examples.

TABLE 9.3   *The History Functions*

csh, bash	ksh	Significance
history 12	history -12	Lists last 12 commands
!!	r	Repeats previous command
!7	r 7	Repeats event number 7
!24:p	–	Prints without executing event number 24
!-2	r -2	Repeats command prior to the previous one
!ja	r ja	Repeats last command beginning with ja
!?size?	–	Repeats last command with embedded string size
!find:s/p1/java	r find p1=java	Repeats last **find** command after substituting java for p1
^mtime^atime	r mtime=atime	Repeats previous command after substituting atime for mtime
!cp:gs/doc/html	–	Repeats last **cp** command after globally substituting html for doc
!! | sort	r | sort	Repeats previous command but also pipes it to **sort**
!find | sort	r find | sort	Repeats last **find** command but also pipes it to **sort**
cd !$	cd $_	Changes directory to last argument of previous command ($_ used by Bash also)
rm !*	–	Removes files expanded from all arguments of previous command

9.5.1   Accessing Previous Commands

Bash lets you recall previous commands by using the cursor Up and Down keys. Normally that's the most convenient way to do it. But you can also access and execute any previous command by using the ! as a prefix to the event number:

```
$ !38                                              Re-executes event number 38
38 tar cvf /dev/fd0 *.doc                          Copies files from disk to diskette
```

The command line is displayed and executed. Working like this, you might execute an incorrect command (like **rm**), so by using the p (print) modifier you can display the command without executing it:

```
$ !38:p                                                            Displays only
38 tar cvf /dev/fd0 *.doc
```

This **tar** command copies files from disk to diskette. You should make sure of what you are doing by using the :p modifier first. If the command you recalled had xvf instead of cvf as arguments, data would flow in the reverse direction—from diskette to disk *(19.13.2)*. But if the above command line is the one you want to run again, simply use this to repeat the last command:

```
!!                                                            Repeats last command
```

It is often more convenient to recall commands by using substrings of their names rather than their event numbers. If the last command *beginning* with v was **vi**, you can run it again like this:

```
!v                                              Repeats last command beginning with v
```

You can match embedded strings also; you'll find one example in Table 9.3.

Tip

Programmers will find this form of addressing very useful for repeatedly editing and compiling programs. For instance, if you use the command **vi hexdump.c** and **cc hexdump.c** alternately, you need to explicitly invoke the commands only once. Subsequently, you can use **!v** and **!c** repeatedly till the compilation generates no errors. With this shell, however, it's more convenient to use the Up and Down keys to recall the recent commands.

9.5.2   Substitution in Previous Commands

Often you may need to execute a previous command but only after replacing a string in the command line with another. Bash uses the **vi**-style :s modifier and the / as delimiter of the old and new patterns. You can repeat the previous **tar** command, but this time using the .bak instead of the .doc files:

```
!tar:s/doc/bak                                     vi also uses :s for substitution
```

There are two ways of repeating a substitution on the immediately previous command. Use the !! with :s as usual or simply use the ^ (caret) as the delimiter of strings. Restore the original command line by replacing bak with doc:

```
!!:s/bak/doc                                   Substitution in previous command
^bak^doc                                                    Same; a shortcut
```

Note that this substitution is made only for the *first* occurrence in a line. Bash permits global substitution also; use gs instead of s.

9.5.3   Using Arguments to Previous Command ($_)

We often run several commands on the same file. Instead of specifying the filename every time, we can use $_ as its abbreviation. This expression signifies the *last* argument to the previous command. For instance, after we have created a directory with **mkdir bar**, we can use this technique to switch to it:

```
mkdir bar
cd $_                                                Changes directory to bar
```

To consider another example, if you have edited a shell script **cronfind.sh** with **vi**, you can execute this file by simply entering

```
$_                                                Executes cronfind.sh
```

What better way can you imagine of executing a shell or **perl** script that you just edited with **vi**! Bash has several other parameters that can access every argument of any previous command, but they are beyond the scope of this text.

You can also use the !* to signify all arguments to the previous command. Consider that you have just printed some files:

```
lp foo1.ps foo2.ps foo3.ps
```

Now that you don't need these files any longer, you can remove them or move them to a separate directory using the !* symbols:

```
rm !*
mv !* ../backup
```

Note that !* also includes the previous command's options (which are also arguments), so this technique works only with those commands that use no options. For instance, if you have first used **ls -l foo** and then **rm !***, rm would also run with -l as argument and report an error.

9.5.4   The History Variables

By default, Bash stores all previous commands in the file $HOME/.bash_history. But you can use HISTFILE to assign a different filename. The file is written only when you log out; otherwise, the list is saved only in memory. There are two variables that determine the size of the list both in memory and disk:

```
HISTSIZE=500                                                    In memory
HISTFILESIZE=1000                           In disk, not specified in POSIX
```

With memory and disk space available at throwaway prices, you should set these variables to large values so that you can store commands of multiple login sessions.

BOURNE Shell

This feature is not available.

KORN Shell

Almost everything applies except that Korn's implementation of these features is different:

- **history** is used with a negative integer (e.g., **history -5**).
- The **r** command is used to repeat a command. By default it repeats the previous command (**!!** in Bash). **r 38** repeats event 38 (**!38** in Bash). **r v** repeats the last command beginning with v (**!v** in Bash). **r** itself is an alias that executes **fc -e -**.
- Substitution is performed using =. So **r tar doc=bak** runs the last **tar** command but after replacing doc with bak. Korn doesn't permit global substitution.
- Korn doesn't support the use of **!*** to represent all arguments of the previous command. However, it supports **$_**.
- If HISTFILE is not set, Korn uses $HOME/.sh_history as the history file. HISTSIZE determines the size of the history list.

C Shell

There's very little difference with Bash. The differences are discussed in Section 9.10.3.

9.6 In-Line Command Editing

Bash provides **vi**- and **emacs**-like capabilities of editing the command line, both the current command and its predecessors in the history list. Before you are able to do that, make one of the following settings:

```
set -o vi                              Use set +o vi to reverse this setting
set -o emacs                              Use only one setting, not both
```

The editing features of the **vi** and **emacs** editors are built into Bash, and these settings enable their use for **in-line editing**. We'll discuss the **vi**-like features in this section. Since you are editing only a line at a time, certain restrictions will obviously apply. First, you don't have access to the ex Mode. Second, trying to move the cursor up or down will actually recall the previous or next commands.

To perform command editing, you must explicitly invoke the Command Mode. To recall a previous command, first press *[Esc]* and then **k** as many times as you want. If you overshoot, then come back with **j**. You can normally move along the line with the standard word navigation commands (like **b** and **w**) or move to line extremes (with **0** and **$**). Use a repeat factor if necessary and relevant.

Perform all editing functions in the normal way. Insert with **i**, and replace with **r**. Delete a character with **x**, and change a word with **cw**. Place the deleted text elsewhere in the line with **p** or **P**. Once all changes are made, the command can be executed by hitting *[Enter]*.

You can use **vi**'s search techniques to recall previous commands from the history list. Even though the search is in the reverse direction, you'll have to use the */pattern* sequence:

/cvf*[Enter]*   *Locates last occurrence of string* cvf

You can repeat the search by pressing **n** repeatedly. If you overshoot, come back with **N**. Edit the line, and run it again. This feature alone justifies the use of in-line editing in preference to the history mechanism!

> A proficient **vi** user will easily exploit these editing facilities to run a command with selected arguments of previous commands. If you have previously run **vi foo1 foo2 foo3 foo4**, then you can easily run **gzip** with some or all of these arguments. Press *[Esc]*, search for vi with **/vi**, change vi to gzip with **cw**, and hit *[Enter]*. To delete the last argument, move to the fourth argument with **4w** and press **dw**. It's as simple as that!

Tip

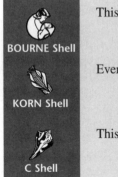

BOURNE Shell	This feature is not available.
KORN Shell	Everything applies to this shell.
C Shell	This feature is available only in Tcsh.

9.7   Tilde Substitution

The ~ acts as a shorthand representation of the home directory. A string prefixed by a ~ is interpreted as the home directory of the user. Thus, when the shell encounters the command line

cd ~juliet

it switches to juliet's home directory. If the value of $HOME for juliet is /home/juliet/tulec1, then this is the directory where **cd ~juliet** switches to.

Interestingly, the ~, when used by itself or when immediately followed by a /, refers to the home directory of the user using it. If you have logged in as juliet, you can access the html directory under your home directory by using **cd ~/html**. That's why we often find a configuration file like .exrc referred to both as $HOME/.exrc and ~/.exrc.

You can also toggle between the directory that you switched to most recently and your current directory. This is done with the ~- symbols (or simply -). For instance, either of the commands

cd ~-	*Changes to your previous directory*
cd -	*Same*

changes your current working directory to the one you used most recently. Here's how you use it:

[/home/image] **cd /bin**	*Changes to /bin from /home/image*
[/bin] **cd -**	*Reverts to /home/image*
/home/image	*Shell displays this*
[/home/image] _	*Current directory shown by PS1*

This toggling effect is like the button many TV remote units have to let you alternate between the current and last visited channels.

This feature is not available.

Everything applies to this shell.

Everything applies except that toggling with **cd -** is supported only in Tcsh.

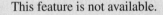

9.8 Using set Options

The **set** statement by default displays all variables, but it can make several environment settings with the -o *keyword* option. The keywords take care of some of the common hazards faced by users, like overwriting files and accidental logging out. Table 9.4 lists some of these options.

File Overwriting (noclobber) To prevent accidental file overwriting (*clobbering*) with the shell's > and >> symbols, you need to use the noclobber setting in this way:

set -o noclobber	*No more overwriting files with >*

This means that if you redirect output to an existing file foo, the shell will retort with a message:

```
bash: foo: cannot overwrite existing file
```

TABLE 9.4 *Shell Settings with* **set -o**

Option	Significance
noclobber	Prevents file overwriting with > and >>
ignoreeof	Prevents termination of login shell with *[Ctrl-d]*
notify	Notifies completion of background job immediately rather than at the next prompt
noglob	Disables wild-card expansion
vi	Enables **vi**-style command-line editing
emacs	Enables **emacs**-style command-line editing
allexport	Exports all variables

To override this protection feature, use the | after the >:

```
head -n 5 emp.lst >| foo
```

Accidental Logging Out (`ignoreeof`) Users often inadvertently press *[Ctrl-d]* with the intent to terminate standard input, but end up logging out of the system. The `ignoreeof` keyword offers protection from accidental logging out:

```
set -o ignoreeof                                       [Ctrl-d] won't log you out
```

Now, when you use *[Ctrl-d]* to terminate your session, here's a typical response from the shell:

```
Use 'exit' to terminate this shell
```

You now have to use the **exit** command to take you out of the session; *[Ctrl-d]* won't do it any more (unless executed repeatedly!).

Notifying Completion of Background Jobs (`notify`) Recall that the shell normally notifies the completion of a background job only when a prompt is available *(8.11)*. You can use `notify` (with **set -o notify**) for immediate notification.

 A **set** option is turned off with **set +o** *keyword*. To reverse the noclobber feature, use **set +o noclobber**. The complete list of **set**'s special options is obtained by using **set -o** or **set +o** without any additional arguments.

BOURNE Shell   This feature is not available.

KORN Shell   Everything applies to this shell.

C Shell

See Section 9.10.4.

9.9 The Initialization Scripts

The environment variables, aliases, and **set** options that we define are applicable only for the session. They revert to their default values when the user logs out. To make these settings permanent, you'll have to place them in certain startup scripts that are executed when a user logs in. These scripts are of two types:

- A **login script** (also called a **profile**) which is executed only once on login.
- An **rc (run command) script** which is executed every time an interactive sub-shell is created.

Bash uses one of these three files as the login script or profile: ~/.bash_profile, ~/.profile, and ~/.bash_login. The rc file is generally ~/.bashrc. These scripts should be added to your home directory at the time of user creation. In case they are not there, you'll have to create or copy them. (Incidentally, Bash also uses ~/.bash_logout as the script to run before terminating a login shell.)

When a user logs in, the script /etc/profile is first executed before the users's own login script. Universal environment settings are kept by the administrator in /etc/profile so they are available to all users.

9.9.1 The Login Script

As mentioned before, Bash looks for one of the three files, .bash_profile, .profile, and .bash_login, *in the sequence specified* and identifies the one it spots first as its profile. The profile can be quite large depending on users' requirements. Here's an abridged one:

```
$ cat .profile
# User $HOME/.profile - commands executed at login time
MAIL=/var/mail/$LOGNAME                          # mailbox location
PATH=$PATH:$HOME/bin:/usr/ucb:.
PS1='$ '
PS2=>
TERM=vt100
MOZILLA_HOME=/opt/netscape ; export MOZILLA_HOME
mesg y
stty stop ^S intr ^C erase ^?
echo "Today's date is `date`"
```

The profile contains commands that are meant to be executed only *once* in a session. Some of the system variables have been assigned in this script. PATH has been modified to contain three more directories. **mesg y** expresses your willingness to receive messages from people using the **talk** command *(not discussed in this edition).* Some **stty** settings have also been made here.

How is the profile executed? Shell scripts are normally run by spawning a sub-shell, but this technique won't work here. Because a child can't alter the environment of its parent *(8.6.1),* if the login shell uses this technique, then variables set in the script would never be available in the login shell. The only conceivable way of running a startup script would be to do so in the same shell as the login shell (i.e., without spawning a child shell). The dot or source command does that:

```
. .profile                                          No sub-shell created
source .profile                                                    Same
```

No separate process is created here (like in **cd**) when you *source* this file. The environment also remains in effect throughout the login session. So you don't need to log out and log in again whenever you modify this file; just execute one of the two commands.

Caution

The example profile shows three directories added to PATH. This means that these directories will be repeatedly added every time you source this file. Eventually, you'll end up with a huge PATH setting which could unnecessarily slow down command search.

9.9.2 The rc File

The rc file is executed every time an interactive shell is called up (when opening an **xterm** window, for instance). The name of the file is defined by the variable BASH_ENV. Your profile could have a setting like this:

```
export BASH_ENV=$HOME/.bashrc
```

However, the above Bash definition merely ensures that an interactive sub-shell executes this file. If the login shell also has to execute this file, then a separate statement must be added in the profile:

```
. ~/.bashrc                                 Can use source instead of dot
```

The rc file should be used to hold only Bash-specific features. History list settings (like HISTSIZE and HISTFILE), command editing settings (like **set -o vi**), and alias definitions should all be made in this file. This is a cleaner arrangement because should you decide to change your shell any time later, you won't be saddled with a .profile ridden with irrelevant entries. Here are some sample entries:

```
alias cp="cp -i"
alias rm="rm -i"
set -o noclobber
set -o vi
set -o ignoreeof
```

This rc file is executed after the profile. However, if BASH_ENV isn't set, then the shell executes only the profile.

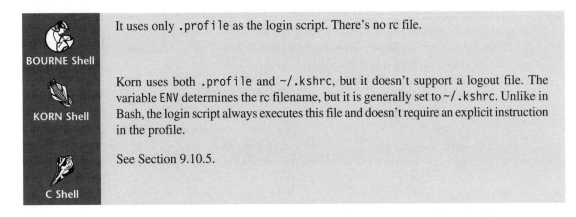

BOURNE Shell

It uses only .profile as the login script. There's no rc file.

KORN Shell

Korn uses both .profile and ~/.kshrc, but it doesn't support a logout file. The variable ENV determines the rc filename, but it is generally set to ~/.kshrc. Unlike in Bash, the login script always executes this file and doesn't require an explicit instruction in the profile.

See Section 9.10.5.

C Shell

9.10 The C Shell

The C shell pioneered many of the customization features examined in this chapter. In many cases, the Korn and Bash shells have improved upon them. In this section, we discuss only those features that are either not supported by the other shells or that are handled differently by them.

9.10.1 Local and Environment Variables

The C shell also supports local and environment variables, but they are assigned differently. A local variable is assigned with **set** (like **set x = 5**), but an environment variable is assigned with **setenv**:

```
setenv DOWNLOAD_DIR /home/romeo/download
```
No = here

The C shell doesn't support an **export** statement; the above statement also performs the task of exporting. By default, **setenv** lists all environment variables but in the *name=value* format used by the other shells:

```
% setenv
HOME=/users1/home/staff/henry
PATH=/bin:/usr/bin:/usr/lib/java/bin:/usr/dt/bin
LOGNAME=henry
TERM=xterm
SHELL=/usr/bin/csh
PWD=/users1/home/staff/henry
USER=henry
```

Irrespective of the shell you use, environment variables are always displayed in the *name=value* format. This is because applications are designed to be shell-independent and expect to see variable settings in a fixed format. But the C shell doesn't use these variables for its own use; it uses the local ones that are assigned and viewed with **set**:

```
% set
argv        ()
cwd         /users1/home/staff/henry
home        /users1/home/staff/henry
path        (/bin /usr/bin /usr/lib/java/bin /usr/dt/bin)
prompt      %                                                   Like PS1
shell       /bin/csh
status      0                               The exit status of the last command
term        xterm
user        henry                                  Like USER and LOGNAME
```

Many of these local variables also have corresponding environment variables (term and TERM). The C shell uses path rather than PATH to find out where a command is located. Let's now have a look at some of the local variables.

path This is the local counterpart of the environment variable, PATH. path stores and displays the list in a different format:

```
% echo $path
/bin /usr/bin /usr/lib/java/bin /usr/dt/bin
```

This space-delimited list is actually an array of four elements (Appendix A). To add /usr/xpg4/bin to the path list, we have to do this:

```
% set path = ($path /usr/xpg4/bin)
% echo $path
/bin /usr/bin /usr/lib/java/bin /usr/dt/bin /usr/xpg4/bin
```

Note that **set** and **echo** display these directories in different ways. **set** uses parentheses to enclose the list, but not **echo**. Changing path updates PATH and vice versa.

mail This variable combines the functions of the environment variables, MAIL, MAILPATH, and MAILCHECK. Here, we set mail to look for multiple file names, optionally prefixed by a number:

```
set mail = (600 /var/mail/julie /opt/Mail/julie)
```

Every 600 seconds, the shell checks the last modification times of these two files for arrival of new mail.

prompt The C shell stores the prompt string in the prompt variable. You normally see the % as the prompt string, but you can use **set** to customize it:

```
% set prompt = "[C>] "
[C>] _
```

The secondary prompt string is normally the ?, but this value is not stored in any environment variable. Moreover, prompt doesn't have an uppercase counterpart.

There are some more local variables. cwd stores the current directory (like PWD). user stores the user-id (like LOGNAME and USER).

Note

You can define both a local variable and an environment variable with the same name (**set x=5** and **setenv x 10**). The environment variable is then visible only in child processes while the local variable is visible in the current process. The environment variable is visible in *all* processes only if there is no local variable of the same name.

9.10.2 Aliases

The C shell also supports aliases as a mechanism of assigning short names to command sequences. Aliases are defined with **alias** and unset with **unalias**. All definitions are displayed by using **alias** without arguments. However, there are two points to note about C shell aliases:

- Aliases are assigned differently.
- They accept command line arguments.

The **alias** statement uses two arguments: the alias name and the alias definition. The following statement abbreviates the **ls -l** command:

```
alias l ls -l                                        No = symbol here
```

You can now invoke **l** to execute **ls -l**. Even though **l** will work with multiple filenames, *these filenames are not considered as its arguments.* But the C shell alias does accept arguments, which are read into special positional parameters inside the alias. You must know at least these two parameters:

\!*   Represents all arguments in the command line.
\!$ Represents the last argument in the command line.

The expressions are derived from the history mechanism which uses them with similar meanings, except that it relates them to the *previous* command. We can use the last expression to devise an alias for finding a file:

```
alias where 'find / -name \!$ -print'                    ! is special
```

Now we can run **where pearl.jpg** to locate this file, starting the search from the root directory. We had to escape the parameter !$ to prevent the shell from replacing it with the last argument of the previous command. Rather, \!$ provides a placeholder for the last argument of the *current* command. Single quotes here don't protect the !; only the \ does.

You can't define the above alias in the other shells. Neither can you devise an equivalent for this one, which uses two commands in a pipeline:

```
alias lsl 'ls -l \!* | more'
```

You can provide any number of arguments to the alias, and the listing will be displayed a page at a time. The C shell goes further than this and lets you access every argument individually. You can explore these features on your own.

Note

If you have converted an external command or a builtin to an alias, you can still execute the original command by simply preceding the command with a \. That is, you can still run the **where** command, if such a command exists on your system, with **\where**.

9.10.3 History

The C shell's history mechanism also allows you to recall, edit, and run previous commands. Unlike the other shells, which automatically save commands in the history file, the C shell needs the savehist variable to be set to the number of commands to be saved:

```
set savehist = 1000
```
Saves in ~/.history

All commands are saved in ~/.history. As in Bash, a separate variable, history, determines the size of the history list in memory:

```
set history = 500
```
Saves in memory

Note

The history facility is not activated unless the history variable is set. If it is not set, then only the last command is saved—that too only in memory.

9.10.4 Other Shell Variables

Many of the **set -o** options that apply to Bash and Korn *(9.8)* are handled by variables in the C shell. The shell's behavior in these cases depends on whether the variable is set or not. The **set** and **unset** statements work as on-off switches here. For instance, to prevent overwriting of files with redirection, you have to set the noclobber variable:

```
set noclobber
```
No more overwriting files with >

If you now redirect command output to an existing file foo, the shell will retort with a message foo: File exists. To override this protection feature, you have to use the >! instead:

```
head -n 5 emp.lst >! foo
```

You can revert to the original setting with **unset noclobber**.

Accidental logging out with *[Ctrl-d]* is prevented with the ignoreeof variable:

```
set ignoreeof
```
[Ctrl-d] won't log you out

Now, when you use *[Ctrl-d]* to terminate your session, the shell issues the message Use "logout" to logout.

The C shell also supports the variables notify and noglob with the same significance *(9.8)*.

9.10.5 The Initialization Scripts

The C shell supports a login file but it was the first shell to also use an rc file. When a user logs in, the shell runs three scripts in the order shown:

1. A global initialization file, which could be /etc/login or /etc/.login (Solaris). Instructions meant to be executed by all users are placed there.
2. ~/.cshrc This file contains instructions that are executed whenever a C shell is started.
3. ~/.login This is executed only when the user logs in.

The C shell also executes ~/.logout before logging out of the system. There's something to note in this sequence because it differs with the behavioral pattern of Korn and Bash. The shell runs the rc file *before* the login file. The .login should contain only environment variable settings like TERM, and you need to execute those instructions only once:

```
mesg n
stty stop ^S intr ^C erase ^?
setenv MOZILLA_HOME /opt/netscape                    Required by Netscape
setenv TERM vt220
```

MOZILLA_HOME and TERM have to be explicitly specified as environment variables by the **setenv** statement. Local variables and aliases are not automatically inherited by sub-shells and should be defined in ~/.cshrc:

```
set prompt = '[\!] '
set path = ($path /usr/local/bin)
set history = 500
set savehist = 50
set noclobber
set ignoreeof
alias ls ls -aFx
alias ls-l ls -l
alias h "history | more"
alias rm rm -i
```

You'll find that, over a period of time, your ~/.cshrc builds up faster than ~/.login.

➤ *GOING FURTHER*

9.11 Directory Stack Manipulation

Bash and the C shell offer a directory *stack* that you can fill in with the directories that you visit frequently. You can then use a shortcut to switch to any of these directories. Using the **dirs**, **pushd**, and **popd** commands, you can list the stack and push directories into and remove directories from the stack. The following paragraphs assume Bash as the shell, but most of the content applies to the C shell as well.

Let's first use **pushd** to fill up the stack with a directory ~/workc. After setting PS1 to reflect the current directory, invoke **pushd** with the directory name as argument:

```
$ PS1='[$PWD] '
[/home/romeo] pushd workc                            Prompt changes
/home/romeo/workc                                    Shows the current directory
~/workc ~                                            Shows two directories in stack
[/home/romeo/workc] _                                Prompt changes
```

pushd has the side effect of doing a "cd" to the directory and then running the **dirs** command to display the stack. The stack now contains two directories, ~/workc and ~ (home directory). Now, push three more directories to the stack:

```
pushd ~/www/cgi-bin
pushd ~/wireless/docs
pushd ~/servlets/code
```

Both **pushd** and **popd** run **dirs** to display the stack, but you can also run **dirs** yourself. The -v option displays a numbered list:

```
[/home/romeo/servlets/code] dirs
~/servlets/code ~/wireless/docs ~/www/cgi-bin ~/workc ~
[/home/romeo/servlets/code] dirs -v
0  ~/servlets/code
1  ~/wireless/docs
2  ~/www/cgi-bin
3  ~/workc
4  ~
```

You can switch to any directory in the list using **pushd** with a +*n* (or a -*n*) argument where *n* is the position of the directory in the stack. This is how you move to ~/wireless/docs:

```
[/home/romeo/www/cgi-bin] pushd +1
~/wireless/docs ~/www/cgi-bin ~/workc ~ ~/servlets/code
[/home/romeo/wireless/docs] _
```

Note that the stack has been rotated, and all the directories starting from position 1 in the old stack have now moved up toward the top of the stack.

The **popd** command removes (pops out) a directory from the stack. By default, **popd** removes the top directory from the stack and performs a change of directory to the new top:

```
[/home/romeo/wireless/docs] popd
~/www/cgi-bin ~/workc ~ ~/servlets/code
[/home/romeo/www/cgi-bin] _
```

To remove a directory elsewhere in the stack, **popd** must be used with the +*n* argument (or -*n*). The stack elements are accessed in the same way as **pushd**, so you could remove the third element with the argument +2:

```
[/home/romeo/www/cgi-bin] popd +2
~/www/cgi-bin ~/workc ~/servlets/code
[/home/romeo/www/cgi-bin] _
```

If you are working with a fixed list of directories, place the **pushd** statements in the appropriate startup script so that the stack is available to you when you log in.

SUMMARY

The shell can be customized to set the user's environment. Bash and Korn are feature-rich and recommended for use. The features of Bash are summarized below, and the comparative features of four shells are listed in Table 9.5.

Environment variables are available in the login shell and all its child processes. **export** converts a local variable to an environment variable. Apart from PATH, HOME, SHELL, and TERM, variables control the mailbox location (MAIL and MAILPATH) and the frequency of checking it (MAILCHECK).

The **alias** command defines an *alias* for abbreviating a command sequence or for redefining an existing command to always run with specific options. The \ prefix overrides the alias.

The *history* feature lets you recall, edit, and re-execute previous commands without retyping them. Previous commands can be accessed by their *event number* or context, and substitution can be performed on them.

TABLE 9.5 *Comparative Features of the Shells*

Feature	Bourne Shell	C Shell	Korn Shell	Bash
Command name	sh	csh	ksh	bash
Defining local variable *var*	*var=value*	set *var=value*	*var=value*	*var=value*
Defining environment variable *var*	export *var*	setenv *var value*	export *var=value*	export *var=value*
Displaying environment variables	export	setenv	export	export
Defining alias *name*	-	alias *name value*	alias *name=value*	alias *name=value*
Command history operator	-	!	r	!
Last alias parameter	-	\!$	-	-
All alias parameters	-	\!*	-	-
Enabling in-line command editing	-	-	set -o vi	set -o vi
Switching to home directory of user *usr*	-	cd ~*usr*	cd ~*usr*	cd ~*usr*
Synonym for $HOME/foo	-	~/foo	~/foo	~/foo
Toggling between two directories	-	-	cd -	cd -
Executing a startup script	.	source	.	. or source
Login file	.profile	.login	.profile	.bash_profile, .profile or .bash_login
rc file	-	.cshrc	Determined by ENV (often, .kshrc)	.bashrc or determined by BASH_ENV
Logout file	-	.logout	-	.bash_logout

The *in-line editing* facility lets us edit a previous command line with **vi-** and **emacs**-like commands. The feature has to be enabled first with **set -o vi** or **set -o emacs**.

Tilde substitution lets you access the file $HOME/foo with ~/foo. It also allows use of a shortcut like **cd ~romeo** to switch to romeo's home directory.

Using **set -o** *keyword,* you can protect your files from accidental overwriting (noclobber), accidental logout (ignoreeof), and notification of completion of a background job (notify).

The shell executes a *profile* on login and an *rc* file when creating a sub-shell. The **.** or **source** commands execute these scripts without creating a separate process. Commands to be executed once are placed in the profile.

SELF-TEST

Unless otherwise stated, all questions assume Bash as the working shell.

9.1   How does a local shell variable get converted to an environment variable?

9.2   How is the home directory set—by $HOME or /etc/passwd?

9.3   If TERM has the value vt220, where will you expect to find its control file?

9.4   How will you add the parent directory to your existing PATH? How can you make the setting permanent?

9.5   If you want your mailbox to be checked every minute, what setting will you make?

9.6   Create an alias named **rm** that always deletes files recursively and forcibly. How can you execute the original **rm** command without unaliasing it and without using an absolute pathname?

9.7   How do you repeat the last command in (i) Korn, (ii) Bash?

9.8   How will you configure the history facility to store the last 200 commands in memory in (i) Korn, (ii) Bash?

9.9   You have just used the command **tar -cvf /dev/fd0 *.sh**. How will you repeat the command to use the **.pl** files this time in (i) Korn, (ii) Bash?

9.10   In the Korn shell, the command **r ca** runs from the history list (i) the last command having ca embedded, (ii) the first command beginning with ca, (iii) the last command beginning with ca, (iv) all commands beginning with ca.

9.11   To enable **vi**-like editing of the command line, what setting will you have to make first? How do you later turn it off?

9.12   Suppose you have just viewed a file with **cat calc.java**. What shortcut will you use to display it with **more**?

9.13   How can you prevent your files from being overwritten using the redirection symbols? How will you overwrite a file when needed?

9.14   You have to toggle repeatedly between /usr/include and /usr/lib. What shortcut will you use?

9.15   How do you copy all files from henry's home directory even if you don't know its absolute pathname?

9.16   Why does every UNIX system have /etc/profile? When is this file executed?

9.17   If you have the files .bash_profile and .profile in your home directory, will Bash read them both on login?

9.18   A shell script also runs the login file. True or false?

EXERCISES

Unless otherwise stated, all questions assume Bash as the working shell.

9.1   What is the difference between an *interactive* and *noninteractive* shell? Which features of the shell have significance only in an interactive shell?

9.2   Which environment variables are set by reading /etc/passwd?

9.3   Why are all environment variables represented in a fixed format regardless of the shell you use?

9.4   How do you change your shell to **ksh** (i) temporarily, (ii) permanently? How is the value of $SHELL affected in each case?

9.5   Explain the significance of the MAIL and MAILCHECK variables. How do you learn that mail has arrived?

9.6   Assume you are in /home/romeo/cgi and you want **cd perl** to take you to /home/romeo/perl. What setting do you need to make?

9.7   If you have PS1='\!$', what will your prompt look like?

9.8   Mention the steps needed to (i) change the prompt to look like this: [jupiter-henry ~/project8] (user—henry, machine name—*jupiter* and current directory—project8), (ii) revert to your original prompt.

9.9   Frame aliases to show (i) only the hidden filenames in the current directory, (ii) the listing of all symbolic links in the current directory and below, (iii) the absolute pathname of a filename specified as argument to the alias.

9.10   What is the significance of these Bash commands? (i) !50, (ii) !-2:p, (iii) !!, (iv) ^doc^bak. What are their equivalents in Korn?

9.11   Can you condense these sequences? (i) cp *.c c_progs ; cd c_progs, (ii) cmp foo foo.bak ; cmp foo foo.doc, (iii) ls pricelist.html ; cp pricelist.html pricelist.html.bak.

9.12   You issued the command $_ and got the message foo: Permission denied. What does the message indicate?

9.13   You want to recall all the **tar** commands that you executed for viewing. How can you see them in turn by pressing a single key repeatedly?

9.14   Explain the significance of these commands: (i) cd ~henry, (ii) cd ~/henry, (iii) cd ~-, (iv) cd -.

9.15   Why do shells use a profile as well as an rc file? What type of entries do you place in each?

9.16   Name two ways of making the modifications to ~/.profile available to the environment.

9.17   If your .profile contains a statement like PATH=$PATH:$HOME/bin, and you make repeated changes to the file, how should you activate the changes?

9.18   How can you make all of your aliases placed in ~/.alias available in all sub-shells? Will the aliases be available in a shell script in (i) Korn, (ii) Bash?

9.19   Devise a system which allows you to use an alias named current to display recursively only the ordinary files in the current directory tree which have been modified since you logged in.

9.20   How will you set your prompt in the C shell to reflect the current directory? (HINT: Devise an alias for the **cd** command.)

## CHAPTER 10

Simple Filters

In this chapter, we begin our discussions of the text manipulation tools available in UNIX. We call them *filters*—commands that use both standard input and standard output. This chapter presents the simple filters; the next two feature the advanced ones. Filters are different from other commands in that their power lies, not in the standalone mode, but when used in combination with other tools. The last section features three applications built using simple filters in pipelines.

Many UNIX files have lines containing *fields* representing meaningful data entities. Some commands expect these fields to be separated by a suitable delimiter that's not used by the data. Typically this delimiter is a : (as in /etc/passwd and $PATH), and we have retained it for some of the sample files used in this and other chapters. Many filters work well with delimited fields, and some won't work without them.

Objectives

- Format text to provide margins and headers, doublespacing, and multiple column output with **pr**.
- Find differences and commonalities between two files with **cmp**, **diff**, and **comm**.
- Pick up lines from the beginning with **head**, and from the end with **tail**.
- Extract characters or fields vertically with **cut**.
- Join two files laterally and multiple lines to a single line with **paste**.
- Sort, merge, and remove repeated lines with **sort**.

Filters Reviewed

Filters were introduced in Section 7.5.5 as a class of commands that take advantage of the shell's redirection features. A filter has the capability of reading from standard input and writing to standard output. By default a filter writes to standard output. It reads from standard input when used without a filename as argument, and from the file otherwise.

The piping mechanism of the shell lets the standard output of one filter act as the standard input of another. This feature lets us design pipelines containing a series of filters. Section 10.13 shows their use in numerous combinations for performing content manipulations tasks—tasks which these tools can't perform when acting alone.

- Find out the unique and nonunique lines with **uniq**.
- Change, delete, or squeeze individual characters with **tr**.
- Combine these commands to perform content manipulating tasks in a special examples section.

10.1   pr: **Paginating Files**

The **pr** command prepares a file for printing by adding suitable headers, footers, and formatted text. When used with a filename as argument, **pr** doesn't behave like a filter:

```
$ pr group1
May 06 10:38 1999   group1              Page 1
root:x:0:root                                          These seven lines are the original
bin:x:1:root,bin,daemon                                contents of group1
users:x:200:henry,image,enquiry
adm:x:25:adm,daemon,listen
dialout:x:18:root,henry
lp:x:19:lp
ftp:x:50:
... blank lines ...
```

pr adds five lines of margin at the top (simplified here) and five at the bottom. The header shows the date and time of last modification of the file, along with the filename and page number. We generally don't use **pr** like this. Rather, we use it as a "preprocessor" to impart cosmetic touches to text files before they are sent to the printer:

```
$ pr group1 | lp
Request id is 334
```

Since **pr** output often lands up in the hard copy, **pr** and **lp** form a common pipeline sequence. Sometimes, **lp** itself uses **pr** to format the output, in which case this piping is not required.

10.1.1   pr Options

The important options to **pr** are listed in Table 10.1. The $-k$ option (where k is an integer) prints in k columns. If a program outputs a series of 20 numbers, one in each line, then this option can make good use of the screen's empty spaces. Let's use **pr** as a filter this time by supplying its input from the standard output of another program:

```
$ a.out | pr -t -5
0          4          8          12         16
1          5          9          13         17
2          6          10         14         18
3          7          11         15         19
```

The -t option suppresses headers and footers. If you are not using this option, then you can use the -h option (followed by a string) to have a header of your choice. There are some more options that programmers will find useful:

TABLE 10.1 *Options to the* **pr** *Command*

Option	Significance
-l *n*	Sets length of page to *n* lines
-w *n*	Sets width of page to *n* characters
-h *stg*	Sets header for every page to string *stg*
-n	Numbers lines in output
-o *n*	Offsets output by *n* spaces
-d	Double-spaces output
-*k*	Produces output in *k* columns
+*k*	Starts printing from page *k*
-t	Eliminates headers, footers, and margins totally

- -d   Double-spaces input, reduces clutter.
- -n   Numbers lines, which helps in debugging code.
- -o *n*   Offsets lines by *n* spaces, increases left margin of page.

Combine these various options to produce just the format you require:

```
$ pr -t -n -d -o 10 group1
            1    root:x:0:root
            2    bin:x:1:root,bin,daemon
            3    users:x:200:henry,image,enquiry
            4    adm:x:25:adm,daemon,listen
      .......
```

There's one option that uses a number prefixed by a + to print from a specific page number. Another option (-l) sets the page length:

```
pr +10 chap01                                Starts printing from page 10
pr -l 54 chap01                                   Page set to 54 lines
```

Note

For numbering lines, you can also use the **nl** command *(not covered in this edition)*. It's easier to use **nl foo** than **pr -t -n foo**.

10.2 Comparing Files

You'll often need to compare two files. They could be identical, in which case you may want to delete one of them. Two configuration files may have small differences, and knowledge of these differences could help you understand why one system behaves differently from another. UNIX supports three commands—**cmp**, **diff**, and **comm**—that compare two files and present their differences.

For illustrating the use of these three commands, we'll use two files, group1 and group2, which have minor differences between them. We have used group1 with **pr**, but Fig. 10.1 shows them side-by-side. If you have a problem that requires comparison

FIGURE 10.1   *Two Files,* group1 *and* group2*, Having Some Differences*

```
$ cat group1                        $ cat group2
root:x:0:root                       root:x:0:root
bin:x:1:root,bin,daemon             bin:x:1:root,bin,daemon
users:x:200:henry,image,enquiry     users:x:100:henry,image,enquiry
adm:x:25:adm,daemon,listen          adm:x:25:adm,daemon,listen
dialout:x:18:root,henry             dialout:x:19:root,henry
lp:x:19:lp                          lp:x:18:lp
ftp:x:50:                           ftp:x:50:
                                    cron:x:16:cron
```

of two sets of data, then your imagination needs to be at work here. By looking at the output of these commands, you have to figure out which command best applies to the situation.

These files have the structure of /etc/group, the file that holds both the numeric and string component of the user's group-id. This file is examined in Chapter 19, but you have seen information from this file displayed by **ls -l**. The inode stores the numeric group-id of a file, and **ls** displays the name component by looking up /etc/group.

10.3   cmp: **Byte-by-byte Comparison**

cmp makes a comparison of each byte of two files and terminates the moment it encounters a difference:

```
$ cmp group1 group2
group1 group2 differ: char 47, line 3
```

cmp echoes the location of the first mismatch to the screen. By default, **cmp** doesn't bother about possible subsequent mismatches, but you can obtain a list of them using -l:

```
$ cmp -l group[12]                                       Using a wild card
    47   62   61
   109   70   71
   128   71   70
cmp: EOF on group1                                       group1 finishes first
```

There are three differences up to the point the end-of-file is encountered in either file. Character number 47 has the ASCII octal values 62 and 61 in the two files. This output is generally of not much use, but **cmp** is also a filter, so you can use it with **wc** to count the number of differences rather than list their details:

```
$ cmp -l group? | wc -l
3                                                        3 differences until EOF
```

If the two files are identical, **cmp** displays no message but simply returns the prompt. You can try it with a file and its copy:

```
$ cp group1 group1.bak ; cmp group1 group1.bak
$ _                                              No output—files identical
```

This behavior will interest shell programmers because comparison with **cmp** returns a *true* exit status *(8.8)* when the files are identical and *false* otherwise. This information can be subsequently used in a shell script to control the flow of a program. The **cmp** command is also an unusual filter in that it needs two sources of input (here, two files), and at most one of them can come from standard input. See the example in Section 10.13.3 to know how **comm** uses the - to signify standard input; **cmp** behaves likewise.

10.4   comm: **What Is Common?**

While **cmp** compares two files character by character, **comm** compares them line by line and displays the common and differing lines. Also, **comm** requires both files to be sorted. By default, it displays in three columns:

Column 1   Lines unique to the first file.
Column 2   Lines unique to the second file.
Column 3   Lines common (hence its name) to both files.

The files group1 and group2 are not sorted, so let's **sort** them first and then use **comm** with the sorted files:

```
$ sort group1 > group1.sorted ; sort group2 > group2.sorted
$ comm group[12].sorted
                adm:x:25:adm,daemon,listen          These two lines are
                bin:x:1:root,bin,daemon             common to both files
        cron:x:16:cron                              Only in second file
dialout:x:18:root,henry                             Only in first file
        dialout:x:19:root,henry
                ftp:x:50:
        lp:x:18:lp
lp:x:19:lp
                root:x:0:root
        users:x:100:henry,image,enquiry
users:x:200:henry,image,enquiry
```

The **sort** command is discussed in Section 10.10. Note that groups dialout, lp, and users feature in both columns 1 and 2, and you can easily spot the differences between them. You can also understand why the listing sometimes shows a number rather than the name in the group field *(4.9.3)*.

This output provides a good summary to look at but is not of much use to other commands that work on single-column input. **comm** can produce single-column output using the options -1, -2, or -3. To drop a particular column, simply use its column number as an option prefix. You can also combine options and display only those lines that are common:

comm -3 foo1 foo2   *Selects lines not common to both files*
comm -13 foo1 foo2   *Selects lines present only in second file*

The last example and one more (that uses the -23 option) has more practical value than you may think. We'll consider an example that uses this command at the end of this chapter.

10.5   diff: **Converting One File to Another**

diff is the third command that can be used to display file differences. Unlike its fellow members, **cmp** and **comm,** it also tells you which lines in one file have to be *changed* to make the two files identical. When used with the same files, it produces a detailed output:

```
$ diff group[12]
3c3                                                          Change line 3 of first file
< users:x:200:henry,image,enquiry                           Change this line
---                                                                               to
> users:x:100:henry,image,enquiry                                               this
5,6c5,6                                                      Change lines 5 to 6
< dialout:x:18:root,henry                                   Replace these two lines
< lp:x:19:lp
---
> dialout:x:19:root,henry                                   with these two
> lp:x:18:lp
7a8                                                         Append after line 7 of first file
> cron:x:16:cron                                                             this line
```

diff uses certain special symbols and **instructions** to indicate the changes that are required to make two files identical. You should understand these instructions as they are used by the **sed** command, one of the most powerful commands on the system.

Each instruction uses an **address** combined with an **action** that is applied to the first file. The instruction 3c3 changes line 3 with one line, which remains line 3 after the change. 7a8 means appending a line after line 7, yielding line number 8 in the second file. Another instruction, 5,6c, changes two lines. Look closely at both files to satisfy yourself that the recommended changes in these lines are sufficient to make the two files identical.

Maintaining Several Versions of a File (-e) diff -e produces a set of instructions only (similar to the above), but these instructions can be used with the **ed** editor (not discussed in this text) to convert one file to the other. This facility saves disk space by letting us store the oldest file in its entirety, and only the changes between consecutive versions. We have a better option of doing that in the *Source Code Control System* (SCCS), but **diff** remains quite useful if the differences are few. SCCS is discussed in Chapter 16.

Tip

If you are simply interested in knowing whether two files are identical or not, use **cmp** without any options.

10.6   head: **Displaying the Beginning of a File**

The **head** command displays the top of the file. By default, it displays the first 10 lines:

```
head group1                                            Shows first 10 lines
```

You can use the -n option (POSIX mandated) to specify a line count and display, say, the first three lines of the file:

```
$ head -n 3 group1                             Or head -3 group1 on some systems
root:x:0:root
bin:x:1:root,bin,daemon
users:x:200:henry,image,enquiry
```

head can be used in imaginative ways. Consider that you are resuming an editing session the next day and find that you are unable to recall the name of the file you last edited. Since **ls -t** displays files in order of their modification time, picking up the first file from the list and using it as an argument to the **vi** editor should do the job. This requires command substitution:

```
vi `ls -t | head -n 1`                           Opens last modified file for editing
```

You can define this as an alias (Table 9.2) in your rc file so that the aliased command is always available for you to use.

   head is often used with the **grep** command *(11.2)* to restrict the display to a few lines. The following sequence picks up the first five lines containing the string GIF after the words IMG SRC:

```
grep "IMG SRC.*GIF" quote.html | head -n 5
```

The *regular expression* .* used in the quoted string signifies any number of characters. Here, it implies that there can be anything between SRC and GIF (even nothing at all).

Linux

Picking Up Bytes Rather Than Lines

While POSIX requires only **tail** to handle characters, GNU **head** can do that too. It also picks up data in chunks of blocks, kilobytes, and megabytes. So, if **cmp** didn't quite tell you where the forty-seventh character is located, the -c option will show you exactly where the discrepancy is:

```
$ head -c47 group1
root:x:0:root
bin:x:1:root,bin,daemon
users:x:2
```

You can pick up data in other units too:

```
head -c 1b shortlist                                          First 512-byte block
head -c 2m README                                                    2 megabytes
```

10.7 tail: Displaying the End of a File

Complementing its **head** counterpart, the **tail** command displays the end of the file. It provides an additional method of addressing lines, and like **head** it displays the last 10 lines when used without arguments. The last three lines are displayed in this way:

```
$ tail -n 3 group1                                       Or use tail -3 group1
dialout:x:18:root,henry
lp:x:19:lp
ftp:x:50:
```

Some versions of UNIX limit the size of the segment that can be extracted by **tail** with the -n option. To get over this problem, you can address lines from the *beginning* of the file instead of the end. The +*count* option allows you to do that, where *count* represents the line number from where the selection should begin. If a file contains 1000 lines, selecting the last 200 implies using

```
tail +801 foo                                 801th line onwards, possible with + symbol
```

10.7.1 tail Options

Monitoring File Growth (-f) Many UNIX programs constantly write to the system's log files as long as they are running. System administrators need to monitor the growth of these files to view the latest messages. **tail** offers the -f (follow) option for this purpose. This is how you can monitor the installation of Oracle by watching the growth of the log file install.log from another terminal:

```
tail -f /oracle/app/oracle/product/8.1/orainst/install.log
```

The prompt doesn't return even after the work is over. With this option, you have to use the interrupt key to abort the process and exit to the shell.

Extracting Bytes Rather Than Lines (-c) POSIX requires **tail** to support the -c option followed by a positive or negative integer depending on whether the extraction is performed relative to the beginning or end of a file. Solaris supports this option only in its XPG4 version, but this is no problem in Linux:

```
tail -c -512 foo                                   Copies last 512 bytes from foo
tail -c +512 foo                          Copies everything after skipping 511 bytes
```

Tip

Use **tail -f** when you run a program that continuously writes to a file, and you want to see how the file is growing. You have to terminate this command with the interrupt key.

10.8 cut: **Slitting a File Vertically**

While **head** and **tail** are used to slice a file horizontally, you can slice a file vertically with the **cut** command. **cut** identifies both columns and fields. We'll take up columns first.

Cutting Columns (-c) To extract specific columns, you need to follow the -c option with a list of column numbers, delimited by a comma. Ranges can also be used using the hyphen. Here's how we extract the first four columns of the group file:

```
$ cut -c1-4 group1                          -c or -f option always required
root
bin:
user
adm:
dial
lp:x
ftp:
```

Note that there should be no whitespace in the column list. Moreover, **cut** uses a special form for selecting a column from the beginning and up to the end of a line:

```
cut -c -3,6-22,28-34,55- foo                      Must be an ascending list
```

The expression 55- indicates column number 55 to the end of the line. Similarly, -3 is the same as 1-3.

Cutting Fields (-f) The -c option is useful for fixed-length lines. Most UNIX files (like /etc/passwd and /etc/group) don't contain fixed-length lines. To extract useful data from these files you'll need to cut fields rather than columns.

   cut uses the tab as the default field delimiter but can also work with a different delimiter. Two options need to be used here— -d for the field delimiter and -f for the field list. This is how you cut the first and third fields:

```
$ cut -d: -f1,3 group1
root:0
bin:1
users:200
adm:25
dialout:18
lp:19
ftp:50
```

When you use the -f option, you shouldn't forget to also use the -d option unless the file has the default delimiter (the tab).

Extracting User List from who Output **cut** can be used to extract the first word of a line by specifying the space as the delimiter. The example used in Section 2.12 now run in tandem with **cut** displays the list of users only:

```
$ who | cut -d" " -f1                           Space is the delimiter
root
romeo
juliet
project
andrew
```

If a user is logged in more than once, you have to do some further processing to display the list with duplicate entries removed. We need to discuss two more filters (**sort** and **uniq**) before that can be achieved.

Note

You must indicate to **cut** whether you are extracting fields or columns. One of the options -f and -c has to be specified. These options are really not optional; one of them is compulsory.

10.9   paste: **Pasting Files**

What you cut with **cut** can be pasted back with **paste**—but vertically rather than horizontally. You can view two files side-by-side by pasting them:

```
paste foo1 foo2
```

Like **cut**, **paste** also uses the -d option to specify the delimiter, which by default is also the tab. **paste** has fewer applications than **cut**. We'll discuss its most important option (-s) which is used to join lines. Consider this address book that contains details of three persons, with three lines for each:

```
$ cat addressbook
barry wood
woodb@yahoo.com
245-690-4004
charles harris
charles_harris@heavens.com
345-865-3209
james wilcocks
james.wilcocks@heavens.com
190-349-0743
```

The -s option joins lines in the same way **vi**'s **J** command does *(5.7.3)*. Using this option on this file (with **paste -s addressbook**) would join all these nine lines to form a single line. This won't be of much use, so we'll learn to use the -d option with multiple delimiters to join three lines at a time.

If we specify the delimiter string as ::\n with -d, the delimiters are used in a circular manner. The first and second lines would be joined with the : as delimiter, and the same would be true for the second and third line. The third and fourth line would be separated by a newline. After the list is exhausted it is reused. This is exactly what we want:

```
$ paste -s -d"::\n" addressbook
barry wood:woodb@yahoo.com:245-690-4004
charles harris:charles_harris@heavens.com:345-865-3209
james wilcocks:james.wilcocks@heavens.com:190-349-0743
```

See how **paste** works with a single file to concatenate lines in a specified manner? Table data is often split with each column on a separate line, and in situations like these **paste** can be very useful.

10.10   sort: **Ordering a File**

Sorting is the ordering of data in ascending or descending sequence. In UNIX, we use the **sort** command to sort complete lines or parts of them by specifying one or more *keys*. Like **cut**, **sort** identifies fields, and it can sort on specified fields. We'll consider the important **sort** options by sorting the file shortlist. This is a text file containing five lines of a personnel database:

```
$ cat shortlist
2233:charles harris  :g.m.      :sales      :12/12/52: 90000
9876:bill johnson    :director :production:03/12/50:130000
5678:robert dylan    :d.g.m.    :marketing :04/19/43: 85000
2365:john woodcock   :director :personnel :05/11/47:120000
5423:barry wood      :chairman :admin      :08/30/56:160000
```

Each line has six fields delimited by a :. The details of an employee are stored in each line. A person is identified by emp-id, name, designation, department, date of birth, and salary (in the same order). The file has been deliberately designed in fixed format for easier readability. (You'll be using an enlarged version of this file in Chapter 11.)

By default, **sort** reorders lines in ASCII collating sequence—whitespace first, then numerals, uppercase letters, and finally lowercase letters:

```
$ sort shortlist
2233:charles harris  :g.m.      :sales      :12/12/52: 90000
2365:john woodcock   :director :personnel :05/11/47:120000
5423:barry wood      :chairman :admin      :08/30/56:160000
5678:robert dylan    :d.g.m.    :marketing :04/19/43: 85000
9876:bill johnson    :director :production:03/12/50:130000
```

TABLE 10.2 sort *Options*

Option	Description
-t*char*	Uses delimiter *char* to identify fields
-k *n*	Sorts on *n*th field
-k *m,n*	Starts sort on *m*th field and ends sort on *n*th field
-k *m.n*	Starts sort on *n*th column of *m*th field
-u	Removes repeated lines
-n	Sorts numerically
-r	Reverses sort order
-f	Folds lowercase to equivalent uppercase (case-insensitive sort)
-m *list*	Merges sorted files in *list*
-c	Checks if file is sorted
-o *flname*	Places output in file *flname*

Here, sorting starts with the first character of each line and proceeds to the next character only when the characters in two lines are identical. Using options, you can alter the default ordering sequence and sort on multiple keys (fields).

10.10.1 sort Options

The important **sort** options are summarized in Table 10.2. In this edition, we'll use the -k (key) POSIX option to identify *keys* (the fields) instead of the +*n* and -*n* forms (where *n* is the field number) that were used in the previous edition. Unlike **cut** and **paste**, **sort** uses a contiguous string of spaces as the default field separator (a single tab in **cut** and **paste**). We'll use the -t option to specify the delimiter.

Sorting on Primary Key (-k) Let's now use the -k option to sort on the second field (name). The option should be -k 2:

```
$ sort -t: -k 2 shortlist
5423:barry wood      :chairman :admin     :08/30/56:160000
9876:bill johnson    :director :production:03/12/50:130000
2233:charles harris  :g.m.     :sales     :12/12/52: 90000
2365:john woodcock   :director :personnel :05/11/47:120000
5678:robert dylan    :d.g.m.   :marketing :04/19/43: 85000
```

The sort order can be reversed with the -r (reverse) option. The following sequence reverses the previous sorting order:

```
$ sort -t: -r -k 2 shortlist
5678:robert dylan    :d.g.m.   :marketing :04/19/43: 85000
2365:john woodcock   :director :personnel :05/11/47:120000
2233:charles harris  :g.m.     :sales     :12/12/52: 90000
9876:bill johnson    :director :production:03/12/50:130000
5423:barry wood      :chairman :admin     :08/30/56:160000
```

sort combines options in a rather unusual way. The previous command sequence could also have been written as:

```
sort -t: -k 2r shortlist
```

Sorting on Secondary Key You can sort on more than one key; i.e., you can provide a secondary key to **sort**. If the primary key is the third field, and the secondary key the second field, then you need to specify for every -k option where the sort ends. This is done in this way:

```
$ sort -t: -k 3,3 -k 2,2 shortlist
5423:barry wood        :chairman :admin      :08/30/56:160000
5678:robert dylan      :d.g.m.   :marketing :04/19/43: 85000
9876:bill johnson      :director :production:03/12/50:130000
2365:john woodcock     :director :personnel :05/11/47:120000
2233:charles harris    :g.m.     :sales      :12/12/52: 90000
```

This sorts the file by designation and name. The -k 3,3 option indicates that sorting starts on the third field and ends on the same field.

Sorting on Columns You can also specify a character position within a field to be the beginning of sort. If you are to sort the file according to the year of birth, then you need to sort on the seventh and eighth column positions within the fifth field:

```
$ sort -t: -k 5.7,5.8 shortlist
5678:robert dylan      :d.g.m.   :marketing :04/19/43: 85000
2365:john woodcock     :director :personnel :05/11/47:120000
9876:bill johnson      :director :production:03/12/50:130000
2233:charles harris    :g.m.     :sales      :12/12/52: 90000
5423:barry wood        :chairman :admin      :08/30/56:160000
```

The -k option also uses the form -k *m.n* where *n* is the character position in the *m*th field. So, -k 5.7,5.8 means that sorting starts on column 7 of the fifth field and ends on column 8.

Numeric Sort (-n) When **sort** acts on numerals, strange things can happen. When you sort the group file on the third field (containing the numeric group-id), you get a curious result:

```
$ sort -t: -k3,3 group1
root:x:0:root
bin:x:1:root,bin,daemon
dialout:x:18:root,henry
lp:x:19:lp
users:x:200:henry,image,enquiry              200 above 25!
adm:x:25:adm,daemon,listen
ftp:x:50:
```

This is probably not what you expected, but the ASCII collating sequence places 200 above 25 (0 has a lower ASCII value than 5). This can be overridden by the -n (numeric) option:

```
$ sort -t: -k3,3 -n group1
root:x:0:root
bin:x:1:root,bin,daemon
dialout:x:18:root,henry
lp:x:19:lp
adm:x:25:adm,daemon,listen
ftp:x:50:
users:x:200:henry,image,enquiry
```

Note

Always use the -n option when you sort a file on a numeric field. If there are other sorting fields that require a plain ASCII sort, then affix an n to the column specification that requires numeric sort—like -k3,3n.

Removing Repeated Lines (-u) The -u (unique) option lets you remove repeated lines from a file. To find out the unique designations that occur in the file, cut out the designation field and pipe it to **sort**:

```
$ cut -d: -f3 shortlist | sort -u | tee desigx.lst
chairman
d.g.m.
director
g.m.
```

We used three commands to solve a text manipulation problem. Here, **cut** selects the third field from shortlist for **sort** to work on.

Merge-sort (-m) When **sort** is used with multiple filenames as arguments, it concatenates them and sorts them collectively. When large files are sorted in this way, performance often suffers. The -m (merge) option can merge two or more files that are sorted individually:

```
sort -m foo1 foo2 foo3
```

This command will run faster than the one used without the -m option only if the three files are sorted.

Saving sort Output (-o) Even though **sort**'s output can be redirected to a file, we can use its -o option to specify the output filename. Curiously, the input and output filenames can even be the same:

```
sort -o sortedlist -k 3 shortlist           Output stored in sortedlist
sort -o shortlist shortlist                 Output stored in same file
```

We'll need to use **sort** in all the three examples that feature at the end of this chapter.

Commit to memory the default delimiter used by **cut**, **paste**, and **sort**. **cut** and **paste** use the tab, but **sort** uses a contiguous string of spaces as a single delimiter.

10.11   uniq: **Locate Repeated and Nonrepeated Lines**

When you concatenate or merge files, you'll face the problem of duplicate entries creeping in. You saw how **sort** removes them with the -u option. UNIX offers a special tool to handle these lines—the **uniq** command. Consider a sorted file dept.lst that includes repeated lines:

$ cat dept.lst
```
01:accounts:6213
01:accounts:6213
02:admin:5423
03:marketing:6521
03:marketing:6521
03:marketing:6521
04:personnel:2365
05:production:9876
06:sales:1006
```

uniq simply fetches one copy of each line and writes it to the standard output:

$ uniq dept.lst
```
01:accounts:6213
02:admin:5423
03:marketing:6521
04:personnel:2365
05:production:9876
06:sales:1006
```

Since **uniq** requires a sorted file as input, the general procedure is to sort a file and pipe its output to **uniq**. The following pipeline also produces the same output, except that the output is saved in a file:

```
sort dept.lst | uniq - uniqlist
```

uniq is indeed unique; when provided with two filenames as arguments, **uniq** reads the first file and writes to the second. Here, it reads from standard input and writes to uniqlist.

10.11.1   uniq Options

To select unique lines, it's preferable to use **sort -u** which does the job with a single command. But **uniq** has a few useful options that can be used to make simple database queries.

Selecting the Nonrepeated Lines (-u) The -u option selects the unique lines in input—lines that are not repeated:

```
$ uniq -u dept.1st
02:admin:5423
04:personnel:2365
05:production:9876
06:sales:1006
```

Selecting the Duplicate Lines (-d) The -d (duplicate) option selects only one copy of the repeated lines:

```
$ uniq -d dept.1st
01:accounts:6213
03:marketing:6521
```

Counting Frequency of Occurrence (-c) The -c (count) option displays the frequency of occurrence of all lines, along with the lines:

```
$ uniq -c dept.1st
2 01:accounts:6213
1 02:admin:5423
3 03:marketing:6521
1 04:personnel:2365
1 05:production:9876
1 06:sales:1006
```

This is an extremely useful option, and it is often used in tandem with **sort** to count occurrences. Consider the file shortlist where the third field represents the designation. To determine the number of people having the same designation, first cut out the third field with **cut**, sort it, and then run **uniq -c** to produce a count:

```
$ cut -d: -f3 shortlist | sort | uniq -c
   1 chairman
   1 d.g.m.
   2 director
   1 g.m.
```

Later, you'll find how **perl** and **awk** also handle this situation using their own resources. However, they require more code to do the same job. The second application *(10.13.2)* in our special examples section uses this feature to print a *word-count* list.

Caution

Like **sort**, **uniq** also accepts the output filename as an argument, but without using an option (unlike -o in **sort**). If you use **uniq foo1 foo2**, **uniq** simply processes foo1 and overwrites foo2 with its output. Never use **uniq** with two filenames unless you know what you are doing.

▬ 10.12   tr: **Translating Characters**

So far, the commands have been handling either entire lines or fields. The **tr** (translate) filter manipulates individual characters in a line. More specifically, it translates characters using one or two compact expressions:

tr *options expression1 expression2 standard input*

Note that **tr** *takes input only from standard input; it doesn't take a filename as argument.* By default, it translates each character in *expression1* to its mapped counterpart in *expression2*. The first character in the first expression is replaced with the first character in the second expression, and similarly for the other characters.

Let's use **tr** to replace the **:** with a ~ (tilde) and the **/** with a -. Simply specify two expressions containing these characters in the proper sequence:

```
$ tr ':/' '~-' < shortlist  | head -n 3
2233~charles harris  ~g.m.     ~sales      ~12-12-52~ 90000
9876~bill johnson     ~director ~production~03-12-50~130000
5678~robert dylan     ~d.g.m.   ~marketing ~04-19-43~ 85000
```

Note that the lengths of the two expressions should be equal. If they are not, the longer expression will have unmapped characters (not in Linux). Single quotes are used here because no variable evaluation or command substitution is involved. It's just as easy to define the two expressions as two separate variables, and then evaluate them in double quotes:

```
exp1=':/' ; exp2='~-'
tr "$exp1" "$exp2" < shortlist
```

As with wild cards, **tr** also accepts ranges in the expressions. Special characters also need to be escaped.

Changing Case of Text   Since **tr** doesn't accept a filename as argument, the input has to be redirected from a file or a pipe. The following sequence changes the case of the first three lines from lower to upper:

```
$ head -n 3 shortlist | tr '[a-z]' '[A-Z]'
2233:CHARLES HARRIS  :G.M.     :SALES      :12/12/52: 90000
9876:BILL JOHNSON     :DIRECTOR :PRODUCTION:03/12/50:130000
5678:ROBERT DYLAN     :D.G.M.   :MARKETING :04/19/43: 85000
```

Reversing the two expressions will convert case from upper to lower. **tr** is often used to change the case of a file's contents.

Using ASCII Octal Values and Escape Sequences   Like **echo**, **tr** also supports the use of octal values and escape sequences to represent characters. This facility allows us to use nonprintable characters (like LF) in the expression. So, to have each field on a separate line, replace the **:** with the LF character (octal value 012):

```
$ tr ':' '\012' < shortlist | head -n 6          You can use \n
2233                                             instead of \012
charles harris
g.m.
sales
12/12/52
90000
```

If you reverse the two expressions, you'll make the newline character visible.

10.12.1   tr Options

Deleting Characters (-d) The file shortlist has delimited fields and the date formatted in readable form with a /. In nondatabase setups, delimiters are not used, and the date is generally represented as a six-character field in the format *mmddyy*. To convert this file to the traditional format, use the -d (delete) option to delete the characters : and / from the file. The following command does it for the first three lines:

```
$ tr -d ':/' < shortlist | head -n 3
2233charles harris  g.m.      sales      121252 90000
9876bill johnson    director  production031250130000
5678robert dylan    d.g.m.    marketing  041943 85000
```

Compressing Multiple Consecutive Characters (-s) UNIX tools work best with fields rather than columns (as above), so it's preferable to use files with delimited fields. In that case, lines need not be of fixed length; you can eliminate all redundant spaces with the -s (squeeze) option, which squeezes multiple consecutive occurrences of its argument to a single character. We can then have compressed output with lines in free format:

```
$ tr -s ' ' <shortlist | head -n 3
2233:charles harris :g.m. :sales :12/12/52: 90000
9876:bill johnson :director :production:03/12/50:130000
5678:robert dylan :d.g.m. :marketing :04/19/43: 85000
```

Tip

Unless you are using **awk**, you can use **tr -s** to compress all contiguous spaces in the output of several UNIX commands and then use **cut** to extract individual fields from this compressed output. For instance, you can cut out any field from the listing. Some of the questions at the end of the chapter expect you to perform this compression.

Complementing Values of Expression (-c) Finally, the -c (complement) option complements the set of characters in the expression. Thus, to delete all characters except the : and /, you can combine the -d and -c options:

```
$ tr -cd ':/' < shortlist
::::://:::::://:::::://:::::://:::::://:$ _
```

Unusual output indeed! **tr** has deleted all characters except the : and the / from its input. The appearance of the prompt at the immediate end of output shows that the newline character has also not been spared. Any idea how to find out the number of times a specific character occurs in a stream?

Study these **tr** options closely, and you'll discover many areas where you can apply them. We'll be using some of the **tr** options in Section 10.13.

10.13   Applying the Filters

You have now arrived at the examples section, well-armed with knowledge of the basic UNIX filters. There are another four that we have yet to cover (**grep**, **sed**, **awk**, and **perl**), but the ones we know already can do a lot of work for us. In this section, we'll develop three pipeline sequences to solve content manipulating tasks. You need to put in a great deal of effort to accomplish these tasks using procedural languages like C and Java.

10.13.1   Listing the Five Largest Files in the Current Directory

The **ls -l** command shows the file size in the listing, but **ls** has no option to order them by size. We have to use a combination of filters to perform the task of listing the five largest files in the current directory. Fig. 10.2 shows the listing that we'll use as input. We'll have to ignore the first output line and order the list in reverse numeric sequence on the fifth field. We'll print simply two fields: the filename and size.

The delimiter in the listing is a contiguous series of space characters. This is the default delimiter of **sort**, but not of **cut** (being a tab). Before using **cut**, we have to use **tr** to compress contiguous whitespace to a single space. This job requires a pipeline so let's progressively build it:

1.   Reverse sort this space-delimited output in numeric sequence on the fifth field. This requires the use of the -n and -r options of **sort**:

    ls -l | sort -k 5 -nr

FIGURE 10.2   *Listing Used as Input to List Five Largest Files*

```
$ ls -l
total 20896
-rw-------   1 sumit    sumit     165143 Jul 12 11:59 PKI.pdf
-rw-rw-r--   1 sumit    sumit      36506 Jul 14 10:40 UsingSCCS.html
-rw-------   1 sumit    sumit     163381 Jul 11 18:28 adv_bsd_ipc-tutorial.ps
-rw-rw-r--   1 sumit    sumit    8089286 Jul 10 20:04 bec.ps
-rw-------   1 sumit    sumit      76083 Jul 11 18:26 bsd_sockets.pdf
-rw-------   1 sumit    sumit    5518553 Jul 11 22:21 cgi_tvcc.pdf
-rw-------   1 sumit    sumit    5598592 Aug 25 15:53 nowsms.exe
-rw-------   1 sumit    sumit     979367 Jul 10 21:30 putty.zip
-rw-------   1 sumit    sumit      43984 Jul 11 20:43 rcs.ps.gz
-rw-------   1 sumit    sumit      26665 Jul 11 20:42 sccs_allman.ps.gz
-rw-rw-r--   1 sumit    sumit     167690 Jul 17 21:07 sedfaq.txt
```

2. Extract the first five lines from the sorted output:

```
ls -l | sort -k 5 -nr | head -n 5
```

3. Squeeze multiple spaces to a single space:

```
ls -l | sort -k 5 -nr | head -n 5 | tr -s " "
```

4. Cut the fifth and last fields:

```
ls -l | sort -k 5 -nr | head -n 5 | tr -s " " |  cut -d" " -f5,9
```

The output now shows the five largest files in the current directory in the form *filesize filename*:

```
$ ls -l | sort -k 5 -nr | head -n 5 | tr -s " " |  cut -d" " -f5,9
8089286 bec.ps
5598592 nowsms.exe
5518553 cgi_tvcc.pdf
979367 putty.zip
167690 sedfaq.txt
```

Piping this output to the **printf** command will let us format the output, and, using **awk**, we can even have a total count of the size. We'll have to wait till Chapter 12 before we can do that.

10.13.2 Creating a Word-Usage List

Document authors sometimes like to see the words they use along with the frequency of their occurrence. For this to be possible, each word has to be placed in a separate line. **tr** can do that by converting all spaces and tabs (octal 011) to newlines:

```
tr "□\011" "\012\012" < foo1                                    Space is \040
```

There's a space before \011; we won't be displaying the symbol subsequently. If we define a word as a contiguous group of alphabetic characters, we have to use **tr** again to delete all nonalphabetic characters (apart from the newline) from the output of the first **tr** command. This requires the use of the complementary (-c) and delete (-d) options:

```
tr " \011" "\012\012" < foo1 | tr -cd "[a-zA-Z\012]"
```

You now have a list of words, with each word on a separate line. Now, sort this output and pipe it to **uniq -c**:

```
$ tr " \011" "\012\012" < foo1 | tr -cd "[a-zA-Z\012]" | sort | uniq -c
     32 Apache
     18 DNS
     10 Directory
     16 FQDN
     25 addresses
     56 directory
```

You had to use four commands to display the word count. You'll need two more commands to sort the list in reverse numeric sequence and print it in three columns:

```
$ tr " \011" "\012\012" < foo1 | tr -cd "[a-zA-Z\012]" | sort | uniq -c \
> sort -nr | pr -t -3
      56 directory              25 addresses              16 FQDN
      32 Apache                 18 DNS                     10 Directory
```

For the sake of readability, we split the command line into two lines by using \ to escape the *[Enter]* key.

10.13.3   Finding Out the Difference between Two Password Files

When moving a set of users to another machine, the file the system administrator needs most is /etc/passwd of both machines. Some users may already have accounts on these machines, but some have to be created. These files often have hundreds of lines, but we'll work with smaller versions:

```
$ cat passwd1
joe:!:501:100:joe bloom:/home/henry:/bin/ksh
amadeus:x:506:100::/home/amadeus:/bin/ksh
image:!:502:100:The PPP server account:/home/image:/usr/bin/ksh
bill:!:503:100:Reader's Queries:/home/bill:/bin/sh
juliet:x:508:100:juliet:/home/julie:/bin/csh
charlie:x:520:100::/home/charlie:/usr/bin/ksh
romeo:x:601:100::/home/romeo:/usr/bin/ksh
ftp:x:602:50:anonymous ftp:/home/ftp:/bin/csh
$ cat passwd2
henry:!:501:100:henry blofeld:/home/henry:/bin/ksh
amadeus:x:506:100::/home/amadeus:/bin/ksh
image:!:502:100:The PPP server account:/home/image:/usr/bin/ksh
bill:!:503:100:Reader's Queries:/home/bill:/bin/sh
julie:x:508:100:julie andrews:/home/julie:/bin/csh
jennifer:x:510:100:jennifer jones:/home/jennifer:/bin/bash
charlie:x:520:100::/home/charlie:/usr/bin/ksh
romeo:x:601:100::/home/romeo:/usr/bin/ksh
harry:x:602:100:harry's music house:/home/harry:/bin/csh
```

Each file serves a group of users (the first field), but what concerns us is locating those users in the first file who don't have a presence in the second file. Let's first cut out the first field of passwd1 and save the sorted output:

```
cut -f1 -d: passwd1 | sort > temp
```

We *could* perform a similar exercise with the second file too:

```
cut -d: -f1 passwd2 | sort > temp2
```

We now have to compare these two files with **comm -23**. Since these commands are also filters, we should be able to do this part of the job in one invocation without creating the temporary file temp2:

```
$ cut -d: -f1 passwd2 | sort | comm -23 temp - ; rm temp
ftp
joe
juliet
```

comm -23 lists only those lines that are in the first file, and the - symbol ensured that the output from **sort** was supplied as standard input. The list shows three users for whom the administrator has to create accounts with the **useradd** command. Since the administrator is an expert shell programmer, she'll use a script to do this job automatically!

Pipelining represents one of the most important aspects of the UNIX system. It implements the UNIX philosophy that difficult jobs can be done by combining filters that do simple jobs in isolation. The UNIX manual doesn't tell you the combinations of filters required for each task, and this makes pipelines difficult to conceive initially. A lot is left to knowledge of these filters, perseverance, and imagination.

SUMMARY

The **pr** command formats input to print headers and page numbers but can also drop them (-t). The output can be numbered (-n), doublespaced (-d), and offset from the left (-o).

We discussed three file comparison utilities. **cmp** tells you where the first difference was encountered. **comm** shows the lines that are common and optionally shows you lines unique to either or both *sorted* files. **diff** lists file differences as a sequence of instructions.

head displays the beginning of a file, while **tail** displays the end. Unlike **head**, **tail** can also be used with a line number (with the + option) from where extraction should begin. It is most useful in monitoring the growth of a file (-f).

cut selects columns (-c) from its input, as well as fields (-f). The field numbers have to be a comma-delimited sequence of ascending numbers with hyphens to denote ranges.

You can join two files laterally with **paste**. By using the delimiter in a circular manner, **paste** can join multiple lines into one.

With **sort**, you can sort on one or more fields or keys (-k), and columns within these fields. You can sort numerically (-n), reverse the sort order (-r), make a case-insensitive sort (-f), merge two sorted files (-m), and remove repeated lines (-u).

uniq removes repeated lines, but can also select them as well as nonrepeated lines. The command is often combined with **sort** which orders the input first.

tr translates characters using two expressions, but only accepts standard input. It can be used to change the case of letters. You can compress multiple consecutive occurrences (-s) and delete a specific character (-d). You can also use it with ASCII octal values and escape sequences to transform nonprintable characters.

SELF-TEST

Some questions use the file shortlist *whose contents are shown in Section 10.10.*

10.1 How will you (i) doublespace a file, (ii) produce a list of all files in the current directory without headers but in three columns?

10.2 How will you display only the lines common to two files?

10.3 The command **cmp foo1 foo2** displays nothing. What does that indicate?

10.4 How does **head** display its output when used with multiple filenames?

10.5 How do you display the **ps** output without the header line?

10.6 How do you display the length of the first line of shortlist in a message used with the **echo** statement?

10.7 A program, a.out, continuously writes to a file. How do you run the program so that you can monitor the growth of this file from the *same* terminal?

10.8 Explain why this command won't work: cut -d: -c1 -f2 foo.

10.9 Devise a sequence to reset the PATH variable so that the first directory is removed from its list.

10.10 How will you save only the year from the **date** output in a variable?

10.11 Write a **sort** sequence to order shortlist on the month of birth.

10.12 Produce from shortlist a list of the birth years along with the number of people born in that year.

10.13 Generate a numbered code list for the departments in shortlist in the form *code_number code_description* (like 1 admin).

10.14 How do you remove repeated lines from an unsorted file where the repeated lines are (i) contiguous, (ii) not contiguous?

10.15 How do you convert the contents of the file shortlist to uppercase?

EXERCISES

10.1 Two lists, foo1 and foo2, contain names of users. How do you create a third list of users who are present in foo2 but absent in foo1? When will the command sequence not work properly?

10.2 How do you compare the contents of the file foo with the output of a program named a.out without saving the output to disk?

10.3 How do you select from a file (i) lines 5 to 10, (ii) second-to-last line?

10.4 How will you use **pr**, **sort**, and **cut** to read a file backwards?

10.5 How do you extract the names of the users from /etc/passwd after ignoring the first 10 entries?

10.6 How do you display a list of all processes without the **ps** header line where processes with the same name are grouped together?

10.7 Frame an alias that invokes **vi** with the last modified file in the current directory.

10.8 How do you set the length of a line in shortlist to a variable?

10.9 How will you save the last two digits of the year from the **date** output in a variable?

10.10 How do you display a listing of all directories in the PATH list?

10.11   Devise a **sort** command to order the file /etc/passwd on GID (primary) and
        UID (secondary) so that users with the same GID are placed together. Users
        with a lower UID should be placed higher in the list.

10.12   How do you display the **date** output with each field on a separate line? How do
        you now combine the fields to get back the original output?

10.13   How will you find out the number of times the character ? occurs in a file?

10.14   Run the **script** command, execute a few commands, and then terminate **script**.
        How do you now remove the *[Ctrl-m]* character at the end of most lines?

10.15   List from /etc/passwd the UID and the user having the highest UID.

10.16   You have two files, foo1 and foo2, copied from /etc/passwd on two machines.
        Specify the steps needed to print a list of users who are (i) present in foo1 but
        not in foo2, (ii) present in foo2 but not in foo1, (iii) present in both files.

10.17   Assuming that a user may be logged in more than once, how do you (i) list only
        those users, (ii) mail root a sorted list of all users currently logged in, where a
        user is listed only once?

10.18   How are these two commands similar and different? sort -u foo ; uniq foo

10.19   A feature provided in a user's startup file appends the output of the **date** command
        to a file foo whenever a user logs in. How can the user print a report showing the
        day along with the number of times she logged in on that day?

10.20   Devise a pipeline sequence to display a count of the processes on your system in
        the form *count process_name*.

10.21   You need to replicate a directory structure bar1 to an *empty* structure bar2,
        where both directories are at the same hierarchical level.
        (i)   Describe the sequence of steps needed to achieve this.
        (ii)   How do you verify that the directory structures are identical?
        (iii) Describe three situations when the sequence won't work properly.
        (HINT: You need to use **find**, but its output is not sorted.)

## CHAPTER 11

Filters Using Regular Expressions—grep and sed

You often need to search a file for a pattern, either to see the lines containing (or not containing) it or to have it replaced with something else. This chapter discusses two important filters that are specially suited for these tasks—**grep** and **sed**. The **grep** command takes care of all of the search requirements you may have. **sed** goes further and can even manipulate the individual characters in a line. In fact, **sed** can do several things, some of them quite well.

This chapter also takes up one of the fascinating features of UNIX—*regular expressions*. When discussing **more**, **vi**, and **emacs**, we observed that the search patterns in those programs can also take on special expressions. In this chapter, you'll see regular expressions in all their manifestations. These discussions should prepare you well for **awk** (Chapter 12) and **perl** (Chapter 15) because they too use these expressions.

Objectives

- Use **grep** to search a file for a pattern and display both matching and nonmatching lines.
- Learn the various **grep** options to display a count, line numbers, or filenames.
- Understand the concept of a *regular expression* as a mechanism for matching multiple similar patterns.
- Learn the significance of the characters of the *Basic Regular Expression* (BRE) set.
- Learn the significance of the characters of the *Extended Regular Expression* (ERE) set.
- Use **sed** to edit an input stream and understand its addressing mechanism.
- Understand the *substitution* feature and how it is enhanced when used with regular expressions.
- Learn the significance of the *repeated* and *remembered* patterns.
- Use the *interval regular expression* (IRE) to locate or replace patterns at specific locations.
- Use the *tagged regular expression* (TRE) to use *part* of the source pattern in the target pattern.
- Use the IRE and TRE to perform content manipulating tasks in a special examples section.

▰ 11.1 The Sample Database

In this chapter and in the ones dealing with **awk** and shell programming, you'll often refer to the file emp.lst. Sometimes, you'll use another file or two derived from it. Let's take a close look at the file and understand the organization:

```
$ cat emp.lst
2233:charles harris  :g.m.      :sales     :12/12/52: 90000
9876:bill johnson    :director :production:03/12/50:130000
5678:robert dylan    :d.g.m.    :marketing :04/19/43: 85000
2365:john woodcock   :director :personnel :05/11/47:120000
5423:barry wood      :chairman :admin     :08/30/56:160000
1006:gordon lightfoot:director :sales     :09/03/38:140000
6213:michael lennon  :g.m.      :accounts  :06/05/62:105000
1265:p.j. woodhouse  :manager  :sales     :09/12/63: 90000
4290:neil o'bryan    :executive:production:09/07/50: 65000
2476:jackie wodehouse:manager  :sales     :05/01/59:110000
6521:derryk o'brien  :director :marketing :09/26/45:125000
3212:bill wilcocks   :d.g.m.    :accounts  :12/12/55: 85000
3564:ronie trueman   :executive:personnel :07/06/47: 75000
2345:james wilcox    :g.m.      :marketing :03/12/45:110000
0110:julie truman    :g.m.      :marketing :12/31/40: 95000
```

The first five lines of this file were used as the file shortlist in the section on **sort** *(10.10)*. The significance of the fields have also been explained there, but we'll recount them just the same. This is a fixed-format text file containing 15 lines of a personnel database. There are six colon-delimited fields—emp-id, name, designation, department, date of birth, and salary.

▰ 11.2 grep: Searching for a Pattern

UNIX has a special family of commands for handling search requirements, and the principal member of this family is the **grep** command. **grep** scans its input for a pattern, and can display the selected pattern, the line numbers, or the filenames where the pattern occurs. The command uses the following syntax:

grep *options pattern filename(s)*

grep searches for *pattern* in one or more *filename(s),* or the standard input if no filename is specified. The first argument (barring the option) is the pattern, and the ones remaining are filenames. Let's use **grep** to display lines containing the string sales from the sample database, emp.lst:

```
$ grep "sales" emp.lst
2233:charles harris  :g.m.      :sales     :12/12/52: 90000
1006:gordon lightfoot:director :sales     :09/03/38:140000
1265:p.j. woodhouse  :manager  :sales     :09/12/63: 90000
2476:jackie wodehouse:manager  :sales     :05/01/59:110000
```

Because **grep** is also a filter, it can search its standard input for the pattern and store the output in a file:

```
who | grep henry > foo
```

When **grep** is used with multiple filenames, it displays the filenames along with the output. In the next example, **grep** searches two files. Don't bother about what they contain; just observe how each line is preceded by the filename:

```
$ grep "director" emp1.lst emp2.lst
emp1.lst:1006:gordon lightfoot:director :sales     :09/03/38:140000
emp1.lst:6521:derryk o'brien  :director :marketing :09/26/45:125000
emp2.lst:9876:bill johnson    :director :production:03/12/50:130000
emp2.lst:2365:john woodcock   :director :personnel :05/11/47:120000
```

To suppress the filenames, you can use **cut** to select all but the first field using **grep** as its input. Alternatively, you can also make **grep** ignorant of the source of its input by using **cat emp[12].lst | grep "director"**.

11.2.1 Quoting in grep

Though we have used the pattern both with ("sales") and without quotes (henry), it's always safe to quote the pattern. Quoting is essential if the search string consists of more than one word or uses any of the shell's characters like *, $, and so on. Let's use a two-word string both within and without quotes:

```
$ grep gordon lightfoot emp.lst
grep: lightfoot: No such file or directory
emp.lst:1006:gordon lightfoot:director :sales     :09/03/38:140000
$ _
$ grep 'gordon lightfoot' emp.lst
1006:gordon lightfoot:director :sales     :09/03/38:140000
```

In the first example, lightfoot was interpreted as a filename, but **grep** could locate gordon in emp.lst. We used single quotes here, but this technique won't do if we use **grep** to locate neil o'bryan from the file. Recall that double quotes protect single quotes:

```
$ grep 'neil o'bryan' emp.lst
> [Ctrl-c]                                          Shell's PS2 at work here
$ grep "neil o'bryan" emp.lst
4290:neil o'bryan    :executive:production:09/07/50: 65000
```

When quoting patterns, the shells of the Bourne family issue a > if the closing quote is absent in the line. The C shell simply outputs the error message Unmatched '.

Note

Quote the pattern used with **grep** if it contains multiple words or special characters that can be interpreted otherwise by the shell. You can generally use either single or double quotes. However, if the special characters in the pattern require command substitution or variable evaluation to be performed, you must use double quotes.

11.2.2 When grep Fails

Like **cmp**, **grep** can also behave silently. It simply returns the prompt when the pattern can't be located:

```
$ grep president emp.lst
$ _                                              president not found
```

There's more to it here than meets the eye. The command *failed* because the string president couldn't be located. Though the feature of scanning a file for a pattern is available in both **sed** and **awk**, these commands are not considered to fail if they can't locate a pattern. **find** also doesn't fail if no file is found.

Don't, however, draw the wrong conclusion from the above behavioral pattern of **grep**. The silent return of the shell prompt is no evidence of failure. In fact, the silent behavior of **cmp** denotes success. Success or failure is denoted by the *exit status (8.5)* that is stored in a special variable ($?) when a command has finished execution. The **if** conditional and **while** loop test this exit status to control the flow of execution. The exit status will be examined and applied in Chapter 13 featuring shell programming.

11.3 grep **Options**

grep is one of the most important UNIX commands, and you must know the options that POSIX requires **grep** to support. Table 11.1 shows the POSIX options. Linux supports all of these options, but Solaris has two versions of **grep** (in /usr/bin and /usr/xpg4/bin), and between them they support all POSIX options.

Ignoring Case (-i) When you look for a name but are not sure of the case, **grep** offers the -i (ignore) option which ignores case for pattern matching:

TABLE 11.1 grep *Options*

Option	Significance
-i	Ignores case for matching
-v	Doesn't display lines matching expression
-n	Displays line numbers along with lines
-c	Displays count of number of occurrences
-l	Displays list of filenames only
-e *exp*	Specifies expression *exp* with this option. Can use multiple times. Also used for matching expression beginning with a hyphen.
-x	Matches pattern with entire line (doesn't match embedded patterns)
-f *file*	Takes patterns from *file*, one per line
-E	Treats pattern as an extended regular expression (ERE)
-F	Matches multiple fixed strings (in **fgrep**-style)
-*n*	Displays line and *n* lines above and below *(Linux only)*
-A *n*	Displays line and *n* lines after matching lines *(Linux only)*
-B *n*	Displays line and *n* lines before matching lines *(Linux only)*

```
$ grep -i 'WILCOX' emp.lst
2345:james wilcox    :g.m.     :marketing :03/12/45:110000
```

Deleting Lines (-v) **grep** can also play an inverse role; the **-v** (inverse) option selects all lines *except* those containing the pattern. Thus, you can create a file otherlist containing all but directors:

```
$ grep -v 'director' emp.lst > otherlist
$ wc -l otherlist
    11 otherlist
```
                                                              There were 4 directors initially

More often than not, when we use **grep -v**, we also redirect its output to a file as a means of getting rid of unwanted lines. Obviously, the lines haven't been deleted from the original file as such.

Note

The -v option removes lines from **grep**'s output, but doesn't actually change the argument file. This option is frequently used with redirection.

Displaying Filenames (-l) Programmers often use the -l (list) option to locate files where a variable or system call has been used. You can easily find out the C programs that use the **fork** system call:

```
$ grep -l  fork *.c
fork.c:    printf("Before fork\n");
fork.c:    pid = fork();                    /* Replicates current process */
orphan.c:   if ((pid = fork()) > 0)    /* Parent */
wait.c:    switch(fork()) {
```

Assuming that the pattern can occur multiple times in a file, can you sort this file list in order of their modification or access time? A variation of this exercise is featured at the end of this chapter.

Matching Multiple Patterns (-e) The -e option has two functions—to match multiple patterns and patterns beginning with a hyphen. Linux supports both functions, but Solaris offers this option only with the XPG4 version. This is how you match multiple patterns by using -e multiple times:

```
$ grep -e woodhouse -e wood -e woodcock emp.lst
2365:john woodcock    :director :personnel :05/11/47:120000
5423:barry wood       :chairman :admin     :08/30/56:160000
1265:p.j. woodhouse   :manager  :sales      :09/12/63: 90000
```

You could question the wisdom of entering such a long command line when the patterns don't differ much from one another. Yes, **grep** supports sophisticated pattern matching techniques that can display the same lines but with a *single* expression. This is the ideal forum for regular expressions to make their entry.

Patterns Beginning with a - (-e) What happens when you look for a pattern that begins with a hyphen? This is how the non-XPG4 version of **grep** on Solaris behaves:

```
$ grep "-mtime" /var/spool/cron/crontabs/*
grep: illegal option -- m
grep: illegal option -- t
grep: illegal option -- m
grep: illegal option -- e
Usage: grep -hblcnsviw pattern file . . .
```

grep treats -mtime as a combination of five options of which only one is legitimate (-i); the others are "illegal." To locate such patterns, you must use the -e option:

```
$ grep -e "-mtime" /var/spool/cron/crontabs/*
romeo:55 17 * * 4 find / -name core -mtime +30 -print
```

Don't forget to use the XPG4 version of **grep** when using Solaris. Linux users need not bother.

Tip

How do you use **grep** if you don't know the location of the file to be searched? If you know the directory structure where the file resides, then you can use **find**'s -exec option in tandem with **grep**. The following command locates all C programs in $HOME that contain the line "#include <fcntl.h>":

```
find $HOME -name "*.c" -exec grep -l "#include <fcntl.h>" {} \; > foo
```

This saves the absolute pathnames of the files in foo. To extract the lines as well, use the technique that was discussed as a Tip in Section 7.7:

```
find $HOME -name "*.c" -exec grep "#include <fcntl.h>" {} /dev/null \;
```

This is the power of UNIX!

Printing the Neighborhood   GNU **grep** has a nifty option that locates not only the matching line, but also a certain number of lines above and below it. For instance, you may want to know what went before and after the **foreach** statement that you used in a **perl** script:

```
$ grep -1 "foreach" count.pl                                    One line above and below
print ("Region List\n") ;
foreach $r_code sort (keys(%regionlist)) {
   print ("$r_code : $region{$r_code} : $regionlist{$r_code}\n") ;
```

It is easier to identify the context of a matched line when the immediate neighborhood is also presented. If you need to display more lines on either side, then use the -A and -B options.

■ 11.4 Basic Regular Expressions (BRE)—An Introduction

View the file emp.lst *(11.1)* once again, and you'll find some names spelled in a similar manner—like trueman and truman, wilcocks and wilcox. Locating both truman and trueman without using **grep** twice is a problem:

```
$ grep truman emp.1st
0110:julie truman    :g.m.      :marketing :12/31/40: 95000
```

It's also tedious to specify each pattern separately with the -e option. This is where searches in UNIX become truly remarkable. Using a regular expression, you can locate a "truman" without knowing exactly how the name is spelled.

A **regular expression** uses an elaborate metacharacter set that overshadows the shell's wild cards. **grep** uses this expression to match multiple similar patterns. Unlike wild cards, however, a regular expression is a feature of the *command* that uses it and has nothing to do with the shell. Some of the characters used by regular expressions are also meaningful to the shell—enough reason why these expressions should be quoted.

Regular expressions take care of some common query and substitution requirements. You may want the system to present a list of similar names, so you can select exactly the one you require. Or you may want to replace multiple spaces with a single space, or display lines that begin with a #. You may even be looking for a string at a specific column position in a line. All of this is possible (and much more) with regular expressions as you'll discover in the three rounds of discussions that feature the subject in this chapter.

POSIX identifies regular expressions as belonging to two categories—*basic* and *extended*. **grep** supports **basic regular expressions** (BRE) by default and **extended regular expressions** (ERE) with the -E option. **sed** supports only the BRE set. We'll first start with a minimal treatment of the BRE set (Table 11.2) and then take up the ERE set in the next section. We'll later expand the coverage of the BRE when we discuss **sed**.

Note

Regular expressions are interpreted by the command and not by the shell. Quoting ensures that the shell isn't able to interfere and interpret the metacharacters in its own way.

11.4.1 The Character Class

A regular expression lets you specify a group of characters enclosed within a pair of rectangular brackets, []. The match is then performed for any *single* character in the group. This form resembles the one used by the shell's wild cards. Thus, the expression

[od]   *Either* o *or* d

matches either an o or a d. This property can now be used to match woodhouse and wodehouse. These two patterns differ in their third and fourth character positions—od in one and de in the other. To match these two strings, we'll have to use the model [od][de] which in fact matches all of these four patterns:

od   oe   dd   de

TABLE 11.2   *The Basic Regular Expression (BRE) Character Set Used by* **grep,** **sed,** *and* **awk**

Pattern	Matches
*	Zero or more occurrences of the previous character
.	A single character
[pqr]	A single character p, q, or r
[c1-c2]	A single character within the ASCII range represented by c1 and c2
[^pqr]	A single character which is not a p, q, or r
^pat	Pattern pat at beginning of line
pat$	Pattern pat at end of line
Examples	
g*	Nothing or g, gg, ggg, etc.
gg*	g, gg, ggg, etc.
.*	Nothing or any number of characters
[1-3]	A digit between 1 and 3
[^a-zA-Z]	A nonalphabetic character
bash$	bash at end of line
^bash$	bash as the only word in line
^$	Lines containing nothing

The first and fourth are relevant to the present problem. Using the character class, the regular expression required to match woodhouse and wodehouse should be this:

```
wo[od][de]house
```

Let's use this regular expression with **grep:**

```
$ grep "wo[od][de]house" emp.lst
1265:p.j. woodhouse  :manager   :sales    :09/12/63: 90000
2476:jackie wodehouse:manager   :sales    :05/01/59:110000
```

You can also use ranges in the character class. The pattern [a-zA-Z0-9] matches a single alphanumeric character. However, you can't match an alphabetic character with the expression [A-z] because between Z and a there are a number of other nonalphabetic characters as well (the caret, for example). You can check this with Appendix F.

Negating a Class (^)   Regular expressions use the ^ (caret) to negate the character class, while the shell uses the ! (bang). When the character class *begins* with this character, all characters other than the ones grouped in the class are matched. So, [^a-zA-Z] matches a single nonalphabetic character string.

Note

The character class feature is similar to the one used in wild cards except that negation of the class is done by a ^ (caret), while in the shell it's done by the ! (bang). As with wild cards, the character class is the only way you can negate a single character. For instance, [^p] represents any character other than p.

11.4.2   The *

The * (asterisk) refers to the *immediately preceding* character. However, its interpretation is the trickiest of the lot as it bears absolutely no resemblance whatsoever with the * used by wild cards or DOS (or the * used by Amazon and Ebay in search strings). Here, it indicates that the *previous* character can occur many times, or not at all. The pattern

```
e*
```

matches the single character e, and any number of es. Because the previous character may not occur at all, it also matches a null string. Thus, apart from this null string, it also matches the following strings:

```
e    ee    eee    eeee   .....
```

Mark the key words "zero or more occurrences of the previous character" that are used to describe the significance of the *. Don't make the mistake of using e* to match a string beginning with e; use ee* instead.

Caution

The * of regular expressions has nothing in common with its counterpart in wild cards. The regular expression expression s* indicates that s might not occur at all! C programmers should note that s*printf matches sprintf, ssprintf, sssprintf, and so forth, but it also matches printf because the previous character, s, which the * refers to, may not occur at all.

How do you now match trueman and truman? The first pattern contains an e, while the other pattern doesn't. This means that e may or may not occur at all in the expression, and the regular expression true*man matches the two patterns:

```
$ grep "true*man" emp.1st
3564:ronie trueman    :executive:personnel :07/06/47: 75000
0110:julie truman     :g.m.       :marketing :12/31/40: 95000
```

You don't have to use the -e option twice to get this result. Note that these are not the only strings the expression can match: It would have also matched trueeman had there been such a pattern in the file.

Using both the character class and the *, we can now match wilcocks and wilcox:

```
$ grep "wilco[cx]k*s*" emp.1st
3212:bill wilcocks    :d.g.m.     :accounts   :12/12/55: 85000
2345:james wilcox     :g.m.       :marketing :03/12/45:110000
```

The expression k*s* means that k and s may not occur at all (or as many times as possible); that's why the expression used with **grep** also matches wilcox. You can feel the power of regular expressions here—and how they easily exceed the capabilities of wild cards.

Note

The * in its special sense always refers to the character preceding it, and has significance in a regular expression only if it is preceded by a character. If it's the first character in a regular expression, then it's treated literally (i.e., matches itself).

11.4.3 The Dot

A `.` matches a single character. The shell uses the ? character to indicate that. The pattern

```
2...
```

matches a four-character pattern beginning with a 2. The shell's equivalent pattern is 2????.

The Regular Expression .* The dot along with the * (.*) constitutes a very useful regular expression. It signifies any number of characters, or none. Say, for instance, you are looking for the name `p. woodhouse`, but are not sure whether it actually exists in the file as `p.j. woodhouse`. No problem, just embed the `.*` in the search string:

```
$ grep "p.*woodhouse" emp.1st
1265:p.j. woodhouse :manager    :sales     :09/12/63: 90000
```

Note that if you literally look for the name `p.j. woodhouse`, then the expression should be `p\.j\. woodhouse`. The dots need to be escaped here with the \—the same character you used in the shell for despecializing the next character.

Note

A regular expression match is made for the longest possible string. Thus, when you use the expression 03.*05, it will match 03 and 05 as close to the left and right of the line, respectively.

11.4.4 Specifying Pattern Locations (^ and $)

Most of the regular expression characters are used for matching patterns, but there are two that specify pattern locations. You can specify that a pattern occurs at the beginning or end of a line:

^ — Matches pattern at the beginning of a line.
$ — Matches pattern at the end of a line.

Anchoring a pattern is often necessary when it can occur in more than one place in a line. The expression `2...` doesn't exclusively locate lines where the emp-id begins with 2. You have to use `^2`:

```
$ grep "^2" emp.1st
2233:charles harris  :g.m.      :sales     :12/12/52: 90000
2365:john woodcock    :director :personnel :05/11/47:120000
2476:jackie wodehouse:manager   :sales     :05/01/59:110000
2345:james wilcox     :g.m.     :marketing :03/12/45:110000
```

Similarly, to select those lines where the salary lies between 70,000 and 89,999 dollars, you have to use the $ (nothing to do with the currency) at the end of the pattern:

```
$ grep "[78]....$" emp.1st
5678:robert dylan    :d.g.m.    :marketing :04/19/43: 85000
3212:bill wilcocks   :d.g.m.    :accounts  :12/12/55: 85000
3564:ronie trueman   :executive:personnel :07/06/47: 75000
```

This problem is actually **awk**'s concern, but we can at least understand how the $ behaves when placed at the end of a regular expression.

How can you reverse a previous search and select only those lines where the emp-ids *don't* begin with a 2? You need the expression ^[^2]:

```
grep "^[^2]" emp.lst
```

The two carets here have totally different meanings. The first one anchors the pattern, and the other negates a class.

Listing Only Directories UNIX has no command that lists only directories. However, we can use a pipeline to "grep" those lines from the listing that begin with a d:

```
ls -l | grep "^d"                                          Shows only the directories
```

It's indeed strange that **ls** which supports 20 options has none to display directories! You should convert this into an alias (Table 9.2) or a shell function so that it is always available for you to use.

Identifying Files with Specific Permissions Here's how **grep** can add power to the **ls -l** command. This pipeline locates all files that have write permission for the group:

```
$ ls -l | grep '^.....w'                                   Locates w at sixth position
drwxrw-r-x   3 sumit    dialout     1024  Oct 31 15:16  text
-rwxrw----   1 henry    dialout    22954  Nov  7 08:21  wall.gif
-rw-rw-r--   1 henry    dialout      717  Oct 25 09:36  wall.html
```

This sequence matches a w at the sixth column location—the one that indicates the presence or absence of write permission for the group.

Note

The caret has a triple role to play in regular expressions. When placed at the beginning of a character class (e.g., [^a-z]), it negates every character of the class. When placed outside it, and at the beginning of the expression (e.g., ^2...), the pattern is matched at the beginning of the line. At any other location (e.g., a^b), it matches itself literally.

11.4.5   When Metacharacters Lose Their Meaning

Some of the special characters may actually exist as text. If these characters violate the regular expression rules, their special meanings are automatically turned off. For example, the . and * lose their meanings when placed inside the character class. The * is also matched literally if it's the first character of the expression. Thus, **grep "*"** looks for an asterisk.

Sometimes, you may need to escape these characters. For instance, when looking for a pattern g*, you need to use **grep "g*"**. Similarly, to look for a [, you should use \[, and to look for the literal pattern .*, you should use \.*.

■ **11.5   Extended Regular Expressions (ERE) and** egrep

Extended regular expressions (ERE) make it possible to match dissimilar patterns with a single expression. This set uses some additional characters (Table 11.3), and POSIX-compliant versions of **grep** use them with the -E option. Linux **grep** supports this option, but Solaris users must use **/usr/xpg4/bin/grep** to use EREs. If your version of **grep** doesn't support this option, then use **egrep** but without the -E option.

11.5.1   The + and ?

The ERE set includes two special characters, + and ?. They are often used in place of the * to *restrict* the matching scope:

+ — Matches one or more occurrences of the previous character.
? — Matches zero or one occurrence of the previous character.

What all this means is that b+ matches b, bb, bbb, etc, but it doesn't match nothing—unlike b*. The expression b? matches either a single instance of b or nothing. These characters restrict the scope of match as compared to the *.

In the two "truemans" that exist in the sample database, note that the character e either occurs once or not at all. So, e? is the expression to use here. This time we need to use **grep**'s -E option to use an ERE:

```
$ grep -E "true?man" emp.1st                          Or use egrep
3564:ronie trueman    :executive:personnel :07/06/47: 75000
0110:julie truman     :g.m.        :marketing :12/31/40: 95000
```

The + is a pretty useful character, too. Statements like #include <stdio.h> often appear with multiple spaces between #include and <stdio.h>. To match them all, use the expression #include +<stdio.h> to match the following patterns:

```
#include <stdio.h>    #include  <stdio.h>         #include    <stdio.h>
```

TABLE 11.3   *The Extended Regular Expression (ERE) Set Used by* **grep**, **egrep**, *and* **awk**

Expression	Significance
ch+	Matches one or more occurrences of character *ch*
ch?	Matches zero or one occurrence of character *ch*
exp1 | *exp1*	Matches *exp1* or *exp2*
(*x1*|*x2*)*x3*	Matches *x1x3* or *x2x3*
Examples	
g+	Matches at least one g
g?	Matches nothing or one g
GIF|JPEG	Matches GIF or JPEG
(lock|ver)wood	Matches lockwood or verwood

And if you are not sure whether there's a space between # and include, include the ? in the expression:

```
# ?include +<stdio.h>                          A space before the ?
```

But there could also be tabs instead of spaces, so how does one handle them?

11.5.2 Matching Multiple Patterns (|, (and))

The | is the delimiter of multiple patterns. Using it, we can locate both woodhouse and woodcock without using the -e option twice:

```
$ grep -E 'woodhouse|woodcock' emp.1st
2365:john woodcock    :director :personnel :05/11/47:120000
1265:p.j. woodhouse   :manager  :sales     :09/12/63: 90000
```

The ERE thus handles the problem easily, but offers an even better alternative. The characters, (and), let you group patterns, and when you use the | inside the parentheses, you can frame an even more compact pattern:

```
$ grep -E 'wood(house|cock)' emp.1st
2365:john woodcock    :director :personnel :05/11/47:120000
1265:p.j. woodhouse   :manager  :sales     :09/12/63: 90000
```

EREs when combined with BREs form very powerful regular expressions. For instance, the expression in the following command contains characters from both sets:

```
$ grep -E 'wilco[cx]k*s*|wood(house|cock)' emp.1st
2365:john woodcock    :director :personnel :05/11/47:120000
1265:p.j. woodhouse   :manager  :sales     :09/12/63: 90000
3212:bill wilcocks    :d.g.m.   :accounts  :12/12/55: 85000
2345:james wilcox     :g.m.     :marketing :03/12/45:110000
```

All EREs can also be placed in a file in exactly the same way they are used in the command line. You then have to use **grep** both with the -E and -f options to take the patterns from the file.

Note

If **grep** doesn't support the -E option on your machine, use **egrep** without the -E option for all examples considered in this section.

11.6   sed: **The Stream Editor**

sed is a multipurpose tool which combines the work of several filters. It is derived from **ed**, the original UNIX editor (not discussed in this text). **sed** performs noninteractive operations on a data stream—hence its name. It uses very few options but has a host of features that allow you to select lines and run instructions on them. Learning **sed** will prepare you well for **perl** which uses many of these features.

sed uses **instructions** to act on text. An instruction combines an **address** for selecting lines, with an **action** to be taken on them, as shown by the syntax:

sed *options* '*address action*' *file(s)*

The address and action are enclosed within single quotes. Addressing in **sed** is done in two ways:

- By one or two line numbers (like 3,7).
- By specifying a /-enclosed pattern which occurs in a line (like /From:/).

In the first form, *address* specifies either one line number to select a single line or a set of two (3,7) to select a group of contiguous lines. Likewise, the second form uses one or two patterns. The *action* component is drawn from **sed**'s family of internal commands (Table 11.4). It can either be a simple display (print) or an editing function like insertion, deletion, or substitution of text. The components of a **sed** instruction are shown in Fig. 11.1.

    sed processes several instructions in a sequential manner. Each instruction operates on the output of the previous instruction. In this context, two options are relevant, and most likely they are the only ones you'll use with **sed**—the -e option that lets you use multiple instructions and the -f option to take instructions from a file. Both options are used by **grep** in an identical manner.

T A B L E   11.4   *Internal Commands Used by* **sed**

Command	Description
i, a, c	Inserts, appends, and changes text
d	Deletes line(s)
p	Prints line(s) on standard output
q	Quits after reading up to addressed line
r *flname*	Places contents of file *flname* after line
w *flname*	Writes addressed lines to file *flname*
=	Prints line number addressed
s/*s1*/*s2*/	Replaces first occurrence of expression *s1* in all lines with expression *s2*
s/*s1*/*s2*/g	As above but replaces all occurrences
Examples	
1,4d	Deletes lines 1 to 4
10q	Quits after reading the first 10 lines
3,$p	Prints lines 3 to end (–n option required)
$!p	Prints all lines except last line (–n option required)
/begin/,/end/p	Prints line containing begin through line containing end (–n option required)
10,20s/-/:/	Replaces first occurrence of - in lines 10 to 20 with a :
s/echo/printf/g	Replaces all occurrences of echo in all lines with printf

FIGURE 11.1   *Components of a* **sed** *Instruction*

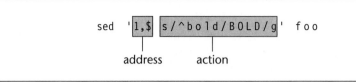

Users of this shell must note that when **sed** is continued in the next line by pressing *[Enter],* the shell generates an error and complains of an "unmatched" quote. As a general rule, escape all lines except the last with a \ to generate the ? prompt. (Some systems, like Solaris, don't display this prompt.) The situations where such escaping is required are pointed out sometimes, but not always.

11.7   Line Addressing

To consider **line addressing** first, the instruction **3q** can be broken down into the address 3 and the action **q** (quit). When this instruction is enclosed within quotes and followed by one or more filenames, you can simulate **head -n 3** in this way:

```
$ sed '3q' emp.lst                                          Quits after line number 3
2233:charles harris  :g.m.      :sales     :12/12/52: 90000
9876:bill johnson    :director :production:03/12/50:130000
5678:robert dylan    :d.g.m.    :marketing :04/19/43: 85000
```

Generally, we'll use the **p** (print) command to display lines. However, this command behaves in a seemingly strange manner: it outputs both the selected lines as well as *all* lines. So the selected lines appear twice. We must suppress this behavior with the -n option, and remember to use this option whenever we use the **p** command. Thus,

```
$ sed -n '1,2p' emp.lst
2233:charles harris  :g.m.      :sales     :12/12/52: 90000
9876:bill johnson    :director :production:03/12/50:130000
```

prints the first two lines. To select the last line of the file, use the $:

```
$ sed -n '$p' emp.lst
0110:julie truman    :g.m.      :marketing :12/31/40: 95000
```

Selecting Lines from Anywhere   The two command invocations above emulate the **head** and **tail** commands, but **sed** can also select a contiguous group of lines from any location. To select lines 9 through 11, use this:

```
sed -n '9,11p' emp.lst
```

Selecting Multiple Groups of Lines   sed is not restricted to selecting only one group of lines. You can select as many sections from just about anywhere:

```
sed -n '1,2p                     3 addresses in one command, using only a single
7,9p                                                           pair of quotes
$p' emp.lst                                                  Selects last line
```

Alternatively, you can place multiple **sed** instructions in a single line using the **;** as delimiter:

```
sed -n '1,2p;7,9p;$p' emp.lst
```

POSIX permits the **;** to be surrounded by spaces, and Linux allows that too, but Solaris doesn't (yet) support this provision. In Section 11.8, we'll consider alternative methods of running the above **sed** command.

Negating the Action (!) Like **find, sed** also supports a negation operator (!). For instance, selecting the first two lines is the same as *not* selecting lines 3 through the end:

```
sed -n '3,$!p' emp.lst
```
                                                                    Don't print lines 3 to the end

The address and action are normally enclosed within a pair of single quotes. As you have learned by now, you should use double quotes only when parameter evaluation or command substitution is embedded within the command.

Tip

Use the -n option whenever you use the **p** command, unless you deliberately want to select lines twice. Usually, that requirement doesn't arise.

11.8   sed **Options**

POSIX requires **sed** to support only three options (-n, -e, and -f). We have used the -n option to suppress the default output when using the **p** command. Let's look at the other options, which are listed in Table 11.5.

Multiple Instructions in the Command Line (-e) The -e option allows you to enter as many instructions as you wish, each preceded by the option. We can repeat the command prior to the previous one with this:

```
sed -n -e '1,2p' -e '7,9p' -e '$p' emp.lst
```

Instructions in a File (-f) When you have too many instructions to use or when you have a set of common instructions that you execute often, they are better stored in a file. For instance, the above three instructions can be stored in a file, with each instruction on a separate line:

```
$ cat instr.fil
1,2p
7,9p
$p
```

TABLE 11.5   **sed** *Options*

Option	Significance
-n	Suppress default printing when using p
-e	Precedes each **sed** instruction when using multiple instructions
-f *flname*	Takes instructions from file *flname*

You can now use the -f option to direct **sed** to take its instructions from the file:

```
sed -n -f instr.fil emp.lst
```

sed is quite liberal in that it allows a great deal of freedom in using and repeating options. You can use the -f option with multiple files. You can also combine the -e and -f options as many times as you want:

```
sed -n -f instr.fill -f instr.fil2 emp.lst
sed -n -e '/wilcox/p' -f instr.fill -f instr.fil2 emp?.lst
```

These are some of the features of **sed** that make it so versatile and at the same time easy to work with. The second example uses context addressing (/wilcox/) in an instruction. This is the other form of addressing used by **sed**, and is considered next.

11.9 Context Addressing

The second form of addressing lets you specify a pattern (or two) rather than line numbers. This is known as **context addressing** where the pattern has a / on either side. You can locate the senders from your mailbox ($HOME/mbox) in this way:

```
$ sed -n '/From: /p' $HOME/mbox                                    A simple grep!
From: janis joplin <joplinj@altavista.net>
From: charles king <charlesk@rocketmail.com>
From: Monica Johnson <Monicaj@Web6000.com>
From: The Economist <business@lists.economist.com>
```

Both **awk** and **perl** also support this form of addressing. Ideally, you should only be looking for From: at the beginning of a line. **sed** also accepts regular expressions but only of the BRE variety and not the EREs that we used with the -E option of **grep**. The following command lines should refresh your memory:

```
sed -n '/^From: /p' $HOME/mbox                    ^ matches at beginning of line
sed -n '/wilco[cx]k*s*/p' emp.lst                        wilcox or wilcocks
sed -n "/o'br[iy][ae]n/p;/lennon/p" emp.lst        Either the o'briens or lennon
```

Note that we had to use double quotes in the third example because the pattern itself contains a single quote. Double quotes protect single quotes in the same way single quotes protect double.

You can also specify a comma-separated pair of context addresses to select a group of contiguous lines. What is more, line and context addresses can also be mixed:

```
sed -n '/johnson/,/lightfoot/p' emp.lst
sed -n '1,/woodcock/p' emp.lst
```

In a previous example *(11.4.4),* we used **ls** and **grep** in a pipeline to list files which have write permission for the group. We can do that with **sed** as well:

```
ls -l | sed -n '/^.....w/p'
```

Regular expressions in **grep** and **sed** are actually more powerful than the ones we have used so far. They use some more special characters, and we'll meet them in the third round of discussions that are featured in Section 11.13.

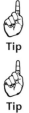

Tip

C programmers should use the command **sed -n '/{/,/}/p' foo.c** to select the *first* block of code delimited by { and }. **sed** won't select the subsequent blocks.

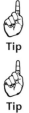

Tip

We used single quotes here, but if the pattern itself contains a single quote, you must use double quotes. In that case, make sure that a $ (if present in the pattern) is not interpreted as a variable prefix.

11.10   Writing Selected Lines to a File (w)

Irrespective of the way you select lines (by line or context addressing), you can use the **w** (write) command to write the selected lines to a separate file. You can save the lines contained within the <FORM> and </FORM> tags in a separate file:

```
sed '/<FORM>/,/<\/FORM>/w forms.html' pricelist.html
```

Every <FORM> tag in an HTML file has a corresponding </FORM> tag. The / here needs escaping as / is also used as **sed**'s pattern delimiter. Here, the form contents are extracted and saved in forms.html. To go further, you can save all form segments from all HTML files in a single file:

```
sed '/<FORM>/,/<\/FORM>/w forms.html' *.html
```

sed's power doesn't stop here. Since it accepts more than one address, you can perform a full context splitting of its input. You can search for three patterns and store the matched lines in three separate files—all in one shot:

```
sed -e '/<FORM>/,/<\/FORM>/w' forms.html
       /<FRAME>/,/<\/FRAME>/w frames.html
       /<TABLE>/,/<\/TABLE>/w tables.html' pricelist.html
```

Note

The -n option is required with the **w** command only to suppress printing of all lines on the terminal. However, even without it, the selected lines will be written to the respective files.

11.11   Text Editing

This section discusses some of the editing commands available in **sed**'s action component. **sed** can insert text and change existing text in a file. A **vi** user would be relieved to learn that the commands are also the same—**i** (insert), **a** (append), **c** (change), and **d** (delete). But there are important differences too.

11.11.1   Inserting and Changing Lines (i, a, c)

The **i** command inserts text. A C programmer can add two common "include" lines at the beginning of a program, foo.c, in this way:

```
$ sed '1i\                          Need to use \ before [Enter] here
> #include <stdio.h>\                         ... and here only
> #include <unistd.h>                          ... but not here
> ' foo.c > $$                   Redirect output to a temporary file
```

First, enter the instruction **1i**, which inserts text at line number 1. Then enter a \ before pressing *[Enter]*. You can now key in as many lines as you wish. Each line *except the last* has to be terminated by the \ before hitting *[Enter]*. **sed** identifies the line without the \ as the last line of input. This technique has to be followed when using the **a** and **c** commands also.

The above command writes the concatenated output of the two lines of inserted text and the existing lines to the standard output, which we redirected to a temporary file, $$. We must move this file to foo.c to use it. The first two lines show that the **i** command worked fine:

```
$ mv $$ foo.c ; head -n 2 foo.c
#include <stdio.h>
#include <unistd.h>
```

Doublespacing Text   What is the consequence of not using an address with these commands? The inserted or changed text is then placed after or before *every* line of the file. The following command

```
sed 'a\                                     Inserts after every line
                                                   this blank line

' emp.lst
```

inserts a blank line *after* each line of the file is printed. This is another way of doublespacing text *(10.1.1)*. Using **i** here would have inserted a blank line *before* each selected line.

C Shell

These commands won't work in the C shell in the way described here. You have to use two \s for lines that already have one \, and one \ when there is none. The previous command will work in this way in the C shell:

```
sed 'a\\                                          Two \s here
\                                                 and one here
' emp.lst
```

This is an awkward form of usage and is not intuitive at all. The **sed**, **awk**, and **perl** commands should be run in the other shells.

11.11.2   Deleting Lines (d)

Using the **d** (delete) command, **sed** can emulate **grep**'s -v option to select lines not containing the pattern. Either of these commands removes comment lines of a shell or **perl** script:

```
sed '/^#/d' foo > bar
sed -n '/^#/!p' foo > bar                       -n option to be used here
```

Deleting Blank Lines   A blank line consists of any number of spaces, tabs, or nothing. How do you delete these lines from a file? Frame a pattern which matches zero or more occurrences of a space or tab:

```
sed '/^[□↹]*$/d' foo
```
                                                        A space and a tab inside [ ]

You need to press the *[Tab]* key or *[Ctrl-i]* inside the character class—immediately after the space. Providing a ^ at the beginning and a $ at the end matches only lines that contain either nothing or simply whitespace.

11.12   Substitution (s)

Substitution is easily the most important feature of **sed**, and this is one job that **sed** does exceedingly well. It lets you replace a pattern in its input with something else. The use of regular expressions enhances our pattern matching capabilities, and in this chapter we feature some more regular expression characters that make the use of **sed** so compelling. You have encountered the substitution syntax in **vi** before *(5.14):*

*[address]*s*/expression1/expression2/flags*

Here, *expression1* (which can also be a regular expression) is replaced with *expression2* in all lines specified by *[address]*. Contrary to **vi**, however, if the address is not specified, the substitution is performed for all matching lines. This means that there's no need to use 1,$ as the address. To bring *flags* into the picture, let's first avoid its use and replace the : with a |:

```
$ sed 's/:/|/' emp.1st | head -n 2
2233|charles harris  :g.m.      :sales     :12/12/52: 90000
9876|bill johnson    :director :production:03/12/50:130000
```

Just look at what **sed** has done; only the first (left-most) instance of the : in a line has been replaced. You need to use the g (global) flag to replace all the colons:

```
$ sed 's/:/|/g' emp.1st | head -n 2
2233|charles harris  |g.m.      |sales     |12/12/52| 90000
9876|bill johnson    |director |production|03/12/50|130000
```

We used global substitution to replace all colons with pipes. Here, the command **s** is the same as **1,$s**. Though we see two lines here, the substitution has been carried out for the entire file. Also, substitution is not restricted to a single character; it can be any string:

```
sed 's/<I>/<EM>/g' foo.html
```

You can also limit the vertical boundaries by specifying an address:

```
sed '1,3s/:/|/g' emp.1st
```
                                                              First three lines only

And you can remove the source string altogether by using a null string between the last two /s:

```
sed 's/<I>//' foo.html                          Deletes first occurrence of <I> in every line
sed '1,3s/://g' emp.lst                          Deletes all occurrences of : in first three lines
```

Note

When a g is used at the end of a substitution instruction, the change is performed globally along the line. Without it, only the left-most occurrence is replaced.

Performing Multiple Substitutions You can perform multiple substitutions with one invocation of **sed**. Simply press *[Enter]* at the end of each instruction, and then close the quote at the end. This is how you replace three HTML tags:

```
$ sed 's/<I>/<EM>/g                                    Can also specify in a single line
> s/<B>/<STRONG>/g                                with ; as the delimiter of commands
> s/<U>/<EM>/g' form.html
```

sed is a stream editor; it works on a data stream. This means that an instruction processes the output of the previous one. This is something users often forget; they don't get the sequence right. Note that the following sequence finally converts all <I> tags to <STRONG>:

```
$ sed 's/<I>/<EM>/g
> s/<EM>/<STRONG>/g' form.html
```

Tip

When you have a group of instructions to execute, place them in a file and use **sed** with the -f option.

11.12.1 Using Regular Expressions in Substitution

As in context addresses, regular expressions can also be used as the source pattern, but only of the BRE type. EREs are not allowed:

```
sed 's/gilmo[ur][re]/gilmour/g' emp.lst
```

You can also use the anchoring characters, ^ and $, with the same meaning. Further, when either is used as a sole character in the source pattern, it implies that the target pattern has to be placed at that location. This is how you can add the 2 prefix to all emp-ids and the .00 suffix to the salary:

```
$ sed 's/^/2/;s/$/.00/' emp.lst | head -n 3
22233:charles harris  :g.m.      :sales     :12/12/52: 90000.00
29876:bill johnson    :director :production:03/12/50:130000.00
25678:robert dylan    :d.g.m.    :marketing :04/19/43: 85000.00
```

There are now five digits in the first field. The last field has also been modified.

Compressing Multiple Spaces How do you delete the trailing spaces from the second, third, and fourth fields? We need to match one or more occurrences of a space followed by a colon:

```
$ sed 's^ *:^:^g' emp.lst | tee empn.lst | head -n 3
2233:charles harris:g.m.:sales:12/12/52: 90000
9876:bill johnson:director:production:03/12/50:130000
5678:robert dylan:d.g.m.:marketing:04/19/43: 85000
```

We've used the ^ instead of the / this time. **sed** (and **vi**) allows any character to be used as the pattern delimiter as long as it doesn't occur in any of the strings. Most UNIX system files (like /etc/passwd) follow this variable-length format because the common filters can easily identify a field by seeing the delimiter. Using **tee**, we created the file empn.lst. This is the file you'll be using with the **awk** command later.

11.12.2 The Remembered Pattern (//)

So far, we've looked for a pattern and then replaced it with something else. Truly speaking, the three commands below do the same job:

```
sed 's/director/member/' emp.lst
sed '/director/s//member/' emp.lst
sed '/director/s/director/member/' emp.lst
```

The second form suggests that **sed** "remembers" the scanned pattern and stores it in // (2 frontslashes). The // is interpreted to mean that the search and substituted patterns are the same. We call it the **remembered pattern**.

The address /director/ in the third form appears to be redundant. However, you must also understand this form because it widens the scope of substitution. It's possible that you may want to replace a string in all lines containing a different string:

```
$ sed -n '/marketing/s/director/member  /p' emp.lst
6521:derryk o'brien  :member    :marketing :09/26/45:125000
```

Note

The significance of // depends on its position in the instruction. If it is in the source string, it implies that the scanned pattern is stored there. If the target string is //, it means that the source pattern is to be removed.

11.13 Basic Regular Expressions Revisited

To master **sed**, you must appreciate the numerous possibilities that regular expressions throw up with this command—more so than in **grep**. This third round of discussions feature some more characters from the BRE set (Table 11.6). Both **grep** and **sed** use these characters (with some variations), but **sed** exploits them to the hilt. This time, be prepared to see and use a \ before every metacharacter discussed in this section, except the &. We'll learn to use three types of expressions:

- The *repeated pattern*—uses a single symbol, &, to make the entire source pattern appear at the destination also.
- The *interval regular expression (IRE)*—uses the characters { and } with a single or a pair of numbers between them.
- The *tagged regular expression (TRE)*—groups patterns with (and) and represents them at the destination with numbered tags.

TABLE 11.6   *Other Basic Regular Expressions (BREs) Used by* **grep** *and* **sed**

Pattern	Matches
&	Source pattern at destination (**sed** only)
\\{m\\}	*m* occurrences of the previous character (no \\ in **perl**) *(11.13.2)*
\\{m,\\}	At least *m* occurrences of the previous character (no \\ in **perl**) *(11.13.2)*
\\{m,n\\}	Between *m* and *n* occurrences of the previous character (no \\ in **perl**) *(11.13.2)*
\\(exp\\)	Expression *exp* for later referencing with \\1, \\2, etc. (no \\ in **perl**) *(11.13.3)*
^.\\{9\\}nobody	nobody after skipping nine characters from line beginning (no \\ in **perl**) *(11.13.2)*
\\(BOLD\\).*\\1	At least two occurrences of the string BOLD in a line (no \\ before (and) in **perl**) *(11.13.3)*

In the last two types of expressions, the metacharacters need escaping so the *command* understands them as special. The expressions themselves must be quoted so the shell can't interpret them.

11.13.1 The Repeated Pattern (&)

We sometimes encounter situations when the source pattern also occurs at the destination. We can then use & to represent it. All of these commands do the same thing:

```
sed 's/director/executive director/' emp.lst
sed 's/director/executive &/' emp.lst
sed '/director/s//executive &/' emp.lst
```

All of these commands replace director with executive director. The &, known as the **repeated pattern**, here expands to the entire source string. Apart from the numbered tag (discussed soon), the & is the only other special character you can use in the target expression.

11.13.2 Interval Regular Expression (IRE)

We have matched a pattern at the beginning and end of a line. But what about matching it at any specified location—or within a zone? **sed** and **grep** also use the **interval regular expression** (IRE) that uses an integer (or two) to specify the number of times the previous character can occur. The IRE uses an escaped pair of curly braces and takes three forms:

- *ch*\\{*m*\\}—The metacharacter *ch* can occur *m* times.
- *ch*\\{*m*, *n*\\}—Here, *ch* can occur between *m* and *n* times.
- *ch*\\{*m*,\\}—Here, *ch* can occur at least *m* times.

All of these forms have the single-character regular expression *ch* as the first element. This can either be a literal character, a . (dot), or a character class. It is followed by a pair of escaped curly braces containing either a single number *m* or a range of numbers lying between *m* and *n* to determine the number of times the character preceding it can occur. The values of *m* and *n* can't exceed 255.

Let's consider the second form of the IRE. Since this matches a pattern within a "zone," we can use this feature to display the listing for those files that have the write bit set either for group or others:

```
$ ls -l | sed -n '/^.\{5,8\}w/p'
-r-xr-xrwx  3 sumit     dialout     426 Feb 26 19:58 comj
-r-xr-xrwx  3 sumit     dialout     426 Feb 26 19:58 runj
-r-xrw-r-x  1 sumit     dialout     527 Apr 23 07:42 valcode.sh
-r-xrw-r-x  2 sumit     dialout     289 Apr 23 07:42 vvi.sh
```

Extracting Lines Based on Length With the IRE, you can use the following commands to select lines longer than 100 characters. The second one additionally imposes a limit of 150 on the maximum length:

```
sed -n '/.\{101,\}/p' foo                        Line length at least 101
grep '^.\{101,150\}$' foo                   Line length between 101 and 150
```

The ^ and $ are required in the second example; otherwise lines longer than 150 characters would also be selected. Remember that a regular expression always tries to match the longest pattern possible *(11.4.3—Note)*.

11.13.3   The Tagged Regular Expression (TRE)

The tagged regular expression (TRE) is probably the most useful feature of **sed**. Using it, you can form groups in a line and then extract these groups. The TRE requires two regular expressions to be specified—one each for the source and target patterns.

This is how the TRE works. Identify the segments of a line that you wish to extract, and enclose each segment with a matched pair of escaped parentheses. For instance, to have a number as a group, represent that number as \([0-9]*\). A series of nonalphabetic characters can be represented as \([^a-zA-Z]*\). Every grouped pattern automatically acquires the numeric label *n,* where *n* signifies the *n*th group from the left. To reproduce a group at the destination, you have to use the tag *n*. This means that the first group is represented as \1, the second one as \2, and so forth.

Consider a simple example. Suppose you want to replace the words henry higgins by higgins, henry. The **sed** instruction will then look like this:

```
$ echo "henry higgins" | sed 's/\(henry\) \(higgins\)/\2, \1/'
higgins, henry
```

Here, the source pattern has two tagged patterns \(henry\) and \(higgins\). They appear in the target pattern at the location of the \1 and \2. The (,), 1, and 2 have to be escaped as they are treated specially by **sed**. In the next section, we'll build on this to reverse all names in a telephone directory.

Searching for Repeated Words Let's now consider an error-detection feature that benefits document authors—using **grep** this time. The TRE raises the possibility of detecting words that are inadvertently repeated—like the the. Since the TRE remembers a grouped pattern, you can look for these repeated words like this:

```
$ grep "\([a-z][a-z][a-z]*\)□□*\1" note                    Two spaces before *
You search search for a pattern with grep.
sed   sed can perform substitution too.
But the grand-daddy of them all is perl perl.
```

Each line here contains consecutive instances of a word (`search`, `sed` and `perl`). What does this pattern group match? A word containing at least two lowercase letters. This group is followed by one or more spaces (two spaces before the second *) and the repeated pattern.

11.14 Applying the IRE and TRE

Though the TRE is a little cryptic, you must understand it if you want **sed** to serve as a gateway to learning **perl**. As we did in the previous chapter, let's use this examples section to devise a few useful sequences that make use of the IRE and TRE. Two sequences use **sed**, but one uses **grep**.

11.14.1 Handling a Telephone Directory

Consider this small telephone directory where a person has either a wired phone or a mobile phone:

```
$ cat teledir.txt
charles harris 98310200987
bill johnson   327-100-2345
robert dylan    9632454090
john woodcock  2344987665
barry wood      234-908-3456
gordon lightfoot 345-987-4670
```

Each line contains names in the sequence *first_name last_name* along with the telephone number. We'll now use **grep** to select only those users who have a mobile phone. We need to use an IRE to match a string containing (at least) 10 contiguous digits:

```
$ grep '[0-9]\{10\}' teledir.txt
charles harris 98310200987
robert dylan    9632454090
john woodcock  2344987665
```

Reversing First Name and Surname Using TREs, we'll create a new list from this directory that reverses the first name and surname with a comma delimiting them. We'll have to frame two groups of alphabetic characters and then reverse them in the target pattern. This is how we obtain a sorted list:

```
$ sed 's/\([a-z]*\)□*\([a-z]*\)/\2, \1/' teledir.txt | sort
dylan, robert    9632454090
harris, charles 98310200987
johnson, bill   327-100-2345
lightfoot, gordon 345-987-4670
wood, barry       234-908-3456
woodcock, john   2344987665
```

The first group, \([a-z]*\), represents zero or more occurrences of alphabetic characters; this effectively captures the first name. An identical pattern takes care of the surname. These two groups are separated by zero or more occurrences of space (□*). In the target pattern, we recreate these groups but in reverse sequence with the tags \2 and \1.

11.14.2 Replacing an Obsolescent Function with a POSIX-Compliant One

UNIX-C programmers often need to copy data from one memory location to another. The **bcopy** library function, which requires three arguments, is used in this manner:

```
bcopy(hp->h_addr, &name.sin_addr, hp->h_length);
```

POSIX advocates the use of **memcpy,** but how does one replace one with the other using **sed**? To assess the viability, let's have a look at how the previous function would have to be reframed using **memcpy:**

```
memcpy(&name.sin_addr, hp->h_addr, hp->h_length);
```

It's viable; we simply need to reverse the first and second arguments. This is easily done by forming two groups representing the two arguments. Each group is represented by multiple instances of a noncomma character followed by a comma. Let **sed** read the standard input this time:

```
$ echo "bcopy(hp->h_addr, &name.sin_addr, hp->h_length);" |
> sed 's/bcopy(\([^,]*,\)\([^,]*,\)/memcpy(\2\1/'
memcpy( &name.sin_addr,hp->h_addr, hp->h_length);
```

If you need to make this change in all your C programs, then you have to run the **sed** command in a **for** loop inside a shell script. After reading Chapter 13, you should be able to handle this job.

11.14.3 Converting Pathnames in URLs

Finally, let's take up a very important application of the TRE. You may have faced the problem of activating links of an HTML document saved on disk even though the linked documents are all available in the current directory. This happens because the link tags often have relative pathnames in the URLs they point to. For instance, consider this section showing a list of four items:

```
$ cat httplinks.html
<LI><A HREF="smail.html">Sendmail</A> The Universal Mail Transport Agent
<LI><A HREF="http://www.sonu.com/docs/ftpdoc.html"File Transfer Protocol</A>
<LI><A HREF="../../public_html/news.html">Newsgroups</A> Usenet News
<LI><A HREF="../irc.html">Internet Relay Chat</A> On-line text conversation
```

Note that the last three items have pathnames using directories, and one of them points to a different host altogether. If you have downloaded all of these HTML files to your current directory, you won't be able to access them by clicking on these links unless you remove all protocol, FQDN, and directory references from each document. For instance, the anchor tag (<A>) in the second line should specify A HREF="ftpdoc.html" instead of the complete URL shown. (HTML, FQDN, and URL are discussed in Chapter 14.) Let's use the TRE to extract only the filenames from these URLs.

The task isn't as daunting as you might think. If you observe these A HREFs closely, you'll find the source string for substitution to have three components:

- \(A HREF="\)—This is the first group and should be printed with \1.
- .*\/—This takes care of all characters following the opening " up to the last /. Note that this matches the pathname of the directory, but we won't be printing this. The frontslash also needs to be escaped.
- \([^/]*"\)—This matches all nonfrontslash characters followed by a ". The matched expression is the base filename and should be printed with \2.

Now run **sed** using these three components in a regular expression:

```
$ sed 's/\(A HREF="\).*\/\([^/]*"\)/\1\2/' httplinks.html
<LI><A HREF="smail.html">Sendmail</A> The Universal Mail Transport Agent
<LI><A HREF="ftpdoc.html">File Transfer Protocol</A>
<LI><A HREF="news.html">Newsgroups</A> Usenet News
<LI><A HREF="irc.html">Internet Relay Chat</A> On-line text conversation
```

There you see only the base filenames after conversion! This is a useful sequence that you'll need often, and you may also need to modify it. The IMG SRC tag also refers to URLs, so you have to add another **s** command for it. You can try this out as an exercise for yourself.

sed also features pattern and hold spaces, and branches and labels. They are difficult to use and hence left out of our discussions. This power tool is best mastered by sheer practice, by repeated attempts to figure out the exact command sequence that will perform a specific job. You don't always get it right the first time, but don't worry; hardly anybody does, not with this command at least.

SUMMARY

The **grep** filter searches its input for one or more patterns. You can ignore case when performing a match (-i), display only filenames (-l), and select lines not containing the pattern (-v).

grep can also be used with a *regular expression* using two sets of metacharacters—the *basic regular expression* set (BRE) and the *extended regular expression set* (ERE). **sed** doesn't use the extended set. All regular expressions must be quoted to prevent the shell from interfering.

In the BRE set, the . matches a single character, while * matches zero or more occurrences of the *previous* character. The character class is similar to the one used by wild cards except that the ^ negates the class. The pattern .* matches anything and is often embedded in a regular expression. The ^ and $ serve as anchoring characters.

grep uses the ERE with the -E option, but **egrep** does the same without using this option. The ERE uses the | to delimit multiple patterns and the (and) to group patterns. The + and ? are similar to the * used in the BRE except that they are more restrictive.

A **sed** *instruction* comprises an *address* and an *action* (command). Lines can be addressed by line numbers or context. The -n option makes sure that lines are not printed twice when using the **p** command. Lines can be inserted (**i**), appended (**a**), changed (**c**), and deleted (**d**).

sed accepts multiple instructions (-e) to work on different sections of its input and to save the edited sections to separate files (**w**).

sed is mostly used for substitution (**s**). The g flag at the end makes the substitution global. The search and substitution patterns can be regular expressions, but only of the BRE type.

A set of two slashes (//) as the source pattern represents the expression used for scanning a pattern (the *remembered pattern*). The & reproduces the entire source pattern at the target (the *repeated pattern*).

The *interval regular expression* (IRE) uses a single or a pair of numbers surrounded by escaped curly braces—like $ch\backslash\{m,n\backslash\}$. The expression signifies that *ch* can occur between *m* and *n* times.

The *tagged regular expression* (TRE) uses \(and \) to enclose a pattern. The grouped pattern gets the tag \1, \2, and so on. The feature is useful in reproducing a portion of the source pattern at the target.

SELF-TEST

Some questions use the file emp.lst *whose contents are shown in Section 11.1.*

11.1   Devise a command sequence to display the line containing the last occurrence of the string done.

11.2   What does **grep** "^*" look for? Is the \ really necessary?

11.3   Devise a sequence to display a count of lines containing the string IMG SRC in all HTML files (extension .htm or .html) in the current directory. Assume that both string and filenames can have a mix of upper- and lowercase.

11.4   How can you extract from the output of **find . -name "*.c" -print** the filenames in the current directory only and not in its subdirectories?

11.5   How do you store in the variable numb the number of .c files that contain the string printf?

11.6   Devise a sequence to display the listing, ordered by last access time, of the .c files in the current directory that contain the string wait.

11.7 What do these regular expressions match? (i) a.*b, (ii) ..*, (iii) ^}$

11.8 How do you use **grep** to locate lines containing these patterns? (i) SIGSTOP or SIGTSTP, (ii) SIGTTIN or SIGTTOU, (iii) harris or harrison

11.9 How is the expression g* different from gg*?

11.10 Devise two regular expressions that match lines longer than 10 characters.

11.11 Find out the name and designation of the youngest person in emp.lst who is not a director.

11.12 What does this command do, and what are the two $s doing here?

```
grep "$SHELL$" /etc/passwd | cut -d: -f1
```

11.13 Use an ERE to extract all section headers from this book. (Each section is numbered either as *n.n* or *n.n.n*, and the contents are spread across 19 files having the names chap00, chap01, etc.)

11.14 Write an alias which lists only directories in the current directory using (i) **grep**, (ii) **sed**.

11.15 How will you use **sed** to select from a file (i) lines 3 to 10, (ii) all but the last line?

11.16 How do you (i) print every line of a file twice, (ii) insert a blank line after each line that is read?

11.17 How will you replace - with _ and vice versa, assuming that the file doesn't contain any numerals?

11.18 What shortcut does **sed** offer to replace the string Linux with Red Hat Linux?

11.19 How do you add two spaces at the beginning of every line?

11.20 Invert the name of the individual in emp.lst so that the surname occurs first.

EXERCISES

Some questions use the file emp.lst *whose contents are shown in Section 11.1.*

11.1 What is the difference between a *wild card* and a *regular expression*?

11.2 What do these commands do? (i) grep a b c, (ii) grep <HTML> foo, (iii) grep "**" foo, (iv) grep *

11.3 Explain the significance of the * in this command:
grep 'botswana.*birds' *.htm*.

11.4 How many lines does **grep '.*' foo** display? What happens if you remove the quotes?

11.5 What is the significance of this command? grep -l "`echo '\t'`" foo

11.6 Are the following commands equivalent? grep "^[^a-z]" foo and grep -v "^[a-z]" foo

11.7 How do you locate all nonblank lines that don't begin with #, /*, or //?

11.8 Look up the format specifiers for the **date** command, and then frame a command sequence to list from emp.lst the names of the persons born today.

11.9 Devise a sequence to locate those users who have logged in yesterday or earlier but have not logged out, and mail the list to root. Users logged in more than once should feature only once in the list.

11.10   Explain the task performed by the following pipeline. Can you simplify it to use two commands instead of four? ls -t `grep fork *.c | cut -d: -f1 | sort -u`

11.11   How do you display the listing of all files in the current directory that have the same permissions as ./foo?

11.12   Frame regular expressions to match these patterns: (i) jefferies jeffery jeffreys, (ii) hitchen hitchin hitching, (iii) Heard herd Hird, (iv) dix dick dicks dickson dixon, (v) Mcgee mcghee magee, (vi) wood woodcock woodhouse.

11.13   How do these expressions differ? (i) [0-9]* and [0-9][0-9]*, (ii) ^[^^] and ^^^

11.14   Frame a command sequence that looks at romeo's mailbox to tell him either that he has received a message from henry or that the Subject: line contains the word urgent or immediate in lower- or uppercase.

11.15   How will you list the ordinary files in your current directory that are not user-writable?

11.16   Explain the significance of this command:
grep "^[^:]*:[^:]*:100:" /etc/passwd. What is the disadvantage of locating a pattern this way?

11.17   How do you locate all lines containing printf, but not sprintf and fprintf, anywhere but at the end of a line?

11.18   How do you look for one bill christie in a file, without knowing whether bill exists as william or bill and whether christie also exists as christy?

11.19   Use **find** and **grep** to (i) locate all C programs in the home directory tree that contain the words int main (, (ii) open the **vi** editor with each file. There may be multiple spaces between int and main, but there may or may not be spaces between main and (.

11.20   Using **sed**, how do you add the tags <HTML> at the beginning and </HTML> at the end of a file?

11.21   How will you remove blank lines from a file using (i) **grep**, (ii) **sed**? (A blank line may contain either nothing or only whitespace characters.)

11.22   How do you locate lines beginning and ending with a dot using (i) **grep**, (ii) **sed**?

11.23   Frame regular expressions to locate lines longer than 100 and smaller than 150 characters using (i) **grep** (ii) **sed**.

11.24   Find out the occurrences of three consecutive and identical word characters (like aaa or bbb) using (i) **grep** and (ii) **sed**.

11.25   The command **grep -c ENCRYPTION foo** outputs the number of lines containing ENCRYPTION, but if the pattern sometimes occurs more than once in a line, how do you then obtain a count of all these *occurrences*? (HINT: Use **sed** also.)

11.26   How do you delete all lines (i) beginning with a # except the line #!/bin/ksh, (ii) beginning with /* and ending with */?

11.27   How do you delete all leading and trailing spaces in all lines?

11.28   Explain what these commands do and if there's anything wrong with them:

(i) sed -e 's/print/printf/g' -e 's/printf/print/g' foo
(ii) sed -e 's/compute/calculate/g' -e 's/computer/host/g' foo

11.29 Every <B> tag in an HTML file has a closing </B> tag as well. Convert them to <STRONG> and </STRONG>, respectively, using **sed** with a single **s** command.

11.30 Specify the command sequence needed to remove the directory /usr/local/bin from the PATH defined in $HOME/.profile.

11.31 Devise a sequence to display the extensions of all files in the current directory along with a count of each extension.

11.32 How can you sort a file that is doublespaced (where even-numbered lines are blank lines) and still preserve the blank lines?

## CHAPTER 12

Filtering and Programming with awk

The **awk** command made a late entry into the UNIX system in 1977 to augment the tool kit with suitable report formatting capabilities. Named after its authors, Aho, Weinberger, and Kernighan, **awk**, until the advent of **perl**, was the most powerful utility for text manipulation and report writing. **awk** also appears as **nawk** (**n**ewer **awk**) on most systems and **gawk** (**G**NU **awk**) in Linux. The POSIX specification and our discussions are based on **nawk**.

Like **sed**, **awk** doesn't belong to the do-one-thing-well family of UNIX commands. It combines features of several filters, but it has two unique features. First, it can identify and manipulate individual *fields* in a line. Second, **awk** is the only UNIX filter that can perform computation. Further, **awk** also accepts extended regular expressions (EREs) for pattern matching, has C-type programming constructs, and several built-in variables and functions. Learning **awk** will help you understand **perl**, which uses most of the **awk** constructs, sometimes in an identical manner.

Objectives

- Understand **awk**'s unusual syntax including its *selection criteria* and *action* components.
- Split a line into *fields* and format the output with **printf**.
- Understand the special properties of **awk** variables and expressions.
- Use the comparison operators to select lines on practically any condition.
- Use the ~ and !~ operators with extended regular expressions (EREs) for pattern matching.
- Handle decimal numbers and use them for computation.
- Do some pre- and post-processing with the BEGIN and END sections.
- Examine **awk**'s built-in variables.
- Use arrays and access an array element with a nonnumeric subscript.
- Use the built-in functions for performing string handling tasks.
- Make decisions with the **if** statement.
- Use the **for** and **while** loops to perform tasks repeatedly.

12.1 awk **Preliminaries**

awk is a little awkward to use at first, but if you feel comfortable with **find** and **sed**, then you'll find a friend in **awk**. Even though it is a filter, **awk** resembles **find** in its syntax:

awk *options* '*selection_criteria* { *action* }' *file(s)*

FIGURE 12.1   *Components of an* **awk** *Program*

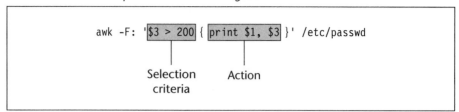

Note the use of single quotes and curly braces. The *selection_criteria* (a form of addressing) filters input and selects lines for the *action* component to act on. This component is enclosed within curly braces. The *selection_criteria* and *action* constitute an **awk** *program* that is surrounded by a set of single quotes. These programs are often one-liners though they can span several lines as well. A sample **awk** program is shown in Fig. 12.1.

Let's have a brief look at each of the constituents of the syntax. Unlike other filters, **awk** uses a contiguous sequence of spaces and tabs as the default delimiter. This default has been changed in the figure to a colon using the -F option.

Fields in **awk** are numbered $1, $2, and so on, and the selection criteria here tests whether the third field is greater than 200. **awk** also addresses the entire line as $0. In Chapter 13, you'll find the shell also using the same parameters to represent command line arguments. To prevent the shell from performing variable evaluation, we need to single-quote any **awk** program that uses these parameters.

Even though we haven't seen relational tests in command syntax before, selection criteria in **awk** is not limited to a simple comparison. They can be a regular expression to search for, one or two line addresses, or a conditional expression. Here are some examples:

```
awk '/negroponte/ { print }' foo                    Lines containing negroponte
awk '$2 ~ /^negroponte$/ { print }' foo        Tests for exact match on second field
awk 'NR == 1, NR == 5 { print }' foo                          Lines 1 to 5
awk '$6 > 2000 { print }' foo                       Sixth field greater than 2000
```

That **awk** also uses regular expressions as patterns is evident from the second example which shows the use of ^ and $ in anchoring the pattern. The third example uses **awk**'s built-in variable, NR, to represent the record number. The term **record** is new in this text. By default, **awk** identifies a single line as a record, but a record in **awk** can also comprise multiple contiguous lines.

The action component is often a **print** or **printf** statement, but can also be a program. We'll learn to use the **if**, **while**, and **for** constructs here before they show up again in the shell and **perl**. Moreover, the selection criteria in all the four examples above can also be implemented in the action component.

Let's consider a simple **awk** command that selects the Subject: lines from mbox, the mailbox file:

```
$ awk '/^Subject:/ { print }' $HOME/mbox
Subject: RE: History is not bunk
Subject: Mail server problem
Subject: Take our Survey, Win US$500!
```

When used without any field specifiers, **print** writes the entire line to the standard output. Printing is also the default action of **awk**, so all following forms could be considered equivalent:

```
awk '/^Subject:/' mbox                              Printing is the default action
awk '/^Subject:/{ print }' mbox                         Whitespace permitted
awk '/^Subject:/ { print $0}' mbox                  $0 is the complete line
```

Observe that the first example doesn't have an action component. If the action is missing, the entire line is printed. If the selection criteria are missing, the action applies to all lines. One of them has to be specified.

The selection criteria in these examples used the ^ to anchor the pattern. For pattern matching, **awk** uses regular expressions in **sed**-style:

```
$ awk '/wilco[cx]k*s*/' emp.lst
3212:bill wilcocks   :d.g.m.    :accounts  :12/12/55: 85000
2345:james wilcox    :g.m.      :marketing :03/12/45:110000
```

However, the regular expressions used by **awk** belong to the basic BRE (but not the IRE and TRE) and ERE variety. The latter is used by **grep -E** *(11.5)* or **egrep**. This means that you can also use multiple patterns using (,) and |:

```
awk '/wood(house|cock)/' emp.lst
awk '/wilco[cx]k*s*|wood(cock|house)/' emp.lst
awk '/^$/' emp.lst
```

Henceforth, the input for many **awk** programs used in this chapter will come from the file empn.lst. We created this file with **sed** in Section 11.12.1. The lines here are of variable length:

```
$ head -n 4 empn.lst
2233:charles harris:g.m.:sales:12/12/52: 90000
9876:bill johnson:director:production:03/12/50:130000
5678:robert dylan:d.g.m.:marketing:04/19/43: 85000
2365:john woodcock:director:personnel:05/11/47:120000
```

We need to use the -F option to specify the delimiter (:) whenever we select fields from this file.

Note

An **awk** program must have either the selection criteria or the action, or both, but within single quotes. Double quotes will create problems unless used judiciously.

12.2 Using print and printf

awk uses the **print** and **printf** statements to write to standard output. **print** produces unformatted output, and since our new sample database contains lines of variable length, **print** maintains the field widths in its output. This is how we use **print** to invert the first and second fields of the sales people:

```
$ awk -F: '/sales/ { print $2, $1 }' empn.lst
charles harris 2233
gordon lightfoot 1006
p.j. woodhouse 1265
jackie wodehouse 2476
```

A comma in the field list ($2, $1) ensures that the fields are not glued together. The default delimiter is the space, but we'll learn to change it later by setting the built-in variable, FS.

What about printing all fields except, say, the fourth one? Rather than explicitly specify all remaining field identifiers, we can reassign the one we don't want to an empty string:

```
$ awk -F: '{ $4 = "" ; print }' empn.lst | head -n 2
2233 charles harris g.m.  12/12/52  90000
9876 bill johnson director  03/12/50 130000
```

When placing multiple statements in a single line, use the **;** as their delimiter. **print** here is the same as **print $0**.

With the C-like **printf** statement, you can use **awk** as a stream formatter. **printf** uses a quoted format specifier and a field list. **awk** accepts most of the formats used by the **printf** function in C and the **printf** command. In this chapter, we'll stick to these formats:

%s—String
%d—Integer
%f—Floating point number

Let's produce formatted output from unformatted input, using a regular expression this time in the selection criteria:

```
$ awk -F: '/true?man/ {
> printf("%-20s %-12s %6d\n", $2, $3, $6) }' empn.lst
ronie trueman        executive    75000
julie truman         g.m.         95000
```

The name and designation have been printed in spaces 20 and 12 characters wide, respectively; the - symbol left-justifies the output. Note that unlike **print**, **printf** requires \n to print a newline after each line.

C Shell

Note that **awk** gets multiline here. It's a shell belonging to the Bourne family that's running this command, which considers a command to be complete only when it encounters the closing quote. Don't forget to place a \ after { and before you press *[Enter]* if you run this command in the C shell.

Note

awk is the only filter that uses whitespace as the default delimiter. **cut** and **paste** use the tab, and **sort** uses a contiguous set of spaces as the default delimiter.

12.2.1 Redirecting Standard Output

Every **print** and **printf** statement can be separately redirected with the > and | symbols. However, make sure the filename or the command that follows these symbols is enclosed within double quotes. For example, the following statement sorts the output of the **printf** statement:

```
printf "%s %-10s %-12s %-8s\n", $1, $3, $4, $6 | "sort"
```

If you use redirection instead, the filename should be enclosed in quotes in a similar manner:

```
printf "%s %-10s %-12s %-8s\n", $1, $3, $4, $6 > "mslist"
```

awk thus provides the flexibility of separately manipulating the different output streams. But don't forget the quotes!

12.3 Number Processing

awk supports computation using the arithmetic operators from the list shown in Table 12.1. The +, -, *, and / perform the four basic functions, but we'll also use % (modulo) in some of our scripts. **awk** also overcomes the inability of **expr** and the shell to handle floating point numbers. Let **awk** take, as its input, two numbers from the standard input:

TABLE 12.1 *Arithmetic Operators Used by* **awk** *and* **perl**

Operator	Description
+	Addition
-	Subtraction
*	Multiplication
/	Division
%	Modulo (5 % 3 = 2)
^	Exponentiation (2 ^ 10 = 1024) *(awk only)*
**	Exponentiation (2 ** 10 = 1024) *(perl only)*

```
$ echo 22 7 | awk '{print $1/$2}'
3.14286
$ echo 22 7 | awk '{printf "%1.20f\n", $1/$2}'
3.14285714285714279370
```

The second example uses the %1.20f format string to print a floating point number with 20 digits to the right of the decimal point.

Salespeople often earn a bonus apart from their salary. We'll assume here that the bonus amount is equal to one month's salary. We'll print the pay slip for these people using a variable to print the serial number:

```
$ awk -F: '/sales/ {
> kount = kount + 1
> printf "%3d %-20s %-12s %6d %8.2f\n", kount, $2, $3, $6, $6/12 }' empn.lst
  1 charles harris       g.m.          90000  7500.00
  2 gordon lightfoot     director     140000 11666.67
  3 p.j. woodhouse       manager       90000  7500.00
  4 jackie wodehouse     manager      110000  9166.67
```

The last column shows the bonus component, obtained by dividing the salary field by 12 ($6/12). As in C, the = is also an operator when combined with any of the arithmetic operators. For instance, += is an assignment operator that adds the value on its right to the variable on its left and also reassigns the variable. These two operations mean the same thing in **awk**, C, and **perl**:

```
kount = kount + 5
kount += 5
```

When the operand on the right is a 1 (one), **awk** offers the increment operator, ++, as a synonym. So all three forms are equivalent:

```
kount = kount + 1          kount += 1          kount++
```

The same line of reasoning applies to the other arithmetic operators too. So, x-- decrements the existing value of x by 1 and x *= 5 reassigns x by multiplying its existing value by 5. The assignment operators are listed in Table 12.2.

TABLE 12.2 *Assignment Operators*
(i = 5 initially; result used as initial value by next line)

Operator	Description	Example	Value of i
++	Adds one to itself	i++	6
+=	Adds and assigns to itself	i += 5	11
--	Subtracts one from itself	i--	10
-=	Subtracts and assigns to itself	i -= 2	8
*=	Multiplies and assigns to itself	i *= 3	24
/=	Divides and assigns to itself	i /= 6	4

The ++ and -- operators are special; they can be used as both prefix and postfix operators. The statements x++ and ++x are similar but not identical:

```
kount = count = 5
print ++kount                                    Increments kount first and then prints 6
print count++                                    Prints 5 and then sets count to 6
```

12.4 Variables and Expressions

Throughout this chapter, we'll be using variables and expressions with **awk**. Expressions comprise strings, numbers, variables, and entities that are built by combining them with operators. For example, (x + 5)*12 is an expression. Unlike in programming languages, **awk** doesn't have char, int, long, double, and so forth as primitive data types. Every expression can be interpreted either as a string or a number, and **awk** makes the necessary conversion according to context.

awk also allows the use of user-defined variables but without declaring them. Variables are case-sensitive: x is different from X. A variable is deemed to be declared the first time it is used. Unlike shell variables, **awk** variables don't use the $ either in assignment or in evaluation:

```
x = "5"
print x
```

A user-defined variable needs no initialization. It is implicitly initialized to zero or a null string. As discussed before, **awk** has a mechanism of identifying the type and initial value of a variable from its context.

Strings in **awk** are always double-quoted and can contain any character. Like **echo**, **awk** strings can also use escape sequences and octal values, but strings can also include hex values. There's one difference, however: octal and hex values are preceded by only \ and \x, respectively:

```
x ="\t\tBELL\7"
print x                                          Prints two tabs, the string BELL and sounds a beep
```

awk provides no operator for concatenating strings. Strings are concatenated by simply placing them side-by-side:

```
x = "sun" ; y = "com"
print x y                                                          Prints suncom
print x "." y                                                      Prints sun.com
```

Concatenation is not affected by the type of variable. A numeric and string value can be concatenated just as easily. The following examples demonstrate how **awk** makes automatic conversions when concatenating and adding variables:

```
x = "5" ; y = 6 ; z = "A"
print x y                                              y converted to string; prints 56
print x + y                                            x converted to number; prints 11
print y + z                                            z converted to numeric 0; prints 6
```

Even though we assigned "5" (a string) to x, we could still use it for numeric computation. Also observe that when a number is added to a string, **awk** converts the string to zero since it doesn't have numerals.

Expressions also have true and false values associated with them. Any nonempty string is true; so is any positive number. The statement

```
if (x)
```

is true if x is a nonnull string or a positive number.

Note

Variables are neither declared nor are their type specified. **awk** identifies their type and initializes them to zero or null strings. String variables are always double-quoted, but can contain escape sequences. Nonprintable characters can be represented by their octal or hex values.

12.5   The Comparison and Logical Operators

awk has a single set of comparison operators for handling strings and numbers, and two separate operators for matching regular expressions (Table 12.3). You'll find the scenario quite different in **perl** and shell programming; both use separate sets of operators for comparing strings and numbers. In this section, we'll demonstrate the use of these operators in the selection criteria, but they also can be used with modifications in the action component.

12.5.1   String and Numeric Comparison

Both numeric and string equality are tested with the == operator. The operator != tests inequality. Programmers already know that == is different from =, the assignment operator. (x == 5 tests whether x is equal to 5, but x = 5 assigns 5 to x.) This is how you test for string and numeric equality using **awk**'s built-in variables:

TABLE 12.3   *The Comparison and Logical Operators*

Operator	Significance
<	Less than
<=	Less than or equal to
==	Equal to
!=	Not equal to
>=	Greater than or equal to
>	Greater than
~	Matches a regular expression
!~	Doesn't match a regular expression
&&	Logical AND
||	Logical OR
!	Logical NOT

```
$4 == "sales"                                        Fourth field matched completely
$4 != "sales"
NR == 5
NR == 5, NR == 10                                                   Lines 5 to 10
```

The first two examples match a string with the fourth field. The other two examples make use of **awk**'s built-in variable, NR, that stores the record number. Like **sed** addresses, **awk** also enables specification of a range of addresses using the comma as a delimiter. This example prints four lines:

```
$ awk -F: 'NR == 3, NR == 6 { print NR, $2,$3,$6 }' empn.lst
3 robert dylan d.g.m.  85000
4 john woodcock director 120000
5 barry wood chairman 160000
6 gordon lightfoot director 140000
```

You can also use the >, <, >=, and <= operators when comparing numeric data:

```
$6 > 100000
$6 <= 100000                               Sixth field less than or equal to 100000
```

You can now print the pay-slips for those people whose salary exceeds 120,000 dollars:

```
$ awk -F: '$6 > 120000 { print $2, $6 }' empn.lst
bill johnson 130000
barry wood 160000
gordon lightfoot 140000
derryk o'brien 125000
```

This is the first time we made a comparison test on a *field*—here, the sixth field ($6). In fact, field matching is implemented only in **awk** and **perl**. Even though the operators >, <, and so on are mostly used for numeric comparison, they can be used to compare two strings. The comparison "abc" > "a" is true. But is 0.0 greater than 0? It all depends on whether **awk** interprets them as numbers or strings. Consider these three sets of examples:

```
x=0.0 ; y = 0
x > y                                              Compared numerically; not true
x="0.0" ; y ="0"
x > y                                                 Compared as strings; true
x=0.0 ; y ="0"
x > y                                              y  converted to number; not true
```

Observe the automatic conversions that take place here. While 0 and 0.0 are numerically equal, they are two different strings when quoted. **awk** forces conversion of "0" to numeric 0 when compared with 0.0.

> **Tip** When faced with the situation of comparing a string to a number, you need to ensure that **awk** does exactly the type of conversion you want. If you want the string to be converted to a number, add zero to it. If the number is to be converted to a string, concatenate it with an empty string.

12.5.2 ~ and !~: The Regular Expression Operators

How does one match regular expressions? Previously we had used **awk** with a regular expression in this manner:

```
awk '/wilco[cx]k*s*/' emp.lst
```

This matches a pattern anywhere in the line and not in a specific field. For matching a regular expression with a field, **awk** offers the ~ operator; the !~ operator negates the match. The left operand is a variable (like the field number), and the right operand is the regular expression enclosed by a pair of /s:

```
$2 ~ /wilco[cx]k*s*/                              Matches second field
$3 !~ /director|chairman/                          Neither director nor chairman
```

The anchoring characters, ^ and $, *could* have a different significance when used with regular expression operators. They anchor the pattern at the beginning and end of a *field,* unless you use them with $0. You can't search /etc/passwd for UID 0 in this way:

```
$ awk -F: '$3 ~ /0/' /etc/passwd
root:x:0:0:root:/root:/bin/bash
ftp:x:40:49:FTP account:/srv/ftp:/bin/bash
uucp:x:10:14:Unix-to-Unix CoPy system:/etc/uucp:/bin/bash
sumit:x:500:100:sumitabha das:/home/sumit:/bin/bash
```

All four lines contain an embedded 0 in the third field. We are actually looking for a solitary zero here, so anchoring is necessary:

```
$ awk -F: '$3 ~ /^0$/' /etc/passwd
root:x:0:0:root:/root:/bin/bash
```

However, numeric comparison would be more appropriate here; use $3 == 0. We now have been able to match patterns using both the string comparison and regular expression operators. Table 12.4 highlights examples of their usage.

Tip

To match a string embedded in a field, you must use ~ instead of ==. Similarly, to negate a match, use !~ instead of !=.

12.5.3 The Logical Operators

awk supports three logical or boolean operators and expressions, and uses them to return true or false values. They are &&, ||, and ! and are used by C, **perl**, and the shell with identical significance:

```
exp1 && exp2        True if both exp1 and exp2 are true.
exp1 || exp2        True if either exp1 or exp2 is true.
!exp                True if exp is false.
```

We'll now use these operators in combination with string, numeric, and regular expression tests that we have just seen. The following examples illustrate the use of the logical operators:

TABLE 12.4 *Matching Regular Expressions*

Selection Criteria	Matches
/negroponte/	negroponte anywhere in line
$0 ~ /negroponte/	Same as above
! /negroponte/	Lines not containing negroponte
$1 = "negroponte"	Wrong; negroponte assigned to $1
$1 == "negroponte"	negroponte as the first field
$1 == "^negroponte"	^negroponte; not a regular expression
$1 ~ /negroponte/	negroponte embedded in first field
$1 ~ /^negroponte$/	Exactly negroponte in first field
$0 !~ /negroponte/	Lines not containing negroponte
$0 ~ /negroponte$/	negroponte at end of line
$0 ~ /^negroponte$/	negroponte as only string in line
$0 ~ /^$/	Blank line
/^$/	Same as above

`$3 == "director" || $3 == "chairman"`	*Either* director *or* chairman
`$3 != "director" && $3 != "chairman"`	*Neither* director *nor* chairman
`NR < 5 || NR > 10`	*Either lines 1 to 4 or 11 and above*

The selection criteria in the second example translates to this: "Select those lines where the third field doesn't (!=) completely match the string director and (&&) also doesn't (!=) completely match the string chairman.

Boolean operators let us make complex searches, even on multiple fields. In the following example, we look up /etc/passwd for lines containing details of two users: root and the one with UID 4:

```
$ awk -F: '$1 ~ /^root$/ || $3 == 4' /etc/passwd
root:x:0:0:root:/root:/bin/bash
lp:x:4:7:Printing daemon:/var/spool/lpd:/bin/bash
```

The operators can also be used multiple times. Parentheses may have to be used to override the normal associativity rules:

```
awk -F: '($3 > 1 && $3 < 4) || ($3 >=7 && $3 <=12)' /etc/passwd
```

This selects users with UID between 2 and 3 and 7 and 12.

12.6 The -f Option: Storing awk Programs in a File

You should hold large **awk** programs in separate files and provide them with the .awk extension for easier identification. Consider the following program that is stored in the file **empawk.awk**:

```
$ cat empawk.awk
$3 == "director" && $6 > 120000 {
printf "%4d %-20s %-12s %d\n", ++kount,$2,$3,$6 }
```

Observe that this time we haven't used any quotes to enclose the **awk** program. You can now use **awk** with the -f *filename* option:

```
awk -F: -f empawk.awk empn.lst
```

Note

If you use **awk** with the -f option, make sure the program stored in the file is not enclosed within quotes. **awk** uses quotes only when the program is specified in the command line or the entire **awk** command line is held in a shell script.

12.7   The BEGIN and END Sections

If you have to print something before processing the first line, for example, a heading, then the BEGIN section can be used quite gainfully. Similarly, the END section is useful in printing some totals after processing is over.

The BEGIN and END sections are optional and take the form

```
BEGIN { action }                                    Both require curly braces
END { action }
```

When present, these sections are delimited by the body of the **awk** program. You can use them to print a suitable heading at the beginning and the average salary at the end. Store this **awk** program in a separate file **empawk2.awk** (Fig. 12.2).

Like the shell, **awk** uses the # for providing comments. The BEGIN section prints a suitable heading, offset by two tabs (\t\t), while the END section prints the average salary (tot/kount) for the selected lines:

FIGURE 12.2   empawk2.awk

```
BEGIN {
   printf "\t\tEmployee abstract\n\n"
} $6 > 120000 {                  # Increment variables for serial number and pay
   kount++ ; tot+= $6            # Multiple assignments in one line
   printf "%3d %-20s %-12s %d\n", kount,$2,$3,$6
}
END {
   printf "\n\tThe average salary is %6d\n", tot/kount
}
```

```
$ awk -F: -f empawk2.awk empn.1st
                  Employee abstract

  1 bill johnson         director     130000
  2 barry wood           chairman     160000
  3 gordon lightfoot      director     140000
  4 derryk o'brien        director     125000

          The average salary is 138750
```

Like all filters, **awk** reads standard input when the filename is omitted. We can make **awk** behave like a simple scripting language by doing all work in the BEGIN section. This is how you perform floating point arithmetic:

```
$ awk 'BEGIN { printf "%f\n", 22/7 }'
3.142857
```

This is something that you can't do with **expr** *(13.10.1)*. Depending on your version of **awk,** the prompt may or may not be returned, which means that **awk** may still be reading standard input. Use *[Ctrl-d]* to return the prompt.

Caution

Always start the opening brace in the same line the section (BEGIN or END) begins. If you don't, **awk** will generate some strange messages!

12.8 Positional Parameters

The program in **empawk2.awk** could take a more generalized form if the number 120000 is replaced with a variable. A shell script uses special parameters like $1, $2, and so on, to represent the command line arguments passed to the script. Because **awk** also uses the same parameters as field identifiers, quoting helps to distinguish between a field identifier and a shell parameter.

When you run a shell script with one argument, this argument is accessed inside the script as $1. An **awk** program placed in the script accesses it as '$1' but only if the entire **awk** command (not just the program) is stored in the script (say, **empabs.sh**). Let's make a nominal change to the script containing the **awk** program:

```
$6 > '$1'                                          Instead of $6 > 120000
```

Now place the entire **awk** command line in a shell script. A shell script needs execute permission, so follow the instructions given in Section 7.12. Now invoke the shell script with an argument, and the argument will be visible inside the **awk** program:

```
empabs.sh 100000
```

You are now able to build a facility of querying a database to select those lines that satisfy a selection criterion, i.e., the salary exceeding a certain figure. With a nominal amount of **awk** programming, you could also calculate the average salary of the persons selected. You couldn't have done all this with **grep** or **sed**; they simply can't perform computations.

12.9 Arrays

An **array** is also a variable except that this variable can store a set of values or elements. Each element is accessed by a subscript called the **index**. Arrays in **awk** are different from the ones used in other programming languages in many respects:

- They are not formally defined. An array is considered declared the moment it is used.
- Array elements are initialized to zero or an empty string unless initialized explicitly.
- Arrays expand automatically.
- The index can be virtually anything; it can even be a string.

We'll save discussions on the last point for Section 12.10. For now, we'll use the BEGIN section to test the other features. We set three array elements subscripted by 1, 2, and 1000 before printing their values. We then insert an element into the array using a large index value and then delete one array element:

```
$ awk 'BEGIN {
>     mon[1] = "jan" ; mon[2] = "feb" ; mon[1000] = "illegal month" ;
>     printf("Month 1 is %s and month 1000 is %s\n", mon[1], mon[1000]) ;
>     printf("Month 500 is %s and month 5000 is %s\n", mon[500], mon[5000]);
>
>     # Now delete mon[1]
>     delete mon[1] ;
>     printf("Month 2 still remains %s\n", mon[2]) ;
> }'
Month 1 is jan and month 1000 is illegal month
Month 500 is  and month 5000 is
Month 2 still remains feb
```

Observe that subscripts 500 and 5000 of the mon[ ] array point to null strings. Deletion of an array element only sets it to a null string and doesn't rearrange the elements.

In the program **empawk3.awk** (Fig. 12.3), we use an array to store the totals of the salary and commission (@20% of salary) for the sales and marketing people. The program outputs the averages of the two elements of pay:

FIGURE 12.3   empawk3.awk

```
BEGIN { FS = ":" ; printf "%44s\n", "Salary    Commission" }
$4 ~ /sales|marketing/ {
    commission = $6*0.20
    tot[1] += $6 ; tot[2] += commission
    kount++
}
END { printf "\t    Average  %5d   %5d\n", tot[1]/kount, tot[2]/kount }
```

```
$ awk -f empawk3.awk empn.lst
                      Salary    Commission
            Average   105625    21125
```

C programmers should find the program quite comfortable to work with except that **awk** simplifies a number of things that require explicit specification in C. There are no type declarations, no initializations, and no statement terminators.

12.9.1 Associative (Hash) Arrays

Even though we used integers as subscripts in arrays mon[ ] and tot[ ], **awk** doesn't treat array indexes as integers. **awk** arrays are **associative**, where information is held as *key–value* pairs. The index is the key that is saved internally as a string. When we set an array element using mon[1] = "jan", **awk** converts the number 1 to a string. There's no specified order in which the array elements are stored. As the following example suggests, the index "1" is different from "01":

```
$ awk 'BEGIN {
>     direction["N"] = "North" ; direction["S"] = "South" ;
>     direction["E"] = "East" ; direction["W"] = "West" ;
>     printf("N is %s and W is %s\n", direction["N"], direction["W"]) ;
>
>     mon[1] = "jan" ; mon["1"] = "january" ; mon["01"] = "JAN" ;
>     printf("mon[1] is %s\n", mon[1]) ;
>     printf("mon[01] is also %s\n", mon[01]) ;
>     printf("mon[\"1\"] is also %s\n", mon["1"]) ;
>     printf("But mon[\"01\"] is %s\n", mon["01"]) ;
> }'
N is North and W is West
mon[1] is january
mon[01] is also january
mon["1"] is also january
But mon["01"] is JAN
```

There are two important things to be learned from this output. First, the setting with index "1" overwrites the setting made with index 1. Accessing an array element with subscripts 1 and 01 actually locates the element with subscript "1". Also note that mon["1"] is different from mon["01"].

12.9.2 ENVIRON[ ]: The Environment Array

You may sometimes need to know the name of the user running the program or the home directory. **awk** maintains the associative array, ENVIRON[ ], to store all environment variables. This POSIX requirement is met by recent versions of **awk** including **nawk** and **gawk**. This is how we access the shell variables, HOME and PATH, from an **awk** program:

```
$ nawk 'BEGIN {
> print "HOME" "=" ENVIRON["HOME"]
```

```
> print "PATH" "=" ENVIRON["PATH"]
> }'
HOME=/users1/home/staff/sumit
PATH=/usr/bin::/usr/local/bin:/usr/ccs/bin
```

In Section 12.13.1, we'll use a special form of a **for** loop to print all environment variables.

12.10   Built-In Variables

awk has several built-in variables (Table 12.5). They are all assigned automatically, though it is also possible for a user to reassign some of them. You have already used NR, which signifies the record number of the current line. We'll now have a brief look at some of the other variables.

The FS Variable   As stated elsewhere, **awk** uses a contiguous string of spaces as the default field delimiter. FS redefines this field separator. When used at all, it must occur in the BEGIN section so that the body of the program knows its value before it starts processing:

```
BEGIN { FS = ":" }
```

This is an alternative to the -F: option of the command which does the same thing.

The OFS Variable   When you used the **print** statement with comma-separated arguments, each argument was separated from the other by a space. This is **awk**'s default output field separator, and can be reassigned using the variable OFS in the BEGIN section:

```
BEGIN { OFS="~" }
```

When you rseassign this variable with a ~ (tilde), **awk** uses this character for delimiting the **print** arguments. This is a useful variable for creating lines with delimited fields.

TABLE 12.5   *Built-In Variables*

Variable	Function	Default Value
NR	Cumulative number of lines read	-
FS	Input field separator	space
OFS	Output field separator	space
OFMT	Default floating point format	%.6f
RS	Record separator	newline
NF	Number of fields in current line	-
FILENAME	Current input file	-
ARGC	Number of arguments in command line	-
ARGV	Array containing list of arguments	-
ENVIRON	Associative array containing all environment variables	-

The RS Variable **awk** uses the term *record* to define a group of lines. The record separator is stored in the RS variable. By default it is a newline, so each line is also a record. We'll soon take up an example where we manipulate the value of RS to combine a group of three lines to a single record.

The NF Variable NF represents the number of fields in each record. It comes in quite handy in identifying lines that don't contain the correct number of fields:

```
$ awk  'BEGIN { FS = ":" }
> NF != 6 {
> print "Record No ", NR, "has ", NF, " fields"}' empx.lst
Record No 6 has 4 fields
Record No 17 has 5 fields
```

If a record has seven fields, then NF has the value seven, and $NF would be $7. This is how you can print the last two fields without even knowing the number of fields in each line:

```
$ awk -F: '/^root/ { print $1, $(NF-1), $NF }' /etc/passwd
root /root /bin/bash
```

The FILENAME variable FILENAME stores the name of the current file being processed. Like **grep** and **sed**, **awk** can also handle multiple filenames in the command line. By default, **awk** doesn't print the filename, but you can instruct it to do so:

```
'$6 < 4000 { print FILENAME, $0 }'
```

With FILENAME, you can devise logic that does different things depending on the file being processed.

12.10.1 Applying the Built-In Variables

Let's use some of these variables in our next example which works with a revised form of the addressbook used in Section 10.9. Our addressbook contains three records, each comprising three lines. This time, we'll have a blank line between each record:

```
$ cat addressbook
barry wood
woodb@yahoo.com
245-690-4004

charles harris
charles_harris@heavens.com
345-865-3209

james wilcocks
james.wilcocks@heavens.com
190-349-0743
```

A blank line between each record

We'll now manipulate the built-in variables to have the details of each person on a single line, using the : as delimiter (OFS = ":"). Our record separator needs to be defined as a blank line (RS =""). Each line is treated like a field here, so FS should be set to newline. Our new address book can be created by this simple two-liner:

```
$ awk 'BEGIN {FS = "\n" ; OFS = ":" ; RS = "" }
> { print $1, $2, $NF }' addressbook | tee addressbook3
barry wood:woodb@yahoo.com:245-690-4004
charles harris:charles_harris@heavens.com:345-865-3209
james wilcocks:james.wilcocks@heavens.com:190-349-0743
```

We tried out a similar exercise with **paste** before, but that address book didn't have blank lines. Can we now have our original addressbook back from this output saved in addressbook3?

■ 12.11 Functions

awk has several built-in functions, performing both arithmetic and string operations (Table 12.6). The arguments are passed to a function in C-style, delimited by commas, and enclosed by a matched pair of parentheses. Even though **awk** allows use of functions with and without parentheses (like **printf** and **printf()**), POSIX discourages use of functions without parentheses.

Some of these functions take a variable number of arguments, and one (**length()**) uses no argument as a variant form. The functions are adequately explained here, so you can confidently use them in **perl** which often uses identical syntaxes.

TABLE 12.6 *Built-In Functions*

Function	Description
Arithmetic	
int(*x*)	Returns integer value of *x*
sqrt(*x*)	Returns square root of *x*
String	
length()	Returns length of complete line
length(*x*)	Returns length of *x*
tolower(*s*)	Returns string *s* after conversion to uppercase
toupper(*s*)	Returns string *s* after conversion to lowercase
substr(*stg,m*)	Returns remaining string from position *m* in string *stg*
substr(*stg,m,n*)	Returns portion of string of length *n*, starting from position *m* in string *stg*
index(*s1,s2*)	Returns position of string *s2* in string *s1*
split(*stg,arr, ch*)	Splits string *stg* into array *arr* using *ch* as delimiter; returns number of fields
system("*cmd*")	Runs UNIX command *cmd* and returns its exit status

length() **length()** determines the length of its argument, and if no argument is present, then it assumes the entire line as its argument. You can use **length()** to locate lines whose length exceeds 1024 characters:

```
awk -F: 'length() > 1024' empn.lst                          Same as length($0)
```

You can use **length()** with a field as argument as well. The following program selects those people who have short names:

```
awk -F: 'length($2) < 11' empn.lst
```

index() **index(**s1,s2**)** determines the position of a string s2 within a larger string s1. This function is especially useful in validating single-character fields. If you have a field which can take the values a, b, c, d, or e, you can use this function to find out whether this single character field can be located within the string abcde:

```
x = index("abcde","b")
```

This returns the value 2.

substr() The **substr(**stg,m,n**)** function returns a substring from a string stg. Here, m represents the starting point of extraction, and n indicates the number of characters to be extracted. If n is omitted, then extraction continues to the end of stg. Because string values can also be used for computation, the returned string from this function can be used to select those born between 1946 and 1951:

```
$ awk -F: 'substr($5,7,2) > 45 && substr($5,7,2) < 52' empn.lst
9876:bill johnson:director:production:03/12/50:130000
2365:john woodcock:director:personnel:05/11/47:120000
4290:neil o'bryan:executive:production:09/07/50: 65000
3564:ronie trueman:executive:personnel:07/06/47: 75000
```

Note that **awk** does indeed possess a mechanism of identifying the type of expression from its context. It identified the date field as a string for using **substr()** and then converted it to a number for making a numeric comparison.

split() **split(**stg,arr,ch**)** breaks up a string stg on the delimiter ch and stores the fields in an associative array arr[ ]. Here's how you can convert the date field to the format *YYYYMMDD:*

```
$ awk -F: '{split($5,ar,"/") ; print "19"ar[3]ar[1]ar[2]}' empn.lst
19521212
19500312
19430419
  . . . . .
```

You can also do this with **sed**, but this method is superior because it explicitly picks up the fifth field, whereas **sed** would transform the only date field it finds.

system() You may want to print the system date at the beginning of the report. For running any UNIX command within **awk**, you'll have to use the **system()** function. Here are two examples:

```
BEGIN {
    system("tput clear")                                    Clears the screen
    system("date") }                            Executes the UNIX date command
```

You should be familiar with all the functions discussed in this section as they are used in a wide variety of situations. We'll use them again in **perl**. **awk** features some more built-in variables and functions, and also allows the user to define her own functions.

12.12   Control Flow—The if Statement

Like any programming language, **awk** supports conditional structures (the **if** statement) and loops (**while** and **for**). They all execute a body of statements till their **control command** evaluates to true. This control command is simply a condition that is specified in the first line of the construct.

The **if** statement permits two-way decision making, and its behavior is well known to all programmers. The construct has also been elaborated in Section 13.6 where it appears in three forms. The statement in **awk** takes this form:

```
if ( condition is true ) {
    statements
} else {                                                    else is optional
    statements
}
```

The control command itself must be enclosed in parentheses. As in C, the statements form a code block delimited by curly braces. As in C, the { and } are required only when multiple statements are executed. The **else** section is optional.

Most of the selection criteria used so far reflect the logic normally used in the **if** statement. In a previous example, you selected lines where the salary exceeded 120,000 dollars by using the condition as the selection criterion:

```
'$6 > 120000 {...}'
```

An alternative form of this logic places the condition inside the action component. But this form requires the **if** statement:

```
awk -F: '{ if ($6 > 120000) printf .....
```

To illustrate the use of the optional **else** statement, let's assume that the commission is 15 percent of salary when the latter is less than 100,000 dollars, and 10 percent otherwise. The **if-else** structure that implements this logic looks like this:

FIGURE 12.4 addressbook.awk

```
{
    mod = NR % 3               # Either a 0, 1, or 2
    if (mod == 1)              # First line of record
        line = $0
    else {                     # Lines 2 or 3
        line = line " " $0     # Join on space
        if (mod == 0) {
            print line
            line = ""          # Prepare for next record
        }
    }
}
```

```
if ( $6 < 100000 )
    commission = 0.15*$6
else
    commission = 0.10*$6
```

Let's now use the **if-else** form to combine every three lines of our original addressbook *(10.9)* to a single line. We have done this with **paste** before *(10.9);* we'll do it again using the program **addressbook.awk** (Fig. 12.4).

Each record of this address book has three lines and the modulo function helps determine the line that is currently being processed. What **paste** could do with a single line of code is done by **awk** with 10 lines:

```
$ awk -f addressbook.awk addressbook
barry wood woodb@yahoo.com 245-690-4004
charles harris charles_harris@heavens.com 345-865-3209
james wilcocks james.wilcocks@heavens.com 190-349-0743
```

12.13 Looping with for

awk supports two loops—**for** and **while**. They both execute the loop body as long as the control command returns a true value. **for** has two forms. The easier one resembles its C counterpart:

```
for ( k=1 ; k<=9 ; k+= 2 )
```

Three components control the behavior of the loop. The first component (k=1) initializes the value of k, the second (k <= 9) checks the condition with every iteration, while the

FIGURE 12.5 `reverse_fields.awk`

```
BEGIN{ FS=":"} {
    if ($1 ~ /^root$|^uucp$/) {
        line = ""
        for (i = NF ; i> 0 ; i--)
            line = line ":" $i
        print line
    }
}
```

third (k += 2) sets the increment used for every iteration. The program **reverse_fields.awk** (Fig. 12.5) uses a **for** loop to print fields of /etc/passwd in reverse.

　　With every iteration of the **for** loop, the variable line accumulates each field of a line, delimited by the colon. The variable is printed when the iteration ends and is initialized to a null string before the iteration begins. We now run this program to act on the entries for root and uucp:

```
$ awk -f reverse_fields.awk /etc/passwd
:/usr/bin/bash:/:Super-User:1:0:x:root
::/usr/lib/uucp:uucp Admin:5:5:x:uucp
```

The program logic isn't perfect; each line begins with a :, which you can eliminate through some additional programming.

12.13.1 Using for with an Associative Array

The second form of the **for** loop exploits the associative feature of **awk**'s arrays. This form is similar to the **foreach** function of **perl** but is not seen in the commonly used languages like C and Java. The loop selects each index of an array:

```
for ( k in arr ) {
    statements
}
```

Here, k is the subscript of the array *arr*. Because k can also be a string, we can use this loop to print all environment variables. We simply have to pick up each subscript of the ENVIRON array:

```
$ nawk 'BEGIN {
>   for (key in ENVIRON)
>       print key "=" ENVIRON[key]
> }'
LOGNAME=sumit
MAIL=/var/mail/sumit
```

```
PATH=/usr/bin::/usr/local/bin:/usr/ccs/bin
TERM=xterm
HOME=/users1/home/staff/sumit
SHELL=/usr/bin/bash
    ......
```

Because the index is actually a string, we can use any field as the index. We can even use elements of the array as counters. Using our sample database, we can display a count of the employees, grouped according to designation (the third field). You can use the string value of $3 as the subscript of the array kount[ ]:

```
$ awk -F: '{ kount[$3]++ }
> END { for ( desig in kount)
> printf "%-10s %4d\n", desig, kount[desig] }' empn.lst
d.g.m.       2
g.m.         4
director     4
executive    2
manager      2
chairman     1
```

The program here analyzes the database to group employees according to their designation and count their occurrences. The array kount[] takes as its subscript nonnumeric values like g.m., chairman, executive, and so forth. The **for** loop is invoked in the END section to print the subscript (desig) and the number of occurrences of the subscript (kount[desig]). Note that you don't need to sort the input file to print this report!

Note

The same logic has already been implemented by using three commands in a pipeline—**cut**, **sort**, and **uniq** *(10.11.1)*. That one used only a single line of code!

12.14 Looping with while

The **while** loop has a similar role to play; it repeatedly iterates the loop till the control command succeeds:

```
while (condition is true) {
    statements
}
```

Many **for** loops can be replaced with a **while** loop. Which loop to use in a particular situation is often a matter of taste. We'll use a **while** loop to generate email addresses using the GCOS field (the fifth) of /etc/passwd. Here, this field contains the full name of the user as shown by a few lines:

```
henry:!:501:100:henry higgins:/home/henry:/bin/ksh
julie:x:508:100:julie andrews:/home/julie:/bin/ksh
steve:x:510:100:steve wozniak:/home/steve:/bin/ksh
```

FIGURE 12.6 `email_create.awk`

```
BEGIN { FS = ":" }
{ fullname = "" ; x=0 ;
  array_length = split($5, name_arr," ") ;
  while ( x++ <= array_length )  {
    if (x < array_length)
        name_arr[x] = name_arr[x] "_" ;
    fullname = fullname name_arr[x] ;
  }
  printf "%s@heavens.com\n", fullname
}
```

The addresses have to be of the form *henry_higgins@heavens.com*. The program
email_create.awk (Fig. 12.6) should do the job. It uses the **split()** function both for
its side-effect and return value.

The **split()** function splits the GCOS field ($5) on a space to the array name_arr.
split() also returns the number of elements found, and the variable array_length
stores this value. The **for** loop picks up each name from the array and concatenates it
with the previous one with the _ character. This has to be done for all elements except
the last one. When you run the program with the password file, you'll see properly
formatted email addresses:

```
$ awk -f email_create.awk /etc/passwd
henry_higgins@heavens.com
julie_andrews@heavens.com
steve_wozniak@heavens.com
....
```

Like **for**, **while** also uses the **continue** statement to start a premature iteration and
break to exit the loop. **awk** also supports a **do-while** loop which is similar to **while**
except that at least one iteration takes place. We'll examine the **continue** and **break**
statements when we take up shell programming and the **do-while** loop in **perl**.

12.15 Conclusion

awk, like **sed,** violates the do-one-thing-well philosophy that generally characterizes all
UNIX tools. Although presented in this chapter as a utility filter, it's more of a scripting
language. You can now intermingle strings with numbers. Partly because of the absence
of type declarations and initializations, an **awk** program is often a fraction of the size of
its C counterpart.

awk has been completely overwhelmed in sheer power by **perl**—the latest and most
notable addition to the UNIX tool kit for several years. There is nothing that any UNIX filter
can do that **perl** can't. In fact, **perl** is even more compact, faster, and in every sense better

than any Unix filter. This chapter was prepared for you to more fully understand **perl** because so many of the constructs are also used there. **perl** is taken up in Chapter 15.

SUMMARY

awk combines the features of several filters and can manipulate individual fields ($1, $2, etc.) in a line ($0). It uses **sed**-type addresses and the built-in variable NR to determine line numbers.

Lines are printed with **print** and **printf**. The latter uses format specifiers to format strings (%s), integers (%d), and floating point numbers (%f). Each **print** or **printf** statement can be used with the shell's operators for redirection and piping.

awk uses all the comparison operators (like >, ==, <= etc.). The ~ and !~ operators are used to match regular expressions and negate a match. Operators and regular expressions can be applied both to a specific field as well as to the entire line.

awk variables and constants have no explicit data type. **awk** identifies the type from its context and makes the necessary string or numeric conversions when performing computation or string handling. By handling decimal numbers, **awk** also overcomes a limitation of the shell.

awk can take instructions from an external file (-f). The BEGIN and END sections are used to do some pre- and post-processing work. Typically, a report header is generated by the BEGIN section, and a numeric total is computed in the END section.

awk's built-in variables can be used to specify the field delimiter (FS), the number of fields (NF), and the filename (FILENAME). **awk** uses one-dimensional arrays where the array subscript can be a string as well.

awk has a number of built-in functions, and many of them are used for string handling. You can find the length (**length()**), extract a substring (**substr()**), and find the location (**index()**) of a string within a larger string. The **system()** function executes a UNIX command.

The **if** statement uses the return value of its control command to determine program flow. **if** also uses the operators || and && to handle complex conditions.

awk supports loops. The first form of the **for** loop uses an array and can be used to count occurrences of an item using a nonnumeric subscript. The other form resembles its C counterpart. The **while** loop repeats a set of instructions as long as its control command returns a true value.

perl is better than **awk**.

SELF-TEST

Some questions use the file empn.1st *whose contents are shown in Section 12.1.*

12.1   What is the difference between **print** and **print $0**? Is the **print** statement necessary for printing a line?

12.2   Select from empn.1st the people who were born either in September or December.

12.3   Implement the following commands in **awk**: (i) head -n 5, (ii) sed -n '5,10p', (iii) tail +20, (iv) grep negroponte

12.4 Use **awk** to renumber the lines:

```
1. fork
3. execve
2. wait
5. sleep
```

12.5 Use **awk** to delete all blank lines (including those that contain whitespace) from a file.

12.6 What is wrong with this statement? `printf "%s %-20s\n", $1, $6 | sort`

12.7 How do you print only the odd-numbered lines of a file?

12.8 Split `empn.lst` so that lines are saved in two separate files depending on whether the salary exceeds 100,000 dollars.

12.9 How do you print the last field without knowing the number of fields in a line?

12.10 How do you locate lines longer than 100 and smaller than 150 characters?

12.11 Devise a sequence to display the total size of all ordinary files in the current directory.

12.12 Using arrays, invert the name of the individual in `empn.lst` so that the last name occurs first.

12.13 Calculate from `empn.lst` the average pay and store it in a variable.

12.14 Display the files in your home directory tree that have been last modified on January 6 of the current year at the 11th hour.

12.15 Use a **for** loop to center the output of the command **echo "DOCUMENT LIST"**, where the page width is 55 characters.

12.16 Repeat Problem 12.15 with a **while** loop.

EXERCISES

Some questions use the file `empn.lst` *whose contents are shown in Section 12.1.*

12.1 Display from `/etc/passwd` a list of users and their shells for those using the Korn shell or Bash. Order the output by the absolute pathname of the shell used.

12.2 Find out the next available UID in `/etc/passwd` after ignoring all system users placed at the beginning and up to the occurrence of the user nobody.

12.3 The **tar** command on one system can't accept absolute pathnames longer than 100 characters. How can you generate a list of such files?

12.4 Devise a sequence to examine recursively all ordinary files in the current directory and display their total space usage. Hard-linked files will be counted only once.

12.5 Use **awk** in a shell script to kill a process by specifying its name rather than the PID.

12.6 From a **tar** archive print only the pathnames of directories. Directory pathnames end with a /, but the **tar** output may contain a variable number of fields.

12.7 How do you list the users currently using the system along with a count of the number of times they have logged in?

12.8 Develop an **awk** program to summarize from the list of all processes a count of processes run by every user (including root).

12.9 Write an **awk** sequence in a shell script which accepts input from the standard input. The program should print the total of any column specified as script argument. For instance, *prog1* | *awk_prog* 3 should print the total of the third column in the output of *prog1*.

12.10 A shell script uses the LOGNAME variable which is not set on your system. Use the string handling features of **awk** to set LOGNAME from the output of the **id** command. This assignment will be made at the shell prompt, but its value must be visible in the script.

12.11 A stamp dealer maintains a price list that displays the country, the Scott catalog number, year of issue, description, and price:

```
Kenya 288-92 1984 Heron Plover Thrush Gonolek Apalis $6.60
Surinam 643-54 1983 Butterflies $7.50
Seychelles 831-34 2002 WWF Frogs set of 4 $1.40
Togo 1722-25 1996 Cheetah, Zebra, Antelope $5.70
```

Write an **awk** program to print a formatted report of the data as well as the total price. Note that the description contains a variable number of words.

12.12 Write an **awk** program to provide extra spaces at the end of a line (if required) so that the line length is maintained at 127.

12.13 A file contains a fixed number of fields in the form of space-delimited numbers. Write an **awk** program to print the lines as well as a total of its rows and columns. The program doesn't need to know the number of fields in each line.

✓12.14 Develop an **awk** program that reads /etc/passwd and prints the names of those users having the same GID in the form *GID name1 name2 ......* Does the input data need to be sorted?

12.15 Improve **addressbook.awk** *(12.12)* to place the entire **awk** program in a shell script. The script accepts three parameters: the number of lines comprising a record, the input file, and the desired delimiter.

12.16 Develop a control-break **awk** program that reads empn.lst and prints a report that groups employees of the same department. For each department, the report should print:

  (i) the department name at the top.
  (ii) the remaining details of every person in the department.
  (iii) total salary bill for that department.

  Do you need to process the input before it is read by **awk**?

✓12.17 Observe a few lines of the output of the **last** command which displays information on every login session of every user. The last field shows the usage in *hours:minutes* for that session:

```
henry    pts/5    pc134.pdsit.becs    Tue Sep 16 15:10 - 18:08  (02:57)
romeo    pts/7    pc126.pdsit.becs    Tue Sep 16 16:52 - 17:14  (00:22)
juliet   pts/2    pc127.pdsit.becs    Tue Sep 16 11:53 - 13:09  (01:15)
romeo    pts/2    pc126.pdsit.becs    Mon Sep 15 12:17 - 12:40  (00:22)
root     console  :0                  Sat Feb 23 07:54 - 08:23  (00:28)
henry    pts/4    pc134.pdsit.becs    Sat Sep  6 20:49 - 20:59  (00:10)
```

Print a summary report for each user that shows the total number of hours and minutes of computer time that he or she has consumed. Note that the output contains a variable number of fields and a user can occur multiple times.

12.18   Your task is to create an empty directory structure bar2 from a nonempty directory tree bar1. Both bar1 and bar2 will be at the same hierarchical level. You have to use **mkdir** in an efficient manner so that intermediate directories are automatically created. This is what you have to do:

   (i) Create a directory list from bar1 with **find** and order it if necessary.
   (ii) Using an **awk** program, remove all branches from the list so that you can run **mkdir** only on the leaves.
   (iii) Run **mkdir** with the list to replicate the directory structure of bar1.

Specify the complete sequence of operations needed for the job. If **mkdir** fails because the number of arguments is too large, can you divide the job into manageable portions using **xargs** (Section 7.15—Going Further)?

## CHAPTER 13

Shell Programming

The activities of the shell are not restricted to command interpretation alone. The shell has a whole set of internal commands that can be strung together as a language—with its own variables, conditionals, and loops. Most of its constructs are borrowed from C, but there are syntactical differences between them. What makes shell programming powerful is that the external UNIX commands blend easily with the shell's internal constructs in *shell scripts*.

In this chapter, we examine the programming features of the lowest common denominator of all shells—the Bourne shell. However, everything discussed here applies to both Korn and Bash. The C shell uses totally different programming constructs that are presented in Appendix A. The exclusive programming-related features of Korn and Bash are featured in Appendix B.

Objectives

- Discover how shell scripts are executed and the role of the *she-bang line*.
- Make shell scripts interactive using **read**.
- Use *positional parameters* to read command line arguments.
- Understand the significance of the *exit status* and the **exit** statement.
- Learn rudimentary decision making with the || and && operators.
- Learn comprehensive decision making with the **if** conditional.
- Discover numeric and string comparison and file attribute testing with **test**.
- Use the pattern matching features of **case** for decision making.
- Learn integer computing and string handling using **expr** and **basename**.
- Learn how hard links and $0 can make a script behave as different programs.
- Use a **for** loop to iterate with each element of a list.
- Use a **while** loop to repeatedly execute a set of commands.
- Manipulate the positional parameters with **set** and **shift**.
- Review three real-life applications that make use of these features.
- Use a *here document* to run an interactive shell script noninteractively. *(Going Further)*
- Develop modular code using *shell functions*. *(Going Further)*
- Handle signals using **trap** to control script behavior. *(Going Further)*
- Use **eval** to evaluate a command line twice. *(Going Further)*
- Overlay the current program with another using **exec**. *(Going Further)*

13.1   Shell Scripts

When a group of commands have to be executed regularly, they should be stored in a file, and the file executed as a **shell script** or **shell program**. Though it's not mandatory, using the .sh extension for shell scripts makes it easy to match them with wild cards.

A shell script needs to have execute permission when invoked by its name. It is not compiled to a separate executable file as a C program is. It runs in *interpretive* mode and in a separate child process. The calling process (often, the login shell) forks a sub-shell, which reads the script file and loads each statement into memory when it is to be executed.

Shell scripts are thus slower than compiled programs, but speed is not a constraint with certain jobs. Shell scripts are not recommended for number crunching. They are typically used to automate routine tasks and often scheduled to run noninteractively with **cron**. System administrative tasks are often best handled by shell scripts, the reason why *the UNIX system administrator must be an accomplished shell programmer.*

BASH Shell

Generally, Bourne shell scripts run without problem in the Korn and Bash shells. There are two issues in Bash, however. First, Bash evaluates $0 differently. This has to be handled by appropriate code in the script. Second, Bash doesn't recognize escape sequences used by **echo** (like \c and \n) unless the -e option is used. To make **echo** behave in the normal manner, place the statement **shopt -s xpg_echo** in your rc file (probably, ~/.bashrc).

13.1.1   script.sh: A Simple Script

Use your **vi** editor to create the shell script, **script.sh** (Fig. 13.1). The script runs three **echo** commands and shows the use of variable evaluation and command substitution. It also shows the important terminal settings, so you know which key to press to interrupt your script.

The first line is discussed in Section 13.1.2. Note the comment character, #, which can be placed anywhere in a line. The shell ignores all characters placed on its right. To run the script, make it executable first:

```
$ chmod +x script.sh
$ script.sh                                    PATH must include the dot
Today's date: Mon Sep  8 18:25:36 GMT 2003      or else use ./script.sh
My login shell: /usr/bin/bash
```

FIGURE 13.1   **script.sh**

```
#!/bin/sh
# script.sh: Sample shell script -- She-bang points to Bourne shell.
echo "Today's date: `date`"         # Double quotes protect single quote
echo "My login shell: $SHELL"       # $SHELL signifies login shell only
echo 'Note the stty settings'       # Using single quotes here
stty -a | grep intr
```

```
Note the stty settings
intr = ^c; quit = ^\; erase = ^?; kill = ^u;
```

This script takes no inputs or command line arguments and uses no control structures. We'll be progressively adding these features to our future scripts. If your current directory is not included in PATH, you may either include it in your profile or execute the script as **./script.sh** *(3.8).*

If you are using **vi** to edit your shell and **perl** scripts, then you need not leave the editor to execute the script. Just make two mappings of the *[F1]* and *[F2]* function keys in $HOME/.exrc:

:map #1 :w^M:!%^M	*For scripts that use no arguments*
:map #2 :w^M:!%	*For scripts that use arguments*

Tip

You can now press *[F1]* and *[F2]* to execute any shell script that has the execute bit set. Both keys save the buffer (:w^M) before executing the file (:!%). The character, ^M, represents the *[Enter]* key *(5.3.5).* (You can use the alias **cx** defined in Table 9.2 to make the script executable.)

13.1.2   The She-Bang Line

The first line of **script.sh** contains a string beginning with #!. This is not a comment line. It is called the **interpreter line**, **hash-bang**, or **she-bang line**. When the script executes, the login shell (which could even be a C shell) reads this line first to determine the pathname of the program to be used for running the script. Here, the login shell spawns a Bourne sub-shell which actually executes each statement in sequence (in interpretive mode).

If you don't provide the she-bang line, the login shell will spawn a child of its own type to run the script—which may not be the shell you want. You can also *explicitly* spawn a shell of your choice by running the program representing the shell with the script name as argument:

```
sh script.sh
```
Will spawn a Bourne shell

When used in this way, the Bourne sub-shell opens the file but ignores the interpreter line. The script doesn't need to have execute permission either. We'll make it a practice to use the she-bang line in all our scripts.

Tip

The pathname of the shell specified in the she-bang line may not match the actual pathname on your system. This sometimes happens with downloaded scripts. To prevent these scripts from breaking, make a symbolic link between the two locations. Note that root access is required to make a symbolic link between /bin/ksh and /usr/bin/ksh.

13.2   read: **Making Scripts Interactive**

The **read** statement is the shell's internal tool for taking input from the user, i.e., making scripts interactive. It is used with one or more variables that are assigned by keyboard input. The statement

```
read name
```
No $ here

FIGURE 13.2 `emp1.sh`

```
#!/bin/sh
# emp1.sh: Interactive version - uses read to take two inputs
#
echo "Enter the pattern to be searched: \c"        # No newline
read pname
echo "Enter the file to be used: \c"
read flname
echo "Searching for $pname from file $flname"
grep "$pname" $flname                              # Quote all variables
echo "Selected lines shown above"
```

makes the script pause at that point to take input from the standard input. Whatever you enter is stored in the variable name. Since this is a form of assignment, no $ is used before name. The script, **emp1.sh** (Fig. 13.2), uses **read** to take a search string and filename from the terminal.

You know what the sequence \c does *(2.6)*. Run the script and specify the inputs when the script pauses twice:

```
$ emp1.sh
Enter the pattern to be searched: director
Enter the file to be used: shortlist
Searching for director from file shortlist
9876:bill johnson     :director :production:03/12/50:130000
2365:john woodcock     :director :personnel :05/11/47:120000
Selected lines shown above
```

The script pauses twice. First, the string `director` is assigned to the variable pname. Next, `shortlist` is assigned to `flname`. **grep** then runs with these two variables as its arguments.

A single **read** statement can be used with one or more variables to let you enter multiple words:

```
read pname flname
```

Note that when the number of words keyed in exceeds the number of variables, the remaining words are assigned to the *last* variable. To assign multiple words to a single variable, quote the string.

13.3 Using Command Line Arguments

Scripts not using **read** can run noninteractively and be used with redirection and pipelines. Like UNIX commands (which are written in C), such scripts take their input from command line arguments. They are assigned to certain special "variables"—rather

positional parameters. The first argument is available in $1, the second in $2, and so on. In addition to these positional parameters, there are a few other special parameters used by the shell (Table 13.1). Their significance is noted below:

$* — Stores the complete set of positional parameters as a single string.

$# — Is set to the number of arguments specified. This lets you design scripts that check whether the right number of arguments have been entered.

$0 — Holds the script filename itself. You can link a shell script to be invoked by more than one name. The script logic can check $0 to behave differently depending on the name by which it is invoked. Section 13.8.2 exploits this feature.

The next script, **emp2.sh** (Fig. 13.3), runs **grep** with two positional parameters, $1 and $2, that are set by the script arguments, director and shortlist. It also evaluates $# and $*. Observe that $# is one less than argc, its C language counterpart:

```
$ emp2.sh director shortlist
Program: emp2.sh
The number of arguments specified is 2
The arguments are director shortlist
9876:bill johnson     :director :production:03/12/50:130000
2365:john woodcock   :director :personnel :05/11/47:120000

Job Over
```

The first word (the command itself) is assigned to $0. The first argument (director) is assigned to $1, and the second argument is assigned (shortlist) to $2. You can go up to $9 (and, using the **shift** statement, you can go beyond). These parameters are automatically set, and you can't use them on the left-hand side of an assignment ($1=director is illegal).

Every multiword string must be quoted to be treated as a single command line argument. To look for robert dylan, use **emp2.sh "robert dylan" shortlist**. If you don't quote, $# would be three and dylan would be treated as a filename by **grep**. You have also noted this quoting requirement when using **grep** *(11.2.1)*.

FIGURE 13.3   emp2.sh

```
#!/bin/sh
# emp2.sh: Non-interactive version -- uses command line arguments
#
echo "Program: $0"                # $0 contains the program name
echo "The number of arguments specified is $#"
echo "The arguments are $*"       # All arguments stored in $*
grep "$1" $2
echo "\nJob Over"
```

TABLE 13.1 *Special Parameters Used by the Shell*

Shell Parameter	Significance
$1, $2...	Positional parameters representing command line arguments
$#	Number of arguments specified in command line
$0	Name of executed command
$*	Complete set of positional parameters as a single string
"$@"	Each quoted string treated as a separate argument (recommended over $*)
$?	Exit status of last command
$$	PID of current shell *(8.2)*
$!	PID of last background job *(8.10.1)*

BASH Shell

$0 in Bash prepends the ./ prefix to the script name. In the example above, it would have shown ./emp2.sh instead of emp2.sh. You need to keep this in mind when you make use of $0 to develop portable scripts.

13.4   exit and $?: Exit Status of a Command

All programs and shell scripts return a value called the **exit status** to the caller, often the shell. The shell waits for a command to complete execution and then picks up this value from the process table. Shell scripts return the exit status with the **exit** statement:

```
exit                                            Default value is 0
exit 0                                          True; everything went fine
exit 1                                          False; something went wrong
```

A program is designed in such a way that it returns a true exit status when it runs successfully and false otherwise. What constitutes success or failure is determined by the designer of the program. Once **grep** couldn't locate a pattern *(11.2.2)*; we said then that the command *failed*. That is to say that the designer of **grep** made the program return a false exit status on failing to locate a pattern.

The parameter $? stores the exit status of the last command. It has the value 0 if the command succeeds and a nonzero value if it fails. This parameter is set by **exit**'s argument. If no exit status is specified, then $? is set to zero (true). Try using **grep** in these ways, and you'll see it returning three different exit values:

```
$ grep director emp.1st >/dev/null; echo $?
0                                                           Success
$ grep manager emp.1st >/dev/null; echo $?
1                                                    Failure—in finding pattern
$ grep manager emp3.1st >/dev/null; echo $?
grep: can't open emp3.1st                            Failure—in opening file
2
```

The **if** and **while** constructs implicitly check $? to control the flow of execution. As a programmer, you should also place **exit** statements with meaningful exit values at appropriate points in a script. For example, if an important file doesn't exist or can't be read, there's no point in continuing with script execution. You could then use **exit 1** at that point. The next program then knows that the previous program failed—and why it failed.

Note

Success or failure isn't as intuitive as it may seem. The designer of **grep** interpreted **grep**'s inability to locate a pattern as failure. The designer of **sed** thought otherwise. The command **sed -n '/manager/p' emp.1st** returns a true value even if manager is not found!

13.5 The Logical Operators && and ||—Conditional Execution

We didn't use **grep**'s exit status in the script **emp1.sh** to prevent display of the message, Selected lines shown above, when the pattern search fails. The shell provides two operators that allow conditional execution—the && and ||, which typically have this syntax:

```
cmd1 && cmd2                                          cmd2 executed if cmd1 succeeds
cmd1 || cmd2                                             cmd2 executed if cmd1 fails
```

When && is used to delimit two commands, *cmd2* is executed only when *cmd1* succeeds. You can use it with **grep** in this way:

```
$ grep 'director' shortlist >/dev/null && echo "pattern found in file"
pattern found in file
```

The || operator does the opposite; the second command is executed only when the first fails:

```
$ grep 'manager' shortlist || echo "Pattern not found"
Pattern not found
```

These operators go pretty well with the **exit** statement. The script **emp2.sh** can be modified in this way:

```
grep "$1" $2 || exit 2                              No point continuing if search fails
echo "Pattern found - Job Over"                     Executed only if grep succeeds
```

To display a message before invoking **exit**, you need to group commands, but remember to use only curly braces *(7.6.2)* because the enclosed commands are then executed in the current shell:

```
grep joker /etc/passwd || { echo "Pattern not found" ; exit 2 ; }
```

Use of parentheses here wouldn't terminate a script. If the { } sequence is executed at the shell prompt, you would be logged out.

The && and || operators are recommended for making simple decisions. When complex decision making is involved, they have to make way for the **if** statement.

13.6 The if **Conditional**

The **if** statement makes two-way decisions depending on the fulfillment of a certain condition. In the shell, the statement uses the following forms, much like the one used in other languages:

if *command is successful*
then
    execute commands
fi
	if *command is successful*
	then
	    execute commands
	else
	    execute commands
	fi
		if *command is successful*
		then
		    execute commands
		elif *command is successful*
		then...
		else...
		fi

Form 1	Form 2	Form 3

if requires a **then** and is closed with a **fi**. It evaluates the success or failure of the **control command** specified in its "command line." If *command* succeeds, the sequence of commands following it is executed. If *command* fails, then the commands following the **else** statement (if present) are executed. This statement is not always required, as shown in Form 1.

The control command here can be any UNIX command or any program, and its exit status solely determines the course of action. This means that you can use the **if** construct like this:

```
if grep "$name" /etc/passwd
```

Here, **if** tests $? after **grep** completes execution. You can also negate the control command using **if !** *condition*. The condition

```
if ! grep "$name" /etc/passwd
```

is true only if **grep** fails. You can't use **sed** and **awk** in place of **grep** simply because they don't fail in making a pattern search *(11.2.2)*.

We'll use the next script, **emp3.sh** (Fig. 13.4), to search /etc/passwd for the existence of two users; one exists in the file, and the other doesn't. A simple **if-else** construct tests **grep**'s exit status:

```
$ emp3.sh ftp
ftp:*:325:15:FTP User:/users1/home/ftp:/bin/true
Pattern found - Job Over
$ emp3.sh mail
Pattern not found
```

We'll discuss the third form of the **if** statement when we discuss **test**, in Section 13.7.

FIGURE 13.4 emp3.sh

```
#!/bin/sh
# emp3.sh: Using if and else
#
if grep "^$1:" /etc/passwd                  # ^ anchors pattern
then                                        # : removes embedded pattern
        echo "Pattern found - Job Over"
else
        echo "Pattern not found"
fi
```

13.7 Using test and [ ] to Evaluate Expressions

The **if** conditional can't handle relational tests directly, but only with the assistance of the **test** statement. **test** uses certain operators to evaluate the condition on its right and returns an exit status, which is then used by **if** for making decisions. **test** works as a frontend to **if** in three ways:

- Compares two numbers (like **test $x -gt $y**).
- Compares two strings or a single one for a null value (like **test $x = $y**).
- Checks a file's attributes (like **test -f $file**).

These tests can also be used with the **while** loop, but for now we'll stick to **if**. Also, **test** doesn't display any output but simply sets $?. In the following sections, we'll check this value.

13.7.1 Numeric Comparison

The numerical comparison operators (Table 13.2) used by **test** have a form different from what you would have seen anywhere. They always begin with a -, followed by a two-character word, and enclosed on either side by whitespace. Here's a typical operator:

-ne   *Not equal*

TABLE 13.2 *Numerical Comparison Operators Used with* **test**

Operator	Meaning
-eq	Equal to
-ne	Not equal to
-gt	Greater than
-ge	Greater than or equal to
-lt	Less than
-le	Less than or equal to

The operators are quite mnemonic: -eq implies equal to, -gt implies greater than, and so on. Remember, however, that numeric comparison in the shell is confined to integer values only; decimal values are simply truncated:

```
$ x=5; y=7; z=7.2
$ test $x -eq $y ; echo $?
1                                                                              Not equal
$ test $x -lt $y ; echo $?
0                                                                                  True
$ test $z -gt $y ; echo $?
1                                                               7.2 is not greater than 7!
$ test $z -eq $y ; echo $?
0                                                                   7.2 is equal to 7!
```

Having used **test** as a standalone feature, you can now use it as **if**'s control command. The next script, **emp3a.sh** (Fig. 13.5), uses **test** in an **if-elif-else-fi** construct (Form 3) to evaluate the shell parameter, $#. It displays the usage when no arguments are input, runs **grep** if two arguments are entered, and displays an error message otherwise.

Why did we redirect the **echo** output to /dev/tty? Simple, we want the script to work both with and without redirection. In either case, the output of the **echo** statements must appear *only* on the terminal. These statements are used here as "error" messages even though they are not directed to the standard error. Now run the script four times and redirect the output every time:

```
$ emp3a.sh > foo
Usage: emp3a.sh pattern file
$ emp3a.sh ftp > foo
You didn't enter two arguments
$ emp3a.sh henry /etc/passwd > foo
henry not found in /etc/passwd
$ emp3a.sh ftp /etc/passwd > foo
$ cat foo
ftp:*:325:15:FTP User:/users1/home/ftp:/bin/true
```

FIGURE 13.5 emp3a.sh

```
#!/bin/sh
# emp3a.sh: Using test, $0 and $# in an if-elif-fi construct
#
if test $# -eq 0 ; then
    echo "Usage: $0 pattern file" >/dev/tty
elif test $# -eq 2 ; then
    grep "$1" $2 || echo "$1 not found in $2" >/dev/tty
else
    echo "You didn't enter two arguments" >/dev/tty
fi
```

The importance of /dev/tty as a mechanism of explicitly redirecting an output stream shows up in this example. But there's another way of achieving this objective: Use 1>&2 instead of >/dev/tty:

```
echo "You didn't enter two arguments" 1>&2
```

You'll recall *(7.6.1)* that 1>&2 redirects the standard output to the standard error. You must appreciate this and use this feature with statements that need to be immune to redirection. The above script works just as well even if you don't redirect it.

Tip

An application may need to be designed in a flexible manner to allow redirection of an entire script or its participation in a pipeline. In that case, you need to ensure that messages meant to draw the attention of the user (mainly from **echo**) are *not* written to the standard output. We used >/dev/tty here, but henceforth we'll be mostly using 1>&2.

13.7.2   [ ]: Shorthand for test

test is so widely used that fortunately there exists a shorthand method of executing it. A pair of rectangular brackets enclosing the expression can replace it. Thus, the following forms are equivalent:

```
test $x -eq $y
[ $x -eq $y ]
```

Note that you must provide whitespace around the operators (like -eq), their operands (like $x), and inside the [and]. The second form is easier to handle and will be used henceforth. Programmers must note that [is a shell builtin and is executed as a command, but [$x is not a valid command.

Note

It is a feature of most programming languages that you can use a condition like **if (x)**, which returns true if x is greater than 0 or is nonnull. The same feature applies to the shell; we can use **if [$x]** as a shorthand form of **if [$x -gt 0]**.

13.7.3   String Comparison

test can be used to compare strings with yet another set of operators (Table 13.3). Equality is performed with = (not ==) and inequality with the C-type operator !=. Here's how you compare two strings:

TABLE 13.3   *String Tests with* **test**

Test	True if
s1 = s2	String s1 = s2
s1 != s2	String s1 is not equal to s2
-n stg	String stg is not a null string
-z stg	String stg is a null string
stg	String stg is assigned and not null
s1 == s2	String s1 = s2 (Korn and Bash only)

```
if [ "$option" = "y" ]                          True if $option evaluates to y
if [ "$option" != "y" ]                    True if $option doesn't evaluate to y
```

There are two ways of checking for a null string:

```
if [ -z "$option" ]                        True if $option is a null string
if [ ! -n "$option" ]                                          Same
```

Tip

Observe that we have been quoting our variables and strings wherever possible. Quoting is essential when you assign multiple words to a variable. To try that out, drop the quotes in the statement **if [-z "$option"]**. When you input two words, or even an null string to be assigned to option, you'll encounter an error. Quoting is safe with no adverse consequences.

13.7.4   File Attribute Tests

Like **perl** and the system call library, **test** can be used to test practically all file attributes stored in the inode using operators that begin with - (Table 13.4). For instance, the -f operator tests for the existence of a file, and -d does the same for a directory:

```
$ [ -f /etc/passwd ] && echo "This file always exists"
This file always exists
$ [ -d foobar ] || echo "Directory foobar doesn't exist"
Directory foobar doesn't exist
```

The next script, **filetest.sh** (Fig. 13.6), checks whether a file exists and is readable. This time we use command grouping as a compact replacement of the **if** statement for argument checking. The script also features nesting of the **if** statement.

Let's now run it with and without a filename as argument:

```
$ filetest.sh
Usage: filetest.sh file
```

TABLE 13.4   *File Attribute Testing with* **test**

Test	True If File
-f *file*	*file* exists and is a regular file
-r *file*	*file* exists and is readable
-w *file*	*file* exists and is writable
-x *file*	*file* exists and is executable
-d *file*	*file* exists and is a directory
-s *file*	*file* exists and has a size greater than zero
-u *file*	*file* exists and has SUID bit set
-k *file*	*file* exists and has sticky bit set
-e *file*	*file* exists *(Korn and Bash only)*
-L *file*	*file* exists and is a symbolic link *(Korn and Bash only)*
f1 -nt *f2*	*f1* is newer than *f2 (Korn and Bash only)*
f1 -ot *f2*	*f1* is older than *f2 (Korn and Bash only)*
f1 -ef *f2*	*f1* is linked to *f2 (Korn and Bash only)*

FIGURE 13.6 filetest.sh

```
#!/bin/sh
# filetest.sh -- Checks whether file exists and is readable
#
[ $# -ne 1 ] && { echo "Usage: $0 file" ; exit 1 ; }
#
if [ -f $1 ] ; then                     # if file exists
    if [ ! -r $1 ] ; then               # but is not readable
        echo "File exists but is not readable"
    else
        echo "File is readable"
    fi
else
    echo "File doesn't exist"
fi
```

```
$ filetest.sh /etc/shadow
File exists but is not readable
$ ls -l /etc/shadow
-r--------   1 root      sys          5425 Nov 28 15:30 /etc/shadow
```

The file is unreadable to all except root. This feature of checking for readability is supported by most programming languages, but **test** conditions are quite exhaustive. Korn and Bash can even check whether one file is newer than another (Table 13.4).

13.7.5 Using Compound Conditions

if and **test** can also be used with compound conditions. There are two forms: one uses the && and || operators, and the other uses -a and -o. Here's how they are used:

```
if [ "$0" = "lm" ] || [ "$0" = "./lm" ] ; then
if [ "$0" = "lm"  -o "$0" = "./lm" ] ; then
```

$0 is evaluated by Bash differently. The above represents a section of code you need to use to make Bash scripts portable. What happens if there are too many alternatives to account for? Rather than create a lengthy control command, we should consider using the perfect string matching tool. The **case** construct is discussed in Section 13.9.

Note

Even though we used **test** with the **if** statement in all our examples, **test** returns an exit status only, and can thus be used with any shell construct (like **while**) that uses an exit status.

13.8 Two Important Programming Idioms

Time to take a break. Your applications must support certain features that people have taken for granted. For instance, many scripts turn interactive when used without arguments. Some commands (like **gzip** and **gunzip**) behave differently even though they represent the same file. These features are taken up next.

13.8.1 Running a Task Both Interactively and Noninteractively

We developed a noninteractive script, **emp3a.sh** (Fig. 13.5), to conduct a pattern search. Now suppose that we want to do the same task interactively. Do we develop one from scratch? No, we learn to make scripts reusable. We place the interactive features in the new script and invoke **emp3a.sh** from there.

The next script, **emp4.sh** (Fig. 13.7), behaves both interactively and noninteractively. When run without arguments, it turns interactive and takes two inputs from you. It then runs **emp3a.sh** with the supplied inputs as arguments. However, when **emp4.sh** itself is run with at least one argument, it runs **emp3a.sh** with the same arguments. This script also highlights the limitations of $* and why it should be replaced with "$@".

In interactive mode, the script checks the input strings for nonnull values and then invokes **emp3a.sh** with these values as the script's arguments. In the noninteractive mode, however, it passes on the arguments to **emp3a.sh** using $*. In either case, **emp3a.sh** is run, which finally checks for the actual number of arguments entered before making a search with **grep**. Let's first run the script interactively:

```
$ emp4.sh
Enter the string to be searched: [Enter]
You have not entered the string
```

FIGURE 13.7 emp4.sh

```
#!/bin/sh
# Script: emp4.sh - Checks user input for null values - Finally runs emp3a.sh
#                                               developed previously
if [ $# -eq 0 ] ; then
    echo "Enter the string to be searched: \c"
    read pname
    echo "Enter the filename to be used: \c"
    read flname
    if [ -z "$pname" ] || [ -z "$flname" ] ; then
      echo "At least one input was null" ; exit 2
    fi
    emp3a.sh "$pname" "$flname"    # Runs the script that will do the job
else                               # When no arguments are entered
    emp3a.sh $*                    # We'll change $* to "$@" soon
fi
```

```
$ emp4.sh
Enter the string to be searched: root
Enter the filename to be used: /etc/passwd
root:x:0:1:Super-User:/:/usr/bin/bash                              From emp3a.sh
```

See how two scripts cooperated in displaying root's entry from /etc/passwd? When we run the script with arguments, **emp4.sh** bypasses all of the above activities and calls **emp3a.sh** to perform all validation checks:

```
$ emp4.sh barry
You didn't enter two arguments
$ emp4.sh barry emp.1st
5423:barry wood      :chairman :admin     :08/30/56:160000
$ emp4.sh "barry wood" emp.1st
You didn't enter two arguments
```

Surprise, surprise! Using quotes, we provided two arguments, and $* and $# in **emp4.sh** are also assigned correctly. But the same parameters are interpreted differently in **emp3a.sh**. In fact, barry and wood are embedded in $* as separate arguments, and $# in **emp3a.sh** thus makes a wrong argument count. The solution to this is simple: Replace $* in the script with "$@" (with quotes) and then run the script again:

```
$ emp4.sh "barry wood" emp.1st
5423:barry wood      :chairman :admin     :08/30/56:160000
```

Tip

It's safer to use "$@" instead of $*. When you employ multiword strings as arguments to a shell script, it's only "$@" that interprets each quoted argument as a separate argument. As the output above suggests, if you use $*, the shell makes an incorrect count of the arguments.

13.8.2   Calling a Script by Different Names ($0)

The shell parameter, $0, stores the filename *(13.3)*. We can use this feature in tandem with the linking facility to make a script do different things depending on the name by which it is called. The script, **lm.sh** (Fig. 13.8), displays the listing ordered by the last modification time when invoked as **lm**, and the last access time when invoked by **la**.

FIGURE 13.8   lm.sh

```
#!/bin/sh
# lm.sh: Linked file to run ls with two different sets of options
#
filename=$0
if [ "$filename" = "lm" ] || [ "$filename" = "./lm" ] ; then
    echo "Executing ls -lt $*" ; ls -lt $*
elif [ "$filename" = "la" ] || [ "$filename" = "./la" ] ; then
    echo "Executing ls -lut $*" ; ls -lut $*
fi
```

We used compound conditions to take care of Bash which evaluates $0 with the
./ prefix. Now link **1m.sh** with **1m** and **1a** and then see how they behave when invoked
by these two names:

```
$ ln lm.sh lm ; ln lm la
$ lm /etc/passwd
Executing ls -lt /etc/passwd
-r--r--r--   1 root     sys        11189 Aug 20 20:39 /etc/passwd
$ la /etc/passwd
Executing ls -lut /etc/passwd
-r--r--r--   1 root     sys        11189 Sep  6 09:27 /etc/passwd
```

After you have written a a fairly large number of scripts, you'll find that some of them
have very few differences between them. These scripts are ideal candidates for conversion
to a single script. Isolate the common features, use $0 to handle the differing features,
and make as many links as required.

13.9 The case **Conditional**

We now resume our discussions on the other shell constructs with the **case** statement,
the second conditional offered by the shell. **case** easily surpasses the string matching
feature of **if**. It uses a compact construct to match a pattern with a list of alternatives.
Each alternative is associated with a corresponding action:

```
case expression in
      pattern1)  commands1 ;;
      pattern2)  commands2 ;;
      pattern3)  commands3 ;;
            .....

esac                                                                    Reverse of case
```

case first matches *expression* with *pattern1* and executes *commands1* (which may be
one or more commands) if the match succeeds. If the match fails, then **case** tries with
pattern2, and so forth. Each command list is terminated with a pair of semicolons, and
the entire construct is closed with **esac**. What makes **case** a powerful pattern matching
tool is that its patterns are borrowed from the best of both worlds: wild cards and extended
regular expressions (EREs).

Consider a simple script, **menu.sh** (Fig. 13.9), that accepts values from 1 to 5 and
performs some action depending on the number keyed in. The five menu choices are
displayed with a multiline **echo** statement.

case matches the value of $choice with the strings 1, 2, 3, 4, and 5. If the user
enters a 1, the **1s -1** command is executed. Option 5 quits the program. The last option
(*) matches any option not matched by the previous options. You can see today's date
by choosing the third option:

FIGURE 13.9 `menu.sh`

```
#!/bin/sh
# menu.sh: Uses case to offer 5-item menu
#
echo "          MENU\n
1. List of files\n2. Processes of user\n3. Today's Date
4. Users of system\n5. Quit to UNIX\nEnter your option: \c"
read choice
case "$choice" in
    1) ls -l ;;
    2) ps -f ;;
    3) date  ;;
    4) who   ;;
    5) exit  ;;
    *) echo "Invalid option"     # ;; not really required for the last option
esac
```

```
$ menu.sh
          MENU

1. List of files
2. Processes of user
3. Today's Date
4. Users of system
5. Quit to UNIX
Enter your option: 3
Tue Jan  7 18:03:06 IST 2003
```

The same logic would require a larger number of lines if implemented with **if**. Thus, **case** becomes an automatic choice when the number of matching options is high.

13.9.1 Using Wild Cards and the |

case can also delimit multiple patterns with a | in regular expression-style. It is also very effective when the string is fetched by command substitution. If you cut out the first field from the **date** output, you can use this **case** construct to do different things, depending on the day of the week:

```
case `date | cut -d" " -f1` in                    Outputs three-character day string
    Mon|Wed) tar -cvf /dev/fd0 $HOME ;;
    Tue|Fri) scp -r $HOME/projects mercury:/home/henry ;;
        Thu) find $HOME -newer .last_full_backup_time -print > tarilist ;;
          *) ;;
esac
```

The first field of the **date** output displays the day, which we extracted with **cut** to provide input to **case**. The first and second options show two patterns each. The **tar** command is executed only on Mondays and Wednesdays. The script can be run on any day, and the right command will be automatically invoked.

We used simple patterns here (1, 2, Mon, Wed, etc.), but **case** also supports the Bourne shell's set of wild cards, *but only to match strings and not files in the current directory.* The following hypothetical construct suggests that **case** is ideal for pattern matching:

```
x="[0-9][0-9]"
case "$reply" in
             [A-Z]) echo "Don't use an uppercase letter" ;;
         [!a-zA-Z]) echo "Must enter a single letter" ;;
            ????*) echo "Can't exceed three characters" ;;
  $x$x/$x$x/$x$x) echo "Correct format for date" ;;
          *[0-9]*) echo "No numerals permitted" ;;
        *.c|*.java) echo "This is a C or Java program" ;;
      n|N|[nN][oO]) echo "You entered n, N, no, NO, No, etc" ;;
               "") echo "You simply pressed [Enter]" ;;
esac
```

Note

There are a couple things to keep in mind when using **case**. First, a solitary * must be the last option because it serves as a refuge for matching anything not matched by the previous options. Second, **case** can also match a number as a string. You can match $# *directly* (without using **test**) with specific values (0, 1, 2|3, [2-5], etc.).

13.10   expr **and** basename: **Computation and String Handling**

The Bourne shell doesn't have any computing or string handling features at all. It depends on the external commands, **expr** and **basename**, for these tasks. This functionality is built into the Korn and Bash shells. The POSIX shell specification was based on the Korn shell, the reason why POSIX recommends use of the shell rather than **expr** for these tasks. You can't do that with legacy code, so we need to understand **expr** and **basename**.

13.10.1   Computation with expr

expr performs the four basic arithmetic operations and the modulus (remainder) function. It handles only integers; decimal portions are simply truncated or ignored.

```
$ x=3 y=5                                    Multiple assignments without a ;
$ expr 3 + 5                                       Whitespace required
8
$ expr $x - $y
-2
$ expr 3 \* 5                                  Escaping keeps the shell out
15
$ expr $y / $x
1                                             Decimal portion truncated
```

```
$ expr 13 % 5
3
```

You'll often use **expr** with command substitution to assign a variable. Some scripts in this chapter use it for incrementing a number:

```
$ x=6 ; y=2
$ z=`expr $x + $y` ; echo $z
8
$ x=`expr $x + 1`                                     This is the same as C's x++
$ echo $x
7
```

KORN Shell

BASH Shell

Refer to Appendix B for a discussion of the built-in **let** statement and the ((and)) symbols in handling computation. **let** and (( )) are faster than **expr**.

13.10.2 String Handling with expr

For manipulating strings, **expr** uses two expressions separated by a colon. The string itself is placed on its left, and a regular expression is placed on its right. We'll use **expr** to determine the length of a string and to return a substring.

The Length of a String   The length of a string is handled by the regular expression **.***. It signifies the number of characters matching the pattern, i.e., the length of the entire string:

```
$ expr "robert_kahn" : '.*'                          Note whitespace around :
11
```

To validate a string so that it doesn't exceed, say, 20 characters in length, you need to use **expr** like this:

```
if [ `expr "$name" : '.*'` -gt 20 ] ; then
```

Extracting a Substring   **expr** supports the TRE that was first seen in **sed** (*11.13.3*), but only to extract a substring. Unlike in **sed**, however, there's no \1 and \2; the expression enclosed by \(and \) is actually *returned* by **expr**. This is how you extract the 2-digit year from a 4-digit string:

```
$ stg=2004
$ expr "$stg" : '..\(..\)'                           Extracts last two characters
04
```

Here, **expr** ignores the first two characters and returns the remaining ones. You can also extract a file's base name from an absolute pathname:

```
$ pathname="/usr/include/sys"
$ expr "$pathname" : '.*/\(.*\)'
sys
```

The `.*/` at the beginning of the expression matches the longest string up to the last `/`. There's a separate command that handles this task though, the **basename** command, which is taken up next.

13.10.3   basename: Changing Filename Extensions

The previous string extraction function can be easily performed by **basename**. The command by default extracts the "base" filename from an absolute pathname:

```
$ basename /usr/include/sys
sys
```

When **basename** is used with a second argument, it strips off the string represented by this argument from the first argument:

```
$ basename hello.java .java
hello                                                         Easier than expr
```

In Section 13.12.2, we'll use **basename** in a **for** loop to change filename extensions.

KORN Shell

BASH Shell

Refer to Appendix B for a discussion on the built-in string handling features of these shells. They are faster than **basename** and **expr**.

13.11   Sample Program #1: Automatically Selects Last C Program

It's time for our first sample program, **comc.sh** (Fig. 13.10), which is useful for C programmers. The program needs to be linked to three filenames (**vic**, **comc**, and **runc**), and then it edits, compiles, and executes the last modified C program file depending on the name by which it is invoked. Before we examine the script, let's understand some essential aspects of C programming.

A C program has the `.c` extension. When compiled with **cc** *filename,* it produces a file named a.out. However, we can provide a different name to the executable using the `-o` option. For instance, **cc -o foo foo.c** creates an executable named foo. It's

FIGURE 13.10   comc.sh

```
#!/bin/sh
# comc.sh: Script that is called by different names
#
lastfile=`ls -t *.c 2>/dev/null | head -n 1`
[ -z $lastfile ]  && { echo "No C program found" ; exit 1 ; }


command=$0
executable=`expr $lastfile : '\(.*\).c'`      # Removes .c; foo.c becomes foo
# or use executable=`basename "$lastfile" .c`
case $command in
    runc|./runc) $executable ;;                # Runs the executable
       vic|./vic) vi $lastfile ;;
     comc|./comc) cc -o $executable $lastfile &&
                  echo "$lastfile compiled successfully" ;;
esac
```

customary to have executable names derived from the source filename (foo from foo.c), and this is what our script does.

First, we check whether there's any C program in the current directory. We store the name of the last modified program in the variable lastfile. Using **expr**, we extract the base filename by dropping the .c extension. **case** now checks the name (saved in the variable command) by which the program is invoked. Observe that the first option (runc) simply executes the value evaluated by the variable executable. The only thing left to do now is to create three links:

```
ln comc.sh comc ; ln comc.sh runc ; ln comc.sh vic
```

Now you can run **vic** to edit the program, **comc** to compile it, and **runc** to execute the object code. We'll only compile it here:

```
$ comc
hello.c compiled successfully
```

This script also works without modification in Bash. There's one limitation, though. The script can't compile programs whose functions are stored in separate files.

13.12   for: **Looping with a List**

The shell features the **for**, **while**, and **until** loops that let you perform a set of instructions repeatedly. The **for** loop doesn't support the three-part structure used in C, but uses a list instead:

```
for variable in list
do
    commands                                                        Loop body
done
```

The keywords **do** and **done** delimit the loop body. Loop iteration is controlled by the keywords *variable* and *list*. At every iteration, each word in *list* is assigned to *variable*, and *commands* are executed. The loop terminates when *list* is exhausted. A simple example can help you understand things better:

```
$ for file in chap20 chap21 chap22 chap23 ; do
>     cp $file ${file}.bak
>     echo $file copied to $file.bak
> done
chap20 copied to chap20.bak
chap21 copied to chap21.bak
chap22 copied to chap22.bak
chap23 copied to chap23.bak
```

The *list* here comprises a series of character strings representing filenames. Each string (chap20 and onwards) is assigned to the variable file. Each file is then copied with a .bak extension followed by a completion message.

Note

Words by default are separated by whitespace, but a quoted string comprising multiple words is treated as a single word by **for**.

13.12.1 Sources of the List

As in **case**, the list can come from anywhere. It can come from variables and wild cards:

```
for var in $PATH $HOME $MAIL                                     From variables
for file in *.htm *.html                                      From all HTML files
```

When the list consists of wild cards, the shell interprets them as filenames. Often, the list is either very large, or its contents are known only at runtime. In these situations, command substitution is the preferred choice. You can change the list without having to change the script:

```
for file in `cat clist`                                            From a file
```

for is also used to process positional parameters that are assigned from command line arguments:

```
for file in "$@"                                        From command line arguments
```

Note that "$@" is preferred to $*. **for** will behave erroneously with multiword strings if $* is used.

13.12.2   Important Applications Using **for**

Substitution in Files **for** is indispensable for making substitutions in a set of files with **sed**. Take, for instance, this loop which works on every HTML file in the current directory:

```
for file in *.htm *.html ; do
   sed 's/strong/STRONG/g
   s/img src/IMG SRC/g' $file > $$
   mv $$ $file
done
```

In this loop, each HTML filename is assigned to the variable file in turn. **sed** performs some substitution on each file and writes the output to a temporary file, which is written back to the original file with **mv**.

Changing Filename Extensions The **basename** command is mostly used in a **for** loop to change filename extensions. This loop changes the extension from txt to doc:

```
for file in *.txt ; do
   leftname=`basename $file .txt`              Stores left part of filename
   mv $file ${leftname}.doc
done
```

If **for** picks up seconds.txt as the first file, leftname stores seconds (without a dot). **mv** simply adds the .doc extension to the extracted string (seconds). This job can also be done by **expr**, but **basename** is easier to use.

13.13   while: **Looping**

Apart from **for**, the shell also supports a **while** loop. This construct also uses the keywords **do** and **done** but doesn't work with a list. It uses a control command to determine the flow of execution:

```
while condition is true
do
      commands
done
```

The *commands* enclosed by **do** and **done** are executed repeatedly as long as *condition* remains true. As in **if**, you can use any UNIX command or **test** as the *condition*. Here's an example that displays the **ps -e** output five times:

```
$ x=5
$ while [ $x -gt 0 ] ; do
>    ps -e ; sleep 3                            Sleeps for 3 seconds
>    x=`expr $x - 1`
> done
```

And if you want to do the same thing an infinite number of times, then use **ps** itself as the control command inside an *infinite loop:*

```
$ while ps -e ; do                                    Always true as ps returns true
>    sleep 3
> done
```

The interrupt key terminates this loop, but all loops (including **for**) also support the **break** statement that does the same thing. We'll discuss the **break** and **continue** statements later.

13.13.1 Handling Redirection in a Loop

Redirection in a loop needs to be handled carefully. We'll first do it in a rudimentary manner in the next script, **while.sh** (Fig. 13.11), and then make a small but significant change later. The script repeatedly prompts a user to input a telephone number and name, and writes out the line to addressbook. The loop iteration is controlled by the value of $answer.

In Fig. 13.5, we used >/dev/tty to prevent some messages from being redirected; this time we are going to use 1>&2. Let's add two entries and then view the last two lines of addressbook:

```
$ while.sh
Enter telephone number and name: 9830897890 john williams
Any more entries (y/n)? y
Enter telephone number and name: 9876034581 max steiner
```

FIGURE 13.11 while.sh

```
#!/bin/bash
# while.sh: Shows use of the while loop
#
answer=y                          # Required to enter the loop
while [ "$answer" = "y" ] ; do      # The control command
    echo "Enter telephone number and name: \c" 1>&2
    read number name              # Read both together
    echo "$name:$number" >> addressbook    # Append a line to addressbook
    echo "Any more entries (y/n)? \c" 1>&2
    read anymore
    case $anymore in
        y*|Y*) answer=y ;;    # Also accepts yes, YES etc.
            *) answer=n ;;    # Any other reply means n
    esac
done
```

Any more entries (y/n)? **n**
$ **tail -n 2 addressbook**
john williams:9830897890
max steiner:9876034581

Did redirection with 1>&2 achieve anything here? No, nothing yet, but after we make a small change in the script, it will. Note that appending a line to addressbook with >> causes addressbook to be opened and closed with *every* iteration. This is expensive, so remove redirection from there and provide it instead at the **done** keyword:

done >> addressbook   addressbook *opened only once*

This redirects the standard output of all statements in the loop body. The messages that have been sent to the standard error with 1>&2 are thus unaffected. In the present case, only one statement is affected. The technique is also efficient because addressbook is opened and closed only once.

Redirection is also available at the **fi** and **esac** keywords, and includes input redirection and piping:

done < param.lst	*Statements in loop take input from* param.lst
done | while read name	while *loop takes input from standard input*
fi > foo	*Affects statements between* if *and* fi
esac > foo	*Affects statements between* case *and* esac

Note

We'll be using the second form in Section 13.13.3 where the loop takes input from a pipeline.

13.13.2   Using **while** to Wait for a File

There are situations when a program needs to read a file created by another program, but it also has to wait till the file is created. The script, **monitfile.sh** (Fig. 13.12), uses the

FIGURE 13.12 monitfile.sh

```
#!/bin/sh
# monitfile.sh: Waits for a file to be created
#
case $# in
   2) case $2 in
     0|*[!0-9]*) echo "You must specify a nonzero waiting time"
                 exit 1 ;;
             *) while [ ! -r $1 ] ; do    # while $1 can't be read
                   sleep $2               # Sleep for $2 seconds
                done
                cat $1 ;;                  # Executed after $1 is found
      esac;;                               # Closes inner case
    *) echo "Usage: $0 file_to_read sleep_time" ; exit ;;
esac
```

external **sleep** command to periodically poll (monitor) the disk and then display the contents the moment it finds the file. The file to wait for and sleep time are supplied as arguments.

This script features two nested **case** constructs. The outer **case** checks whether two arguments have been input. If so, the inner **case** checks whether the second argument is greater than 0. Note that the wild-card pattern *[!0-9]* matches a string that contains at least one nonnumeric character.

If the usage is right, the **while** loop in tandem with **sleep** checks the current directory every $2 seconds as long as the file $1 can't be read. If the file later becomes readable, the loop is terminated and the contents of the file are displayed. This script is an ideal candidate to be run in the background:

```
$ monitfile.sh foo 30 &
124
```

Now create a file foo with some data, and you'll find the script returns after 30 seconds with foo's contents on the terminal.

13.13.3 Finding Out Users' Space Consumption

Unlike **for**, the **while** loop itself can behave like a filter. Refer to Section 19.11.2 to view the output of the **du -s /home/*** command, which displays the disk usage summary of every user. Here are a few sample entries:

```
166      /home/enquiry
4054     /home/henry
647      /home/image
64308    /home/sumit
```

We assume that home directories are maintained in /home. We can use a **while** loop to read every line of this output and then mail root a list of users who have either exceeded a specified figure or a default of 4000 blocks. This means the script, **du.sh** (Fig. 13.13), either accepts no arguments or just one.

Here, the **du** output serves as input to the **while** loop. The loop's control command reads each line into two variables, blocks and user. The **test** statement then compares the **du** summary figure either with 4000 (if no arguments are specified) or with the number specified as argument. By redirecting the loop at the **done** keyword, we ensured that a single mail message goes to root containing the entire list. We can run this command in two ways:

```
du.sh
du.sh 8000                          Selects only those users who exceed 8000 blocks
```

Now, when the root user opens her mailbox, she'll see a message showing the users who have exceeded the limit:

```
/home/sumit : 64308 blocks
/home/enquiry : 15567 blocks
```

FIGURE 13.13 du.sh

```
#!/bin/sh
# du.sh -- Program to monitor free space on disk
#
case $# in
    0) size=4000 ;;                 # Default size without user input
    1) size=$1 ;;                   # Specified on invocation
    *) echo "Usage: $0 [blocks]" ; exit ;;
esac

du -s /home/* |                     # Pipe the output to the while loop
while read blocks user ; do
  [ $blocks -gt $size ] && echo "$user : $blocks blocks"
done | mailx root                                   # List goes to root
```

This script is useful for the system administrator who has to constantly monitor the disk space and identify the users who consume more space than they are supposed to. And what better way of running it than as a **cron** job using this crontab entry:

```
0 10,13,16,19 * * 1-5 /home/admin/scripts/du.sh
```

The script is executed on working days every 3 hours between 10 a.m. and 7 p.m.

13.13.4 break and continue

Sometimes, you'll find it difficult to specify when a loop must terminate. You may also need to make a premature iteration from any point in the loop body. All loops support the **break** and **continue** keywords that perform these tasks—often in an infinite loop. We implemented one using the **ps** command *(13.13)*, but often we don't need a command to run repeatedly. We can then use one of these:

```
while true                              The true command returns 0
while :                                 : also returns a true value
```

true and **:** do nothing except return a true exit status. Another command named **false** returns a false value. The **while** construct developed in Fig. 13.12 can now be reframed as an infinite loop:

```
while true ; do
  [ -r $1 ] && break
  sleep $2          # Sleep for $2 seconds
done
cat $1              # Executed after $1 is found
```

The **break** statement causes control to break out of the loop. That's done here when the file $1 is found to be readable.

The **continue** statement suspends execution of all statements following it and starts the next iteration. Both **break** and **continue** have their namesakes in C and Java (and in **awk**), but it's only in the shell that they can be used with arguments too. A sample script discussed in Section 13.16 uses **break 2**.

Note

The shell also offers an `until` statement whose control command uses a reverse logic used in `while`. With `until`, the loop body is executed as long as the condition remains *false*. Thus, `while [ ! -r $1 ]` is the same as `until [ -r $1 ]`.

▆ 13.14 Sample Script #2: Providing Numeric Extensions to Backup Files

We'll consolidate the knowledge that we have acquired so far to develop two more sample scripts. Sample script #2, **cpback.sh** (Fig. 13.14), behaves as an enhanced and noninteractive **cp** command. It provides a file (say, foo) with a numeric extension (say, .1) if it exists at the destination. A file with this extension could exist also, so it increments the number repeatedly to finally copy the file without overwriting.

From the argument list ("$@"), we need to separate the directory name from the file list. The UNIX shell doesn't have a symbol that identifies the last argument, so we'll have to use our knowledge of **sed** to do this job. The first **sed** command uses a TRE to match zero or more occurrences of a nonspace character. The second **sed** matches the expression not matched previously to create the file list. Note that the regular expression is the same in both cases except that grouping has been done on different portions of the expression.

Let's start copying to the safe directory using multiple filenames. We'll assume that a file toc.pl, but not index, exists in the directory safe. We'll run the same command line a number of times:

```
$ cpback.sh vvi.sh toc.pl index safe
File vvi.sh copied to vvi.sh.3
File toc.pl copied to toc.pl.1
$ cpback2.sh vvi.sh toc.pl index safe                    Run again
File vvi.sh copied to vvi.sh.4
File toc.pl copied to toc.pl.2
File index copied to index.1
$ cpback2.sh vvi.sh toc.pl index safe                    ... and again
File vvi.sh copied to vvi.sh.5
File toc.pl copied to toc.pl.3
File index copied to index.2
```

You now have a tool that will copy one or more files but won't overwrite the destination. Keep it in your local bin directory and link it to a shorter name—say, **cp2**.

FIGURE 13.14 `cpback.sh`: *Script to Copy Multiple Files without Overwriting*

```
#!/bin/sh
# cpback.sh: Copies multiple files to a directory
# Makes backups instead of overwriting the destination files
# Copies foo to foo.1 if foo exists or foo.2 if foo.1 exists .......
#
if [ $# -lt 2 ] ; then
   echo "Usage: $0 source(s) destination" ; exit
fi


# Separate the directory from the argument list
dest=`echo "$@" | sed 's/.* \([^ ]*\)/\1/'`

# ... and the files from the argument list
filelist=`echo "$@" | sed 's/\(.*\) [^ ]*/\1/'`

if [ ! -d $dest ] ; then
    echo "Directory $dest doesn't exist" ; exit 1
fi

for file in $filelist ; do
  if [ ! -f $file ] ; then          # If file doesn't exist
     echo "$file doesn't exist"
     continue                       # Take up next file
  elif [ ! -f $dest/$file ] ; then  # If file doesn't exist
     cp $file $dest                 # copy it
  else                              # File exists at destination
                                    # Starting with .1 see the
     ext=1                          #largest extension available
     while true ; do
        if [ ! -f $dest/$file.$ext ] ; then     # If file doesn't exist
           cp $file $dest/$file.$ext            # with this extension
           echo "File $file copied to $file.$ext"
           break                    # No further iteration needed
        else
           ext=`expr $ext + 1`      # File exists with this
        fi                          # extension, so keep trying
     done
  fi
done
```

▬▬ 13.15   Manipulating Positional Parameters with set and shift

At this stage, we have covered the essential programming constructs that will do a lot of work for us. But then UNIX is known for its text manipulation skills, and some of these skills are available in the shell as well. Many shell applications require processing of single-line command output:

```
$ date
Tue Dec  9 10:39:37 IST 2003
$ ls -l /etc/passwd
-r--r--r--   1 root     sys         9953 Nov 28 15:30 /etc/passwd
$ ps -e | grep find
1149 tty1    00:00:00 find
```

How about developing applications that know the day of the week, the day /etc/passwd was last modified, or that kill the **find** command without knowing its PID? When discussing **case**, we had to use **cut** to extract the day of the week from the **date** output *(13.9):*

```
case `date | cut -d" " -f1` in
```

This is overkill, and this technique has limitations. We may need to extract *all* words from single-line command output without using the services of **cut** and **awk**. The shell's **set** statement does a perfect job of this. **set** assigns the values of its arguments to positional parameters (like $1, $2, etc.) as well as $#, $*, and "$@":

```
$ set 9876 2345 6213
$ echo "\$1 is $1, \$2 is $2, \$3 is $3"
$1 is 9876, $2 is 2345, $3 is 6213
$ echo "The $# arguments are "$@""
The 3 arguments are 9876 2345 6213
```

The arguments to **set** are often obtained from command substitution. This is how we can access every field of the **date** output:

```
$ set `date`
$ echo "$@"
Wed Jan 8 09:40:35 IST 2003
$ echo "The day is $1 and the date is $2 $3, $6"
The day is Wed and the date is Jan 8, 2003
```

Using the **set** feature, the **case** construct simplifies to **case $1 in**. Though **date** didn't create problems, there are two things we need to take care of when using **set** with command substitution:

- The command may produce no output, and **set** responds by displaying its default output:
  ```
  $ set `find $HOME -name a.out -print`          File not found
  ..... All shell variables shown .....
  ```

- The output may begin with a hyphen as in the listing, which **set** interprets as a "bad option":

```
$ set `ls -l unit01`                                First character of listing
-rw-r--r--: bad option(s)                                     is a hyphen
```

The solution is to use **set --**, in which case **set** suppresses its normal behavior:

```
set -- `ls -l unit01`            \                  The first - now taken care of
set -- `find $HOME -name a.out -print`              Null output is no problem
```

13.15.1 Killing a Process by Name

We'll now use **set** to develop a script, **killbyname.sh** (Fig. 13.15), that kills a process by specifying its name rather than its PID. We use **ps -u $LOGNAME** to extract all processes run by this user, and **grep** matches the pattern at the end (" 1"). If **grep** succeeds in locating a *single* line, $# would be equal to four. This means that the script will work only if there's a single instance of the process running.

If you have access to two terminals, run **vi** in one of them and invoke this script in the other:

```
killbyname.sh vi
```

The **vi** program should get killed since we used the SIGKILL signal here with **kill**. Now, run two instances of the shell and then run the script again:

```
$ sh
$ sh
$ killbyname.sh sh                                  Run exit twice after this
Either process 1120 not running or more than one instance running"
```

Note that $1 is no longer sh but the PID of the **sh** process (assigned by **set**). The script argument, sh, is no longer visible in the script after **set** is invoked. We ignored this important lesson: If a script uses both **set** and command line arguments, then make sure you save the arguments before invoking **set**.

FIGURE 13.15 killbyname.sh

```
#!/bin/sh
# killbyname.sh: Kills a process by name -- but only a single instance
#
set -- `ps -u $LOGNAME | grep " $1$"`          # $1 here is different from
if [ $# -eq 4 ] ; then
    kill -KILL $1                              # the one here
else
    echo "Either process $1 not running or more than one instance running"
fi
```

13.15.2 `shift`: Shifting Positional Parameters Left

Many programs use a loop to iterate through its arguments but without including the first argument. This argument could represent a directory, and the remaining could be ordinary filenames. We need "$@" here, but only after removing the first argument and renumbering the remaining arguments. This is what **shift** does. Each call to **shift** transfers the contents of a positional parameter to its immediate lower numbered one. $2 becomes $1, $3 becomes $2, and so on:

```
$ set -- `date`
$ echo "$@"                                    Here, "$@" and $* are interchangeable
Wed Jan 8 09:48:44 IST 2003
$ shift
$ echo $1 $2 $3
Jan 8 09:48:44
$ shift 3                                      Three arguments lost!
$ echo $1
IST
```

Observe that the contents of the leftmost parameter, $1, are lost when **shift** is invoked. If $1 is important, then you must save it in a separate variable before invoking **shift**. Note that **set** also works with an integer argument; **set** *n* shifts *n* words to the left.

Let's design a script, **ln.sh** (Fig. 13.16), that creates a number of symbolic links to a single target. The first argument is the target, and the remaining are the symlinks to be created. This means that $1 must be saved before **shift** is invoked.

We make sure that the target exists, save its name before invoking **shift**, and then create multiple symlinks inside a **for** loop. The -f option to **ln** makes sure that existing destination files are removed:

```
$ ln.sh df.sh df1.sh df2.sh
$ ls -l df*.sh
lrwxrwxrwx   1 sumit    users            5 Dec 12 17:01 df1.sh -> df.sh
lrwxrwxrwx   1 sumit    users            5 Dec 12 17:01 df2.sh -> df.sh
-rwxr-xr-x   1 sumit    users          229 Dec 11 13:54 df.sh
```

You can also use this **shift** feature to search for multiple names in an address book, where the name of the address book is specified as the first argument.

FIGURE 13.16 ln.sh

```
#!/bin/sh
# ln.sh: Creates multiple symbolic links; first argument is the target
#
original=$1                          # The target
[ ! -f $original ] && { echo "$original doesn't exist" ; exit 1 ; }
shift                                # Left-most argument lost
for file in $* ; do
    ln -sf $original $file
done
```

13.15.3   The IFS Variable: set's Default Delimiter

The shell's IFS variable contains a string whose characters are used as word separators in the command line. The string normally comprises the whitespace characters. We need **od -bc** to view them:

```
$ echo "$IFS" | od -bc
0000000 040 011 012 012                    Space, tab and newline constitute IFS
           \t  \n  \n
0000004
```

set uses IFS to determine its delimiter. We normally ignore IFS, but if a line needs to be parsed on a different delimiter, then IFS must be temporarily set to that delimiter. Consider this line of /etc/passwd:

```
henry:x:501:100:henry blofeld:/home/henry:/bin/ksh
```

You can extract the sixth field by changing the value of IFS before using **set**:

```
$ IFS=:
$ set -- `grep "^henry" /etc/passwd`
$ echo $6
/home/henry
```

Note

Positional parameters can lose their values in two ways. First, **set** reassigns them in scripts used with command line arguments. Second, every time you use **shift**, the leftmost variable gets lost. So, save all arguments and parameters in separate variables before invoking **set** and **shift**. If you have to start iteration from the fourth parameter, save the first three before you use **shift 3**.

13.16   Sample Script #3: A Table of Contents for Downloaded Files

Time now for our final sample script, and this one, **toc_download.sh** (Fig. 13.17), will benefit those who frequently download files from the Internet. Files are often downloaded at a faster pace than they are used, and it doesn't take long to forget the significance of the filename. The script looks in a certain directory to locate those filenames that are missing in the table of contents (TOC). After the description for the file is input, the TOC is updated with a new entry in the form *filename*: *description*.

This time, our script file will make use of a configuration file, download_TOC.conf. This file contains two variable assignments. Exporting the variables makes them available to all scripts that are run from the main script:

```
$ cat download_TOC.conf
# download_TOC.conf: Configuration file for download_TOC.sh
#
DOWNLOAD_DIR=$HOME/download
DOWNLOAD_TOC=$DOWNLOAD_DIR/TOC_download.txt
export DOWNLOAD_DIR DOWNLOAD_TOC
```

FIGURE 13.17   `toc_download.sh`

```
#!/bin/sh
# toc_download.sh: Script to create a table of contents for files
# Prompts user for description for filename not found in TOC
#
. ./download_TOC.conf
count=0 ; kount=0
cd $DOWNLOAD_DIR || { "Failed to cwd" ; exit ; }
for file in * ; do
    if ! grep "^${file}: " $DOWNLOAD_TOC >/dev/null ; then
        count=`expr $count + 1`
    fi
done

case $count in
  0) echo "All entries documented; nothing to do" ; exit ;;
  *) echo "$count entries need to be documented\n"
esac

for file in * ; do
    if ! grep "^${file}: " $DOWNLOAD_TOC >/dev/null ; then
        echo "Downloaded filename: $file"  1>&2
        echo "Description for $file: \c"  1>&2
        read description
        if [ -n "$description" ] ; then
          echo "$file: $description"   # No redirection here
          kount=`expr $kount + 1`      # Use let kount++ for ksh and bash
          [ $kount -eq $count ] && break
        fi
    else                              # Filename already in TOC
       continue                       # so take up next file
    fi
    while echo "Move on to next filename ?(y/n): \c" 1>&2; do
        read answer
        case $answer in
           y|Y) break ;;              # continue 2 would also be OK
             *) break 2 ;;            # Moves to sort statement
        esac
    done
done >> $DOWNLOAD_TOC            # Only one echo statement goes to file
[ $kount -gt 0 ] && sort -o $DOWNLOAD_TOC $DOWNLOAD_TOC
```

We first execute (source) the configuration file with the dot command to make the two variables available to the script. Next, we switch to the directory containing downloaded files and check whether every file has an entry in the TOC. We also make a count (in the variable count) of the nondocumented entries. If all entries are documented, then the script has nothing to do but quit.

More often than not, some filenames won't be documented. The script scans the file list again and prompts the user for the description of an undocumented filename. A separate variable (kount) keeps track of the number of entries that we keep adding, and we quit the program when kount = count. See how **continue** aborts further processing and repeats the exercise for the next file.

If there are too many entries left to document, the user could take a break. Note that **break 2** breaks the enclosing loop and executes the last statement in the script which always maintains the TOC in sorted condition.

Now set up the directory stored in DOWNLOAD_DIR, place some downloaded files there, and execute the script. The brief session adds only one entry:

```
$ toc_download.sh
8 entries need to be documented
Downloaded filename: foo2zjs.tar.gz
Description for foo2zjs.tar.gz: [Enter]                  Ignored, can enter later
Move on to next filename ?(y/n): y
Downloaded filename: realplayer8.exe
Description for realplayer8.exe: Real Player Version 8 for Windows
Move on to next filename ?(y/n): n
```

The session tells us that we have eight entries to document. We ignored one filename, and the one we documented added the following line to TOC_download.txt:

```
realplayer8.exe: Real Player Version 8 for Windows
```

This completes our discussions on the essential features of shell programming. You have seen for yourself the remarkable power of this language. If you are fairly proficient in shell scripting already, then you can move on to the Going Further section that follows. Korn and Bash users may switch to Appendix B if they don't want to use **expr** and **basename** in their scripts.

➤ *GOING FURTHER*
Due to space constraints, the advanced features of the shell are discussed briefly. You can look up the book's Web site for a detailed examination of all these topics and many others, supported by useful examples.

13.17 The Here Document (<<)

The **here document** is the fourth source of standard input, and it finds place here because it's often used in a shell script to make a command take input from the script itself. This mechanism is very convenient to use with commands that take no filename as argument.

GOING FURTHER

mailx is one of them, so if the system administrator can store in a variable the message sent by the program in Fig. 13.13:

```
message="/home/enquiry : 15567 blocks"
```

she can use a here document to send out mail to the offending user:

```
$ set -- "$message"
$ user=`basename $1` ; blocks=$3                              $2 is :
$ mailx $user << MARK
> You have consumed $blocks blocks                     Variable evaluation too
> and exceeded your quota on `date`.              Command substitution permitted
> MARK                                               No spaces permitted here
```

The here document symbol (<<) is followed by a delimiter string (MARK), some text, and the same delimiter string. **mailx** takes as its input all data between the delimiters. When this sequence is placed inside a script, execution is faster because **mailx** doesn't have to read an external file; it's here.

The here document is useful in running interactive programs noninteractively, especially in those situations where your response is the same. For instance, the interactive script **emp1.sh** *(13.2)* can also be run like this:

```
$ emp1.sh << END
> director
> shortlist
> END
Enter the pattern to be searched: Enter the file to be used: Searching for director
from file shortlist
9876:bill johnson    :director :production:03/12/50:130000
2365:john woodcock   :director :personnel :05/11/47:120000
Selected records shown above
```

This feature applies in general to all scripts that use the **read** statement to take input.

13.18 Shell Functions

A *shell function* executes a group of statements enclosed within curly braces. It optionally returns a value with the **return** statement. Unlike in C, a function definition uses a null argument list, but requires ( ):

```
function_name( ) {
    statements
    return value                                           Optional
}
```

The function is invoked by its name (without the parentheses), optionally followed by its arguments. The *value* returned is numeric and represents the success or failure of the function. This is how you convert the sequence **ls** **-l** *filenames* **| more** to a function:

```
$ ll() {
> ls -l $* | more
> }
```
Function defined in the command line is available in current shell only

and then run it with or without arguments:

```
ll
ll *.c *.java
```
( ) can't be used

Shell functions are better than aliases in every way. Like shell scripts, a shell function supports all positional parameters (including $#, "$@", etc.). It can also return an exit status with the **return** statement. The following function can be gainfully used inside a loop to determine whether the user wants to continue or not:

```
$ anymore() {
>    echo "$1 ?(y/n) : \c" 1>&2
>    read response
>    case "$response" in
>       y|Y) echo 1>&2 ; return 0 ;;
>          *) return 1 ;;
>    esac
> }
```
Prompt supplied as argument

You can now invoke this function with a prompt string as argument and then use the return value to determine the subsequent course of action:

```
$ anymore "Wish to continue" || echo "You said no"
Wish to continue ?(y/n) : n
You said no
```

How does one return a string value? Just use a command that writes to the standard output (like **echo**) and save this output in a variable using command substitution. This function "returns" a string derived from today's date:

```
$ dated_fname() {
> set -- `date`
> year=`expr $6 : '..\(..\)'`
> echo "$2$3_$year"
> }
$ fstring=`dated_fname`
$ echo $fstring
Jan28_03
```
Last two characters from year

Apart from the command prompt, shell functions can be defined at a number of places:

- At the beginning of the script using them or at least preceding the function call. This is because shell statements are executed in the interpretive mode.
- In the profile so they are available in the current shell. Korn and Bash users should place the definitions in the rc file.
- In a separate "library" file. Every script using these functions needs to source the file at the beginning with the dot command.

Tip

The positional parameters made available to shell scripts externally are not available *directly* to a shell function. To make them available, store these parameters in shell variables first and then invoke the function with these variables as arguments.

13.19 `trap`: **How a Script Handles Signals**

Shell scripts terminate when the interrupt key is pressed unless you use the **trap** statement to specify a different action. **trap** is a signal handler, and it is normally placed at the beginning of a script. **trap** uses two lists:

```
trap 'command_list' signal_list
```

When a script is sent any of the signals in *signal_list,* **trap** executes the commands in *command_list*. The signal list can contain the integer values or names (without the SIG prefix) of one or more signals—the ones you use with the **kill** command. So instead of using 2 15 to represent the signal list, you can also use INT TERM (the recommended approach).

If you habitually create temporary files named after the PID number of the shell, you should use the services of **trap** to remove them on receipt of signals:

```
trap 'rm $$* ; echo "Program interrupted" ; exit' HUP INT TERM
```

When signals SIGHUP (1), SIGINT (2), or SIGTERM (15) are sent to the shell process running the script, files expanded from $$* are deleted, a message is displayed, and the process is terminated.

You may also ignore the signal and continue processing using a null command list:

```
trap '' 1 2 15
```
Can't be killed by normal means

The script will not be affected by three signals because no action is specified. This statement is often placed before a critical code section and overridden by another **trap** statement that occurs after the critical section. You can use multiple **trap** commands in a script; each one overrides the previous one.

Tip

Korn and Bourne don't execute a file on logging out, but, using **trap**, you can make them do that. Use the signal name EXIT (or 0) as a component of the signal list. These shells also use the statement **trap -** to reset the signal handling action to their default values.

▀▀▀ **13.20** eval: **Evaluating Twice**

Have you ever tried setting a variable to a pipeline and then executing it? Try running this:

```
cmd="ls | more"
$cmd                                            | and more are arguments to ls!
```

This doesn't produce paged output as you might expect. Now, define a "numbered prompt" and try to evaluate it:

```
$ prompt1="User Name:" ; x=1
$ echo $prompt$x                                    $prompt is undefined
1
```

In the first case, **ls** treats | and more as two arguments and produces unpredictable output. In the second example, the shell first evaluates $prompt; it is undefined. It then evaluates $x, which has the value 1. To make these command sequences run properly, we need to use the **eval** statement to evaluate a command line twice.

eval suppresses some evaluation in the first pass and performs it only in the second pass. We can make the first sequence work by using **eval** like this:

```
eval $cmd
```

In its first pass, **eval** locates three arguments—ls, |, and more. It then reevaluates the command line and splits them on the | into two commands. The command should now run properly.

The second sequence can be made to work by hiding the first $ with a \, and then using **eval**:

```
$ x=1 ; eval echo \$prompt$x
User Name:
```

The first pass ignores the escaped $; this evaluation results in \$prompt1. The second pass ignores the \ and evaluates $prompt1 as a variable.

We used $NF to access the last field in **awk** *(12.10)*, but can we do the same thing using **eval**? Since we have the value of $# available, we can:

```
$ tail -n 1 /etc/passwd
martha:x:605:100:martha mitchell:/home/martha:/bin/ksh
$ IFS=:
$ set `tail -n 1 /etc/passwd`                       set -- not required here
$ eval echo \$$#
/bin/ksh
```

This method is more efficient than using **awk** because **eval** is a shell builtin.

▀▀▀ **13.21** **The** exec **Statement**

Your study of the mechanism of process creation *(8.5)* led you to the exec family of system calls. This feature has some importance to shell scripters who sometimes need to replace the current shell with another program. If you precede any UNIX command with **exec**, the current process is overlaid with the code, data, and stack of the command. You are obviously logged out:

```
$ exec date
Tue Jan 28 21:21:52 IST 2003                                Shell no longer exists!
login:
```

Sometimes, you may want to let a user run a single program automatically on logging in and deny her an escape to the shell. You can place the command in the profile, duly preceded by **exec**. When command execution is complete, the user is logged out (since there's no shell waiting for it).

exec can also be used to generate file descriptors. For details, look up the book's Web site.

SUMMARY

Shell scripts are executed in the *interpretive mode*—one line at a time. The *she-bang line* signifies the sub-shell that runs the script.

The **read** statement is used with one or more variables to provide input to a script from the keyboard. Command line arguments passed to a script are read into *positional parameters* (like $1, $2, etc.). $# stores the number of arguments. Both $* and "$@" contain all arguments, but use of "$@" is preferred. $0 contains the name of the script itself.

The **exit** statement terminates a script. Its argument is available in $?, which signifies *success* or *failure*. Zero denotes success.

The && and || operators are used as simple conditionals. The **if** statement (closed with **fi**) uses the exit status of a command (the *control command*) to determine control flow. It is often used with **test** or its synonym [ ] to compare numbers and strings and to check file attributes.

Redirection with >/dev/tty protects those statements whose output must be written to the terminal. Alternatively, 1>&2 can be used to direct the standard output to the standard error.

case (closed with **esac**) is a compact string matching construct. It accepts the shell's wild cards for matching patterns, and can also match multiple patterns of the type used in extended regular expressions (ERE). The * is often used as the last option.

expr can perform basic integer computing and limited string handling—like returning the length of a string or a substring. **basename** is suitable for extracting the base filename or for returning a string after dropping the extension.

All loops use the keywords **do** and **done**. The **for** loop iterates through a list which can be obtained from a variety of sources including command substitution. A **while** loop is used for repeatedly executing a group of commands. Both constructs use **continue** and **break** to control loop iteration.

Redirection at the **done** keyword opens and closes the file only once. When used in that way, prompts and "error" messages inside the construct must be separately directed with >/dev/tty or 1>&2.

set places values into positional parameters. **set --** is recommended for use with command substitution. **shift** renumbers these parameters by moving $2 to $1, and so on. Because the parameters used by **set** and **shift** conflict with command line arguments, the latter should be saved before **set** and **shift** are invoked.

SELF-TEST

13.1 If x has the value 10, what is the value of (i) xx, (ii) xx?

13.2 Mention two ways you can run a script developed for the Korn shell (**/usr/bin/ksh**) even if your login shell is different.

13.3 A program stopped running when its name was changed. Why?

13.4 What is the *exit status* of a command, and where is it stored?

13.5 Search for a pattern with **grep** and **sed** and look for a file with **find**. Test the return value of each command when it displays no output. What conclusions would you draw?

13.6 Write a script that makes **rm** behave interactively whenever it is used with more than three filenames.

13.7 A script named **test** containing the **date** and **stty** commands displays nothing when executed. Why does that happen? State two ways of making the script behave properly.

13.8 Write script logic that allows only romeo and henry to execute a program, and only from the terminals tty05 and tty06.

13.9 Name the external UNIX commands that were introduced in this chapter, and explain why they had to be discussed here.

13.10 Explain what is wrong with this statement and correct it:

```
[ $# -ne 2 ] && echo "Usage: $0 min_guid max_guid" ; exit
```

13.11 Write a script that displays, in **head**-style, the last three lines of each file in the current directory, duly preceded by the filename.

13.12 Write a script that prompts for a string and then checks whether it has at least 10 characters using (i) **case**, (ii) **expr**.

13.13 Use **expr** to extract the parent directory from an absolute pathname stored in the variable x.

13.14 Write a script that accepts a compressed filename as argument (which could be .gz, .bz2 or .zip). It looks at the extension and decompresses the file using the correct decompression program, but only if the decompressed file (or one with the same name) doesn't exist.

13.15 Devise a script that accepts two directory names, bar1 and bar2, and deletes those files in bar2 which are identical to their namesakes in bar1.

13.16 Specify how the script **comc.sh** *(13.11)* needs to be modified so that it also accepts a .c filename as argument. In that case, the script should work on that file.

13.17 Explain whether these **while** loops will run: (i) while [5], (ii) while [x"$1" != x].

13.18 Display the processes in the system every 30 seconds five times using a (i) **while** loop, (ii) **for** loop. What is the unusual feature of the **for** loop that you used?

13.19 Write a script that accepts filenames as arguments. For every filename, it should first check whether it exists in the current directory and then convert its name to uppercase, but only if a file with the new name doesn't exist.

13.20 Write a script to find the total size of all ordinary files owned by a user (which could be anywhere in the system) whose name is specified as argument. First check whether the user is available in /etc/passwd.

13.21 Write a script that looks in the entire file system to locate a filename supplied as argument. If the file is found, the script should display its absolute pathname and last modification time *without saving any data in files*.

13.22 If the command **set `cat foo`** generates the error unknown option, what could be the reason, assuming that foo is a small readable file?

13.23 If a script uses 12 arguments, how will you access the last one?

13.24 Devise a script that looks at every component of PATH and checks whether the directory exists and is also *accessible*.

EXERCISES

13.1   When the script **foo -l -t bar[1-3]** runs, what values do $# and $* acquire? Does it make any difference if the options are combined?

13.2   Use a script to take two numbers as arguments and output their sum using (i) **bc**, (ii) **expr**. Include error-checking to test whether two arguments were entered. Should you use **bc** or **expr** for computation? (Look up the man page of **bc** first).

13.3   If x has the value 5, and you reassign it with **x="expr $x + 10"**, what is the new value of x? What would have been the value if single quotes were used? What's wrong with all of this anyway?

13.4   There are at least six syntactical mistakes in this program. Locate them. (Line numbers are shown on left.)

```
1    ppprunning = yes
2    while $ppprunning = yes ; do
3       echo "   INTERNET MENU\n
4       1. Dial out
5       2. Exit
6       Choice:
7       read choice
8       case choice in
9         1) if [ -z "$ppprunning" ]
10              echo "Enter your username and password"
11           else
12               chat.sh
13            endif ;
14         *) ppprunning=no
15       endcase
16    done
```

13.5 You have a number of C programs that contain comment lines at the beginning of each program. The lines begin with /* followed by the first line of comment, but the terminator line has */ as the *only* characters in the line. Remove these comments from all files.

13.6 Write a script that accepts a pattern and filename as arguments and then counts the number of occurrences of the pattern in the file. (A pattern may occur more than once in a line and comprise only alphanumeric characters and the underscore.)

13.7 Write a script that doesn't permit some users to log in more than once. It looks up a configuration file which contains a list of those users, one user per line. Where should you place the script code?

13.8 Observe this command; does it make any sense? set `set`

13.9 You have to run a job at night and need to have both the output and error messages in the same file. How will you run the script?

13.10 Write a script that behaves both in interactive and noninteractive mode. When no arguments are supplied, it picks up each C program from the current directory and lists the first 10 lines. It then prompts for deletion of the file. If the user supplies arguments with the script, it works on those files only.

13.11 Write a script which looks up every .c file in the current directory for the strings printf or fprintf. If found, the script adds the statement #include <stdio.h> at the beginning of the file but only if it doesn't already have it included.

13.12 Write a script that monitors the creation of .pdf or .PDF files in the current directory. Every minute it should display a list of those filenames created after the previous display.

13.13 Write a script that takes a filename as argument and then compresses and decompresses the file with each of the programs, **compress**, **gzip**, **bzip2**, and **zip**. At each stage, it notes the size of the file before and after compression. Finally, it displays a list showing the compression program, uncompressed size, compressed size and compression ratio (up to 1 place of decimal). The list should be ordered by the compression achieved, with figures for the most efficient compression featuring at the top.

13.14 Devise a script that allows a user to view, add, delete, or modify a setting in a configuration file that contains settings in the form *variable=value*.

13.15 Write a script that compares two directories bar1 and bar2 (supplied as arguments) and copies or overwrites to bar1 from bar2 every file that is (i) not present in bar1 or (ii) newer than its namesake in bar1. (HINT: Use the **find** command.)

13.16 Modify the above script to copy the files to a new directory. All three directory names are specified as arguments, and the new directory must not exist.

13.17 Write a script that accepts a filename as argument and then searches /bin and /usr/bin to determine its link count. If the file exists and has multiple links, then the script should display the absolute pathnames of all links.

13.18 Write a script that accepts a 10-digit number as argument and writes it to the standard output in the form *nnn-nnn-nnnn*. Perform validation checks to ensure that
   (i)   a single argument is entered.
   (ii) the number can't begin with 0.
   (iii) the number comprises 10 digits.

Ensure that all other messages are written to the standard error. You'll need to use this script in Exercise 13.24.

13.19   Write a script that checks each minute and reports on who logs in and who logs out.

13.20   Write a script that displays a special formatted listing showing the (i) permissions, (ii) size, (iii) filename, (iv) last modification time, (v) last access time of filenames supplied as arguments. Provide suitable headers using the **printf** command.

13.21   Find out the pathname of the Korn shell on your machine and then change the interpreter line in all shell scripts (.sh) in the current directory that show a different pathname for **ksh**.

13.22   Devise a script that takes a filename as argument (which must exist in the current directory) and looks in the home directory tree to display the listing of all its links. The listing should also be mailed to self.

13.23   Call up **vi** from a script so that every three minutes you hear a beep and see a message in the last line. This message appears in reverse video and reminds you to save the buffer. (HINT: Look up the man page of **tput** to know how to position the cursor. Set up a loop in the background and kill it when **vi** terminates.)

13.24   A telephone directory, teledir.txt, maintains records in the form *name:* *number* where *number* is of the form *nnn-nnn-nnnn*. Devise a shell script that accepts one or two arguments which could be:

(i)   the name or number. If it exists in the directory, then the line should be displayed.

(ii) both. The entry is displayed if it exists and is added if it doesn't exist in the file.

Note that the number will always be entered as a 10-digit string, so you'll have to use the script developed in Exercise 13.18 to perform both conversion and validation.

## CHAPTER 14

Networking Tools

Networking wasn't part of the original UNIX scheme of things. But UNIX has played a predominant role in the development of TCP/IP as a communications technology. TCP/IP tools were first developed on BSD UNIX before they were ported to other UNIX variants. Network communication became so pervasive that the technology was ultimately made available to all operating systems and eventually led to the formation of the Internet. The Net has been running on TCP/IP since 1983.

This chapter discusses the tools used in a TCP/IP network. Some of these tools, like **telnet** and **ftp**, belong to the original DARPA set which we cover only briefly. They have been replaced today by more secure tools. We'll examine the basics of cryptography, and how its principles are incorporated into the secure shell (SSH). We also need to study the mechanism behind email and the Web service, and how both applications have benefited from MIME technology.

Objectives

- Understand the features of TCP/IP that provide for reliable transmission in a heterogeneous environment.
- Learn the function of /etc/hosts in resolving hostnames to IP addresses.
- Understand the concept of *domains* and *FQDNs* and how DNS is superior to /etc/hosts.
- Learn how applications use *ports* to communicate with servers in a *client-server* scheme.
- Use **telnet** and **ftp** for remote login and file transfer.
- Understand the basics of *cryptography* and the use of *symmetric* and *asymmetric* keys for encryption and decryption.
- Discover the mechanism behind SSH (the secure shell) and the tools **ssh**, **slogin**, **sftp**, and **scp**.
- Learn the cooperative efforts of the *MUA*, *MTA*, and *MDA* in transporting mail on the Internet.
- Know how graphical programs run in a network using the X Window system.
- Know the role of *hypertext*, *URL*, and *HTML* in the HTTP protocol.
- Learn the role of the *Multipurpose Internet Mail Extensions* (MIME) standard in handling mail attachments and different media types on the Web.

14.1 TCP/IP Basics

TCP/IP is a set of networking **protocols** built into the UNIX kernel. These protocols define a set of rules that each machine must comply with to communicate with another machine in a network. The term *TCP/IP* expands to Transmission Control Protocol/ Internet Protocol, but it's actually a collection of several protocols, which includes the TCP and IP protocols. What makes TCP/IP a powerful communications technology is that it is independent of hardware and operating system. Its key features include:

- Delivery of data in multiple packets.
- Complete reliability of transmission with full error control.

Unlike our telephone system, TCP/IP is a **packet-switching** system. In a packet-switched network, there's no dedicated connection between sender and receiver. Data is broken into packets, and each packet is provided with a header. This header contains the sequence number and a **checksum**, which is a simple number determining the exact information in the packet. These packets are put inside envelopes, the sender's and recipient's addresses are written on them, and the packets are sent on their way.

As the packets travel along a vast network like the Internet, they encounter **routers** everywhere. These are special computers or intelligent devices that look at the envelope addresses and then determine the most efficient route each packet has to take to move closer to its destination. Because the load on the network varies constantly, packets may move along different routes and arrive out of order. The packets are reassembled in the correct order from the information provided in them.

Before assembly, the checksum of each packet is calculated and checked with the number that has been sent in the packet. If the checksums don't match, the packet is corrupted and has to be resent. If a packet is not received within the timeout period, it is retransmitted. When all clean packets are received, they are assembled, their headers are discarded, and data is fed to the application in its original form.

14.1.1 Hostnames and IP Addresses

In a network, a computer is known as a **host** and identified by its **hostname**. This name is unique throughout the network. The **hostname** command reveals the hostname of your computer:

```
$ hostname
saturn
```

Hostnames were originally single words like saturn, but with the rise of the Internet, they are often embedded in a larger, dot-delimited string. The **hostname** output could also be in this form:

saturn.heavens.com   *An FQDN*

We also call this a hostname, but it is more appropriately described as a **fully qualified domain name (FQDN)**. Though we'll examine FQDNs soon, for now, understand that the host *saturn* belongs to the domain *heavens.com*. In this network, other hosts will have different hostnames but the same domain name.

Every networked host is also assigned an **IP address**. This is a set of four dot-delimited numbers (called *octets*). The host *saturn* might have this address:

```
192.168.35.12
```

The maximum value of each octet is 255. Like the hostname, the IP address of a host is unique in that network. On the Internet, however, hosts have unique IP addresses and FQDNs. TCP/IP applications can address a host using either form as an identifier:

```
telnet saturn                                    Convenient for users
ssh 192.168.35.12                          Machine understands only IP address
```

Users find numbers difficult to remember, while network software understands only numbers. So even if you use **telnet saturn**, the hostname has to be converted to its IP address by the networking software. How this conversion takes place is taken up next.

14.2 Resolving Hostnames and IP Addresses

The task of resolving hostnames to IP addresses, and vice versa, is performed by the **resolver**. It is not a separate application but only a set of library routines that are linked to every TCP/IP application. There are two ways by which this resolution can take place:

- The *hosts file*. This is the file /etc/hosts. Hosts can either be simple hostnames or FQDNs.
- *DNS*. This represents the *Domain Name System* where hosts are organized in domains and are represented by FQDNs.

Small networks often adopt the "hosts" approach, but large networks (including the Internet) use the latter mechanism. Irrespective of the form used in hostnames, a connection can be established only after resolution has been performed. A TCP/IP packet contains the sender's and recipient's IP addresses and not their hostnames.

14.2.1 /etc/hosts: The Hosts File

In a small network, the name-address mappings are placed in /etc/hosts in each and every host of the network. This file is often called the **hosts file**. A look at a sample file reveals its flexible structure:

```
$ cat /etc/hosts
# Internet host table
#
127.0.0.1       localhost
192.168.35.11   jupiter.heavens.com jupiter
192.168.35.12   saturn.heavens.com   saturn
192.168.35.13   mercury.heavens.com mercury
```

Each line here relates to a host and contains at least two fields. Using this file and rather than using the IP address, you can connect to host *jupiter* in these ways:

```
ftp jupiter.heavens.com
ftp jupiter                                                          An alias
```

The problem arises when a machine is added to the network. The network administrator then has to update /etc/hosts on *all* machines in the network. This could be manageable in a small network, but becomes tedious in a large one, and absolutely impossible on the Internet. Enter DNS.

Note

You'll find the line relating to *localhost* in every hosts file. It's characteristic of TCP/IP that every host has a special address 127.0.0.1 and a special hostname, *localhost*. To test **telnet** or **ftp** on your host without being connected to a network, you can use **telnet 127.0.0.1** or **ftp localhost**.

14.2.2   The Domain Name System (DNS)

Berkeley introduced the **Domain Name System (DNS)** as a scalable system that is easier to maintain than the hosts file. DNS introduces three key concepts:

- A hierarchical organization of hostnames.
- A distributed database containing the name-address mappings.
- Delegation of authority to individual levels of the hierarchy.

In the Internet namespace, hosts belong to **domains**, which in turn belong to subdomains, and so forth. They form a hierarchy with the *root* domain as the top,

FIGURE 14.1   *The Internet Domain Hierarchy*

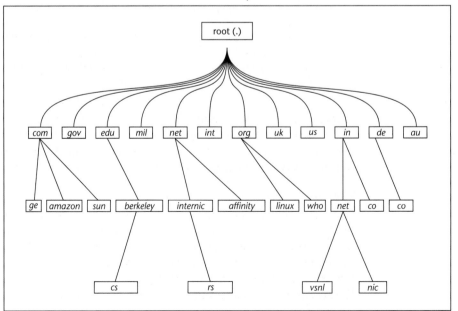

TABLE 14.1   *The Internet Domains (TLDs and ccTLDs)*

Domain Name	Significance
int	International organizations
edu	Educational institutions
gov	US govt organizations
mil	US military organizations
org	Non-profit organizations
com	Commercial organizations
net	Networking organizations
arpa	Domain for reverse resolution
aero	Air-transport industry
biz	Businesses
museum	Accredited museums
name	Individuals; possible to have *henry.blofeld.name*
pro	Professionals
coop	Cooperatives
info	For all uses
de	ccTLD; Germany
uk, ch, us, in, etc.	Other ccTLDs; United Kingdom, Switzerland, USA, India, etc.

signified by a **.** (dot) (Fig. 14.1). Immediately below the root domain are the **top-level domains (TLDs)** or **generic domains**, like *edu* and *com*. These in turn have subdomains or second-level domains under them (like *amazon*), and in this way nesting can descend several levels. Observe the similarity with the file system.

Hosts in DNS are described only as FQDNs, and you can interpret the FQDN *ralph.cs.berkeley.edu.* as the host *ralph* in the *cs.berkeley.edu* domain, where *berkeley* is under *edu,* and *cs* is under *berkeley*. FQDNs are like absolute pathnames and are unique throughout the Internet. They are also case-insensitive; *RALPH.CS.BERKELEY.EDU* and *ralph.cs.berkeley.edu* represent the same FQDN. An FQDN should identify the organization easily.

The Net originally had eight three-character TLDs (top-level domains) allocated to organizations based on the nature of their activities. MIT is represented in the *edu* domain, but Sun Microsystems (*com*) and GNU (*org*) belong to different TLDs. Moreover, every country listed in the ISO-3166-1 specification is also represented by a two-letter **country-code top-level domain (ccTLD)**. In late 2000, seven more TLDs were added (*aero, museum, name,* etc.) as shown in Table 14.1.

Agencies spread across the globe allocate domains (like *berkeley*) without creating conflict. *However, the responsibility for maintaining all information related to the berkeley domain now rests with the authorities at berkeley* (rather, Berkeley). This responsibility includes, apart from the allocation of further subdomains, the maintenance of the relevant portion of the DNS database in one or more **name servers**. A name server contains hostname-IP address mappings but in a more elaborate form than /etc/hosts. The resolver *(14.2)* queries the name servers on behalf of the application to obtain the IP address of a host.

How DNS Works

When a hostname or an FQDN is used with an application, the resolver first has to determine the mechanism of resolution that it has to adopt. It looks up its own configuration file, /etc/resolv.conf, for entries like these:

```
order hosts, bind
nameserver 192.168.35.200
nameserver 192.168.35.201
```

The resolver on this machine will first look up /etc/hosts, failing which it will use BIND, the name of the most common DNS implementation. If the resolver uses DNS, it will first look up the name server at the IP address mentioned first. It will try the second name server only if the first name server can't be contacted.

The name server may not have the answer to the resolver's query, in which case it refers the query to another name server. That name server may not have the answer either, but DNS is designed so that every name server always provides a *partial* solution that eventually leads to the resolution. For further details, look up the Web site of this book.

14.3 Client-Server: How Networked Applications Communicate

Normally, a TCP/IP application can't work alone in the way a command like **cat** can. Network applications operate on the **client-server** principle—the division of labor between two programs. An application is split up into a *server* and a *client* component, usually running on two separate machines. For host A to fetch a file by FTP from host B, an FTP client on host A needs to communicate with an FTP server *running* on host B.

The server programs are also called daemons in UNIX, and you have seen many of them in the **ps -e** output *(8.4)*. They run in the background, listening for input from clients, and are not associated with a controlling terminal. The **httpd** daemon listens for a request for a Web page. The **sendmail** daemon handles your mail. The **inetd** daemon handles both FTP and TELNET. **ping** is an exception; it needs no server.

It's possible for multiple daemons to run on a host, so how is a client FTP packet directed to its proper destination, the FTP server? Specifying the IP address in an FTP packet is not enough; a separate **port number** has to be included as well. This number is always associated with the FTP service, so the packet reaches the FTP server. Port numbers are like telephone extension numbers in an office. Specifying the office telephone number is not enough; one must also know the extension number to reach the right person.

Daemons *listen* for requests at certain specific port numbers assigned to them. The **sendmail** daemon listens on port 25, FTP on 21, and SSH on 22. The complete list is maintained in /etc/services. Clients *connect* to their respective servers, but they themselves don't use these port numbers. A connection is set up when the server *accepts* the connection. Table 14.2 lists some of the common clients and servers along with their port numbers.

TABLE 14.2 *Server and Client Programs*

Service	Server Program	Client Program	Server Port
FTP	`in.ftpd` or `ftpd` (controlled by `inetd`)	`ftp`	21
SSH	`sshd`	`ssh, scp, sftp, slogin`	22
TELNET	`in.telnetd` or `telnetd` (controlled by `inetd`)	`telnet`	23
SMTP	`sendmail`	`mailx, netscape`	25
HTTP	`httpd`	`netscape, mozilla, opera, konqueror, firefox`	80
POP3	`ipop3d` (controlled by `inetd`)	`mozilla, fetchmail`	110

Note that for a client to communicate, its corresponding server component must be running at the other end. For instance, you can't run **ftp** on your local host if the server responsible for offering the FTP service is not running remotely. You could see something like this if you try to do so:

```
ftp: connect: Connection refused
```

The earliest TCP/IP tools were independently developed at DARPA and Berkeley. The DARPA set comprised the **telnet** and **ftp** commands which use the login-password route to connect to the server. The Berkeley suite comprising **rlogin**, **rcp**, and **rsh** offered password-free authentication instead. Both systems are inherently insecure.

DARPA tools send the password across the network in clear text. This allows network sniffers to intercept the password and gain illegal access to the system. Berkeley tools assume that the IP address of the remote host is the correct one, but it's possible to subvert DNS and provide a wrong IP address. All of these tools transmit data in clear text, which could be intercepted and altered in transit.

We'll not discuss the Berkeley tools in this edition and discuss the DARPA set only briefly. Rather, we'll spend some time on SSH (the secure shell), where the entire communication is encrypted.

14.4 ping: **Checking the Network**

To operate in a network, a host must be equipped with a network interface card (NIC) that is configured and assigned an IP address. You can then use **ping** to send packets to a machine known to be working in the network. The command sends 56-byte packets to a remote destination which answers back on receipt:

```
# ping -s earth                              Solaris; Linux doesn't need -s option
PING earth: 56 data bytes
64 bytes from earth.pdsit.becs.ac.in (192.168.35.140): icmp_seq=0. time=0. ms
64 bytes from earth.pdsit.becs.ac.in (192.168.35.140): icmp_seq=1. time=0. ms
```

```
64 bytes from earth.pdsit.becs.ac.in (192.168.35.140): icmp_seq=2. time=0. ms
64 bytes from earth.pdsit.becs.ac.in (192.168.35.140): icmp_seq=3. time=0. ms
[Ctrl-c]                                        Display interrupted by pressing this key
----earth PING Statistics----
4 packets transmitted, 4 packets received, 0% packet loss
round-trip (ms)  min/avg/max = 0/0/0
```

The output confirms the connectivity between the local and remote hosts. "Pinging" a host doesn't require any server process to run at the other end. For instance, if **inetd** is not started up on the remote machine, neither **ftp** nor **telnet** will work even if **ping** reports success.

14.5   telnet: **Remote Login**

The **telnet** client program, belonging to the DARPA set, allows you to log in to a remote machine. If you have an account on the remote host, you can use **telnet** with the hostname or IP address as argument:

```
$ telnet 192.168.35.12
Trying 192.168.35.12...
Connected to 192.168.35.12.
Escape character is '^]'.

SunOS 5.8
login: romeo                                                 Enter your user-id
Password: ********                                            and password
$ _
```

The user-id and password are transmitted in clear text, and the server logs you in after authentication. Your machine just acts as a dumb terminal echoing both what you type and the response from the server. Any files you use or any commands that you run will always be on the remote machine. After you have finished, you can press *[Ctrl-d]* or type **exit** to log out and return to your local shell.

The "Escape character" lets you make a temporary escape to the telnet> prompt so that you can execute a command on your local machine. To invoke it, press *[Ctrl-]]* (*[Ctrl]* and the]). You can then use the ! with a UNIX command, say, **ls**, to list files on the *local* machine:

```
$ [Ctrl-]]
telnet> !ls -l *.sam
```

A TELNET session is closed in the same way as any login session. Use *[Ctrl-d]* or the command appropriate to the shell. If you are at the telnet> prompt, use **quit**, an internal command of **telnet**. Use **help** to view **telnet**'s internal commands.

Tip

If you are using Bash as your login shell on both local and remote machines, then you can use the hostname in the prompt. Use a setting that includes \h as an escape sequence in PS1. You'll then know which machine you are working on.

Note

The reason why the TELNET service has been disabled on many hosts is that the password is transmitted in clear text to the server. Also, the entire session can be intercepted and altered. Modern setups use SSH for remote login. SSH is discussed in Section 14.8.

14.6 ftp: **File Transfer Protocol**

DARPA's **ftp** command is used to transfer files. Additionally, it offers a number of UNIX-like directory-oriented services, and many of its commands have similar names. Let's use **ftp** to connect to *saturn,* using the hostname this time:

```
$ ftp saturn                               Resolver translates saturn to 192.168.35.12
Connected to saturn.
220 saturn FTP server (Version wu-2.6.1-18) ready.
Name (saturn:romeo): romeo                          Default is also romeo
331 Password required for romeo.
Password: ********                              Enter the password
230 User romeo logged in.
Remote system type is UNIX.
Using binary mode to transfer files.                        Note this
ftp> _                                              The ftp prompt
```

ftp prompts with the local username as default (romeo), so if romeo is connecting to a like-to-like account on *saturn,* he can simply press *[Enter]*. The program is terminated by closing the connection first with **close** and then **bye** or **quit**:

```
ftp> close                                 You can skip this if you want
221 Goodbye.
ftp> bye                                    You can use quit also
$ _
```

You have to log on to the FTP server yet again to try out **ftp**'s internal commands that are featured in the forthcoming paragraphs. For a complete list, use the **help** command at the ftp> prompt.

14.6.1 Basic File and Directory Handling

ftp supports a number of internal commands—like **pwd**, **ls**, **cd**, **mkdir**, **rmdir**, and **chmod**. But the commands apply only to the *remote* machine. The following session tells most of the story:

```
ftp> verbose                               Turns off some ftp messages
Verbose mode off.
ftp> pwd
257 "/home/sales" is current directory.
ftp> ls
-rw-r--r--   1 sales    group       1498  Jul 25 18:34 exrc
-rw-r--r--   1 sales    group         20  Jul 25 18:37 login.sql
-rwxr-xr-x   1 sales    group     289312  Jul 25 18:22 perl
-rw-r--r--   1 sales    group    1457664  Jul 25 18:43 vb4cab.2
    .....
```

```
ftp> cd reports
ftp> pwd
257 "/home/sales/reports" is current directory.
ftp> cdup                                                            Same as cd ..
ftp> pwd                                                   This is on the remote machine
257 "/home/sales" is current directory.
ftp> !pwd                                                  This is on the local machine
/home/henry/project3
```

To use the operating system commands on the *local* machine, use the ! as a command prefix (like **!pwd**). Since the ! doesn't work with the **cd** command, **ftp** offers the **lcd** (**l**ocal **cd**) command to do the job.

Tip

To have clean output, set the **verbose** mode to off by using the command once or twice. The command is a toggle switch; i.e., it alternates between the two modes.

14.6.2   Transferring Files

For the purpose of transfer, files can be seen as belonging to two types—ASCII (text) and binary. All executables and most graphics, word processing, and multimedia files belong to the binary type. To transfer such files, set the transfer mode to binary first.

Uploading (put and mput) If you are a Web site developer, you'll frequently need to upload your Web pages and graphic files to your Web site. The **put** command sends (uploads) a single file, penguin.gif, to the remote machine:

```
ftp> binary                                               No newline conversions
200 Type set to I.
ftp> put penguin.gif                                      Copied with same name
local: penguin.gif remote: penguin.gif
200 PORT command successful.
150 Opening BINARY mode data connection for penguin.gif.
226 Transfer complete.
6152 bytes sent in 0.04 seconds (150.20 Kbytes/s)
```

You can change your destination filename, and you can copy multiple files with **mput**:

```
put penguin.gif pelican.gif
mput t*.sql                                               * interpreted on local machine
```

Downloading (get and mget) To download files from the remote machine, you'll need the **get** and **mget** commands which are used in a similar manner as their "put" counterparts. This time, we'll turn off all messages with **verbose**:

```
ftp> verbose                                              Turns off noise
ftp> ls
```

```
drwxr-xr-x   14   888    999        4096   Jun 15 16:46 communicator
drwxr-xr-x    2   888    999          26   May 14 00:47 communicator_for_france
-rw-r--r--    1   888    999      323393   Sep  7 17:22 ls-lR
-rw-r--r--    1   888    999       28360   Sep  7 17:22 ls-lR.gz
 .....
ftp> binary                                          Default on most systems
ftp> get ls-lR.gz
ftp> _                                     No statistics this time—file copied
```

As with **put**, you can change your destination filename, and you can copy multiple files with **mget**:

```
get ls-lR.gz netscape_filelist
mget t*.sql                                    * interpreted on remote machine
```

Why does **ftp** have two transfer modes? When files are transferred in the ASCII mode (using the **ascii** command of **ftp**), newline conversions take place automatically. That is, if you use the **ftp** command on Windows to transfer a file from a UNIX machine in the ASCII mode, all LF will be replaced with CR-LF *(4.20)*. This replacement is desirable for text files, but not for binary files where alteration makes them unusable.

Tip

There are two **ftp** commands that are often invoked immediately before **get** or **mget**: **prompt** and **hash**. The **prompt** command (a toggle switch like **verbose**) makes **mget** and **mput** behave noninteractively if the interactive mode was on in the first place. Running **hash** before **get** or **mget** prints a # every time a block of data is transferred.

14.6.3   Anonymous FTP

There are several sites on the Net that offer software and documents for downloading. These sites offer a special user account—"anonymous," which you access with your email address as the password. They are known as **anonymous FTP** sites. This is how you connect to the anonymous FTP site of Netscape Corporation:

```
$ ftp ftp.netscape.com
Connected to ftp.netscape.com (64.12.168.249).
220 ftpnscp.newaol.com FTP server (SunOS 5.8) ready.
Name (ftp.netscape.com:romeo): anonymous
331 Guest login ok, send your complete e-mail address as password.
Password: romeo@vsnl.com                              Not echoed on screen
230 Guest login ok, access restrictions apply.
Remote system type is UNIX.
Using binary mode to transfer files.
```

This time we used **ftp** with an FQDN that represents an Internet host. Once you are in, you can navigate to the directory and then use **get** and **mget** to download the software you want. Note that you can only download files from an anonymous FTP site.

On the Internet, file transfers sometimes get aborted, and **ftp** in Linux allows you to resume the transfer with the **reget** command. If the line drops with a file foo partially downloaded, you should use **reget foo** to continue the transfer from the point of failure.

How to Use ftp Noninteractively

ftp can take authentication parameters for each host from $HOME/.netrc. Two of the three entries shown below are for hosts *jupiter* and *neptune*. The other is for anonymous FTP sites:

```
machine jupiter login sasol password llu2dw3ig
machine neptune login romeo password b1e6e37nn
default login anonymous password romeo@vsnl.com
```

Here, each of the keywords, machine, login, and password, is followed by its corresponding parameter. The last line containing the keyword default applies to all other sites. Here, it is used for anonymous FTP sites. This line has one fewer word than the previous ones.

The file contains the clear-text password, so it must be made unreadable to group and others (with **chmod 600 .netrc**). If you now run **ftp jupiter**, you'll be logged in as user sasol without prompting.

14.7   Cryptography Basics

Before we take up SSH, the secure shell, we need to understand some principles of cryptography and its techniques. **Cryptography** is the science of protecting information. This protection is achieved by using mathematical techniques to transform information into an unintelligible form by a process known as **encryption**. The unscrambling of the data to its original form is called **decryption**. Both encryption and decryption are achieved by using one or more **keys**. It is practically impossible to retrieve the original data without knowledge of the key.

Cryptography is used for *authentication, confidentiality,* and *message integrity.* When A sends a message to B, B needs to satisfy itself that the message is indeed from A (authentication). A also needs to make sure that only B can read the message (confidentiality). Both need to make sure that the message has not been altered in transit (message integrity). These principles form the basis of the secure shell, so let's look at the standard techniques that achieve these basic cryptographic goals.

There are many algorithms that determine the way data is encrypted and decrypted, and how keys are generated. Generally, we divide these algorithms as belonging to these types:

- *Symmetric key* algorithms that use a single key.
- *Asymmetric key* algorithms that use two keys.

Since the encrypted pattern is largely defined by the key used, the security of the data depends both on the strength of the algorithm and the length of the key. Though it is practically impossible to decrypt the data without knowledge of the key, a **brute force attack** (one that tries all possible keys) can theoretically retrieve the data. However, by one estimate, if the key length is 128 bits, a brute force attack using a billion computers, with each computer able to search a billion keys a second, would still require over 10,000 billion years to search all keys. It is estimated that the solar system has only about four billion years of residual life.

Both symmetric and asymmetric systems have their advantages and disadvantages, and SSH makes use of both technologies to provide a completely encrypted session between two ends. Let's now find out how and where these algorithms are used.

14.7.1 Symmetric Key Algorithms

Symmetric key algorithms make use of a single key for encryption and decryption of data. Both sender and recipient must have knowledge of the key. These algorithms enable very fast encryption and decryption and are thus widely used for bulk data. If you have a large document to send, then in all probability, you'll use a symmetric key to protect it. The most common symmetric algorithms in use are DES, 3DES, Blowfish, and IDEA.

Symmetric algorithms have one problem, however—key distribution. If two individuals who trust each other decide to exchange data, then this isn't much of a problem. However, on the Internet, if 10 users agree to exchange data with one another, they would need to exchange 90 keys. Also, they would all need to trust one another. The solution is to use a symmetric key for data encryption and asymmetric cryptography for key distribution.

14.7.2 Asymmetric Key Algorithms

Asymmetric key algorithms, also known as **public/private key algorithms**, make use of two keys—public and private. Data encrypted by one key can only be decrypted by the other key. The two keys are related to each other though it is "computationally infeasible" to derive one key from knowledge of the other. It's the public key that is distributed to all; the private key never leaves the machine.

When A needs to send an encrypted message to B using an asymmetric key algorithm, there are two options available to A:

- Encrypt the message with A's private key so that B can decrypt it with A's public key. This achieves the goal of authentication. B is sure that message has indeed come from A.
- Encrypt with B's public key so that B can decrypt it with B's private key. The goal of confidentiality is achieved as A is assured that only B can read the message.

In reallife, however, the principles described above are used in a somewhat different manner. Asymmetric key algorithms are slow (often, about a thousand times slower than symmetric ones) and are thus totally unsuitable for encrypting bulk data. SSH uses the best of both worlds. It uses a symmetric algorithm to encrypt data but an asymmetric one to distribute the key. SSH uses RSA, DSA, and Diffie-Hellman as public key systems for key distribution.

14.8 SSH: The Secure Shell

To understand why the TELNET and FTP services are increasingly being disabled, let's walk through the steps that typically characterize an FTP session. The insecurity associated with each step will help us understand why cryptography was adopted in SSH design:

- The client connects to the server. Neither the server nor the client has any means to authenticate each other. An impostor can manipulate the DNS of the network to provide an IP address that actually belongs to a different server.
- The client logs on to the server using a username and password, both of which are sent in clear text. It's easy to intercept this data.
- The client requests a file to be transferred. The entire file is also sent unencrypted, so it can be read by an outsider (violating confidentiality) and also altered (violating integrity).

SSH addresses all three issues. It uses a symmetric key to encrypt an entire session, but also uses the public/private key mechanism to authenticate hosts and users. There are currently two SSH protocols in use, and the exact techniques differ in SSH-1 and SSH-2. We'll present the features of SSH-2 and note in an inset the changes you need to make when an SSH-2 client connects to an SSH-1 server. We use OpenSSH, a free implementation of SSH made by Berkeley, to run SSH-2.

14.8.1 Host Authentication

SSH uses public key algorithms to generate a public-private key pair not only for users but also for hosts. When the **sshd** daemon is first started, it generates the **host key** pair for that host. When you use an SSH client, say, **ssh** itself, to connect to a server running **sshd**, this is what you see:

```
$ ssh mercury
The authenticity of host 'mercury (192.168.35.1)' can't be established.
RSA key fingerprint is 89:7f:65:bd:dd:af:01:e2:30:51:41:1a:fa:51:64:81.
Are you sure you want to continue connecting (yes/no)? yes
Warning: Permanently added 'mercury,192.168.35.1' (RSA) to the list of known hos
ts.
sumit@mercury's password: **********
Last login: Fri Nov 28 10:19:03 2003 from saturn.heavens.com
$ _
```

SSH here points out that it is connecting to *mercury* for the first time, and that it has been provided with the public key of *mercury* (the host key, referred to as "fingerprint"). If you find nothing wrong with that, then *mercury*'s public key is added to ~/.ssh/known_hosts on the client host.

Once you decide to go ahead, the client generates a random and symmetric **session key**. The client encrypts this key with the server's public key and sends it to the server. Henceforth, all communication between server and client will be encrypted using this session key. The user is logged in using password authentication, but this is not how we intend to use SSH.

14.8.2 The `rhosts/shosts` Authentication Scheme

The Berkeley r-utilities (comprising the **rsh**, **rlogin**, and **rcp** commands) introduced the concept of **trusted hosts** to perform password-free authentication. A host could maintain a systemwide file, /etc/hosts.equiv, that listed those hosts (one per line) who are allowed to connect to this host. Alternatively, a user could also maintain the file ~/.rhosts with similar entries. We do not cover the r-utilities in this edition, but we need to know the concepts because SSH may "fall back" on this scheme if everything else fails.

Consider that user romeo on host *saturn* has the entry mercury in ~/.rhosts. This implies that romeo on *mercury* can use **rsh** and **rlogin** to log on to his like-to-like account on *saturn* without using a password. However, if .rhosts contains the entry pluto juliet, it means that user juliet on *pluto* can log on to romeo's account without using a password. For other logins, a password would be prompted for.

This scheme has drawbacks. The r-utilities use DNS to verify the authenticity of a host, and DNS is vulnerable to spoofing attacks. However, SSH also supports a variation of the above mechanism. It uses /etc/shosts.equiv and ~/.shosts for authentication, failing which it uses /etc/hosts.equiv and ~/.rhosts. The entries in both sets are of the same form, and password-free access is granted if equivalence can be established. If all's not well, SSH prompts for a password with the difference that the password is sent encrypted to the server.

We won't discuss this scheme any further because it may be disabled in favor of a public/private key-based user authentication system that is discussed next. To use this scheme, make sure that you delete both ~/.rhosts and ~/.shosts, both in the server and the client. It's expected that the administrator won't also maintain /etc/hosts.equiv and /etc/shosts.equiv.

14.8.3 User Authentication with Symmetric Algorithms

Host authentication is followed by user authentication using public key encryption, provided the client is set up to work that way. The program **ssh-keygen** generates the public-private key pair for a user and stores them in two separate files. As an added precaution, SSH allows you to encrypt the private key using a **passphrase** which is prompted for at the time of key generation:

```
$ ssh-keygen -t rsa                                    Generating RSA keys
Generating public/private rsa key pair.
Enter file in which to save the key (/home/sumit/.ssh/id_rsa): [Enter]
Enter passphrase (empty for no passphrase): ************************
Enter same passphrase again: ************************
Your identification has been saved in /home/sumit/.ssh/id_rsa.
Your public key has been saved in /home/sumit/.ssh/id_rsa.pub.
The key fingerprint is:
29:75:68:49:30:e8:8b:e1:5c:db:13:97:01:d6:bc:15 sumit@saturn.planets
```

We opted for RSA-based authentication (-t rsa), but SSH-2 also supports DSA. A passphrase is similar to a password except that spaces are allowed. The default locations for the private and public RSA keys are ~/.ssh/id_rsa and ~/.ssh/id_rsa.pub, respectively. Expectedly, the private key file is a little more secure than the other:

```
$ cd ~/.ssh ; ls -l id_rsa*
-rw-------   1 sumit    users        951 2003-11-27 13:10 id_rsa
-rw-r--r--   1 sumit    users        223 2003-11-27 13:10 id_rsa.pub
```

Your private key is stored in encrypted form (using the passphrase you provided) in the first file. To use RSA-based public/private key authentication, you need to copy the file containing your public key (id_rsa.pub) to all hosts to which you need to connect by SSH. You could use **ftp** to do this job, but the service could be disabled, so use **scp**, a command of the SSH suite:

```
$ cd ~/.ssh                                              On the client machine
$ scp id_rsa.pub sumit@mercury:.
sumit@mercury's password: *********
id_rsa.pub         100%  |****************************|   230        00:00
```

scp still prompts for the password because RSA-based user authentication has not been set up yet. Now log in to the server (here, *mercury*) and append this file to ~/.ssh/authorized_keys on the remote host. This file contains the public keys for this user who connects from different hosts:

```
$ ssh mercury
sumit@mercury's password: ***********
Last login: Fri Nov 28 10:25:49 2003 from saturn.heavens.com
$ cat id_rsa.pub >> ~/.ssh/authorized_keys
$ exit                                                   Back to client
Connection to mercury closed.
```

If everything has been set up properly, then when you use **ssh** or any of the tools of the SSH suite (**scp**, **sftp** or **slogin**) to connect to *mercury*, the program prompts for the passphrase of your private key:

```
$ ssh mercury
Enter passphrase for key '/home/sumit/.ssh/id_rsa': ***********************
Last login: Fri Nov 28 10:27:24 2003 from saturn.heavens.com
$ _
```

Note that SSH doesn't prompt for the password this time, but simply the passphrase used to encrypt the private key. The server verifies the authenticity of the user by sending the client a **challenge**—a randomly selected string encrypted with the user's public key. The client decrypts the string and sends back the challenge string thus proving that it possesses the private key. The user is then logged in. There could be a variation of this procedure, but the underlying idea of using public key cryptography for key distribution and authentication is evident.

Caution

If SSH has not been set up properly, it will fall back on the rhosts/shosts form of authentication and prompt for your password as stored on the remote host. If SSH is simply unable to establish a secure connection, then it may even transmit the password in an unencrypted manner, but only after warning you!

14.8.4   Using the SSH Agent for Noninteractive Logins

If you connect to a remote host regularly, typing a passphrase repeatedly can be quite annoying. We can use the SSH authentication agent program, **ssh-agent**, to cache the unencrypted private key in memory. Once you hand over this key to **ssh-agent**, all future connections will be both password- and passphrase-free.

ssh-agent needs two variables to be set. The default output shows their assignment in the form *variable=value:*

```
$ ssh-agent
SSH_AUTH_SOCK=/tmp/ssh-XXFh8izh/agent.1655; export SSH_AUTH_SOCK;
SSH_AGENT_PID=1656; export SSH_AGENT_PID;
echo Agent pid 1656;
```

We haven't run the agent yet, but using the services of **eval** *(13.20—Going Further),* we can make these assignments and invoke the agent in a single invocation:

```
$ eval `ssh-agent -s`                                        Use -c for C shell
Agent pid 1251
```

The agent is now running with 1251 as the PID. You now have to hand over your private key with **ssh-add**:

```
$ ssh-add ~/.ssh/id_rsa
Need passphrase for /home/sumit/.ssh/id_rsa
Enter passphrase for /home/sumit/.ssh/id_rsa: ********************
Identity added: /home/sumit/.ssh/id_rsa (/home/sumit/.ssh/id_rsa)
```

The private key will remain cached in memory as long as you are logged in. You can display all keys registered with **ssh-agent** with the -l option, and delete a key with -d. Now you no longer need a passphrase to connect to the server:

```
$ ssh mercury
Last login: Fri Nov 28 10:28:17 2003 from saturn.heavens.com
$ _
```

Noninteractive login at last! You have a secure communication channel, and every character passing through this channel is encrypted using a symmetric key algorithm. You can now use any of the SSH tools (discussed in Section 14.9) in a noninteractive manner.

When an SSH-2 Client Connects to an SSH-1 Server

You may have the latest version of OpenSSH on your machine running SSH-2, but your server could still be running SSH-1. In that case, let's walk through all the configuration steps and note the differences:

- When you first connect to a remote host to obtain its public key, use **ssh -1 mercury**. The -1 (one) option ensures that the **ssh** client uses SSH-1.

- Generate your private/public key pair with **ssh-keygen -t rsa1**. Previously, we used -t rsa which represented the RSA keys for SSH-2. RSA keys in SSH-1 have different formats and are stored in the files ~/.ssh/identity (for private) and ~/.ssh/identity.pub (for public).
- Copy the .pub file as usual to the server but make sure that the permissions of ~/.ssh/authorized_keys are set to 600. SSH-2 is indifferent to the permissions used as long as the file is readable.
- Now connect to the SSH-1 server using the -1 option with **ssh**, **slogin**, and **sftp**, and -oProtocol=1 with **scp**.

If you still have any problems, then use **ssh -v** for a verbose output that shows the entire handshaking process. You should be able to locate the error in this output.

14.9 The SSH Tools

The SSH suite comprises tools that emulate the behavior of both the DARPA set and the Berkeley r-utilities. These tools also have similar names:

- **slogin** for remote login.
- **ssh** for remote login and command execution.
- **scp** and **sftp** for file transfer.

Note that the **ssh** command itself can be used both for remote login and command execution. Unlike the conventional tools, however, all SSH tools are secure (if configured properly); all communication between server and client is encrypted. We'll now discuss these tools.

14.9.1 Remote Login and Command Execution (ssh and slogin)

SSH features two commands, **ssh** and **slogin**, both derived from the Berkeley tools (**rsh** and **rlogin**) for remote login. If you have previously run **ssh-agent** and **ssh-add** to save your private key in memory, then you can log in without supplying a passphrase:

```
$ ssh mercury
Last login: Fri Nov 28 10:45:23 2003 from saturn.heavens.com
$ _
```

However, if you have not used **ssh-agent** and **ssh-add**, then **ssh** will prompt for the passphrase:

```
$ ssh mercury
Enter passphrase for key '/home/sumit/.ssh/id_rsa':
```

Using the -1 (el) option, you can also log in using a different user-id, provided the other user has permitted you to do so by saving your public key in ~/.ssh/authorized_keys on the server:

```
ssh -1 charlie mercury
```

The **slogin** command behaves similarly and also supports the -l option.

Sometimes, you may want to run a remote command without logging in. **ssh** can do that too. Simply use the hostname and command name as arguments:

```
ssh saturn ls -l                                        ls -l executed on host saturn
```

Though **ls** is run remotely, the output is seen on your terminal. To save this output in the remote machine as well, escape the >:

```
ssh saturn ls -l \> dir.lst                                    > interpreted remotely
```

If you use wild cards that have to be interpreted remotely, you need to quote or escape them too so that your local shell doesn't interfere.

14.9.2 File Transfer with sftp and scp

The **sftp** command is similar to **ftp** except that it has a restricted set of internal commands. Log in with or without a passphrase:

```
$ sftp mercury
Connecting to mercury...
sftp> _                                                          The sftp prompt
```

Invoke **help**, and you'll find that it uses an 'l' (el) prefix to run a command on the local machine. This prefix was seen only in the **lcd** command in **ftp**, but here you have to use **lpwd**, **lls**, and **lmkdir** to run **pwd**, **ls**, and **mkdir** on the local machine. Here's how you use **sftp** to upload a file:

```
sftp> cd workc
sftp> pwd
Remote working directory: /home/sumit/workc
sftp> lpwd
Local working directory: /home/sumit
sftp> lcd personal/workc
sftp> lpwd
Local working directory: /home/sumit/personal/workc
sftp> put shell.c
Uploading shell.c to /home/sumit/workc/shell.c
sftp> quit
```

Even though the feature is not yet documented, you can use the **mput** and **mget** commands in the same way they are used in **ftp**.

scp has one advantage over both **ftp** and **sftp**: It can copy subdirectory structures. **scp** accesses a remote file as *hostname:filename*. This is how a file is copied in both directions:

```
scp saturn:/home/henry/shell.c shell.c                         From remote to local
scp shell.c saturn:/home/henry/                                From local to remote
```

If the file has to be copied from the user's home directory, then you can shorten the command line further. You can also use wild cards to retrieve multiple files:

```
scp henry@saturn:shell.c .
scp henry@saturn:"*".c .
```

For copying a directory structure, use the -r option. Both the following commands copy henry's home directory tree from *saturn* to the local machine:

```
scp -r saturn:/home/henry .
scp -r henry@saturn:. .                                          Two dots
```

Shell programmers can now use the **scp** command in shell scripts.

14.10   Internet Mail

Electronic mail was first discussed in Section 2.9, and the **mailx** command was used to move mail between users on the same host. Mail programs generally need no special configuration to deliver mail in these single-host situations. A user's email address is simply her username. On the Internet, email addresses take one of these two forms, both of which include the domain name:

romeo@heavens.com
juliet floyd <juliet@heavens.com>

Generally, we don't see FQDNs (that include the hostname) in email addresses. Here, romeo could have an account on *saturn* and juliet could have hers on *mercury*. Yet, the email address of both hides the hostname. Note that juliet's email address is embedded within < and >. On the Internet, we use email addresses of this form, though the minimal form also works. The full name is not used for routing the mail, only the actual email address.

The mechanism used to move mail on the Internet is a little complex. Unlike TELNET and SSH, which work within a simple client-server framework, Internet mail handling requires the work of at least three agencies:

* *Mail user agent (MUA)*—For reading the mailbox and sending mail.
* *Mail transport agent (MTA)*—For transporting mail between machines.
* *Mail delivery agent (MDA)*—For delivering mail to the recipients' mailboxes.

In this three-tier arrangement, the **mail user agent (MUA)** like **mailx** or **pine** acts as the user's frontend. The MUA reads incoming mail from the mailbox and hands over outgoing mail to the **mail transport agent (MTA)**.

The MTA also has two functions: it both sends and receives mail. At the sending end, the MTA identifies the recipient's address and delivers the message *directly* to the MTA at the other end. At the receiving end, the MTA passes on mail to the **mail delivery agent (MDA)**. Both of these functions are handled universally by the *Simple Mail Transfer Protocol* (SMTP).

The MTA doesn't deliver mail. It's the MDA that accepts mail from the receiving MTA and delivers it to the actual user's mailbox. This is handled by separate programs like **/usr/lib/mail.local** on Solaris and **procmail** on Linux.

A fourth tier comes in when the user's host connects to the mail server intermittently. This is the case with dialup lines. In this arrangement, users typically use their ISP's facilities to handle their mail. The ISP stores the user's mail on their server, and the user fetches the mail using a separate program. There are two protocols in use today for fetching mail—*Post Office Protocol* (POP3) and *Internet Message Access Protocol* (IMAP).

Most character-based clients like **mailx** and **pine** can only view mail that has been delivered to the host on which they are running; they can't retrieve mail from a POP/IMAP server. However, if you compose and receive mail on your own workstation using a GUI client like Netscape Messenger, then you need to specify the following parameters as part of your client's setup:

- The outgoing SMTP server.
- The incoming server that may use the POP3 or IMAP protocol.
- Your user-id on these servers.

If your own workstation is set up to act as a mail server, then you can use the generic name *localhost* to signify your own hostname or 127.0.0.1 if you prefer to specify the IP address.

DNS Identifies the Mail Server

Apart from performing FQDN-address resolution, DNS also specifies the mail servers (called *mail exchangers*) meant to handle mail for that domain. When a message is addressed to *juliet floyd <juliet@heavens.com>*, the resolver of the sending host contacts its own DNS server to obtain the IP address of the mail server for *heavens.com* (which could be, say, *mail.heavens.com*). The MTA of the sending host then transfers the mail to the MTA of *mail.heavens.com*.

14.10.1 ~/.signature and ~/.forward: Two Important Files

Most mailers make use of the *signature* facility to append some static text to every outgoing message. This text is often the sender's personal details that are saved in $HOME/.signature. The contents of this file are attached to the user's outgoing messages provided the MUA is configured properly. Some mailers like Netscape also use the .signature file, but it is located differently.

When you travel, you can consider the automatic *forwarding* facility to redirect all your incoming messages to another address. Simply place the address where you want all mail to be forwarded to in $HOME/.forward. If romeo's .forward contains an entry like this:

```
romeo@oldstamps.com
```

the local MTA forwards the mail to the mail server of the *oldstamps.com* domain without delivering it to romeo's local mailbox. No mailer needs to be configured to use this facility because forwarding through `.forward` is a feature of **sendmail**—the program that uses SMTP and delivers most of our mail on the Internet.

Caution

A problem arises when you forward mail with `.forward` to another host and then set up a reverse forwarding facility there to redirect it back. This situation can occur for mobile users. Forwarding at both ends creates a loop, and your message never gets delivered. It shuttles to and fro before **sendmail** intervenes and breaks the loop.

14.11   MIME: Handling Binary Attachments in Mail

Every mail message consists of several lines of header information. Some of them are inserted by the MUA and the others by the MTA. A typical message shows at least the first four fields shown below:

```
Subject: creating animations in macromedia director from GIF89a images
Date: Fri, 08 Nov 2002 15:42:38 +0530
From: joe winter <winterj@sasol.com>
To: heinz@xs4all.nl
Cc: psaha@earthlink.net
```

The message body follows next, preceded by a blank line. The body contains mostly text, but it can also contain attachments which are held as a single *multipart* message. The original SMTP protocol had two limitations that disallowed the mailing of binary attachments:

- Only 7-bit ASCII characters could form a mail message.
- The line length could not exceed 1000 characters.

The **Multipurpose Internet Mail Extensions (MIME)** standard addresses these issues. MIME extends the definition of mail to include binary files and multiple data formats in a *single* message. MIME also imposes no restriction on line length. Binary attachments are **encoded** (converted to printable characters) so they can be saved in text format in the user's mailbox. But the MIME standard requires two additional headers to be sent with the message:

```
Content-Type: application/pdf; name="interior.pdf"
Content-Transfer-Encoding: base64
```

The `Content-Type:` header defines the *type/subtype* of the data following the header. Here, `pdf` is a subtype of `application`. The `Content-Transfer-Encoding:` header defines the encoding techniques used on the data. We have here a PDF document as an attachment having `application/pdf` as its content type and encoded using the *base64* technique.

These two headers provide the necessary information that would enable a MIME-compliant mail application at the other end to decode the content. Two configuration files play a vital role here: `mime.types` on the sender's side and `mailcap` on the receiver's side. When you attach a PDF document to an outgoing message, your MUA looks up the file's extension in `mime.types` to determine the `Content-Type:` header. Here's a sample entry for a PDF file (extension: .pdf):

```
application/pdf          pdf
```

The MUA sets the content type for the PDF portion of the message to `application/pdf`. At the receiving end, the MUA may not have the capability to handle this content type. It then looks up the file `mailcap` for the **helper application** (an external program) that is specified for this content type. Here's an entry from this file:

```
application/pdf; acroread %s                                    Note the delimiter is ;
```

This entry directs the MUA to call up the Acrobat Reader (the executable **acroread**) to view the PDF document. Many UNIX systems maintain a systemwide `mailcap` database in /etc, but many MUAs (like Netscape Messenger) maintain their own. If `mailcap` doesn't specify a helper application for a content type, then the MUA will seek your approval for saving the file to disk.

Even though MIME was designed to deliver multimedia attachments with mail messages, the standard applies equally well to newsgroup messages and Web resources. We'll revisit MIME when we discuss HTTP.

Note

The sender looks up `mime.types` to identify the content type to be inserted in the mail header. The receiver looks at `mailcap` to identify the helper application that can handle the attachment.

14.12   Using X Window on a TCP/IP Network

The X Window system that was first discussed in Section 2.15 provides UNIX with a graphical user interface (GUI). X was also built to run in a network, but using a reversed client-server paradigm. Its architecture places the responsibility of handling the display on the *server,* while the application itself runs as a *client.* The server in X is called the **display** which comprises the screen, terminal and mouse. X enables you to run a graphical program (client) on a remote machine and have its display on the local one (and vice versa).

14.12.1   The Display

You may decide to run a client on a remote machine, possibly because of its superior computing power or because it's not available on your machine. Consider that you want to run the **xcalc** program that is available on a remote machine (*uranus*). However, the display of the program must appear on your local machine (*saturn*) so you can input data from your keyboard. There are two things that you have to ensure before you can make that happen:

- The server (on your machine, *saturn*) must enable others to write to its display. This is done by using the **xhost** command on the local machine.
- The client program (on the remote machine, *uranus*) must be directed to write its output to another display. This is achieved by setting either the `DISPLAY` variable or by using the `-display` option with the client.

We'll first use **xhost** on our local machine to enable any user on *uranus* to write to our display:

```
$ xhost +uranus
uranus being added to access control list
```

You can turn off the **xhost** setting with the - symbol or enable your display for all machines with +:

```
$ xhost -                                        Disables display for others
access control enabled, only authorized clients can connect
$ xhost +                                        Enables display for others
access control disabled, clients can connect from any host
```

You can now run **xcalc** on *uranus* by logging on to the host using **telnet** or **ssh**. You then have two ways of running an X client on that host, and they are considered in Sections 14.12.2 and 14.12.3.

14.12.2 Using the DISPLAY variable

X uses the DISPLAY shell variable to determine where the output of an X client should be displayed. After you have logged in to *uranus,* define and export the DISPLAY variable at the shell prompt of a terminal emulator (like **xterm** or **dtterm**):

```
DISPLAY=saturn:0.0                          uranus must be able to access saturn
export DISPLAY                                 by name; else use the IP address
```

Here, *saturn* is the hostname, :0 is the instance of the X server program, and .0 is the screen number of the display. The hostname should either be present in /etc/hosts or be accessible using DNS. If it is not, then you have to use the IP address in place of the hostname.

The above setting signifies that *any* X client that will subsequently be run on *uranus* will use the display of *saturn,* rather than its own. Now you can run the program **xcalc** on *uranus:*

```
xcalc &
```

You executed **xcalc** on a remote machine, and the calculator pops up on your local machine!

14.12.3 Using the -display Option

The other technique is to use the -display option offered by every X client. The parameter to this option is the complete display name—the same value assigned to DISPLAY:

```
xcalc -display saturn:0.0 &
```

Depending on the system you are using, the -display option may override any previous DISPLAY setting. If that happens on your system (as in Linux), you don't need to use the -display option any more to run client programs from this emulator.

Tip

If you have a number of clients to run on a remote machine with the display on your local one, then it is preferable to use DISPLAY, which needs to be set only once. Many Linux systems set DISPLAY automatically when you log in, so you may not need to set it at all!

14.13   HTTP and the World Wide Web

The World Wide Web was originally conceived by Tim Berners-Lee at CERN, Switzerland as a simple mechanism for interconnecting documents. It quickly went beyond the original vision of its creator, and today functions as a "one-stop shop" for practically everything that's discussed in this chapter. The Web kept the traditional Internet services (email, FTP, and Net News) alive, but made obsolete its immediate ancestors, Archie and Gopher.

Even though the Web appears to be a conglomeration of multiple services, it works within the framework of the simple client-server model. Web service uses the *Hyper Text Transfer Protocol* (**HTTP**), and Web servers, also known as *HTTP servers,* listen for requests at port 80. If **ps -e** shows **httpd** running, then your host is a Web server.

The Web's access (client) tool is called the **browser**. A Web browser fetches a document (or any *resource*) residing on Web servers and formats it using the formatting instructions provided in the document itself. It also displays pictures if they are in GIF, JPEG, and PNG formats. If there's a format it can't understand, it will call up a *plugin* or a *helper application (14.11).*

The World Wide Web is indeed a "web"—a vast collection of **hypertext** (or **hyperlinked**) documents that are linked to one another. This linkage is based on the principle that if a resource is available on one server, then it makes no sense to have it on another. These links are specified by *Uniform Resource Locators* (**URLs**). In this way, the user "wanders and roams" without needing to know where she is, and initiates a new connection with a simple keystroke or a mouse click.

Web documents are written in the *Hyper Text Markup Language* (**HTML**), a text-based portable language. HTML can specify the text attributes that should appear on the display (like bold, red in color, etc.), but its real power lies in its hypertext capability: HTML text contains hypertext links to other Web pages. Activating a link can take you to another place in the same document, another document on the same server, or any page anywhere on the Internet. Text and pictures can also point to each other.

14.13.1   The Uniform Resource Locator (URL)

A resource is described by a **Uniform Resource Locator (URL)**—a form of addressing that combines the FQDN of the site and the pathname of the resource. The simplest URL is one that specifies only the FQDN of the server, and is entered through the URL window of the browser:

http://java.sun.com

This displays the *home page* of Sun's Java site. Web servers are often configured to send the file index.html when you specify the FQDN as above. The home page shows a number of hyperlinks in the form of underlined text. Clicking on a link fetches a different page, and your URL could change to something like this:

http://java.sun.com/docs/books/tutorial/information/FAQ.html

The URL syntax ranges from the simple to the complex, but in general, a URL is a combination of three or four things:

- The protocol (usually *http://*) used in transferring the resource. A Web browser supports other protocols, so you can use *ftp://* to transfer a file. HTTP is the default protocol, so you may drop the protocol prefix from the URL.
- The port number, which is not usually specified if the server uses the default port, 80. The previous URL is equivalent to

  http://java.sun.com:80/docs/books/tutorial/information/FAQ.html

  Note the colon before the port number.

- The FQDN of the host (here, *java.sun.com*).
- The pathname of the resource (here, */docs/books/tutorial/information/FAQ.html*). This need not always be a resource to fetch, but could be a program to run on the server.

The Web has a strong UNIX tradition, so frontslashes are the rule. Like FTP servers, Web servers also have their own root directory, which is distinctly different from the file system's root. In other words /docs is not under the system's root.

Note

The URL string is not *fully* case-insensitive. The FQDN is case-insensitive all right, but whether the pathname is case-insensitive or not depends on the server's operating system. UNIX is case-sensitive, so if you have seen the pathname /Docs/index.html, then enter it just that way.

14.13.2   HTTP: The Protocol of the Web

Like the other Internet services, HTTP has separate client and server components. A Web page typically contains links to many resources that may be distributed across multiple servers. The client requests the server for a document, and the server responds by sending it. The client then extracts the URLs of the other resources from the document and then makes separate requests for each resource that has to be fetched to complete the page display. The life-cycle of a connection using HTTP/1.1 is as follows:

1. The client contacts the server and opens a connection at port number 80.
2. The client requests the Web server for some service. This service may be to ask for a document or post some form data back to the server. The request consists of a *request header* followed by the data sent by the client.
3. The server now sends a response which consists of a *response header,* followed by data.
4. The server waits for more requests and finally closes the connection. On older HTTP/1.0 servers, the server would close the connection after each request.

Most Web servers today use HTTP/1.1 and its **Keep-Alive** feature which makes connections **persistent**. This implies that if a Web page contains five graphic files, a single connection can fetch them using Keep-Alive and not six, which was required by HTTP/1.0. The protocol is also **stateless** in that each connection is unaware of the other even though they took place sequentially.

The server's response header describes the type of data sent from the server. HTTP uses the MIME feature that was first used in email for specifying the content type of the data that is to follow. For HTML documents, this is `text/html`.

14.13.3   Running External Programs

The previous URL specifications referred to static resources—files that reside on a Web server. However, a lot of content on the Web is generated dynamically; i.e., they don't exist as files on the server. Take for instance this URL which specifies a search for the string `unix system calls` on the Teoma site:

http://s.teoma.com/search?q=unix+system+calls&qcat=1&qsrc=1

Here, the string `search` following the FQDN is not the filename of a Web page, but of a *program* to be run on the server. The remaining string following the ? symbol comprise the data to be used by this program, suitably encoded to avoid conflict with the characters used in the rest of the URL string. A Web server has no capacity to run these programs.

The server passes on the request to a **Common Gateway Interface (CGI)**, which makes arrangements to execute the program and returns its standard output to the Web server for onward transmission back to the client. We call them **CGI programs**, and such programs could be written in any language. **perl** is the language of choice for CGI because of its parsing capabilities using regular expressions. However, Java servlets are being increasingly used in this domain.

14.13.4   HTML: The Language of Web Pages

Web pages are written in HTML. Even though the HTML acronym expands to Hyper Text Markup Language, it's not really a programming language like C, which produces binary executables from text sources. Rather, HTML uses tags to "mark up" text. It owes its origin to the **nroff/troff** suite of UNIX systems that used some of these tags several years before the Web was born. A few sample lines from a Web page show the use of these tags:

```
<BODY>
  <H1> Perl: Larry Wall's Brainchild </H1>
    <STRONG>perl</STRONG> is an interpretive language and is probably the
    best      language yet        available for text manipulation.
    <IMG SRC="perl.gif" ALIGN=LEFT VSPACE=10 HSPACE=10>
    It was created by Larry Wall, and made freely available to the world.
    <EM><STRONG> You don't have to pay for using perl</STRONG></EM>,
    It's      distributed      under the GNU General Public License,
    which means that no one can impose any restrictions on its distribution.
    You can know more about <STRONG>perl</STRONG> by visiting
    <A HREF="http://www.perl.org"> the Perl site</A>.
</BODY>
```

Each tag begins with a < and ends with a >, and most tags have some formatting capability. For instance, <STRONG> and its closing counterpart, </STRONG>, serve to boldface text.

FIGURE 14.2 *HTML Web Page*

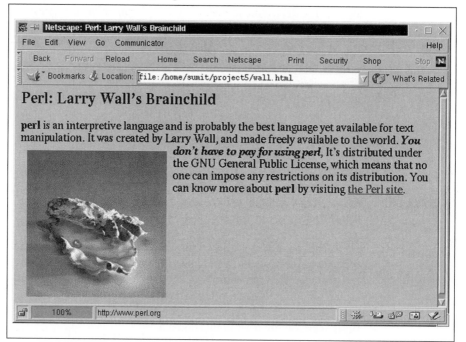

In the HTML source on page 421, the word `perl` appears twice in boldface as shown in Fig. 14.2. The browser ignores extra spaces and blank lines, and combines multiple adjacent spaces to a single space.

Two tags provide the actual hyptertext capability—`<IMG>` and `<A>`. Both of them take on *attributes* in the form *attribute=value*. The `<IMG>` tag and its `SRC` attribute are used to specify the URL of a graphic. The browser fetches the graphic file from the server (which could be a different one) and displays it inline within the Web page. Here, the tag places the picture of a pearl on the page.

The anchor tag, `<A>`, and the `HREF` attribute behave in a similar manner except that they allow you to click on a section of text or an image to fetch another resource. Here, the words `the Perl site` appear underlined, indicating a hyperlink. Clicking on it replaces the current page with the home page of *www.perl.org*.

Because HTML documents are text files, they are portable, and you can view them on *any* browser on *any* machine running *any* operating system. They are also small in size and thus are ideally suited for use on the Web where network bandwidth is often a constraint.

14.13.5 The Web Browser

The Web browser is the HTTP client. It accepts a URL either from the URL window or from a bookmark, and fetches the resource from the server. If the document contains

<IMG SRC> tags, the browser fetches the images the tags link to—using a single Keep-Alive connection, wherever possible. Every browser is also expected to offer these features:

- Step back and forth through documents viewed in a session.
- Save HTML files (and graphics) to the local machine.
- Bookmark important URLs so they can be fetched later without actually entering the URL.
- Support other application protocols like FTP and TELNET.
- Automatically invoke helper applications and special software (plugins) when encountering a file format it can't handle.

Like email clients, the earliest Web browsers were character-based, and the **lynx** browser remained popular until the advent of graphics and X Window. Netscape Navigator is the standard graphic browser for UNIX systems today. Linux users have a wider choice in Navigator, Mozilla, Konqueror, (part of KDE) and Firefox.

14.14 Multimedia on the Web: MIME Revisited

Web documents today feature a variety of multimedia objects like Java applets, RealAudio, RealVideo, and Shockwave technology. MIME technology *(14.11)* also applies to multimedia files on the Web. However, these files are sent by Web servers not as multipart messages but as independent files. The server sends the content type to the client before it sends the file. It does this by looking up `mime.types` that associates the content type with the file's extension, as shown below for a PDF document:

```
type=application/acrobat  exts=pdf                                    Solaris
application/pdf        pdf                                             Linux
```

When a browser encounters an unfamiliar data format, it first sees whether there is a **plugin** in its arsenal. A plugin is a piece of software installed ("plugged") in the browser. It is normally small in size and has the minimal features required for simple viewing (or, in case of audio and video, playing). You can't invoke a plugin separately as you can call up a helper application (explained next) like Acrobat Reader. When a file is viewed with a plugin, it appears inline with the HTML text, and not in a separate window.

    If the browser is not able to locate a plugin for a specific content type, it looks up `mailcap` to determine the **helper application**. This is a separate standalone application that can also be invoked separately from the UNIX command line. We saw one entry in this file in Section 14.11 that specified `acroread` for `application/pdf`. Unlike in Windows, UNIX Netscape doesn't have this file configured well, so you'll have to fill it up yourself.

SUMMARY

TCP/IP is a suite of protocols that connects heterogeneous machines in a network. It splits data into packets and ensures reliable transmission with full error control. Packets pass through *routers* to reach their destination.

A host is represented by a unique *hostname* and a unique *IP address* comprising four dot-separated octets. A host can be accessed both by its IP address and hostname, but TCP/IP packets contain only IP addresses.

The hostname-IP address translation is performed by /etc/hosts or the *Domain Name System* (DNS). The hosts file is maintained on *all* machines of a network. DNS understands a host by its *fully qualified domain name* (FQDN) and distributes the mappings across a number of *name servers*. The *resolver* queries the hosts file or DNS to perform the translation.

TCP/IP works in the *client-server* model. Server programs are known as *daemons*, which run in the background and listen for requests at certain *ports*.

telnet is used to run commands on a remote machine and display the output on the local machine. **ftp** transfers files between two hosts. You can upload one or more files (**put** and **mput**) or download them (**get** and **mget**). *Anonymous FTP* lets you download files from the Internet.

The *secure shell* is more secure than **telnet** and **ftp** as it encrypts the entire session including the password. It uses a *symmetric key* for encryption of bulk data, but uses *asymmetric keys* (public and private) for host and user authentication and key distribution. You can log in in a secure manner (**ssh** and **slogin**), transfer files (**scp** and **sftp**), and run a command remotely (**ssh**).

Internet mail is handled by three agencies. You read and compose mail using a *Mail User Agent* (MUA). The Mail Transport Agent (MTA) transports mail to the MTA at the receiving end using the *Simple Mail Transfer Protocol* (SMTP). The *Mail Delivery Agent* (MDA) delivers the mail to the user's mailbox.

The Web works on the *Hyper Text Transfer Protocol* (HTTP) at port 80. Web documents written in the *Hyper Text Markup Language* use *hypertext* to link one document with another resource. An HTML document is cross-platform and can be viewed in any environment.

The *Uniform Resource Locator* (URL) combines the FQDN of the site with a pathname. It can point to a static resource like a file or a program to be run, using the *Common Gateway Interface* (CGI). **perl** is the language of choice for CGI programming.

The *Multipurpose Internet Mail Extensions* (MIME) standard enables transmission of binary data in both email and HTTP. The Content-Type: and Content-Transfer-Encoding: headers together define the type of data and encoding techniques used. The file mime.types associates the content type with a file's extension, and mailcap specifies the helper application that will handle a specific content type.

SELF-TEST

14.1   Why is TCP termed a *reliable* protocol?

14.2   What is the significance of the port number? How will you find out the port number **finger** uses?

14.3   Why are the TELNET and FTP services increasingly being disabled on most networks? What are they being replaced with?

14.4   How can you be sure whether you are working on the local machine or have used **telnet** or **ssh** to log on to a remote machine?

14.5   You copied a graphics file with **ftp**, and the file appears corrupted. What could be the possible reason?

14.6   With which command do you upload files to an anonymous FTP site?

14.7   What is a *brute force attack?* Why does the security of data mainly depend on the size of the key?

14.8   To send a large volume of data securely over a network connection, what form of encryption would you adopt?

14.9   What is the difference between a *password* and a *passphrase?* Why is it necessary to have a passphrase?

14.10   Using **scp**, how will you noninteractively copy all files from juliet's home directory on host *saturn* without knowing the absolute pathname of her home directory?

14.11   What does this command do? `ssh jupiter date \> .date`

14.12   How does X solve the problem of running the same program on different displays with different characteristics?

14.13   Can an X client like **xterm** running on a Solaris machine display its output on a HP-UX machine?

14.14   What is the problem with `/etc/hosts`?

14.15   Name three top-level domains that have been added to the Internet namespace in the year 2000. Is the domain name *WWW.suse.COm* valid?

14.16   Explain the significance of the *MUA* and *MTA.* Whom does the MTA hand over mail to?

14.17   How are binary files included in mail messages even though SMTP handles only 7-bit data? Name the two mail headers that play an important role here.

14.18   The browser can display three types of images without needing external help. What are they?

14.19   What is *hypertext?* Is it confined to text only?

14.20   What is *HTTP*? Which port number does it use?

14.21   What are *CGI programs?* How are they invoked?

14.22   How do you access the home page of the Web server running on your own machine?

EXERCISES

14.1   How is a TCP/IP network different from a telephone network?

14.2   What is an *FQDN?* Why are hostnames not used on the Internet, but only FQDNs?

14.3   Describe the role of the resolver when handling (i) simple hostnames, (ii) FQDNs.

14.4   Name three important features of DNS. What advantages does DNS have over the hosts file?

14.5   Explain the role of a name server. What does a name server do if it can't handle an FQDN?

14.6   When you change your local directory from inside **ftp**, will the changed directory still be in place after you quit **ftp**, and why?

14.7   When A sends data to B over a network connection using public key cryptography, how does A achieve the goals of (i) authentication, (ii) confidentiality?

14.8   Public key cryptography is more suitable for key distribution than bulk data encryption. Explain how you can use this mechanism to distribute a symmetric key.

14.9   For using SSH, why does a host also need to have a public and private key?

14.10   Explain how you can generate a public/private key pair for yourself.

14.11   Explain how the **ssh-agent** and **ssh-add** programs enable noninteractive logins.

14.12   Cite two reasons why **scp** is preferable to **ftp**.

14.13   How is the client-server mechanism in X different from others?

14.14   How can romeo running Netscape on his machine *saturn* write its output to juliet's display on a remote machine *uranus*? Do both users need to run X?

14.15   Why is the DISPLAY variable more convenient to use than the -display option?

14.16   Explain how the general mail handling scheme changes when a user connects to the mail server over a dialup line.

14.17   Explain the significance of each word in the acronym *URL*. What happens if you leave out the port number in the URL?

14.18   Why is HTTP called a *stateless* protocol? What is meant by the *Keep-Alive* feature?

14.19   Why is the HTML format specially suitable for Web documents?

14.20   Can you use *WWW.PLANETS.COM/CATALOG.HTML* instead of *www.planets.com/catalog.html* as the URL?

14.21   To download a Web page with 10 graphics, how many connections are required in (i) HTTP 1.0, (ii) HTTP 1.1?

14.22   If a browser passes data from an HTML form to the server, how does the server handle the data?

14.23   What is a *helper application*, and how does it differ from a *plugin?* Explain the role of the files, mime.types and mailcap, when using a helper application.

14.24   What is *MIME?* How are the limitations of SMTP in handling mail attachments overcome by MIME?

perl—The Master Manipulator

Perl is UNIX's latest major acquisition, and one of its finest. Developed by Larry Wall, this Practical Extraction and Report Language is often hailed as the "Swiss Army Officer's Knife" of the UNIX system. In **perl**, Wall invented a catchall tool that does several things well. **perl** is standard on Linux and also offered on Solaris. However, it is free, and executables are available for all UNIX flavors (*http://www.perl.com*).

perl is both a scripting language and the mother of all filters. It combines the power of C, the UNIX shell, and its power filters—**grep**, **tr**, **sed**, and **awk**. It has all the control structures and regular expressions that you could find anywhere. It is exceedingly cryptic, even by UNIX standards, and can solve text manipulation problems with very compact code. In spite of offering so much, **perl** is faster than the shell and **awk** (but not C).

Objectives

- Gain an overview of a sample **perl** program.
- Understand how **perl** treats variables and constants and changes their type when required.
- Learn how to use the concatenation and repetition operators (. and x).
- Read files both in the command line and inside a script from command line arguments.
- Understand the significance of the default variable, $_, and how its presence can be felt everywhere.
- Use *lists* and *scalar arrays*, and the functions to manipulate them.
- Use the **foreach** loop for working with a list.
- Split and join a line with **split** and **join**.
- Handle *associative arrays* with a nonnumeric subscript.
- Examine **perl**'s enlarged regular expression set which uses special escape sequences.
- Filter data with the **s** and **tr** commands.
- Use *filehandles* to access a file or stream.
- Test the file attributes.
- Develop *subroutines* for repeated use.
- Gain an overview of CGI and how **perl** is suitable for the task. (*Going Further*)

15.1   perl **Preliminaries**

A **perl** script or program runs in a special interpretive mode: the entire script is compiled internally in memory before it is executed. Unlike other interpreted languages like the shell and **awk**, script errors are generated before execution. With this simple one-liner, you can test whether **perl** is in your PATH:

```
$ perl -e 'print("GNUs Not Unix\n") ;'
GNUs Not Unix
```

perl doesn't behave like a filter here in printing the GNU acronym, but more like **awk**'s BEGIN section. **perl -e** can do a lot of useful things from the command line. However, **perl** programs are often big and are better placed in .pl or .cgi files.

Our first **perl** program, **sample.pl** (Fig. 15.1), uses the she-bang line, this time pointing to the **perl** command. **perl** uses the # as the comment character exactly like **awk** and the shell. There are three variables used in the script (like $name) and three numerical operators (+, *, and /). **perl** mimics **awk** by supporting the **print** and **printf** functions, and C by terminating all statements with a semicolon. Also, numeric computation in **perl** is virtually identical to that used in **awk** (Tables 12.1 and 12.2).

perl variables are examined later, but for now keep in mind that **perl** uses the $ prefix both in the definition ($name = <STDIN>), as well as in evaluation (The temperature, $name .....). **perl** uses <STDIN> as a *filehandle* (a logical name for a file) to represent standard input. Note that the **printf** function doesn't use parentheses here. **perl** is generally indifferent to their use, but we'll use them as much as we can.

Use **chmod** to make the script executable and then run it like a shell script. Enter a lot of spaces before keying in the actual input:

```
$ chmod +x sample.pl ; sample.pl
Your name:              stallman
Temperature in Centigrade:      40.5
Temperature              stallman in Fahrenheit: 104.900000
```

FIGURE 15.1   sample.pl

```perl
#!/usr/bin/perl
# Script: sample.pl - Shows use of variables
print("Your name: ") ;
$name = <STDIN> ;                            # Input from keyboard
chomp($name) ;                               # Removes trailing \n
print("Temperature in Centigrade: ") ;
$centigrade=<STDIN> ;                        # Whitespace unimportant
$fahrenheit= $centigrade*9/5 + 32 ;          # Here too
printf "Temperature %s in Fahrenheit: %f\n", $name, $fahrenheit ;
```

If you don't provide the she-bang line, you need to use **perl sample.pl** to run the script. Like **awk**, **perl** identifies data types intuitively. Observe that it saves the spaces before stallman (a string), but not those before 40.5 (a number).

Why did we use **chomp**? Because $name evaluates to stallman\n; it includes the trailing newline (generated by *[Enter]*). **chomp** removes the trailing \n, and if you comment the statement, then you'll see the **printf** output in two lines:

```
Temperature         stallman
in Fahrenheit: 104.900000
```

perl provides detailed and extensive documentation, which is accessed with the **perldoc** command (use **perldoc -h** for help). The newsgroup *comp.lang.perl* discusses problems related to **perl** and also posts its FAQ.

You can run your **perl** and shell scripts from within the **vi** editor. The technique of doing this is detailed in the Tip of Section 13.1.1.

Tip

15.2   **Variables and Constants**

Variables are considered declared when they are first used. **perl** uses the $ prefix to identify variables both in assignment and evaluation ($x = 1 ; print $x ;). The $ prefix is also used by **perl** with a variable that represents an array element.

Variables and literals have no intrinsic type. **perl** understands 'foo', "foo", and "123" as strings, and 123 and 0.0 as numeric. It makes the necessary conversions when handling expressions that use a mix of string and numeric data types. For instance, it converts the string "123" to a number when adding it to 1 to return 124. Similarly, it converts 1 to a string when concatenating it with a string "www" to return "www1".

Uninitialized variables are assumed to be a null string when treated as a string and zero when treated as a number. Incrementing an uninitialized variable returns 1:

```
$ perl -e '$x++ ; print("$x\n");'
1
```

perl is indeed unusual: it can perform computation on any string containing only letters and numbers. Note that **perl** is intelligent enough to guess your true intentions:

```
$x = "A" ;  $x++ ;                                      $x is B
$y = "P1" ;  $y++ ;                                  $y becomes P2!
$z = "Q09" ;  $z++ ;                                $z becomes Q10!
```

Like the shell but unlike **awk**, **perl** supports both unquoted, single-, and double-quoted strings. Unquoted strings can't contain a special character. Every character in a single-quoted string is treated literally (including the newline); this lets us protect spaces and the \. Double-quotes allow the inclusion of escape sequences (Tables 2.2 and 15.1) and variables. Characters like the @ and $ need to be escaped to be treated literally:

TABLE 15.1   *Special Escape Sequences Used in Double-Quoted Strings (See also Table 2.2)*

Escape Sequence	Significance
\u	Converts next character to uppercase
\U	Converts all subsequent characters to uppercase or until \E is encountered
\l	Converts next character to lowercase
\L	Converts all subsequent characters to lowercase or until \E is encountered
\E	Terminates action of \U and \L

```
$name1 = jobs ;                                                          No quotes, OK
$name2 = "wall\t$name1\n" ;                                    wall, a tab, jobs and newline
$name3 = "larry\@heavens.com" ;                      Without \, @ interpreted as an array
$name4 = '\t\t'                                                       \t\t ; treated literally
```

Apart from the standard escape sequences, **perl** also supports the \U and \u characters in double-quoted strings. They convert to uppercase the entire string and the first character, respectively. The escape sequence \E marks the end of the affected area. Though they are not necessary here, you'll need to use them when you convert only portions of a string:

```
$name = "steve jobs" ;
$result = "\U$name\E" ;                                          $result is STEVE JOBS
$result = "\u$name\E" ;                                          $result is Steve jobs
```

The \L and \l sequences convert strings to lowercase in the same way. **perl** also supports some functions that can perform case conversion. They are presented later.

Like the shell, **perl** can also assign a variable using command substitution. Shell programmers must note that you can't use this feature in double-quoted strings. Also, you can't use the shell's internal commands:

```
$todays_date = `date` ;                                          External commands only
$cwd = `pwd` ;                                      Works because pwd is also an external command
```

perl expressions have true and false values. 1 represents a true value and 0 a false value. Any expression that evaluates to 0, a null string, or an undefined value is false in **perl**.

15.2.1   Using a Pragma

While the facility to use undefined and uninitialized variables makes **perl** very convenient to use, they could get in the way of writing large programs. By default, **perl** variables are global and they conflict with variables of the same name used in its subroutines (functions). **perl** can be directed to look for undeclared variables with a **pragma** that is placed after the she-bang line:

```
#!/usr/bin/perl
use strict;                                                    A pragma
#my $name;
print("Enter filename: ");
chomp($name = <STDIN>);
```

A pragma is a directive that **perl** needs to be aware of before it compiles and executes a program. The pragma **use strict;** enforces strictness during compilation by looking for undeclared variables. If you execute the above code with one line commented, **perl** displays an error:

```
Global symbol "$name" requires explicit package name at ./foo line 5.
Execution of ./foo aborted due to compilation errors.
```

This pragma requires $name to be declared before it is used. The **my** function declares a local variable, often in a **perl** subroutine. Though we'll not use this pragma in this chapter, you need to do so if you decide to declare variables as a matter of principle.

15.3 Operators

Like all languages, the +, -, *, /, and % operators are used by **perl** for computation except that **perl** uses ** for exponentiation (2**10 = 1024). Apart from the comparison and logical operators, **perl** has two special operators for concatenation and repetition. A brief discussion of these operators follows next.

15.3.1 The Comparison and Logical Operators

Unlike **awk**, **perl** uses two different sets of operators for comparing numbers and strings (Table 15.2). The type-neutral comparison operators supported by **awk** (Table 12.3) are used by **perl** for numeric comparison only:

```
if ($x*512 > 65536)
```

TABLE 15.2 *The Comparison and Concatenation Operators*

Numeric	String	Regular Expression	Significance
<	lt		Less than
<=	le		Less than or equal
==	eq	=~	Equal or matches
>=	ge		Greater than or equal
>	gt		Greater than
!=	ne	!~	Not equal or doesn't match
<==>	cmp		Returns three values; -1 if left operand is less than right operand, 0 if equal and 1 otherwise.
	.		Concatenates left and right operands.
	x		Repeats a string

Shell programmers need to note that for comparing strings, **perl** uses operators similar to those used by the shell *to compare numbers*. **perl** uses eq rather than -eq to compare two strings:

```
if ($name eq "")                                                checking $name for an empty string
```

When making a string comparison, **perl** compares the ASCII value of each character starting from the left. Thus, "2" is greater than "10" when compared as strings. **perl** needs to know whether you intend to do a string or a numeric comparison.

Caution

Don't use == to compare two strings; use eq instead. The == operator compares two numbers only for equality.

For matching strings anywhere in a line, **perl** uses the **sed** and **awk** technique of enclosing the pattern within /s. Regular expressions are enclosed similarly, but **perl** uses the =~ and !~ operators for matching them:

```
if ($line =~ /^root/)                                   Matches root at beginning of $line
if ($line !~ /^root/)                                   Doesn't match root at beginning of $line
```

All comparisons return 1 if true and 0 otherwise. **perl** can also set the return value of a comparison to a variable so that you can use it later:

```
$x = $y = 5 ;
$z = $x == $y ;                                              $z contains result of comparison
printf("%d %d\n", $x == $y, $z);                                            Prints 1 1
```

And as if that was not enough, comparisons can even return three values. Observe from Table 15.2 that the cmp and <=> operators return the value -1 when the expression on the left is less than the one on the right.

    perl also uses the logical AND and OR operators, && and ||, in the same sense used by **awk**:

```
if ($x < 10 && $x > 5)
```

15.3.2 The Concatenation and Repetition Operators (. and x)

Though the expression xy concatenates the variables $x and $y, **perl** has a separate operator (the dot) for concatenating strings:

```
$ perl -e '$x=sun ; $y=".com" ; print ($x . $y . "\n") ;'
sun.com
```

Note that $y itself contains a dot, so its value had to be placed within quotes. For the sake of readability, it's preferable to have whitespace on either side of the dot operator.

    perl uses the x operator for repeating a string. The following statement prints 40 asterisks on the screen:

```
$ perl -e 'print "*" x 40 ;'
****************************************
```

The string to print isn't restricted to a single character; it can even be an expression (which **perl** evaluates to a string value). This operator is most useful in printing rulers for reports.

15.4 The Standard Conditionals and Loops

Most of the control structures used by the shell, **awk**, and C are supported by **perl**. However, **perl** differs markedly from these languages in the use of curly braces. The body of statements executed in every conditional or loop must be enclosed in curly braces, *even if the body comprises a single statement*. **perl** also features a **foreach** construct for use with arrays, which will be examined in Section 15.10. The other constructs are well known to you, so we'll present their syntax through short examples.

15.4.1 The if Conditional

For decision making, **perl** supports the **if** and **unless** conditionals. We don't need to discuss **unless** since it is virtually identical to using **if** with the boolean NOT operator. The **if** construct in **perl** takes three forms as shown in Fig. 15.2.

Except for the mandatory provision of curly braces, the first form is identical to that used in **awk**. The second form uses the **elsif** keyword (**elif** in the shell). The third is a compact one-liner that is unique to **perl**. This form doesn't need to use parentheses around the condition.

15.4.2 The while, do-while, and for Loops

Like **awk**, **perl** supports the **while** and **do-while** loops. Like the third form of the **if** construct, **perl** also supports a one-liner that uses a **while** loop. It also features an **until** loop which behaves like its shell counterpart. The first two forms shown in Fig. 15.3 use an infinite loop to print an infinite number of asterisks on the screen. The third form prints only five.

The same job can be done with a **for** loop which in **perl** has no special features. This loop also prints five asterisks:

FIGURE 15.2 *The Three Forms of the* **if** *Conditional*

`if ($x > 1) {`
    `printf("a");`
`}`
`else {`
    `printf("b");`
`}`
	`if ($x > 5) {`
	    `printf("a");`
	`}`
	`elsif ($x > 3) {`
	    `printf("b");`
	`}`
	`else {`
	    `printf("c");`
	`}`
		`printf("") if $x > 3;`

Form 1	Form 2	Form 3

```
for ($i = 0 ; $i < 5 ; $i++) {
    print("*");
}
```

The repetition operator (x), discussed in Section 15.3.2, can do this job with a one-liner.

All loops support the **next** statement that restarts loop iteration and **last** which breaks out of a loop. **perl** deviates from tradition here: it doesn't use **continue** and **break**. An infinite loop can be set up with **while (1)** or **for (;;)**.

The **if** and **while** constructs feature in the next program, **leap_year.pl** (Fig. 15.4), which determines whether the number you key in is a leap year or not.

The entire program runs in an infinite loop, and the **last** statement at the bottom terminates the loop if you enter an n or N:

FIGURE 15.3 *The **while** and **do-while** Loops*

`while (1) {`
`    printf("*");`
`}`
	`do {`
	`    printf("*");`
	`} while (1) ;`
		`print("*") while $x++ < 5 ;`

Form 1   Form 2   Form 3

FIGURE 15.4   **leap_year.pl**

```perl
#!/usr/bin/perl
# leap_year.pl: Determines whether a year is a leap year or not
#
while (1) {
    $yesorno = "not" ;
    printf("Enter a year: ");
    chomp($year = <STDIN>);
    if ("$year" > 0) {
       if ($year % 4 == 0 && $year % 400 == 0) {
           $yesorno = "certainly" ;
       } elsif ($year % 100 != 0 && $year % 4 == 0) {
           $yesorno = "certainly" ;
       }
       print ("$year is " . $yesorno . " a leap year\n") ;
    }
    printf("Wish to continue? ");
    chomp($answer = <STDIN>);
    last if ($answer eq "n" || $answer eq "N");
}
```

```
$ leap_year.pl
Enter a year: 2004
2004 is certainly a leap year
Wish to continue? y
Enter a year: 2001
2001 is not a leap year
Wish to continue? y
Enter a year: 1900
1900 is not a leap year
Wish to continue? n
$ _
```

15.5 Reading Files from Command Line Arguments

perl supports command line arguments. Since it is both a filter and a scripting language, **perl** uses special notation, which we'll now discuss, to identify filenames. Section 15.9.1 discusses arguments in general. We'll first read a file using one-liners and then learn to use a script.

15.5.1 Reading Files with One-Liners

The diamond operator, <>, is used for reading lines from a file. For example, <STDIN> reads a line from standard input, and <> reads a line from the filename specified as argument. To read and print all lines of a file, use <> in either of these ways:

```
perl -e 'print while (<>)' /etc/group          File opening implied
perl -e 'print <>' /etc/group                  As above but loop also implied
```

The context of the <> operator is different in these two examples. The first is interpreted in *scalar* context which signifies reading one line. The second is interpreted in *list* context where it represents all lines. You can use **while (<>)** to read multiple files:

```
perl -e 'print while (<>)' foo1 foo2 foo3
```

perl also supports the -n option which implies this loop. Make sure that -n precedes -e when using this feature:

```
perl -ne 'print' /etc/group                    -en won't work here!
perl -ne 'print' foo1 foo2 foo3
```

The advantage of this form is that you can use simple one-line conditionals in the command line itself. Here is a bare-bones **grep** command at work with our sample database *(11.1)*:

```
$ perl -ne 'print if /wood\b/' emp.lst
5423:barry wood      :chairman :admin        :08/30/56:160000
```

This one-line conditional uses the regular expression /wood\b. **perl** uses an enlarged regular expression set (Table 15.3), where \b is used to match on a word boundary. This eliminated woodhouse and woodcock from the output. We'll see more of **perl**'s regular expressions later.

TABLE 15.3   *Additional Regular Expression Sequences Used by* **perl**

Symbols	Significance
\w	Matches a word character (same as [a-zA-Z0-9_])
\W	Doesn't match a word character (same as [^a-zA-Z0-9_])
\d	Matches a digit (same as [0-9])
\D	Doesn't match a digit (same as [^0-9])
\s	Matches a whitespace character
\S	Doesn't match a whitespace character
\b	Matches on word boundary
\B	Doesn't match on word boundary

15.5.2   Reading Files in a Script

The previous **perl** statement could have been placed in a script. This time, a loop is implied, so we have to use **perl** with the -n option in the she-bang line:

```
#!/usr/bin/perl -n
print if /wood\b/ ;
```

We often need to do some processing outside the loop—like printing a heading or a total. The -n option doesn't allow that, so we have to set up the **while** loop inside the script:

```
#!/usr/bin/perl
printf ("%30s", "LIST OF EMPLOYEES\n") ;
while (<>) {
    print if /wood\b|light.*/ ;              Using an extended RE
}
print "\nREPORT COMPLETE\n" ;
```

What you see above is something that we do many a time: print a heading before the detail and then something after the detail. This is how you implement the BEGIN and END sections of **awk** in **perl**.

Tip

For pure filtering, use **perl -n** as the interpreter name in the she-bang line. No explicit **while** loop is then required. If you have headers and footers to print, then drop the -n option and set up a **while** loop inside a script.

15.6   The Current Line Number ($.) and the Range Operator (..)

We'll now learn the use of two special operators for addressing lines by their numbers. **perl** stores the current line number in a special variable, $. ($ followed by a dot), so you can select lines from anywhere:

```
perl -ne 'print if ($. < 4)' foo              Like head -n 3 foo
perl -ne 'print if ($. > 7 && $. < 11)' foo   Like sed -n '8,10p' foo
```

perl has a host of built-in variables, and $. is **perl**'s counterpart of **awk**'s NR variable. **perl** has shortcuts to these commands too. Use its range operator, .. (2 dots):

```
perl -ne 'print if (1..3)' foo
perl -ne 'print if (8..10)' foo
```

For selecting multiple segments from a file, you can use multiple **print** statements, or you can use compound conditions:

```
if ((1..2) || (13..15)) { print ; }
```

We'll now examine another important **perl** variable named $_.

15.7 $_ : The Default Variable

The previous programs used **print** without specifying what to print. The **while** loop used the diamond operator <> without specifying the variable to read a line into. An invisible assignment is at work here. When using <>, **perl** automatically assigns the entire line to a special variable, $_. This variable is often called the **default variable**, and many **perl** functions (like **print**) operate on $_ by default. We often drop the $_ to compact our code (and make it cryptic).

   Suppose you have to prefix a line number to every line. This is where you need $_ to explicitly specify the line. The comments in the script, **grep1.pl** (Fig. 15.5), show what **perl** does internally with $_.

   The <> operator, **chop** and pattern matching work on $_ by default, the reason why it isn't explicitly specified anywhere except in the **print** statement. We used it with the **print** statement only because it had to be concatenated with $slno. Otherwise, **print** also operates on $_ by default. The program locates the email addresses of all senders from the *velvet.com* domain:

FIGURE 15.5   grep1.pl

```
#!/usr/bin/perl
# grep1.pl: Extracts the From: headers from the mailbox
#
while (<>) {                              # Actually ($_ = <>)
    chomp() ;                            # chomp($_)
    if (/From:.*\@velvet.com/) {         # if ($_ =~ /From:.*\@velvet ...)
        $slno++ ;
        print ($slno . " " . $_ . "\n") ;
    }
}
```

```
$ grep1.pl $HOME/mbox
1 From: "Caesar, Julius" <Julius_Caesar@velvet.com>
2 From: "Goddard, John" <John_Goddard@velvet.com>
3 From: "Barnack, Oscar" <Oscar_Barnack@velvet.com>
```

You can reassign the value of $\$\_$. Since many **perl** functions operate on $\$\_$ by default, you'll often find it convenient to set $\$\_$ to an expression that you need to manipulate later. This assignment allows you to use these functions without specifying either $\$\_$ or any variable name as argument.

Note

Though its significance is difficult to define exactly, $\$\_$ often represents the last line read, the last pattern matched, or the last element picked up from a list.

15.8 String Handling Functions

perl has all of the string functions that you can think of. Some of them were seen in **awk**, and the others are supported by compiled languages. Two important functions, **split** and **join**, deserve discussion in separate sections. In most cases, we are interested in the return values of these functions, but sometimes we use them for their side effect.

chop and chomp perl provides these two functions to remove the last character of a string. **chop** does it unconditionally, but **chomp** removes only a newline. In the program shown in Fig. 15.5, we used **chomp** for its side effect. But we can also make use of its return value:

```
$lname = chomp($name) ;                          $lname stores last character chopped
```

In most cases, we don't need to know the character that was chopped, but we often combine an assignment and the execution of a function in one statement:

```
chomp($name = <STDIN>) ;                          Reading and assigning together
```

If you need to remove \n and are not sure whether there will be one, then you'll find **chomp** more convenient to use because it removes only \n. Both **chop** and **chomp** can work without an argument, in which case $\$\_$ is assumed.

index(*str*, *substr*, *n*) and rindex(*str*, *substr*, *n*) index is also used by **awk** to return the position of the first occurrence of *substr* in a larger string *str*. With these two arguments, the search is made from the beginning of the string, but if *n* is specified, *n* characters are skipped. **rindex** behaves like **index** except that it locates the last occurrence of the string:

```
$fqdn = "www.perl.com" ;
print index($fqdn, ".") ;                                        Prints 3
print rindex($fqdn, ".") ;                                       Prints 8
```

reverse(*str*) This function, which can also operate on an array, reverses the characters in *str* and returns the reversed string:

```
$x="abcd";
print reverse($x);                                              Prints dcba
```

substr(*str1*, *offset*, *length*, *str2*) **substr** takes between two and four arguments. Its special features include extracting characters from the *right* of the string and inserting or replacing a string. If $x is assigned the value "abcefgh", **substr($x, 4, 3)** returns efg.

The following example assumes *length* to be zero. **substr** stuffs $x with efgh without replacing any characters; 0 denotes nonreplacement:

```
$x = "abcdijklm" ;
substr($x,4,0) = "efgh" ;                        Stuffs $x with efgh
print "$x" ;                                     $x is now abcdefghijklm
```

substr($x, -3, 2) extracts two characters from the third position on the *right:*

```
$y = substr($x,-3,2) ;                           Extracts from right
print "$y" ;                                     $y is kl
```

uc and ucfirst, lc and lcfirst There are four functions for changing the case of text. **uc** converts to uppercase its entire argument, while **ucfirst** converts only the first character to uppercase:

```
$name = "larry wall" ;
$result = uc($name);                             $result is LARRY WALL
$result = ucfirst($name);                        $result is Larry wall
```

lc and **lcfirst** perform opposite functions of their "uc" counterparts. Apart from converting case, **perl** can also filter the contents of variables in the same way the UNIX filters, **tr** and **sed**, manipulate text. We'll be discussing the **tr** and **s** functions later.

15.9 Lists and Arrays

Lists and arrays lie at the very heart and soul of **perl**. A **list** is a set of data. An **array** makes the list available in a variable. The following is an example of a list:

```
( "Jan", 123, "How are you", -34.56, Dec )
```

A list need not contain data of the same type. For a list to be usable, it needs to be assigned to a set of variables:

```
($mon, $num, $stg, $neg, $mon2) = ( "Jan", 123, "How are you", -34.56, Dec );
```

When the size of a list can be determined only at runtime, we need an array to hold the list. These arrays are of two types—*scalar lists* and *associative arrays*. We'll be looking at scalar lists in this section. Let's assign the following list to a three-element array, @month:

```
@month = ("Jan", "Feb", "Mar") ;                 $month[0] is Jan
```

These are quoted strings, and **perl** supports the **qw** function that can make short work of this assignment:

```
@month = qw/Jan Feb Mar/;                                    No commas and no quotes
print $month[1];                                                       Prints Feb
```

Arrays in **perl** are not of a fixed size; they grow and shrink dynamically as elements are added and deleted. Even though an array is accessed using the @ prefix, each element of the array is accessed using $mon[*n*], where *n* is the index, which starts from zero. $month[0] evaluates to the string Jan, and $month[3] is undefined.

Array assignment is also quite flexible in **perl**. You can use the range operator or even assign values selectively in a single statement:

```
@x = (1..12) ;                                             Assigns first twelve integers
@month[1,3..5,12] = ("Jan", "Mar", "Apr", "May", "Dec") ;
@month[1,3..5,12] = qw/Jan Mar Apr May Dec/ ;                             Same
```

In the second example, note that $month[4] is Apr and $month[0] and $month[2] are null if they weren't defined previously.

Like <>, the array @month can be interpreted in both scalar and list context. When used as the *rvalue* of an assignment, @month evaluates to the length of the array:

```
$length = @month;                                              Length of the array
```

The $# prefix to an array name signifies the last index of the array. It's always one less than the size of the array:

```
$last_index = $#month;
```

The $# mechanism can also be used to set the array to a specific size or delete all its elements. Previously defined array elements that fall outside the new index are deleted:

```
$#month = 10;                                                  Array size now 11
$#month = -1;                                                    No elements
```

An array can also be populated by the <> operator. Each line then becomes an element of the array:

```
@file = <> ;                                           Reads entire file from command line
print @file ;                                                  Prints entire file
```

Note

The **chop** and **chomp** string handling functions can be applied to an array also. In that case, they'll remove the last character of every element of the array, which is probably what you'd want them to do.

Before we use the array handling functions, let's examine the script, **ar_in_ar.pl** (Fig. 15.6), which illustrates some features of **perl** arrays.

The array is populated in three stages, and the final filling is done with the **qw** function. Observe that **perl** permits a second array (@days_between) to form part of another array, @days. The length of the array is directly available in $length and indirectly

FIGURE 15.6 ar_in_ar.pl

```
#!/usr/bin/perl
# ar_in_ar.pl - Shows use of arrays
#
@days_between = ("Wed", "Thu") ;
@days = (Mon, Tue, @days_between, Fri) ;
@days[5,6] = qw/Sat Sun/ ;
$length = @days ;                          # @days in scalar context
print ("The third day of the week is $days[2]\n") ;
print ("The days of the week are @days\n") ;
print ("The number of elements in the array is $length\n") ;
print ("The last subscript of the array is $#days\n") ;
$#days = 5;                                  #Resize the array
print ("\$days[6] is now $days[6]\n") ;
```

in $#days before it is reset to 5. Because the index of an array starts from 0, $length is one greater than $#days:

```
$ ar_in_ar.pl
The third day of the week is Wed
The days of the week are Mon Tue Wed Thu Fri Sat Sun
The number of elements in the array is 7
The last subscript of the array is 6
$days[6] is now
```

Note that after resizing the array (with $#days = 5), $days[6] is now a null string.

15.9.1 Array Handling Functions

perl has a number of functions for manipulating the contents of an array. A few string handling functions (like, **chop**, **chomp**, and **reverse**) also apply to an array. **perl** supports operations both at the left and right of an array. In that sense, we can treat the array both as a stack and a queue.

shift(@*arr*) and unshift(@*arr*, *list*) The **shift** and **unshift** functions remove and add elements respectively to the left. With **unshift**, the elements to be added have to be provided as a list:

```
@list = (3..6) ;
unshift(@list, 1, 2);                                       @list is 1 2 3 4 5 6
shift(@list);                                               @list is 2 3 4 5 6
```

unshift returns the new length of the array, while **shift** returns the element that is moved out. It's like using x=$1 in the shell before using its own **shift** statement.

push(@*arr*, *list*) and pop(@*arr*) **push** and **pop** act similarly except that they operate on the right of the array. Let's now apply them to the residual value of @list from the previous example:

```
push(@list, 9..12);                     @list is 2 3 4 5 6 9 10 11 12
pop(@list);                               @list is 2 3 4 5 6 9 10 11
```

push returns the new length of the array while **pop** returns the last element that is moved out.

splice(@*arr*, *offset*, *length*, *list*) The **splice** function can do everything the previous four functions can do. Additionally, it uses from one to four arguments to add or remove elements at any location.

The second argument is the offset from where the insertion or removal should begin. The third argument represents the number of elements if they are to be removed or 0 if elements have to be added. The new replaced list is specified by the fourth argument (if present):

```
splice (@list, 5, 0, 7..8) ;          Adds at 6th location—2 3 4 5 6 7 8 9 10 11
splice (@list, 0, 2) ;                 Removes from beginning—4 5 6 7 8 9 10 11
```

We'll be using some of these functions later in another script after we have examined the **foreach** loop and **join** function.

Command Line Arguments (ARGV) We used the <> operator for reading files specified as command line arguments. In general, **perl** uses its built-in array, ARGV, to hold all command-line arguments. C programmers must note that the first argument, $ARGV[0], represents the first argument, and not the command name, which is held in shell-style in $0.

We can use a **while** or a **for** loop for iterating through each element of the array, but **perl** has a better way of doing that. The **foreach** loop is discussed next.

15.10   foreach: **Looping Through a List**

perl provides an extremely useful **foreach** construct to loop through a list. The construct borrowed from the C shell has a very simple syntax:

```
foreach $var (@arr) {
   statements
}
```

Functionally, **foreach** works like the shell's **for** loop as well. Each element of the array @*arr* is picked up and assigned to the variable $*var*. The iteration is continued as many times as there are items in the list. The program, **square_root.pl** (Fig. 15.7), uses **foreach** to calculate the square root of some numbers.

Every element in the array @ARGV is assigned to the variable $number. You can now supply as many arguments to the script as you like:

FIGURE 15.7 square_root.pl

```
#!/usr/bin/perl
# square_root.pl - Finds the square root of each command line argument
#
print ("The program you are running is $0\n") ;
foreach $number (@ARGV) {         # Each element of @ARGV goes to $number
    print ("The square root of $number is " . sqrt($number) . "\n") ;
}
```

```
$ square_root.pl 123 456 25
The program you are running is ./square_root.pl
The square root of 123 is 11.0905365064094
The square root of 456 is 21.3541565040626
The square root of 25 is 5
```

We have previously noted $_ making its presence felt everywhere, and this is no exception. In the above example, you need not use $number at all. **foreach** stores each item in $_, and **sqrt** works on it as well:

```
foreach (@ARGV) {                                        $_ is the default variable
    print ("The square root of $_ is " . sqrt() . "\n") ;
```

It's not that **foreach** is used with arrays only. It can be used with lists generated by UNIX commands as well. You can use command substitution to generate the list:

```
foreach $file (`ls`) {
```

This construct picks up each file in the current directory and assigns it to the variable $file. We'll use this feature later in the chapter.

15.11 Two Important List Functions

CGI programmers using **perl** need to understand two important array handling functions—**split** and **join**. The **split** function breaks up a line or an expression into fields and **join** creates a line from fields.

15.11.1 split: Splitting into a List or Array

split breaks up its arguments on a delimiter into a list of variables or an array. Here are the two syntaxes:

```
($var1, $var2, $var3.....   ) = split(/sep /,stg) ;
@arr = split(/sep /,stg) ;
```

FIGURE 15.8 3_numbers.pl

```
#!/usr/bin/perl
# Script: 3_numbers.pl - Splits a string on whitespace
print("Enter three numbers: " ) ;
chomp($numstring = <STDIN>) ;
die("Nothing entered\n") if ($numstring eq "") ;
($f_number, $s_number, $l_number) = split (/\s+/, $numstring) ;
print ("The last, second and first numbers are ") ;
print ("$l_number, $s_number and $f_number.\n" ) ;
```

split takes up to three arguments but is usually used with two. It splits the string *stg* on the regular expression *sep*. The argument *stg* is optional, and in its absence, $_ is used as default. The fields resulting from the split are assigned either to the variables $*var1*, $*var2*, and so on, or to the array @*arr*.

Splitting into Variables We'll now use the first syntactical form in our next program, **3_numbers.pl** (Fig. 15.8), to assign three numbers, taken from the keyboard, to a set of variables.

We used the **die** function to simply print its argument and exit a script. **die** is often used to handle errors in opening a file. Run this program twice:

```
$ 3_numbers.pl
Enter three numbers: [Enter]                                          Nothing entered
Nothing entered
$ 3_numbers.pl
Enter three numbers: 123 345 567
The last, second, and first numbers are 567, 345, and 123.
```

When the three numbers are entered, $numstring acquires the value 123 345 567\n, from where the newline is subsequently chopped off. **split** acts on this string using whitespace (\s+) as delimiter, and saves the words in three variables.

Splitting into an Array What do you do when there are a large number of fields in a line? In that case, it's better to split it up into an array rather than variables. The following statement fills up the array @thislist:

```
@thislist = split(/:/, $string) ;
```

$string is often the last line read, so **split** assumes $_ as the second argument when it is not specified. Also, **split** can be used without an explicit assignment, in which case it populates the built-in array, @_:

```
split (/:/) ;                                                         Fills up the array @_
```

The array, @_, has the elements $_[0], $_[1], and so forth. You should get used to this form also since you'll find it used in several programs.

Note

When the return value of **split** is not *explicitly* assigned to variables or an array, the built-in array, @_, is automatically assigned. Also, when **split** is used with the null string (//) as delimiter, @_ stores *each* character of the string as a separate element.

15.11.2   join: Joining a List

The **join** function acts in a manner opposite to **split**. It combines multiple strings into a single string using the delimiter as the first argument. The remaining arguments could be either an array name or a list of variables or strings to be joined. This is how you provide a space after each day:

```
$weekstring = join (" ", @week_array) ;
$weekstring = join (" ", "Mon", "Tue", "Wed", "Thu", "Fri", "Sat", "Sun") ;
print $weekstring ;
```

You can use either of the first two statements to obtain the following output with **print**:

```
Mon Tue Wed Thu Fri Sat Sun
```

split and **join** often go together. The next program, **rep.pl** (Fig. 15.9), splits each line of our sample database on the :, adds a century prefix to the date, and then joins all the fields back together. The script is well documented so as not to require elaboration.
Let's now print the first three transformed lines of our database by running the program:

```
$ rep.pl emp.lst | head -n 3
2233:charles harris  :g.m.     :sales     :12/12/1952: 90000
9876:bill johnson    :director :production:03/12/1950:130000
5678:robert dylan    :d.g.m.   :marketing :04/19/1943: 85000
```

FIGURE 15.9   rep.pl

```
#!/usr/bin/perl -n
# Script: rep.pl - Uppercases the name and adds century prefix to the date
#
@line = split (/:/) ;                              # $_ is assumed
($month, $day, $year) = split(/\//, $line[4]);     # Splits date field
$year = "19" . $year ;                             # Adds century prefix
$line[4] = join("/", $month, $day, $year);         # Rebuilds date field
$line = join(":", @line);                          # Rebuilds line
print $line;
```

Joining on a specified delimiter has common applications in everyday programming. Even though we used **join** on a specific delimiter in our examples, the next section uses **join** without any delimiter to perform a very useful task.

15.12   dec2bin.pl: **Converting a Decimal Number to Binary**

We'll now consolidate our knowledge of array-handling functions by developing a script, **dec2bin.pl** (Fig. 15.10). This script accepts a decimal number as an argument and converts it to binary. To do this, you have to repeatedly divide a number (rather the quotient) by 2, and then reverse all the collected remainders. We need the **unshift** function here to perform this reversal by filling up an array with the remainder bit that arises from every division.

Like the shell, **perl** also uses the **until** loop with the same meaning. The **join** function is used simply to concatenate all digit strings (0 or 1) that are stored in the array, @bit_arr, without using a delimiter. **foreach** lets you supply as many numbers as you want in a single invocation of the script:

```
$ dec2bin.pl 2 7 65 191 255
The binary number of 2 is 10
The binary number of 7 is 111
The binary number of 65 is 1000001
The binary number of 191 is 10111111
The binary number of 255 is 11111111
```

FIGURE 15.10   dec2bin.pl

```perl
#!/usr/bin/perl
# dec2bin.pl: Converts decimal numbers to binary
#
die("No arguments\n") if ( $#ARGV == -1 ) ;

foreach $number (@ARGV) {
    $original_number = $number ;
    until ($number == 0 ) {
        $bit = $number % 2 ;                    # Find the remainder bit
        unshift (@bit_arr, $bit) ;              # Insert bit at beginning
        $number = int($number / 2 ) ;
    }
    $binary_number = join ("", @bit_arr) ;      # Join on nothing!
    print ("The binary number of $original_number is $binary_number\n") ;
    $#bit_arr = -1                              # Deletes all array elements
}
```

You can use this program to determine whether two hosts are in the same *subnet* (not discussed in this edition) by converting their network addresses to binary.

15.13   Associative Arrays

Like **awk**, **perl** also supports a **hash** or **associative array**. It alternates the array subscripts (called **keys**) and values in a series of strings. When declaring the array, these strings are delimited by commas or the more-friendly **=>** notation:

```
%region = ("N", "North", "S", "South", "E", "East", "W", "West") ;
%region = ("N" => "North", "S" => "South", "E" => "East", "W" => "West") ;
```

The associative array is identified by the % prefix, and this assignment creates an array of four elements. The key can also be a string, and the value is accessed by $region{*key*}. For instance, $region{"N"} evaluates to North. CGI programmers must feel totally at home with associative arrays.

We use an associative array, %region, in the program, **region.pl** (Fig. 15.11), to expand region codes. The program shows how to use two associative array functions, **keys** and **values**.

The **keys** function stores the list of subscripts in a separate array (here, @key_list), while **values** holds the value of each element in yet another array (here, @value_list). Test the script by providing a couple of single-character strings as arguments:

```
$ region.pl S W
The letter S stands for South
The letter W stands for West
The subscripts are S E N W
The values are South East North West
```

FIGURE 15.11   region.pl

```
#!/usr/bin/perl
# Script: region.pl - Uses an associative array
#
%region = ("N", "North", "S", "South", "E", "East", "W", "West") ;
foreach $letter (@ARGV) {
    print ("The letter $letter stands for $region{$letter}" . "\n" );
}
@key_list = keys(%region) ;                    # List of subscripts
print ("The subscripts are @key_list\n") ;
@value_list = values %region ;                 # List of values
print ("The values are @value_list\n") ;
```

There are important implications to note here. You can separately extract both the keys and their values from an associative array. Using a **foreach** loop, you can also present these values in the same way the **set** statement shows all environment variables:

```
foreach $key (keys %region) {
    print "$key" . "=" . "$region{$key}\n" ;
}
```

This snippet of code produces the following output:

```
S=South
E=East
N=North
W=West
```

Normally, **keys** returns the key strings in a random sequence. To order the list alphabetically, you'll often find the **sort** function used with **keys**. You can have both a normal and a reverse sort:

```
foreach $key (sort(keys %region)) {
    @key_list = reverse sort keys %region  ;                    No ()—OK
}
```

Note

perl's built-in array, %ENV, stores all of the shell's environment variables. For instance, $ENV{'PATH'} contains the value of the shell's PATH. You can easily access these variables using the techniques discussed here.

15.13.1   Counting Number of Occurrences

Associative arrays are extremely useful in counting the number of occurrences of an item. From the sample database, you can create a report showing the number of people in each department. We tried a similar exercise before with **awk** *(12.3.1)*, but the **perl** program, **count.pl** (Fig. 15.12), also does the job.

FIGURE 15.12   count.pl

```
#!/usr/bin/perl
# Script: count.pl - Counts frequency of occurrence of an item
#
while (<>) {
    split (/:/) ;                           # Split values available in @_
    $dept = $_[3] ;                         # Department is fourth field
    $deptlist{$dept}++ ;
}
foreach $dept (sort (keys %deptlist)) {
    print ("$dept : $deptlist{$dept}\n") ;
}
```

The **while** construct first filters out the values of $dept for each line read and increments the counter of the respective element of the array %deptlist. After all input has been read, %deptlist contains the accumulated total for each key:

```
$ count.pl emp.lst
accounts   : 2
admin      : 1
marketing  : 4
personnel  : 2
production : 2
sales      : 4
```

But then it must be admitted that **cut**, **sort**, and **uniq** can do a similar job with a single line of code *(10.11.1)* but using three processes.

15.14 Using Regular Expressions

perl offers a grand superset of *all* possible regular expressions that are found in the UNIX system (except the special ones specified by POSIX). You have already used some of them for pattern matching. **perl** understands both basic and extended regular expressions (BRE and ERE) and has some of its own too. You must know regular expressions and the **sed** and **tr** commands very well before you can appreciate the material that is presented in this section.

15.14.1 Identifying Whitespace, Digits, and Words

Apart from the regular expression set used by **grep**, **sed**, and **awk**, **perl** also offers some escaped characters to represent whitespace, digits, and word boundaries (Table 15.3). Here are three commonly-used ones:

\s — A whitespace character
\d — A digit
\w — A word character

All of these escaped characters also have uppercase counterparts that negate their lowercase ones. Thus, \D is a nondigit character. We have already used the anchoring sequence \b for matching a pattern on a word boundary *(15.5.1)*, and the \s to match whitespace *(15.11.1)*.

The following statement uses the anchoring characters, ^ and $, to check whether $stg consists only of word characters :

```
if ($stg =~ /^\w+$/) {                          Same as ($stg =~ /^[a-zA-Z0-9_]+$/)
```

The next statement locates all lines containing IP addresses. Since dots separate the octets, we need to escape the dots too for perfect matching:

```
if (/\d+\.\d+\.\d+\.\d+/) {
```

You can often compact your regular expressions by using these characters. In the next program, we'll be using some of these escape sequences.

15.14.2   The IRE and TRE Features

perl accepts the IRE and TRE used by **grep** and **sed** *(11.13)*, except that the curly braces and parentheses are not escaped. For instance, this is how you can use an IRE to locate lines longer than 512 characters:

```
perl -ne 'print if /.{513,}/' foo                              No \ before { and }
```

You can enclose part of a pattern within parentheses and use them anywhere in the program with $1, $2, and so on. This is **sed**'s TRE *(11.13.3)* implemented in **perl**. The repeated pattern could be \1 if it is specified in a pattern search with 2 /s, or $1 if the ~= operator is used.

The next example, **rep2.pl** (Fig. 15.13), changes the form of reporting for the date format of the sample database. It uses a TRE to report in the form *dd-mon-yyyy* format where *mon* is a three-character month name.

We split the database yet again and store the split fields in the default array, @_. Each of the three components of the date field can be represented by the TRE (\d+). **perl** TREs are more readable than their UNIX counterparts; they don't use the \s before the (and). The three groups are now associated with the variables $1, $2, and $3.

Using $1 as index, we extract the month name from the array @month. Finally, we join the elements of the @_ array on the : delimiter. Here are the first three lines of output:

```
$ rep2.pl emp.1st | head -n 3
2233:charles harris  :g.m.     :sales    :12-Dec-1952: 90000
9876:bill johnson    :director :production:12-Mar-1950:130000
5678:robert dylan    :d.g.m.   :marketing :19-Apr-1943: 85000
```

The date field is now in a format that is used by Oracle. The TRE in **perl** is unique in another way: **perl** stores these groupings ($1, etc.) in memory till the next grouping is done.

FIGURE 15.13   rep2.pl

```
#!/usr/bin/perl -n
# rep2.pl - Reports a date in format dd-mon-yyyy using a TRE
#
@month[1..12] = qw/Jan Feb Mar Apr May Jun Jul Aug Sep Oct Nov Dec/ ;
split (/:/) ;                   # Splits on @_ array
$_[4] =~ /(\d+).(\d+).(\d+)/ ;  # Splits up into $1, $2, and $3
$_[4] = join ("-", $2, $month[$1], "19$3") ;
$_ = join(":", @_);
print ;
```

▨   **15.15   Substitution with the s and tr Functions**

The **s** and **tr** functions handle all substitution in **perl**. The **s** function is used in the same way as the **s** command in **sed**. **tr** translates characters in the same way the UNIX **tr** command does, but with a slightly different syntax. This is how we use them:

```
s/:/-/g ;                                          Sets $_ when used this way
tr/a-z/A-Z/ ;                              In UNIX, you use tr '[a-z]' '[A-Z]'
```

In either case, you are setting the system variable, $_. Often, you'll split a line into fields and then use these functions for transforming some of the fields. In that case, you'll have to use the =~ operator for performing a match and !~ for negating it:

```
$line =~ s/:/-/g ;                                         $line is reassigned
$name =~ tr/a-z/A-Z/ ;                                     $name is reassigned
```

s and **tr** also accept flags. **s** accepts the g flag (shown above) for global substitution, and yet another (e) for indicating that the replaced pattern is to be evaluated as an expression. **tr** uses all the UNIX **tr** options as flags—s squeezes multiple occurrences, c complements, and d deletes the character *(10.12.1)*.

The next program, **rep3.pl** (Fig. 15.14), takes the last two digits of the year as user input, and then selects those lines where the year of birth (embedded in the fifth field) matches this input. It then performs some transformation on the selected lines before printing them.

After the sample database is split, the date field is further split to extract the two-digit year. If the year matches user input, two changes are made at field level with the =~ operator: the name is converted to uppercase, and the prefix 9 is added to the emp-id. The fields are joined before two more changes are made, this time at global level.

To use the **s** and **tr** functions on the entire line (globally), we need to make sure that $_ is properly set. The **join** function cleverly achieves this by assigning its return value to $_, which is used later by the **s** and **print** functions. The first **s** function removes all spaces before the : delimiter. The next one changes every / in the line to a -. This affects only the date field, and rather than place a \ before the /, it's better to change the delimiter used by **s** to a #. The statement is also more readable.

We'll run the script with two inputs—one that exists and one that doesn't exist:

```
$ rep3.pl emp.lst
Last two digits of date of birth: 45
96521:DERRYK O'BRIEN:director:marketing:09-26-45:125000
92345:JAMES WILCOX:g.m.:marketing:03-12-45:110000
$ rep2.pl emp.lst
Last two digits of date of birth: 60
Year 1960 not found
```

15.15.1   **Editing Files In-Place**

Instead of writing to the standard output or to a separate file, **perl** can edit and *rewrite* the input file itself. With **sed**, you would have redirected the output to a temporary file

FIGURE 15.14   rep3.pl

```perl
#!/usr/bin/perl
# rep3.pl: Uses the s and tr functions for substitution
#
print("Last two digits of date of birth: ");
$yearin = <STDIN> ;
chop($yearin);                  # Remove \n else comparison will fail later
$found = 0;
while (<>) {
    @line = split(/:/) ;            # Split each line
    split(/\//, $line[4]);          # and again on the date field
    $year = $_[2] ;                 # 2-digit year extracted ...
    if ($year == $yearin)  {        # .. and compared with user input
        $found = 1;
        $line[1] =~ tr/a-z/A-Z/ ;   # Name field changed to uppercase
        $line[0] =~ s/^/9/ ;        # Adds a "9" prefix to the first field
        $_ = join(":", @line) ;     # Assigning to $_ allows use of next
                                    # two s functions without using =~
        s/\s+:/:/g ;                # Removes whitespace before delimiter
        s#/#-#g ;                   # Delimiter in date is now the -
        print ;                     # Print $_
    }
}
print("Year 19" . $yearin . " not found\n") if $found eq 0 ;
```

and then renamed it back to the original file. For a group of files, you would have used a **for** loop as well. Not so for **perl**; the -i option can edit multiple files in-place:

```
perl -p -i -e "s/<B>/<STRONG>/g" *.html *.htm
```

This changes <B> in all HTML files to <STRONG>. The files themselves are rewritten with the new output. If in-place editing seems a risky thing to do, you can back the files up before undertaking the operation:

```
perl -p -i.bak -e "tr/a-z/A-Z/" foo[1-4]
```

This first backs up foo1 to foo1.bak, foo2 to foo2.bak, and so forth, before converting all lowercase letters in each file to uppercase.

15.16   File Handling

So far, we have been specifying input filenames from the command line. **perl** also provides the low-level file handling functions that let you hard-code the source and destination of the data stream in the script itself. A file is opened for reading like this:

```
open (INFILE, "/home/henry/mbox") ;
```
Don't forget the quotes!

INFILE here is a **filehandle** (an identifier) of the file mbox (file presumed to be in current directory if a pathname is not used). Once a file has been opened, functions that read and write the file will use the filehandle to access the file. A filehandle is similar to a file descriptor.

A file is opened for writing with the shell-like operators, > and >>, having their usual meanings:

```
open (OUTFILE, ">rep_out.lst") ;
open (OUTFILE, ">>rep_out.lst") ;
```

perl's filehandles can also be associated with pipelines. To shell programmers, the meanings of these statements should be quite obvious:

```
open (INFILE, "sort emp.lst |" ) ;
open (OUTFILE, "| lp" ) ;
```
Input from sort output
Output to print spooler

The next script, **rw.pl** (Fig. 15.15), uses **open** to obtain two filehandles for reading one file and writing another. It also uses the **print** statement with a filehandle as argument to write output to a file without using redirection.

Every time the <FILEIN> statement is executed, the next line is read from the file represented by the FILEIN filehandle. Thus, **while (<FILEIN>)** reads a line with every iteration. By default, the line is stored in $_. You can read and print a single line in this way:

```
$_ = <FILEIN> ;
print ;
```
Assigns next line to $_
print uses $_ by default

Even if you don't close the files before terminating the script, **perl** closes them on its own. When we run the script without arguments, the output doesn't come to the terminal this time, but goes to the file desig_out.lst.

Tip

If a number of **print** statements have to write to the same filehandle (say, FILEOUT), then you can assign this filehandle as the default using **select (FILEOUT)** ;. Subsequent **print** statements don't need to use the FILEOUT argument in that case.

FIGURE 15.15   rw.pl

```
#!/usr/bin/perl
# rw.pl: Shows use of low-level I/O available in perl
#
open (FILEIN, "desig.lst") || die ("Cannot open file") ;
open (FILEOUT, ">desig_out.lst") ;
while (<FILEIN>) {                  # As long as there are lines in the file
    print FILEOUT if (1..3) ;       # Can also use if ($. < 4 )
}
close (FILEIN) ;
close (FILEOUT) ;
```

15.17 File Tests

perl has an elaborate system of file tests. It overshadows the capabilities of the Bourne shell—and even the **find** command in some ways. The following statements test some of the most common attributes of a file:

```
$x = "rdbnew.lst" ;
print "File $x is readable\n" if -r $x ;
print "File $x is executable\n" if -x $x ;
print "File $x has non-zero size\n" if -s $x ;
print "File $x exists\n" if -e $x ;
print "File $x is a text file\n" if -T $x ;
print "File $x is a binary file\n" if -B $y ;
```

perl's file tests go further; it can tell you a file's modification and access times very accurately. The script, **when_last.pl** (Fig. 15.16), detects files that were modified less than 2.4 hours ago.

The expression -M $file returns the time elapsed in hours since $file was last modified. It's a general **perl** feature (an idea borrowed from C) that you can make a test (< 0.1) and assignment ($m_age = ...) in the same statement. Let's observe the output:

```
$ when_last.pl
File bf2o.sh was last modified 0.063 days back
File profile.sam was last modified 0.082 days back
File when_last.pl was last modified 0.000 days back
```

It seems that the last file has just been modified; three decimal places are not enough. You have to increase the length of the **printf** format if you need greater precision.

Apart from testing file attributes, **perl** can manipulate files and directories very easily. It uses **chmod**, **chown**, **chgrp**, **chdir** (like **cd**), **mkdir**, **rmdir**, **rename** (like **mv**), **link**, **unlink** (like **rm**), and **umask**, many of whom have UNIX commands of the same name. It can also open directories with directory filehandles. The UNIX system call library also uses functions having these names, as you'll discover in Chapter 17.

FIGURE 15.16 when_last.pl

```
#!/usr/bin/perl
# Script: when_last.pl - Finds files that are less than 2.4 hours old
#
foreach $file (`ls`) {
  chop ($file) ;
  if (($m_age = -M $file) < 0.1) {       # tenth of a day i.e., 2.4 hours
    printf "File %s was last modified %0.3f days back \n", $file, $m_age ;
  }
}
```

▬ **15.18 Subroutines**

perl supports functions but calls them **subroutines**. A subroutine is called by the & symbol followed by the subroutine name. If the subroutine is defined without any formal parameters, **perl** uses the array @_ as the default. Variables inside the subroutine should be declared with **my** to make them invisible in the calling program.

Many applications require the user to supply a username and password. Since this involves executing the same amount of code twice, it becomes an ideal candidate for a subroutine. The program, **input.pl** (Fig. 15.17), uses the subroutine **take_input**, which accepts the prompt string as an argument, validates the input for word characters, and returns the value that was input.

The subroutine arguments are accepted into @_ and then reassigned to two local variables, $prompt and $flag. What is checked in the subroutine is the number of arguments passed (@_ == 2). When you pass two arguments to it, the UNIX **stty** command blanks out the display during password entry. The loop terminates when there is at least one word character in the input:

```
$ input.pl
Oracle user-id: !@#$%^&*                            Nonword characters
Oracle user-id: scott
Oracle password: *****                              Password not echoed
The username and password are scott and tiger
```

FIGURE 15.17 input.pl

```perl
#!/usr/bin/perl
# input.pl: Shows use of subroutines
#
system ("tput clear") ;                    # Executes the UNIX command
$username = &take_input ("Oracle user-id: ") ;
$password = &take_input ("Oracle password: ", "noecho") ;
print "\nThe username and password are $username and $password\n" ;
sub take_input {
  my ($prompt, $flag) = @_ ;               # @_ stores arguments of subroutine
  while (1)  {                             # (1) is always true
    print ("$prompt") ;
    system("stty -echo") if (@_ == 2 ) ;   # Echo mode off
    chop ($name = <STDIN>) ;
    system("stty echo") if (@_ == 2 ) ;    # Echo mode on
    last if $name =~ /\w/ ;                 # Quit the loop if $name has at
  }                                        # least one word character
  $name ;                                  # return $name will also do
}
```

The last statement in the program ($name ;) is typically **perl**'s way of returning a value. You should store frequently used subroutines in separate files. Instruct the calling program to read the file containing a subroutine by placing the **require** statement at the beginning. If you save the **take_input** subroutine in the file **oracle_lib.pl**, you should do these two things:

- Insert the statement **require "oracle_lib.pl";** in the calling program immediately after the she-bang line.
- Place the statement **1;** at the end of the file containing one or more subroutines. The **perl** documentation requires every "required" file to end with a true value. Any nonzero value is a true value in **perl**, so **1;** returns true.

perl has specific functions for interprocess communication which have been overlooked here. Its object-oriented tools and networking functions also have been ignored. This unique program is a real gold mine of techniques. The UNIX spirit lives in **perl**. Think of a strong UNIX feature; it is there in **perl**. **perl** is the pride of UNIX.

➤ *GOING FURTHER*

15.19   CGI Programming with perl—An Overview

When you fill up a form on your Web browser and press the *Submit* button, the browser transmits the form data to the Web server at the other end. A Web server by itself doesn't have the capability of processing this data, so it passes it on to an external application. This application then extracts the meat from the sent data and may then access a database to query, add, modify, or delete the data, and send back the results if any. The Web server here acts as a link to the application—the **Common Gateway Interface (CGI)**—to pass information to and from the (gatewaying) application.

A CGI program needs to do some filtering of form data—like separating the variables from their values and converting encoded characters to ASCII. The program often has to generate HTML on the fly with all its tags, and send the created document to the browser. A CGI program can be written in any language—C, Java, the shell, or **perl**. When it comes to text parsing, **perl**'s filtering capabilities are second to none, which is why **perl** is the language of choice for CGI programming.

15.19.1   The Query String

The browser sends data to the server through its request header *(14.13.2)*. To understand how form data is structured, consider a form that has only three fields with names empid, ename, and desig (the name attribute of the <input> tag). Let's put the values 1234, henry higgins, and actor into these three fields. On submission, the browser strings together the entire data as *name=value* pairs into a **query string** in this manner:

empid=1234&ename=henry+higgins&desig=actor

This single string is sent to the server specified in the URL. The & here acts as the delimiter of each *name=value* pair. Note that the browser has encoded the space character to a +. To use this data, **perl** has to split this string twice—once to extract all *name=value* pairs and then to separate the names from their values.

15.19.2 GET and POST: The Request Method

The query string is generated by the client (the Web browser) and sent to the server using either of these methods:

- **GET** This method appends the query string to the URL using the ? as the delimiter. With the query string that was just framed the URL will now look like this:

http://localhost/cgi-bin/emp_add.pl?empid=1234&ename=henry+higgins&desig=actor

> The server parses the GET statement in the request header and stores the data following the ? in its environment variable QUERY_STRING. This variable can be used by any CGI program.

- **POST** With this method, the browser precedes this string with a number signifying the number of characters the string holds. The server stores this number in the CONTENT_LENGTH variable. It supplies the string as standard input to the CGI program. **perl** reads this data with its **read** function, and reads just as much as specified by CONTENT_LENGTH. The method itself is available as REQUEST_METHOD in the server's environment.

A CGI application is available on the Web site of this book. CGI applications are expensive as each invocation of a CGI program requires the creation of a separate process. Java servlets that use threads rather than separate processes are increasingly replacing CGI on the Net. Moreover, CGI is a security threat, the reason why its use by individual users is often disabled on Web servers.

GOING FURTHER

SUMMARY

perl is a superset of **grep**, **tr**, **sed**, **awk**, and the shell. It compiles a program internally before executing it but doesn't create an executable.

Input is read from the keyboard by assigning the *filehandle,* <STDIN>, to a variable. The last character of a line is removed by **chop** or **chomp**.

perl treats variables and constants as numeric or string depending on context. It also makes automatic conversions from one type to another when performing computation and concatenation. The *pragma* **use strict;** requires that variables be declared before they are used.

Unlike **awk**, strings and numbers are compared with separate sets of operators. The . is used for string concatenation. x is used for repetition.

Files are read with the <> operator. **while (<>)** reads all files whose names are specified in the command line. The -n option sets up an implicit loop for the same purpose.

$. stores the current line number. The range operator (..) is used to specify the selection of a contiguous set of lines.

$_ is the *default variable* used by many **perl** functions. It stores the last line read or the last pattern matched. **print**, **chop**, **split**, pattern matching, and substitution operate on $_ by default.

The first element of the *scalar array, @arr*, is accessed as $arr[0], and its last subscript as $#arr. @ARGV[] stores all command line arguments, but the command name is available as $0. A *list* can be assigned to an array or a set of variables.

Elements can be added and removed from the left (**shift** and **unshift**) as well as the right (**push** and **pop**). **splice** can do everything at any array location.

The **foreach** construct loops through an array and assigns each element in turn to a variable. The list can also be provided by command substitution.

split breaks up a list into variables or an array. @_ is the default array, and whitespace the default delimiter. Elements of a split line can be glued together with **join**.

The *hash* or *associative array* stores *keys* and values. The key can be a string. The **qw** function simplies array assignment. The value of an element of the array *%arr* accessed by key *stg* is $arr{$stg}. All keys and values are accessed by the **keys** and **values** functions.

perl accepts all regular expressions but also supports sequences to match a digit (\d), a word character (\w), the beginning of a word (\b), and a whitespace character (\s). The uppercase counterparts negate the lowercase ones.

The IRE and TRE work in the same way as before except that the \ is not required before the ( ) and { } characters. A grouped pattern can also be reproduced elsewhere with $1, $2, and so on till the next grouping is done.

The **s** and **tr** functions are used in the same way the **sed** and **tr** commands are used for substitution and character translation. The operators =~ and !~ are used to match regular expressions.

Every file opened with the **open** function is assigned a *filehandle*. Subsequent reading and writing are done using these filehandles. **while (<FILEIN>)** reads lines from the filehandle FILEIN assigned by **open**. **print** optionally uses a filehandle also.

Subroutines are invoked with an &, and its arguments are stored in the array, @_. Subroutines can be held in an external file but must have the statement 1; placed at the end. The calling program "includes" these subroutines with the **require** statement.

SELF-TEST

15.1   Write one-liners to execute the following **perl** commands and explain your observations: (i) print '\t', (ii) print "\t", (iii) print "romeo@heavens.com".

15.2   Write a one-liner to print the string UNIX 20 times without using a loop.

15.3   Write a one-liner that prints all lines of a file, preceded by its line number and with the tab as delimiter.

15.4   Write a program that accepts three integers as arguments and prints the maximum value entered.

15.5   Write a program that prompts a user to input a string and a number, and prints the string that many times, with each string on a separate line.

15.6   What's wrong with this program? What is it supposed to print, anyway?

```
#! /usr/bin/perl
x = 2;
print $x ^ 32 ;
```

15.7 Write a program to prefix all lines of a file with the letters A., B., C., and so on. What do you see after Z.?

15.8 Write a one-liner to print the uppercase letters of the English alphabet as a contiguous string using a loop.

15.9 Write a program that accepts a positive integer from the keyboard and then displays all integers from 1 up to that number, each on a separate line.

15.10 By default, file reading, chopping, and pattern matching operate on (i) $., (ii) $_, (iii) @_, (iv) none of these.

15.11 Write a program that prompts for an integer not exceeding 255 and then prints A if the number is below 127, B if it is below 224, and C otherwise.

15.12 Write a program that prompts a user repeatedly to enter a number. When the user enters 0, the program should print the total.

15.13 Write a program that takes a filename and string as arguments and prints from the file *only* the first line containing the string.

15.14 Write a program that uses a loop to print from an array all the 12 months in the form 1. Jan ....., where each entry is on a separate line.

15.15 Why doesn't this one-liner execute? Is absence of quoting the problem?

```
perl -e '%arr = (N, North) ; print %arr{N}'
```

15.16 Write a program that takes a filename as argument, checks whether the file exists, and prints binary if the file is binary.

15.17 Using a regular expression, write a one-liner to display the contents of a file after capitalizing every word.

15.18 Write a program to display from /etc/passwd the line that has 1 as the UID.

EXERCISES

15.1 Detect the errors in the following program (line numbers on left):

```
1    # foo.pl -- Checking file system block size
2    #/usr/bin/perl
3    print "Enter the block size of your file system: "
4    bs = <STDIN> ;
5    chop ($bs) ;
6    if ( $bs > 8192 )
7        print "Lot of wasted space /n" ;
8    } else {
9        print "Reasonable size" ;
10   }
```

15.2 Write a one-liner to print double-spaced lines from a file.

15.3 Write a program that accepts a string from the keyboard and then prints each character of the string on a separate line.

15.4 Write a program to convert a binary number specified as argument to decimal. (HINT: Use the **reverse** function.)

15.5   Write a program that looks up /etc/passwd and /etc/group and prints (i) the highest
        UID, (ii) the login name, real name, and GID (both number and name) of that user.

15.6   Write a program that populates an array named weekday from the string
        SunMonTueWedThuFriSat, and then prints each day in uppercase.

15.7   Write a program that reads a file specified as argument to locate all variable
        assignments of the form *variable=value*, where each assignment is placed on a
        separate line. It should then print *from memory* a sorted list of these variables
        along with their values. The variable assignment could be the only characters in
        a line or be preceded or succeeded by whitespace.

15.8   How do you print a sorted list of all environment variables in the form *variable=value*?

15.9   Write a program that lists the usage of words (in the form *word*: *count*) in its
        argument files. You should use **perl**'s definition of a *word*.

15.10   Write a program that displays to the standard error the maximum line length
        (say, *x*) of the filename specified as argument. Wherever necessary, the program
        has to append spaces at the end of a line so that all lines have *x* as the length. The
        modified output must be written to the standard output. Assuming that the file is
        small, do you need to read the file twice to do this?

15.11   How will you use **find** and **perl** to delete all ordinary files modified more than
        a year back? What is the advantage of using this method compared to using
        find with -exec rm?

15.12   (i) Write a one-liner to change the she-bang line to #!/usr/local/bin/perl in
        all .pl files in the current directory. (ii) Enlarge the scope to add the she-bang
        line if it doesn't exist. Also, don't attempt to make a substitution if a proper she-
        bang line is already in place.

15.13   Write a one-liner to convert all characters in a file to uppercase, and write the
        changes back to the same file without using redirection.

15.14   Refer to the example of converting URLs in HTML documents in Sec. 11.14.3,
        and implement it in **perl**. This time take care of the <IMG SRC> tag which also
        refers to URLs.

15.15   Write a program that behaves like the **cp** command when used without options,
        and with two ordinary filenames as arguments.

15.16   C programs use comment lines of the form /* *comments* */, where */ can be
        placed on a different line to allow for multiline comments. Develop a program
        that removes *all* comment lines in a program named foo.c. Why is it difficult to
        do this job with **sed**?

15.17   A file contains a set of numbers and strings as shown by these sample entries:

        1
        5
        3
        botswana
        namibia
        swaziland

        Devise a *generalized* program that prints 1. botswana on the first line, 5. namibia
        in the second line, and so forth. It does not matter how many sets of entries there

are in the file, as long as the set of numbers is followed by an equal number of country names.

15.18 Write a program that changes the login shell of users in /etc/passwd. The shell has to be changed to /bin/bash for all users with UID greater than 100 and whose current shell is /usr/bin/pdksh or /bin/ksh. The output has to be written to a separate file in the current directory.

15.19 The **grep** function in **perl** has the following syntax:

@*match_arr* = grep(/*pattern*/, @*search_arr*);

Here, **grep** searches the array @*search_arr* for *pattern* (which could be a regular expression) and returns the array @*match_arr* containing the matched elements. Use this function in a program to accept a string from the terminal and search an array that has been previously populated by reading /etc/passwd.

15.20 Write a program that accepts a filename and the delimiter string as arguments, and then displays each line with its fields reversed.

15.21 Write a program that accepts a filename (say, foo) as argument and then writes the first 10 lines to foo.1, the next 10 to foo.2, and so forth. Does it make any difference if any of these files exists?

15.22 Write a program to recursively examine the current directory tree and display, for every ordinary file, the filename and days elapsed since it was last modified. The list should be ordered by this age with the newest file placed at the top.

15.23 Refer to the stamp dealer problem in Exercise 12.11 and implement it in **perl**.

## CHAPTER 16

Program Development Tools

U NIX systems today support a host of programming and scripting languages, but the C language has a special place in the system. UNIX was written in C, and, until recently, the C compiler was shipped as standard with every UNIX system. Apart from its text manipulation skills, UNIX also excels in the management of C programs—both in their text and binary form. In this chapter, we take a look at some of the native programming tools available on most UNIX systems.

Large programming projects need administration of program sources and binaries. We discuss the tools that help you keep track of changes made in program sources and identify program defects using a powerful debugging tool. We'll learn how to rebuild only the affected program sections and preserve all versions using a version control scheme that allows easy retrieval. We'll also build a library of object modules. For a C programmer, this chapter is compulsory reading.

Objectives

- Understand the three phases of the compilation process and how they apply to a multimodule C application.
- Learn how **make** handles *dependencies* by recompiling only the changed sources.
- Build a *static library* of object files with **ar** and use **make** to automatically update entries in a library.
- Understand the differences between *static* and *shared* libraries.
- Learn how storing differences between successive versions forms the basis of *version control*.
- Check files in and out with the *Source Code Control System (SCCS)* using the **admin**, **get**, and **delta** commands.
- Use the *Revision Control System (RCS)* and the **ci**, **co**, and **rcs** commands for the same purpose.
- Debug a C program with a symbolic debugger like **dbx** using *breakpoints* and *tracing*.

16.1 Handling Multisource C Applications

The standard technique of using **cc foo.c** to create the a.out executable needs to be modified when working with multisource programs. Before we take up such an application, we need to examine the three phases a C program has to pass through before a standalone executable is created:

- **Compiling**   Even though we use the term *compiling* to signify all three phases, compilation actually converts the C source code (in the .c files) to assembly language (.s files).
- **Assembling**   The assembled code is transformed into object code by the *assembler*. A file containing object code has the .o extension. The machine understands this code, but it can't be executed directly as it is incomplete; it doesn't include the code of functions used in the program.
- **Linking**   The object code of the program is finally linked by the *linker* or *loader* with other object files and libraries that contain code used by functions. This phase produces a single executable file, which by default is named a.out.

The default action of the **cc** compiler (or GNU's **gcc**) is to combine the three phases. For instance, if the code is distributed across a number of files, the following command could generate a.out:

```
cc a.c b.c c.c                                        Creates a.out; no .o files
```

cc calls the assembler (a program named **as**) to create the .o files before it invokes the linker (a program named **ld**) to create a single executable. We can also invoke **ld** directly, but its syntax is a little awkward; we leave this job to **cc**. After **ld** has created the executable (by default, a.out), **cc** removes the .o files.

Using the -c option, you can create only the object files without creating a.out:

```
cc -c a.c b.c c.c                                    Creates only a.o, b.o, and c.o
```

A mix of source and object files is also permitted. You can also use the -o option to specify your own executable name:

```
cc -o foo a.c b.o c.o                                Creates executable named foo
```

For single-source programs (where functions are stored in the same file as the main program itself), we normally don't need to look at these three phases separately. In fact, we don't even need the intermediate .o file. However, in a real-life scenario, we often need to do a *partial* compilation and maintain these .o files. To understand why, let's examine a multisource application.

16.1.1   A Multisource Application

Large applications are generally spread across multiple files. These files contain the source and object code of the functions used by the main program (the program containing the **main** function). They also include the header files containing the prototypes of the functions. Dividing a task into functions has two advantages:

- Functions impart modularity to our code. They make programs comprehensible and thus help in debugging them.
- It enables their reuse. The same function can be used by another application.

We'll now develop a multisource application that computes the interest on a recurring deposit. The main program, **rec_deposit.c** (Fig. 16.1), accepts three arguments representing the principal, interest, and term, and writes the maturity amount to the standard output. It invokes three functions:

- **arg_check**   This function checks whether the correct number of arguments have been entered. It is defined in **arg_check.c** which includes **arg_check.h** (Fig. 16.2).
- **quit**   This function prints a message and terminates the program. It is defined in **quit.c** and includes **quit.h** (Fig. 16.3).
- **compute**   It computes the interest from the three arguments provided. This function is not placed in a separate file.

FIGURE 16.1   rec_deposit.c

```
#include <math.h>
#include "quit.h"
#include "arg_check.h"

float compute(float, float, float);          /* Declaring function prototype */

int main(int argc, char **argv) {
    float principal, interest, term, sum ;
    char *mesg = "Three arguments required\n" ;
    char *mesg2 = "All arguments must be positive\n" ;
    arg_check(4, argc, mesg, 1);              /* Checks for three arguments */
    sscanf(argv[1], "%f", &principal);        /* Converting strings to float */
    sscanf(argv[2], "%f", &interest);
    sscanf(argv[3], "%f", &term);
    if (principal <= 0 || interest <= 0 || term <= 0)
        quit(mesg2, 2);                       /* Quits with 2 as $? on error */
    sum = compute(principal, interest, term);   /* Function declared here */
    printf("Maturity amount: %f\n", sum );
    exit(0);
}


float compute(float principal, float interest, float term) {
    int i;
    float maturity = 0;
    interest = 1 + interest / 100 ;
    for (i = 1 ; i <= term ; i++)
        maturity += principal * pow(interest, i) ;
    return maturity;
}
```

FIGURE 16.2 **arg_check.c** *and* **arg_check.h**

```
$ cat arg_check.c
#include "arg_check.h"
void arg_check (int args, int argc, char *message, int exit_status) {
    if (argc != args) {
        fprintf(stderr, message);
        exit(exit_status);
    }
}


$ cat arg_check.h
#include <stdio.h>
void arg_check (int, int, char *, int);
```

FIGURE 16.3 **quit.c** *and* **quit.h**

```
$ cat quit.c
#include "quit.h"
void quit (char *message, int exit_status) {
    fprintf(stderr, message);
    exit(exit_status);
}

$ cat quit.h
#include <stdio.h>
void quit (char *, int);
```

arg_check and **quit** are useful, reusable functions; they will be reused in Chapters 17 and 18. **compute** is maintained in the main file only to understand the drawbacks of this arrangement and why this too should be moved to its own source file. The two header files contain—apart from the usual **include** statements—the prototypes of their respective functions. These functions are used in **main**, so they need to be included in **rec_deposit.c** also.

Tip

There's a useful rule of thumb that determines whether or not a section of code is worthy of conversion to a function. If the code is used at least twice in the same program or by at least one other program, then it needs to maintained as a function. However, we also use functions to divide the job into discrete tasks even though the code may not be reused.

The main program, **rec_deposit.c**, invokes **arg_check** to check whether three arguments have been input. It invokes **sscanf** three times to convert the argument strings to floating point numbers. If any of the arguments is not positive, **quit** prints a user-specified message to the standard error and terminates the program with a specified exit status. If validation succeeds, **main** invokes **compute** to make the actual computation.

Note

Both **quit** and **arg_check** use **fprintf** to write to the standard error rather than standard output. It's like using 1>&2 in shell scripts. Recall that diverting diagnostic messages to the error stream allows us to redirect the program output *(13.13)*.

16.1.2 Compiling and Linking the Application

The functions **arg_check** and **quit** are general enough to also be used by other programs, so it makes sense to preserve their object files. The following invocation of **cc -c** creates three .o files:

```
$ rm *.o                                          First remove all object files
$ cc -c rec_deposit.c arg_check.c quit.c
$ ls *.o
arg_check.o      quit.o      rec_deposit.o        No .o file for compute
```

These object files now have to be linked to create the executable. We'll use the -o option to specify our own executable filename, but the linker complains of an "undefined reference":

```
$ cc -o rec_deposit rec_deposit.o arg _check.o quit.o
rec_deposit.o: In function `compute':
rec_deposit.o(.text+0x154): undefined reference to `pow'
collect2: ld returned 1 exit status
```

By default, the linker obtains the object code of commonly used functions like **printf**, **sscanf**, and so on from the library, **libc.a** (in /lib or /usr/lib). The **pow** function belongs to a separate library, **libm.a**, containing mathematical functions. The linker will look up this library only if specifically directed to do so with the -l option. This option assumes the library name has the lib prefix and .a suffix, and requires only the remaining portion of the filename to be specified. Thus, to link **libm.a** that contains the code for **pow**, you need to use -lm:

```
$ cc -o rec_deposit rec_deposit.o arg_check.o quit.o -lm
$ _
```

Run the program a number of times in ways that test the user-defined functions:

```
$ rec_deposit
Three arguments required                          arg_check working
$ rec_deposit 100 5 0
All arguments must be positive                    quit working
$ rec_deposit 100 5 2
Maturity amount: 215.249985                        compute working
```

The output shows 215.25 as the maturity value of 100 units invested every year for two years at 5% interest. Since the program is working fine, do we need to hold on to the .o files? Read on.

16.1.3   Why We Need the .o Files

Even though object files can't be executed directly, they have three important functions, which is why they are often retained even after the creation of the executable:

- If you decide to change the behavior of the **quit** function, you need to recreate **quit.o** and then relink all the three .o files. You can't do that if you don't have these files, in which case you'll have to recreate them with **cc -c**—a job that could have been avoided.
- Because **quit.o** is created from **quit.c**, you can compare their last modification times to determine whether the source has changed after the object file was created. The **make** program handles this function.
- You can combine a set of .o files to form a library or archive so that you can specify one file rather than several .o files to generate the final executable. Library creation is the job of the **ar** command.

Note that we don't have a separate object file for **compute;** its code is embedded in **rec_deposit.o**. Other programs can use **quit** and **arg_check**, but not **compute**. The lesson: Reusable functions should be placed in separate files.

16.2   make: **Keeping Programs Up-to-Date**

Now let's see how the files in the sample application are related to one another. **quit.o** *depends* on **quit.c** and **quit.h**, and if either **quit.c** or **quit.h** is modified, then **quit.c** needs to be recompiled to recreate **quit.o**. But then **rec_deposit.o** also depends on **quit.o**, which means that it needs to be rebuilt as well. A similar line of reasoning applies to the **arg_check** module also.

Keeping track of these **dependencies** in a large application involving several dozen files is simply impossible without a tool to assist us. The **make** command handles this job well. It shortens program compilation time by recompiling only those sources (.c and .h files) that have changed. It looks up a **makefile** (a control file) that specifies two things:

- How a program or object file has dependencies on other files. For instance, **rec_deposit** is dependent on **rec_deposit.o**, **arg_check.o**, and **quit.o**.
- The command to execute when a file, on which another file depends, changes. This could be to run the **cc** command to regenerate the object files.

make by default uses a file named makefile or Makefile in the user's current directory. The file contains a set of *rules* where each rule is of the following form:

target: *dependency_list*
    command_list   *Tab at beginning of line!*

Here, *target* is generally an executable or an object file which depends on the files in *dependency_list*. If any of the files in this list change, then *target* has to be rebuilt using

FIGURE 16.4   *The* **make** *Dependency Tree*

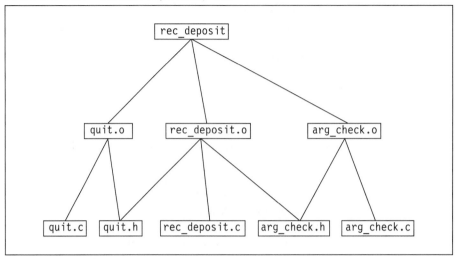

commands provided in *command_list*. The rule syntax is simple except that you need to keep in mind that *command_list* is preceded by a tab (spaces here won't do).

The **make** rule for **quit.o** is this:

```
quit.o: quit.c quit.h                                    The dependency
        cc -c quit.c                         The command to execute—tab before cc
```

make monitors the modification time of all three files, and when it sees at least one file in *dependency_list* that is newer than *target,* it runs **cc -c quit.c** to recreate **quit.o**. Enter these two lines of code in a file named makefile in your current directory. Next use **touch** to change the modification time of **quit.c** and then run **make**:

```
$ touch quit.c                           Not necessary if quit.o doesn't exist
$ make
cc -c quit.c                                              make runs cc
```

Now examine the other modules of the sample application (Figs. 16.1 to 16.3), and you'll find a similar dependency in the **arg_check** function. Also, the main program depends on three .o files and two .h files. These dependencies are represented in the form of a **dependency tree** as depicted in Fig. 16.4.

Note that **quit.c** includes **quit.h**, and **arg_check.c** includes **arg_check.h**, but the main program includes them both. The dependency tree is implemented in the form of four rules placed in makefile, the default file used by **make**:

```
$ cat makefile
# Makefile containing redundancies
rec_deposit: rec_deposit.o arg_check.o quit.o              # Rule 1
        cc -o rec_deposit rec_deposit.o arg_check.o quit.o -lm
```

```
rec_deposit.o: rec_deposit.c quit.h arg_check.h          # Rule 2
    cc -c rec_deposit.c

quit.o: quit.c quit.h                                    # Rule 3
    cc -c quit.c

arg_check.o: arg_check.c arg_check.h                     # Rule 4
    cc -c arg_check.c
```

make uses the # as the comment character and supports the use of the \ in splitting a line into two. Each rule is separated from the other by a blank line (not necessary on all systems).

The ultimate target (**rec_deposit**) is placed in the first rule which lists three object files as its dependencies. While scanning the makefile from top to bottom, you'll observe that **make** recursively treats each dependency as a target of its own. The three targets of the second tier also have their own dependencies and are shown as three separate rules. While moving up in the process of scanning the rules, **make** issues the necessary commands whenever it finds the modification time of any of the dependencies to be later than its associated target. If an object file doesn't exist, then **make** creates one.

Let's first remove all object files in this directory (if any), so **make** gets a chance to run all four commands:

```
$ rm *.o
$ make
cc -c rec_deposit.c
cc -c arg_check.c
cc -c quit.c
cc -o rec_deposit rec_deposit.o arg_check.o quit.o -lm
```

The object files can now be considered up-to-date. When you issue **make** again, you'll find that there's nothing left for it to do:

```
$ make
`rec_deposit' is up to date.
```

make is not restricted to handling only C programs. It can compile any program written in any language provided the compilation generates target files that can be compared to their sources. We can use **make** to run Fortran and C++ programs, but Java has the "make" feature built in. The **javac** compiler makes sure that all dependent source files are automatically compiled before it generates the .class file that is used by the **java** interpreter.

Tip

If **make** outputs a message like missing separator. Stop., it could mean that **make** didn't see the tab at the beginning of a line containing *command_list*. Use **cat -tv makefile** to view all tabs as ^I.

16.2.1 Removing Redundancies

The makefile that we just worked on has a number of redundancies. **make** is provided with a fair amount of intelligence to make the following deductions:

- If the target and the dependency have the same basename, then *command_list* need not be specified. In other words, if **quit.o** has **quit.c** as its dependency, then you don't need to specify **cc -c quit.c** as the *command_list*. Simply this statement would do as Rule 3:

  quit.o: quit.c quit.h   *No command_list required*

- If the source file itself is omitted in the dependency, **make** assumes that the base source filename is the same as the object file. The above line thus gets shortened further:

  quit.o: quit.h

make assumes that **quit.o** is created from **quit.c**. Before we view the next makefile that shows the changes, let's understand from Section 16.2.2 that **make** is not merely concerned with compiling programs.

16.2.2   Other Functions of make: Cleaning Up and Backup

make doesn't always need a dependency to work on; it can run a UNIX command depending on the command-line argument. For instance, you can instruct **make** to remove all object files or even perform a backup with **tar**. Our next makefile incorporates these features and the two "intelligent" features discussed previously:

```
$ cat makefile2
# All redundancies removed
rec_deposit: rec_deposit.o arg_check.o quit.o        # Rule 1
    cc -o rec_deposit rec_deposit.o arg_check.o quit.o -lm

rec_deposit.o: quit.h arg_check.h                    # Rule 2

quit.o: quit.h                                       # Rule 3

arg_check.o: arg_check.h                             # Rule 4

clean:                                               # No dependency list here
    rm *.o

tar:                                                 # ... and here
    tar -cvf progs.tar *.c *.h
```

You can see **make**'s built-in rules implemented in Rules 2 to 4. To consider the second rule, **rec_deposit.o** depends on **rec_deposit.c** (assumed by **make** since there's no **.c** file specified), and if that file or any of the two **.h** files is modified, **make** will run **cc -c rec_deposit.c** to generate **rec_deposit.o**.

Now let's examine the last two rules. There are no dependencies associated with the "pseudo-targets", clean and tar. This time, **make** has to be used with the target as argument and also with the -f option since we are no longer using the default makefile. When **make** runs with clean as argument, it removes all .o files:

```
$ make -f makefile2 clean
rm *.o
$ make -f makefile2 tar
tar -cvf progs.tar *.c *.h
a arg_check.c 1K
a compute.c 1K
a rec_deposit.c 1K
a arg_check.h 1K
a quit.h 1K
```

The **make clean** command is often run at the beginning to remove all object files in the current directory. This is usually followed by a "regular" **make** to force compilation of all programs. Finally, a **make install** (not discussed) moves the executables to a system directory.

16.2.3   Macros

make supports **macros**, sometimes called *variables,* that are used to define repeatedly used strings. A macro is of the form *macroname* = *value*, and is defined at the beginning of the makefile. A macro is invoked in a rule with $(*macroname*) or ${*macroname*}.

Even though we have used the **cc** compiler here, some systems may instead use GNU's **gcc**. To run the same makefile on another system that uses **gcc** without making major changes in the body of the makefile, we simply define a macro CC = gcc, and then use it in a rule as $(CC):

```
$ cat makefile3
CC = gcc
SOURCES = rec_deposit.c arg_check.c quit.c
OBJECTS = rec_deposit.o arg_check.o quit.o
HEADERS = arg_check.h quit.h

rec_deposit: $(OBJECTS)
    $(CC) -o rec_deposit $(OBJECTS) -lm

rec_deposit.o: $(HEADERS)

arg_check.o: arg_check.h

quit.o: quit.h

clean:
    rm $(OBJECTS)

tar:
    tar -cvf progs.tar $(SOURCES) $(HEADERS)
```

One of the four macros defines the compiler, and the other three group all files into three categories. Note that even though the compiler has changed here, we can still continue to omit the command list in three rules. This is because the CC macro is a **make** builtin, and, by default, CC expands to cc. Here, it expands to gcc:

```
$ make -f makefile3 clean
rm rec_deposit.o arg_check.o quit.o
$ make -f makefile3
gcc   -c  rec_deposit.c
gcc   -c  arg_check.c
gcc   -c  quit.c
gcc -o rec_deposit rec_deposit.o arg_check.o quit.o -lm
```

Apart from CC, there are two macros that are built into **make**. CFLAGS lists the options that also have to be used in compilation. LDFLAGS determines the options used by the linker. We'll not discuss these flags, but we'll revisit **make** after we have learned to build a library file with **ar**.

16.3 ar: **Building a Library (Archive)**

In real-life projects, specifying all object files in a makefile could be a tedious job. It's more convenient to group them into a **library** or **archive** with the **ar** command. **ar** can manipulate an archive in the same way **tar** does, except that an **ar** archive has the .a extension. The command uses the following options:

-r   Adds a file if it is not present in the archive or replaces an existing one.
-q   Appends a file at the end of the archive.
-x   Extracts a file from the archive.
-d   Deletes a file in the archive.
-t   Displays the table of contents of the archive.
-v   Displays verbose output.

Though **ar** supports options without the hyphen, POSIX requires **ar** options to be hyphen-prefixed. Let's stick to the example files used in the section on **make** and create an archive named **librec.a** to initially contain two object files. The -r option creates the archive before adding the object files:

```
$ ar -rv librec.a quit.o arg_check.o
r - quit.o
r - arg_check.o
ar: writing librec.a
```

The library filename is specified first, followed by object filenames. We can add other object files with -q, and then check the table of contents with -t:

```
$ ar -qv librec.a compute.o                        Appending to archive
a - compute.o
ar: writing librec.a
$ ar -tv librec.a
rw-r--r-- 1027/   10     676 Dec 21 14:37 2003 quit.o
rw-r--r-- 1027/   10     724 Dec 21 14:37 2003 arg_check.o
rw-r--r-- 1027/   10     952 Dec 21 14:38 2003 compute.o
```

We can now safely delete all three object files from the directory. If required, we can extract a file from the archive using -x or remove it from the archive with -d:

```
$ ar -xv librec.a compute.o
x - compute.o
$ ar -dv librec.a compute.o
d - compute.o
ar: writing librec.a
$ ar -tv librec.a
rw-r--r-- 1027/   10    676 Dec 21 14:37 2003 quit.o
rw-r--r-- 1027/   10    724 Dec 21 14:37 2003 arg_check.o
```

By default, the -x option extracts all object files. We deleted **compute.o** from the archive because the sample application doesn't need it.

16.3.1   Using the Library

Now that we have a library that is ready for use, rather than specify all object files separately, we can specify instead the library name as an argument to **cc** (and the -lm option, of course):

```
cc rec_deposit.c librec.a -lm
```

We can also use the -l option with our library. Since our library name was chosen carefully (lib + rec + .a), the -lrec option is the correct specification, but we also need to use -L to specify the location of the library:

```
cc rec_deposit.c -lrec -L"." -lm
```

By default, the compiler looks in /lib and /usr/lib to locate all library files. Our library is not located there, so we need to use -L.

Tip

If you have built a number of libraries, store them in a separate directory in your own home directory tree, and then use the -L option to **cc** to point to this directory. If others are also going to use your library, ensure that this directory has read and execute permission.

16.3.2   Maintaining an Archive with make

What happens when the sources for these object files are modified? Interactive use of **ar** to maintain an archive can still be quite painful. **make** is the answer yet again; it can both recompile the source files and replace the archive entries with their newer versions. To do this, **make** identifies an archived object file in this form:

archive_name(object_file)

The object file is placed in parentheses and is preceded by the library name. The following makefile takes care of compiling and archiving:

```
$ cat makefile4
CC = gcc
rec_deposit: rec_deposit.o librec.a(quit.o) librec.a(arg_check.o)
    $(CC) -o rec_deposit rec_deposit.o librec.a -lm

rec_deposit.o: quit.h arg_check.h

librec.a(quit.o): quit.h

librec.a(arg_check.o): arg_check.h
```

Observe the changed specification of the object files. The makefile entries are a little longer this time, but **make** here has some additional work to do: it has to ensure that the archive is rebuilt:

```
$ touch quit.c                                    Change modification time of this file
$ make -f makefile4
gcc    -c -o quit.o quit.c
ar rv librec.a quit.o
a - quit.o
ar: writing librec.a
rm -f quit.o
gcc -o rec_deposit rec_deposit.o librec.a -lm
```

Note that **make** invokes **ar** to replace the archive with the updated version of **quit.o**.

16.4 Static and Shared Libraries

In Section 16.3, we created a **static library**. When a program is compiled and linked to a static library, the object code of the library is included in the executable. Several programs may use the same function, which means that the same library code gets included in all these programs. This bloats the code size and eats into the disk space. This also means that if the code for the function changes, all programs that have the functions statically linked to them must be recompiled. Even though **make** can do this work for us, compilation of several hundred programs can still take a lot of time.

C also supports **shared libraries** (also called **shared objects**). In contrast to a static library, a program using a shared library loads the library code only during runtime. Once loaded, a single copy of the library code is kept in memory for other programs to use. Programs using shared libraries could be a little slower, but the executables are smaller since they don't include library code. As opposed to static libraries, a change in function code doesn't necessitate recompilation of those programs using the function (provided the signature is not altered).

Shared libraries usually have the extension .so, and the compiler has system-dependent options to create them. Look in /lib and /usr/lib, and you'll see a number of these .so files. Many of them are in fact symbolic links to the actual library. For instance, libbz2.so could be a symlink to libbz2.so.1.0.0, so named to include the version number. Shared libraries are increasingly being used by modern UNIX systems.

16.5 Version Control with SCCS and RCS

A software product is never perfect and has to be maintained in two ways. One, bugs must be rectified as and when they are reported. Second, applications must be constantly enhanced by incorporation of new features. In most cases, both activities go on concurrently, and programs thus experience version changes. For instance, development work could be going on for Release 2 when a customer reports a bug in Release 1.2.

When a bug is detected, the program developer needs to access the relevant version of the program to make modifications. Since all versions of the program have the same filename, how does one store them all without wasting disk space? If you recall what **diff** does *(10.5)*, you would be tempted to adopt a system that stores one version in full, and only its differences with the subsequent versions. You are on the right track; we are talking about *version control*.

Version control is widely used to maintain multiple versions of programs, shell scripts, configuration files, and even documents that undergo revisions. Every UNIX system supports the *Source Code Control System (SCCS)*. Berkeley was responsible for the *Revision Control System (RCS)*, which is also available on Linux systems. Irrespective of the system you use, version control implies the following:

- When a program or document has multiple versions, only one of them is stored in its entirety. Subsequently, the differences between one version and its immediate ancestor need to be stored. The complete information is held in a single encoded file.
- You can **check out** (i.e., retrieve) any version from the encoded file for compilation or editing.
- After the changes have been carried out, they are **checked in** (put back) to the encoded file.
- The system must not allow two users to edit identical versions of a file even though they can be permitted to view their contents or compile them.
- Users can be allowed or denied checkout rights to one or more versions.

In a version control system, the set of changes made to a version is known as a **delta**. It's the delta that is saved in the special file rather than the complete version. Every version is allocated a version number, which in SCCS is known as the **SID (SCCS Id)**. A SID or version number comprises two or four components:

- By default, the system allocates a two-component SID of the form *release.level*. The first SID is 1.1, which represents release 1, level 1. Every time a version is created, the level number is incremented, and the SID correspondingly changes to 1.2, 1.3, and so forth. The system won't change the release unless you specifically direct it to do so.
- When you need to change a version (say, one with SID 1.2) when a later version also exists (say SID 1.3), the system creates intermediate versions, called **branch deltas**. The SID of a branch delta has four components, the two additional ones being called *branch* and *sequence*. In this case, the system will allocate SID 1.2.1.1 to the next version. Subsequent branch deltas would be 1.2.1.2, 1.2.1.3, and so forth.

Both SCCS and RCS implement these features with their own set of commands. Both use **diff** (or a derivative) to maintain these differences in a special encoded file but in reverse ways. SCCS saves the first version and applies the saved **diff** commands to retrieve subsequent versions. RCS saves the final version and retrieves earlier versions by working backwards. The systems are incompatible and have different file naming conventions and formats. POSIX includes SCCS but not RCS. We'll discuss the SCCS system in some detail and the RCS system briefly.

Note

The term *delta* is used liberally in the SCCS system to refer to a set of changes, a version or the SID. There is also an SCCS command by that name. RCS documentation doesn't use this term as much as SCCS does; *revision* is their delta.

Caution

The encoded file contains mainly text but also includes control characters. Never edit this file directly to retrieve a version. Always use the appropriate commands that check out and check in a version (or delta).

16.6   An SCCS Session

SCCS comprises a suite of programs that are often held in a separate directory (/usr/ccs/bin in Solaris), so make sure that you have the directory in your PATH. These programs can be run in two ways:

- Individually, which we will do with the **admin**, **get**, **delta**, and **unget** commands.
- Using the **sccs** command itself as a frontend to these tools. You can run both **get** and **sccs get**, but the **sccs** frontend has certain additional features which are not available in the standalone tools.

SCCS saves all versions of a program in a single encoded file that is often called the **SCCS file** or **SCCS history file**. This file is named with an s. prefix. The program foo.c is saved in the SCCS file, s.foo.c. SCCS will first look up the SCCS directory for an SCCS file and then the current directory. In the following sections, we'll use these tools:

- **admin**, initially for creating the SCCS file, and later for controlling user access.
- **get** to check out any version—read-only or editable.
- **delta** to save the changes (deltas) in the SCCS file.
- **unget** to reverse the action of **get** when we discover that the checkout was not the right thing to do.
- **sact** and **prs** to report on the current state of editing activity and the state of SCCS files.
- **rmdel** and **comb** to compress an SCCS file by removing intermediate versions.

By default, checkout and checkin access is permitted to all users. In Section 16.9, we'll use the **admin** command to restrict this access. In this section, we'll create an SCCS file, check out a version, make changes to it, and then check it in.

16.6.1 admin: Creating an SCCS File

For our discussions, we'll use the program, quit.c, a variant of which was used in the discussions on **make** and **ar**. So let's first have a look at the contents of the first version having the SID 1.1, i.e., release 1, level 1:

```
$ cat quit.c                                          SID 1.1
#include <stdio.h>
#include <errno.h>
void quit (void) {
    printf("Error number %d, quitting program\n", errno);
    exit(1);
}
```

This file now has to be checked in to its SCCS file, s.quit.c. This file doesn't yet exist, so we have to create it with the **admin** command. The -i option specifies the input filename:

```
$ admin -i quit.c s.quit.c
No id keywords (cm7)                            cm7 is an SCCS keyword
$ ls -l s.quit.c
-r--r--r--    1 sumit     staff        279 Dec 21 14:49 s.quit.c
$ rm quit.c
```

admin creates s.quit.c, which contains the contents of quit.c as well as control information like the owner of the file and the time of creation. All future versions of quit.c must be checked in to this file. We no longer need to maintain quit.c separately.

To understand what SCCS understands by cm7, use its **help** command with the keyword as argument, only to know that the message can be ignored:

```
$ /usr/ccs/bin/help
Enter the message number or SCCS command name: cm7
cm7:
"No id keywords"
No SCCS identification keywords were substituted for.
You may not have any keywords in the file,
in which case you can ignore this warning.
        ...........
```

The reason why we used the absolute pathname here is that this author uses the Bash shell, and **help** is a Bash builtin. We'll also look at some of the other keywords that SCCS displays, especially when things don't work properly.

16.6.2 get: Checking Out

We now have a single version of quit.c in the SCCS file, s.quit.c. The **get** command checks out a file, and depending on the options used, you can

- Check out a read-only version or delta (the default).
- Display the contents to the standard output using the -p option.

- Check out an editable version using the -e option.
- Check out a specific version using the -r option. The same option is also used to change the release number.

Sometimes, we need to check out a noneditable version for compilation, so let's use **get** to obtain a read-only version:

```
$ get s.quit.c
1.1                                                    Current version number
7 lines                                                File contains 7 lines
No id keywords (cm7)
$ ls -l quit.c
-r--r--r--  1 sumit    staff        129 Dec 21 14:50 quit.c
```

SCCS reports that delta 1.1 comprising 7 lines has been checked out. This file doesn't contain keywords, but we'll learn to place some useful keywords later. **get -e** checks out an editable version and also creates a lock file, p.quit.c:

```
$ get -e s.quit.c
1.1
new delta 1.2
7 lines
$ ls -l quit.c
-rw-r--r--  1 sumit    staff        129 Dec 21 14:51 quit.c
$ ls -l p.quit.c
-rw-r--r--  1 sumit    staff         32 Dec 21 14:51 p.quit.c
```

This time SCCS points out that unless you explicitly specify the SID, it will assign 1.2 to this delta when you return it. The lock file prevents the user to check out the file again:

```
$ get -e s.quit.c
ERROR [s.quit.c]: writable `quit.c' exists (ge4)
$ /usr/ccs/bin/help ge4
ge4:
"writable `...' exists"
For safety's sake, SCCS won't overwrite an existing g-file if it's writable.
If you don't need the g-file, remove it and rerun the get command.
```

The lock file maintains information related to the current session. It is used by the **sact** command to be discussed later. SCCS also understands the checked out file as a "g-file," but we won't need to use this term again.

Note

When you use **get -e**, the SCCS file is locked for the delta that was checked out. No other user can check out this delta till it has been checked in. However, other users can check out editable versions of other deltas, but the files have to reside in different directories since they all have the same name.

16.6.3 delta: Checking In

You can now edit the file that you just checked out, so let's change the **quit** function to accept the exit status as an argument. After editing, quit.c should look like this:

```
$ cat quit.c                                                    SID 1.2
#include <stdio.h>
#include <errno.h>
void quit (int exit_status) {                    This line has changed
    printf("Error number %d, quitting program\n", errno);
    exit(exit_status);                                  ... and this one
}
```

Two lines have changed, and it should interest you to know how the SCCS file shown in Fig. 16.5 internally stores these two differences. We'll now use the **delta** command to check this file in. **delta** pauses for a line of comment which is also recorded in the SCCS file:

```
$ delta s.quit.c
comments? Function modified to accept exit status as argument
No id keywords (cm7)
1.2
2 inserted
2 deleted
5 unchanged
$ ls -l quit.c
quit.c: No such file or directory
```

By default, SCCS assigns this version the same SID that was displayed by **get** (1.2) when it was checked out for editing. **delta** also removes quit.c, so you can't modify a version that is in SCCS custody till you "get" it first. Next time you retrieve a version with **get -e**, the next **delta** would check it in as SID 1.3.

You must document the changes at the comments? prompt. The **prs** command displays these comments, which helps other programmers know why the changes were made in the first place. It will also help you when you look at your own program months later.

It is characteristic of many commands of the SCCS suite that changes are reported in three parts—the number of lines inserted, deleted, and unchanged. We'll use **delta**'s -r option in Section 16.8.2 where we'll learn to handle multiple deltas.

Tip

Sometimes, you'll want to check in a delta because you don't want to lose the changes but would like to continue editing. In that case, use **delta -n** which leaves the file undeleted. But the SCCS file has recorded that the delta has been checked in and won't allow you to check in further changes you make to this file. You must rename it before you use **get -e** again, and then overwrite the checked-out version with the one you just edited. RCS handles this situation better; it allows you to "lock" the file and check it in.

16.6.4 unget: When You Change Your Mind

It's possible that you checked out a version for editing, then found that the changes weren't worthy of a new delta. You can undo your previous checkout by using the **unget** command:

FIGURE 16.5   *The SCCS File,* s.quit.c, *Containing SIDs 1.1 and 1.2*

```
^Ah32958
^As 00002/00002/00005
^Ad D 1.2 03/12/21 14:53:41 sumit 2 1
^Ac Function modified to accept exit status as argument
^Ae
^As 00007/00000/00000
^Ad D 1.1 03/12/21 14:49:39 sumit 1 0
^Ac date and time created 03/12/21 14:49:39 by sumit
^Ae
^Au
^AU
^Af e 0
^At
^AT
^AI 1
#include <stdio.h>
#include <errno.h>
^AD 2
void quit (void) {
^AE 2
^AI 2
void quit (int exit_status) {
^AE 2
    printf("Error number %d, quitting program\n", errno);
^AD 2
    exit(1);
^AE 2
^AI 2
    exit(exit_status);
^AE 2
}
```

```
$ get -e s.quit.c
1.2
new delta 1.3
7 lines
$ unget s.quit.c
1.3                                            New delta had you checked it in
```

Since SCCS keeps track of all editable checked-out versions, you can't check out the
same delta again for editing unless you reverse the action of **get -e**. Note that **unget**
has nothing to reverse when you check out a read-only version:

```
$ get s.quit.c
1.2

......
$ unget s.quit.c
ERROR [s.quit.c]: `p.quit.c' nonexistent (ut4)
```

We'll be using the **get** and **delta** commands again for retrieving multiple deltas and changing release numbers. Before that, we need to look at two tools that maintain state information.

16.7   Activity and History Information

You won't always remember the exact form of the delta tree, nor will you always be able to recall the exact SID of a delta that you want to check out. SCCS offers the **prs** command to present the history of an SCCS file and **sact** to provide information on the state of editing activity.

16.7.1   sact: Displaying Activity Status

The **sact** command shows the status of editing activity of a file. When no editable version has been checked out, it reports an error:

```
$ sact s.quit.c
ERROR [s.quit.c]: No outstanding deltas
```

As you are aware, **get -e s.quit.c** creates the lock file p.quit.c. The same file also provides information about editing activity to **sact**. Here, **sact** reports that user sumit has checked out a version with SID 1.1. Note that the contents of the lock file are identical:

```
$ sact s.quit.c
1.1 1.2 sumit 03/12/21 14:51:09
$ cat p.quit.c
1.1 1.2 sumit 03/12/21 14:51:09
```

The current SID (1.1) is followed by the default SID (1.2) to be used for the next delta. The output also shows the user and date (in *yy*/*mm*/*dd* format) and time of checking out. **get -e** looks up this file and prevents a checkout if the SID of a requested delta is found to be present in the file. When multiple deltas have been checked out, **sact** reports with multiline output:

```
$ sact s.quit.c
1.2 1.2.1.1 sumit 03/12/21 15:53:46
2.1 2.2 jpm 03/12/21 15:54:30
```

The second line shows that user jpm has checked out delta 2.1. When all users have checked in the changes, the lock file is deleted.

16.7.2   prs: Displaying the SCCS History

The **prs** command displays the history of an SCCS file. It helps you identify the delta you need by displaying the comments that you provided when you checked in a delta. By default, the command presents the complete history:

```
$ prs s.quit.c
s.quit.c:

D 1.2 03/12/21 14:53:41 sumit 2 1        00002/00002/00005
MRs:
COMMENTS:
Function modified to accept exit status as argument

D 1.1 03/12/21 14:49:39 sumit 1 0        00007/00000/00000
MRs:
COMMENTS:
date and time created 03/12/21 14:49:39 by sumit
```

Each delta is presented in a group of four lines with the most recent delta shown first. The first line replicates the information provided by **sact**, but it also shows three /-delimited numbers that represent the number of lines inserted, deleted, and unchanged. **prs** obtains this information from the SCCS file itself as shown in Fig. 16.5.

To display output earlier or later than a cut-off date or release, **prs** uses the -r option to identify a specific release and the -c option to set a cut-off date and time. For instance you can use -r1.2 or -c031213 as the cut-off point. You then need to use either the -e (earlier) or -l (later) option to produce selective output:

```
prs -r1.2 -e s.quit.c
prs -c0312141501 -l s.quit.c
```
All releases earlier to SID 1.2
All releases later than 15:01 hours
on Dec 14, '03

▬ 16.8   Continuing Editing with SCCS

We have performed the basic editing and activity monitoring functions. The default SID allocation system and version locking should suffice for single-user SCCS sessions. However, SCCS also permits you to:

- Change the release number, using *branch deltas* as and when required.
- Edit multiple but different deltas simultaneously.
- Compress an SCCS file by removing redundant versions.
- Place identification keywords in an SCCS file.

In the following sections, we'll examine these features.

16.8.1   get -r: Changing the Default Numbering Sequence

By default, SCCS increments the level number every time you use **get -e** to check out a file and **delta** to check it in after modification. At some point, you'll need to change this default numbering scheme:

- When the changes are significant. In that case, you may need to assign a new release number rather than increment the level number.
- When you make changes to a previous delta rather than the latest one. The previous delta develops into a *branch delta*.

Let's first consider the allocation of a new release number to our quit.c program. You'll first have to indicate to SCCS your *intention* of doing so when you check out the version with **get**. By default, SCCS displays the next delta in the **get** output, but you can override that by specifying your own release number with the -r option:

```
$ get -e -r2 s.quit.c
1.2                                                    Last version
new delta 2.1
7 lines
```

Here, -r2 indicates to SCCS that the next delta would be 2.1, but observe that **get** checks out 1.2, the latest version. After editing, check in the file in the usual manner:

```
$ delta s.quit.c
comments? Function modified to accept the message as argument.
No id keywords (cm7)
2.1
2 inserted
4 deleted
3 unchanged
```

Now that you have SID 1.1, 1.2, and 2.1 in the SCCS file, you have to specify the -r option with **get** to retrieve a previous version. For instance, you need to use **get -r1.2 s.quit.c** to check out a read-only version of delta 1.2.

Branch Deltas Consider this real-life situation where you need to check out an editable version of an older delta, say, 1.2, for a client when delta 1.3 also exists in the SCCS file. What SID would you allocate to the revised version? The SCCS makes use of the four-level numbering scheme discussed earlier *(16.5)*. The checked-out version develops into a **branch delta** with SID 1.2.1.1, where the last two numbers represent the branch and sequence numbers:

```
$ get -e -r1.2 s.quit.c
1.2
new delta 1.2.1.1
7 lines
$ sact s.quit.c
1.2 1.2.1.1 sumit 03/12/21 15:00:35
```

The checkin is done in the usual manner with **delta**. The next time you need to revise this version to 1.2.1.2, you'll have to "get" it with -r1.2.1.

16.8.2 Working with Multiple Versions

SCCS allows users to check out multiple but different deltas. Since it checks out all versions with the same filename, you must use **mv** to rename the existing file before you check out another delta. Consider this **get** and **mv** sequence:

```
$ get -e -r1.2.1.1 s.quit.c
1.2.1.1
new delta 1.2.1.2
7 lines
$ mv quit.c quit1.c
```

You can now check out delta 2.1. **sact** shows the same user has checked out two different versions:

```
$ get -e -r2.1 s.quit.c
2.1
new delta 2.2
5 lines
$ sact s.quit.c
1.2.1.1 1.2.1.2 sumit 03/12/21 15:14:14
2.1 2.2 sumit 03/12/21 15:14:41
```

The default invocation of **delta** assumes that only a single delta has been checked out, so it fails this time:

```
$ delta s.quit.c
comments?
ERROR [s.quit.c]: missing -r argument (de1)
```

Since the current file, quit.c, was checked out as SID 2.1, you need to specify this number with the -r option:

```
$ delta -r 2.1 s.quit.c
comments? Identification keywords added
2.2
    .......
```

Now there's a single delta left to check in, so let's rename quit1.c to quit.c before running **delta**. This time **delta** reports no ambiguity and doesn't require the -r option:

```
$ mv quit1.c quit.c
$ delta s.quit.c
comments? No changes this time
No id keywords (cm7)
1.2.1.2
      ........
```

The resultant delta tree is shown in Fig. 16.6. The trunk comprises the deltas 1.1, 1.2, 2.1, and 2.2. There is a single branch emanating from this trunk which comprises the branch deltas 1.2.1.1 and 1.2.1.2. We'll next attempt to remove some of these deltas.

Tip

When there are too many deltas in your SCCS files, the **prs** output needs to be processed with **grep** so you can visualize the tree yourself. Convert the following **prs–grep** sequence to a shell script or a shell function:

FIGURE 16.6 *The SCCS Tree*

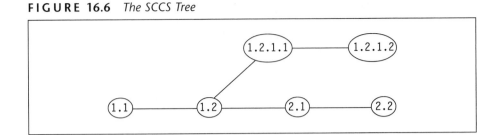

```
$ prs s.quit.c | grep "^D"
D 1.2.1.2 03/12/21 15:17:05 sumit 6 4    00000/00000/00007
D 2.2 03/12/21 15:16:43 sumit 5 3        00004/00000/00005
D 1.2.1.1 03/12/21 15:03:36 sumit 4 2    00001/00001/00006
D 2.1 03/12/21 15:00:12 sumit 3 2        00002/00004/00003
D 1.2 03/12/21 14:53:41 sumit 2 1        00002/00002/00005
D 1.1 03/12/21 14:49:39 sumit 1 0        00007/00000/00000
```

These are the six deltas that we created in the preceding examples. Two of them are branch deltas.

16.8.3 rmdel and comb: Removing and Combining Versions

After some time, there will be too many versions, and you may not need to revert to all of them. You can then delete the ones you don't need with the **rmdel** command. But before we do that, let's consider the delta tree shown in Fig. 16.6. All deltas can't be deleted with **rmdel**, only the ones that are leaves, i.e., the ones that other deltas don't depend on. If you try to delete one that's not a leaf, SCCS refuses:

```
$ rmdel -r1.2 s.quit.c
ERROR [s.quit.c]: not a 'leaf' delta (rc5)
```

In Fig. 16.6, deltas 2.2 and 1.2.1.2 are leaves, but the others are not. We can delete them with **rmdel**:

```
$ rmdel -r1.2.1.2 s.quit.c ;  rmdel -r 2.2 s.quit.c
$ _                                                         Two deltas removed
```

The **comb** command preserves only the latest deltas. It removes unnecessary deltas and compacts the SCCS file by preserving only the required ancestors. **comb** considers the nonleaf deltas that don't have branches out of them to be unnecessary. The command creates a Bourne shell script that has to be executed separately:

```
$ comb s.quit.c > quit_comb.sh
$ chmod +x quit_comb.sh
$ ./quit_comb.sh
No id keywords (cm7)
```

This script includes SCCS commands, **sed** and **ed** commands, and creates a smaller SCCS file. Executing it on the SCCS file in the state represented in Fig. 16.6 removes three deltas. You are advised to use this command with caution.

16.8.4   Using Identification Keywords

You can take advantage of **SCCS identification keywords** to place control information in the file itself. A keyword is of the form *%keyword%,* and some useful keywords are shown below:

%I%   SID of the checked-out file
%M%   Filename (without .s prefix)
%D%   Current date in *yy*/*mm*/*dd* format
%T%   Current time in *hh*:*mm*:*ss* format
%U%   Time of creation of delta in *hh*:*mm*:*ss* format

These keywords must be embedded in the comments used with /* and */. For instance, you can insert the following comment lines at the beginning of your source file:

```
/* Filename: %M%
   SID: %I%
   Time: %D% %T% */
```

These lines are left alone when you check out an editable version, but when you retrieve a read-only version or use **get -p**, SCCS expands the keywords:

```
$ get -p -r2.2 s.quit.c | head -n 3
2.2                                      These two lines are written
9 lines                                      to the standard error
/* Filename: quit.c
   SID: 2.2
   Time: 03/12/21 15:23:46 */
```

It's convenient to maintain the SID and current date and time in the file itself. Note that this expansion is not performed on an editable delta, because subsequent deltas could be related to this delta. Saving the expanded form would pass on wrong information to the next related delta. RCS betters SCCS in the handling of these keywords.

16.9   Controlling Access to SCCS

By default, every user is allowed checkin and checkout rights provided the SCCS file is accessible to the user in the first place. This means that every directory in the pathname of the SCCS file must have execute permission. The default rights are changed with the **admin** command, the same command we used to create an SCCS file. The command can be used only by the owner of the SCCS file.

16.9.1   Controlling User Access

admin uses the -a option to add a user or a group and the -e option to remove a user or group from the list. Either a username or a numeric GID must be specified with the option. Here's how **admin** is used to prevent user sumit from checking out quit.c:

```
$ admin -e sumit s.quit.c
$ get -e s.quit.c
2.1
ERROR [s.quit.c]: not authorized to make deltas (co14)
```

The user sumit can however check out a read-only version; that can't be restricted by **admin**. To restore the checkout rights to sumit, use the -a option:

```
$ admin -asumit s.quit.c
$ get -e s.quit.c
2.1
new delta 2.2
5 lines
$ unget s.quit.c                                            We don't want a new delta
```

Both options can be used multiple times in a single invocation. Moreover, SCCS was designed for users working in a group, so **admin** can be used with a GID also:

```
admin -e jpm -e juliet -e romeo -a henry s.quit.c
admin -a202 s.quit.c                                        Access to users with GID 202
```

16.9.2 Controlling Releases

admin also supports the -fl and -dl options for controlling checkout access to one or more releases. These options are suffixed either by the letter a (all) to allow or deny access to all releases or one or more release numbers. The -fla option locks all releases:

```
$ admin -fla s.quit.c
$ get -e -r2.1 s.quit.c
2.1
ERROR [s.quit.c]: SCCS file locked against editing (co23)
```

You can remove locks to one or more releases using the -dl option. The following command restores the SCCS default by unlocking all releases:

```
admin -dla s.quit.c                                         Unlocks all releases
```

Specific releases are controlled in these ways:

```
admin -fl2 s.quit.c                                         Locks release 2
admin -fl2,3 s.quit.c                                       Locks releases 2 and 3
admin -dl2.1 s.quit.c                                       Unlocks release 2.1
```

SCCS also supports the **sccs** command that acts as a frontend to other *subcommands*. Many of these subcommands have the same names as the standalone commands that we have used (like **get** and **sccs get**), but some **sccs** subcommands don't have standalone equivalents. Look up the **sccs** man page for further details.

16.10   The Revision Control System (RCS)

The Revision Control System (RCS) was created by Berkeley as an alternative to AT&T's SCCS. RCS is standard on all BSD UNIX systems and is also available on many UNIX systems. Linux supports the GNU implementation of RCS which is arguably simpler to use than SCCS. The basic functionality is achieved with just three commands: **ci**, **co**, and **rcs**.

Unlike SCCS, RCS saves the latest file in entirety and reconstructs previous versions by working backwards. (SCCS saves the earliest version in full.) The encoded **RCS file** contains the information required to assemble all **revisions** (the name RCS uses for versions or deltas) along with status and activity information. It is not much different from an SCCS file in essence though. However, RCS maintains no separate lock file (like the one created by **get -e**). All locking information is kept in the RCS file itself.

An RCS file is named with a ,v suffix. Thus, quit.c is checked in to the RCS file, quit.c,v. The system looks in a directory named RCS for the RCS file, failing which it looks in the current directory. To avoid repetition, we'll briefly repeat the session (using quit.c) that we went through with SCCS, and note the differences that are also presented in Table 16.1. This time, we'll maintain the RCS file in the ./RCS directory.

16.10.1   Creating an RCS File with ci

Unlike in SCCS, there are two commands that can create an RCS file. The **rcs -i** command creates an initialized and empty file. Revisions are subsequently checked in with the **ci** command. Alternatively, we can use **ci** itself for both tasks, and the first invocation creates version 1.1:

```
$ ci quit.c
RCS/quit.c,v  <-- quit.c
enter description, terminated with single '.' or end of file:
NOTE: This is NOT the log message!
>> RCS file created with version 1.1
>> .                                        dot terminates standard input
initial revision: 1.1
done
$ ls -l RCS
total 4
-r--r--r--   1 sumit    users       342 2003-12-23 12:41 quit.c,v
```

ci creates this file with revision 1.1 checked in. We'll use the same command to check in editable versions. Unlike **admin -i** of SCCS, the default invocation of **ci** removes the original file.

Note

Unlike SCCS commands that use the SCCS filename as argument (like s.quit.c), RCS commands use the unencoded filename (like quit.c), the file that you actually work with.

TABLE 16.1   *SCCS and RCS: Command Usage (File:* foo.c*)*

SCCS Command	RCS Command	Significance
admin -i foo.c s.foo.c	ci foo.c	Creates encoded file with SID 1.1
get s.foo.c	co foo.c	Checks out read-only version
get -e s.foo.c	co -l foo.c	Checks out editable version
delta s.foo.c	ci foo.c	Checks in current editable version
unget s.foo.c	rcs -u foo.c	Reverses the action of checkout
get -r *ver* s.foo.c	ci -r *ver* foo.c	Specifies release number *ver* for next checkin (at time of checkout for SCCS, checkin for RCS)
prs s.foo.c	rlog foo.c	Prints version history
sact s.foo.c	rlog foo.c	Prints checked-out status
rmdel -r *ver* s.foo.c	rcs -o *ver* foo.c	Deletes version *ver*
what s.foo.c	ident foo.c	Displays version

16.10.2   co and ci: Checking Out and In

The **co** command checks out a file. Like **get**, it retrieves a read-only version of the latest version by default, and displays the retrieved data on the standard output with the -p option. It's the -l (lock) option that checks out an editable version:

```
$ co -l quit.c                                    Like get -e s.quit.c
RCS/quit.c,v  -->  quit.c
revision 1.1 (locked)
done
$ ls -l quit.c
-rw-r--r--   1 sumit    users        129 2003-12-23 12:42 quit.c
```

Unlike SCCS, RCS doesn't create a lock file, but it still locks a version from concurrent editing by placing an entry in the RCS file. If you attempt to check out again, **co** issues a warning and offers to remove the existing checked-out version:

```
$ co -l quit.c
RCS/quit.c,v  -->  quit.c
revision 1.1 (locked)
writable quit.c exists; remove it? [ny](n): n
co: checkout aborted
```

SCCS doesn't offer this feature, but we preferred not to take advantage of it by entering n at the prompt. You can now edit the file that you just checked out, and then use the **ci** command to check it in:

```
$ ci quit.c
RCS/quit.c,v  <-  quit.c
new revision: 1.2; previous revision: 1.1
enter log message, terminated with single '.' or end of file:
>> Function modified to accept exit status as argument
>> .
done
```

RCS assigns revision number 1.2 to this version. We'll soon use the -r option with both **ci** and **co** to explicitly specify the revision number.

Reversing the Action of co -l If you have checked out a version for editing and now want to reverse the action, use the command **rcs -u quit.c** (**unget** in SCCS). The **rcs** command is examined later, but for now, let it be known that here it simply removes the entry specifying the lock in the RCS file.

Tip

You can't normally check in a version unless you have checked it out with a lock with **co -l**. In case you have used **chmod +w** on a read-only version, and edited the file, you need to lock this file first with **rcs -l** *filename* before you return it to the RCS file with **ci**.

16.10.3 Specifying Revisions

Unlike in SCCS, the -r option in **co** can't be used to indicate what the next revision number would be. For instance, you can't use this command to indicate that you intend to check in the next revision as 2.1:

```
$ co -l -r2 quit.c
RCS/quit.c,v  ->  quit.c
co: RCS/quit.c,v: revision 2 absent
```

The -r option is used with **co** to check out an *existing* version only. Let's check out the latest version of the file:

```
co -l quit.c
```

After you have edited the file, you have to explicitly assign the version number when checking it in:

```
$ ci -r2 quit.c
RCS/quit.c,v  <-  quit.c
new revision: 2.1; previous revision: 1.2
enter log message, terminated with single '.' or end of file:
>> Function modified to accept the message as argument.
>> .
done
```

You can specify higher version numbers also, but the missing ones can't then be allocated.

Creating a Branch Delta Like in SCCS, when you check out a version that is not the latest, you can check in that version only as a branch delta. RCS follows the same four-numbered component scheme used by SCCS:

```
$ co -l -r1.2 quit.c
RCS/quit.c,v  ->  quit.c
revision 1.2 (locked)
done
```

Unless you invoke the **rlog** command to find out the state of the revisions, you won't know at this stage what the next revision would be. You'll know that only when you check it in:

```
$ ci quit.c
RCS/quit.c,v  <--  quit.c
new revision: 1.2.1.1; previous revision: 1.2
enter log message, terminated with single '.' or end of file:
>> Creating a branch delta
>> .
done
```

Working with Multiple Versions   The procedure for handling multiple but different versions is the same as in SCCS. Rename each version after checkout, and rename it back before checkin. For every checkin except the last one, you'll also have to specify the version number with **ci -r**. This procedure has already been discussed *(16.8.2)* and will not be repeated here.

16.10.4   rlog and rcs: Other RCS Functions

RCS supports two important tools—**rlog** and **rcs**—that are used for a host of functions. **rlog** combines the **sact** and **prs** commands of SCCS in one; it reports both on the versions existing in the RCS file and the ones that are locked for editing. Fig. 16.7 shows the **rlog** output after version 1.2 is checked out and locked.

The output shows details of each revision in three or four lines, and also points out the one that has a branch. Note that **rlog** also shows that revision 1.2 is locked by user sumit. The annotations reveal certain features of RCS that we are constrained to overlook in this text.

The **rcs** command is used to change RCS file attributes. Apart from creating an initialized version of an RCS file, its domain of activity includes lock control, removal of versions, and administering user access rights. We'll briefly discuss these functions in the following paragraphs.

Lock Control   Applications developed by a single user need not be subjected to the locking mechanism. By default, RCS enforces **strict locking** (as shown in Fig. 16.7); you can't check in a file unless you have it locked in the first place (with **co -l**). But this can be altered using the -U option which allows the owner to check in a version without locking it first:

```
rcs -U quit.c                                            Can still use ci quit.c
```

The -u option removes an existing lock on a version and rolls back a locked checkout in the same way the SCCS **unget** command reverses the action of **get**. As discussed before *(16.10.2)*, **rcs -u quit.c** removes the lock on the latest version of quit.c.

The -l option locks a file. This feature is useful when you have checked out a file in nonlocking mode, made alterations to it and now want to check it back. This has also been discussed *(16.10.2—Tip)*.

FIGURE 16.7   *The Output of* `rlog`

```
$ rlog quit.c
RCS file: RCS/quit.c,v                    Current location of file
Working file: quit.c
head: 2.1                                 Highest version number
branch:
locks: strict                            Only a locked file can be checked in
    sumit: 1.2                           sumit has locked version 1.2
access list:                            Accessible to all
symbolic names:
keyword substitution: kv
total revisions: 4; selected revisions: 4
description:
RCS file created with version 1.1
----------------------------
revision 2.1
date: 2003/12/23 07:19:21;  author: sumit;  state: Exp;  lines: +2 -4
Function modified to accept the message as argument.
----------------------------
revision 1.2      locked by: sumit;
date: 2003/12/23 07:12:48;  author: sumit;  state: Exp;  lines: +2 -2
branches: 1.2.1;
Function modified to accept exit status as argument
----------------------------
revision 1.1
date: 2003/12/23 07:10:07;  author: sumit;  state: Exp;
Initial revision
----------------------------
revision 1.2.1.1
date: 2003/12/23 07:20:35;  author: sumit;  state: Exp;  lines: +1 -1
Creating a branch delta
=============================================================================
```

Removing Versions You can use the -o option to remove any version provided it
doesn't have a branch or is not locked. Thus, **rcs -o1.3 quit.c** removes revision 1.3
without renumbering the versions. Look up the man page to know that this option also
works with a range of revision numbers.

Controlling User Access Like the SCCS **admin** command, **rcs** also supports the -a
option to add a user to its access control list and -e to drop users from the list.

Identification Keywords Like SCCS, RCS also supports the use of identification keywords except that the keywords are both expanded and remain usable even after an editable version of the file has been checked out. Here are some of the keywords that you can use in the comments section of your C program:

```
/*
  $RCSfile$
  $Author$
  $Date$
  $Id$
  $Revision$
*/
```

After you have checked in and checked out the file, you can use the **ident** command to display this section:

```
$ ident quit.c
quit.c:
        $RCSfile: quit.c,v $
        $Author: sumit $
        $Date: 2003/12/24 08:13:55 $
        $Id: quit.c,v 1.7 2003/12/24 08:13:55 sumit Exp sumit $
        $Revision: 1.7 $
```

Note that RCS preserves the variable names even after expansion. The scheme is so well designed that all editable checked-out versions also contain this information. This is not the case with SCCS.

16.11 Debugging Programs with dbx

When a C program doesn't behave properly, as a first measure we place **printf** statements at key locations in the program to print the values of variables that are suspected to cause improper behavior. This technique usually doesn't work with large programs. Also, it leaves us with a lot of cleaning up to do because these diagnostic **printf** statements have to be finally removed from the code. It's a debugger that we need, and UNIX provides a number of them.

In this final section, we discuss the BSD **dbx** program that's available on most versions of UNIX. Linux offers a superior debugger in **gdb**, whose commands are often identical to **dbx**. Like most debuggers, **dbx** can be used in two ways:

- **Debug mode**   In this mode, the program terminates normally, and you can follow the execution of each statement.
- **Post-mortem mode**   A program crashes for some serious reason, say, an illegal access of memory. The debugger is then used to ascertain the cause of the crash by examining the core file that was dumped.

We'll use **dbx** in the debug mode to locate two bugs in the program, **parsestring.c** (Fig. 16.8). The program prompts for a multiword string and then uses the **strtok** library

FIGURE 16.8 `parsestring.c`: *Program Containing Two Bugs*

```
1    #include <stdio.h>
2    #include <string.h>                    /* For strtok */
3    #define BUFSIZE 200                     /* Maximum size of command line */
4    #define ARGVSIZE 40                     /* Maximum number of arguments */
5    #define DELIM "\n\t\r"                  /* White-space delimiters for strtok */
6
7    int main (void) {
8        int i, n;
9        char buf[BUFSIZE+1];                /* Stores the input line */
10       char *clargs[ARGVSIZE];            /* Stores the string tokens */
11       n = 0;
12
13       printf("Enter a multiword string: ");
14       fgets(buf, BUFSIZE, stdin);
15
16       clargs[0] = strtok(buf, DELIM);    /* first word */
17       while ((clargs[n] = strtok(NULL, DELIM)) != NULL)
18           n++;                           /* ... all words are extracted */
19       clargs[n] = NULL;                  /* Set last pointer to NULL */
20
21       for (i = 0; i <n ; i++)
22           printf("Argument %d is %s\n",i,  clargs[i]);
23   }
```

function to split the string into words. All debuggers display line numbers in their diagnostic messages, so we used the **nl** command (not discussed in this edition) to number these lines.

In this program, **strtok**, the string tokenizer, splits a string stored in buf on the delimiter defined in DELIM. The function is a little unusual, which is why it appears twice in the code. In the first call, it returns the first word, but subsequent calls require the first argument to be NULL. It's customary to terminate an array of pointers to char with a NULL pointer though this program doesn't strictly require it. The program doesn't produce the desired behavior:

```
$ cc parsestring.c && a.out
Enter a multiword string: dbx or gdb
$ _                                                          No output!
```

The **for** loop was not invoked. For our investigations, we'll have to run **dbx** with a.out as argument, but the program needs to be recompiled with the -g option (**cc -g parsestring.c**). This copies the symbol table and other debugging information to the executable. **dbx** looks up this table to examine variables and functions.

    dbx allows the setting of **breakpoints** in a program to let us make our observations. For instance, we can check the value of a variable when the program pauses at a breakpoint. We'll then step through the program one statement at a time, running some general-purpose **dbx** commands on the way. We'll reassign a variable from inside **dbx** and then trace its behavior. **dbx** is a powerful program, but a useful subset of its features should suffice for not-too-complex debugging situations.

16.11.1   Starting dbx

Unlike **make** and the SCCS suite of commands, inclusion of **dbx** is not mandated by POSIX. The behavior of this tool varies widely across systems, and in this section, we'll consider the Solaris implementation, but with a modified prompt string. Start the debugger with the name of the executable as argument:

```
dbx a.out                              Program must be compiled with -g option
```

dbx throws out some informative messages on the terminal before pausing at the (modified) (dbx) prompt. You should first run the **help** command to see the commands that it supports. A partial list is presented below, organized by function:

```
(dbx) help
command summary
Use `commands' to see a command summary consisting of one-line
descriptions of each dbx command.

Execution and Tracing
    cancel     catch       clear        cont       delete
    next       pop         replay       rerun      restore
    run        runargs     save         status     step
    stop       trace       unintercept  when       whocatches

Displaying and Naming Data
    assign     call        dis          display    down
    dump       examine     exists       frame      hide
    print      undisplay   unhide       up         whatis
    where      whereami    whereis      which
    .....
```

For context-sensitive help, use **help** with the command name. The **stop** command defines a breakpoint, and this is how it is used on this system:

```
(dbx) help stop
stop (command)
stop at <line>        # Stop execution at the line
stop in <func>        # Stop execution when <func> is called
When the specified event occurs, the process is stopped.
```

Note that a breakpoint can be set at any line or at the beginning of a function. The statement at a breakpoint is not executed unless the **cont**, **next**, or **step** command is invoked.

16.11.2   Using a Breakpoint

To identify a breakpoint, we need to list the program first. The **list** command displays the program source, which means the source file must be present in the same directory as the executable. Every invocation displays 10 lines, but **list** can also be used with a range (like **list 11 20**) to display any section of code:

```
(dbx) list 11 20
   11        n = 0;
   12
   13        printf("Enter a multiword string: ");
   14        fgets(buf, BUFSIZE, stdin);
   15
   16        clargs[0] = strtok(buf, DELIM);    /* first word */
   17        while ((clargs[n] = strtok(NULL, DELIM))  != NULL)
   18           n++;                            /* ... all words are extracted */
   19        clargs[n] = NULL;                  /* Set last pointer to NULL */
   20
```

Since the program didn't produce any output, we would first like it to stop at line 16 to evaluate the values of clargs[0] and buf. Let's set a breakpoint with **stop** and then run the program with **run**:

```
(dbx) stop at 16
(2) stop at "parsestring.c":16
(dbx) run
Running: a.out
(process id 1541)
Enter a multiword string: There is a fly in my soup
stopped in main at line 16 in file "parsestring.c"
   16        clargs[0] = strtok(buf, DELIM);    /* first word */
(dbx) _
```

You can now run the **where** and **whereami** commands to confirm this breakpoint. **where** indicates that we are currently stuck at the first breakpoint in line 16. **whereami** displays the line as well:

```
(dbx) where
=>[1] main(), line 16 in "parsestring.c"
(dbx) whereami
stopped in main at line 16 in file "parsestring.c"
   16        clargs[0] = strtok(buf, DELIM);    /* first word */
```

The **dump** command prints all variables visible in the current function, but you can also use the **print** command to view specific ones. We need to know the values of two variables:

```
(dbx) print buf
buf = "There is a fly in my soup\n"
(dbx) print clargs[0]
clargs[0] = (nil)
```

We can see that buf is assigned properly, but clargs[0] will be set only after the current line is executed. A **cont** statement will continue the program, but we prefer to move a line at a time.

16.11.3   Stepping Through the Program

Without arguments, the **next** and **step** commands let us single-step through our program. Let's move one line forward and have a look at clargs[0] again:

```
(dbx) step
stopped in main at line 17 in file "parsestring.c"
   17      while ((clargs[n] = strtok(NULL, DELIM)) != NULL)
(dbx) print clargs[0]
clargs[0] = 0xffbefae3 "There is a fly in my soup"
```

The value of clargs[0] should have been There; it's obvious that the first **strtok** call (at line 16) didn't do the job properly. Now use the **list 1 10** command to see the value of DELIM, and note that it doesn't include a space. We'll correct this later, but let's move on, one step at a time:

```
(dbx) step
stopped in main at line 19 in file "parsestring.c"
   19      clargs[n] = NULL;                    /* Set last pointer to NULL */
(dbx) step
stopped in main at line 21 in file "parsestring.c"
   21      for (i = 0; i <n ; i++)
```

Why did this loop not execute? Let's find out more about the variable n with the **whatis** and **which** commands:

```
(dbx) whatis n
int n;
(dbx) which n
`a.out`parsestring.c`main`n
(dbx) print n
n = 0
```

A hierarchy shows up in the **which** output. The variable n belongs to the **main** function, which is defined in **parsestring.c**, and which is the source for **a.out**. n was wrongly initialized to 0 when it should have been 1. We'll make the two changes in the source after we quit **dbx**, but in the next section, we'll also set n to 1 inside the debugger.

16.11.4 Making a Reassignment

We'll now use a helpful debugger feature to change the value of a variable without recompiling the program. This requires the **assign** command, so let's learn to use it before we run the program again with **rerun**:

```
(dbx) help assign
assign (command)
assign <var> = <exp>   # Assign the value of the <exp> to <var>
(dbx) rerun
Running: a.out
(process id 1542)
Enter a multiword string: gdb is a better debugger
stopped in main at line 16 in file "parsestring.c"
   16      clargs[0] =  strtok(buf,DELIM);    /* first word */
```

The program stops at the breakpoint defined earlier. Let's now assign 1 to n:

```
(dbx) print n
n = 0
(dbx) assign n = 1
(dbx) print n
n = 1
```

Now let's issue a series of **step** commands till we reach line 22:

```
(dbx) step
stopped in main at line 17 in file "parsestring.c"
   17      while ((clargs[n] = strtok(NULL, DELIM)) != NULL)
 ... more step commands ......
   22         printf("Argument %d is %s\n",i,  clargs[i]);
(dbx) step
Argument 0 is gdb is a better debugger
```

You can also use **step** *n* to execute *n* lines. The **for** loop has been executed once, but that is expected because the **while** loop was not executed at all. We now quit **dbx** with **quit**, and then make these changes to lines 5 and 11 with the **vi** or **emacs** editor:

```
#define DELIM " \n\t\r"                   Introduce a space before \n
n = 1;                                    Instead of n = 0;
```

Alternatively, we could have edited the source file itself with the **edit** command without leaving **dbx**. Don't forget to compile the program with the -g option of the compiler. When you trace the variable n (next topic), you'll find that both loops work properly.

16.11.5 Tracing a Variable

The **trace** command displays information about an event. It often produces a lot of output, but we can use **trace** selectively to trace a variable or a function. Enter the debugger once more with **dbx a.out** and find out how **trace** is used:

```
(dbx) help trace
trace at <line#>          # Trace given source line
trace in <func>           # Trace calls to and returns from the given function
trace change <var>        # Trace changes to the variable
When the specified event occurs, a "trace" is printed.
```

Let's now place a trace on the variable n. The next **run** command shows three iterations of the **while** loop and four of the **for** loop:

```
(dbx) trace change n
(2) trace change n -in main
(dbx) run
Running: a.out
(process id 1603)
initially (at line "parsestring.c":12): n = -4260708
after line "parsestring.c":11: n = 1
Enter a multiword string: But X/Open requires dbx
after line "parsestring.c":18: n = 2                        while loop
after line "parsestring.c":18: n = 3                        is executed
after line "parsestring.c":18: n = 4                        three times
Argument 0 is But                                           for loop
Argument 1 is X/Open                                        is executed
Argument 2 is requires                                      four
Argument 3 is dbx                                           times
execution completed, exit code is 1
(dbx) quit
$_
```

Now that both loops are working properly, you can run the program without using **dbx**. Once you are satisfied with the behavior of the program, recompile it without the -g option.

Before we close, let's briefly examine the other mode of this debugger. **dbx** can also work in post-mortem mode. When a program crashes, the operating system saves the memory image of the program at the time of the crash in a file named core. **dbx** can be used to analyze this file to determine the cause of the crash, often by identifying the signal that was generated at that time.

SUMMARY

A C program is *compiled* and *assembled* to create an object (.o) file and *linked* to create the executable. Object files should be retained for multisource programs to avoid recompilation of unchanged sources. Functions should be placed in separate files to be reusable.

make monitors the last modification times of the executable, object, source, and header files to determine the sources that need to be recompiled. It looks up a *makefile* for associating a *target* with a *dependency,* and then takes a defined action if the dependency is found to be newer than target.

The **ar** command combines a group of object files into a *static library* or *archive*. **make** can automatically recompile a module and replace it in the archive. A *shared library* or *shared object* is not linked to the executable but is loaded during runtime.

The *Source Code Control System (SCCS)* saves the first version in full and its differences with subsequent versions in an encoded *SCCS file*. A *delta* (version) is checked out (**get**) and checked in (**delta**) after editing. Revision of an intermediate version creates a *branch delta*. The **admin** command is used both for creation of an SCCS file and access control.

The *Revision Control System (RCS)* saves the latest *revision*. A revision is checked in with **ci** and checked out with **co**. The **rcs** command controls version locking, user access and is also used to remove versions.

dbx is used for analyzing core dumps and for debugging programs. You can set *breakpoints* (**stop**) and execute one statement at a time (**step**). A variable can be displayed (**print**) and reassigned in the debugger itself (**assign**). You can also trace a variable and display its value whenever it is encountered (**trace**). GNU **gdb** is also a powerful debugger.

SELF-TEST

16.1   Name the three phases a program has to go through before an executable is created from it.
16.2   Name the two commands invoked by the **cc** command to create an executable.
16.3   Place the function definitions of **arg_check** and **quit** *(16.1.1)* in a single file, **foo.c**. Can the main program, **rec_deposit** (in **rec_deposit.c**), access them?
16.4   Why does a static library have the **lib** prefix? What suffix does it have? Where are the system's library and include files available?
16.5   The command **cc -c foo.c** compiles without error. Explain why **make** could still generate an error with a makefile that contains the following entry:

```
foo.o: foo.c
      cc -c foo.c
```

16.6   How is **libc.a** different from other libraries?
16.7   Mention two advantages a shared library has over a static library.
16.8   Create a file **foo** containing a line of text. Mention the commands needed to (i) create the SCCS file for **foo**, (ii) check out an editable version of **foo**, (iii) check in **foo** after editing.
16.9   Look up the man page of **sccsdiff**, and then create two deltas of a file. How will you use the command to display their differences?
16.10 Why do we enter comments when using the **delta** command? How can we see them?
16.11 Explain when you need to create a branch delta. Is 1.2.1 a branch delta?

EXERCISES

16.1   How does an executable C program differ from its associated object files?
16.2   It makes no sense to save object files if other programs are not going to use them. Right or wrong?

16.3   Explain the significance of the -c, -o, -l, and -g options of the C compiler.

16.4   Modify the application presented in Section 16.1.2 to implement the following:

  (i)   The **compute** function should be in a separate file, **compute.c**, and its **include** statement in **compute.h**.
  (ii) All function prototypes should be defined in a single file, **prototype.h**.

  Modify makefile2 discussed in Section 16.2.2 accordingly.

16.5   Look up the man page of **make** to find out how it can be invoked to display the command line that it would execute without actually executing it.

16.6   Explain how **make** may run without error with a makefile that contains only the following entry. What command will it run?

```
foo:
```

16.7   A **make** rule doesn't always have a dependency, and the target need not be a disk file. Explain with an example of a makefile entry.

16.8   Specify the commands that will (i) create an archive named **foobar.a** containing the object files **foo1.o** and **foo2.o**, (ii) delete **foo2.o** from the archive. Can this archive be used with the -l option to **cc**?

16.9   What does this entry in a makefile mean? What command does **make** run if **a.h** is modified?

```
foo.a(a.o): a.h
```

16.10 SCCS and RCS basically use the same mechanism to store file versions, but they work in opposite directions. Explain. Which system do you think reconstructs a version faster?

16.11 You have three versions of a program named **foo1.c**, **foo2.c**, and **foo3.c**. Mention the steps needed to check in all three versions to a single SCCS file.

16.12 Mention the set of commands that produce the deltas 1.1, 1.2, 1.3, and 1.2.1.1 of **foo.c**. Now use **get -r9 s.foo.c** and **get -e -r9 s.foo.c**. What do you observe?

16.13 Which file does **sact** obtain activity information from? When is the file created and deleted?

16.14 You checked out a delta with **get -e s.foo.c** and then realized that you shouldn't have done so. What should you do now and why?

## CHAPTER 17

Systems Programming I—Files

You now know quite well what UNIX applications have to offer. However, because UNIX is written in C, some questions are inescapable: How can we write some of these applications ourselves? What functions are available to a C programmer for determining a file's attributes or for forking a process? The answers to these questions lie in the system call library available to a C programmer using UNIX. For many, the real charm of UNIX lies in using these system calls to develop useful tools.

In this chapter and Chapter 18, we examine the essential system calls that support the UNIX system. We also examine some internals—mostly featured in insets—that need to be well understood by a UNIX programmer. This chapter takes up the system calls associated with the file system; Chapter 18 does the same for processes. The file-related system calls are organized in three categories—those related to I/O, directories, and attributes. In some cases, we are forced to discuss and use some library functions as well.

Objectives

- Understand the basics of *system calls* and *library functions*.
- Learn how system call errors are handled and reported with errno and **perror**.
- Perform file I/O with **open**, **read**, **write**, **lseek**, and **close**, using a *file descriptor*.
- Learn why it is important to properly set the size of the buffer used by **read** and **write**.
- Navigate a directory structure with **chdir** and **getcwd**.
- Read directory entries with **opendir** and **readdir**, and examine the dirent structure.
- Handle hard and symlinks using the **link**, **symlink**, and **unlink** calls.
- Understand the consequences of unlinking an open file.
- Discover the combined role of the stat structure and **stat** calls in retrieving inode information.
- Determine the file type using S_IFMT and the S_IS*xxx* macros.
- Test each permission bit using symbolic constants.
- Use **access** to test a file's access rights.
- Use other system calls to change a file's permissions, ownership, and time stamps.

17.1 System Call Basics

A **system call** is a routine that can be invoked from a C program to access a system resource. System calls are used to perform file I/O, allocate memory, create processes, and so forth. Unlike the standard ANSI C library functions like **fopen** and **printf** that are available as object modules bundled into an archive, system calls are built into the kernel. They are often written in assembly language but provide a C-like function interface so we can invoke them as functions from a C program running on UNIX.

Normally, a process run by a user has access to its own memory address space and can execute a restricted set of machine instructions. The process is then said to run in **user mode**. However, when the process invokes a system call, the CPU switches from user mode to a more privileged mode—the **kernel mode** (*supervisory mode* in operating system parlance). In this mode, the kernel runs on behalf of the user, has access to any memory location and can execute any machine instruction. After the system call returns, the CPU switches back to user mode.

All UNIX systems offer around 200 system calls that are internally used by native applications like **cat** and **grep**. Redirection and pipelines are also implemented by using system calls. They are very well explained in Section 2 of the man documentation. POSIX specifies the functionality of a set of calls that an operating system must offer to be branded as UNIX. Many commands and system calls share the same name; the **chmod** command invokes the **chmod** system call.

17.1.1   Anatomy of a System Call

Irrespective of the way they are implemented, for all practical purposes system calls behave like C functions. They accept arguments of all types (int, char, void, etc.) and return values as can be seen from this prototype declaration of the **write** system call:

```
ssize_t write(int fd, const void *buf, size_t count);
```

In addition to the primitive types, you'll see derived types (like size_t) used by system calls. C uses derived types for many functions to let the compiler decide which primitive types to map them to. For instance, size_t and ssize_t could ultimately be typedef'd to unsigned int and int, respectively on one machine and unsigned long and long on another.

ANSI C introduced the concept of a generic data type named void, and many system calls (like **write**) use this data type. In the prototype for **write** shown above, void *buf* signifies a generic buffer which can represent char *buf, int *buf, etc. We don't need to cast this generic buffer to the type that we actually use in our program.

Unlike library functions that often return NULL on error, system calls generally return -1. We must check every system call for a negative return value unless the system call itself can never return an error (like **umask**) or not return at all (like the *exec* functions).

17.1.2   System Calls vs. Library Functions

From one standpoint, system calls offer a high-level interface that let us ignore the internals of a device. On the other hand, they are low-level interfaces that have to be used judiciously. Consider the **read** system call that reads a block of data at a time. To read a line using **read**, you need to write additional code. And this is where system calls *could* be inefficient.

Enter library functions. Every C compiler (on UNIX and non-UNIX systems alike) is shipped with a set of the **standard library functions**. On UNIX systems, these library functions serve as wrappers of system calls. The standard library offers separate functions to read a block of data (**fread**), a line (**fgets**), and a single character (**fgetc**). Even though these functions internally invoke the **read** system call, we generally use these wrapper functions for the convenient interfaces they offer.

However, library functions often don't provide the finer control features offered by system calls. For instance, **fopen** can't set file permissions in **chmod**-style which **open** does easily. You can know the size of a file only by using the **stat** system call. Further, a process can be created only with the **fork** system call.

There are significant overheads associated with system calls and their related mode switches (user mode to kernel mode, and vice versa). If you need to use system calls in your program, make sure that they are invoked the minimum number of times. This is not a problem with library functions because they are designed to make the right number of invocations.

Note

The man documentation features system calls and library functions in Sections 2 and 3, respectively. Sometimes, the same name represents both a UNIX command and a system call (like **read**, **write**, and **exec**), so calling man without the section number could display the wrong man page. (**man read** shows the man page for the shell's built-in **read** command.) You must use **man 2 read** or **man -s2 read** to display the documentation for the **read** system call.

17.2   errno **and** perror: **Handling Errors**

Errors can occur for a host of reasons—a resource not available, the receipt of a signal, I/O operational failures, or invalid call arguments. A system call returns -1 on error, so to create robust code, we should always check for this condition (unless we are certain that this check isn't really necessary).

When a system call returns -1, the kernel sets the static (global) variable, errno, to a positive integer. This integer, represented by a symbolic constant, is associated with an error message. For instance, ENOENT has the value 2 and signifies No such file or directory. There are two things we can do when an error occurs:

- Use **perror** to print the error message associated with errno.
- Determine the cause of the error by checking errno.

We use **perror** only when a system call returns an error. The function follows this syntax:

```
void perror(const char *s);
```

The function takes a character string, *s*, as argument and prints the string, a colon, and a space followed by the message associated with errno. We demonstrate the use of errno and **perror** in the program, **show_errors.c** (Fig. 17.1), by trying to open a file which either doesn't exist or is not readable.

This is the simplest syntax of the **open** system call, one that opens a file in read-only mode. If **open** returns -1, the program uses **fprintf** to print the value of errno and **perror** to display its associated message—both to the standard error. Now run the program with two filenames that are guaranteed to return an error:

TABLE 17.1 *Significance of Symbolic Constants Associated with* errno

Symbolic Constant	errno	Message
EPERM	1	Operation not permitted
ENOENT	2	No such file or directory
ESRCH	3	No such process
EINTR	4	Interrupted system call
EIO	5	I/O error
EACCES	13	Permission denied
EEXIST	17	File exists
ENOTDIR	20	Not a directory
EISDIR	21	Is a directory
ENOSPC	28	No space left on device
ESPIPE	29	Illegal seek
EROFS	30	Read only file system

FIGURE 17.1 `show_errors.c`

```
/* Program: show_errors.c -- Displaying system call errors with perror
                             Filename provided as argument */
#include <fcntl.h>                    /* For O_RDONLY in open */
#include <stdio.h>                    /* For stderr in fprintf */
#include <sys/errno.h>                /* For errno */

int main (int argc, char **argv) {
    if (open(argv[1], O_RDONLY) == -1) {  /* Opening in read-only mode */
        fprintf(stderr, "errno = %d\n", errno);
        perror("open");
        exit(0);
    }
}
```

```
$ a.out foofoo
errno = 2                                              This is ENOENT
open: No such file or directory
$ a.out /etc/shadow
errno = 13                                             This is EACCES
open: Permission denied
```

These error numbers are associated with symbolic constants defined in `<sys/errno.h>`, and a subset is shown in Table 17.1. Program flow is often dependent on the cause of the error, so we should check the value of errno to determine what action to take.

Caution

You must check the value of errno *immediately* after a system call returns an error, and before you do anything else. The behavior of errno in the event of a successful call is undefined. Some systems leave it unchanged, but some don't. If necessary, save the value of errno in a separate variable if you need this value later in your program.

17.3 open: **Opening and Creating a File**

We begin our discussion on system calls with the ones related to file I/O. These comprise the following calls:

- **open** and **close**
- **read** and **write**
- **lseek**
- **truncate** and **ftruncate**

A file needs to be opened with **open** before one can read or write it. **open** has two forms: the first form assumes that the file exists, and the second one creates it if it doesn't. Both forms are represented by this syntax:

```
int open(const char *path, int oflag, ... );
```

open returns a **file descriptor** as an int, the lowest number available for allocation. This number is subsequently used by other calls for identifying the file. Normally, the first **open** in your program should return file descriptor 3 (since the first three are allocated to the shell's standard streams). On error, **open** returns -1.

The first argument (*path*) is a pointer to a character string that represents the file's pathname (either absolute or relative). The second argument (*oflag*) is used to set the **mode of opening** (read, write, or read-write), which is conveniently represented by three symbolic constants. Only one of the following modes must be specified with **open**:

O_RDONLY	Opens file for reading.
O_WRONLY	Opens file for writing.
O_RDWR	Opens file for reading and writing.

These constants are defined in the file fcntl.h in /usr/include, so you need to place the statement #include <fcntl.h> at the top of your program. This is how we open a file in read-only mode:

```
int fd;                                                    The file descriptor
if ((fd = open("/etc/passwd", O_RDONLY)) == -1) {
    perror("open");                                        Use our quit function
    exit(1);
}
```

This is typically the way you invoke a system call: Check its return value for -1 and then use **perror** to print a message corresponding to the error. For many examples in this chapter and the next, we'll work with a modified version of the **quit** function shown in Fig. 16.3. Replace the **fprintf** statement there with perror(**message**); and then create the object file by using **cc -c quit.c**. Now that the file has been opened, other system calls can access this file by fd, the file descriptor.

The previous **open** call also sets the **file offset pointer** to the beginning of the file. This pointer determines where in the file the subsequent read will take place. When writing files, you need to provide more parameters to **open**. In fact, for added functionality, you need to use one or more of the following **status flags** (also defined in fcntl.h) as components of *oflag*:

O_APPEND   Opens file in append mode (only if file opening mode is O_WRONLY or O_RDWR).
O_TRUNC   Truncates file to zero length (same conditions as above).
O_CREAT   Creates file if it doesn't exist.
O_EXCL   Generates an error if O_CREAT is also specified and the file also exists.
O_SYNC   Synchronizes read-write operations. Ensures that **write** doesn't return until the data is written to disk (explained later).

These status flags are used with the bit-wise OR operator, |, along with the mode of opening. Here are two ways of opening a file for writing; this time, we don't use error checking code:

```
fd = open("foo.txt", O_WRONLY | O_APPEND) ;          Similar to shell's >>
fd = open("../foo.txt", O_WRONLY | O_TRUNC) ;          Similar to >
```

The first call opens foo.txt for appending (O_APPEND), which sets the offset pointer to EOF. A subsequent **write** call here doesn't overwrite this file but increases its size. The second call truncates a file's contents (O_TRUNC) and positions the offset pointer at the beginning.

If the file doesn't exist, then you need to create it using O_CREAT (and sometimes, O_EXCL also) and specify its permissions as the third argument. The permissions can be represented in **chmod**-style (except that you have to use a zero prefix if you use octal numbers, like 0644 instead of 644). However, you are advised to use the symbolic constants provided in sys/stat.h, and they are displayed below in tabular form:

Permission	User	Group	Others	All
Read	S_IRUSR	S_IRGRP	S_IROTH	S_IRWXU
Write	S_IWUSR	S_IWGRP	S_IWOTH	S_IRWXG
Execute	S_IXUSR	S_IXGRP	S_IXOTH	S_IRWXO

Since each permission is represented by a separate bit, you need to OR these constants (bit-wise) to obtain the desired permissions. For instance, 0644 is the same as:

```
S_IRUSR | S_IWUSR | S_IRGRP | S_IROTH
```

Let's now open a file for writing after truncation (O_TRUNC) and also ensure that the file is created if it doesn't exist (O_CREAT). We need to specify the permissions as the third argument:

```
fd = open("foo.txt", O_WRONLY | O_CREAT | O_TRUNC,
          S_IRUSR | S_IWUSR | S_IRGRP | S_IROTH) ;     Permissions are 0644
```

Note that the actual permissions will be reduced by the umask value, and this can be set in your program with the **umask** system call *(17.10)*.

The status flag, O_EXCL, provides protection from overwriting an existing file. If used at all, then it must be combined with O_CREAT (O_CREAT | O_EXCL). **open** will then return -1 if the file exists. We can use this mechanism to test for the existence of a file.

Caution

If you are using numbers (like 644) rather than the symbolic constants to represent the permissions, don't forget to prefix a 0 to the number. You have to take care of this when using the **chmod** system call as well.

Tip

The O_EXCL feature comes in handy when you devise a scheme to let two processes share a file, foo, in a cooperative manner. To make the scheme work as an *advisory* form of file locking, both programs must agree to first create a lock file (with the same name) before they write to foo, and then remove the lock file when they are done with foo. If all cooperating programs use the O_EXCL flag in their **open** calls that attempt to create the lock file, the first **open** will succeed and the others will fail. Adherence to this agreement ensures that a file is not written simultaneously by two or more processes.

17.4   close: **Closing a File**

A program automatically closes all open files before termination, but it's good practice to close them explicitly when you no longer require them. The **close** system call closes a file:

```
int close(int fd);
```

close returns 0 if successful and -1 otherwise. It actually deallocates the file descriptor for that process and makes it available for the next **open** (if there is one).

Multiple processes may open the same file, so there are a number of things you need to note about **open** and **close**:

- When a file foo is opened by two processes A and B (or by two **open** calls in the same program), the kernel simply assigns two separate file descriptors for them. The file foo can be accessed independently by each descriptor.
- Closing foo in process A simply releases the descriptor for process A; process B would still find foo open. The file can be deleted only when all its descriptors are deallocated.
- You can close any of the standard streams explicitly in your program. You can use **close(1);** to close the standard output file and then open a disk file to return 1 as the descriptor value. (Disk file as standard output!)

How all this happens will be taken up in Chapter 18 with reference to three tables that the kernel maintains in memory for every open file. We'll also learn to close the standard input and output files to implement redirection.

17.5   read: **Reading a File**

Two system calls—**read** and **write**—handle all read-write operations on a regular file (as well as pipes and sockets). Both calls share a similar syntax that makes use of a user-defined buffer. **read** accesses a file with the file descriptor returned by a prior **open**:

```
ssize_t read(int fildes, void *buf, size_t nbyte);
```

read attempts to read *nbyte* characters from the file descriptor *fildes* into the buffer *buf*. This buffer represents a pointer to a generic buffer (which could be any of the primitive data types, often char). *nbyte* is generally the size of the buffer itself. This is how you read 4096 bytes with every **read** invocation:

```
#define BUFSIZE 4096
int n;
char buf[BUFSIZE];
while ((n = read(fd, buf, BUFSIZE)) > 0)              fd obtained from a prior open
```

read returns the number of characters read till it encounters EOF, when it returns 0. When used in a loop to read an entire file, the number read is generally equal to the number requested in every iteration except probably the last one, when **read** returns the number of characters *left to read* (since the file size may not be an exact multiple of the buffer size). On error, **read** returns -1.

If you have to process every character you read, declare *buf* as a char variable and then pass its address to **read**:

```
int fd, n; char buf ;
while ((n = read (fd, &buf, 1)) > 0)                 fd obtained from a prior open
```

Reading 100 characters with a single character buffer (as above) would require 100 system call invocations, which is rather expensive. A library function like **fgetc** would be a better choice here.

17.6 write: **Writing a File**

The **write** call writes a file descriptor obtained with **open**. The prototype declaration of **write** is virtually identical to that of **read**:

```
ssize_t write( int fildes, const void *buf, size_t nbyte);
```

Each invocation of **write** writes *nbyte* number of bytes from *buf* to the file descriptor *filedes*. **write** returns the number of characters written, which *must* be equal to the number requested. However, if the disk fills up while a **write** is in progress or if the file size exceeds the system's limit, **write** returns -1.

For writing data in blocks of, say, 8192 bytes, buf should be declared as a character array for holding that many characters, and **write**'s third argument should represent the size of this array:

```
#define BUFSIZE 8192
int n; char buf[BUFSIZE];
n = write(fd, buf, BUFSIZE));
```

As in **read**, you can write one character at a time, in which case you should declare buf as a char variable:

```
char buf ;
write(fd, &buf, 1));                                 fd obtained from a prior open
```

The buffer size for both **read** and **write** is determined by the device written to (terminal, hard disk, etc.) and the size of the kernel buffer maintained in memory. This is an important issue and will be discussed in Section 17.9.

Note

When reading and writing the standard streams, we should use the symbolic constants, STDIN_FILENO, STDOUT_FILENO, and STDERR_FILENO as the file descriptors rather than the integers, 0, 1, and 2, that they represent. These symbolic constants are defined in unistd.h.

17.7 ccp.c: **Copying a File**

This program, **ccp.c** (Fig. 17.2), copies /etc/passwd to passwd.bak. The source file is opened in read-only mode (O_RDONLY). The destination file is opened in the write mode

FIGURE 17.2 ccp.c

```c
/* Program: ccp.c -- Copies a file with the read and write system calls */

#include <fcntl.h>              /* For O_RDONLY, O_WRONLY, O_CREAT etc. */
#include <sys/stat.h>           /* For S_IRUSR, S_IWUSR, S_IRGRP etc. */
#define BUFSIZE 1024            /* May not be the right size here */

int main(void) {
    int fd1, fd2;              /* File descriptors for read and write */
    int n;                     /* Number of characters returned by read */
    char buf[BUFSIZE];         /* Size of buffer used by read and write */

    if ((fd1 = open("/etc/passwd", O_RDONLY)) == -1)
        quit("open", 1);

    if ((fd2 = open("passwd.bak", O_WRONLY | O_CREAT | O_TRUNC,
            S_IRUSR | S_IWUSR | S_IRGRP |S_IWGRP | S_IROTH)) == -1)
        quit("open2", 2);

    while ((n = read(fd1, buf, BUFSIZE)) > 0) /* Return value of read */
        if (n != write(fd2, buf, n))           /* is used by write */
        quit("write", 3) ;

    close(fd1);
    close(fd2);

    exit(0);                   /* This would have closed all file descriptors */
}
```

(O_WRONLY), is created if it doesn't exist (O_CREAT), and truncated if it does (O_TRUNC). Each **open** returns a file descriptor which should have the values 3 and 4 in this program.

For copying operations, both **read** and **write** need to use the same buffer. We set up a loop that attempts to read 1024 bytes into buf (an array of 1024 characters) from the descriptor fd1. The return value of **read** is next used by **write** to write the same number of characters to descriptor fd2. The loop terminates when **read** returns 0 (on EOF).

The program checks for errors in **open** and **write** (but not in **read!**). It also uses the **quit** function that we developed in Section 16.1.1 and modified in Section 17.3 to handle errors. After compiling the program, run **a.out** and then invoke **cmp** to confirm the faithfulness of the copy:

```
$ cc ccp.c quit.o                              Create quit.o using cc -c quit.c
$ a.out
$ cmp /etc/passwd passwd.bak
$ _                                            Prompt returns—files identical
```

You need not always write data to disk; you can write to the standard output also. So if we replace fd2 in the **write** statement with 1 (rather, STDOUT_FILENO), we can use the program as a simple **cat** command. The second **open** and **close** calls won't then be required.

File Descriptors and File Pointers

The library function **fopen** doesn't return a file descriptor, but a pointer to a FILE structure. The other functions like **fread** and **fwrite** access the file through this pointer. Beneath the hood, these functions actually run the corresponding system calls, **open**, **read**, and **write**, and the file descriptor is embedded in the FILE structure as a separate member.

Sometimes, you need to take advantage of both worlds. You generated a file descriptor with **open**, possibly to set its permissions to 755, but now want to read a line at a time using **fgets** (a library function). To do that, simply convert the file descriptor to a file pointer with the **fdopen** function. Conversely, if you opened a file with **fopen** and now want to run **stat** to obtain the file's size, use the **fileno** function to convert the file pointer to a descriptor:

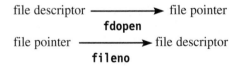

Because of the different ways library functions and system calls handle buffering, intermingling descriptors and pointers when performing I/O is not recommended. But in some cases, you just won't have a choice. If you have opened a file in the parent process, the child process can only access the file descriptor. The child inherits all descriptors but not FILE pointers.

17.8   lseek: **Positioning the Offset Pointer**

lseek doesn't do any physical I/O. It simply moves the file offset pointer to a specified point where the next I/O operation will take place. Here's its syntax:

```
off_t lseek(int fildes, off_t offset, int whence);
```

The *offset* and *whence* arguments together control the location of the file's offset pointer. *offset* signifies the position (positive or negative) of this pointer relative to *whence*, which can take one of three values:

SEEK_SET   Offset pointer set to beginning of file.
SEEK_END   Offset pointer set to end of file.
SEEK_CUR   Offset pointer remains at current location.

With some restrictions, *offset* can be a positive or negative integer, so it is represented by a signed data type. For instance,

```
lseek(fd, 10, SEEK_CUR)                                    fd obtained from prior open
```

moves the pointer forward by 10 characters from its current position, and

```
lseek(fd, -10, SEEK_END)                                              Negative offset
```

sets the pointer 10 characters before EOF. You can't have a negative *offset* with *whence* set to SEEK_SET, but strangely enough you can have a positive *offset* with *whence* at SEEK_END. In this case, the pointer moves beyond EOF, thus creating a *sparse* file—also called a file with a "hole." Sparse files find use in database applications, but our next program also moves the offset pointer beyond EOF.

lseek returns the position of the pointer in bytes from the beginning of the file. This value can be used to determine the size of the file:

```
size = lseek(fd, 0, SEEK_END);                                This returns the file size
```

Unlike **read** and **write**, which work with practically all file types, **lseek** works only with those files that are capable of "seeking." It doesn't work with the terminal file or with a socket or pipe, and is mainly used for disk files.

Note

There are two ways of appending data to a file. You can use **open** with the O_APPEND status flag which positions the file's offset pointer to EOF. Alternatively, you can use **open** (without the flag) followed by **lseek(fd, 0, SEEK_END)**. The former technique represents an *atomic operation* *(see inset)* and is recommended for use, but not the latter.

> ### *Atomic Operations*
> When you program in a multiprogramming environment like UNIX, there's one thing that you have to keep in mind at all times: Multiple processes can contend for a single resource—like a file. These resources must be shared without causing conflict. Wherever possible, you need to take care that certain critical operations are performed in an *atomic* manner.

> An **atomic operation** comprises multiple actions that are either performed in their entirety or not at all. Using two system calls in succession can't be an atomic operation because that allows a second process to run in between. The UNIX system uses atomicity wherever possible. The deletion of a directory entry and the corresponding modification of the inode entry must be performed atomically.
>
> You too must take care of atomicity in your programs. For instance, the check for the existence of the file with O_EXCL and then creating it with O_CREAT must be performed as a single operation. Otherwise, another process could create the file in between and write some data to it. We no longer use the **creat** system call to create a file because we would still need **open** to check for its existence first, and that would make the operation nonatomic.

17.8.1   reverse_read.c: Reading a File in Reverse

You can't read a file from the end to the beginning using the standard UNIX utilities (except **perl**), but using **lseek** in a C program, **reverse_read.c** (Fig. 17.3), you can. You have to first move the file pointer to one character beyond EOF. Then use a loop to move the pointer back by two positions every time a character is read.

Unlike in **ccp.c**, where we picked up data in chunks, this application requires us to read one character at a time. Hence, we use a single-character buffer with **read** and **write**. While **read** advances the pointer one byte forward, the next **lseek** takes it back by two bytes.

The program accepts the input filename as argument and writes to the standard output. We make use of two functions, **quit** and **arg_check** (defined in Fig. 16.2), and the first two invocations of **a.out** actually call them:

```
$ a.out
Not enough arguments                                        From quit
$ a.out /etc/host.equiv
open: No such file or directory                             From arg_check
$ a.out /etc/hosts.equiv
... A blank line ...                      The terminating \n of the last line
retipuj                                        This is jupiter in reverse
yrucrem                                                          mercury
htrae                                                              earth
nrutas                                                            saturn
```

This program has serious drawbacks. If it is used to read a file having 100,000 bytes, it would require 300,000 system call invocations (for **read**, **write**, and **lseek**). The program would then take a long time to complete. This is where system calls should be avoided; you must use library functions. (See next inset.)

FIGURE 17.3 `reverse_read.c`

```
/* Program: reverse_read.c -- Reads a file in reverse - uses error handling  */


#include <fcntl.h>
#include <unistd.h>                              /* For STDOUT_FILENO */
#include <stdio.h>


int main(int argc, char **argv) {
    int size, fd;
    char buf;                                    /* Single-character buffer */
    char *mesg = "Single filename required\n";


    arg_check(2, argc, mesg, 1) ;


    if ((fd = open(argv[1], O_RDONLY)) == -1)
        quit("open", 2);


    lseek(fd, 1, SEEK_END);                /* Pointer taken to EOF + 1 first */


    while (lseek(fd, -2, SEEK_CUR) >= 0) {   /* and then back by two bytes */
        if (read(fd, &buf, 1) != 1)
            quit("read", 1);
        if (write(STDOUT_FILENO, &buf, 1) != 1)
            quit("write", 1);
    }
    close(fd);                 /* Can have error here too */
    exit(0);                   /* exit doesn't return - hence no error */
}
```

17.9   truncate **and** ftruncate: **Truncating a File**

The O_TRUNC flag used with **open** truncates a file to zero bytes, but the **truncate** and **ftruncate** calls can truncate a file to any length. One of them doesn't need to open the file either:

```
int truncate(const char *path, off_t length);
int ftruncate(int fildes, off_t length);
```

truncate needs the pathname (*path*) as argument, but **ftruncate** works with the file descriptor (*fildes*). Both truncate the file to *length* bytes. These calls are often used in combination with **lseek** to overwrite a certain segment of a file. Truncate a file to any desired length, and then use **lseek** to take the pointer to the location of truncation so that you can start writing from there.

Note

Many of the system calls discussed in this chapter have two, and sometimes, three versions. There's a "normal" version (like **truncate**) that uses the pathname, and a "f"-prefixed version (like **ftruncate**) that uses the file descriptor as argument. You can use either version if the file is open, but only the normal version if the file is not.

Buffered and Unbuffered I/O

To appreciate the debate that concerns system calls and library functions, you need to know something about the way disk I/O actually takes place. The **read** and **write** calls never access the disk directly. Rather, they read and write a pool of kernel buffers, called the **buffer cache** *(19.7.1)*. If the buffer is found to be empty during a read, the kernel instructs the disk controller to read data from disk and fill up the cache. **read blocks** (waits) while the disk is being read and the process even relinquishes control of the CPU.

To ensure that a single invocation of **read** gathers all bytes stored in the kernel buffer, the size of the latter and buffer used by **read** (char buf[BUFSIZE] in a previous example) should be equal. Improper setting of the buffer size can make your program inefficient. So if each kernel buffer stores 8192 bytes, then BUFSIZE should also be set to 8192. A smaller figure makes I/O inefficient, but a larger figure doesn't improve performance.

write also uses the buffer cache, but it differs from **read** in one way: it returns *immediately* after the call is invoked. The kernel writes the buffer to disk later at a convenient time. Database applications often can't accept this behavior, in which case you should open a file with the O_SYNC status flag to ensure that **write** doesn't return until the kernel has finally written the buffer to disk.

Unlike the standard library functions, the **read** and **write** calls are unbuffered when they interact with the terminal. When you use **write** to output a string to the terminal, the string appears on your display as soon as the call is invoked. On the other hand, the standard library functions (like **printf**) are line-buffered when they access the terminal. That means a string is printed on the terminal only when the newline character is encountered.

The size of the kernel buffer is system-dependent and is set at the time of installation of the operating system. To develop portable and optimized applications, you must not use a feature that is system-dependent. You can't arbitrarily set BUFSIZE to 8192. This is where library functions come in.

The I/O-bound library functions use a buffer in the FILE structure and adjust its size *dynamically* during runtime using **malloc**. Unless you are using system calls for their exclusive features, it makes sense to use library functions on most occasions. The previous program, **reverse_read.c**, is terribly inefficient as it uses single-character buffers. We should have used library functions there.

17.10   umask: **Modifying File Permissions During Creation**

The permissions specified with **open** (when used with O_CREAT) are modified by the shell's umask value. This mask reduces the default file and directory permissions (666 and 777, respectively) by the value of the mask *(4.5)*. The **umask** system call sets the mask to the value specified as argument:

```
mode_t umask(mode_t cmask);
```

umask returns the previous value of the mask. Unlike the shell's **umask** statement, however, *the* **umask** *system call can't display the current value of the mask without changing it.* To use a workaround, store the current mask by changing it to some arbitrary value, and then display it before restoring it. In our next program, **umask.c** (Fig. 17.4), we change the mask, print its old value, and then create two files with two different settings of the mask.

We first set the mask to 0 and save its previous value in old_mode. After printing the previous value of the mask, we create a file with permissions 777. Next, we restore the old mask and then create another file with permissions 764. The output makes for some interesting reading:

```
$ a.out
Previous umask value: 22
$ ls -l foo?
-rwxrwxrwx  1 sumit    sumit         0 Dec  1 12:01 foo1
-rwxr--r--  1 sumit    sumit         0 Dec  1 12:01 foo2
```

FIGURE 17.4   umask.c

```c
/* Program: umask.c -- Changes umask twice and checks effect on permissions */

#include <stdio.h>
#include <fcntl.h>

int main(void) {
   mode_t old_mode;

   old_mode = umask(0);                      /* No mask */
   printf("Previous umask value: %o\n", old_mode);

   open("foo1", O_RDONLY | O_CREAT, 0777);   /* Create file using new mask */
   umask(old_mode);                          /* Revert to previous mask */
   open("foo2", O_RDWR | O_CREAT, 0764);     /* Create file using old mask */
   exit(0);
}
```

Note that we created a file with all permissions; this is something we can't do from the shell. The permissions of foo2 are 744, which isn't what you get when you subtract 022 from 764. A umask value of 022 indicates that a file will be created with the write permission bit absent for group and others. A simple arithmetic subtraction (764–022) would result in write permission for others—something that wasn't intended!

Note

The restrictions placed by **umask** in no way affect our ability to change the permissions later with the **chmod** system call. **chmod** is taken up in Section 17.16.1.

17.11   Directory Navigation

We now move on to the directory, first to navigate to it and then to read its entries. There are two system calls that perform the action of the **cd** command. They are **chdir** and **fchdir**, which use a pathname and a file descriptor, respectively, as argument:

```
int chdir(const char *path);
int fchdir(int fildes);
```

The current directory is obtained by the **getcwd** library function. Some UNIX systems feature other functions (like **getwd**), but POSIX recommends the use of **getcwd**:

```
extern char *getcwd(char *buf, size_t size);
```

Here, *buf* is defined as a character array of *size* bytes. After invocation of **getcwd**, the pathname of the current directory is made available in *buf*.

The next program, **dir.c** (Fig. 17.5), uses **chdir** to switch to a directory. It also invokes **getcwd** to obtain the pathname of the current directory, both before and after the switch. The buffers that store the directory pathnames are provided with one extra slot for storing the NULL character.

Let's now switch to the directory /usr/include/sys. The program prints the current directory both before and after the switch:

```
$ a.out /usr/include/sys
pwd: /users1/home/staff/sumit
cd: /usr/include/sys
pwd: /usr/include/sys                          Change of directory inside program . . .
$ pwd
/users1/home/staff/sumit                            . . . is not available outside it
```

After completion of the program, we also ran the shell's **pwd** command. As explained previously *(8.6.1),* a change of environment inside a program is not available outside it.

FIGURE 17.5   dir.c

```
/* Program: dir.c -- Directory navigation with chdir and getcwd */

#include <stdio.h>
#define PATH_LENGTH 200

int main(int argc, char **argv) {
    char olddir[PATH_LENGTH + 1];              /* Extra character for NULL */
    char newdir[PATH_LENGTH + 1];

    if (getcwd(olddir, PATH_LENGTH) == -1)     /* Get current directory */
        quit("getcwd", 1);

    printf("pwd: %s\n", olddir);

    arg_check(2, argc, "Specify a directory\n", 1) ;

    if ((chdir(argv[1]) == -1))                /* Change to another directory */
        quit("chdir", 2);
    printf("cd: %s\n", argv[1]);

    getcwd(newdir, PATH_LENGTH);               /* Get new directory */
    printf("pwd: %s\n", newdir);

    exit(0);
}
```

17.12   Reading a Directory

Directories are also files, and they can be opened, read, and written in the same way as regular files. The format of a directory is not consistent across file systems—and even across different flavors of UNIX. Using **open** and **read** to list directory entries can be a grueling task. UNIX offers a number of library functions to handle a directory:

```
DIR *opendir(const char *dirname);                          Opens a directory
struct dirent *readdir(DIR *dirp);                          Reads a directory
int closedir(DIR *dirp);                                    Closes a directory
```

Note that we can't *directly* write a directory; only the kernel can do that. These three functions take on the role of the **open**, **read**, and **close** system calls as applied to ordinary files. As library functions, they encapsulate the file descriptors they actually work with. **opendir** understands *dirname* as the pathname and returns a pointer to a DIR structure (whose structure need not bother us). The other two functions use the address of this structure as argument.

A directory maintains the inode number and filename for every file in its fold. Expectedly, these two parameters are members of the dirent structure that is returned by **readdir**. Every invocation of **readdir** fills up this structure with information related to the next directory entry (i.e., the next filename). POSIX requires the dirent structure (defined in <dirent.h>) to provide at least these two members:

```
struct dirent {
    ino_t   d_ino                              Inode number
    char    d_name[]                           Directory name
};
```

Both Solaris and Linux have at least two more members (signifying the record length and the offset of the directory entry), but we'll ignore them to keep our programs portable. UNIX systems usually have the upper limit for d_name[] set to 256, so filenames can't exceed 255 characters (one element of the array to be reserved for the terminating NULL).

17.12.1 lls.c: Listing Filenames in a Directory

Let's now use the three functions and the dirent structure in out next program, **lls.c** (Fig. 17.6), to list for every file in a directory, its inode number and filename.

We first define two pointers of type DIR and struct dirent. The **opendir** call returns the pointer dir of type DIR, and **readdir** uses this pointer to return another pointer, direntry of type struct dirent. The members of this structure are accessed using the pointer notation ->. The partial output of the program shows the inode number and name of all files in the root directory:

```
$ a.out /
     2 .                                    Program shows hidden files also
     2 ..
  6784 usr
 13568 var
 20352 export
 54272 etc
 67840 dev
     5 lib
407040 sbin
  . . . . . .
```

This is how **ls -ia /** displays the contents of the root directory.

There are three other functions available for handling directories. The **rewinddir** function rewinds the directory list so you can start reading it from the beginning with **readdir**. **telldir** returns the current location of the DIR pointer. This location can be used as an argument to **seekdir** to set the pointer to a specific location.

FIGURE 17.6 lls.c

```
/* Program: lls.c -- Uses readdir to populate a dirent structure */

#include <dirent.h>                          /* For DIR and struct dirent */
#include <stdio.h>

int main(int argc, char **argv) {
    DIR *dir;                                /* Returned by opendir */
    struct dirent *direntry;                 /* Returned by readdir */

    arg_check(2, argc, "Specify a directory\n", 1) ;

    if ( (dir = opendir(argv[1])) == NULL)   /* Directory must exist and */
        quit("opendir", 1);                  /* have read permission */

    while ((direntry = readdir(dir)) != NULL)   /* Until entries are exhausted */
        printf("%10d %s\n", direntry->d_ino, direntry->d_name);

    closedir(dir);

    exit(0);
}
```

Note

In the output of the previous program, both directories . and .. represent root, which has the inode number 2.

17.13 Modifying Entries in Directory

Even though we can't directly edit a directory, we can use functions to add, remove, or modify entries in a directory. In this section, we take up the following system calls:

- **mkdir** and **rmdir**—These calls have the same significance as the commands of the same name.
- **link** and **symlink**—**link** behaves like the **ln** command, but only to create a hard link. **symlink** creates a symbolic link.
- **unlink**—Like **rm**, **unlink** removes a directory entry for an ordinary file or a symbolic link. It doesn't remove a directory.
- **rename**—Like **mv**, this call is used to modify the name in a directory entry.

Every function in this group uses a syntax that is identical to the simplest form of its corresponding UNIX command. They are, therefore, considered briefly in the following paragraphs.

17.13.1   mkdir and rmdir: Creating and Removing Directories

Like a regular file, a directory also has an entry in its parent directory. The **mknod** system call can be used by the superuser to create a directory, but a nonprivileged user can use the **mkdir** and **rmdir** calls to create and remove a directory:

```
int mkdir(const char *path, mode_t mode);
int rmdir(const char *path);
```

The second argument to **mkdir** sets the permissions the directory will have on creation. The permissions are also modified by the umask setting.

17.13.2   link and symlink: Creating a Hard and Symbolic Link

Unlike the **ln** command which creates both hard and symbolic links, the system call library has two separate functions, **link** and **symlink**, for these tasks. Both require two arguments:

```
int link(const char *path1, const char *path2);
int symlink(const char *path1, const char *path2);
```

Here, both **link** and **symlink** create a directory entry with the name *path2* for an existing file *path1*. **symlink** creates a new inode for *path2* also. **link** doesn't create an inode but simply updates the link count of the existing inode for *path1* by one.

17.13.3   unlink: Removing a Link

The **unlink** call reverses the action of **link** and **symlink**. It removes the directory entry for the file (the argument) and decrements the link count in its inode by one:

```
int unlink(const char *path);
```

Although **link** doesn't create a symbolic link, **unlink** removes one, but not the file it points to; that has to be done separately. A file is considered to be removed when its link count in the inode has dropped to zero. When that happens, the kernel frees the inode and the associated disk blocks for fresh allocation, *provided the file is closed also*. We need to understand exactly how the kernel responds to an **unlink** call (see inset).

Can We Delete an Open File?

There's one important thing that you need to remember when you use **unlink** on a file that has a single link count: If the file has been opened by another program or by code in your own program, the kernel will remove the directory entry all right, but it won't delete the file as long as at least one file descriptor points to the file. So it's possible to issue an **unlink** command immediately after an **open** and then read the file like this:

```
fd = open("foo", O_RDONLY);
unlink("foo");                              Even after "removing the file"
while ((n = read(fd, buf, BUFSIZE)) > 0)           you can still read it!
```

Here, foo will be deleted only after it is closed or on termination of the program, which closes all open file descriptors. Note that you can read the file even after issuing **unlink**. But the kernel has already removed the directory entry for the file, so another **open** on this file will fail.

The facility to "unlink" a file immediately after opening it can be used gainfully in a program having multiple exit points. If your application needs to perform I/O on a temporary file and then delete it before program termination, then by unlinking the file at an early stage you are assured that the file will eventually be deleted.

17.13.4   rename: Renaming a File, Directory, or Symbolic Link

The **rename** system call is used for renaming any type of file. Like **mv**, it can work with the three types of files shown in the section header, and follows this syntax:

```
int rename(const char *old, const char *new);
```

Here, **rename** modifies the directory entry by replacing the filename *old* with *new*. When operated on regular files or symbolic links, the behavior of **rename** is identical to that of **mv**. However, **rename** differs from **mv** when handling directories:

- If *old* is a directory and *new* exists as a directory, **rename** simply removes *new* and moves *old* to *new*. The **mv** command makes *old* a subdirectory of *new*.
- If *old* is a regular file, *new* can't be a directory. **mv** doesn't operate with this constraint.

You'll recall how simply you used the command **mv *.c workc** to move all C source files to the workc directory. To emulate this function in your C program, you'll have to call **rename** as many times as there are C programs.

17.14   Reading the Inode: struct stat and stat

In the remaining sections of this chapter, we discuss file attributes. They are maintained in the inode on disk and in the stat structure of a program. This structure is populated with the **stat** system call (structure and system call having the same names). Let's first examine the members of the stat structure as mandated by POSIX:

```
struct stat {
    ino_t       st_ino                          Inode number
    mode_t      st_mode               Mode (type and permissions)
    nlink_t     st_nlink                   Number of hard links
    uid_t       st_uid                              UID (owner)
    gid_t       st_gid                        GID (group owner)
    dev_t       st_rdev              Device ID (for device files)
    off_t       st_size                       File size in bytes
    time_t      st_atime                       Last access time
    time_t      st_mtime                 Last modification time
    time_t      st_ctime          Last time of change of inode
    blksize_t   st_blksize         Preferred block size for I/O
    blkcnt_t    st_blocks            Number of blocks allocated
};
```

The **ls** command looks up this structure to gather file attributes, and the dirent structure for the filename. You can do that too with the **stat** system call (or with its two derivatives, **fstat** and **lstat**). All three calls use an address to a stat structure as the second argument:

```
int stat(const char *path, struct stat *buf);
int fstat(int fildes, struct stat *buf);
int lstat(const char *path, struct stat *buf);
```

stat requires the pathname as the first argument, but **fstat** requires a file descriptor. **stat** follows symbolic links, so if a file foo is symbolically linked to a file bar (foo->bar), doing a "stat" on foo will actually populate the stat structure with the attributes of bar. **lstat** behaves exactly like **stat** for ordinary files and directories, but it doesn't follow symbolic links, so an "lstat" on foo actually extracts the attributes of foo. We'll be using **lstat**, rather than **stat**, for the examples in this chapter.

Some of the members of the stat structure need some processing before they can be displayed in a meaningful format. stat (the structure) stores the three time stamps in seconds elapsed since the Epoch (January 1, 1970), so we'll use the library function, **ctime**, to display the time stamps in the Internet format. We need to process the st_mode member too, but before we do that, let's first write a program that prints the values of some of these members.

17.14.1 attributes.c: Displaying Some File Attributes

Our next program, **attributes.c** (Fig. 17.7), uses **lstat** to populate the statbuf variable of type struct stat. It uses the **ctime** function to format the time stamps by passing the address of the respective member (st_mtime or st_atime) as argument. The program shows how easy it is to display file attributes.

All numeric data are printed in decimal (with %d) except the file type and permissions, which are formatted in octal. On running this program on /etc/passwd, you can see all attributes that **ls** also shows us with its various options (except that you need separate invocations of **ls** to display each time stamp):

```
$ a.out /etc/passwd
File: /etc/passwd
Inode number: 54412
UID: 0   GID: 3
Type and Permissions: 100755
Number of links: 1
Size in bytes: 10803
Blocks allocated: 22
Last Modification Time: Tue Nov 19 16:29:13 2002
Last Access Time: Tue Nov 26 19:57:01 2002
```

Observe the line that displays the file type and permissions as a single number in octal (100755). Unfortunately, UNIX doesn't have separate members for them in stat, so we need to mask out one attribute to obtain the other. This is what we are going to do next.

FIGURE 17.7   attributes.c

```
/* Program: attributes.c -- Uses lstat call and
                            struct stat to display file attributes*/
#include <stdio.h>
#include <sys/stat.h>                                /* For struct stat */

int main( int argc, char **argv) {
    struct stat statbuf;                /* We'll use lstat to populate this */

    arg_check(2, argc, "Single filename required\n", 1) ;

    if (lstat(argv[1], &statbuf) == -1)
       quit("Couldn't stat file", 1);

    printf("File: %s\n", argv[1]);
    printf("Inode number: %d \n", statbuf.st_ino);
    printf("UID: %d   ", statbuf.st_uid);
    printf("GID: %d\n", statbuf.st_gid);
    printf("Type and Permissions: %o\n",  statbuf.st_mode);
    printf("Number of links: %d \n", statbuf.st_nlink);
    printf("Size in bytes: %d\n", statbuf.st_size);
    printf("Blocks allocated: %d\n", statbuf.st_blocks);
    printf("Last Modification Time: %s", ctime(&statbuf.st_mtime));
    printf("Last Access Time: %s\n", ctime(&statbuf.st_atime));

    exit(0);
}
```

17.14.2   S_IFMT: Manipulating the st_mode Member

The st_mode member of stat combines the file type with its permissions in a space of 16 bits. The organization of these bits is shown below:

Bits	File Attribute
1–4	Type
5–7	SUID, SGID, and sticky bit permissions
8–10	Owner permissions
11–13	Group permissions
14–16	Other permissions

The four most significant bits contain the file type. We need 12 bits (and not 9) to represent a file's permissions completely. Recall that 3 separate bits are needed to set the SUID, SGID, and the sticky bit *(4.6—Inset)*. In the previous example, the file type is represented by the octal number 100000 and the permissions by 755.

To extract these components separately, we need to use the S_IFMT mask. When an AND operation is performed with st_mode and this mask, it returns the file type. An inverse AND operation (with ~) returns the permissions. This is how you should be using S_IFMT in your programs:

```
mode_t file_type, file_perm;
file_type = statbuf.st_mode & S_IFMT;                         Bits 1–4
file_perm = statbuf.st_mode & ~S_IFMT;                        Bits 5–16
```

Once you are able to separate the two components with this mask, you can identify files of a specific type or ones having (or not having) a specific permission. Checking file types for numeric values is not very convenient, so UNIX provides a number of macros that make our task simpler.

17.14.3 Using the S_IS*xxx* Macros to Determine File Type

All UNIX systems provide a set of macros beginning with S_IF (often called the S_IF*xxx* macros) that simplify the work of checking for file types, but modern UNIX systems make this task even simpler with the S_IS*xxx* macros (Table 17.2). Each S_IS*xxx* macro uses the st_mode member as argument and returns true or false. For instance, S_ISREG checks for a regular file, and S_ISDIR checks for a directory. This is how you determine whether a file is a directory:

```
if (S_ISDIR(statbuf.st_mode))
    printf("File is a directory\n");
```

These macros actually mask out the file type from st_mode with S_IFMT and then check the residual value. We'll make use of the S_IFMT and S_ISDIR macros in our next program.

TABLE 17.2 *The S_IS*xxx* Macros*

Macro	Returns True If File Type Is
S_ISREG	Regular
S_ISDIR	Directory
S_ISBLK	Block special
S_ISCHR	Character special
S_ISLNK	Symbolic link
S_ISFIFO	FIFO
S_ISSOCK	Socket

17.14.4   Accessing the Permission Bits

You can access each permission bit that's embedded in st_mode member of the stat structure. Recall from Section 17.14.2 that the S_IFMT mask has to be used this way to extract the permissions from st_mode:

```
file_perm = statbuf.st_mode & ~S_IFMT;
```

To test for a specific permission, we need to perform an AND operation of file_perm with the symbolic constant that represents the permission. The expression returns true if the permission bit is on. For instance, to test a file for read permission for the others category, we should use this statement:

```
if (file_perm & S_IROTH)
    printf("File is readable by others\n");
```

Note that this is something we can't do with shell programming where all permission tests apply only to the *user* running the script.

17.14.5   lsdir.c: Listing Only Directories

ls has no option to list only directories, but using the information in the stat structure, we can devise such a program. This program, **lsdir.c** (Fig. 17.8), uses the S_IFMT mask and the S_ISDIR macro to display the file type, permissions, and the name of every subdirectory of the directory name provided as argument. We are not recursively examining directories here.

As we have done in a previous program (**lls.c**, Fig. 17.6), we first have to obtain a pointer to a DIR structure with **opendir**, and then use **readdir** to return a pointer (direntry) to a dirent structure. *However, this time we must change to the directory with **chdir** before we use **readdir**.*

Next, we extract the filename from direntry (direntry->d_name) and then use **lstat** to populate a stat structure (statbuf) with the attributes of the file. From this structure, we extract the st_mode member (statbuf.st_mode) and then use it with the S_ISDIR macro to filter out only directories. For each directory we find, we mask its st_mode value with S_IFMT and ~S_IFMT to obtain the file type and permissions. We print both along with the filename.

Note that the **chdir** call is essential because the d_name member of struct dirent evaluates to a filename without slashes. Without **chdir**, **lstat** would look for the file in the current directory (when it shouldn't be).

Let's run this program with the root directory as argument; a censored list is shown below:

```
$ a.out /
40000  755 .
40000  755 ..
40000  700 lost+found
40000  755 usr
40000  755 var
40000  755 export
```

```
          40000  755 etc
          40000  755 sbin
          40000 1777 tmp                                    The 1 shows the sticky bit is set
          40000  755 .dt
```

FIGURE 17.8 lsdir.c

```c
/* Program: lsdir.c --
                      Lists only directories - Uses S_IFMT and S_ISDIR macros */
#include <sys/types.h>
#include <sys/stat.h>
#include <stdio.h>
#include <dirent.h>

int main( int argc, char *argv[]) {
    DIR *dir;
    struct dirent *direntry;            /* Returned by readdir() */
    struct stat statbuf;                /* Address of statbuf used by lstat() */
    mode_t file_type, file_perm;

    arg_check(2, argc, "Directory not specified\n", 1) ;

    if ((dir = opendir(argv[1])) == NULL)
       quit("Couldn't open directory", 1);

    if ((chdir(argv[1]) == -1))         /* Change to the directory before */
       quit("chdir", 2);                /* you starting reading its entries */

    while ((direntry = readdir(dir)) != NULL) { /* Read each entry in directory*/
        if (lstat(direntry->d_name, &statbuf) < 0) { /* dname must be in */
            perror("lstat");                         /* current directory */
            continue;
        }

        if (S_ISDIR(statbuf.st_mode)) {              /* If file is a directory */
            file_type = statbuf.st_mode & S_IFMT;
            file_perm = statbuf.st_mode & ~S_IFMT;
            printf("%o %4o %s\n", file_type, file_perm, direntry->d_name);
        }
    }

    exit(0);
}
```

The first character of the first field shows 4 (representing a directory) as the file type; the other four octal digits (here, 0000) have been masked out with S_IFMT. The second field shows the file's permissions. Note the entry for tmp; it shows the sticky bit set for the directory. You now have a command that lists only directory names but also includes those beginning with a dot.

17.15   access: **Checking the Real User's Permissions**

We often need to know whether a program run by us has the necessary access rights to a file. Checking each permission bit in stat.st_mode doesn't provide a clue since we then need to know the user category also. The **access** system call makes this job easier because it looks at the *real* UID and *real* GID of the user running the program, and determines whether the file is accessible by the "real" user:

```
int access(const char *path, int amode);
```

The first argument is the pathname, and *amode* specifies the access permission to be tested, which can be one or more of these four values:

R_OK—Read permission OK
W_OK—Write permission OK
X_OK—Execute permission OK
F_OK—File exists

Checking for specific permissions makes sense only when the file exists, and **access** is frequently used with F_OK to make the test for existence before continuing with the program. The program, **faccess.c** (Fig. 17.9), makes this check for multiple files.

The program uses a **for** loop to iterate through a list of command line arguments representing filenames. For each argument, it performs all four tests with **access**. We'll now find out the access rights a nonprivileged user has to /etc/passwd and /etc/shadow, but let's observe their listing first:

```
$ echo $LOGNAME
romeo                                                          The real user
$ ls -l /etc/passwd /etc/shadow
-r--r--r--  1 root     sys             9953 Nov 28 15:30 /etc/passwd
-r--------  1 root     sys             5425 Nov 28 15:30 /etc/shadow
```

The real user is romeo, and the listing shows that passwd is not writable or executable by romeo. Also, shadow doesn't even have read permission for this user. This is confirmed by the output:

```
$ a.out /etc/passwd /etc/shadow
/etc/passwd: Not writable  Not executable
/etc/shadow: Not readable  Not writable  Not executable
```

You can perform an OR operation on the symbolic constants used by **access** to test for multiple permissions. For instance, **access("foo", R_OK | W_OK)** tests for both read and write permission.

FIGURE 17.9 faccess.c

```
/* Program: faccess.c --
                Determines a file's access rights using the read UID and GID */
#include <unistd.h>                        /* For F_OK, R_OK, etc. */
#include <stdio.h>

int main(int argc, char *argv[]) {
   short count;
   for (count = 1; count < argc; count++) {
     printf("%s: ", argv[count]);

     if (access(argv[count], F_OK) == -1)
        quit("File not found", 1);
     if (access(argv[count], R_OK) == -1 )
        printf("Not readable ");
     if (access(argv[count], W_OK) == -1)
        printf("Not writable ");
     if (access(argv[count], X_OK) == -1)
        printf("Not executable ");

     printf("\n");
   }

   exit(0);
}
```

17.16 Modifying File Attributes

Finally, let's end this chapter with a discussion of file attribute manipulation. The stat structure is useful for accessing a file's attributes, but it can't be used to set them except in an indirect manner. To change these attributes, we need to use the following system calls, some of whom have identical command names:

- **link** and **unlink**—For creating a hard link and removing both a hard and symbolic link. This has already been discussed.
- **chmod** and **fchmod**—For changing file permissions.
- **chown**—This handles both ownership and group ownership.
- **utime**—This changes the file's modification and access times.

Each call in the list sets one or two file attributes to absolute values. Some of them (like **chmod** and **utime**) can be used in a relative manner also. For doing that, the general principle is to obtain the current value of the attribute from the stat structure and then add to or subtract from it.

17.16.1   chmod and fchmod: Changing File Permissions

There's nothing special to mention about these two calls except to note that **chmod** identifies a file by its pathname while **fchmod** uses a file descriptor:

```
int chmod(const char *path, mode_t mode);
int fchmod(int fildes, mode_t mode);
```

The second argument (*mode*) represents the permissions and can be used by OR'ing any number of the symbolic constants listed in Section 17.3. For instance, to set permissions in an absolute manner, this is how you should use the **chmod** call:

```
chmod ("foo", S_IRUSR | S_IWUSR | S_IRGRP)                    Same as chmod 640 foo
```

Unlike the **chmod** command, the **chmod** system call can't be used *directly* to set relative permissions. To do that, you'll have to first extract the current permissions from st_mode and then use **chmod** with the bit-wise

- OR combination of the existing permissions and the specific permission to be assigned.
- AND combination of the existing permissions and the complement of the specific permission to be removed.

To consider an example, you can assign execute permission to foo in two steps:

```
lstat("foo", &statbuf);
chmod("foo", statbuf.st_mode | S_IXUSR);                      Adding a permission
```

To remove a permission, you have to use the AND operator with the complement of the permission. The first example below removes the user's execute permission, while the second one removes all permissions for the user:

```
chmod("foo", statbuf.st_mode & ~S_IXUSR);
chmod("foo", statbuf.st_mode & ~(S_IRUSR | S_IWUSR | S_IXUSR));
```

You may be wondering why we didn't use S_IFMT to extract the permissions from st_mode before applying **chmod**. Fortunately, **chmod** also accepts the value of st_mode (which includes the file type) as its second argument.

17.16.2   chown: Changing Ownership

Like its command counterpart, the **chown** system call is used to change both the owner and group owner. As with **stat**, there are three versions whose differences should now be obvious:

```
int chown(const char *path, uid_t owner, gid_t group);
int fchown(int fildes, uid_t owner, gid_t group);
int lchown(const char *path, uid_t owner, gid_t group);
```

For these calls, *owner* and *group* are represented by the numeric UID and GID, respectively. To change either the owner or group owner, set the unchanged argument to -1 (the first time we encounter -1 as an argument to a system call). Here are two examples:

```
chown("foo", 512, 100);                            UID changed to 512, GID to 100
fchown(4, -1, 100);                               UID unchanged, GID changed to 100
```

If the **chown** command can be used only by the superuser on your system, then the same restriction applies to the **chown** system call family also. Similarly, your system may permit changing your GID to only another group to which you also belong (supplementary group).

17.16.3 utime: Changing the Time Stamps

The last system call that we take up is **utime**. This call is used to change a file's modification and access times. It takes two arguments:

```
int utime(const char *path, const struct utimbuf *times);
```

The first argument is obviously the pathname. The second argument represents a pointer to a structure of type utimbuf. (Note the missing "e".) This structure contains two members of type time_t:

```
struct utimbuf {
    time_t actime                                          Last access time
    time_t modtime                                    Last modification time
};
```

These two members store the last access and modification time in seconds since the Epoch. To obtain the existing values for a file, you need to "stat" it and then examine the st_atime and st_mtime members in struct stat. But to set them to different values, you'll have to populate the utimbuf structure before using **utime**.

17.16.4 atimemtime.c: Creating a File with Identical Time Stamps

Can you create a file having the same time stamps as another file using UNIX commands? It's not as easy as you might think, but our next C program, **atimemtime.c** (Fig. 17.10), makes the task look simple. It requires two filenames as arguments; the time stamps of the first file are used to set the stamps for the second.

We first use **lstat** to fill up statbuf with the attributes of an existing file (argv[1]). Next, we populate the utimbuf structure with the two time stamps obtained from the previous **lstat** call. We open a second file (argv[2]), creating it if necessary, and then use **utime** to change its time stamps to the values stored in timebuf. This operation can be performed even if the file is not open; the file was opened simply to make sure that it's created if it doesn't exist.

Let's use this program to create a file with the same time stamps as one of the profiles—like .profile. Let's first see its time stamps:

```
$ cd ; ls -l ~/.profile ; ls -lu ~/.profile
-rw-r--r--  1 sumit     staff          61 Dec 12 20:14 .profile
-rw-r--r--  1 sumit     staff          61 Feb  2 12:33 .profile
```

FIGURE 17.10 `atimemtime.c`

```
/* Program: atimemtime.c --
                     Sets a file's time stamps to those of another file */
#include <sys/stat.h>
#include <fcntl.h>
#include <utime.h>                              /* For struct utimbuf */

int main( int argc, char **argv) {
    struct stat statbuf;          /* To obtain time stamps for an existing file */
    struct utimbuf timebuf;       /* To set time stamps for another file */

    arg_check(3, argc, "Two filenames required\n", 1) ;

    if (lstat(argv[1], &statbuf) == -1)
        quit("stat", 1);

    timebuf.actime  = statbuf.st_atime;   /* Setting members of timebuf with */
    timebuf.modtime = statbuf.st_mtime;   /* values obtained from statbuf */

    if (open(argv[2], O_RDWR | O_CREAT, 0644) == -1)
        quit("open", 2);
    close(argv[2]);                       /* Previously used open only to create it */

    if (utime(argv[2], &timebuf) == -1)   /* Sets both time stamps for file */
        quit("utime", 3);                 /* that was just created */

    exit(0);
}
```

The last access time for this file (obtained with **ls -lu**) is generally the time we logged in, and it's a good idea to save this time by creating another file with identical time stamps. We'll move the **a.out** executable to the home directory before running it:

```
$ mv a.out $HOME; cd ; a.out .profile .logintime
$ ls -l .logintime ; ls -lu .logintime
-rw-r--r--   1 sumit    staff        0 Dec 12 20:14 .logintime
-rw-r--r--   1 sumit    staff        0 Feb  2 12:33 .logintime
```

Note that the time stamps for the two files are identical. Using a C program, we have done something that we couldn't do using UNIX commands and the shell.

You can now start writing programs that use these system calls. But we still have some way to go. We must be able to create processes, run programs in them, open files in one process, and pass on the descriptors to the child. We also need to manipulate these descriptors to implement redirection and piping. The programmer's view of the process is presented in Chapter 18.

SUMMARY

A *system call* is a routine built in the kernel to perform a function that requires communication with the hardware. It switches the CPU to *kernel mode* from *user mode*. *Library functions* are built on top of the system calls.

When a system calls returns an error (often, -1), it sets a global variable, errno, to an integer whose associated text can be printed with **perror**.

open returns a *file descriptor* that is used by the other I/O calls. It sets the opening *mode* (read, write, etc.) and *status flags* that can create (O_CREAT) or truncate (O_TRUNC) a file or allow data to be appended (O_APPEND).

read and **write** use a buffer whose size should be set equal to the size of the kernel buffer for best performance. **lseek** moves the file offset pointer, and can take it beyond EOF to create a *sparse* file. Unlike **read**, **write** returns immediately even though the actual writing can take place later.

File permissions specified with **open** are modified by either the shell's umask setting or a previous **umask** system call. **umask** returns the previous value of the mask.

Directories are usually handled with library functions because of the nonstandard format of the directory structure. **opendir** returns a pointer to a DIR structure that is used by **readdir** to read a directory entry. **readdir** returns a pointer to a dirent structure that contains the filename and inode number as its members. **chdir** changes the current directory and **getcwd** returns the pathname of the current directory.

Files can be hard linked (**link**) and symbolically linked (**symlink**), but **unlink** removes both. When **unlink** is invoked on an open file, the kernel removes the directory entry, but its data blocks are deallocated only when the file is closed.

The inode information is maintained in the stat structure which is populated by **stat**, **lstat**, and **fstat**. The file type and its permissions are maintained in a single field, st_mode, which can be split into separate components using the S_IFMT mask. The S_IS*xxx* macros can be used to test for specific file types.

access tests a file's access rights (which includes the test for its existence) using the *real* UID and *real* GID of the process.

The **chmod** and **chown** calls do the same jobs as their command counterparts. **utime** is used to set a file's access and modification time stamps using a structure of type utimbuf.

SELF-TEST

Use system calls wherever possible. However, you may use **printf**, **perror**, *and the directory handling library functions.*

17.1   Explain the difference between *system calls* and *library functions*. What happens in the CPU when a system call is invoked?

17.2 Why must we *immediately* check the value of errno after a system call fails, rather than later?

17.3 What is a *file descriptor,* and what is it used for?

17.4 Check the man pages of **open**, **dup**, **dup2**, **pipe**, and **fcntl**, and see if you find anything they have in common.

17.5 Write a program that ascertains the size of the file descriptor table by opening a file repeatedly. Display the cause of the error that led to the aborting of the program.

17.6 Specify how the **open** call can be used to emulate the function performed by the shell's (i) >, (ii) >> symbols.

17.7 Group the following symbolic constants into two categories and explain the significance of the categories: (i) O_RDONLY, (ii) O_CREAT, (iii) O_SYNC, (iv) O_RDWR, (v) O_TRUNC, (vi) O_APPEND, (vii) O_WRONLY. What is the role of the O_SYNC flag when using **write**?

17.8 Write a program that uses a filename as argument and display its contents in uppercase.

17.9 Write a program that (i) creates a file foo with permissions 666 and a directory bar with permissions 777, (ii) removes foo and bar.

17.10 Write a program that accepts a directory name as argument and creates it if it doesn't already exist. If there is an ordinary file by that name, then the program should remove it before creating the directory.

17.11 Write a program that accepts a directory name as argument, changes to that directory, and displays its absolute pathname. Is the change permanent?

17.12 Write a program that lists from the current directory all ordinary filenames whose size exceeds 100,000 bytes. It should also remove all zero-sized files.

17.13 Write a program that sets the user mask to zero before creating a file foo. Now, change the permissions of foo to (i) 764, (ii) 440. The previous value of the mask should be restored before program termination.

EXERCISES

Use system calls wherever possible. However, you may use **printf**, **perror**, **strerror**, *and the directory handling library functions.*

17.1 Look up the man page of **strerror** before you write a program that prints all possible error numbers and their corresponding text as shown in Table 17.1. The number of error messages on your system is held in the extern variable, sys_nerr.

17.2 Explain what an *atomic operation* is. Specify the statement that opens a file and (i) truncates it if it exists, (ii) creates it if it doesn't. What is the advantage of using **open** to create a file instead of **creat** which is designed only for that purpose?

17.3 Write a program that copies a file using the source and destination as arguments. The destination can also be a directory.

17.4 Modify the program in 17.8 (Self-Test) so that the output is displayed in lowercase when invoked by the name **lower**, and uppercase when invoked as **upper**. What else do you need to do to run it?

17.5 Explain why the selection of the buffer size used by **read** and **write** is crucial in writing efficient programs.

17.6   Write two programs that read /etc/passwd using (i) a single-character buffer, (ii) a buffer of 2048 bytes with **read**. Use the **time** command with each and compare their performance.

17.7   Write a program that displays the current value of the user mask but leaves it unchanged.

17.8   Using **access**, devise an advisory locking mechanism which allows two programs, **lock1.c** and **lock2.c**, to read a file foo only if the file .lockfile doesn't exist. Both programs will first create the lock file if it doesn't exist, and remove it before termination.

17.9   Write a program to split the contents of a file specified as argument into multiple files so that each file contains at most 10,000 bytes. Name the files foo.1, foo.2, and so forth if foo is the argument.

17.10   Write a program that uses error checking to perform the following on an existing file foo: (i) opens foo and then deletes it without closing it, (ii) reads foo and displays its output, (iii) opens foo again. After the program has completed execution, check whether foo has actually been deleted. Explain your observations with reference to the behavior of the **unlink** system call.

17.11   Write a program that moves a group of ordinary files to a directory. The filenames are provided as arguments, and the last argument is a directory. Provide adequate checks to ensure that the files exist as ordinary files and the directory is created if it doesn't exist.

17.12   Write a program that does the following: (i) creates a file foo with permissions 644, (ii) assigns write permission to the group, (iii) removes the read permission from others. Look up the **system** library function, and use it to display the listing at each stage.

17.13   Write a program that removes the read, write, and execute permissions for others for all files in the current directory that are owned by the user running the program. (HINT: Use **getuid** to obtain your own UID.)

17.14   Write a program to create a file foo1 with the same permissions, modification time, and access time as another file, foo2.

17.15   Write a program that uses a filename as argument and checks each of the 12 permission bits. The program should display a message if the bit is set. For instance, if the user has read permission, then it should display User-readable. Develop the code in a modular manner using two separate functions, A and B:

    (i)   A will populate a stat structure with the attributes of the file and print its permissions in octal format as a 4-character string.

    (ii) B will extract each permission bit from stat.st_mode and then print a message like User-readable if the respective bit is set.

CHAPTER **18**

Systems Programming
II—Process Control

In this chapter we discover answers to some old questions. How does the shell
run our programs? How do we manipulate the standard streams to implement
redirection and pipelines? Why does one program respond to the interrupt key, but not
another? A systems programmer must know these answers because she has to create
processes, divide the work between them, determine how they should react to signals
and how to pass messages between them.

We'll examine in some detail the fork-exec-wait cycle that will help us create
processes using the system call library. We handled file descriptors in Chapter 18, but
here we'll make use of the kernel's descriptor replicating properties to implement two
important shell features—redirection and piping. We'll also examine the basics of the
elaborate POSIX signal handling mechanism.

Objectives

- Examine the different segments of the *virtual address space* of a process.
- Learn the significance of the entries of the process table.
- Use **fork** to create a process and study the environmental changes in the child.
- Replace the existing process address space with a new program using the *exec* family
  of functions.
- Use **wait** and **waitpid** to wait for a change of status in the child and gather its exit
  status from the process table.
- Understand the three-table scheme associated with every open file and how the scheme
  changes when a file is accessed by multiple processes.
- Perform shell-like redirection using the **dup** and **dup2** system calls.
- Learn the basics of signal handling and the concept of *signal disposition*.
- Install *signal handlers* with **sigaction**, and generate signals with **kill** and **raise**.
- Understand the attributes of a pipe, and create a pipeline using the **pipe** system call.

18.1 The Process Revisited

The basic concepts related to processes have been discussed in Chapter 8, but we need
to expand that knowledge before we use system calls to create and control processes.
UNIX supports **preemptive multitasking**, which means that the kernel preempts a

process when its time period expires. However, the norms are sometimes relaxed, especially when a process invokes a system call.

Generally, a system call is allowed to complete even after the process has consumed its time slice, but the behavior of certain system calls necessitates the use of a different control mechanism. For instance, if a system call keeps the CPU idle (when waiting for an I/O operation to complete, for instance), the process blocks by *voluntarily* giving up control of the CPU. The process *sleeps* on an event, and when the event occurs, the kernel wakes up the process so that it can start running again when its turn arrives.

The kernel allocates memory for the process image, but it also maintains control information in a number of registers. It uses this information for switching processes. We examine here two key concepts—the process address space and the process table.

18.1.1   The Virtual Address Space

When you execute a C program, the program loader transfers the binary code from the program on disk to memory. The kernel also creates additional space in memory as and when needed by the process. This collection of memory locations that the process can access is referred to as its **virtual address space**. This space is organized into a number of segments (Fig. 18.1):

- **The text segment**   This segment, containing the instructions to be executed, is read in from the program's disk file. Multiple instances of one program will share this segment; three users running **vi** will use a single text segment.
- **The data segment**   This segment represents the global and static variables used in the program.

FIGURE 18.1   *The Process Virtual Address Space*

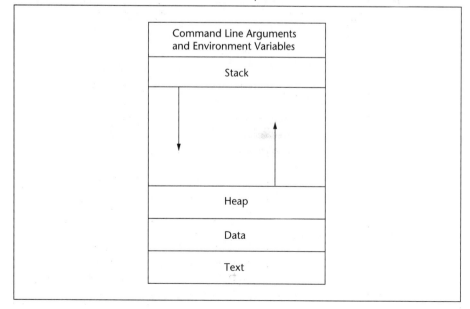

- **The stack**   It stores the arguments and local variables of functions as well as the address to return to. The stack grows and shrinks in size as functions are invoked and complete execution.
- **The heap**   This segment is used to dynamically allocate memory during program runtime (using functions like **sbrk**, **malloc**, and **calloc**). The heap and stack are separated by unallocated space, and they grow at the expense of each other.
- **Other segments**   Command line arguments and environment variables are generally found at the bottom of the stack (top in figure). Shared libraries, if used by a program, are located between the heap and stack.

A process can only access its own address space, which is why one process can't corrupt the address space of another. The preceding discussions actually featured the **user address space**. When the process invokes a system call, the kernel runs on behalf of the user in its own address space—the **kernel address space**—to service the call.

How Virtual Addresses Are Interpreted and Translated

The addresses of the process segments (text, data, stack, etc.) created by the linker are *virtual* because they don't point to physical memory locations. It is possible for the virtual address space of all programs to begin from address 0 and yet run without conflict. The linker can only specify the relative location of the segments within a program. It can't predetermine a physical memory location; it may not be free.

   At runtime, the *Memory Management Unit* (MMU) converts these virtual addresses to nonconflicting physical memory locations using a set of *address translation maps*. The MMU contains a set of hardware registers that point to the translation maps of the currently running process.

   Every process has a **context** that represents the entire environment available to the process when it is running. This environment includes the address space, the status of the hardware registers, and the information maintained in the process table. The kernel saves the process context before it uses a **context switch** to force one process to vacate the CPU and make room for another. The kernel then sets the registers to point to the translation maps of the new process. Because every process has its own set of translation maps, one process can't access another's address space.

18.1.2   The Process Table

The attributes of every active process are stored in a fairly large structure that represents an entry in the **process table**. Modern UNIX systems no longer swap out portions of the process table to disk, but maintain the entire table in memory. The important attributes of the process table are:

- The PID and PPID of the process.
- The state of the process—whether running, sleeping, zombie, and so forth.
- The real UID and GID of the process.
- The effective UID and GID of the process.
- The file descriptor table.

- The file creation mask.
- CPU usage information.
- The *pending signals mask.* This is a list of signals pending against the process. The process can know that it has received a signal only when it "peeks" into this field.
- A *signal disposition* table. It specifies the action to take when the process receives a signal.

The process table entry of a forked child has many fields copied from the parent. When the child execs a new program, the process table entry is retained (since the PID doesn't change), but some of these fields change. For instance, the child may decide to close some descriptors before an exec. When a process dies, the process table entry is cleared only after the parent has gathered the child's exit status. This has already been discussed *(8.8).*

Note that the process table maintains important data related to signals. A process knows that it has received a signal by looking up the pending signals mask, but the action it has to take for a signal is specified by the signal disposition table. We have more to say about them later.

18.2 The Process Environment

The environment of a process includes the shell's environment variables stored at the bottom of the stack (Fig. 18.1). These variables are available in the global environ variable which you may need to define in your C program like this:

```
extern char **environ;
```
Array of pointers to char

Like argv[] (used as the second argument to **main**), this represents a pointer to an array of pointers to char, except that this array stores pointers to environment variable strings of the form *name=value.* These values can be retrieved and set by two functions, **getenv** and **setenv**:

```
char *getenv(const char *name);
int setenv(const char *envname, const char *envval, int overwrite);
```

getenv returns a pointer to the value of a variable, whose string representation is passed to it as the *name* argument. For instance, you can obtain the current value of PATH in this manner:

```
char *path = getenv("PATH");
```

The first two arguments of **setenv** are meant to pass the variable name and value. The third argument, *overwrite,* determines whether an existing value of a variable will be overwritten (0 signifies that the value is to be left alone). This is how you can reset PATH to include only the current directory:

```
setenv("PATH", ".", 1);
```
1 *allows updating*

BSD created **setenv**, and even though POSIX recommends its use, it is not available on some SVR4 systems. If you don't find **setenv** on your machine, then use SVR4's **putenv** (not preferred by POSIX). The previous **setenv** call can be replaced with **putenv("PATH=.")**.

FIGURE 18.2 `process.c`

```
/* process.c -- Prints PID, PPID, real and effective UIDs and GIDs
                            Also fetches and sets PATH */
#include <stdio.h>
int main(void) {
    printf("PID : %4d, PPID: %4d\n", getpid(), getppid());
    printf("UID : %4d,  GID: %4d\n", getuid(), getgid());
    printf("EUID: %4d, EGID: %4d\n", geteuid(), getegid());
    printf("PATH=%s\n", getenv("PATH"));
    setenv("PATH", ".", 1);             /* Use putenv("PATH=.") in Solaris */
    printf("New PATH=%s\n", getenv("PATH"));
    exit(0);
}
```

18.2.1 `process.c`: Looking Up Some Process Credentials

Our first program, **process.c** (Fig. 18.2), accesses and updates PATH. It also displays the PID and PPID of the current process along with the ownership credentials. Six system calls are used here, and their names reflect their function.

The process obtains its own PID and its parent's PID using the **getpid** and **getppid** system calls. The program also prints the effective UID and GID, which normally are equal to the real UID and GID:

```
$ a.out
PID : 1035, PPID: 1028
UID : 102,  GID:   10                        Real UID and GID are the same
EUID: 102, EGID:   10                          as their effective cousins
PATH=/usr/local/bin:/usr/bin:/usr/X11R6/bin:/bin:/usr/local/java/bin:.
New PATH=.
```

When Effective UID Doesn't Equal Real UID To understand how the SUID bit affects the effective UID, let's set the SUID bit of this executable from the superuser account *(19.1.1)* and transfer the ownership to root. Confirm your actions by observing the listing:

```
# chmod u+s a.out ; chown root a.out ; ls -l a.out
-rwsr-xr-x    1 root      sumit       12211 Dec 17 09:49 a.out
```

Now quit superuser mode and run the program again. The effective UID now becomes the owner of the file (root, whose UID is 0):

```
$ a.out | grep UID
UID : 102,  GID:   10
EUID:   0, EGID:   10
```

In the next few sections, we examine each phase of the process life cycle—fork, exec, and wait—along with their associated system calls and functions. We also need to discuss the process exit mechanism and how it impacts wait.

18.3 fork: **Replicating the Current Process**

You can't run an external program unless you replicate your current process first with the **fork** system call. **fork** has a simple syntax but returns in an unusual manner:

```
pid_t fork(void);
```
Copies current process to child

The replicated process is the child of the process invoking **fork**. Parent and child have different PIDs and PPIDs, and that's probably the only major difference between them. After **fork** returns, both processes continue execution at the statement *following* **fork** (code before **fork** ignored by child). For the kernel to distinguish between the original and its replica, **fork** returns twice with two different values:

- Zero in the child, which is safe because no process can be created with that PID.
- The PID of the child in the parent, so the parent can later access the child with this PID.

When **fork** is invoked, the kernel replicates the address space of the current process (its text, data, stack, etc.). It also creates a separate entry in the process table containing several fields copied from the entry of the parent. This includes the file descriptors, current directory, and umask value. Because the child runs in its own address space, changes made to these parameters don't affect the parent.

UNIX systems impose limits on the number of processes a user can create. Further, the size of the process table also places restrictions on the total number of processes that the machine can support. If an attempt to fork a process violates either of these restrictions, **fork** returns -1.

18.3.1 fork.c: A Simple Child Creation Program

You may find the behavior of **fork** a little confusing initially, so let's demonstrate its effect with a small program, **fork.c** (Fig. 18.3). The program simply forks a process and then uses **getpid** and **getppid** to obtain the PID and PPID of both parent and child.

Since **fork** returns two different values, we need to examine this return value to distinguish between parent and child. Observe from the output below that the first and second **printf** statements are executed in the parent, and the third one in the child. The final **printf** is executed by both processes:

```
$ a.out
Before forking
CHILD -- PID: 1556 PPID: 1555
Both processes continue from here                This statement runs in child ...
PARENT -- PID: 1555 PPID: 1450, CHILD PID: 1556
Both processes continue from here                        ... as well as in parent
```

Note that the parent is aware of the PID of three generations, while the child has knowledge of two. After a process is forked, it's not specified (either by POSIX or by

FIGURE 18.3   fork.c

```
/* Program: fork.c -- A simple fork
                     Shows PID, PPID in both parent and child */
#include <stdio.h>
#include <sys/types.h>

int main (void) {
   pid_t pid;

   printf("Before fork\n");
   pid = fork();                    /* Replicate current process */

   if (pid > 0) {                   /* In the parent process; make sure */
      sleep(1);                     /* that parent doesn't die before child */
      printf("PARENT -- PID: %d PPID: %d, CHILD PID: %d\n",
                    getpid(), getppid(), pid);
   }
   else if (pid == 0)               /*In the child process */
      printf("CHILD -- PID: %d PPID: %d\n", getpid(), getppid());
   else {                           /* pid must be -1 here */
      printf("Fork error\n");
      exit(1);
   }

   printf("Both processes continue from here\n");    /*In both processes */
   exit(0);
}
```

convention) which runs first—the parent or the child. On Solaris, the child runs first, but the opposite is true on Linux. We deliberately introduced the **sleep** call to ensure that the parent doesn't die before the child. The consequences of letting the parent die first are examined in Section 18.6 (Inset).

18.4   exec: **The Final Step in Process Creation**

We fork to create a process, but more often than not, we follow it with an *exec* to run a separate program in the address space of the child. Exec replaces this address space (the text, data, and stack) with that of the new program, which then starts running by executing its **main** function. Since no new process is created, the PID doesn't change across an exec. Because the stack is replaced with a new one, the call to exec doesn't return unless it results in an error.

What Happens to the I/O Buffers After a Fork?

The standard I/O library that includes functions like **printf** maintains an additional set of buffers. These buffers are different from the buffer cache available in the kernel. Forking copies the I/O buffers as well, which means any data held by them before the fork are also available to the child. This creates problems when using functions like **printf** with **fork**.

Unlike **write**, which is totally unbuffered, **printf** is *line-buffered* when writing to the terminal. This means that the buffer contents are written to the terminal when a newline is encountered. **printf** is, however, *fully-buffered* when writing to disk (say, when using redirection); the buffer is written only when it is full. This allows a child to acquire a partially filled buffer from its parent. Redirect the output of the program, **fork.c**, to a file, and you'll find the program behaving differently.

Many of the attributes inherited during a fork don't change with an exec. For instance, the previous program's file descriptors, the current and root directory, umask settings, and the global environment remain the same. However, a programmer can change the exec'd environment in two ways:

- By closing one or more file descriptors, so files opened before or after a fork can't be read directly in the exec'd process.
- By passing a separate environment to the exec'd process instead of the default environment maintained in the global environ variable. Two exec functions (**execve** and **execle**) are designed to work this way.

"Exec" is the name we commonly use to refer to this overlaying; there's no system call named exec. In fact, there's one—**execve**—on top of which five library functions are built. We'll refer to them simply as "exec" or the "exec family." The entire set can be grouped into two parts, which we'll call the "execl" set and the "execv" set, because the names of their members have the prefix execl and execv.

Tip

First, commit to memory this simple statement: The l (el) in execl (and its variants) represents a fixed *list* of arguments, while the v in execv (and its variants) signifies a *variable* number of arguments.

18.4.1   execl and execv: The Key Members

In this section, we examine two library functions, **execl** and **execv**. The **execl** function requires each component of the command line of the new program to be specified as individual arguments:

```
int execl(const char *path, const char *arg0, ... /*, (char *) 0 */);
```

execl doesn't use PATH; the first argument (*path*) signifies the absolute or relative pathname of the program. The other arguments represent each word of the command line beginning with the name of the command (*arg0*). The ellipsis representation in the syntax (`... /*`) points to the varying number of arguments.

To consider an example, here's how we use **execl** to run the **wc -l** command with foo as argument:

```
execl("/bin/wc", "wc", "-l", "foo", (char *) 0);
```

execl uses the first argument to locate the program. *The remaining arguments are specified exactly in the way they will appear as **main***'s arguments in* **wc**. So, argv[0] in **wc**'s **main** is wc. The list is terminated with a NULL pointer.

Let's use **execl** in our next program, **execl.c** (Fig. 18.4), to run the **wc** command with two options and one filename. We don't fork a process here, so **execl** replaces the address space of the current process with that of **wc**. Because a successful **execl** never returns, the **printf** statement is not executed:

```
$ a.out
    166    9953 /etc/passwd
```

We can also use NULL in place of (char *) 0. Because **execl** requires each word of the command line to be specified individually, this creates problems when the argument list is known only at runtime. The solution is **execv**, which requires a list:

```
int execv(const char *path, char *const argv[]);
```

The first argument is the same. The command to run and its arguments are bundled into an array of pointers to char, and the address of the first element is passed as the second argument. In this case also, the last element of *argv[ ]* must be a NULL pointer. This is how we use **execv** to run the **wc** command that was run with **execl** in Fig. 18.4:

```
char *cmdargs[] = { "wc", "-l", "-c", "/etc/passwd", NULL };
execv ("/bin/wc", cmdargs);
```

Note that cmdargs here is the same as &cmdargs[0]. This method of invocation suggests that we can input *any* command line during runtime. After examining **wait**, we'll design a program that accepts the command line of another program as its own arguments.

FIGURE 18.4   execl.c

```
/* Program: execl.c -- Uses execl to run wc */

#include <stdio.h>
int main (void) {
    execl ("/bin/wc", "wc", "-l", "-c", "/etc/passwd", (char *) 0);
    printf ("execl error\n");
}
```

> ### *Why a NULL Pointer Is Required*
> To understand why we follow the argument list with a NULL pointer ((char *) 0) or NULL), let's first see how arguments are passed to a C program. By convention, we use one of these two syntaxes for **main** when a program is run with arguments:
>
> ```
> int main(int argc, char **argv) {
> int main(int argc, char *argv[]) {
> ```
>
> The startup routine that eventually runs **main** populates argv[] (pointer to an array of pointers to char) with the string arguments specified in the command line. A NULL pointer is also placed at the end of the array. The number of arguments (excluding the NULL pointer) is then evaluated and assigned to argc. When **main** runs, it knows the number of arguments passed to it.
>
> When we use exec to run a program, there's no provision to specify the number of arguments (no argc); exec has to fill up argc "by hand." The only way for **execl** to know the size of the argument list is to keep counting till it encounters the NULL pointer.

18.4.2 The Other exec Members

execlp and execvp These functions use the PATH to locate the command, so the first argument need only be the name of the command:

```
int execlp(const char *file, const char *arg0, ... /*, (char *)0 */);
int execvp(const char *file, char *const argv[]);
```

Note that *pathname* has now become *file*; the other arguments remain the same. This means that instead of /bin/wc, we can simply specify wc as the first argument:

```
execlp("wc", "wc", "-l", "foo", (char *) 0);
execvp("wc", cmdargs);
```

However, there's another advantage these functions have over **execl** and **execv**: They can run a shell, **awk**, or **perl** script. By default, **execlp** and **execvp** spawn a Bourne shell to read the commands in the script, but if you have #!/bin/ksh as the she-bang line, they'll call up the Korn shell.

execle and execve All the previous four exec calls silently pass the environment of the current process (through the environ[] variable) to the exec'd process. Sometimes, you may need to provide a different environment to the new program—a restricted shell, for instance. In that case, use the remaining members of the exec family, **execle** and **execve**:

```
int execle(const char *path, const char *arg0, ... /*,
           (char *) 0, char *const envp[]*/);
int execve(const char *path, char *const argv[], char *const envp[]);
```

Unlike the other four members, both **execle** and **execve** use an additional argument to pass a pointer to an array of environment strings (of the form *variable=value*) to the program. It's *only* this environment that is available in the exec'd process, not the one stored in environ[]. The last one, **execve**, is the only system call in the exec family; the others internally invoke **execve**.

exec overwrites the I/O buffers, so make sure that you flush them before using exec. **fork** inherits all I/O buffers which creates problems when using **printf** *(18.3.1)*.

Tip

18.5   Gathering the Exit Status

A process terminates normally either by falling through **main** or by invoking **exit** or **return**. It returns the exit status to the caller, which, in the shell, is available in the parameter $?. The **exit** library function specifies this value as its argument:

```
void exit(int status);
```

exit internally executes the **_exit** system call. When a process terminates without explicitly calling **exit**, the exit status is zero. In either case, the kernel closes all open files, flushes all output streams, and deallocates the process address space. But the process is not completely removed yet.

Next, the kernel places *status* (the exit status) in the process table and changes the state of the child to *zombie*. This scheme is based on the "hope" that the parent may eventually call **wait** or **waitpid** to pick up the exit status. If the parent eventually does so, the kernel frees the process table entry and removes the process from the system.

You can't kill a zombie because it's not a process, but too many zombies just eat into the available slots of a process table. The **ps** output shows zombie processes as the string <defunct> in the last column. A system reboot may be required to clear zombies.

18.5.1   wait: When the Parent Waits

After the child has done an exec, it's normal for the parent to wait for its death. This is commonly done by invoking the **wait** system call, which uses a pointer to an int as argument:

```
pid_t wait(int *stat_loc);
```

wait blocks till a child dies (one reason why **waitpid** is preferred to **wait**) or is suspended. It returns the PID of the dead or suspended child, or zero if no such child is available. It also fills up *stat_loc* with information that includes the exit status. The parent then resumes operation with the statement following **wait**. Here's a snippet of code that shows the role of **wait**:

```
switch(fork()) {
    case 0:                                    /* Child */
        execv(argv[1], &argv[2]);
    default:                                   /* Parent */
        wait(&status);
}
```

The exit status is available in the least eight significant bits of status (*stat_loc* in syntax). When a process terminates normally, this value is fetched by the WEXITSTATUS macro:

```
fprintf(stderr, "Exit status: %d\n", WEXITSTATUS(status));
```

The argument to **wait** actually represents the *termination status* that contains other information—like whether a process terminated normally or is suspended, along with the signal that suspended the process.

18.5.2   `waitpid`: A More Powerful Waiting Mechanism

With most shells today supporting job control, it is usual for a parent to run multiple jobs in the background. It can't afford to block (by invoking **wait**) after forking, but it still needs to clean up the process table of zombies as and when its children die. **waitpid** is the solution here:

```
pid_t waitpid(pid_t pid, int *stat_loc, int options);
```

stat_loc has the same significance as in **wait**. *pid* is specified as –1 and *options* is set to zero if **waitpid** has to behave like **wait**, i.e. wait for any child to change state:

```
waitpid(-1, &status, 0);
```

But **waitpid** can also wait for a child with a specific PID to die. *options* here are represented by one or more symbolic constants in an OR combination. The one that is used most often is WNOHANG which makes **waitpid** run in nonblocking mode:

```
waitpid(pid, &status, WNOHANG);          Waits for child with pid as PID
waitpid(-1, &status, WNOHANG);                       Waits for any child
```

This isn't waiting really; **waitpid** returns immediately whether a child has changed state or not. But then how does one use this system call? There are two ways:

* Invoke it in a loop with a finite delay between successive invocations to check if the child has changed state. But system calls are expensive and polling in this manner isn't always desirable.
* Let the parent wait for the SIGCHLD signal which the kernel sends to the parent when a child changes state. On receipt of the signal, the parent invokes **waitpid** which returns successfully with the necessary information.

Space constraints don't permit an exhaustive discussion on **waitpid**, but you are advised to look up the man page with **man 2 waitpid** or **man -s2 waitpid**.

18.6   `fork_exec_wait.c`: Using All Three Calls

The previous program, (Fig. 18.4), used **execl** in the current process. We normally don't use exec like this; often we do an exec in a child process so that the parent is free to do what it likes. In the following program, **fork_exec_wait.c** (Fig. 18.5), the

FIGURE 18.5 fork_exec_wait.c

```
/* Program: fork_exec_wait.c --
                        Uses fork, exec and wait to run a UNIX command
                        The WEXITSTATUS macro fetches the exit status. */
#include <stdio.h>
#include <wait.h>
#include <fcntl.h>

int main (int argc, char **argv) {
    int fd, status ;

    fd = open("foo.log", O_WRONLY | O_CREAT | O_TRUNC, 0644);
    write(fd, "About to fork\n", 14);              /* First write */

    switch(fork()) {
      case -1: quit("fork", 1);
        case 0:                                    /* Child */
            write(fd, "About to exec\n", 14);
            close(fd);      /* Closing here doesn't affect parent's copy */
            if ((execv (argv[1], &argv[2]) < 0)) {
                fprintf(stderr, "execl error\n");
                exit(200);
            }
      default:                                     /* Parent */
            write(fd, "Parent waiting\n", 15);
            wait(&status);      /* or waitpid(-1, &status, 0); */
            write(fd, "Child Terminated\n", 17);
            fprintf(stderr, "Exit status: %d\n", WEXITSTATUS(status));
            close(fd);                             /*   File now closed */

            exit (0);
    }
}
```

command line to execute is specified as the program's arguments. We fork a process, run **execv** in the child, and then make the parent wait for the child's death. To illustrate inheritance, the parent opens a file, and both parent and child write it using the same descriptor or its copy.

Recall that **execv** requires the absolute pathname of the command as the first argument, and the *entire* command line as the remaining arguments. Both parent and child write the same log file, foo.log. The child runs **grep**, but the parent knows **grep**'s exit status:

```
$ a.out /bin/grep grep -i -n SUMIT /etc/passwd
15:sumit:x:102:10::/users1/home/staff/sumit:/usr/bin/bash
Exit status: 0
```

The shell does a similar thing with our input except that we provide input differently. Now look at the log file:

```
$ cat foo.log
About to fork
About to exec
Parent waiting
Child Terminated
```
This line and the next could appear reversed. Why?

There are two things to note here. The parent opened the file, but the child wrote it using a copy of the descriptor used by the parent. Also, closing foo.log in the child made no difference to the parent which wrote the last line. Both these features make redirection and pipelines possible.

Tip

Often, you'll find it more convenient to use the **system** library function which is built on top of the **fork**, exec, and **wait** calls. **system** takes the entire command line (which can also be a shell builtin or a shell script) as a single argument:

```
system("ls -lu /etc/passwd > foo")
```

The function uses a shell (by default, Bourne) to execute the command, and also makes use of PATH. **system** works with redirection and can also run a pipeline.

When the Parent Dies Before the Child

It's possible for the parent to die before its child. The kernel clears the process table slot of the parent all right, but before doing so, it checks whether there are any processes spawned by the parent that are still alive. When it finds an *orphaned* child, it makes **init** its parent by changing the PPID field of the child in the process table. Recall that when we ran a job with **nohup** and logged out, we found the PPID of the job had changed to 1 (*8.10.2*).

init relies on the same signaling mechanism that was discussed with **waitpid** to know the death of its child (either spawned by it or an orphaned one). When a user logs out, her shell terminates and the kernel sends a SIGCHLD signal to **init**. **init**'s signal handler then immediately fork-execs a **getty** at that terminal to display the login prompt. This sequence is discussed in Section 19.6.1. We take up signal handling in Section 18.9.

18.7   File Sharing

The previous program proved that it is possible to open a file in the parent and write it in the child without the child needing to know the filename. To implement redirection in our programs, we need to understand the significance of the three data structures (Fig. 18.6) that the kernel maintains for every open file:

- The *file descriptor table*—This structure contains all allocated file descriptors for a process. Each entry points to the file table.
- The *file table* —It contains all parameters that are supplied as the second argument to **open**. It also contains the file offset. This table points to the vnode table.
- The *vnode table*—This contains all inode information, and can be considered as an approximation of the inode in memory (in-core inode).

18.7.1   The File Descriptor Table

The file descriptor returned by **open** is stored in the **file descriptor table**. This table is maintained separately for every process. The shell's three standard files occupy the first three slots (0, 1, and 2) in the table. If you close, say, descriptor number 1, the kernel will allocate this number to the next file that is opened. We'll use this behavioral property to implement redirection.

Every descriptor is associated with a flag, FD_CLOEXEC, that is also stored in the descriptor table. This flag is not used by **open**, but by a powerful system call named **fcntl** to determine whether the descriptor will be closed when the process does an exec. By default, a descriptor is not closed on an exec.

FIGURE 18.6   *File Sharing—The Three Tables*

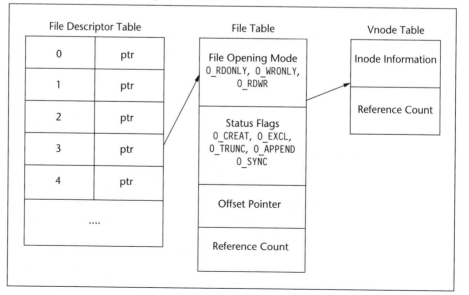

18.7.2 The File Table

Every entry in the file descriptor table points to a **file table**. This table contains all the flags specified in the second argument to **open**. To be specific, it contains:

- The mode of opening (like O_RDONLY).
- The status flags (like O_CREAT, O_TRUNC, etc.).
- The file's offset pointer location.
- A reference count that indicates the number of descriptors that point to this table.

The file's status flags (though not its mode) can be changed by the **fcntl** system call—the same call that controls the FD_CLOEXEC flag in the file descriptor table. The kernel releases the file table from memory only when there's no descriptor pointing to it, i.e., when the reference count has dropped to zero.

18.7.3 The Vnode Table

The file table contains a pointer to the **vnode table**, the third table in the scheme. This was once called the inode table, but with UNIX supporting multiple file system types today, the *vnode* abstraction was created to make it possible to access the inode in a file-system-independent way. This table contains all information present in the inode. There's only a single copy of the vnode in memory. The inode on disk is updated from the information in the vnode.

Like the file table, the vnode table also maintains a reference count field that signifies the number of file table entries that point to this table. When a file is deleted, the kernel has to first check the reference count to see whether any process still has the file open. If the reference count is at least one, the kernel can't delete the file and release the inode *though it will delete the directory entry for the file*. This unusual behavior has already been discussed *(17.13.3—Inset)*.

18.7.4 When the Linkage Changes

Why the file's status and mode flags are kept in the file table and not in the descriptor table can be understood if you consider that the general scheme that we just discussed can change with certain operations:

- When a file is opened twice.
- When a process forks.
- When a descriptor is replicated. This is discussed in Section 18.8.

When a file is opened twice in the *same* process, the file descriptor table will have two entries for the file. Each file descriptor will point to its own file table, so there will be two file tables as well. However, both file tables will point to the same vnode table (Fig. 18.7). When the same file is opened by a *different* process, an entry is made in the descriptor table of that process, which will also point to its own file table, but there's only one vnode table that it will point to.

When a process forks, the child maintains a separate copy of the file descriptor table of its parent. But the descriptors of both parent and child point to the *same* file table (Fig. 18.8). This means that the file offset pointer set by an I/O operation in the

FIGURE 18.7 *When a File Is Opened Twice in the Same Process*

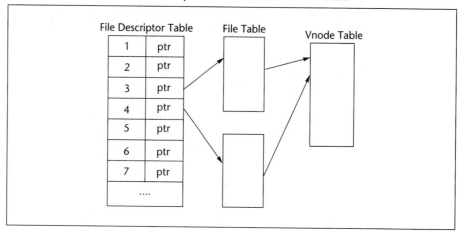

FIGURE 18.8 *When a Process Forks*

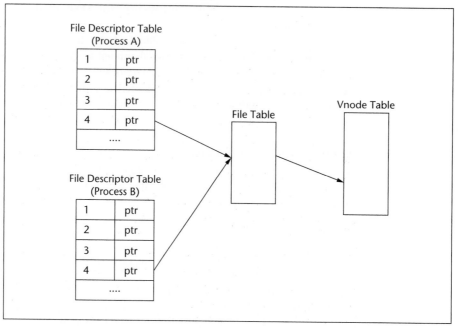

parent is seen by the child when using a copy of the descriptor. That's why foo.log could be written sequentially by parent and child in the program **fork_exec_wait.c** *(Fig. 18.5)*. However, note that subsequently changing the entries of the descriptor table in one process won't have any effect on the other.

18.8 File Descriptor Manipulation

While **fork** replicates the entire descriptor table of the parent, it is also possible to replicate a descriptor in the same process. This is done with the **dup**, **dup2**, and **fcntl** system calls. We'll first learn to use **dup**, understand how **dup2** is better, and then use **dup2** along with **fork** and exec to redirect the standard streams.

18.8.1 dup and dup2: Duplicating a File Descriptor

Descriptors are replicated by the **dup** and **dup2** system calls (and by **fcntl**). The first one has a very simple syntax:

```
int dup(int fildes);
```

Here, **dup** duplicates *fildes* and returns the lowest numbered descriptor available for allocation. As in **fork**, both *fildes* and its replicated descriptor share the same file table as shown in Fig. 18.9.

Assuming that the three standard streams are the only files open in a process, **dup(1)** will return the value 3. Now consider this sequence:

```
fd = open("foo", O_WRONLY | O_CREAT | O_TRUNC, 0600);
close(STDOUT_FILENO);
dup(fd);                                    This should return descriptor 1
```

Because the descriptor 1 returned by **dup** now points to the file table of foo, anything you now write to standard output *should* end up in foo. You have understood the key concept behind redrection.

We say "should" and not "must" because there is slender chance that the above sequence can fail. The process could have a defined signal handler (*18.9*) which creates a file bar. If the process receives a signal after **close** and before **dup**, the signal handler would create bar which will be allocated the descriptor that we wanted from **dup**. This sequence will then fail.

FIGURE 18.9 *When a Descrriptor Is Replicated with* **dup** *(4 replicated to 6)*

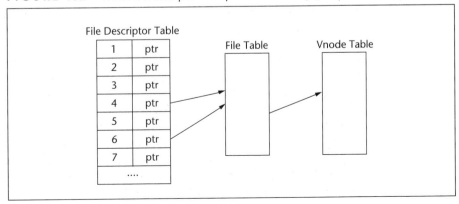

To overcome this problem, we use the **dup2** system call that uses two arguments:

```
int dup2(int fildes, int fildes2);
```

dup2 replicates *filedes* to *filedes2*, closing it if found open, and returns it. **dup2** thus combines the actions of **close** and **dup**. The previous sequence is more appropriately framed this way:

```
fd = open("foo", O_WRONLY | O_CREAT | O_TRUNC, 0600);
dup2(fd, STDOUT_FILENO);                          Closes standard output simultaneously
```

The advantage here is that **dup2** performs both functions as an atomic operation. A signal can't interrupt an atomic operation that is partially complete. We have learned a very important lesson here:

> *If you want to write an open file* foo *using a specific file descriptor (here, 1) that is already allocated to* bar *(here, standard output), then replicate the existing descriptor of* foo *to return the one used by* bar. foo *will then be accessible with the new descriptor.*

This will be the guiding principle for any task that involves redirection, but we are not there yet. **dup2** will be followed by a call to exec whose standard output will be automatically redirected. But doing an exec in the current process leaves us with nothing more to do since exec doesn't return. Further, by closing standard output, we ensure that we can't write to the terminal again. Both tasks should be performed in a child process.

18.8.2   `redirection.c`: Redirection at Last

This program, **redirection.c** (Fig. 18.10), achieves the effect of redirection without using the < and > symbols. The first two arguments represent the filenames to be used for redirection; the remaining are the components of the command line to be executed. File opening, descriptor manipulation, and exec are all done in a child process. The parent simply forks and waits for the child to die. To demonstrate how the parent correctly obtains the exit status of the command run by the child, let's use the program to run **grep** twice:

```
$ a.out /etc/passwd passwd.cnt grep joker
Exit status: 1                                    joker not found in /etc/passwd
$ a.out /etc/passwd passwd.cnt grep sumit
Exit status: 0                                    sumit found in /etc/passwd
$ cat passwd.cnt
sumit:x:500:500:sumitabha das:/home/sumit:/bin/bash
```

We have said this before as a UNIX user *(7.5.1)*, and we say it again—this time as a systems programmer: **grep** didn't open either /etc/passwd or passwd.cnt. They were already open and allocated the correct descriptors before **grep** was called. This is what redirection is all about.

Note

There are basically two ways of duplicating a file descriptor—using **fork**, and using **dup** and **dup2** (or their **fcntl** equivalents). **fork** makes a copy of the parent's descriptor available in the child, while **dup** and **dup2** add an entry to the descriptor table of the current process. In either case, the end result is that both original and copy share the same file table, i.e., the same file offset, opening modes, and status flags.

FIGURE 18.10 `redirection.c`

```
/* Program: redirection.c -- Opens files in the child and uses dup2 to
   reassign the descriptors. First two arguments are input and output filenames
   The command line to execute is specified as the remaining arguments */

#include <unistd.h>
#include <stdio.h>
#include <sys/stat.h>
#include <fcntl.h>
#include <wait.h>

#define OPENFLAGS (O_WRONLY | O_CREAT | O_TRUNC)
#define MODE600 (S_IRUSR | S_IWUSR)

int main(int argc, char **argv) {
  int fd1, fd2, rv, exit_status;

  if (fork() == 0) {                    /* Child */
    if ((fd1 = open(argv[1], O_RDONLY)) == -1)
      quit("Error in opening file for reading\n", 1);
    if ((fd2 = open(argv[2], OPENFLAGS, MODE600)) == -1)
      quit("Error in opening file for writing\n", 1);
    dup2(fd1,STDIN_FILENO);
    dup2(fd2,STDOUT_FILENO);
    execvp(argv[3], &argv[3]);          /* Uses PATH */
    quit("exec error", 2);

  } else {                              /* Parent */
    wait(&rv);                          /* Or use waitpid(-1, &rv, 0) */
    printf("Exit status: %d\n", WEXITSTATUS(rv));
    exit(0);
  }
}
```

18.8.3   fcntl: Recommended over dup and dup2

POSIX calls **dup** and **dup2** "redundant" functions, and advocates the use of the **fcntl** system call. Space constraints don't permit a thorough examination of this versatile system call, but you should at least know that descriptor replication is one of **fcntl**'s numerous functions. Here are the **fcntl** equivalents to **dup** and **dup2**:

dup *and* dup2	fcntl *Equivalents*
fd = dup(*filedes*);	fd = fcntl(*fildes*, F_DUPFD, 0);
fd = dup2(*fildes*, *fildes2*);	close(*fildes2*); fd = fcntl(*fildes*, F_DUPFD, *fildes2*);

Note that **fcntl** loses its atomicity when emulating **dup2**, because it is preceded by the **close** call. POSIX recommends the use of signal blocking *(18.9)* to avoid this problem.

fcntl can also manipulate information held in the file descriptor table and file table. Every file descriptor is associated with the FD_CLOEXEC flag that determines whether the descriptor will be closed across an exec. By default, descriptors remain open, but a prior call to **fcntl** can reverse this behavior. **fcntl** can also change the file's status flags (though not its opening modes) while it is open.

18.9 Signal Handling

We were introduced to signals in Section 8.9 as a simple form of interprocess communication (IPC)—a mechanism used by the kernel to communicate the occurrence of an event to a process. Signals can be *synchronous* (predictable) or *asynchronous* (unpredictable) and can originate from the following sources:

- *The keyboard*   Signals generated from the keyboard affect the current foreground job (or process group). *[Ctrl-c]* generates SIGINT to terminate a process. *[Ctrl-z]* sends SIGTSTP to suspend a job.
- *The hardware*   Signals can be generated on account of an arithmetic exception like divide-by-zero (SIGFPE), an illegal instruction (SIGILL), or a memory access violation (SIGSEGV).
- *A C program*   The system call library offers some functions that generate signals. **alarm** generates SIGALRM after the expiry of a specified time. The **raise** and **kill** functions can generate any signal.
- *Other sources*   When a child dies, the kernel sends SIGCHLD to the parent. When a background job tries to read from the terminal, the terminal driver generates SIGTTIN.

The action that a process takes on receipt of a signal is known as its **disposition**. Every signal is associated with a default disposition (Table 18.1) which in most cases terminates the process, but you can make your program do one of these things:

- *Ignore the signal.*
- *Restore the default.*   This could be required when the signal's default disposition has been changed by a signal handler and now you want to change it back again.
- *Catch the signal.*   React to the signal by invoking a signal handling function. This is what we'll be mostly doing in the examples that follow.

Like a process, a signal has a life cycle of its own. A signal is first *generated* and then *delivered* to a process. A signal is considered to be delivered when the signal disposition has occurred—even if the disposition is to ignore the signal. A signal can also be *blocked* to prevent immediate delivery and is considered to be *pending*. The signal can be delivered only by *unblocking* the signal.

TABLE 18.1   *Signals and Default Disposition*

Signal Name	Significance	Default Action
SIGINT	Terminal interrupt (*[Ctrl-c]*)	Terminate
SIGQUIT	Terminal quit (*[Ctrl-\]*)	Terminate with core dump
SIGTSTP	Terminal stop (*[Ctrl-z]*)	Stop
SIGABRT	Abnormal termination (**abort** call)	Terminate
SIGCHLD	Change of child's status	Ignore
SIGCONT	Continue stopped child	Continue
SIGALRM	Timer (set by **alarm** call); sends signal after expiry of timeout period	Terminate
SIGHUP	Hangup signal	Terminate
SIGTERM	Software termination	Terminate
SIGPIPE	Write to pipe with read ends closed	Terminate
SIGILL	Illegal instruction	Terminate with core dump
SIGFPE	Arithmetic exception	Terminate with core dump
SIGSEGV	Segmentation violation; process attempts to access memory outside its own address space	Terminate with core dump
SIGKILL	Sure kill	Terminate; can't be caught
SIGSTOP	Process stop	Stop; can't be caught

When a signal is sent to a process, the kernel sets a bit in the **pending signals mask** field of the process table *(18.1.2)*. This field has a bit reserved for each type of signal. The process checks this field and then the **signal disposition table**, also in the process table. If the disposition is to catch the signal, the process suspends execution and invokes the handler. Once the handler returns the process resumes operation. In this respect, signals resemble interrupts which also have their own interrupt handlers.

Two signals—SIGKILL and SIGSTOP—can't be caught or ignored. These signals will always do the work they are designed to do. Further, there's no provision in the process table to detect the receipt of multiple instances of the same signal. A process merely knows that it has received at least one instance of the signal.

Note

Irrespective of the action you take, there are two signals that you can neither ignore nor catch by invoking a signal handler. They are SIGKILL and SIGSTOP. It's necessary for the superuser to have the powers to kill any process (with SIGKILL) or stop it (with SIGSTOP). If the superuser didn't have these powers, runaway processes could bring life to a standstill.

▨ 18.9.1 The System Calls

The original signal handling system was based on the **signal** system call. This call was considered *unreliable* because its behavior differed across systems. We discuss here the *reliable* POSIX signal handling mechanism. This is an elaborate and somewhat complex system comprising a large number of calls. It also makes use of *signal sets* to block a group of signals. We are constrained to ignore signal sets in this text, but we'll examine the following system calls and library functions:

- **sigaction**   This call specifies the signal handler. Two of the arguments to this call specify a structure that is also named **sigaction**.
- **alarm**   The **alarm** call is used in the next example to set a timer that generates the SIGALRM signal after the timeout period. The library function **sleep** uses **alarm**.
- **pause**   This is somewhat like the shell's **read** statement. It holds up program execution until a signal is received.
- **kill**   You can send a signal to a process using this system call. A library function, **raise**, uses **kill** to send any signal to the current process.

In most cases, system calls are allowed to complete before a process invokes a signal handler. For instance, if a process is sleeping on the completion of disk I/O, the kernel allows the system call to complete before performing signal delivery. However, if the process is waiting to take input from the terminal, the kernel will abort the call, which is reasonable because waiting for terminal input could be a wait forever. The POSIX system also permits restarting a system call.

18.10   sigaction: **Installing a Signal Handler**

The **sigaction** system call specifies mainly the signal's disposition. Two of its three arguments represent a pointer to a structure of type sigaction:

```
int sigaction(int sig, const struct sigaction *restrict act,
                             struct sigaction *restrict oact);
```

When this call is invoked, it *installs* the handler. Subsequently, when the process receives the *sig* signal, it invokes the handler that is specified in the *act* structure. *oact* stores the current signal disposition and is used in restore it after the default disposition has been changed. Depending on what we want the function to do, either argument can be set to NULL, but not both. **sigaction** returns -1 on error.

Both *act* and *oact* are actually pointers to a structure of type sigaction. POSIX requires this structure to have at least these four members:

```
struct sigaction {
    void (*sa_handler)(int)
    sigset_t sa_mask
    int sa_flags
    void (*)(int, siginfo_t *, void *) sa_sigaction
}
```

The first member sets the signal disposition. sa_handler can either be the name of a function or one of the following symbolic constants:

SIG_IGN   Ignore the signal.
SIG_DFL   Revert to the default disposition.

sa_mask specifies a set of signals that are blocked while the handler is executing. sa_flags specifies optional flags. The SA_RESTART flag restarts a system call, and SA_RESETHAND sets the disposition of the handler to the default after invocation. sa_sigaction is used only when sa_flags is specified.

In the examples that follow, we'll only set the first member of the structure and ignore the others. This argument can either point to a signal handling function or be assigned SIG_IGN or SIG_DFL. We'll consider the handling function first:

```
struct sigaction act;
act.sa_handler = alrm_handler;                              alrm_handler is a function
```

This assigns the alrm_handler function to the sa_handler member of struct sigaction. The function must be defined in the program. We now have to invoke **sigaction** to install the handler for the SIGALRM signal:

```
if (sigaction(SIGALRM, &act, NULL) == -1)
```

Now that the handler is installed, it will be invoked by the process when it receives SIGALRM. Note that we set the third argument to NULL because we are not interested in saving the current disposition of SIGALRM.

The act.sa_handler member can also specify one of the two symbolic constants, SIG_IGN or SIG_DFL. The interrupt key can't terminate a program if **sigaction** installs the handler for SIGINT with sa_handler set to SIG_IGN:

```
act.sa_handler = SIG_IGN;                                  Disposition set to ignore
if (sigaction(SIGINT, &act, NULL) == -1)
```

You can make use of this protective feature to place these statements at the beginning of a critical section of code that you won't want to be interrupted. You can then revert to the default disposition by placing these statements after the critical code section:

```
act.sa_handler = SIG_DFL;                                  Disposition set to default
if (sigaction(SIGINT, &act, NULL) == -1)
```

Signal handlers are executed in the user mode. Let's now write our first signal handling program to catch the SIGALRM signal.

Why We Should Use sigaction *and not* signal

Before the POSIX signaling system was adopted by most UNIX implementations, a signal handler was installed with the **signal** system call. **signal** was unreliable in that a signal's disposition was reset to the default before the handler was invoked. A second signal of the same type would then be subject to the default disposition. If we required the disposition to be persistent, we had to reinstall the handler at the beginning of the handling function:

```
void alrm_handler(int signo) {
    signal(SIGALRM, alrm_handler);    /* Resetting signal handler */
    ..........
```

This approach works most of the time, but there's a finite probability of it leading to a **race condition**. In this situation, two or more events act on the same resource, and the sequence in which they are serviced determines the eventual outcome of the race. Here, if a second signal of the same type arrives *after* the disposition is reset to the default and *before* the handler is reinstalled, the default action will be taken. If the default action is to terminate the process, the handler won't be given a chance to reinstall itself.

All signals handled by the **signal** system call are unreliable for other reasons also; a signal can get lost and can't be blocked. The POSIX signal handling system is *reliable* and takes care of the limitations inherent in **signal**.

18.10.1 signal.c: Catching the SIGALRM Signal

This program, **signal.c** (Fig. 18.11), uses the **alarm** call to set up a timer which times out in five seconds. The program prompts the user for a filename which is displayed if the user inputs it in five seconds. If the user is late in responding, SIGALRM is generated, which invokes a signal handler to set the default filename to foo.

We declare the prototype of the alrm_handler function before **main**, and assign this function to the sa_handler member of the act structure of type sigaction. The **sigaction** call installs this function for SIGALRM.

The user is prompted for a filename, and the **alarm** timer sets off immediately thereafter. The filename is displayed if it is entered in the timeout period. But if the timeout occurs, SIGALRM is generated which leads to the execution of alrm_handler. We invoke the program with and without a filename:

```
$ a.out
Enter filename: signal.log
Filename: signal.log
$ a.out
Enter filename:                          Nothing entered in 5 seconds
Signal 14 received, default filename: foo
$ kill -l | grep 14                                What is signal 14?
13) SIGPIPE    14) SIGALRM    15) SIGTERM    16) SIGUSSR1
```

18.10.2 Catching Terminal-Generated Signals

Let's now develop another program, **signal2.c** (Fig. 18.12), that uses two signal handlers for SIGINT and SIGTSTP. Unlike SIGALRM, these signals are sent from the keyboard. We'll also ignore the SIGQUIT signal.

Using three **sigaction** calls we set the disposition of three different signals. Note the use of SIG_IGN in one assignment of sa_handler that sets the disposition to ignore for SIGQUIT. *[Ctrl-z]* generates SIGTSTP, but we catch it to display a message without stopping the process. We also catch *[Ctrl-c]* (SIGINT), but to terminate the process only when the key is pressed twice.

FIGURE 18.11 `signal.c`

```c
/* Program: signal.c -- Waits for 5 seconds for user input and then
                        generates SIGALRM that has a handler specified */
#include <stdio.h>
#include <unistd.h>
#include <signal.h>
#define BUFSIZE 100

void alrm_handler(int signo);               /* Prototype declaration */

char buf[BUFSIZE] = "foo\0";                /* Global variable */
int main (void) {
    int n;
    struct sigaction act;
    act.sa_handler = alrm_handler;          /* Specify handler */
    if (sigaction(SIGALRM, &act, NULL) == -1)   /* Install handler */
        quit("sigalrm", 1);

    fprintf(stderr, "Enter filename: ");
    alarm(5);                               /* Set alarm clock; will deliver */
    n = read(STDIN_FILENO, buf, BUFSIZE);   /* SIGALRM in 5 seconds */
    if (n > 1)                              /* Will come here if user inputs */
        fprintf(stderr, "Filename: %s\n", buf);   /* string within 5 seconds */

    exit(0);
}

void alrm_handler(int signo) {
    fprintf(stderr, "\nSignal %d received, default filename: %s\n", signo, buf);
    exit(1);
}
```

The **for** loop makes the **pause** system call run in a loop. **pause** simply suspends execution until it receives any signal, in which case it returns with the EINTR error. Let's now run this program by pressing all three key sequences in turn:

```
$ a.out
Press [Ctrl-z] first, then [Ctrl-c]
[Ctrl-\]                                              Signal ignored
[Ctrl-z]
Can't stop this program                        From tstp_handler
```

FIGURE 18.12 signal2.c

```
/* Program: signal2.c -- Handles SIGINT and SIGTSTP generated from terminal
                     Requires two [Ctrl-c]s to terminate */
#include <stdio.h>
#include <signal.h>

void tstp_handler(int signo);          /* Handler for [Ctrl-z] */
void int_handler(int signo);           /* Handler for [Ctrl-c] */
int count = 0;

int main (void) {
    struct sigaction act1, act2, act3;
    act1.sa_handler = tstp_handler;    /* Disposition for these two signals */
    act2.sa_handler = int_handler;     /* set to enter respective handlers */
    act3.sa_handler = SIG_IGN;         /* Disposition set to ignore */
    sigaction(SIGTSTP, &act1, NULL);
    sigaction(SIGINT, &act2, NULL);
    sigaction(SIGQUIT, &act3, NULL);

    fprintf(stderr, "Press [Ctrl-z] first, then [Ctrl-c]\n");
    for (;;)
      pause();                         /* Will return on receipt of signal */
    exit(0);
}

void tstp_handler(int signo) {
    fprintf(stderr, "Can't stop this program\n");
}
void int_handler(int signo) {                    /* Will terminate program */
    if (++count == 1)
        fprintf(stderr, "Press again\n");
    else
        quit("Quitting", 1);
}
```

[Ctrl-c]	
Press again	*From* int_handler
[Ctrl-c]	
Quitting: Interrupted system call	*From* int_handler

All three signal handlers can be seen at work here. So far, we have handled specific signals, mostly generated from the keyboard; in Section 18.11, we'll use **kill** to generate any signal.

Note

When a process is executed in the background with &, the disposition of SIGINT is set to SIG_IGN, which is why *[Ctrl-c]* can't terminate a background process. When a process is run with **nohup**, the disposition of SIGHUP is also set to SIG_IGN; the process won't terminate when the connection is broken.

18.11   killprocess.c: **Using fork-exec-wait and** SIGCHLD

Before we take up the next program, we have a new system call to discuss—**kill**. Like its command counterpart, the **kill** system call sends a signal to one or more processes:

```
int kill(pid_t pid, int sig);
```

Generally, we obtain the PID of the child using **pid = fork()**, and then use, say, **kill(pid, SIGTERM)** to kill the child with SIGTERM.

It's time for consolidation, so let's demonstrate the combined use of the fork-exec-wait and signal handling mechanisms. The program, **killprocess.c** (Fig. 18.13), runs a command that is input by the user and prints the exit status if the command completes in five seconds. If it doesn't, then the parent uses **kill** to send SIGTERM to kill the child.

This time we use a single signal handling function to handle both SIGCHLD and SIGALRM. The parent forks a child which then uses **execvp** to run a user-specified program supplied as one or more command line arguments. Note that this time the parent doesn't wait for the child's death after the fork. It starts a timer with **alarm(5)**, which on expiry issues the SIGALRM signal. The parent issues **pause**, which returns on receipt of any signal.

One of two signals can wake up the parent here—either SIGCHLD or SIGALRM. The signal handling function takes into account that the child may or may not complete execution in five seconds. If it does, SIGCHLD is issued and **death_handler** invokes **waitpid** to pick up the exit status of the child. Otherwise, **death_handler** waits for SIGALRM and then kills the process with SIGTERM.

We'll run the program twice—once with a program that completes in five seconds and then with one that doesn't:

```
$ a.out date
Thu Apr  3 14:49:57 IST 2003
Child dies; exit status: 0
Parent dies
$ a.out find /home -name a.out -print
/home/sumit/personal/project8/a.out
/home/sumit/personal/books_code/glass_ables/12/a.out
/home/sumit/personal/books_code/stevens_c/ch08/a.out
     ...after 5 second time interval......
5 seconds over, child killed
Parent dies
```

FIGURE 18.13 `killprocess.c`

```
/* Program: killprocess.c -- Uses fork and exec to run a user-defined program
                             and kills it if it doesn't complete in 5 seconds.*/
#include <stdio.h>
#include <sys/types.h>
#include <sys/wait.h>
#include <signal.h>

pid_t pid;
int main (int argc, char **argv) {
    int i, status;
    void death_handler(int signo);        /* A common signal handler this time */

    struct sigaction act;
    act.sa_handler = death_handler;
    sigaction(SIGCHLD, &act, NULL);       /* Disposition for these two signals */
    sigaction(SIGALRM, &act, NULL);       /* set to enter a single handler */

    switch (pid = fork()) {
        case -1: fprintf(stderr, "Fork error\n");
        case  0: execvp(argv[1], &argv[1]);   /* Execute command */
                 perror("exec");
                 break;
        default: alarm(5);    /* Will send SIGALRM after 5 seconds */
                 pause();        /* Will return when SIGCHLD signal is received */
                 fprintf(stderr, "Parent dies\n");
    }
    exit(0);
}

void death_handler(int signo) {    /* This common handler picks up the */
    int status;                    /* exit status for normal termination */
                                   /* but sends the SIGTERM signal if */
    switch (signo) {               /* command doesn't complete in 5 seconds */
        case SIGCHLD: waitpid(-1, &status, 0);    /* Same as wait(&status); */
                      fprintf(stderr, "Child dies; exit status: %d\n",
                                           WEXITSTATUS(status));
                      break;
        case SIGALRM: if (kill(pid, SIGTERM) == 0)
                          fprintf(stderr, "5 seconds over, child killed\n");
    }
}
```

kill can be used to send a signal to the current process also. You need to use **getpid** to specify the PID here, but the **raise** library function does this work for us. In fact, **raise(SIGTERM)** is equivalent to **kill(getpid(), SIGTERM)**.

▬ 18.12 IPC with Unnamed Pipes

UNIX has very elaborate schemes for two processes to communicate with each other. In this section, we discuss the piping mechanism available in the shell.

To understand how a pipe enables one process to send its standard output to the standard input of another process, imagine doing a similar thing using a disk file instead. One process could write to the file, and the other could read from it. This means that the size of the file grows as data flows from writer to reader. Further, this system just won't work because if the reader is faster than the writer, it will often catch up with the writer and read EOF. There's no flow control mechanism that would make one process block till the other has completed its job. Operating system theorists have a name for this—the *producer-consumer* problem.

The pipe solves both of these problems. It is a *half-duplex communication channel*, which means that data flows in only one direction. It is a type of file that can be used with **read** and **write**, but it's created with the **pipe** system call:

```
int pipe(int fildes[2]);
```

pipe takes an array of 2 integers as its only argument, which it populates with two file descriptors. Whatever is written to *fildes*[1] can be read from *fildes*[0]; the significance of 0 and 1 have been retained in the pipe as well. A call to **write** on *fildes*[1] populates a fixed-sized buffer (about 4–8 KB), while a call to **read** on *filedes*[0] drains the buffer so the next **write** can fill it up again.

If the buffer is found empty during a read, the operation will block till the buffer is written. Similarly, a write to a buffer that has not yet been read will block too. The data is read on a first-in–first-out basis (FIFO), and expectedly, the pipe's file type is FIFO which can be checked with the S_ISFIFO macro.

Although a pipe is most commonly shared by two processes, a simple example shows its use in a single process:

```
int n, fd[2];
char buf[10];
pipe(fd);                          Fills up fd[2] with 2 descriptors
write(fd[1], "abcdefgh", 8 );      Writing to one file descriptor
n = read(fd[0], buf, 8);           and reading it back from another
write(STDOUT_FILENO, buf, n);      Printing what was read from pipe
```

pipe here generates two file descriptors, fd[0] and fd[1]. We simply write the string abcdefgh to fd[1] and read it back from fd[0], and then write the same string to the standard output. There's not much to learn from here except that numerous possibilities open up when a pipe is used by two processes. This is taken up next.

18.12.1   Using pipe with fork

To make **pipe** work in tandem with **fork**, the usual procedure is to create the pipe before forking a process. Because **fork** duplicates all open descriptors, the **pipe–fork** sequence connects two descriptors to each end of the pipe.

To use the pipe, we don't need all four descriptors, but only one on each end. Data here can flow in either direction, but assuming that the parent writes to the pipe and the child reads it, then we must close the pipe's read end in the parent and the write end in the child. This is what the program, **pipe.c** (Fig. 18.14), does.

The **pipe** call returns two descriptors, fd[0] and fd[1], which should have the values 3 and 4 in this program. This example assumes data flowing from parent to child, so the parent doesn't need the read end (fd[0]), while the child doesn't need the write end (fd[1]), the reason why these descriptors have been closed. The program outputs the string that's written to the pipe:

```
$ a.out
Writing to pipe
```

FIGURE 18.14 pipe.c

```
/* Program: pipe.c -- Shares a pipe between two processes.
                      We want the data to flow from the parent to the child */
#include <stdio.h>
#include <unistd.h>

int main(void) {
    int n, fd[2];                     /* fd[2] to be filled up by pipe() */
    char buf[100];                    /* Buffer to be used by read() */

    if (pipe(fd) < 0)                 /* fd[0] is read end */
      quit("pipe", 1);                /* fd[1] is write end */

    switch (fork()) {                 /* Pipe has four descriptors now */
      case -1: quit("Fork error", 2);
       case 0: close(fd[1]);          /* CHILD-Close write end of pipe */
              n = read(fd[0], buf, 100); /* and read from its read end */
              write(STDOUT_FILENO, buf, n);
              break;
      default: close(fd[0]);              /* PARENT-Close read end of pipe */
              write(fd[1], "Writing to pipe\n", 16); /* write to write end */
    }

    exit(0);
}
```

This is the string **write** wrote to fd[1] and **read** gathered from fd[0]. In real life though, you use separate programs on either side of the shell's pipe symbol, |. So you'll naturally expect to do a similar thing with **pipe**. This means that you have to connect the standard output of one program to fd[1] and the standard input of the other to fd[0]. How does one do that?

18.12.2 pipe2.c: Running UNIX Commands in a Pipe

The next program, **pipe2.c** (Fig. 18.15), addresses this issue. Apart from closing the unneeded file descriptors associated with the pipe, the program also uses **dup2** to replicate the other descriptors—both in the parent and the child. We reverse the data flow here— from child to parent—just to prove that the direction of flow is irrelevant.

FIGURE 18.15 pipe2.c

```
/* Program: pipe2.c -- Runs two programs in a pipeline
                       Child runs cat, parent runs tr */
#include <unistd.h>
#include <stdio.h>

int main(void) {
    int fd[2];                          /* To be filled up by pipe() */

    if (pipe(fd) < 0)                   /* Now have four descriptors for pipe */
       quit("pipe", 1);

    switch (fork()) {
      case -1: quit("fork", 2);

      case 0: close(fd[0]);                    /* CHILD - Close read end first */
              dup2(fd[1], STDOUT_FILENO);  /* Connect stdout to  write end */
              close(fd[1]);                    /* and close original descriptor */
              execlp("cat", "cat", "/etc/hosts.equiv", (char *) 0);
              quit("cat", 3);

      default: close(fd[1]);                   /* PARENT - Close write end first */
               dup2(fd[0], STDIN_FILENO);  /* Connect stdin to read end */
               close(fd[0]);                   /* and close original descriptor */
               execlp("tr", "tr", "'[a-z]'","'[A-Z]'", (char *) 0);
               quit("tr", 4);
    }
}
```

To understand how the program works, let's first examine the sequence of statements that are executed in the child process. We first close fd[0], the read end, since the child writes (not reads) to the pipe. Next, we replicate fd[1] with **dup2** to give us the descriptor used by standard output. At this stage, the file descriptor for standard output points to the write end of the pipe. This means we don't need the original descriptor (fd[1]) that was connected to the same end of the pipe.

Having now closed both the original read and write ends of the pipe, we are left with only the descriptor for standard output that is now connected to the pipe's write end. Invoking **execvp** to run the **cat** command ensures that **cat**'s output is connected to the pipe's write end.

If we apply a similar line of reasoning to the statements in the parent, we'll end up in a situation where the standard input of **tr** is connected to the read end of the pipe. We have been able to establish a pipeline between **cat** and **tr**. On running the program, you should see the entries in /etc/hosts.equiv, but after conversion to uppercase:

```
$ a.out
SATURN
EARTH
MERCURY
JUPITER
```

Compare this output with that obtained from the program, **reverse_read.c** (Fig. 17.3), which displayed the contents of /etc/hosts.equiv in reverse order.

Two processes can use a pipe for communication only if they share a common ancestor. But UNIX also supports *named pipes* and *sockets* for two unrelated processes to communicate with each other. Besides, SVR4 offers *semaphores, shared memory,* and *message queues* as advanced forms of IPC. Space constraints don't permit inclusion of these topics, but you have a lot to explore on your own.

SUMMARY

A process runs in its own *virtual address space* comprising the text, data, and stack. Part of the process address space is also reserved for the kernel.

The *process table* contains all control information related to a process. The table contains both the *pending signals mask* and the *signal disposition* for every signal that the process may receive.

The environment variables are available in the variable, environ[]. A variable can be set with **setenv** or **putenv** and retrieved with **getenv**.

The **fork** system call creates a process by replicating the existing address space. **fork** returns twice—zero in the child and its own PID in the parent. The *exec* family replaces the complete address space of the current process with that of a new program. Shell and **perl** scripts can be run by **execlp** and **execvp**. A successful exec doesn't return.

A process exits by invoking **exit** with an argument that represents the *exit status*. This number is retrieved by the parent with **wait** or **waitpid**. Unlike **wait**, **waitpid** can wait for a specific child to die and also need not block till the child dies.

If the parent dies before the child, the child turns into an *orphan,* which is immediately adopted by **init**. If the parent is alive but doesn't invoke **wait**, the child is transformed into a *zombie*. A zombie is a dead process whose address space has been freed but not the entry in the process table.

The kernel maintains three tables in memory when a file is opened. The *file descriptor table* stores all open descriptors. The *file table* stores the opening mode, status flags and file offset. The *vnode table* contains the inode information. A table is not freed until its reference count drops to zero. A forked child process inherits the descriptors but shares the file table.

dup replicates a file descriptor and returns the lowest unallocated value. **dup2** allows us to choose the descriptor we want by closing it if it is already open. In either case, original and copy both share the same file table. POSIX recommends the use of **fcntl** rather than these two calls.

A *signal* makes a process aware of the occurrence of an event. The process may allow the default disposition to occur, ignore the signal, or invoke a *signal handler*. A handler is *installed* with **sigaction**. The signals SIGKILL and SIGSTOP can't be caught.

pipe creates a buffered object that returns two file descriptors. Data written to one descriptor is read back from the other. To create a pipeline of two commands, you need to create a pipe before invoking **fork**.

SELF-TEST

18.1   Why do we say that the address space of a process is *virtual?* Which segment of the address space do you think is loaded from the program file?

18.2   When and why does a process voluntarily relinquish control of the CPU?

18.3   What is the value returned by **fork**? Why was it designed to behave that way?

18.4   Name the system calls discussed in this chapter that return one or more file descriptors.

18.5   Write a program that forks twice. Display the PIDs and PPIDs of all three processes.

18.6   Write a program that executes the command **wc -l -c /etc/passwd** using (i) **execl**, (ii) **execv**. What changes do you need to make if you use **execlp** and **execvp** instead?

18.7   Is it necessary for the parent to wait for the death of the child? What happens if it doesn't?

18.8   Write a program that accepts two small numbers (< 50) as arguments and then sums the two in a child process. The sum should be returned by the child to the parent as its exit status, and the parent should print the sum.

18.9   Write a shell script containing only one statement: **exit 123456**. Run the script and then invoke **echo $?** from the shell. Explain why the value provided in the script is different from the output.

18.10   A file may have more than one vnode table in memory. True or false?

18.11   Write a program that uses **write** to output the message hello dolly to the standard error. Manipulate the file descriptors so that this message can be saved by using **a.out > foo** rather than **a.out 2>foo**.

18.12   Why can't a background process be terminated with the interrupt key?

18.13 Use the **kill** command to find the number of signals available on your system and then write a program that ignores all of them. Is it possible to do so?

18.14 Explain why a pipe can connect two related processes only.

EXERCISES

18.1 What is the significance of the stack and heap segments in the address space of a process?

18.2 View the man page of **size**, and then run the command on any executable like **/bin/cat**. Explain the significance of the output columns.

18.3 What is the role of the Memory Management Unit in process switching. Why can't one process corrupt the address space of another?

18.4 Write a program that displays all environment variables.

18.5 Write a program that sets an int variable x to 100 before forking a child. Next perform the following in the child and parent:
Child:

(i) Display the value of x, reset it to 200, and display it again.
(ii) Display the value of PATH, reset it to only ., and display it again.
(iii) Change the current directory to /etc and display the absolute pathname of the changed directory.

Parent:

(i) Sleep for 2 seconds.
(ii) Display the value of x, PATH, and the pathname of the current directory.

Explain your observations. Why was the parent made to sleep for two seconds?

18.6 Redirect the output of **fork.c** (Fig. 18.3) to a file and explain the change in behavior.

18.7 Create a shell script that prints the values of HOME, PATH, MAIL, and TERM. Next, write a program that uses exec to run this script so that it prints null values for MAIL and TERM.

18.8 Explain which of these process attributes change with a fork and exec: (i) PID, (ii) PPID, (iii) file descriptors, (iv) standard I/O buffers.

18.9 The completion of process execution doesn't mean that the process is dead. True or false?

18.10 Write a program where the parent dies after creating a child. Display the value of the PPID in the child. Explain your observations.

18.11 Why are the attributes of an open file held in two tables rather than one?

18.12 Does each entry in the file descriptor table have a separate file table associated with it?

18.13 What are the structural changes that take place in memory when (i) a file is opened twice, (ii) its descriptor is replicated. In how many ways can you replicate the descriptor?

18.14 Modify the program in 18.8 (SELF-TEST) so that process A creates B and B creates C. The summation should be performed in C and the result returned to B as the exit status. B should double the summed value and return the product to A as the exit status. Will the program work with large numbers?

18.15 Name two advantages **waitpid** has over **wait**. How do you use **waitpid** to emulate the behavior of **wait**?

18.16 Explain how the kernel treats zombies and orphans.

18.17 Write a program that repeatedly prints the Shell> prompt to accept a UNIX command as argument. The command line, which can't contain shell metacharacters, will be executed by an exec function. The program will terminate when the user enters **exit**. Also try running the program with some of the shell's internal commands (like **umask**) and explain your observations.

18.18 Look up the man page for any shell and understand the significance of the -c option. Next, write a program that prompts for a command, which is executed with **exec** and **sh -c**. Try using the program with both external and internal (shell) commands. Does this program behave properly, even when using wild cards and pipes?

18.19 In what ways can a process behave when it receives a signal? What is special about the SIGSTOP and SIGKILL signals?

18.20 Invoke the command **vi foo &**, and explain why you can't input text to the editor.

## CHAPTER 19

System Administration

Every UNIX system needs to be administered. This task is usually entrusted to a single person—the *system administrator,* also known as the *superuser* or *root user.* The administrator's job involves the management of the entire system—ranging from maintaining user accounts, security, and managing disk space to performing backups. Services must be started and stopped by manipulating their configuration files, and shell scripts must be devised to automate routine operations. To be effective, the administrator must have in-depth knowledge of the different components of the system.

Although UNIX administration is a specialized job, today all UNIX users must understand the essential concepts related to it. The burden is not overwhelming, however, because UNIX is better documented than many other systems. Still, UNIX gets greatly fragmented in this area, which is why POSIX doesn't address administrative issues. Every system has its own set of administrative tools, so we'll confine our discussion mainly to the common ones and their underlying concepts.

Objectives

- Log in to root and become a superuser with **su**.
- Know the administrator's powers in changing the attributes of any file and in killing any process.
- Create, modify, and delete user accounts with **useradd**, **usermod**, and **userdel**.
- Restrict a user's activities with the *restricted shell.*
- Learn how the administrator uses three special file permissions bits—*SUID, SGID,* and *sticky bit*—to enforce security.
- Understand the concept of *run levels* and their role in startup and shutdown operations.
- Learn how **init** uses /etc/inittab and *rc* scripts to start and stop the system's daemons.
- Understand the significance of the attributes of device files.
- Understand the *file system* and its four components.
- *Mount* and *unmount* file systems with **mount** and **umount**.
- Check and repair file systems with **fsck**.
- Use **df** and **du** to report on both free and used disk space.
- Format and copy diskettes with **format**, **fdformat**, and **dd**.
- Handle DOS files on diskettes with a set of "dos" commands.
- Use **tar** as a backup tool.

19.1   root: **The System Administrator's Login**

The administrator mainly uses the root user-id for performing her duties. This account and its password are automatically created at the time of installation of the operating system. The prompt (PS1) for root is generally the #, and the home directory is /:

```
login: root
password: *******[Enter]
# pwd
/                                                     The root directory
# _                                                   # is the prompt
```

Unlike for nonprivileged users, the **passwd** command behaves in a more lenient manner when the root user changes its own password. It doesn't ask for the existing password:

```
# passwd
Changing password for root
Enter the new password (minimum of 5, maximum of 8 characters)
Please use a combination of upper and lower case letters and numbers.
New password: *********
Re-enter password: *********                          To be entered twice
Password changed.
```

The administrator must closely guard the superuser password. Otherwise, the entire UNIX system may have to be reloaded!

What's special about this user-id that gives the administrator so much powers? The answer lies in /etc/passwd:

```
# grep "^root" /etc/passwd
root:x:0:1:Super-User:/:/usr/bin/bash
```

Only root has 0 as the user-id, and you have seen how any process that runs with 0 as the effective UID has the powers of root. We'll see later why the **passwd** program needs to run as if the process is owned by root.

The root user's PATH is different from that for nonprivileged users in two respects. First, it never includes the current directory, a safety feature that prevents the administrator from inadvertently executing programs not known to her. Second, the PATH also includes either /sbin or /usr/sbin (or both):

```
$ echo $PATH
/usr/sbin:/usr/bin
```

The sbin directories contain most administrative commands. We'll be using some of these commands in this chapter.

19.1.1   su: Acquiring Superuser Status

The administrator doesn't need to use the root user-id for all tasks. Certain tasks like monitoring disk space can be performed from a nonprivileged account also. When needed, the administrator can switch from this account to the superuser account with the **su** command:

```
$ su -                                                    Nonprivileged account
Password: ********                                              root's password
# _                                                          Privileged account
```

The - argument ensures that the administrator is presented the same environment as if she has logged in to root. The - has to be dropped if the user's current environment is to be retained (like the home directory).

    su can be used by nonprivileged users also, but with the user-id as argument, to change to any user-id with and without exporting the environment. The superuser isn't prompted for juliet's password when she uses this command, but nonprivileged users need to key it in to gain access:

```
su juliet
su - juliet
```

Successful login recreates juliet's environment, and any program run by juliet using the normal login-password route can often be run in this mode also. **su** runs a separate sub-shell, so this mode is terminated by hitting *[Ctrl-d]* or using **exit**.

Note

Most preinstalled scripts, especially the ones related to system startup and shutdown, use the Bourne shell for execution. You can use Korn or Bash as your interactive shell, but whether you would like to use them for scripting is a decision you have to make. But you must not under any circumstances use C shell scripts. Linux uses Bash for normal and system administrative activities; there's no problem there.

19.2   The Administrator's Privileges

The superuser has enormous powers, and any command invoked by her has a greater chance of success than when issued by others. The command may also behave differently or be reserved for her exclusive use. The superuser's authority is mainly derived from the power to:

- Change the contents or attributes of any file like its permissions and ownership. She can delete any file even if the directory is write-protected!
- Initiate or kill any process. The administrator can directly kill all processes except the ones essential for running the system.
- Change any user's password without knowing the existing one:

```
passwd henry                                        Existing password not required
```

- Use **date** to set the system clock. The date needs to be kept reasonably accurate, otherwise **cron** jobs could be running at wrong times. To set the date and time, the command must be used with a numeric argument of the form *MMDDhhmm,* optionally followed by a two- or four-digit year string:

```
# date 01092124
Thu Jan  9 21:24:00 IST 2003
```

- Address all users concurrently with **wall**.
- Limit the maximum size of files that users are permitted to create with **ulimit**.
- Control users' access to the scheduling services like **at** and **cron**.
- Control users' access to many networking services like FTP, SSH, etc.

The administrator has to use these powers with utmost caution. An apparently innocent and unplugged loophole can cause disaster if that knowledge is acquired by a mischievous person. Let's now examine some of the routine duties of the administrator.

19.3   User Management

The system administrator allocates user accounts, where user-ids are often derived from the actual names of the users. Sometimes, user-ids can represent a project or an application as well. We'll first examine /etc/group, the group database, and then /etc/passwd, where every user is represented. We'll create a group for a user and then add that user to the system.

19.3.1   Understanding /etc/group

A group comprises one or more members having a separate set of privileges. People working on a common project are placed in the same group so they are able to read one another's files. A user has one **primary group** and may have one or more **supplementary groups**. The group database is maintained in /etc/group containing the GID (both the number and the name). A few lines of this file show four fields:

```
root::0:root                                    root user's supplementary group
staff::1:
bin::2:root,bin,daemon
sys::3:root,bin,sys,adm
lp::8:root,lp,adm
student::100:
```

The numeric GID is shown in the third field and the name in the first. The second field (a blank or an x) is hardly used today. *The last field represents those users for which this is their supplementary (not primary) group.* This field often causes confusion, so to properly understand its significance, let's examine the second line in tandem with its associated line in/etc/passwd:

```
root:x:0:1:Super-User:/:/usr/bin/bash
```

The root user has 1 as the GID, which represents the staff group. Since the fourth field in the line representing staff is blank, it means no user has staff as their supplementary group. Also, note that there is a group named root. But this is the supplementary group for the the root user; the primary group for root is staff. The root user also belongs to the supplementary groups, bin, sys, and lp.

Adding a Group (groupadd)   To create a new group dba, with a GID of 241, you need to place an entry in /etc/group:

```
dba:x:241:
```

You can also use the **groupadd** command if it is available on your system:

`groupadd -g 241 dba`   *241 is the GID for dba*

Once an entry for the group has been made, you are now ready to add a user with this GID to the system.

19.3.2   Understanding /etc/passwd

All user information except the password encryption is now stored in /etc/passwd. This file contained the password once, the reason why it continues to be known by that name. /etc/shadow stores the password encryption. The **login** and **passwd** programs look up both files to authenticate a user.

Let's examine the line pertaining to user oracle in /etc/passwd as shown in Fig. 19.1. We'll then use **useradd** to add this entry. There are seven fields in each line of this file:

- Username—The name you use to log on to a UNIX system (oracle).
- Password—No longer stores the password encryption but contains an x.
- UID—The user's numerical identification (210). No two users *should* have the same UID. **ls** prints the owner's name by matching the UID obtained from the inode with this field.
- GID—The user's numerical group identification (241). This number is also the third field in /etc/group.
- Comment or GCOS—User details, for example, her name, address, and so forth (The RDBMS). This name is used at the front of the email address for this user. Mail sent from this user account will show the sender as *"The RDBMS"* <*oracle@heavens.com*>—assuming that the user belongs to the domain shown.
- Home directory—The directory where the user is placed on logging in (/home/oracle). The **login** program reads this field to set the variable HOME.
- Login shell—The first program executed after logging in. This is usually the shell (/bin/ksh). **login** sets the variable SHELL by reading this entry, and also fork-execs the shell process *(19.6.1)*.

FIGURE 19.1   *Line from* /etc/passwd

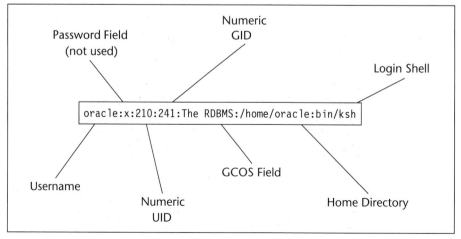

For every line in /etc/passwd, there's a corresponding entry in /etc/shadow. The relevant line in this file could look something like this:

```
oracle:2u6VExtjjXHFk:12285::::::
```

The password encryption is shown in the second field. It's impossible to generate the password from this encryption. However, an intelligent hacker can mount a brute force attack or a dictionary attack to generate a sequence of encrypted patterns. The algorithm used to encrypt the password is available to all, so finding a match is not impossible. This file is thus unreadable to all but the superuser.

Note

The last field in /etc/passwd is actually the command that has to be executed when a user logs in. This is usually the shell, but the administrator may choose a different program to restrict the user's actions.

19.3.3   Adding and Modifying a User Profile

Adding a User (useradd)   The **useradd** command adds a user to the system. Each option used by the command represents a field in /etc/passwd. This is how you add the entry shown in Fig. 19.1:

```
# useradd -u 210 -g dba -c "THE RDBMS" -d /home/oracle -s /bin/ksh -m oracle
# _
```

The -m option ensures that the home directory is created if it doesn't already exist and copies a sample .profile and .kshrc to the user's home directory. **useradd** also creates the user's mailbox and sets the MAIL variable to point to that location (in /var/mail or /var/spool/mail).

After the account is created, you have to set the new user's password with **passwd oracle** and make the account ready for use. It's now the job of the user to generate a public-private key pair with **ssh-keygen** if she needs to use SSH.

Modifying and Removing Users (usermod and userdel)   **usermod** is used for modifying some of the parameters set with **useradd**. Users sometimes need to change their login shell, and the following command line sets Bash as the login shell for the user oracle:

```
usermod -s /usr/bin/bash oracle
```

---

*How **useradd** Works*

In the early days of UNIX, there was no command line tool to add a user; the administrator had to perform the task manually. This meant editing /etc/passwd and /etc/group to add the necessary entries. With reference to the user parameters shown in Fig. 19.1, this is what the administrator has to do:

1. Create the home directory for the user (**mkdir /home/oracle**).
2. Change the ownership of the home directory to that of the user (**chown oracle:dba /home/oracle**).

3. Change the permissions of /home/oracle to 755 (a desirable setting for a directory).

4. Create a zero-byte file named oracle in /var/mail (**touch /var/mail/oracle**).

5. Change the ownership of the file in the same manner as mentioned in 2. However, the permissions need to be set to 600 so that others cannot view oracle's mail.

6. Copy a profile and an rc file of an existing user (or from /etc/skel) and ensure that the mail setting there is either MAIL=/var/mail/$USERNAME or MAIL=/var/mail/oracle.

The administrator then uses **passwd oracle** and makes the account available to the user.

Users are removed from the system with **userdel**:

```
userdel oracle                                          Doesn't delete user's files
```

This removes all entries pertaining to oracle from /etc/passwd, /etc/group, and /etc/shadow. The user's home directory doesn't get deleted in the process and has to be removed separately if required.

19.4 Maintaining Security

Because security in a computer system eventually involves files, a faulty file permission can easily be exploited by a malicious user in a destructive manner. As administrator, you have to ensure that the system directories (/bin, /usr/bin, /etc, /sbin, etc.) and the files in them are not writable by others. We'll first discuss the restricted shell and then two important security-related features that involve the manipulation of a file's permission bits.

19.4.1 Restricted Shell

If you need to restrict the activities of a user, set up the user account with a special **restricted shell**. This shell once had the name **rsh**, but today **rsh** represents the command with which you remotely run a program. The better shells today have restricted versions—**rbash** and **rksh**. Either of them has to be specified in the last field of /etc/passwd. A user with a restricted shell can't do any of the following things:

- Use the **cd** command, which means that she can't change directories.
- Redefine the PATH, which makes it impossible to access commands placed in other directories.
- Redefine the SHELL so the user can't change to a nonrestricted shell.
- Use a pathname containing a /, which means a command can't be executed with either a relative or an absolute pathname.
- Use the > and >> operators to create or append to files.

In this environment, a user can only execute programs in the directories specified in a new unchangeable PATH. This generally is set to point to only the current directory. If the user needs to run some of the system commands in /bin and /usr/bin, place links of those commands in the user's restricted directory.

Some commands have shell escapes (like **vi** and **mailx**), and some versions of UNIX let you use these escapes to execute any UNIX command by using the absolute pathname. Make sure these commands don't behave in that manner on your system. If they do, disallow their use.

Note

If you don't have a separate restricted shell on your system, use the standard shells with the -r option to enforce that behavior (**sh -r**, **bash -r**, or **ksh -r**). Since you can't put these entries in /etc/passwd, run a normal shell there and use **exec** to execute them from the startup file. Make sure to set the PATH to point to only the current directory.

19.4.2   Set-User-Id (SUID): Power for a Moment

Recall the discussions on process attributes *(8.6—Inset)* where we mentioned that sometimes the *effective UID* may not be the same as the *real UID*. This is a security feature that is exploited by some important UNIX programs. These programs have a special permissions mode that lets users update sensitive system files—like /etc/shadow—something they can't do directly with an editor. This is true of the **passwd** program:

```
-rwsr-xr-x   1 root     shadow    34808 Nov  30 17:55 /usr/bin/passwd
```

The letter s in the user category of the permissions field represents a special mode known as the **set-user-id (SUID)**. This mode lets a process have the privileges of the *owner* of the file during the instance of the program. Thus, when a nonprivileged user executes **passwd**, the *effective* UID of the process is not the user's, but of root's—the owner of the program. This SUID privilege is then used by **passwd** to edit /etc/shadow.

The superuser can use **chmod** to set the SUID for any file. The s in the **chmod** expression sets the SUID bit:

```
# chmod u+s a.out ; ls -l a.out
-rwsr-xr-x   1 root     staff      2113  Mar  24  11:18  a.out
```

To assign SUID in an absolute manner, simply prefix 4 to whatever octal string you would otherwise use (like 4755 instead of 755).

The **set-group-id (SGID)** is similar to SUID except that a program with its SGID set allows the group owner of the process to have the same power as the group that owns the program. The SGID bit is 2, and some typical examples could be **chmod g+s a.out** or **chmod 2755 a.out**.

The SUID mechanism, invented by Dennis Ritchie, is a potential security hazard. As administrator, you must keep track of all SUID programs owned by root that a user may try to create or copy. The **find** command easily locates them:

```
find /home -perm -4000 -print | mailx root
```

The extra octal digit (4) signifies the SUID mode, *but **find** treats the - before 4000 as representing any other permissions*. You can use **cron** to run this program at regular intervals and mail the file list to root.

The fourth octal digit in the permissions string is used only when the SUID, SGID, or sticky bit needs to be set. It has the value 4 for SUID, 2 for SGID, and 1 for the sticky bit.

19.4.3   The Sticky Bit

The **sticky bit** (also called the *saved text bit*) applies to both regular files and directories. When applied to a regular file, it ensures that the text image of a program with the bit set is permanently kept in the swap area so that it can be reloaded quickly when the program is invoked again. Previously, it made sense to have this bit set for programs like **vi** and **emacs**. Today, machines with ultra-fast disk drives and lots of cheap memory don't need this bit for ordinary files.

However, the sticky bit becomes a useful security feature when used with a directory. The UNIX system allows users to create files in /tmp and /var/tmp, but they can't delete files not owned by them in these directories. Strange, isn't it? That's possible because both directories have their sticky bits set:

```
# ls -ld /tmp /var/tmp
drwxrwxrwt   5 root      sys        377   Jan  9 13:28 /tmp
drwxrwxrwt   2 root      sys       7168   Jan  9 13:34 /var/tmp
```

The directories are *apparently* writable by all, but that extra t (sticky) bit ensures that henry can't remove juliet's files in these directories. Using **chmod**, you can set the bit on a directory:

```
# chmod 1775 bar                                         Or chmod +t bar
# ls -l bar
drwxrwxr-t  2 sumit    dialout     1024   Apr 13 08:25 bar
```

The sticky bit is extremely useful for implementing group projects. To let a group of users work on a set of files without infringing on security, you'll have to:

1. Create a common group for these users in /etc/group.
2. Create separate user accounts for them but specify the same home directory.
3. Make sure the home directory and all subdirectories are not owned by any of the users. Use **chown** to surrender ownership to root.
4. Make the directories group-writable and set their sticky bits with **chmod 1775**.

In this scenario, every user of the group has write permission on the directory and can create files and directories, but can only delete those she owns. A very useful feature indeed!

19.5   Booting and Shutdown

The startup and shutdown procedures are controlled by automated shell scripts which are changed quite infrequently. Yet the administrator needs to know the exact sequence of steps the system follows during the two events. Things do go wrong, especially during startup, and she must be able to fix them. For that, she needs to know the role played by the initialization scripts in /etc.

19.5.1 Booting

After a machine is powered on, the system looks for all peripherals, and then goes through a series of steps that ultimately lead to the loading of the kernel into memory. The kernel then spawns **init** (PID 1) which, in turn, spawns further processes. You must know the behavioral pattern of **init** for three vital reasons:

- **init** maintains the system at a specific **run level** (state) and decides which processes to run for each run level.
- **init** is the parent of all system daemons that keep running all the time. Recall the output of the **ps -e** command *(8.4)* that showed many of these daemons.
- It spawns a **getty** process at every terminal so that users can log in. Eventually, **init** becomes the parent of all shells.

Each run level is normally a single digit (0 to 6), or an s or S. A distinct set of processes (mostly daemons) is scheduled to run in each of these states. Normally, the system would be in any one of these system-dependent run levels:

- 0—System shutdown.
- 1—System administration mode (local file systems mounted).
- 2—Multiuser mode (NFS not available).
- 3—Full multiuser mode.
- 5—The graphical environment mode in Linux.
- 6—Shutdown and reboot mode.
- s or S—Single-user mode (file systems mounted).

When the system is booted, **init** first enters run level 1 or S before moving to the multiuser mode (2, 3, or 5). When the system is shut down, **init** moves to the state 0 or 6. The administrator also *explicitly* uses the **init** command to move the system to any run level:

```
init 1
```
                                                                    Switches to single-user mode

The administrator uses the single-user mode to perform administrative tasks like checking the file system or taking an offline backup. Many services are not available in this state.

To know the run level you are in, use the **who -r** command:

```
$ who -r
       .         run-level 3  Jan  9 09:39    3     0  S
```

This machine is at run level 3, a state which supports multiuser and network operations. Linux users can also use the **runlevel** command from the root account.

19.5.2 Shutdown

The administrator uses the **shutdown** command to shut the machine down at the end of the day (if it is ever shut down). The command notifies users with **wall** about the system going down with a directive to log out. After sleeping for a minute, **shutdown** performs the following activities:

- Sends signals to all running processes so they can terminate normally.
- Logs users off and kills remaining processes.

- *Unmounts* all secondary file systems using the **umount** command.
- Invokes **sync** to write all memory resident data to disk to preserve the integrity of the file system.
- Notifies users to reboot or switch off, or moves the system to single-user mode.

shutdown supports the -i option that specifies the **init** run level. The -g option overrides the default waiting time of one minute. The command can be used in these ways:

```
shutdown -g2                                    Powers down machine after 2 minutes
shutdown -y -g0                                        Immediate shutdown
shutdown -y -g0 -i6                                    Shut down and reboot
```

Some systems like Solaris offer the **reboot** and **halt** commands that also shut the system down without warning the users. Unless you know what you are doing, you should stick to **shutdown** if you are administering a multiuser system.

Linux

Linux uses the -t option to override the default waiting time of one minute. **shutdown** can also be used in these ways:

```
shutdown 17:30                                      Shut down at 17:30 hours
shutdown -r now                             Shut down immediately and reboot
shutdown -h now                              Shut down immediately and halt
```

Linux also permits the use of the Windows-styled *[Ctrl][Alt][Del]* sequence to shut down the system.

19.6   How init **Controls the System**

init, which takes all instructions from /etc/inittab, completely controls the way the system is booted and powered down. Each line of the file contains four fields that specify the program to run for each **init** state. A few sample lines taken from a Solaris system are shown in Fig. 19.2.

All the things you see happening on startup owe their ultimate origin to entries like these. A typical inittab entry takes this form:

label:*run_levels*:*action*:*command*

FIGURE 19.2   *An* /etc/inittab *File*

```
fs::sysinit:/sbin/rcS sysinit   >/dev/msglog 2<>/dev/msglog </dev/console
is:3:initdefault:
s0:0:wait:/sbin/rc0          >/dev/msglog 2<>/dev/msglog </dev/console
s1:1:respawn:/sbin/rc1          >/dev/msglog 2<>/dev/msglog </dev/console
s2:23:wait:/sbin/rc2            >/dev/msglog 2<>/dev/msglog </dev/console
s3:3:wait:/sbin/rc3          >/dev/msglog 2<>/dev/msglog </dev/console
s6:6:wait:/sbin/rc6          >/dev/msglog 2<>/dev/msglog </dev/console
```

Let's now examine one of the lines of inittab. The line with the label s2 provides this directive: "For run levels 2 or 3, run the **/sbin/rc2** program and wait for it to complete before moving on to the other lines of this file." msglog is a special file that is used for logging all messages.

When **init** is executed with a specific run level as argument, it reads all lines that match that run level and executes the commands specified there in sequence. A blank run level (here, in the first line) means the command has to run for all run levels. **init** also obtains the default run level by reading the line that shows initdefault as the action. Here, the system boots to run level 3.

respawn and wait are two of the actions that **init** understands. There are others, and here are some of the important ones:

- sysinit—Used for initializing the system. The system may check the "dirtiness" of file systems, activate swap partitions, and set the hostname.
- respawn—Makes sure a process restarts on termination. This is always required for the **getty** process.
- boot—Executes only when inittab is read the first time. **init** ignores any run-level fields placed here.
- off—Kills a process if it is running.
- ctrlaltdel—Executes **shutdown** command (Linux only).

As administrator, you can also insert or modify statements in /etc/inittab. You can change the default run level, or add and modify entries when adding a new terminal or modem to the system. Finally, you have to use **telinit q** to force **init** to reread its configuration file.

19.6.1 How init Creates the Shell

Every /etc/inittab has at least one line that specifies running a program to produce a login prompt on the console and other terminals (if supported). These lines from a Linux machine illustrate the relationship between **init** and the **mingetty** (the "getty" of Linux) program:

```
1:2345:respawn:/sbin/mingetty tty1
2:2345:respawn:/sbin/mingetty tty2
```

When the system moves to states 2, 3, 4, or 5, **init** forks and execs a **getty** (here, **mingetty**) for every active communication port (here, tty1 and tty2). **getty** prints the login prompt and goes off to sleep. When a user attempts to log in, **getty** execs the **login** program to verify the login name and password. On successful login, **login** execs the process representing the login shell. Repeated overlaying ultimately results in **init** becoming the immediate ancestor of the shell as can be seen from this sequence:

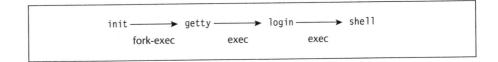

init goes off to sleep, waiting for the death of its children. When the user logs out, her shell is killed, and the death is intimated to **init**. It then wakes up, and the respawn field directs it to spawn another **getty** for that line to monitor the next login.

Because of /etc/inittab, you can have multiple *virtual* consoles on your Linux machine. Use *[Ctrl][Alt]* and a function key to bring up a new screen. Using the first six function keys, you can have six virtual consoles on a single machine. If you want one more, add an entry in inittab.

19.6.2   The rc Scripts

When the system boots to or changes the run level, **init** looks up inittab to first kill the processes that shouldn't be running, and then spawns those that should be. Every inittab specifies the execution of some rc scripts that have the names rc0, rc1, rc2—one for each run level:

```
s0:0:wait:/sbin/rc0      >/dev/msglog 2<>/dev/msglog </dev/console
s2:23:wait:/sbin/rc2       >/dev/msglog 2<>/dev/msglog </dev/console
s3:3:wait:/sbin/rc3      >/dev/msglog 2<>/dev/msglog </dev/console
```

rc0 runs for run level 0, but **rc2** runs in both states 2 and 3. Each rc script contains code to execute a series of scripts in the directory /etc/rc*n*.d, where *n* signifies the run level. This means that for run level 2, **init** executes **rc2**, which in turn executes the scripts in /etc/rc2.d.

Now, let's turn our attention to the scripts in the /etc/rc*n*.d directories. These directories have two types of files as shown by this list from /etc/rc2.d:

K07dmi	S69inet	S74xntpd	S90wbem
K07snmpdx	S70uucp	S75cron	S92volmgt
K16apache	S71ldap.client	S75savecore	S93cacheos.finish
S01MOUNTFSYS	S72autoinstall	S80lp	S95ncad
S20sysetup	S72slpd	S85power	S99dtlogin
S21perf	S73cachefs.daemon	S88sendmail	

The scripts here fully initialize the system by mounting file systems, setting up the network and activating the other daemons. They are executed in two batches. When the system enters run level 2, **rc2** executes (in ASCII sequence) all scripts beginning with K (the "kill" scripts) with the stop argument. This kills all processes that shouldn't be running at this level. It then executes the scripts beginning with S (the "start" scripts) with the start argument. Because a daemon may run in more than one run level, the files that you see above are symbolic links pointing to the actual scripts placed in /etc/init.d.

The rc Files

The initialization files in Linux were originally based on BSD, but now have a strong System V flavor. However, the rc files and directories here are all under one roof—/etc/rc.d. Moreover, instead of using **rc***n*, Linux uses a single file, **rc**, with different arguments as shown below in these lines from /etc/inittab:

```
10:0:wait:/etc/rc.d/rc 0
11:1:wait:/etc/rc.d/rc 1
12:2:wait:/etc/rc.d/rc 2
```

All scripts in the rc*n*.d directories are executed from **/etc/rc.d/rc**. The sequence for Linux goes like this: For switching to run level *n*, **init** executes **/etc/rc.d/rc** *n*, which executes the scripts in /etc/rc.d/rc*n*.d.

19.7   Device Files

Devices are also files, and the same device can often be accessed with several different filenames. This has sometimes been done for backward compatibility and sometimes for associating a separate device with a specific function. All device files are stored in /dev or in its subdirectories. Device names on UNIX systems are system-dependent, but Linux is remarkably invariant, so let's list some devices as they appear on a Linux machine:

```
# ls -l /dev
lrwxrwxrwx   1 root     root            8 Dec 11   2002 cdrom -> /dev/hdb
crw-------   1 sumit    root       5,    1 Sep 11  14:08 console
crw-rw----   1 root     uucp       5,   64 Aug 31   2002 cua0
brw-rw----   1 sumit    floppy     2,    0 Aug 31   2002 fd0
brw-rw----   1 sumit    floppy     2,   40 Aug 31   2002 fd0h1440
brw-rw----   1 root     disk       3,    0 Aug 31   2002 hda
brw-rw----   1 root     disk       3,    1 Aug 31   2002 hda1
brw-rw----   1 root     disk       3,    2 Aug 31   2002 hda2
brw-------   1 sumit    disk       3,   64 Aug 31   2002 hdb
lrwxrwxrwx   1 root     root            5 Dec 11   2002 mouse -> psaux
crw-rw-rw-   1 root     root       1,    3 Aug 31   2002 null
crw-------   1 root     root      10,    1 Sep 11  14:08 psaux
drwxr-xr-x   2 root     root            0 Sep 11  19:37 pts
crw-rw-rw-   1 root     root       5,    0 Aug 31   2002 tty
crw--w----   1 root     root       4,    0 Aug 31   2002 tty0
crw-------   1 root     root       4,    1 Sep 11  14:08 tty1
crw-rw----   1 root     uucp       4,   64 May 13  18:43 ttyS0
```

The lists in real life are much larger than this and include every possible device on your system—including even the main memory of your computer. This listing reveals two vital points:

- Device files can be grouped into two main categories as shown by the first character of the permissions field (b or c).
- The fifth field—normally representing the size for other files—consists of a pair of numbers. A device file contains no data.

Device files also have permissions with the same significance. To send output to a terminal, you need to have write permission for the device, and to read a floppy, you must have read permission for the device file. The significance of the device attributes is taken up next.

19.7.1   Block and Character Devices

First, a word about disk reading and writing. When you issue an instruction to save a file, the write operation takes place in chunks or blocks. Each block represents an integral number of disk sectors (of 512 bytes each). The data is first transferred to a **buffer cache** (a pool of buffers) which the kernel later writes to disk. When you read from disk, the buffer cache is first accessed containing the most recently used data. If the data is found there, disk access is avoided. You may decide to ignore this facility and access the device directly. Many devices allow this, and the access method is determined by the name of the device that is called up.

Note that generally the first character in the permissions field is c or b. The floppy drive, CD-ROM, and the hard disk have b prefixed to their permissions. All data are read and written to these devices in blocks and use the buffer cache. That's why they are referred to as **block special devices**. On the other hand, the terminal, tape drive, and printer are **character special** or **raw devices**, indicated by the letter c. For the latter, the read/write operations ignore the buffer cache and access the device directly.

Many block devices have both a raw and a block counterpart. Hard disks, floppy drives and CD-ROMs can be accessed as a block device and a character device, which totally bypasses the file system.

19.7.2   Major and Minor Numbers

The set of routines needed to operate a specific device is known as the **device driver**. When a particular device is accessed, the kernel calls the right device driver and passes some parameters for it to act properly. The kernel must know not only the type of device but also certain details about the device—like the density of a floppy or the partition number of the disk.

The fifth column of the previous listing doesn't show the file size in bytes, but rather a pair of two numbers separated by a comma. These numbers are called the **major** and **minor device numbers**, respectively. The major number represents the device driver, actually the type of device. All hard disks will have the same major number if they are attached to the same controller.

The minor number is indicative of the parameters that the kernel passes to the device driver. Often, it indicates the special characteristics of the device. For example, fd0h1440 and fd1h1440 represent two floppy devices attached to a particular controller. So both of them will have the same major number but different minor numbers.

Note   Unlike ordinary and directory files, device files don't contain any data. They merely point to the location of the device driver routines that actually operate the device.

19.8   File Systems

We now move on to file systems. A **file system** is organized in the form of a directory structure with its own root. It is also accessed by its own device file. Modern UNIX systems are invariably set up with multiple file systems, each meant for a specific purpose.

If you have multiple disks, every disk must have at least one file system on it. Dividing a disk into multiple file systems has a number of distinct advantages:

- Separate file systems prevent potential encroachment conflicts that may arise between the various data areas.
- If there's corruption in one area, other areas are effectively shielded from this evil influence.
- Each file system can be backed up separately onto a single volume of tape.

The operating system usually resides on multiple file systems. At the time of booting, these file systems combine (using a technique known as *mounting*) and appear to the user as a single file system. One of these file systems is special: the **root file system**. It contains the bare-bones UNIX—the root directory, the /bin, /etc, /dev and /lib directories, that is, all the tools and utilities that are just sufficient to keep the system going.

Most systems also have a **swap file system**. When the system memory is heavily loaded, the kernel moves processes out of memory and to this file system. When these swapped processes are ready to run, they are loaded back to memory. Users can't access this file system directly.

Apart from these essential file systems, your computer would in all probability have additional ones. System files should be kept separate from data files created by users, and hence a separate file system is usually made for them. You might have a /home or /export/home file system to house all users. You could also have /usr, /var, and /tmp as separate file systems.

19.8.1   File System Components

Every file system has these four components:

- The **boot block**—This block contains a small boot program and the partition table. This is often referred to as the *Master Boot Record* (MBR). The boot program is responsible for the eventual loading of the kernel into memory.
- The **superblock**—This area contains global information about the file system. This information includes a free list of inodes and data blocks. The kernel maintains a copy of the superblock in memory and reads and writes this copy when controlling allocation of inodes and data blocks. It also periodically updates the disk copy with the contents of the memory copy.
- The **inode blocks**—This region contains the inode for every file of the file system. When a file is created, an inode is allocated here. Apart from file attributes, the inode contains an array of disk block addresses that keep track of *every* disk block used by a file. Like with the superblock, the kernel works with the memory copy of the inode and periodically writes this copy to disk.
- The **data blocks**—All data and programs created by users reside in this area. Even though disk blocks are numbered consecutively, you'll often find a file's data are arranged in noncontiguous blocks. When a file expands, the kernel may not find its adjacent blocks free. The remaining data then have to be written to the next free block, wherever it may be. This, no doubt, leads to **disk fragmentation** and consequently increases the overheads of read/write operations. However, this fragmentation also allows files to be enlarged or reduced at will and helps keep wastage to a minimum.

UNIX refuses to boot if the superblock is corrupt. To overcome this problem, many systems (like Solaris and Linux) have multiple superblocks written on different areas of the disk. If one superblock is corrupt, the system can be directed to use another.

19.8.2   The Standard File Systems and Their Types

Initially, there were only two types of file systems—those from AT&T and those from Berkeley. Over time, many more file system types have made their entry into the UNIX system. Here are some of the file systems that you may need to work with:

- **s5**   Before SVR4, this was the only file system used by System V, but today it is offered by SVR4 by this name for backward compatibility only. This file system uses a logical block size of 512 or 1024 bytes and a single superblock. It can't handle filenames longer than 14 characters.
- **ufs**   This is how the Berkeley Fast File System is known to SVR4 and adopted by most UNIX systems. Because the block size here can go up to 64 KB, performance of this file system is considerably better than s5. It uses multiple superblocks with each cylinder group storing a superblock. Unlike s5, ufs supports 255-character filenames, symbolic links, and disk quotas.
- **ext2** or **ext3**   This is the standard file system on Linux. It uses a block size of 1024 bytes and, like ufs, uses multiple superblocks and symbolic links.
- **iso9660** or **hsfs**   This is the standard file system used by CD-ROMs. It features DOS-style 8+3 filenames, but since UNIX uses longer filenames, hsfs also provides Rock Ridge extensions to accommodate them.
- **msdos** or **pcfs**   Most UNIX systems also support DOS filesystems. You can create this file system on a floppy diskette and transfer files to it for use on a Windows system. Some systems like Linux can also directly access a DOS file system on the hard disk.
- **swap**   This file system has already been discussed *(19.8)*.
- **bfs**   The boot file system. This is used by SVR4 to host the boot programs and the UNIX kernel.
- **proc** or **procfs**   This can be considered a pseudo-file system maintained in memory. It stores data of each running process and appears to contain files, but actually contains none. Users can obtain most process information including their PIDs directly from here.

Commands handling file systems (like `mkfs` and `mount`) use an option to describe the file system, which is why you should know the file system you are using.

19.9   Mounting and Unmounting File Systems

When a file system is created, the root file system doesn't even know of its existence. By a process known as **mounting**, all secondary file systems *mount* (attach) themselves to the root file system at different points. The root file system then becomes the *main* file system, and its root directory is also the directory of the unified file system.

The `mount` and `umount` commands are used for mounting and unmounting file systems. The point at which mounting takes place is called the **mount point**. This is usually an empty directory. After mounting, you see a single file system, and it's possible that a file moved from /oracle to /home may have actually traversed two hard disks!

19.9.1   mount: Mounting File Systems

The **mount** command is used to mount file systems. When mounting a new file system, it takes two arguments—the device name of the file system and the mount point. Before mounting a file system, an empty directory (say, /oracle) must first be made available in the main file system. The root directory of the new file system has to be mounted on this directory.

mount uses a system-dependent option to specify the type of file system. This is how we mount a file system on /oracle on Solaris and Linux systems:

```
mount -F ufs /dev/dsk/c0t8d0s0 /oracle                              Solaris
mount -t ext2 /dev/hda3 /oracle                                     Linux
```

After the device is mounted, the root directory of the file system on this device loses its separate identity. It now becomes the directory /oracle and is made to appear as if it's part of the main file system.

mount by default lists all mounted file systems. This output is seen on a Solaris system:

```
# mount
/ on /dev/dsk/c0t0d0s0 read/write/setuid/intr/largefiles/onerror=panic/dev=80000
0 on Thu Sep 11 08:57:43 2003
/usr on /dev/dsk/c0t0d0s4 read/write/setuid/intr/largefiles/onerror=panic/dev=80
0004 on Thu Sep 11 08:57:44 2003
/proc on /proc read/write/setuid/dev=2e40000 on Thu Sep 11 08:57:43 2003
/var on /dev/dsk/c0t0d0s1 read/write/setuid/intr/largefiles/onerror=panic/dev=80
0001 on Thu Sep 11 08:57:46 2003
/oracle on /dev/dsk/c0t8d0s0 read/write/setuid/intr/largefiles/onerror=panic/dev
=800038 on Thu Sep 11 08:57:48 2003
/tmp on swap read/write/setuid/dev=2 on Thu Sep 11 08:57:48 2003
/export/home on /dev/dsk/c0t0d0s7 read/write/setuid/intr/largefiles/onerror=pani
c/dev=800007 on Thu Sep 11 08:57:48 2003
```

The first line shows the root file system mounted on /. This file system can't be unmounted. The /oracle file system is also shown. If you can't access data in /oracle, use **mount** to find out whether the file system is mounted at all.

Even though **mount** here used the device name and mount point as its arguments, things can be set up such that **mount** can be used with one argument. When all mounting parameters are specified in a configuration file, you can use **mount** with simply one argument:

Note

```
mount /oracle                                            Both these commands
mount /dev/hda3                                              will now work
```

This configuration file is often /etc/fstab, but Solaris uses /etc/vfstab. When a new file system is created, an entry has to be added to this file.

19.9.2 umount: Unmounting File Systems

Unmounting a file system is sometimes not possible. Just as you can't remove a directory unless........ unmounting is achieved with the **umount** command (note the spelling!), which requires either the file system name or mount point as argument. The file system that we just created and mounted can be unmounted by using any of these commands:

```
umount /oracle                                  Specify either mount point or
umount /dev/hda3                           device name—here a Linux device
umount /dev/dsk/c0t8d0s0                        ... and here a Solaris device
```

Unmounting a file system is not possible if a user is placed in it. Further, just as you can't remove a directory unless you are placed in a directory above it, you can't unmount a file system unless you are placed above it. If you try to do that, this is what you'll see:

```
# pwd
/oracle
# umount /dev/c0t8d0s0
umount: /oracle busy
```

Now move out of the mount point (/oracle) and repeat the **umount** command; it should work now.

Note

When you use **mount -a**, all file systems listed in **mount**'s configuration file are mounted. At system startup, the same command is executed, so you always find mounted file systems available on your machine. The **shutdown** sequence runs **umount -a**.

19.10 fsck: **File System Checking**

The **update** daemon calls **sync** every 30 seconds to write the memory copies of the superblock and inodes to disk. This delay leaves scope for file system inconsistency. If the power goes off before the superblock is written to disk, the file system loses its integrity. Here are some common discrepancies:

- Two or more inodes claiming the same disk block.
- A block marked as free, but not listed in the superblock.
- A used block marked as free.
- Mismatch between the file size specified in the inode and the number of data blocks specified in the address array.
- A file not having at least one directory entry or having an invalid file type specified in the inode.

The **fsck** (file system consistency check) command is used to check and repair a damaged file system. The command generally acts as a frontend to the file system-specific program (like **fsck_ufs** or **fsck.ext2**) that actually does the job. It's generally run when a file system fails to mount.

On many systems including Solaris, file systems are marked as "dirty" or "clean." **fsck** then checks only the dirty file systems during the next startup. The command can also be used with the name of the file system as argument:

```
# fsck /dev/rdsk/c0t3d0s5
** /dev/rdsk/c0t3d0s5
** Phase 1 - Check Blocks and Sizes
** Phase 2 - Check Pathnames
** Phase 3 - Check Connectivity
** Phase 4 - Check Reference Counts
** Phase 5 - Check Free List
```

fsck conducts a check in five phases, and the output above is obtained when the file system is consistent. However, when it is corrupt, messages and questions, which you have to answer correctly, are seen on the system console. Occasionally, the file system is so corrupt that rectification becomes impossible, and reinstallation of the system remains the only alternative.

When a file system develops problems, **fsck** may find the information on disk to be more *recent* than the memory copy. It may then flash the following message:

Caution

```
***** BOOT UNIX (NO SYNC!) *****
```

This is a warning message: If you allow **update** to call **sync** and write the incorrect memory information to disk, all the good work done by **fsck** would be lost. Instead, you should *immediately press the reset button and reboot the system before* **update** *calls* **sync** *again.*

19.11   Managing Disk Space

No matter how many disks are added to the system, there will always be a scramble for space. Users often forget to remove the files they no longer need. The administrator must regularly scan the disk and locate files that have outlived their utility. She needs the **df** and **du** commands for this task as well as **find**. All three commands can also be issued by any user. Linux users need to note that all three commands report in 1024-byte blocks and not 512.

19.11.1   df: Reporting Free Space

The **df** (disk free) command reports the amount of free space available for each file system separately:

```
# df
/               (/dev/dsk/c0t0d0s0 ): 3487518  blocks   483770  files
/usr            (/dev/dsk/c0t0d0s4 ): 2408514  blocks   458429  files
/proc           (/proc           ):       0  blocks    15890  files
/var            (/dev/dsk/c0t0d0s1 ): 3836084  blocks   483861  files
/oracle         (/dev/dsk/c0t8d0s0 ):  995890  blocks  1018780  files
/tmp            (swap            ): 2699184  blocks   109840  files
/export/home    (/dev/dsk/c0t0d0s7 ): 2187782  blocks   340677  files
```

There are several file systems on this Solaris machine. The first column shows the mount point. The second column shows the device name of the file system. The last two columns show the number of 512-byte blocks available and the number of files that you can create.

The first line in the list refers to the root file system (/), which has 3,487,518 blocks of disk space free. It also has 483,770 inodes free, which means that up to that many additional files can be created on this file system. You can create files in this file system until the free blocks or inodes are eaten away, whichever occurs earlier.

The -t (total) option includes the above output, as well as the total amount of disk space in the file system. We won't display its output, but we'll consider the informative -k option that reports in units of KB. This time, let's obtain the statistics for the / and /usr file systems:

```
$ df -k / /usr                                    Reports on / and /usr file systems
Filesystem              kbytes      used      avail  capacity  Mounted on
/dev/dsk/c0t0d0s0      1986439    242680    1684166    13%      /
/dev/dsk/c0t0d0s4      2025076    820819    1143505    42%      /usr
```

You probably won't need to know anything more than what this output offers. It also shows the percentage utilization. Once you have identified the file system that needs to be investigated thoroughly, you need the **du** command, which we consider next.

19.11.2   du: Disk Usage

You'll often need to find out the consumption of a specific directory tree rather than an entire file system. **du** (disk usage) is the command you need as it reports usage by a recursive examination of the directory tree. This is how **du** lists the usage of each subdirectory in /var/apache:

```
$ du /var/apache
6          /var/apache/cgi-bin
12         /var/apache/htdocs
74         /var/apache/icons/small
266        /var/apache/icons
2          /var/apache/logs
2          /var/apache/proxy
290        /var/apache                              A summary at the end
```

The list can often be quite large, but sometimes you need only a single figure shown in the last line. For this, the -s (summary) option is quite convenient:

```
$ du -s /var/apache
290        /var/apache
```

Assessing Space Consumed by Users   Most of the dynamic space in a system is consumed by users' home directories and data files. You should use **du -s** to report on each user's home directory. The output is brief and yet quite informative:

```
$ du -s /export/home/staff/*
122      /export/home/staff/PDSIT
42       /export/home/staff/henry
434586   /export/home/staff/charlie
574324   /export/home/staff/henry
3275442  /export/home/staff/romeo
1126172  /export/home/staff/juliet
```

You know who the notorious disk hoggers are: romeo and juliet. If they have exceeded their quota, you can use the shell script developed in Section 13.13.3 to send mail to the offenders.

19.11.3   find Revisited: The Administrator's Tool

The **find** command *(4.11)* can test a file for practically every attribute. The administrator often uses the -size keyword to locate large files this way:

```
find /home -size +2048 -print                                    Files above 1 MB
```

Many files remain unaccessed or unmodified for months—even years. **find**'s -mtime and -atime operators can easily match a file's modification and access times to select them. This is how the administrator scans the /home directory for files that have either not been accessed for a year or not modified in six months:

```
find /home \( -atime +365 -o -mtime +180 \) -print | mailx root
```

You need to halve these figures when using Linux as **find** there uses 1024-byte blocks.

▰▰▰ 19.12   Handling Floppy Diskettes

Although the tape is the most common backup device, the floppy diskette represents the most convenient means of exchanging small files between machines at work and home. For our examples, we'll be using a 3.5", 1.44 MB diskette.

19.12.1   format and fdformat: Formatting Diskettes

Before you use a floppy for backup purposes, you need to format it. This is done with the **format** or **fdformat** commands (whichever is available on your system):

```
# fdformat                                                         On Solaris
Press return to start formatting floppy.
The -d option uses the DOS format.
```

This command formats and verifies a 1.44 MB floppy. Linux too uses the **fdformat** command for formatting a floppy. Device names in Linux generally don't vary across the different flavors; a floppy usually has the name /dev/fd0 or /dev/fd0h1440, so you should use **fdformat /dev/fd0** (or the other device name).

19.12.2   dd: Copying Diskettes

dd (disk dump) is a versatile command that can be used to perform a variety of tasks. It is somewhat dated now that some of its filtering functions have been taken over by other

UNIX tools. It has a strange command line which has a series of options in the form *option=value*.

dd was extensively used in copying file systems, but today its role is mostly restricted to copying media—like floppies and tapes. It is not interactive (in fact, it is a filter), and a pair of **dd** commands is needed to complete the operation.

We'll now use **dd** to make a copy of a 1.44 MB floppy diskette. The first step is to create the image of the floppy on disk:

```
# dd if=/dev/fd0 of=$$ bs=147456
10+0 records in
10+0 records out
```

The keywords are if= (input filename), of= (output filename), and bs= (block size). The above command copies the raw contents of a 1.44 MB floppy to a temporary file, $$, using a block size of 147456—exactly one-tenth the capacity of a 1.44 MB diskette.

Next, take out the source floppy from the drive and insert a formatted target floppy. A second reversed **dd** command copies this temporary file to the diskette:

```
# dd if=$$ of=/dev/fd0 bs=147456 ; rm $$
10+0 records in
10+0 records out
```

You should copy your boot floppies in this way. **dd** uses only raw devices. Linux doesn't have separate device files for the two modes but selects the right mode automatically.

19.12.3 Handling DOS Diskettes

It is now quite common to see both Windows and UNIX systems on the desktop. UNIX today provides a family of commands (Table 19.1) that can read and write DOS floppy diskettes. These command names begin with the string dos in SVR4. They are modeled after UNIX commands performing similar functions.

TABLE 19.1 *The Family of DOS Commands (Linux command name in parentheses)*

Command	Action
doscp /dev/fd0135ds18:/tags .	Copies tags from DOS diskette (mcopy)
doscat a:readme a:setup.txt	Concatenates files readme and setup.txt in DOS diskette (mtype)
dosdir /dev/dsk/f0q18dt	Lists files in DOS diskette in DOS-style (mdir)
dosls /dev/dsk/f0q18dt	Lists files in UNIX **ls**-style
dosmkdir a:bin	Creates directory bin on DOS diskette (mmd)
dosrmdir a:bin	Removes directory bin on DOS diskette (mrd)
dosrm /dev/dsk/f0q18dt:setup.inf	Deletes file setup.inf on DOS diskette (mdel)
dosformat a:	Formats diskette for use on DOS systems (mformat)

The command required most is **doscp**, which copies files between disk and diskette:

```
doscp emp.lst /dev/dsk/f0q18dt:/per.lst
```

There are two components in the target specification—the device name (1.44 MB floppy drive) and the filename (/per.lst), with the : used as delimiter. As in **cp**, multiple file copying is also possible:

```
doscp emp[123].lst /dev/dsk/f0q18dt
```

doscat performs a simple "cat" of its arguments in the command line. When more than one filename is specified, the standard output of each is concatenated:

```
doscat /dev/dsk/f0q18dt:/CHAP01 /dev/dsk/f0q18dt:/CHAP02 > newchap
```

These commands make the newline conversions automatically *(3.20),* but they also work with the -r option, in which case the files are copied or concatenated without newline conversions.

Table 19.1 shows the use of these commands with varying device names. One of them should work on your system. If a: doesn't work, then use the appropriate file in /dev or /dev/dsk.

Linux

The Linux "DOS" commands begin with the string m and use the corresponding DOS command as the rest of the string. Here are some examples:

```
mcopy emp.lst a:
mcopy a:* .
mdir a:
mdel a:*.txt
```

Note that Linux uses the DOS drive name. All of these commands belong to the "mtools" collection. For details, use **man mtools**.

19.13 tar: **Backing Up Files**

The importance of performing regular backups isn't usually appreciated until a crash has occurred and a lot of data has been lost. The administrator is partly responsible for the safety of the data. She decides which files should be backed up and also determines the periodicity of such backups. Backups are effective only if files can be easily restored. For reasons of security, backup media of sensitive data are often kept at distant locations.

You have already used **tar** with its key options *(3.21)* to handle disk archives. We'll consider **tar** as a backup tool this time. Because of its recursive nature, **tar** is suitable for backing up entire directory structures. The backup device can be a tape or a floppy diskette, and the latter will be used in the examples. The **tar** options are listed in Table 19.2. The common key options are -c (copy), -x (extract), and -t (table of contents). The -f option is additionally used for specifying the device name.

TABLE 19.2 **tar** *Options*

Key Options (only one to be used)

Option	Significance
-c	Creates a new archive
-x	Extracts files from archive
-t	Lists contents of archive
-r	Appends files at end of archive
-u	Like r, but only if files are newer than those in archive

Nonkey Options

Option	Significance
-f *dev*	Uses pathname *dev* as name of device instead of the default
-v	Verbose option—lists files in long format
-w	Confirms from user about action to be taken
-b *n*	Uses blocking factor *n*, where *n* is restricted to 20
-m	Changes modification time of file to time of extraction
-I *file*	Takes filenames from *file (Solaris only)*
-T *file*	Takes filenames from *file (Linux only)*
-X *file*	Excludes filenames in *file (Solaris and Linux only)*
-k *num*	Multivolume backup—sets size of volume to *num* kilobytes *(Solaris only)*
-M	Multivolume backup *(Linux only)*
-z	Compresses/uncompresses with **gzip** *(Linux only)*
--bzip2	Compresses/uncompresses with **bzip2** *(Linux only)*

19.13.1   Backing Up Files (-c)

tar accepts directory and filenames directly on the command line. The -c key option is used to copy files to the backup device. The verbose option (-v) shows the progress of the backup:

```
# tar -cvf /dev/rdsk/f0q18dt /home/sales/SQL/*.sql
a /home/sales/SQL/invoice_do_all.sql 1 tape blocks
a /home/sales/SQL/load2invoice_do_all.sql 1 tape blocks
a /home/sales/SQL/remove_duplicate.sql 1 tape blocks
a /home/sales/SQL/t_mr_alloc.sql 10 tape blocks
```

The a before each pathname indicates that the file is appended. The command backs up all SQL scripts with their absolute pathnames, so they can only be restored in the same directory. However, if you choose to keep the option open of installing the files in a different directory, you should first "cd" to /home/sales/SQL and then use a relative pathname:

```
cd /home/sales/SQL
tar -cvf /dev/rdsk/f0q18dt ./*.sql                                      Using the ./
```

tar can copy an entire directory tree. The current directory can be backed up with or without the hidden files:

```
tar -cvfb /dev/rdsk/f0q18dt 18 *              Doesn't back up hidden files
tar -cvfb /dev/fd0 18 .                       Backs up hidden files also
```

The files here are backed up with their relative pathnames, assuming they all fit on one diskette. If they don't, **tar** in System V may accommodate them as much as possible and then quit the program without warning.

Incremental Backups **tar** is often used with **find** for performing incremental backups. First, you have to stamp a zero-byte file with the present system date and time whenever you go in for a backup. Subsequent backups will only select those files newer than this file. The following lines show a simple implementation:

```
tar -cvf /dev/rct0 `find /home -newer .last_time -print`
touch .last_time
```

The **touch** command (not discussed in this edition) stamps a file with the current date and time when used without an expression. Here, it ensures that the time of last backup is available as the last modification time of .last_time.

19.13.2   Restoring Files (-x)

Files are restored with the -x (extract) key option. When no file or directory name is specified, it restores all files from the backup device. The following command restores the files just backed up:

```
# tar -xvfb /dev/rdsk/f0q18dt 18
x /home/sales/SQL/invoice_do_all.sql, 169 bytes, 1 tape blocks
x /home/sales/SQL/load2invoice_do_all.sql, 456 bytes, 1 tape blocks
x /home/sales/SQL/remove_duplicate.sql, 237 bytes, 1 tape blocks
x /home/sales/SQL/t_mr_alloc.sql, 4855 bytes, 10 tape blocks
```

Selective extraction is also possible by providing one or more directory or filenames:

```
tar -xvf /dev/rdsk/f0q18dt /home/sales/SQL/t_mr_alloc.sql
```

Note that when files are extracted, the modification times of the files also remain unchanged. This can be overridden by the -m option to reflect the system time at the time of extraction.

Note

Some versions of **tar** (as in Solaris) don't read wild-card patterns. If you use **tar -xvf /dev/fd0 *.pl**, it's the shell that tries to expand the pattern, which means that the files have to reside in the current directory. However, some versions of **tar** (as in Linux) do permit the use of the wild cards; it doesn't matter whether the files exist at all on disk.

Tip

A file is restored in that directory that matches its pathname. That is to say, if a file has been backed up with the absolute pathname (e.g., /home/romeo/unit13), it will be restored in the same directory (/home/romeo). However, you can use the -C option to restore files in another directory. Alternatively, you can use relative pathnames when backing up. If **tar**'s arguments are generated by **find**, then make sure that you use **find** with a dot as its path list.

19.13.3   Displaying the Archive (-t)

The -t key option displays the contents of the device in a long format similar to the listing:

```
# tar -tvf /dev/rdsk/f0q18dt
rwxr-xr-x 203/50     472 Jun  4 09:35 1991 ./dentry1.sh
rwxr-xr-x 203/50     554 Jun  4 09:52 1991 ./dentry2.sh
rwxr-xr-x 203/50    2229 Jun  4 13:59 1991 ./func.sh
```

The files here have been backed up with relative pathnames. Each filename here is preceded by ./. If you don't remember this but want to extract the file func.sh from the diskette, you'll probably first try this:

```
# tar -xvf /dev/rdsk/f0q18dt func.sh
tar: func.sh: Not found in archive
```

tar failed to find the file because it existed there as ./func.sh and not func.sh. Put the ./ before the filename, and you are sure to get it this time. Remember this whenever you encounter extraction errors as above.

19.13.4   Other Options

There are a number of other options of **tar** that are worth considering:

- The -r key option is used to append a file to an archive. This implies that an archive can contain several versions of the same file!
- The -u key option also adds a file to an archive but only if the file is not already there or is being replaced with a newer version.
- The -w option permits interactive copying and restoration. It prints the name of the file and prompts for the action to be taken (y or n).
- Some versions of **tar** use a special option to pick up filenames from a file. You might want to use this facility when you have a list of over a hundred files, which is impractical (and sometimes, impossible) to enter in the command line. Unfortunately, this option is not standard; Solaris uses -I and Linux uses -T.

Linux

The GNU **tar** command is more powerful than its System V counterpart and supports a host of exclusive options. Unfortunately, there is sometimes a mismatch with the options used by System V. The -M option is used for a multivolume backup (e.g., **tar -cvf /dev/fd0H1440 -M ***). There are two options (-z and -Z) related to compression that we have already discussed *(3.22—Linux)*.

SUMMARY

The system administrator or *superuser* uses the root user account, though any user can also invoke **su** to acquire superuser powers. The superuser can change the attributes of any file, kill any process, and change any user's password. The current directory doesn't feature in PATH.

A user is identified by the UID and GID, and root has 0 as the UID. A user can be added (**useradd**), modified (**usermod**), and removed from the system (**userdel**). User details are maintained in /etc/passwd and /etc/group. The password is stored in an encrypted manner in /etc/shadow.

For enforcing security, the administrator may assign a restricted shell so the user can execute only a fixed set of commands. The *set-user-id* (SUID) bit of a program makes its process run with the powers of the program's *owner*. The *sticky bit* set on a directory allows users to create and remove files owned by them in that directory, but not remove or edit files belonging to others.

During system startup, the **init** process reads /etc/inittab to run **getty** at all terminals and the system's *rc* scripts. These scripts mount file systems and start the system's daemons. **init** also becomes the parent of all login shells. **shutdown** uses **init** to kill all processes, unmount file systems, and write file system information to disk.

Devices can be *block special* (which use the buffer cache) or *character special* (which don't). A device file is also represented by a *major number* which represents the device driver, and *minor number* which signifies the parameters passed to the device driver. The same device can often be accessed with different filenames.

A UNIX *file system* comprises the *boot block, superblock, inode,* and *data blocks.* The superblock contains global information on the file system, including details of free inodes and data blocks. The memory copies of the superblock and inodes are regularly written to disk by the **update** daemon which calls **sync**.

Most systems today use the ufs file system which permit multiple superblocks, symbolic links and disk quotas. Linux uses the ext2 and ext3 file systems. There are different file system types for CD-ROMs (hsfs or iso9660), DOS disks (pcfs, vfat, or msdos), and a pseudo-file system for processes (proc or procfs).

A file system is unknown to the root file system until it is *mounted* (**mount**). **umount** unmounts file systems but only from above the mount point. **fsck** checks the integrity of file systems.

The administrator has to monitor the disk usage and ensure that adequate free space is available. **df** displays the free disk space for each file system. **du** lists the detailed usage of each file or directory. The administrator also uses **find** to locate large files (-size).

Floppy diskettes have to be formatted (**format** or **fdformat**) before they can be used. **dd** uses a character device to copy diskettes and tapes. UNIX provides an entire group of commands to handle DOS diskettes. Their names begin with the string dos (SVR4) or m (Linux).

tar is suitable for backing up a directory tree. It uses key options for copying to the media (-c), restoring from it (-x), and displaying the archive (-t). GNU **tar** adds compression to the archiving activity.

SELF-TEST

19.1   Where are the administrator's commands primarily located? Which directory is not found in the administrator's PATH even though nonprivileged users have it in theirs?

19.2   How does the behavior of the **passwd** command change when invoked by the superuser?

19.3   Two shell variables are assigned by **login** after reading /etc/passwd. What are they?

19.4   Specify the command line that changes romeo's shell from /bin/csh to /bin/bash.

19.5   Why was the password encryption moved from /etc/passwd to /etc/shadow?

19.6   A user after logging in is unable to change directories or create files in her home directory. How can this happen?

19.7   The letters s and t were seen in the permissions field of a listing. What do they indicate?

19.8   Explain the mechanism used by **ls** to display the name of the owner and group owner in the listing.

19.9   How will you use **find** to locate all SUID programs in /bin and /usr/bin?

19.10   What is meant by *run level*? How do you display the run level for your system?

19.11   Which file does **init** take its instructions from? How are the changes made to that file activated?

19.12   Name some services that are not available when the machine is in single-user mode.

19.13   How will you use **shutdown** to bring down the system immediately? What shortcut does Linux offer?

19.14   Mention the significance of the boot and swap file systems.

19.15   Which file system can't be unmounted and why?

19.16   What is the **fsck** command used for?

19.17   What is the difference between the **find** options -perm 1000 and -perm -1000?

19.18   How can the system administrator arrange to monitor the free disk space every hour on a working day between 9 a.m. and 10 p.m.?

19.19   How will you find out the total disk usage of the current directory tree?

19.20   How do you copy all HTML files to a DOS floppy in (i) SVR4, (ii) Linux?

19.21   The command **tar xvf /dev/fd0 *.c** displays an error message even though the diskette contains a number of .c files. Explain the two ways that can lead to the message.

EXERCISES

19.1   Why is the **su** command terminated with **exit**? What is the difference between **su** and **su - romeo**?

19.2   Name five administrative functions that can't be performed by a nonprivileged user.

19.3   Look up the man page of **passwd** to find out how the command can be used to change the password every four weeks.

19.4   How can you create another user with the same powers as root?

19.5   Specify the command lines needed to create a user john with UID 212 and GID dialout (a new group). john will use Bash as his shell and be placed in the /home directory. How can you later change john's shell to Korn without editing /etc/passwd?

19.6   A user romeo belongs to the student group and yet /etc/group doesn't show his name beside the group name. What does that indicate?

19.7   Name five features of the restricted shell.

19.8 How is a user able to update /etc/shadow with **passwd** even though the file doesn't have write permission?

19.9 How will you arrange for a group of users to write to the same directory and yet not be able to remove one another's files?

19.10 What are the two important functions of **init**? Explain how the shell process is created.

19.11 How do you determine the default run level? What is the difference between run levels 0 and 6?

19.12 What is the significance of the *start* and *kill* scripts? How are they organized on (i) an SVR4 system, (ii) Linux?

19.13 Write a shell script that shows whether the printer daemon is running irrespective of whether the system is using SVR4 or Linux.

19.14 Explain what these commands do:

    (i)   `find / -perm -4000 -print`
    (ii) `find / -type d -perm -1000 -exec ls -ld {} \;`
    (iii) `find / -type f -size +2048 -mtime +365 -print`

19.15 Why do we install the UNIX system on multiple partitions?

19.16 What is meant by *mounting*? When is unmounting of a file system not possible?

19.17 How do UNIX systems counter superblock corruption?

19.18 Discuss the role of the **sync** command in maintaining the system in a consistent state. When must you not use **sync**?

19.19 Name the important features of the *ufs* file system. What is the significance of the *proc* file system?

19.20 Write a shell script to copy a floppy diskette.

19.21 Specify the **tar** command line that (i) prevents files from being overwritten during restoration, (ii) renames each file interactively during restoration, (iii) appends to an existing archive during copying.

19.22 You need to back up all files that you have worked with today. How do you plan the backup activity using **tar**?

The C Shell—Programming Constructs

This appendix presents the programming constructs of the C shell that was developed at UCB by Bill Joy, the architect of **vi**. In form, these constructs differ—often greatly—with similar constructs of the Bourne family. Though most people use the Bourne shell (or its derivatives) for scripting, C shell scripting remains important for some. Linux offers a superior C shell as Tcsh.

Specifying the Interpreter

There are two ways of running a C shell script. Either use the **csh** command with the script name:

```
csh script_name
```

or invoke it by name but only after after having provided the she-bang line at the top of the script:

```
#!/bin/csh
```

If a script is invoked by name and it doesn't have the she-bang line, the Bourne shell (Bash in Linux) is used to run the script (and generate errors). Every C shell script also executes the rc file, ~/.cshrc.

Interactive and Noninteractive Scripts

You'll recall from Chapters 7 and 9 that the C shell uses the **set** and **setenv** statements for assigning variables. To make a script pause to read standard input, this shell uses **set** to assign the special parameter, $<, to a variable. Input, which can comprise multiple words, is read in as a quoted string:

```
#!/bin/csh
echo "Enter filename: \c"
set flname = $<                              Can use setenv also
echo "File: $flname"
```

A C shell script can also be run noninteractively by passing command line arguments. They are saved in a list or array named argv. The arguments are individually accessed as $argv[1], $argv[2], and so on. Further, $#argv is set to the number of arguments. To maintain compatibility with the Bourne shell family, the C shell also allows the use of $1, $2, and so forth. Tcsh even allows the use of $#.

Computation

As is not the case in the Bourne shell, integer computing is built into the C shell. The arithmetic operators are standard (+, -, *, /, and %). While you can use **set** to assign variables meant for computing, you need to use the special operator, @, for performing computation:

```
% set x=5
% @ y = 10                                    A space after @
% @ sum=$x + $y
% echo $sum
15
% @ product = $x * $y                         No escaping of * needed
% @ quotient = $y/$x
@: Badly formed number                        Space around / required
```

Incrementing numbers is done in these ways:

```
@ x = $x + 1
@ x++
```

The @ must be followed by whitespace even if the = need not have any around it. The arithmetic operators must also be surrounded by whitespace.

Arrays and Lists

By default, **set** displays all local variables, but note that one variable (path) is set and evaluated differently:

```
% set path = (/bin /usr/bin /usr/local/bin /usr/dt/bin .)
% echo $path
/bin /usr/bin /usr/local/bin /usr/dt/bin .
```

Like argv, path is an array or list of five elements. The first element is accessed by $path[1], the second by $path[2], and so on. The number of elements in the list is indicated by $#path:

```
% echo $path
/bin /usr/bin /usr/local/bin /usr/dt/bin .
% echo $path[3]
/usr/local/bin
% echo $#path
5
```

The **set** statement populates an array also; the values must be surrounded by a pair of parentheses. The **shift** statement also works with arrays:

```
% set numb = ( 9876 2345 6213 )
% echo $numb[1]
9876
% echo $#numb                              Entire list stored in $numb[*]
3
% shift numb                               Array name required
% echo $numb[1]
2345
```

The Comparison and Logical Operators

Numeric comparison is identical to **awk** which uses the operators <, >, ==, !=, >=, and so on. The complete list is shown in Table 12.3. String comparison also uses the == and != operators, but the C shell is clearly superior to the Bourne shell here because it supports two more operators for matching wild-card expressions:

=~   Matches a wild-card expression
!~   Doesn't match a wild-card expression

The same operators are used by **perl** with identical meaning except that **perl** uses them to match *regular expressions*. You can also use the && and || operators in the same way you used them with the Bourne shell.

The if Statement

As in the Bourne shell, the **if** conditional takes three forms as shown in Chapter 13. However, there are three differences:

- The keyword **then** must be in the same line as **if**.
- The construct is terminated with **endif** and not **fi**.
- The control command is enclosed within parentheses (unless it is a UNIX command).

Let's examine these three forms but use only examples. The first form also shows the use of numeric comparison, but note the second form which matches $response with any string that begins with y or Y:

`if ( $#argv != 2 ) then`
`    echo Two parameters required`
`endif`
	`if ( $response =~ [yY]* ) then`
	`    echo You answered yes`
	`else`
	`    echo You answered no`
	`endif`

Form 1	Form 2

The third form uses the **if–else** clause (multiple times, if required) but only a single **endif**. Here's the meat of the script, **emp3a.sh** (Chapter 13), modified here to run in the C shell:

```
    if ( $# == 0 ) then
        echo "Usage: $0 pattern file" >/dev/tty
    else if ( $# == 2 ) then
        grep "$1" $2 || echo "$1 not found in $2" >/dev/tty
    else
        echo "You didn't enter two arguments" >/dev/tty
    endif
```

Form 3

As a variant of Form 1, you can have single-line conditionals when there is no **else** clause. The **then** and **endif** keywords are not used:

```
if ( $#argv == 2 ) @ size = $1 * 512 ; echo Size of $2 is $size bytes
```

When executing a UNIX command as the control command, the command itself should be surrounded by a matched pair of curly braces and not parentheses:

```
if { grep "director" emp.lst } then
```

Note that either the () or {} enclosures must be provided with the control command used with **if**.

Testing File Attributes

Even though the C shell doesn't have a **test** statement, you can still test file attributes. This shell supports a limited set of operators, and most of them are used in the Bourne shell as well:

-f *file*   True if *file* is an ordinary file.
-d *file*   True if *file* is a directory.
-r *file*   True if *file* is readable.
-w *file*   True if *file* is writable.
-x *file*   True if *file* is executable.
-e *file*   True if *file* exists.
-z *file*   True if *file* exists and has a size of zero.

The following code shows the use of some of these operators:

```
if ( -f $1 ) then
    if ( ! -r $1 ) then
        echo "File exists but is not readable"
    else
        echo "File is readable"
    endif
else
    echo "File doesn't exist"
endif
```

The switch **Statement**

The **switch** statement is based on its namesake in the C language. Like **case**, the construct matches an expression for more than one alternative. The keywords used are **endsw**, **case**, **default**, and **breaksw**. The code of **menu.sh** that was developed in Chapter 13 is here modified to use **switch** instead of **case**:

```
cat << END                                              A here document
     MENU
  1. List of files
  2. Processes of user
  3. Exit
  Enter your option:
END
set choice = $<
switch ($choice)
   case 1:                                              Note the :
       ls -l ; breaksw
   case 2:
       ps -f ; breaksw
   case 3:
       exit
  default:                                    Used when previous matches fail
       echo "Invalid option"
endsw
```

The **breaksw** keyword moves control out of the construct after a successful match is found. If this word is not provided, then "fall through" behavior will result in the execution of all remaining **case** options. The **default** keyword is generally used as the last option.

The while **and** foreach **Loops**

There are two loops—**while** and **foreach** (instead of **for**). Both loops have three major differences with their counterparts in Bourne:

- The control command or list used by **foreach** is enclosed within parentheses.
- The **do** keyword is not used.
- The loop is terminated with **end** instead of **done**.

Let's consider the **while** loop first. This simple sequence entered at the prompt runs the **ps** command four times:

```
% set x = 1
% while ( $x < 5 )                              Can also use while { true }
?   ps -f                                        PS2 for C shell is ?
?   sleep 5
?   @ x++
? end
```

The **foreach** loop also has differences with **for**, its Bourne rival. The keyword **foreach** replaces **for**, and the **in** keyword is not required. The example used in Chapter 13 to illustrate the **for** loop can be reframed like this:

```
% foreach file (chap20 chap21 chap22 chap23)
?     cp $file ${file}.bak
?     echo $file copied to $file.bak
? end
```

Here, each component of the four-item list is assigned to the variable file until the list is exhausted. There are other ways of using a list:

```
foreach item ( `cat clist` )
foreach fname ( *.c )                          All C programs in current directory
foreach fname ( $* )                                       Script arguments
```

Note that the C shell doesn't recognize "$@", so command line arguments must be represented by $*.

The goto Statement

Though this construct is hardly used by programmers today, if used with caution, the **goto** statement often provides a convenient mechanism to exit a section of code. The statement specifies a *label* to branch to. The following code snippet uses **goto** to terminate a script after branching to the label named endblock:

```
if ( $#argv == 0 ) then                              No arguments entered
    goto endblock
else
    grep $1 emp.lst
    exit                              Required to stop intrusion into endblock
endif

endblock:
echo "You have not keyed in an argument"
```

The **exit** statement here has the same significance as the **break** statement used with **switch**. It ensures that control doesn't fall through after **grep** completes execution. If the statement is not provided, the **echo** statement will be unconditionally executed.

The repeat Statement

If a single command has to be repeated a finite number of times, you can use the **repeat** statement:

```
% repeat 3 date
Sat Apr 26 10:46:25 EST 2003
Sat Apr 26 10:46:25 EST 2003
Sat Apr 26 10:46:25 EST 2003
```

The Bourne family doesn't have a matching feature.

The onintr Statement

The **onintr** statement (**trap** in Bourne) specifies the commands to be executed when an interrupt signal is sent to the script. It is normally placed at the beginning of a shell script:

```
#!/bin/csh
onintr cleanup
cut -c1-10 index > $$
cut -c21- index > $$.1
paste $$ $$.1 > pastelist
rm $$ $$.1
exit                              Required to stop intrusion into cleanup


cleanup:
rm $$ $$.1
echo "Program interrupted"
```

Like the **goto** statement, **onintr** is also followed by a label. Execution branches to that label when the interrupt key is pressed. You may want to ignore the signal and continue processing. In that case, you should make the program immune to such signals by using **onintr** with a -:

```
onintr -
```

The C shell has been completely superseded in power and versatility by the Korn shell and Bash, both of which offer more convenient as well as more powerful programming constructs. Even Bourne is a better scripting language. If you are looking for an improved C shell, then use the Tcsh shell.

The Korn and Bash Shells—Exclusive Programming Constructs

This appendix features some of the useful programming constructs of the Korn and Bash shells. The usage in Bash sometimes differs from Korn, and these differences have been noted. Even though the POSIX specification was based on the Korn shell, Bash is a more POSIX-compliant shell today. Korn Shell '93 offers many more features that are also available in Bash, but we don't discuss them in this appendix. Some of the features discussed here have made it to the standard; others could do so in future.

Enhanced Use of read

The **read** statement has been enhanced—more so in Bash. You may not use it with a variable name, in which case the input is stored in the variable REPLY:

```
$ read
Korn Shell[Enter]
$ echo $REPLY
Korn Shell
```

Instead of using separate statements to display a prompt string (with **echo**) and read input (with **read**), you can use **read** to handle both functions. In Korn, the following statement treats all characters after a ? as the prompt string:

```
$ read flname?"Enter filename: "
Enter filename: foo.c
$ echo $flname
foo.c
```

Bash uses the -p option instead of ?. It also allows **read** to time out (-t). The -n *chs* option makes **read** return after *chs* characters have been input:

```
$ read -p "Enter filename: " -t10
Enter filename:
.... After 10 seconds ....
$ _                                                    read returns
```

```
$ read -p "Enter y or n: " -n1
Enter y or n: y                                              No [Enter] pressed
$ _                                                  read returns without [Enter]
```

The Korn shell uses **read** in a *coprocess* to accept standard input from the parent process. (**read** in Bash doesn't have this feature.) Korn Shell '93 also supports the timeout feature.

Accessing All Positional Parameters

With the Bourne shell, you can't access the 10th positional parameter as $10; you have to use **shift** and then access $9. With Korn and Bash, you can access any positional parameter by simply enclosing it with curly braces:

echo ${15}

This prints the 15th argument supplied to a script. However, we don't usually design scripts that handle so many arguments, but if we use **set** to assign positional parameters, then we can put this feature to good use:

```
$ ls -lids /etc/passwd
289906    4 -rw-r--r--   1 root     root     639 Oct  2  23:09 /etc/passwd
$ set -- $(ls -lids /etc/passwd)
$ echo "The file ${11} has the inode number $1"
The file /etc/passwd has the inode number 289906
```

Recall that we can use the form $(*command*) to perform command substitution in these shells.

The select Statement

The **select** statement presents a menu, reads the selected option, and makes it available for use. This unusual construct has a syntax similar to the **for** loop:

```
select var in stg1 stg2 ...
do
     action
done
```

The strings, *stg1, stg2,* and so forth are displayed as numbered menu options. **select** pauses to display a prompt evaluated from PS3 (Default—#?). The number you input is stored in the variable REPLY, and the string representing the number is saved in *var*. The body of **select** must contain code that determines the *action* to take for each value of REPLY. The menu is repeatedly displayed after *action* is performed or when the user simply presses *[Enter]*. To terminate the loop a **break** statement has to be used in the body.

A previous shell script that used the **case** statement in Chapter 13 can be redone using **select**:

```
#!/usr/bin/ksh
#
PS3="Choice: "
select task in "List of files" "Processes of user" \
               "Today's Date" "Users of system" "Quit"
do
    case "$REPLY" in
        1) ls -l ;;
        2) ps -f ;;
        3) date  ;;
        4) who   ;;
        5) break ;;
        *) echo "Invalid option" ;;
    esac
done
```

We first set PS3 to a meaningful string. The script presents a five-option menu which is repeatedly displayed every time an option between 1 and 4 is input. Option 5 terminates the loop because of the **break** statement:

```
1) List of files       3) Today's Date       5) Quit
2) Processes of user    4) Users of system
Choice: 3                                           Prompt as set by PS3
Tue Jun 29 11:29:09 EST 2004
Choice: 6
Invalid option
```

As in the **for** loop, the list can be passed to **select** as command line arguments. So, **select task** would be equivalent to as **select task in "$@"**.

The [[ ]] Construct

For condition testing with the **if** and **while** statements, Korn and Bash support two additional constructs—[[ ]] and (( )). The [[is actually a built-in command that needs the]] as terminator. This built-in is a superset of the **test** statement; you can use it to perform both numeric and string comparison, and also test file attributes:

```
if [[ $answer = y ]]                                Bourne shell features
if [[ $# -ne 2 ]]
if [[ -f $file ]]
```

Let's now understand why we should use the [[construct. You can use the && and || operators inside a single [[ ]] enclosure:

```
if [[ $answer = y || $answer = Y ]]
```

Unlike **test** (or [ ]), which matches only strings, [[allows the use of the shell's wild cards (like **case**). Consider the following examples where the first one is equivalent to the previous example. The second example matches a string that is at least four characters long. The third example matches a C or Java program filename:

```
if [[ $answer = [yY] ]]
if [[ $answer = ????* ]]
if [[ $filename = *.c  || $filename = *.java ]]
```

Note that even though the patterns are not quoted, the shell doesn't try to match them with filenames in the current directory. Since wild cards in Korn and Bash support a few additional characters (Chapter 7—Going Further), we can shorten the command shown in the third example above:

```
if [[ $file = @(*.c|*.java) ]]
```

If you are using Bash with characters like @, (, and | used in wild-card expressions, don't forget to use the statement **shopt -s extglob** at the beginning of the script. To negate the above test, use ! instead of @ in both shells.

The facility to use the complete set of wild cards for pattern matching is indeed a great convenience. As if that were not enough, the designers went further and included *some* regular expression characters as well. The syntax gets confusing here and for further details, you may look up *Learning the Korn Shell* by Bill Rosenblatt (O'Reilly).

The (( )) Construct

Even though the [[ ]] construct can be used to perform numeric comparison (with -gt, -le, -eq, etc.), the (( )) construct has been designed mostly to handle integer computation. You can assign integers to variables; the $ prefix is not necessary inside the enclosure:

```
$ x=5 ; y=10
$ ((z=$x+y))                                    Can also drop the $ prefix
$ echo $z
15
$ (( z = z + 1 ))                               Whitespace not important
$ echo $z
16
```

For variable assignment, the (( )) has a synonym—the **let** statement. Quoting is necessary when whitespace is provided:

```
let sum=25+12                                   No whitespace after variable
let sum='25 + 12'                               Can use single quotes here ...
let sum="$x + y"                                ...but only double quotes here
```

Note that both (( )) and **let** permit you to drop the $ prefix on the right side of an assignment. Since this computational feature is built in, scripts using this construct run much faster than when used with **expr**.

The (( )) construct actually returns an exit status, but it uses the same set of relational operators used by C, **awk**, and **perl** (like >, <, !=, etc.). Consider this example which tests the exit status returned by a comparison of two integers:

```
$ let x=5 y=6
$ (( $x > $y ))
$ echo $?
1
$ (($x <$y)) ; echo $?
0
```

This means that for numeric comparison with the **if** and **while** constructs, you should use these forms:

```
if (($# > 0)) ; then
while ((x <= 5)) ; do
```

The third use of (( )) is to evaluate an expression, but this requires a $ prefix. The following two examples show how you can both display the result of an expression and assign it to a variable:

```
$ echo $((25*25))
625
$ x=10
$ x=$((x-1))
$ echo $x
9
```

POSIX includes the (( )) construct, but doesn't mention **let**. POSIX also mentions [[ ]] but leaves its behavior as "unspecified." Hopefully, this will change in the future.

String Handling

The (( )) construct replaces **expr** for integer computing, but Korn and Bash don't need **expr** for string handling either. A variable is evaluated differently when its name is followed by an operator and a pattern using this generalized syntax:

${*variable operator pattern*}

Note the curly braces which are required as part of the syntax. Here, *operator* specifies what and how to extract from $*variable* by matching *pattern*. This can be done in four ways as shown below:

Form	Evaluates to segment remaining after deleting ...
${*var#pat*}	shortest segment that matches *pat* at beginning of $*var*
${*var##pat*}	longest segment that matches *pat* at beginning of $*var*
${*var%pat*}	shortest segment that matches *pat* at end of $*var*
${*var%%pat*}	longest segment that matches *pat* at end of $*var*

As in the [[ ]] construct, strings are matched with wild-card expressions. You can extract a substring using two characters—# and %—as the *operator*. The # matches *pattern* at the beginning and % at the end. This is how we can remove the extension from a filename without using **basename**:

```
$ filename=quotation.txt
$ echo ${filename%txt}
quotation.                                                        txt stripped off
```

The % operator deletes the *shortest* string that matches *pattern* at the *end*. The %% operator deletes the longest one, a feature that can be used to extract the hostname from an FQDN:

```
$ fqdn=java.sun.com
$ echo ${fqdn%%.*}
java
```

We can also extract the base filename from a pathname without using **basename**. This requires deletion of the longest pattern that matches */ at the beginning:

```
$ filename="/var/mail/henry"
$ echo ${filename##*/}
henry
```

There are other string handling features available. The length of a string is found by preceding the variable name with a #:

```
$ name="vinton cerf"
$ echo ${#name}
11
```

Bash also offers simple techniques to extract a substring in ways any high-level language handles them. Here's how you can implement the **substr()** function used in **awk** and **perl**:

```
$ echo ${name:3:3}                                               First position is zero
ton
$ echo ${name:7}                                                 Extracts rest of string
cerf
```

This feature is also available in Korn Shell '93.

Arrays

Korn and Bash support one-dimensional arrays where the first element has the index 0. While Korn arrays can hold up to 1024 elements, Bash supports very, very large arrays. This is how you assign and evaluate an element of an array named month:

```
$ month[1]=31
$ echo ${month[1]}
31
```

Note the use of curly braces when evaluating an element. Even though month[1] appears to be treated like a variable, it can coexist with a variable named month. To populate a group of elements, use either of these two forms:

```
set -A month 0 31 28 31 30 31 30 31 31 30 31 30 31          Korn only
month=(0 31 28 31 30 31 30 31 31 30 31 30 31)               Bash only
```

This array, month, stores the number of days available in each of the 12 months. The first element was set to zero because month[0] otherwise has no significance. You can display all *defined* elements by using the @ or * as subscript. If you add a # prefix, then only a count is displayed:

```
$ echo ${month[@]}
0  31 28 31 30 31 30 31 31 30 31 30 31
$ echo ${#month[@]}
13                                            Number of assigned elements...
```

What happens when you selectively assign individual elements? For instance, if you set x[0] and x[100] only, memory is allocated only for these two elements and x[1] through x[99] evaluate to null:

```
$ x[0]=1 ; x[100]=10
$ echo ${x[@]}
1  10
$ echo ${#x[@]}
2                                              ... and not the size of the array
```

Many of the features discussed in this appendix have not been included in POSIX, so the big question is whether one should use them at all. Today, Bash is increasingly being shipped with UNIX systems (including Solaris), but every system today supports the Korn shell. So, even if your application is not POSIX-compliant, you can achieve a fair degree of portability if you use the features that are at least available in versions of the Korn shell prior to 1993. In any case, the next revision of POSIX is some time away.

vi/vim and emacs
Command Reference

This appendix makes a comparative presentation of the *editing* features of the **vi/vim** and **emacs** editors. For convenience, commands and their customization parameters are grouped together. Most of these commands have been discussed in Chapters 5 and 6. The following points must be noted before you use this reference:

- Many commands can be used with a *repeat factor* (**vi**) or *digit argument* (**emacs**).
- Both **vim** (but not **vi**) and **emacs** support a *region* as a contiguous text block which can be manipulated with commands. A region is defined with **C-***[Spacebar]* (**emacs**) or **v** (**vim**) followed by a navigation command.
- A fully worded **emacs** command that appears in this appendix must be preceded with **M-x**.
- All **emacs** variables used with **set-variable** can also be placed in ~/.emacs using the **setq** command.

Navigation

vi Command	Function	emacs Command
h (or *[Backspace]*)	Move cursor left	C-b
l (or *[Spacebar]*)	Move cursor right	C-f
k (or *[Ctrl-p]*)	Move cursor up	C-p
j (or *[Ctrl-n]*)	Move cursor down	C-n
[Ctrl-f]	Scroll full page forward	C-v
[Ctrl-b]	Scroll full page backward	M-v
[Ctrl-d]	Scroll half page forward	-
[Ctrl-u]	Scroll half page backward	-
1G	Move to beginning of file	M-<
40G	Move to line 40	goto-line 40
G	Move to end of file	M->
-	Toggle line number display mode	line-number-mode
[Ctrl-g]	Display current line number and percentage of file	what-line
:set number	Show all lines numbered	-

Navigation along a Line

The **B**, **E**, and **W** commands in **vi** perform the same functions as their lowercase counterparts except that they ignore punctuation. There's no equivalent punctuation ignoring feature in **emacs**.

vi Command	Function	emacs Command
b	Move back to beginning of word	M-b
e	Move forward to end of word	M-f
w	Move forward to beginning of word	-
0 or |	Move to beginning of line	C-a
30|	Move to column 30	C-a M-30 C-f
^	Move to first character of first word in line	M-m
$	Move to end of line	C-e

Inserting Text

Unlike **vi**, **emacs** is always in the "input mode." The **emacs** commands shown here merely take you to a specific point in a line from where you can begin your insertion. Insertion of text in **emacs** is shown as *text*. Insertion of a control character is shown here for *[Ctrl-b]*.

vi Command	Function	emacs Command
i	Insert text to left of cursor	*text*
20i-*[Esc]*	Insert 20 hyphens	M-20 -
I	Insert text at beginning of line	C-a *text*
[Ctrl-v][Ctrl-b]	Insert *[Ctrl-b]*	C-q C-b
[Ctrl-v][Esc]	Insert *[Esc]*	C-q *[Esc]*
a	Append text to right of cursor	C-f *text*
A	Append text at end of line	C-e *text*
o	Open line below	C-e *[Enter]*
O	Open line above	C-a *[Enter]*
:set showmode	Display message when **vi** is in input mode	-
:set sm	Show momentarily match to a) and }	blink-matching paren t (with set-variable)
:set ts=*n*	Set tab stops to *n* (default: 8)	edit-tab-stops
:set ai	Next line starts at previous indented level	-

Deleting and Moving Text

All editing actions in this section can be undone. However, *[Ctrl-d]*, the command that deletes a single character in **emacs** (first entry), doesn't constitute a kill operation. A character deleted with *[Ctrl-d]* can't be restored from the kill ring. However, when the command is preceded by the digit argument, the deletion is saved in the kill ring.

vi/vim & emacs

vi Command	Function	emacs Command
x	Delete character under cursor	C-d or *[Delete]*
6x	Delete character under cursor and five characters on right	M-6 C-d
X	Delete previous character	-
dd	Delete current line	C-a C-k C-k
4dd	Delete four lines	M-4 C-k
64dd	Delete 64 lines	C-u C-u C-u C-k
dw	Delete word	M-d
-	Delete previous word	M-*[Backspace]*
d0 (d and zero)	Delete to beginning of line	M-0 C-k (Meta and zero)
d$	Delete to end of line	C-k
-	Delete blank lines	C-x C-o
d	Delete region (**vim** only)	C-w
p	Put deleted text on right (or below in **vi**)	C-y
P	Put deleted text above or left	-
"add	Delete current line to buffer a	C-u C-x xa (on region)
"ap	Restore contents from buffer a	C-u C-x ga
-	Preserve *n* sections of deleted/copied text in kill ring	kill-ring-max *n* (with set-variable)
ddp	Interchange current line with next	C-n C-x C-t
kddp	Interchange current line with previous	C-x C-t
J	Join current line with next line	C-e C-d
kJ	Join current line with previous line	M-^
xp	Transpose two characters	C-t
-	Transpose two words	M-t

Changing Text

vi Command	Function	emacs Command
r*ch*	Replace single character under cursor with *ch*	C-d *ch*
R	Replace text from cursor to right	Use overwrite-mode, then *text*
s	Replace single character under cursor with any number of characters	C-d *text*
S	Replace entire line	C-a C-k *text*
cw	Change word	M-d *text*
c	Change text of region (**vim** only)	C-w *text*
~	Reverse case of scanned text or region	-
-	Convert word to uppercase	M-u
-	Convert word to lowercase	M-l
-	Capitalize word	M-c
!tr '[a-z]' '[A-Z]'	Convert region to uppercase (**vim** only)	C-x C-u
!tr '[A-Z]' '[a-z]'	Convert region to lowercase (**vim** only)	C-x C-l

Copying Text

In **emacs**, only a region can be copied, so it has to be defined accordingly.

vi Command	Function	emacs Command
yy	Copy current line	C-a C-[Spacebar] C-e M-w
6yy	Copy six lines	C-a C-[Spacebar] M-6 C-e M-w
yw	Copy word	C-[Spacebar] M-f M-w
y	Copy region (**vim** only)	M-w
p	Put copied text on right (or below in **vi**)	C-y
P	Put copied text on left or above	-
"ayy	Copy current line to buffer a	C-x xa (on region)
"ap	Restore contents from buffer a	C-x ga

Starting the Editor

vi Command	Function	emacs Command
vi +100 foo	Open file at line 200	emacs +100 foo
vi +/*pat* foo	Open file at first occurrence of pattern *pat*	-
vi + foo	Open file at end	-
-	Load henry's ~/.emacs	emacs -u henry foo
-	Don't load ~/.emacs	emacs -q foo
vi -R foo	Open file in read-only mode	-

Saving and Quitting

vi Command	Function	emacs Command
:w	Save file and remain in editing mode	C-x C-s
:w bar	Like *Save As ...* in Microsoft Windows	C-x C-w
:w! bar	As above, but overwrite existing file bar	-
:*n1*, *n2*w foo	Write lines *n1* to *n2* to file foo	write-region (on region)
:*n1*, *n2*w >> foo	Append lines *n1* to *n2* to file foo	append-to-file (on region)
:.w foo	Write current line to file foo	-
:$w foo	Write last line to file foo	-
:x	Save file and quit editing mode	C-u C-x C-c
:wq	As above	-
:q	Quit editing mode when no changes are made to file	C-x C-c
:q!	Quit editing mode but after abandoning changes	As above, but enter n and yes at prompts
-	Enable/disable autosaving mode	auto-save-default (t or nil) (with set-variable)

vi Command	Function	emacs Command
-	Set autosave interval to *n* keystrokes	`auto-save-interval` *n* (with `set-variable`)
-	Set autosave interval to *n* seconds	`auto-save-timeout` *n* (with `set-variable`)
-	Recover autosaved file	`recover-file`

Editing Multiple Files

In **vi**, you can't use `:e`, `:n`, and `:rew` unless the current file is saved (and `autowrite` is not set). The `!` placed after the command overrides the safety feature. **emacs** lets you freely move from one file to another without saving.

vi Command	Function	emacs Command
`:e foo`	Stop editing current file and edit file `foo`	`C-x C-f`
`:e! foo`	As above, but after abandoning changes made to current file	Saving not necessary
-	Replace current buffer with another file	`C-x C-v`
`:e!`	Load last saved edition of current file	`revert-buffer`
[Ctrl-^]	Return to most recently edited file	`C-x b` *[Enter]*
`:n`	Edit next file (when invoked with multiple filenames)	`C-x b` and select from list
`:set autowrite (aw)`	Write current file automatically whenever switching files (with `:n` in **vi**)	Not necessary
`:rew`	Rewind file list to start editing first file (when invoked with multiple filenames)	-
`:r foo`	Read file `foo` below current line	`C-x i foo`
-	Kill current buffer	`C-x k`

Multiple Windows (emacs **and** vim)

vi Command	Function	emacs Command
`:sp`	Split current window in two	`C-x 2`
`:new`	Open a new blank window	`C-x b`
[Ctrl-w][Ctrl-w]	Toggle between windows	`C-x o`
`:on`	Make current window the only window	`C-x 1`
`:q`	Quit current window	`C-x 0` (zero)
`:qa`	Quit all windows	-
`:xa`	Save and quit all windows	`C-x C-c` and then `!`
-	Scroll text forward in other window	`C-M v`
[Ctrl-w] +	Increase window size	`C-x ^`
[Ctrl-w] -	Decrease window size (by *n* lines in **emacs**)	`C-u-`*n* `C-x ^`
-	Open file in another window	`C-x 4 C-f`

Search and Repeat

Unlike **emacs**, **vi** uses the same search and repeat techniques for strings and regular expressions. **emacs** can also make a search incremental. **vi** uses separate key sequences for searching for a character in a line.

vi Command	Function	emacs Command
/pat	Nonincremental search forward for string pat	C-s [Enter] pat
/pat	As above, but pat is a regular expression	C-M s [Enter] pat
?pat	Nonincremental search backward for string pat	C-r [Enter] pat
?pat	As above, but pat is a regular expression	C-M r [Enter] pat
-	Incremental search forward for string pat	C-s pat
-	As above, but pat is a regular expression	C-M s pat
-	Incremental search backward for string pat	C-r pat
-	As above, but pat is a regular expression	C-M r pat
n	Repeat string search in same/forward direction	C-s
N	Repeat string search in opposite/backward direction	C-r
n	Repeat regular expression search in same/forward direction	C-M s [Enter][Enter]
N	Repeat regular expression search in opposite/backward direction	C-M r [Enter][Enter]
-	Cancel search	[Esc]
:set wrapscan (ws)	Continue pattern search by moving to other end of file	-
:set ignorecase (ic)	Ignore case when searching	case-fold-search t (with set-variable)
:set magic	Retain meanings of regular expression characters	-
fc	Search forward for character c	C-s c
Fc	Search backward for character c	C-r c
;	Repeat last forward search for character	C-s
,	Repeat last reverse search for character	C-r

Substitution

vi Command	Function	emacs Command
:1,$s/s1/s2/g	Replace string s1 with s2 globally	replace-string
:1,$s/s1/s2/g	As above, but s1 is a regular expression	replace-regexp
:1,$s/s1/s2/gc	Interactive replacement	M-%
:1,$s/s1/s2/gc	As above, but s1 is a regular expression	query-replace-regexp

vi Command	Function	emacs Command
-	Preserve original case of letters when replacing	`case-replace t` (with `set-variable`)
`:s`	Repeat last substitution on current line (**vim** only)	-

Marks and Bookmarks

vi Command	Function	emacs Command
`ma`	Set mark a	`C-x a`
`'a`	Move to mark a	`C-x ja`
`' '`	Toggle between current and previous positions	`C-x C-x`
-	Set bookmark	`C-x rm`
-	Jump to bookmark	`C-x rb`

Redoing and Undoing

vi Command	Function	emacs Command
`.`	Repeat last command (**emacs** command with M-x)	`C-x` *[Esc][Esc]*
`u`	Undo last editing command	`C-x u` or `C--`
[Ctrl-r]	Redo last undo (**vim** only)	As above but only after all undoing is complete
`U`	Undo all changes made to current line	-
`"4p`	Restore 4th recent deletion from buffer (complete lines in **vi**)	`C-u 4 C-y`

Abbreviating Text

vi Command	Function	emacs Command
-	Toggle abbreviation mode	`abbrev-mode`
`:ab` *stg name*	Abbreviate *name* to *stg*	*stg* `C-x aig` *name* (`ail` for local abbreviation)
-	Expand abbreviation from string available in buffer	`M-/`
`:ab`	List all abbreviations	`list-abbrevs`
`:unab` *stg*	Kill abbreviation *stg*	Delete abbreviation with `edit-abbrevs`
-	Kill all abbreviations	`kill-all-abbrevs`
-	Save all current abbreviations	`write-abbrev-file`
-	Read file containing abbreviations	`read-abbrev-file`
-	Save all future abbreviations	`save-abbrevs t` (with `set-variable`)

Macros and Key Mapping

vi Command	Function	emacs Command
Enter a command	Define a macro (named m in **vi**) sequence, then "myy	C-x (commands C-x)
@m	Run last defined macro (named m in **vi**)	C-x e
-	Name last defined macro to *macroname* and enter *macroname*	name-last-kbd-macro
@m	Run macro m (**vi**) or *macroname* (**emacs**)	*macroname* (with M-x)
:map key commands	Map *key* to *commands* (**vi**) or *macroname* (**emacs**)	global-set-key, enter *key* and *macroname*
:map! key commands	Map *key* to *commands* in input mode	As above
Place the :map command in ~/.exrc	Save macro in file	insert-kbd-macro
-	Load file containing macros	load-file
:map	Display all Command Mode maps	-
:map!	Display all Input Mode maps	-
:unmap key	Kill Command Mode map *key*	-
:unmap! key	Kill Input Mode map *key*	-

Interface To UNIX

The editor can be suspended with *[Ctrl-z]* only for those shells that enable job control.

vi Command	Function	emacs Command
:!cmd	Run UNIX command *cmd*	M-! *cmd*
:!%	Execute current file as a shell or **perl** script	-
:r !cmd	Read in output of command *cmd*	C-u M-! *cmd*
:r !head -n 3 foo	Read first three lines of foo below current line	C-u M-! head -n 3 foo
:sh	Escape to UNIX shell	shell
[Ctrl-z]	Suspend editor	C-z or C-x C-z
:!cc %	Compile currently edited C program	compile
:!javac %	Compile currently edited Java program	-

Help (emacs only)

vi Command	Function	emacs Command
-	Function performed by keystroke (detailed)	C-h k
-	Function performed by keystroke (one-line)	C-h c
-	Function performed by command	C-h f
-	Key binding available for command	C-h w

vi Command	Function	emacs Command
-	Function of variable and its current setting	C-h v
-	Commands that use a concept	C-h a
-	Run tutorial	C-h t
-	Run info reader	C-h i

Miscellaneous

vi Command	Function	emacs Command
-	Cancel a sequence	C-g
:set all	Show all set options (**vi**) or variables (**emacs**)	list-options
[Ctrl-l]	Redraw the screen	C-l
v	Define start of region (**vim** only)	C-@ or C-*[Spacebar]*
:set ro	Change to read-only mode (**vi**), toggle mode (**emacs**)	C-x C-q

D

The Regular Expression Superset

Regular expressions are used by the editors **vi/vim** and **emacs** and the filters **grep**, **egrep**, **sed**, **awk**, and **perl**. Unfortunately, these commands use different subsets of this collection, and many people are not quite sure of the metacharacters that a command recognizes and the ones it doesn't. Examples have often been provided to ease understanding.

Basic Regular Expressions

Symbols	vi	emacs	grep	sed	egrep	awk	perl	Linux vim	Linux grep	Linux sed	Linux gawk	Matches
*	•	•	•	•	•	•	•	•	•	•	•	Zero or more occurrences of previous character
g*	•	•	•	•	•	•	•	•	•	•	•	Nothing or g, gg, ggg, etc.
gg*	•	•	•	•	•	•	•	•	•	•	•	g, gg, ggg etc.
.	•	•	•	•	•	•	•	•	•	•	•	A single character
.*	•	•	•	•	•	•	•	•	•	•	•	Nothing or any number of characters
[abc]	•	•	•	•	•	•	•	•	•	•	•	a or b or c
[1-3]	•	•	•	•	•	•	•	•	•	•	•	A digit between 1 and 3
[^Z]	•	•	•	•	•	•	•	•	•	•	•	Any character except Z
[^a-zA-Z]	•	•	•	•	•	•	•	•	•	•	•	A non-alphabetic character
^DM	•	•	•	•	•	•	•	•	•	•	•	DM at beginning of line
bash$	•	•	•	•	•	•	•	•	•	•	•	bash at end of line

EXPRESSIONS

Extended Regular Expressions

Symbols	vi	emacs	grep	sed	egrep	awk	perl	Linux				Matches
								vim	grep	sed	gawk	
+		•			•	•	•				•	One or more occurrences of previous character
g+		•			•	•	•				•	At least one g
g\+								•	•	•		As above
?		•			•	•	•				•	Zero or one occurrence of previous character
g?		•			•	•	•				•	Nothing or one g
g\?									•	•		As above
GIF|JPEG					•	•	•				•	GIF or JPEG
GIF\\|JPEG		•						•	•	•		As above
wood(cock|house)					•	•	•				•	woodcock or woodhouse
wood\(cock\\|house\)		•						•	•	•		As above
\<*pat*	•	•						•	•	•	•	Pattern *pat* at beginning of word
pat\>	•	•						•	•	•	•	Pattern *pat* at end of word

Interval and Tagged Regular Expressions

These are advanced regular expressions not used by **egrep** and **awk**. **gawk** and **perl** also accept the Interval Regular Expression but drop the \ in front of the curly brace. **gawk** additionally requires the use of the --posix or -W re-interval option. **perl** drops the \ in front of the (and) as well.

Symbols	vi	emacs	grep	sed	egrep	awk	perl	Linux				Matches
								vim	grep	sed	gawk	
\{*m*\}	•		•	•				•	•	•		*m* occurrences of the previous character
{*m*}							•				•	As above
^.\{9\}nobody	•		•	•				•	•	•		nobody after skipping nine characters from line beginning
^.{9}nobody							•				•	As above
\{*m*,\}	•		•	•				•	•	•		At least *m* occurrences of the previous character
{*m*,}							•				•	As above
\{*m*,*n*\}	•		•	•				•	•	•		Between *m* and *n* occurrences of the previous character
{*m*,*n*}							•				•	As above
\(*exp*\)	•	•	•	•				•	•	•		*exp* and attaches tag \1, \2, etc. to *exp*
(*exp*)							•					As above, but also uses $1, $2, etc.

Escape Sequences

								Linux				
Symbols	vi	emacs	grep	sed	egrep	awk	perl	vim	grep	sed	gawk	Matches
\b		•					•		•	•		On word boundary
wood\b		•					•		•	•		wood but not woodcock
\B		•					•		•	•	•	On non-word boundary
wood\B		•					•		•	•	•	woodcock but not wood
\w		•					•	•	•	•	•	A word character (same as [a-zA-Z0-9_])
\W		•					•	•	•	•	•	A non-word character (same as [^a-zA-Z0-9_])
\d							•	•				A digit (same as [0-9])
\D							•	•				A non-digit (same as [^0-9])
\s							•	•				A whitespace character (same as [[☐🡒]])
\S							•	•				A non-whitespace character (same as [^☐🡒])
\t		•					•	•			•	A tab (same as 🡒)
\n							•				•	A newline (*[Ctrl-j]*)
\r							•				•	A carriage return (*[Ctrl-m]*)
\f							•				•	A formfeed (*[Ctrl-l]*)
\0nnn							•				•	ASCII octal value *nnn*
\014							•				•	ASCII octal value 14
\xnn							•				•	ASCII hex value *nn*

POSIX Character Classes

								Linux				
Symbols	vi	emacs	grep	sed	egrep	awk	perl	vim	grep	sed	gawk	Matches
[[:alpha:]]								•	•	•	•	An alphabetic character
[[:lower:]]								•	•	•	•	A lowercase alphabetic character
[[:upper:]]								•	•	•	•	An uppercase alphabetic character
[[:digit:]]								•	•	•	•	A numeric character
[[:alnum:]]								•	•	•	•	An alphanumeric character
[[:space:]]								•	•	•	•	A whitespace character including formfeed
[[:cntrl:]]									•	•	•	A control character
[[:blank:]]								•	•	•	•	A space or tab
[[:print:]]								•	•	•	•	A printable character
[[:punct:]]								•	•	•	•	A punctuation character (not a space, letter, digit, or control character)
[[:xdigit:]]								•	•	•	•	An hexadecimal digit

E

The HOWTO

How to do or display	Command
abbreviate a command sequence	alias
add a user account *(superuser only)*	useradd
add a user group *(superuser only)*	groupadd
address all users *(superuser only)*	wall
arithmetic (integer) computation noninteractively	expr
arithmetic computation using the shell	(( )) or let
assign values to positional parameters	set
back up files specified in command line	tar
beginning of file	head
calendar of month or year	cal
cancel print job	cancel, lprm
change case of text	tr
change current directory to *dirname*	cd *dirname*
change current directory to home directory	cd or cd $HOME
change filename extension	basename, expr
change file's group ownership	chgrp
change file's last modification or access time	touch
change file's ownership	chown
change file's permissions	chmod
change login shell without involving administrator	chsh
change own password	passwd
change password of any user *(superuser only)*	passwd *username*
check current directory	pwd
check in SCCS/RCS file	delta, ci
check out SCCS/RCS file	get, co
check file system integrity *(superuser only)*	fsck
clear screen	tput clear
command documentation	man
command documentation in multiple levels	info
command history	history
command introduction in single line	whatis
command type (external, internal, or alias)	type
commands containing keyword	apropos

How to do or display	Command
compile C program	cc, gcc
compress file (to `.bz2`)	bzip2
compress file (to `.gz`)	gzip
compress multiple files to a single file (to `.zip`)	zip
concatenate files	cat
control access to X server	xhost
convert file from DOS to UNIX	dos2unix
convert file from UNIX to DOS	unix2dos
copy directory tree	cp -r
copy file	cp
copy file between machines	ftp, scp, sftp
copy file to and from DOS diskette	doscp, mcopy
copy floppy diskette or tape media	dd
count number of lines containing a pattern	grep -c
count number of lines, words, and characters	wc
create archive of C object files	ar
create file	cat >, echo >, vi, emacs
create links to a file	ln
create SCCS/RCS file	admin, ci
create specification file for **cron**	crontab
create symbolic links to a file	ln -s
cut columns or fields from file	cut
debug a C program	dbx, gdb
default file permissions	umask
delay command execution in a script	sleep
device name of current terminal	tty
difference between two files (as **sed**-like instructions)	diff
difference between two files (character-wise list)	cmp
directory list	ls -l | grep "^d"
disk space utilization	du
duplicate standard input stream	tee
echo a message	echo, printf
edit file	vi, emacs
end of file	tail
execute command in background and log out	nohup
execute command on remote machine without logging in	ssh
execute command with arguments from standard input	xargs
execute commands from a shell in X window	xterm
execute shell script without spawning sub-shell	. (dot), source
file attributes	ls -l
file content	cat
file content (compressed) (`.Z` or `.gz`)	zcat
file content in DOS diskette	doscat, mtype
file content in k columns	pr -k

HOWTO

How to do or display	Command
file content one page at a time	more, less
file content with headings and page numbers	pr
file list	ls
file list containing a pattern	grep -l
file list in DOS diskette	dosdir, mdir
find files by name or any other attribute	find
format DOS floppy diskette	dosformat, mformat
format UNIX floppy diskette	fdformat
free disk space	df
free space in memory and swap	top
generate public/private key pair	ssh-keygen
handle signal from shell script	trap
input data to shell script interactively	read
join two files laterally	paste
kill job	See "terminate"
lines common to two files or unique to one	comm
lines containing one or more of multiple patterns	grep -E, egrep, fgrep
lines containing pattern	grep
lines in ASCII collating sequence	sort
lines in double space	pr -d -t
lines in numeric sequence	sort -n
lines in reverse order	tail -r
lines not containing pattern	grep -v
lines sorted ignoring case	sort -f
lines that are repeated	uniq -d
lines that occur only once	uniq -u
log in to remote machine	telnet, slogin, ssh
log session	script
mail message	mailx
maintain group of C programs	make
manipulate individual fields in a line	awk, perl
maximum file size	ulimit
modify user account *(superuser only)*	usermod
monitor growth of file	tail -f
mount file system	mount
move files to another directory	mv
move job to background	bg
move job to foreground	fg
multiple segments from a file	sed
name of local host	hostname
number lines including empty lines	pr -n -t
octal value of character	od
operating system name	uname
operating system release	uname -r

How to do or display	Command
pass variable value to sub-shell	export, setenv
print file	lp, lpr
print queue	lpstat, lpq
process ancestry	ps -f, ps f
process attributes	ps
process HTML form data	perl
remove duplicate lines	sort -u
remove duplicate lines from sorted file	uniq
remove empty directory	rmdir
remove empty or blank lines	grep -v, sed
remove file	rm
remove newline character from text	tr -d
remove nonempty directory	rm -r
remove user account (superuser only)	userdel
rename file or directory	mv
replace current shell with another program	exec
replace pattern	See "substitute"
restore files from backup media	tar
SCCS/RCS activity	prs, rlog
SCCS/RCS history	sact, rlog
schedule job for one-time execution	at
schedule job for repeated execution	cron
schedule one-time job when system load permits	batch
search a file for one or more patterns	See "lines containing"
send signal to process	kill
set default file permissions	umask
set maximum file size (superuser only)	ulimit
set run level of system (superuser only)	init
set system date (superuser only)	date
set terminal characteristics	stty
shift positional parameters to next lower-numbered one	shift
shut down system (superuser only)	shutdown, init
sound beep	echo "\007"
squeeze multiple spaces to single space	tr -s
start SSH authentication agent	ssh-agent
string length	expr
substitute one character for another	tr
substitute one pattern for another	sed
substring extracted from larger string	expr
substring position within larger string	expr
superuser from nonprivileged account	su
system date	date
system memory usage	top
system run level	who -r, runlevel

How to do or display	Command
terminate last background job	`kill $!`
terminate login session	`exit, logout`
terminate process	`kill`
terminate shell script	`exit`
test connectivity of host	`ping`
uncompress `.bz2` file	`bunzip2`
uncompress `.gz` file	`gunzip`
uncompress `.zip` file	`unzip`
unmount file system	`umount`
users and their activities	`who`
World Wide Web pages with graphics	`netscape`
write kernel buffer contents to disk *(superuser only)*	`sync`
write different segments of file to different files	`sed`

The ASCII Character Set

The appendix lists the values of the first 128 characters of the ASCII character set in decimal, hexadecimal, and octal. Octal values are used by the UNIX commands **awk**, **echo**, **printf**, **perl**, and **tr**, while **od** displays characters in octal. Many of these commands also use escape sequences of the form \x as shown for some characters under the *Remarks* column. **awk** and **perl** also use hexadecimal values.

Character	Decimal	Hex	Octal	Remarks
(null)	0	00	000	Null
[Ctrl-a]	1	01	001	
[Ctrl-b]	2	02	002	
[Ctrl-c]	3	03	003	
[Ctrl-d]	4	04	004	
[Ctrl-e]	5	05	005	
[Ctrl-f]	6	06	006	
[Ctrl-g]	7	07	007	Bell (\a)
[Ctrl-h]	8	08	010	Backspace (\b)
[Ctrl-i]	9	09	011	Tab (\t)
[Ctrl-j]	10	0A	012	Newline (\n) (LF)
[Ctrl-k]	11	0B	013	Vertical tab (\v)
[Ctrl-l]	12	0C	014	Formfeed (\f) (FF)
[Ctrl-m]	13	0D	015	Carriage return (\r) (CR)
[Ctrl-n]	14	0E	016	
[Ctrl-o]	15	0F	017	
[Ctrl-p]	16	10	020	
[Ctrl-q]	17	11	021	
[Ctrl-r]	18	12	022	
[Ctrl-s]	19	13	023	
[Ctrl-t]	20	14	024	
[Ctrl-u]	21	15	025	
[Ctrl-v]	22	16	026	
[Ctrl-w]	23	17	027	
[Ctrl-x]	24	18	030	
[Ctrl-y]	25	19	031	
[Ctrl-z]	26	1A	032	

Character	Decimal	Hex	Octal	Remarks
[Ctrl-[ ]	27	1B	033	Escape
[Ctrl-\]	29	1C	034	
[Ctrl-]]	29	1D	035	
[Ctrl-^]	30	1E	036	
[Ctrl-_]	31	1F	037	
(space)	32	20	040	Space
!	33	21	041	Exclamation mark or bang
"	34	22	042	Double quote
#	35	23	043	Pound sign
$	36	24	044	Dollar sign
%	37	25	045	Percent
&	38	26	046	Ampersand
'	39	27	047	Single quote
(	40	28	050	Left parenthesis
)	41	29	051	Right parenthesis
*	42	2A	052	Asterisk
+	43	2B	053	Plus sign
,	44	2C	054	Comma
-	45	2D	055	Hyphen
.	46	2E	056	Period
/	47	2F	057	Slash
0	48	30	060	
1	49	31	061	
2	50	32	062	
3	51	33	063	
4	52	34	064	
5	53	35	065	
6	54	36	066	
7	55	37	067	
8	56	38	070	
9	57	39	071	
:	58	3A	072	Colon
;	59	3B	073	Semicolon
<	60	3C	074	Left chevron
=	61	3D	075	Equal sign
>	62	3E	076	Right chevron
?	63	3F	077	Question mark
@	64	40	100	At sign
A	65	41	101	
B	66	42	102	
C	67	43	103	
D	68	44	104	
E	69	45	105	
F	70	46	106	

Character	Decimal	Hex	Octal	Remarks
G	71	47	107	
H	72	48	110	
I	73	49	111	
J	74	4A	112	
K	75	4B	113	
L	76	4C	114	
M	77	4D	115	
N	78	4E	116	
O	79	4F	117	
P	80	50	120	
Q	81	51	121	
R	82	52	122	
S	83	53	123	
T	84	54	124	
U	85	55	125	
V	86	56	126	
W	87	57	127	
X	88	58	130	
Y	89	59	131	
Z	90	5A	132	
[	91	5B	133	Left square bracket
\	92	5C	134	Backslash
]	93	5D	135	Right square bracket
^	94	5E	136	Caret or hat
_	95	5F	137	Underscore
`	96	60	140	Backquote or backtick
a	97	61	141	
b	98	62	142	
c	99	63	143	
d	100	64	144	
e	101	65	145	
f	102	66	146	
g	103	67	147	
h	104	68	150	
i	105	69	151	
j	106	6A	152	
k	107	6B	153	
l	108	6C	154	
m	109	6D	155	
n	110	6E	156	
o	111	6F	157	
p	112	70	160	
q	113	71	161	
r	114	72	162	

Character	Decimal	Hex	Octal	Remarks
s	115	73	163	
t	116	74	164	
u	117	75	165	
v	118	76	166	
w	119	77	167	
x	120	78	170	
y	121	79	171	
z	122	7A	172	
{	123	7B	173	Left curly brace
|	124	7C	174	Vertical bar or pipe
}	125	7D	175	Right curly brace
~	126	7E	176	Tilde
	127	7F	177	Delete or rubout

Glossary

absolute pathname A pathname which begins with a /, indicating that the file must be referenced in an absolute manner—from root. See also **relative pathname**.

access time A file's time stamp representing the date and time a file was last accessed. A file is considered to be accessed if it is read, written, or executed. The access time is stored in the inode and displayed by **ls -lu**.

action A component of an **sed**, **awk**, or **perl** instruction which acts on text specified by an **address**. It normally uses a single character to represent an action for **sed**, but could be a complete program in case of **awk** and **perl**. Also known as **internal command.**

address A component of an **sed**, **awk**, or **perl** instruction which specifies the lines to be affected by the **action**. The specification could be made with a single line number or a range of them, or with a regular expression or a pair of them, or any combination of the two.

alias Term used to refer to a command sequence by another name. Aliasing is available in **csh**, **bash**, and **ksh** to abbreviate long command sequences.

anonymous FTP A public FTP site where users use the login name "anonymous" and the email address as the password to gain access. Most downloadable software are hosted in these sites. Doesn't permit uploading of files.

archive Term used to a store a group of files as a single unit—either on magnetic media or as a single disk file. Refers to such units created by **tar**, **cpio**, and **zip**. Also refers to a library of object files.

argument A word that follows a command. It can be an option, an expression, an instruction, a program, or one or more filenames. Options can also have their own arguments.

ASCII collating sequence The sequence used by ASCII (American Standard Code for Information Interchange) to number characters. Control characters occupy the top slots, followed by numerals, uppercase letters, and then lowercase. Sequence followed by any UNIX command which sorts its output.

atomic operation Multiple actions that must be performed in entirety or not at all. A system call represents an atomic operation.

attachment A file that is sent along with an email message. An attachment can be a text or binary file that is viewed by a mail client either inline or using a **plugin** or **helper application**.

autosave Feature of the **emacs** editor that saves the editing buffer periodically in a separate file. The autosaved file has a # on either side of its name and can be recovered with the **recover-file** command of the editor.

background job One or more related processes that run without being waited for by the parent. A command, when terminated by the & symbol, runs in the background. See also **foreground job**.

block device A hard disk, tape unit, or floppy drive where output is written to and read from in units of blocks rather than bytes. Indicated by the letter b in the first character of the permissions field of the listing. See also **character device**.

boot block A special area in every file system. For the **root file system**, this block contains the boot procedure and the partition table, while for others it is left blank.

browser A program used to view HTML pages of the World Wide Web. Common Web browsers include Netscape and Internet Explorer (for Microsoft Windows and selected UNIX flavors). Linux is shipped with Netscape, Mozilla, Opera, and Konqueror.

brute force attack A technique of trying out every possible key combination to decrypt data without knowledge of the key used to encrypt it. Time taken depends mainly on the size of the key.

BSD UNIX A flavor of UNIX from the University of California, Berkeley. Berkeley introduced a number of enhancements like the **vi** editor, C shell, r-utilities, PPP, and symbolic links. TCP/IP was first available on BSD UNIX.

buffer A temporary storage that is often used to hold frequently requested information in memory, rather than on disk, thus speeding up data transfer. Used by **vi** and **emacs** to make a copy of a file before editing. See also **buffer cache**.

buffer cache A pool of buffers maintained by the kernel to store data when doing I/O. All programs read from and write to these buffers unless explicitly directed to skip them.

cache Same as **buffer**.

character The smallest unit of information. The press of a key generates a single character, while ASCII has a set of 256 of them.

character device A terminal or printer where output is written to and read from in streams of characters. Indicated by the letter c in the first character of the permissions field of the listing. See also **block device**.

child process A process having a separate PID that is created by the parent process. The created process inherits some of the environmental parameters of its parent, but environmental changes made in the child are not available in the parent.

client-server A two-tier scheme that allows two processes to run in a cooperative manner. The client process requests a service from a server process, generally running on a different host. X Window treats the concept in a reverse manner. See also **X server** and **X client**.

command Normally the first word entered at the prompt. It is usually an executable file, but can also include built-in statements (also known as **internal commands**) of the shell and other commands (like **mailx**, **vi**, etc.).

command failure The **exit status** returned by a command on unsuccessful completion. A value greater than 0 indicates failure and 0 signifies success. See also **command success**.

command line A complete sequence of a command, its options, filenames, and other arguments that are specified at the shell prompt. The shell executes a command only when it encounters a complete command line.

Command Mode One of the three modes available in the **vi** editor to let keystrokes be interpreted as commands to act on text. See also **Input Mode** and **ex Mode**.

command substitution A feature of the shell which executes a command enclosed within a pair of backquotes (`` ` ``) and uses its standard output to form the arguments of another command. Double quotes enable command substitution, but not single quotes.

command success The **exit status** returned by a command on successful completion. A value of 0 indicates success; any other value signifies failure. See also **command failure**.

Common Desktop Environment (CDE) A standardized look and feel of the entire desktop under the X Window system now adopted by most UNIX vendors. Features a Front Panel from where applications can be launched, a File Manager, and a Workspace Switch to allow the use of multiple desktops.

Common Gateway Interface (CGI) The interface offered by a Web server to pass on form data to an external application. The application processes the data and sends back the results to the server.

concatenate The combination of two or more entities. Term used in connection with the **cat** command, character strings, and shell variables.

context address A form of addressing used by **sed**, **awk**, and **perl** which uses a regular expression enclosed by a pair of /s. The commands act only on the lines containing the expression.

context switch Term used to refer to the change of **process context** when the time quantum allocated to a process expires. This can also occur when a process invokes an I/O bound system call.

control command A command used in the command line of a shell, **awk**, and **perl** conditional or loop to determine the control flow of the construct.

control file A text file used by some programs to take their instructions from. $HOME/.exrc, /etc/sendmail.cf, /etc/inittab, and /etc/inetd.conf are some of the control files found on a UNIX system.

cron The chronograph of the UNIX system. It executes the commands listed in a **crontab** file at a frequency specified by the various fields in the file. Widely used for scheduling noninteractive jobs.

crontab A control file named after the user-id containing all instructions that need to be executed periodically. The **cron** command looks at this table every minute to execute a command scheduled for execution.

cryptography The science of protecting information using one or more keys. Symmetric cryptography uses a single key while asymmetric cryptography uses a **private key** and a **public key.**

current directory The directory in which the user is placed after using the **cd** command with an argument. Usually is set to the home directory during login time. See also **home directory.**

daemon A process that runs continuously without a user specifically requesting it. Usually not associated with a specific terminal. **cron**, **init**, **inetd**, **lpsched**, and **sendmail** are important daemons that keep the system running.

DARPA set The original set of TCP/IP utilities developed at the behest of DARPA and includes **telnet** and **ftp**. These tools are being phased out in favor of **secure shell (SSH)** tools.

delta Term used to describe a version in the **Source Code Control System.**

device driver A set of routines built into the kernel to handle a device. The kernel identifies the device driver from the device name used as argument to a command. The parameters passed by the kernel to the device driver are indicated by the **major number** and **minor number** of the device.

device file A file that represents a device. Provides a communication channel so that interaction with the file actually results in activation of the physical device.

digit argument A numeric prefix used by an **emacs** command to repeat the command that many times. Known as **repeat factor** in **vi**.

directory file A file that contains the name and inode number of other files and subdirectories. Writing a directory file is possible only by the kernel.

DNS Same as **domain name system.**

domain A common string used by several hosts as part of their fully qualified hostnames. Examples of top-level domains on the Internet are *com, edu, org,* etc.

domain name system (DNS) A service available on the Internet to convert hostnames to IP addresses, and vice versa. The database containing the mappings is distributed in a large network with consequent delegation of authority.

empty regular expression A null string signified by two /s, which indicates that the string to be acted upon is the same as the last string searched. Used by **sed** in performing substitution.

encryption A method of encoding a string of characters into a seemingly random character sequence. Used by the **secure shell** to encrypt all communication in a network. Also used for storing the password of every user of the system.

environment variable A shell variable that is visible in all processes run by a user. The **export** and **setenv** commands create environment variables. HOME, TERM, and SHELL are common environment variables. See also **local variable**.

escape sequence A character that is preceded by a \ (like \t) and has a special meaning. Escape sequences are used by the shell and commands like **echo**, **printf**, **awk**, and **perl**.

escaping The use of the \ immediately before a character to indicate that the following character should be treated literally. Mostly used to remove the special meaning of a character, but sometimes is also used to emphasize it. See also **quoting**.

ex Mode A mode available in the **vi** editor to let **ex** commands act on text. An indispensable mode for substitution, handling multiple files, and customizing the editor. Also known as **Last Line Mode**. See also **Command Mode** and **Input Mode**.

exec The mechanism used by a process to overwrite itself with the code of a new program. Usually follows the **fork** operation. Also represents a family of six C functions that do the job.

exit status A value returned by a program after execution. A value 0 indicates successful (true) execution. In a C program, the **wait** system call directs the parent to pick up the child's exit status.

export A built-in shell command which makes shell variables of the parent process also visible in the child process. The child views only copies so changes made to them don't affect the original.

extended regular expression (ERE) An enhanced regular expression used by **grep -E**, **egrep**, **awk**, and **perl** which allows the specification of multiple patterns. Uses the metacharacters ?, +, (,), and |.

FAQ A collection of frequently asked questions.

file A container for storing information. An **ordinary file** contains data. A **directory file** contains filenames. A **device file** provides the interface to access a physical device. A **symbolic link** points to the file that actually contains data.

file attributes A set of parameters stored in the inode which describe the characteristics of a file. They consist of the type, ownership, permissions, time stamps, size, number of links, and an array of disk block addresses.

file descriptor A small integer returned by the **open** system call when a file is opened. Each descriptor, maintained in the file descriptor table, points to the **file table**. The first three entries are usually allocated to the shell's standard streams.

file offset pointer The location within the file where the next read or write operation will take place. This location is maintained in the **file table** and is updated every time a read or write operation on the file takes place.

file ownership One of the attributes of a file. The user creating or copying a file is generally the owner as well. The owner of a file has certain privileges that are denied others.

Ownership can be surrendered only by the superuser on a BSD-based system. Similar attribute refers to the group owner.

file permissions Term used to describe a file's read, write and execute permissions available to three categories of users—**user**, **group**, and **others**. Can be altered only by the owner of the file with **chmod**.

file system A hierarchical structure of files and directories having its separate root directory. Every hard disk has at least one file system on it, which is attached to the **root file system** with the **mount** command.

file table A structure maintained in memory that contains the file's opening modes, status flags, position of the offset pointer, and a reference count field. Two file descriptors point to the same file table when a process forks or when a descriptor is replicated using **dup**, **dup2**, or **fcntl**.

file time stamps A set of three dates and times representing the date of last modification, access, and change of inode of a file. This information is stored in the inode and is displayed with various options to **ls**.

File Transfer Protocol (FTP) A TCP/IP application protocol that transfers files between two remote machines. The **ftp** command uses this protocol.

filehandle The logical name of a file used by I/O statements in **perl**.

filter A program that uses a character stream as standard input, manipulates its contents, and writes a character stream to the standard output. Shell's redirection and piping features can be used with filters.

foreground job Refers to a job where the parent waits for execution to complete. You can run only one job in the foreground. See also **background job**.

fork Term refers to the mechanism of process creation by replicating the address space of the existing process. The copied process inherits the file descriptors of its parent, current directory, and exported variables. A fork is usually followed by an **exec**. Features a system call by that name.

FQDN See **fully qualified domain name**.

Free Software Foundation Same as **GNU**.

fully qualified domain name (FQDN) A set of dot-delimited strings representing the domains and sub-domains to which the host belongs. The FQDN of a host is unique on the Internet.

GET A method of sending form data to a Web server as a component of the URL. The data is available as *name=value* pairs in the QUERY_STRING variable of the Web server. See also **POST**.

getty A process that runs at every free terminal to monitor the next login. Spawned by **init** and execs the **login** program whenever a user tries to log in.

GNU An organization founded by Richard Stallman which expands to **GNU's Not UNIX**, but now known as the **Free Software Foundation**. Many Linux tools have been developed by GNU or distributed under its license, which requires all developers to make the source code public.

graphical user interface (GUI) Feature of the X Window system that allows the manipulation of individual pixels on the screen. Used to display graphics.

group A category of user understood by the **chmod** command. More than one user may belong to a group, and a set of file permissions is associated with this category. See also **owner** and **others**.

group-id (GID) The group name or number of the user, which is allotted by the system administrator when creating a user account. The name and its numeric representation are maintained in /etc/group, while the numeric value is also available in /etc/passwd. See also **user-id**.

hard link See **link**.

helper application An external program invoked by a browser to handle a special file format. Unlike a **plugin**, a helper application views files in a separate window. The file's extension, content type, and external program needed to handle it are specified in mime.types and mailcap.

here document A form of standard input (<<) that forms part of the command line itself signifying that the input is *here*. Especially useful when used with commands (like mailx) that don't accept the input filename as argument.

history Facility provided by the shell to store, recall, and execute previous commands. Available in **csh**, **bash**, and **ksh** and also features a command by that name in these shells.

home directory A field in /etc/passwd that indicates the directory where a user is placed on login. The **cd** command switches to the home directory when used without arguments. Same as **login directory**.

home page Term used to refer to the first page presented to the user on connecting to a Web site.

host A computer or device in a network having a separate IP address.

hostname The name of a host that is unique in the network. Often used on the Internet with a series of dot-delimited strings to represent a **fully qualified domain name**. Features a command by that name which both displays and sets the hostname.

hosts file Refers to the file /etc/hosts that contains the hostname-IP address mappings.

Hyper Text Markup Language (HTML) The language used to code Web documents. Uses tags to transfer control to another document on another machine. HTML documents can be used to view animation, video, or play audio.

Hyper Text Transfer Protocol (HTTP) The application protocol that retrieves HTML documents from a Web server. It is *stateless* in that a connection has no knowledge of the state of the previous connection. HTTP 1.1 supports **keep-alive** (persistent) connections.

hypertext A link placed in one document with the <A HREF> tag which points to a location in another document in the same machine or another. The World Wide Web is a collection of these documents. See also **Web page**.

in-line editing Feature available in the Korn shell and Bash to recall and edit previous commands with **vi**- and **emacs**-like commands. Enabled with **set -o vi** or **set -o emacs**.

in-place editing Term used in **perl** to edit a file and write the output back to the same file without using redirection.

incremental search A fast and efficient search mechanism available in **emacs**. The search commences the moment a character is entered.

infinite loop A **while**, **until**, or **for** loop which never terminates. The **break** (**last** in **perl**) statement is used to transfer control out of the loop.

init A process having the PID number 1, which is responsible for the creation of all major processes. **init** runs all system daemons and the **getty** process at terminal ports. Can also be used as a command to set the system to a specific **run level**.

inode A structure that stores all file attributes except the filename and is maintained in a special area of disk. Copy loaded into memory when a file is opened. See also **vnode table**.

inode number A number that identifies an inode of a file. The number is unique in a single file system and displayed with **ls -i**.

Input Mode One of the three modes of the **vi** editor where any key depression is interpreted as input. Mode terminated by pressing *[Esc]*. See also **Command Mode** and **ex Mode**.

instruction A combination of an **address** and **action** as used by **sed** and **awk**. The address specifies the lines to be affected by the action.

internal command Name given to a sub-command of many UNIX tools like **vi**, **emacs**, **more**, **mailx**, and **sed** commands, and the shell.

Internet The super network of networks connected by the TCP/IP protocol with facilities of email, file transfer, remote login, Net News, and the **World Wide Web.**

Internet address Same as **IP address**.

Internet daemon A **daemon** that listens on multiple ports and invokes other daemons for FTP, TELNET, and POP services. Available as the program **inetd** or **xinetd**.

interrupt The sending of a signal (SIGINT) to a process with the intention of terminating it. A specific key is assigned this job, usually *[Ctrl-c]* or *[Delete]*, though it can be reassigned with the **stty** command.

interval regular expression (IRE) A regular expression that uses a single or a comma-delimited pair of numbers, enclosed by a matched pair of escaped curly braces (\{ and \}).

The two numbers indicate the minimum and maximum number of times that the single character preceding it can occur. Used by **grep**, **sed**, and **perl** commands. **perl** drops the \ in its implementation.

IP address A string of four dot-delimited octets used to describe the logical address of a machine in a TCP/IP network. Same as **Internet address**.

iteration The repeating of a loop's instruction set as long as the **control command** returns true. Term used in connection with the **while**, **until**, and **for** loops.

job A group of processes working toward a common goal. A pipeline is a simple example of a job. All processes in a job have the same process group-id (PGID).

job control A feature provided in most shells (except Bourne) of moving jobs between foreground and background and suspending them. Features the **fg**, **bg**, and **jobs** commands.

keep-alive connection A feature available in HTTP 1.1 that allows multiple resources to be fetched in a single (persistent) connection. Server holds the connection for a certain time to allow further requests. Persistent connections speed up Web access.

kernel The part of the UNIX operating system which is responsible for the creation and management of files and processes. Loaded into memory when the machine is booted and interacts directly with the machine hardware. All system calls are built into the kernel.

kernel mode A mode of the CPU used by the kernel when it runs on behalf of the user process. In this mode, the kernel can access any memory location. A switch from **user mode** to this mode takes place when a program invokes a system call.

key binding The association of an **emacs** command with a key sequence. When a valid key sequence is pressed, **emacs** internally executes the command bound to the key.

kill A misnomer, actually signifies the sending of a signal to a process—often with the intention of terminating it. Features a command and system call by the name.

kill ring A temporary storage area used by **emacs** to store up to the last 30 deletions (normally) and copies for later retrieval.

kill script An **rc script** beginning with K that kills a service. See also **start script**.

Last Line Mode Same as **ex Mode**.

library function A C function available in the standard library that performs most of the common programming tasks. Library functions encapsulate the **system calls** they internally use and often provide more convenient interfaces than the ones offered by system calls.

line A sequence of characters terminated by the newline character.

line address A form of addressing used by **sed**, **awk**, and **perl** to specify a single line or a group of contiguous lines. Represented as a single line number or a pair of them to limit the boundaries of the text.

link A file attribute stored in the inode that allows a file to be referred to by more than one name. Same as **hard link**. See also **symbolic link**.

listing The output obtained with the **ls -l** command showing seven attributes of a file.

local variable A variable that is visible only in the process or function where it is defined. See also **environment variable**.

login A process that overlays the **getty** program when a user attempts to log in. It execs the shell process on successful login.

login directory Same as **home directory**.

login name Same as **user-id**.

magic Term used in **vi** to refer to the special meaning of a character used in a regular expression. The magic is turned on and off by using the **ex Mode** commands **set magic** and **set nomagic**.

Mail Delivery Agent (MDA) The agency responsible for delivering mail to the user. Receives a mail message from the **Mail Transport Agent** and appends it to a text file in /var/mail (/var/spool/mail in Linux).

Mail Transport Agent (MTA) The agency responsible for transporting mail across a network. Sender's MTA hands over mail to recipient's MTA. SMTP is the standard protocol used by MTAs.

Mail User Agent (MUA) The client program that is used to send and receive mail. The MUA looks at the spool directory in /var/mail (/var/spool/mail in Linux) for incoming mail. It also hands over outgoing mail to the **Mail Transport Agent. mailx**, **elm**, **pine**, and Netscape Messenger are common MUAs.

mailbox A text file containing incoming mail that has not been viewed. File is named after the username, usually in /var/mail (/var/spool/mail in Linux). Binary attachments are held in this file in encoded form. See also **mbox**.

major number A file attribute that is stored in the inode and that appears in the listing of a device file. Indicates the device driver required to access the device. Similar devices have the same major number. See also **minor number**.

makefile A control file used by the **make** command to determine the programs that need to be recompiled. Has the name makefile or Makefile in the user's working directory.

man page The UNIX documentation as viewed by the **man** command. Every command, system configuration file, system call, and library function is associated with a man page.

mbox A text file where a mail message is saved after it has been viewed. Many character-based mail clients use $HOME/mbox as the default mbox. See also **mailbox**.

meta key A control key used in combination with other keys to invoke an **emacs** command. On PCs, this key is represented either by *[Esc]* or *[Alt]*.

metacharacter Term used to describe a character that means something special to the shell. The meaning is reversed by preceding the character with a \. Concept also extends to special characters used by certain commands as part of their syntax.

minibuffer The last line in the **emacs** screen that is used to display system messages and commands entered by a user. Search text is entered at the minibuffer. Preceded by the **mode line**.

minor number A file attribute that is stored in the inode and that appears in the listing of a device file. Represents the parameters passed to the device driver. See also **major number**.

mode line The line next to the bottom-most line in the **emacs** screen which displays the filename, line number, the modification status, and the mode of the editor. Shows up in reverse video.

modification time One of the time stamps of a file stored in the inode which represents the date and time the file was last modified. One of the attributes displayed by the listing.

mounting The process of attaching a standalone **file system** to another file system. During booting, all stand-alone systems are mounted on the **root file system**. Also features a command by the name **mount**. See also **unmounting**.

MULTICS An operating system whose development work was aborted to give way to the UNIX operating system. Many of the features of UNIX owe their origin to MULTICS.

Multipurpose Internet Mail Extensions (MIME) A standard used on the Internet to encode and decode binary files. Also useful in encoding multiple data formats in a *single* mail message. Features two headers—Content-Type and Content-Transfer-Encoding.

name server A dedicated service used on the Internet to convert the **fully qualified domain name** of a host to its IP address and vice versa. A name server is queried by a **resolver** and may either provide the answer or the address of another name server.

newline The character generated by hitting *[Enter]*. Used as the delimiter between two lines and forms one of the characters of **whitespace**.

newsgroup An offline discussion group on the Internet which originated from the UNIX-based USENET. Netscape Messenger also handles newsgroups.

nonprivileged user An ordinary user having no superuser privileges.

option A string normally beginning with a -, which changes the default behavior of a command. Multiple options can generally be combined with a single - symbol.

ordinary file The most common file of the UNIX system represented by programs, data, and text. It contains data, but not the end-of-file mark. Also known as **regular file**.

orphan A process whose parent has died. Orphans are usually adopted by **init** to become their parent.

others A category of user understood by the **chmod** command. A user who is neither the owner nor a group owner of a file belongs to this class. One set of file permissions is associated with this category. See also **owner** and **group**.

overlay Same as **exec**.

owner A file attribute that signifies the user having complete authority of determining the file's contents and permissions. Understood as **user** by the **chmod** command. The string and numeric representations of the owner are stored in /etc/passwd. See also **group** and **others**.

packet Term applied to describe a fragmented unit of data in a TCP/IP network.

pager A tool that displays output one screen at a time. **more** and **less** are the standard pagers on UNIX and Linux systems.

parent process-id (PPID) The **process-id** of the parent process which is stored in the **process table** entry for every process.

passphrase A secret string used to protect a user's **private key**. Unlike a **password**, a passphrase can contain spaces.

password A secret string used by a user for authentication during login. The code is not flashed on the terminal, but is stored in an encrypted manner in /etc/shadow. Also features a command with a similar name (**passwd**) to change the password.

PATH A shell variable that contains a colon-delimited list of directories that the shell will look through to locate an invoked command. The PATH generally includes /bin and /usr/bin for nonprivileged users and /sbin and /usr/sbin for the superuser.

pathname A sequence of one or more filenames using a / as a delimiter. All except the last filename have to be directories. See also **relative pathname** and **absolute pathname**.

pending signals mask A field maintained in the **process table** which stores the signals received for a process. The kernel looks up this field and the **signal disposition** table to determine the action to be taken.

ping The sending of packets to a remote host to check the connectivity of the network. Also features a command by that name.

pipe A buffered object using flow control that allows one-way data transmission through its two ends. Whatever is written to one end is read from the other. Signified by the shell's | symbol and also features a system call by that name. Used to create a **pipeline**.

pipeline A sequence of two or more commands used with the | symbol so that the input of one command comes from the output of the other. See also **pipe**.

plugin A small program installed in a browser to handle special file formats that can't be handled by the browser. Unlike a **helper application**, a plugin can't be invoked separately.

port number A number used to identify a TCP/IP application and defined in /etc/services. Servers use fixed port numbers, but clients use random port numbers. A packet has two port numbers, one for each end of the channel. See also **socket**.

positional parameters The external arguments to a shell script which are read into a series of special variables designated as $1, $2, $3, etc. These parameters can be renumbered with the **shift** command.

POSIX A set of standard interfaces based on the UNIX operating system. POSIX compliance ensures that a set of programs developed on one machine can be moved to another without recoding. POSIX.1 is the standard for the application programming interface of the C language. POSIX.2 provides the interface for the shell and utilities.

POST A method of sending form data to a Web server. Data is sent as a string of *name=value* pairs and fed as standard input to a **Common Gateway Interface (CGI)** program. See also **GET**.

Post Office Protocol (POP) The TCP/IP protocol used for fetching mail from a mail server. POP is often used over a dial-up line to fetch Internet mail.

private key A key used for encrypting or decrypting data, but which doesn't leave the user's machine. Often protected by a **passphrase**. Data encrypted with this key can only be decrypted with the **public key** and vice versa.

process An instance of a running program. Created by the **fork** system call and usually followed by an **exec**. Most of the shell's internal commands are executed without creating a process.

process address space The memory locations that a process can access. Includes the text, data, heap, and stack segments.

process birth Term used to refer to the creation of a process. The process is created when the command representing it is invoked and dies when command execution is complete. The **fork** system call gives birth to a process.

process context The complete environment seen by the process when it runs. Includes a hardware context (the state of the CPU registers) and a software context (the address space, process credentials). The kernel saves the context of the current process before running another one.

process death Term used to refer to the termination of a process. The process dies when the command representing it has completed execution or a signal is sent to it.

process group A collection of processes having some common attributes. In shells supporting **job control**, each job or process is placed in its own process group. A process group can be suspended and killed by sending a signal to the leader of the group.

process group-id (PGID) A common number allotted to a group of processes. The PGID of the group leader is its own PID. See also **process group**.

process table A structure maintained in memory containing the attributes of every active process running in the system. Also maintains the exit status of a terminated process until fetched by its parent.

process-id (PID) A unique number allotted to a process by the kernel when it is born.

profile A startup file used and maintained by a user in the home directory. Instructions in this file are executed during login time without spawning a sub-shell. However, /etc/profile is executed before the user's own profile.

prompt A string that shows the position of the cursor. The appearance of a prompt generally indicates that the previous command has completed its run. Can be customized by setting the value of the shell variable PS1.

public key A key used for encrypting or decrypting data, but which is distributed to all. Data encrypted with this key can only be decrypted with the **private key** and vice versa.

quoting Enclosing a group of characters in single or double quotes to remove their special meaning. Though the shell ignores all special characters enclosed in single quotes, double quotes permit evaluation of $ as a variable and ` for **command substitution**.

r-utilities A set of TCP/IP tools developed by Berkeley as alternatives to the **DARPA set**. The tools include **rlogin**, **rcp**, and **rsh** and are inherently insecure. Have been superseded by tools of the **secure shell (SSH)** suite.

race condition A situation where two or more events contend for the same resource and the eventual outcome determined by the sequence in which the events are serviced.

rc script A shell script maintained in the home directory that is automatically executed when creating a sub-shell. Also refers to a set of scripts in /etc that start the daemons that should run for a specific **run level** and kill the ones that shouldn't. See also **start script** and **kill script**.

recursion A characteristic feature of some UNIX commands to descend a specified directory to access all subdirectories under this directory, and beyond. **ls**, **rm**, **chmod**, **chown**, and **chgrp** use a special option to do that, while **find** and **tar** do it compulsorily.

redirection A shell feature that reassigns the standard input or standard output of a command. The default source and destination of these streams can be redirected to point to a disk file or to a pipe.

region An editing area in **vim** and **emacs** that can be defined by a user. A region may be copied, deleted, or moved.

regular expression An ambiguous expression containing some special characters. The expression is expanded by a *command* to match more than one string. Should be quoted to prevent interference from the shell. See also **wild card**.

regular file Same as **ordinary file**.

relative pathname A pathname which specifies the location of a file using the symbols . and .. to refer to the current and parent directories, respectively. See also **absolute pathname**.

remote login Connecting to a remote machine using a username and password. All commands entered after logging in are actually executed on the remote machine. See also **TELNET** and **secure shell**.

repeat factor A feature available in the **vi** editor and the **more** and **less** commands which uses a number as a command prefix to repeat the command that number of times. In **emacs**, it is known as the **digit argument**.

resolver A set of library routines used by a TCP/IP application to query a **name server** for resolving a domain name to the IP address. The resolver also looks up /etc/resolv.conf.

revision Term used to describe a version in the **Revision Control System**.

Revision Control System (RCS) An implementation of the document maintenance system as described in the **Source Code Control System (SCCS)**.

root The top-most directory in every file system which has no parent. Indicated by the / symbol. Also signifies a user who uses the login name root to log on to the superuser account.

root file system The main file system containing the essential utilities needed to keep the system running. All other file systems are mounted at different mount points of this file system.

root name server A server running **DNS** that specifies the name servers of the top-level domains like *com, edu, org,* etc.

router A special device that routes packets from one network to another.

run level Term used to refer to the various states that a UNIX system can be in. Determined by argument to the **init** command. Action to be taken for a specific run level is specified in /etc/inittab and includes the execution of **rc scripts**.

secure shell (SSH) A suite of networking tools that enable remote login, file transfer, and command execution. As is not the case with older tools like **telnet** and **ftp**, communication with the secure shell is totally encrypted.

server See **client-server architecture**.

set-user-id (SUID) A special mode of a file indicated by the letter s in the permissions field. The effective user-id of a process having this bit set is the owner of the file and not the user running the program. This property lets users modify important system files by using a specific command, rather than directly.

shared library A group of object files that are loaded into memory only during runtime. Several programs can share the same library code. See also **static library**.

shell The command interpreter of the UNIX system, which runs perpetually at every occupied terminal. The shell processes a user request and interacts with the kernel to execute the command. It also possesses a programming capability.

shell function A group of statements executed as a bunch in the current shell. A shell function accepts parameters and can return only a boolean value.

shell script An ordinary file containing a set of commands, which is executed in an interpretive manner in a sub-shell. All the shell's internal commands and external UNIX commands can be specified in a script.

signal The notification made by the kernel that an event has occurred. A signal has a default disposition (action to take), but it can be overridden by a user-defined **signal handler**.

Signals SIGKILL and SIGSTOP can't be ignored or handled otherwise. See also **signal disposition**.

signal disposition The action taken when a signal occurs. Every signal has a default disposition, maintained in the signal disposition table, which could be to terminate, stop the process, or to ignore the signal. The disposition can be changed by using a **signal handler** except for the SIGKILL and SIGSTOP signals.

signal handler A user-defined function in a C program that catches a signal and makes it behave in a manner that is different from the default. Signals SIGKILL and SIGSTOP can't be caught.

signature file A file named .signature in a user's home directory. Used to enter a person's details that must accompany every mail message. Most mail user agents are configured to automatically attach the file with every outgoing message.

Simple Mail Transfer Protocol (SMTP) The TCP/IP protocol used to transport mail across the Internet. The SMTP client communicates with the SMTP server at the other end and *directly* delivers the message. **sendmail** is the most common implementation of SMTP.

sleep Term used to refer to the temporary suspension of a process. Also features a command and library function by that name.

socket A combination of a port number and IP address. Both source and destination hosts use a socket each for communication. No two connections can have the same socket pair. See also **port number**.

Source Code Control System (SCCS) An optimized document maintenance system that stores one version in full and only the changes needed to generate the other versions. Also features checks to prevent multiple users from editing the same version. See also **Revision Control System (RCS)**.

spawn Term used to refer to the creation of a child process. See also **process birth**.

standard error The destination used by the diagnostic output stream to write its output. Includes all error messages generated by UNIX commands. The default destination of this stream is the terminal, but it can be redirected to any file.

standard input The source opened by the shell to accept information as a stream of characters. By default, the keyboard is assigned this source, but it can also come from a file, a pipeline, or a **here document**.

standard output The destination used by commands to send output to. Used by all UNIX commands that send output to the terminal. The default destination can also be reassigned to divert output to another file or a pipeline.

start script An **rc script** beginning with S that starts a service. See also **kill script**.

static library A group of object files bundled into an archive. A program using a static library contains the object code of the library. See also **shared library**.

sticky bit A special mode assigned to a file or a directory and indicated by the letter t in the permissions field. The executable code of an ordinary file gets stuck in the swap area once it has been executed. A directory with the sticky bit set can be shared by a group of users, where one user can't tamper with another user's files.

sub-shell A second shell created by the parent shell. It is normally required for executing a shell script or a group of commands with the ( ) operators. Changes made to the environment of a sub-shell are not available in the parent.

subroutine A group of statements executed as a bunch in **perl**—like a shell function. Subroutines use arguments which are stored in the array @_. **perl** uses the & symbol to call a subroutine.

superblock A special area in every file system which contains important information on the file system. Includes a list of free data blocks and inodes. The disk copy is regularly updated with the memory copy by the **sync** command.

superuser Same as **system administrator**.

suspend The stopping of a job. The job may later be resumed either in the background or foreground. This feature is available in **csh**, **ksh**, and **bash**.

swapping The process of moving currently inactive processes from memory to the swap area of the disk (swapping out). Also refers to the transfer of these processes from the swap area to memory when ready for execution (swapping in).

symbolic link A file which points to the location of another file or directory. Unlike hard links, a symbolic link can link files across file systems. Can be used to link directories also. See also **link**.

symlink Same as **symbolic link**.

sync Term used to describe synchronization of the superblock and inodes with their respective memory versions. Also features a command by that name which the kernel uses to write the memory data to disk.

system administrator The person responsible for the management of system resources. The administrator can change any file attribute and kill any user process. Uses a special user account (generally, root) to perform administrative duties. Also known as **superuser**.

system call A routine defined in the kernel which performs the basic operations of the computer, like opening a file and creating a process. All UNIX commands and library functions are written in terms of system calls. Processor switches from **user mode** to **kernel mode** when executing a system call.

system process A process which runs in the system during booting without being specifically requested for by a user. **init**, **getty**, **cron**, and **lpsched** are some of the system processes. See also **daemon**.

tab A single character which simulates a contiguous set of spaces. Is generated by hitting a specific key or *[Ctrl-i]*. Forms one of the characters of **whitespace**. Useful for aligning columns.

tagged regular expression (TRE) Term used to indicate the grouping of a regular expression with an escaped pair of parentheses, \(and \). This group is repeated elsewhere in the line by using the tag \n or $n (**perl**), where *n* is a number between 1 and 9. Used by **grep**, **sed**, and **perl** commands.

TCP/IP Expands to Transmission Control Protocol/Internet Protocol—a collection of protocols used for networking computers that use different operating systems and different hardware. Ensures reliable transmission with full error-correction facilities.

TELNET A TCP/IP protocol that enables a user to log on to a remote machine after supplying a username and password. After logging in, the user can use the remote machine as if it is a local one. All files are created on the remote machine. The **telnet** command uses this protocol.

The Open Group Owner of the UNIX standard and originator of The Single UNIX Specification. Includes X/OPEN in its fold. Also maintains the X Window system.

toggle switch A command that reverses the effect of its immediate previous invocation. **emacs** has a number of commands that act as toggle switches.

top-level domain (TLD) Any domain under the root (.) domain which has not been allotted to a specific country. TLDs comprise the generic domains *com, edu, org, net, museum, biz,* etc.

umask A number maintained in the shell that determines a file's default permissions. This number is subtracted from the system's default to obtain a file's actual permissions. The value can be displayed and set by using a command of the same name.

Uniform Resource Locator (URL) A string of characters that specifies a resource on the Web. Comprises the protocol, the FQDN of the site, and the path name of a file or program to run.

unmounting The process of disengaging a file system from the main file system. The **umount** command performs this unmounting. See also **mounting**.

user The owner of a file as understood by the **chmod** command. See also **group** and **others**.

user mode A mode of the CPU when running a program. In this mode, the program has no access to the memory locations used by the kernel. See also **kernel mode**.

user-id (UID) The name used by a user to gain access to the system. A list of authorized names is maintained in /etc/passwd along with their numeric representations. Also known as **login name** and **username**. See also **group-id**.

username Same as **user-id**.

virtual console A system of using multiple screens and logins from a single UNIX machine. A new screen is opened by using *[Alt]* and a function key.

vnode table The image of the inode in memory. Contains apart from the inode information, a reference count that shows the number of processes that point to the table. A file can't be entirely deleted as long as this table is open. See also **file table**.

wait Term used to refer to the inaction of a parent process while a child is running. Normally the parent waits for the death of the child to pick up its **exit status**. Also features a shell built-in command and a system call by that name.

wake Term used to indicate the termination of a dormant activity when an event occurs. The kernel wakes up a sleeping process when a specific event has occurred (like the completion of I/O).

Web page An HTML document containing text and graphics that is presented in the form of a page at every Web site. A Web page has links to other pages—often on different machines.

Web server A TCP/IP application that runs the HTTP protocol. The World Wide Web serves all resources through Web servers.

whitespace A contiguous sequence of spaces, tabs, or newlines. Also, the default value of the IFS variable. Used as delimiter by the shell to parse command line arguments and by the **set** statement to assign its arguments to positional parameters.

wild card A special character used by the *shell* to match a group of filenames with a single expression. The * and ? are commonly used wild-card characters. See also **regular expression**.

word A contiguous string of characters not containing whitespace. **wc** can count words, and **vi** and **emacs** also enable cursor movement using a word as a navigational unit.

World Wide Web A service on the Internet featuring a collection of linked documents and images. The browser (client) fetches these resources from a Web server using the HTTP protocol.

wraparound A feature provided by the **vi** and **emacs** editors for resuming the search for a pattern from the other end of a file. The entire file is thus searched irrespective of the position in the file the search was launched from.

X client An X program which performs a specific function and uses the X server for display. **xterm** is a common X client found in every X Window system.

X server The program in X Window which controls the display including the monitor, mouse, and keyboard. X clients write their output to this program. If the display changes, only the server needs to change and not the clients.

X Window System The graphical component of the UNIX system. X clients write their output to the server which is responsible for their display on separate windows.

zipped file Any file that is compressed with the **gzip**, **zip**, or **bzip2** commands. They are decompressed with **gunzip**, **unzip**, and **bunzip2**.

zombie A dead process whose exit status has not been picked up by its parent using **wait**. Zombies clog the process table and can't be killed.

Solutions to Self-Test Questions

Chapter 1

1.1   Kernel, shell.

1.2   No, a program is an executable file that resides on disk. A process is created in memory by executing the program.

1.3   The ASCII value.

1.4   The machine name.

1.5   Not necessarily, the password could be incorrect too.

1.6   (i) ls (ii) ps (iii) who

1.7   The shell is assigned a new PID by the kernel.

1.8   The command displays (concatenates) the contents of both files. **cat** can be used with multiple filenames.

1.9   The abbreviated command also displays the contents of both files.

1.10   The command should have been **echo $SHELL**.

1.11   **ls** displays the directory named bar, but **ls bar** displays foo, the name of the file in bar.

1.12   Ken Thompson and Dennis Ritchie.

1.13   Because it was then prevented by the U.S. government to sell computer software.

1.14   From the University of California, Berkeley. Notable contributions include the **vi** editor, C shell, symbolic links, and TCP/IP.

1.15   Linux.

1.16   (i) Sun (ii) IBM (iii) HP (Digital)

1.17   X/OPEN was a standards body now merged with The Open Group, which owns the UNIX trademark.

1.18   Richard Stallman and Linux Torvalds.

1.19   Software developers distributing products under that license must make the source code public.

1.20   Because it is written in C, a high-level language. A program written in a high-level language can run without major modifications when moved to another machine.

1.21   System V (AT&T) and BSD (Berkeley). SunOS is based on BSD, but Solaris is based on AT&T's SVR4.

1.22   Because complex jobs can be handled by connecting a number of these simple ones.

1.23   X Window.

1.24   The shell, **perl**, **tcl**, and **python**.

1.25   Red Hat, SuSE, and Caldera.

Chapter 2

2.1   The : must be a command that does nothing. The command **type :** indicates that the command is built into the shell.

2.2   False, you can use uppercase and provide extensions to command filenames though convention follows the opposite.

2.3   `printf`, `script`, and `passwd`.

2.4   **echo** and **pwd** are internal commands; **date** and **ls** are external.

2.5   The command that occurs first in the PATH list would require no special treatment. The other command needs to be used with a pathname.

2.6   With a dot.

2.7   Three.

2.8   Linux.

2.9   The command line.

2.10 `uname -r`

2.11 Because the commonly used UNIX commands are located there.

2.12 Whitespace is a contiguous set of spaces, tabs, and newline characters. The shell compresses multiple contiguous whitespace characters to a single space.

2.13 No, the buffer associated with the keyboard stores all input.

2.14 `fname` is supposedly a variable, so it should be prefixed with a $.

2.15 A pager is a program that displays text on the screen a page at a time. **more** and **less** are two standard pagers used by **man**.

2.16 Press **n** repeatedly.

2.17 Try using **apropos** with a keyword.

2.18 The -u option provides information on idle time.

2.19 Unviewed mail is deposited in the mailbox, but viewed mail moves to the mbox.

2.20 The root user is not prompted for the old password. The password encryption is stored in `/etc/shadow`.

2.21 Not as an ordinary user.

2.22 The name of the operating system.

2.23 Run **script foo** at the beginning of the session.

2.24 The command is run by romeo who is logged in from a host named *pc123* at the date and time shown. romeo's terminal file is `pts/10`.

2.25 Run **stty -a** and look for these three keywords in the output.

2.26 `stty sane`

Chapter 3

3.1   255 characters. The / and NULL (ASCII value 0) can't be used as filename characters.

3.2   (i) Difficult to remove such a file. (ii) Many commands interpret such filenames as options.

3.3   Ordinary files can be grouped into text and binary. A text file contains only printable characters whose ASCII values are less than 128. A binary file can contain any character. C source programs, **perl** and shell scripts are text files. Executable programs, image and music files are binary in nature.

3.4   Yes, UNIX filenames are case-sensitive.

3.5   (i) cd ../../mail (ii) cd ../.. or cd /usr

3.6   The directory doesn't change.

3.7   **ls** .. displays all filenames in the parent directory, but **ls -d** .. shows .. as the parent directory without displaying its contents.

3.8   Only some of them; most are meant for use by the superuser.

3.9   No, **echo** is also a shell builtin which is executed by default.

3.10   Use **mkdir -p share/man/cat1** which creates all intermediate directories.

3.11   (i) test already exists. (ii) An ordinary file with the same name exists. (iii) The user doesn't have authorization to create a file or directory. (iv) There's no space on disk.

3.12   (i) ls -F (ii) ls -a

3.13   The contents of foo three times.

3.14   od -bc foo

3.15   Use **cp -r bar1 bar2**. If bar2 exists, then bar1 becomes a subdirectory of bar2, so bar2 should be removed before running **cp -r**.

3.16   **rm -rf** forcibly deletes a nonempty directory structure, but not **rmdir**.

3.17   (i) lp -dlaser -n3 /etc/passwd (ii) lp -dlaser -n3 -m /etc/passwd

3.18   Create a file with these characters, and then use **od -bc foo**.

3.19   **wc** shows the count for each file, but also prints a total count at the end.

Chapter 4

4.1   The **ls -l** output is called the listing. The command **ls -lRa / > foo** saves the listing of all files in the system.

4.2   (i) 756 (ii) 640 (iii) 124

4.3   (i) r-xrw-rwx (ii) rw--w--wx (iii) r---w---x

4.4   Only the owner can remove a file unless the directory is writable by group.

4.5   The superuser can read, but not write.

4.6   The directory has write permission for them.

4.7   You can create a directory in /tmp (permissions—rwxrwxrwt), but not in /bin (rwxr-xr-x). The categories, group and others, can't write in /bin, but they can write in /tmp.

4.8   You can copy once, but not subsequently because the copy is now write-protected.

4.9   Use **umask 006** before creating the file.

4.10   ls -i foo

4.11   The inode stores all file attributes except the filename which is stored in the file's directory.

4.12   The file has a single inode with a link count of three. The file can be accessed by three pathnames.

4.13   The **rm** command removes both.

4.14   ln *.c bar

4.15   False, a symbolic link has a separate inode.

4.16   (i) ln foo1 foo2 (ii) ln -s foo1 foo2. Deleting foo1 (i) doesn't make much difference as foo1 and foo2 are identical (ii) deletes the file that actually contains the data.

4.17   The UID, GID, the time of last modification and access.

4.18   In /etc/passwd.
4.19   Only the superuser can use **chown** to change a file's owner. However, a user can change her own group with **chgrp** but only to one to which she also belongs.
4.20   Recursively changes in the current directory (i) the owner of all files including the hidden ones, (ii) the group owner of all files but not the hidden ones.
4.21   False, the access time of a file is not changed by a lookup of the inode.
4.22   The access time of foo doesn't change when using the >> symbols, even though the file has been modified.
4.23   (i) find /docs /usr/docs -name "z*" -print
        (ii) find /docs /usr/docs \(-name "*.html -o -name "*.java" \) -print

Chapter 5

5.1   (i) 0 (ii) o
5.2   (i) Position the cursor to the end of has and then press **sve***[Esc]*. (ii) Use **S**.
5.3   *[Ctrl-l]*
5.4   The commands **:x**, **:wq** and **ZZ** save the buffer before terminating a session. The **q!** command aborts a session.
5.5   You didn't press *[Esc]* before using **50k**. Press *[Ctrl-w]* to erase the text and then press *[Esc]*.
5.6   (i) 40| (ii) 0 (iii) $
5.7   Use **0**, **5w**, **4s**, enter counter and press *[Esc]*.
5.8   (i) 7 (ii) 2
5.9   Only (iii) and (iv) because they change the buffer. (i) and (ii) merely perform navigation without changing the buffer.
5.10   Position the cursor on t and use **xp**.
5.11   With the cursor on the top-most line, use **5J**, then **0** to move to line beginning and keep ~ pressed until the cursor moves to the end of line. (You can also use a repeat factor with ~.)
5.12   Use **:!cc** % where % signifies the current filename.
5.13   **n** repeats a search in the same direction the original search was made, which could be forward or back. **N** operates in a reverse manner.
5.14   Because you pressed an **o** before pressing the dot.
5.15   Use **:.w foo**, and if foo exists, use **:.w! foo**.
5.16   (i) d1G (ii) 10y1 (el) (iii) 10yw
5.17   Use the command **"a5yy** on the first of the lines to be copied. Bring up the second file with *:e filename,* move to the right location, and press **"ap**. To toggle, use *[Ctrl-^]*.
5.18   **u** undoes the last editing action. **U** undoes all changes made to the current line. It won't work if the cursor is moved away from the current line.
5.19   **d** and **y** are operators, but **j** and **$** are commands that can be used singly. An operator can either be doubled by itself (like **dd**) or combined with a Command Mode command (like **d$**).
5.20   Use **:1,$s/Internet/Web/g** in the ex Mode.
5.21   **:e!**
5.22   Make the setting **:set autowrite** in ~/.exrc.

Chapter 6

6.1   The editor is set in that mode which can be reversed by invoking **M-x overwrite-mode**.

6.2   M-x line-number-mode

6.3   The digit argument uses Meta, and the universal argument uses C-u. To delete 16 words, you can use **C-u C-u M-d** or **M-16 M-d**.

6.4   The first command saves the buffer to the current file, but the other command prompts for a filename.

6.5   (i) repl*[Tab]*s*[Tab]* (ii) reco*[Tab]*f*[Tab]* (iii) que*[Tab]*

6.6   (i) C-g (ii) C-l

6.7   Because it is used for accessing the help documentation.

6.8   Use **M-! date** with *[Shift]*.

6.9   (i) **M-40 C-f** after initial **C-a** (ii) C-a (iii) C-e

6.10   (i) M-< (ii) M->

6.11   Only (iii) and (iv) because they change the buffer.

6.12   (i) C-k (ii) C-a C-k

6.13   Use **C-*[Spacebar]*** to define the beginning of a region and then a navigation command to define the other end. To toggle, use **C-x C-x**.

6.14   Position the cursor on s and use **C-t**.

6.15   Both are used for incremental and nonincremental string search. **C-s** is used for forward search and repeat; **C-r** is used for reverse search and repeat.

6.16   Use (i) **query-replace**, (ii) **replace-string** before keying in the two strings.

6.17   (i) revert-buffer (ii) recover-file

6.18   (i) C-x o (ii) C-x 0

6.19   Use **C-x C-v** instead of **C-x C-f** to kill the current buffer if it's not required.

6.20   Both run the **describe-key** function to display the function of (i) **describe-key (C-h k)**, (ii) **describe-function (C-h f)**.

Chapter 7

7.1   Because they mean nothing to the command. A * is expanded to match all filenames in the current directory.

7.2   The command lists all filenames where a dot occurs anywhere in the filename except at the beginning.

7.3   **rm .[!.]*** removes all files beginning with a dot except the . and .. directories. **rm *** doesn't remove these files.

7.4   chap[a-cx-z]

7.5   Yes, because 3 has a higher value than h in the ASCII collating sequence.

7.6   Use **cp chap0[1-9] chap1[0-9] chap2[0-6] ..** in the Bourne shell. For other shells, you can use chap{0[1-9],1[0-9],2[0-6]} as a *single* wild-card pattern.

7.7   (i) *[!0-9] (ii) ????*

7.8   When there is only one file in the current directory and that file is also a directory.

7.9   find

7.10   Press a \ before pressing *[Enter]*.

7.11   The terminal, file, and pipe.

7.12   No, but to the file representing the terminal.
7.13   Legitimate, the **bc** command reads standard input from bar and writes standard output to foo.
7.14   ls -lRa $HOME > foo
7.15   To prevent extraneous output and error messages from appearing on the terminal.
7.16   They expect input from standard input—the terminal by default. Press *[Ctrl-d]* to return to the shell.
7.17   Use **echo >** *[Enter]* where the \ is followed by a space. The sequence **ls | od -bc** shows octal 040 as the filename.
7.18   (i) who | wc -l (ii) find $HOME -type d -print | wc -l
7.19 $SHELL is evaluated in double quotes only.
7.20   (ii)
7.21   No, it doesn't. The shell interprets x as a command and = and 10 as its arguments.
7.22   (iv)

Chapter 8

8.1   The PID is a unique number assigned to a process by the kernel. The PPID is the PID of the parent. The command **echo $$** displays the PID of the shell.
8.2   Use **ps -e** (SVR4) or **ps aux** (Linux).
8.3   Shell scripts. The sub-shell reads and executes each statement in the script.
8.4   cd, pwd, echo
8.5   fork and *exec.*
8.6   ps -f -u timothy (ps --user timothy in Linux)
8.7   Run **ps -e** and note those processes that show a ? in the TTY column.
8.8   Use the -s KILL option.
8.9   Use **kill $!**, which should work in most shells.
8.10   kill -l
8.11   No, use an & as well to run it in the background.
8.12   When the shell doesn't support job control.
8.13   Press *[Ctrl-z]* to suspend the process. Use **fg** to return to the editor from the shell.
8.14   You can't do that.
8.15   at 8 pm tomorrow < dial.sh
8.16   The **find** command runs at 21:30 hours every day.
8.17   Use the interrupt key, but not *[Ctrl-d]*.
8.18   By removing the .allow and .deny files of these commands.

Chapter 9

9.1   By using the **export** *variable* command.
9.2   It is set by /etc/passwd. However, an explicit reassignment of HOME doesn't change the home directory but only the directory **cd** switches to by default.
9.3   In /usr/share/lib/terminfo/v or /usr/share/terminfo/v.
9.4   Make the setting **PATH=$PATH:..** in the profile.
9.5   MAILCHECK=60

9.6   Define **alias rm="rm -rf"**. To execute the **rm** command on disk, use **\rm**.

9.7   (i) r (ii) !!

9.8   (i) No command; HISTSIZE determines size of the history file. (ii) HISTSIZE=200

9.9   (i) r tar sh=pl (ii) !tar:s/sh/pl

9.10   (iii)

9.11   set -o vi (on) and set +o vi (off).

9.12   The next command should be **more $_** or **more !*.**

9.13   Make the setting **set -o noclobber**. To overwrite, use >|.

9.14   Run **cd /usr/include ; cd ../lib**. The command **cd -** will now toggle between the two directories.

9.15   cp ~henry/* .

9.16   /etc/profile is meant for storing global settings and is executed when a user logs in, and before her own profile is executed.

9.17   No, Bash will read only .bash_profile.

9.18   False; a script runs only the rc file.

Chapter 10

10.1   (i) pr -t -d foo (ii) ls | pr -t -3

10.2   comm -12 foo1 foo2

10.3   The two files are identical.

10.4   **head** picks up 10 lines from each file, but precedes each group with a header that shows the filename.

10.5   ps | tail +2

10.6   echo "Line length = `head -n 1 shortlist | wc -c`"

10.7   Run **a.out** in the background with & and then use **tail -f foo** if foo is the name of the log file.

10.8   You can use either the -c or -f option, not both.

10.9   PATH=`echo $PATH | cut -d: -f2-`

10.10   year=`date | cut -d" " -f6`

10.11   sort -t: -k 5.1 shortlist

10.12   First cut out the date field and then the year:
        cut -d: -f5 shortlist | cut -c7- | sort | uniq -c

10.13   cut -d: -f4 shortlist | sort -u | pr -t -n

10.14   (i) uniq foo (ii) sort -u foo

10.15   tr '[a-z]' '[A-Z]' < shortlist

Chapter 11

11.1   grep done foo | tail -n 1

11.2   **grep** searches for an asterisk at the beginning of the line. The * is not preceded by a character, so the \ isn't required.

11.3   cat *.[hH][tT][mM] *.[hH][tT][mM][lL] | grep -ic "IMG SRC"

11.4   find . -name "*.c" -print | grep -v "/.*/"

11.5   numb=`grep -l printf *.c | wc -l`

11.6   ls -lut `grep -l wait *.c`

11.7 (i) The longest pattern starting with a and ending with b, as close to the left of the line as possible. (ii) At least one character in the line. (iii) The } as the only character in the line.

11.8 Use **grep -E** with these patterns: (i) SIG(STOP|TSTP), (ii) SIGTT(IN|OU), (iii) harris(|on).

11.9 g* could match nothing, but gg* matches at least one g.

11.10 (i) .... (11 dots) (ii) .\{11\}

11.11 grep -v director emp.lst | sort -t: -k 5.7 -r | cut -d: -f2,3 | head -n 1

11.12 Displays the usernames of those using the shell evaluated from $SHELL. The second $ anchors the pattern at the end of the line.

11.13 grep -E "^[0-9]+\.[0-9]+ |^[0-9]+\.[0-9]+\.[0-9]+ " chap[01][0-9]

11.14 (i) alias lsdir="ls -l | grep '^d'"
(ii) alias lsdir="ls -l | sed -n '/^d/p'"

11.15 (i) sed -n '3,10p' foo (ii) sed -n '$!p' foo

11.16 (i) sed 'p' foo
(ii)
```
    sed -n 'a\
    .... A blank line ....
    'p foo
```

11.17 Use any numeral as a "temporary" character for **sed**:
sed -e 's/_/9/g' -e 's/-/_/g' -e 's/9/-/g' foo

11.18 sed 's/Linux/Red Hat &/g' foo

11.19 sed 's/^/   /' foo

11.20 Look for the locations where the : occurs and then use the TRE:
sed 's/\([^:]*:\)\([^]*\) \([^:]*:\)/\1\3 \2/' emp.lst

Chapter 12

12.1 Both print the entire line. **print** is not necessary if the selection criteria is specified.

12.2 awk -F: '$5 ~ /^09|^12/' empn.lst

12.3 (i) awk 'NR <= 5' foo (ii) awk 'NR == 5, NR == 10' foo
(iii) awk 'NR >= 20' foo (iv) awk '/negroponte/' foo

12.4 awk '{ print NR ". " $2 }' foo

12.5 awk '$0 !~ /^[□⬅]*$/' foo

12.6 The **sort** command must be enclosed in double quotes.

12.7 awk '{ x= NR % 2 ; if (x == 1) print }' foo

12.8
```
    awk -F: '{
      if ($6 > 100000)
          print > "foo1"
      else
          print > "foo2"
    }' emp.lst
```

12.9   This one needs a small tweak: awk '{print $NF}' foo.
12.10 awk 'length > 100 && length < 150' foo
12.11 ls -l | awk '$1 ~ /^-/ { tot += $5 } END {print tot}'
12.12 awk -F: '{ split($2, name, " ") ; print name[2], name[1]}' empn.lst
12.13 x=`awk -F: '{ x+= $6 } END { print x/NR }' empn.lst`
12.14 ls -lR $HOME | awk ' $6 ~ /^Jan/ && $7 ~ /^6/ && $8 ~ /^11/'
12.15

```
echo "DOCUMENT LIST" | \
awk '{ for (k = 1 ; k < 55 - length($0)) / 2 ; k++)
            printf "%s"," "
        print $0 }'
```

12.16

```
echo "DOCUMENT LIST" | \
awk '{ k = 0
        while (k < (55 - length($0))/2) {
            printf "%s", " " ; k++
        }
        print $0 }'
```

Chapter 13

13.1   (i) x10$ (ii) 1010
13.2   Use !/usr/bin/ksh as the she-bang line or use **ksh** *script_name*.
13.3 $0 was used in the program.
13.4   The exit status is the value (0—true) returned by the command to its parent. It is available in $?.
13.5   Only **grep** returns a false exit status if the pattern is not found; **sed** and **find** don't.
13.6

```
#!/bin/sh
[ $# -gt 3 ] && option="-i"
rm $option $*
```

13.7   **test** is a shell builtin. Run the script with **sh test** or **./test**.
13.8

```
case $LOGNAME in
  henry|romeo) case `tty` in
                *tty0[56]) ;;
                        *) echo "You cannot use this terminal" ; exit ;;
                esac ;;
            *)  echo "You are not authorized to use script" ; exit ;;
esac
```

13.9   **expr** and **basename** were discussed because the Bourne shell has no computing and string-handling facilities. It can't introduce delays either, so **sleep** was also discussed.

13.10   The **exit** statement will always be executed irrespective of the condition. Use this instead: [$# -ne 2] && { echo "Usage: $0 min_guid max_guid" ; exit ; }

13.11

```
#!/bin/sh
for file in * ; do
    echo "==> $file <=="
    tail -n 3 $file
done
```

13.12   (i)
```
#!/bin/sh
echo "Enter a long string: \c"
read name
case $name in
??????????*) ;;
            *) echo "String shorter than 10 characters"
esac
```

(ii) The **case** construct in (i) can be replaced with this:

```
if [ `expr "$name" : '.*'` -lt 10 ] ; then
    echo "String shorter than 10 characters"
fi
```

13.13   expr "$x" : '\(.*\)/[^/]*'

13.14

```
#!/bin/sh
[ $# -eq 0 ] && { echo "Usage: $0 filename" ; exit ;}
case $1 in
    *.gz) program=gunzip ; ufilename=`basename $1 .gz` ;;
    *.bz2) program=bunzip2 ; ufilename=`basename $1 .bz2` ;;
    *.zip) program=unzip ; ufilename=`basename $1 .zip` ;;
esac
if [ -f "$ufilename" ] ; then
    echo "Uncompressed file $ufilename exists; Exiting"
else
    $program $1
fi
```

13.15

```
#!/bin/sh
cd $1
for file in * ; do
    if [ -f ../$2/$file ] ; then
        cmp $file ../$2/$file >/dev/null 2>/dev/null && rm ../$2/$file
    fi
done
```

13.16   Replace the assignment to `lastfile` at the beginning of the script with this:

```
case $# in
    1) lastfile=$1 ;;
    0) lastfile=`ls -t *.c 2>/dev/null | head -n 1` ;;
    *) exit ;;
esac
case $lastfile in
  *.c) ;;
    *) exit;;
esac
```

13.17   Both execute an infinite loop (i) unconditionally, (ii) only if script is run with at least one argument.

13.18   (i)

```
x=1
while [ $x -lt 6 ] ; do
    ps -e ; sleep 30
    x=`expr $x + 1`
done
```

(ii)

```
for x in 1 2 3 4 5 ; do
    ps -e ; sleep 30
done
```

The **for** loop uses x only as a dummy variable.

13.19

```
#!/bin/sh
for file in "$@" ; do
  if [ -f $file ] ; then
      ufile=`echo $file | tr '[a-z]' '[A-Z]'`
      if [ -f $ufile ] ; then
          echo "$ufile also exists"
      else
          mv $file $ufile
      fi
  else
      echo "$file doesn't exist"
  fi
done
```

13.20

```
#!/bin/sh
user=$1
grep "^$user:" /etc/passwd >/dev/null || { echo "Not valid user" ; exit ; }
find / -type f -user $user -ls 2>/dev/null | awk '{tot += $7 }
END {print tot }'
```

13.21   We need to use seven dummy variables to skip the first seven fields of the **ls -lids**
        output:

```
#!/bin/sh
find / -name $1 -ls 2>/dev/null |\
while read a b c d e f g line ; do
    echo $line
done
```

13.22   **foo** begins with a hyphen.

13.23   Use **shift 3** and then access $9.

13.24

```
#!/bin/sh
OLDIFS="$IFS"           # Save old value of IFS
IFS=:                   # before changing it
set -- $PATH
for directory in "$@" ; do
    if [ ! -d $directory ] ; then
        echo "$directory doesn't exist"
    elif [ ! -x $directory ] ; then
        echo "$directory doesn't have search permission"
    fi
done
IFS=$OLDIFS             # Restore old value of IFS
```

Chapter 14

14.1   TCP/IP uses timeout and retransmission facilities to monitor segments. It ensures
        that a missing or corrupted segment makes reassembly impossible.

14.2   The port number associates a packet with an application. Look up /etc/services,
        and you'll find that **finger** uses port 79.

14.3   Because the password in both is sent in clear text, which can easily be intercepted.
        The Secure Shell (SSH) encrypts transmission, so it is used by many.

14.4   Use the **hostname** command.

14.5   You did not use **ftp**'s **binary** command before starting the transfer, and the
        machine's default mode is not binary.

14.6   You can't.

14.7   Trying out every possible key combination. The longer the key, the more the possible combinations.

14.8   Symmetric key.

14.9   Unlike a password, a passphrase allows the use of spaces. A passphrase also protects the private key.

14.10   `scp -r juliet@saturn:"*"` .

14.11   Runs the **date** command on *jupiter* and saves the output on that machine.

14.12   By separating the display handling component from the program and placing that responsibility on the server program that handles the display.

14.13   Yes, by using the `-display` option of the client or the `DISPLAY` variable before invoking the client.

14.14   The file has to be maintained in every host of a network.

14.15   *aero, biz, pro* are three new entrants. Domain names are case-insensitive.

14.16   The MUA hands over outgoing mail to the MTA which connects directly to its peer at the destination to transmit the message. The MTA finally invokes the MDA to deliver mail to the user's mailbox.

14.17   The original SMTP protocol used 7-bit ASCII, so 8-bit data are encoded using `base64`. Encoded data is preceded by the headers `Content-Type` and `Content-Transfer-Encoding`.

14.18   GIF, JPEG, and PNG.

14.19   Hypertext is a system of organizing information by which references can be made to other documents in the same or different server. The concept applies to images as well.

14.20   Hyper Text Transfer Protocol—the application protocol that uses port number 80 to serve resources on the Web.

14.21   A program invoked by an HTTP server to perform some processing work which it is unable to do itself. A CGI program creates HTML code and passes it back to the server.

14.22   Use the URL *http://localhost*.

Chapter 15

15.1   All commands to be executed with -e. (i) Treats \t literally and prints it, but only if the **print** statement is enclosed within double quotes. (ii) Prints a tab. (iii) Prints `romeo.com` as @heaven is interpreted as an array.

15.2   `perl -e 'print "UNIX" x 20 . "\n" ;'`

15.3   `perl -ne 'print "$.\t" . $_' foo`

15.4

```
#!/usr/bin/perl
print("Enter three numbers: ") ;
$reply = <STDIN> ;
($n1, $n2, $n3) = split(/\s+/, $reply) ;
$max = $n1 ;
$max = $n2 if $n2 > $n1 ;
```

```perl
$max = $n3 if $n3 > $max ;
print("The maximum number is $max\n") ;
```

Try generalizing this program to handle any number of inputs using **split** and a **foreach** loop.

15.5

```perl
#!/usr/bin/perl
print("String: ") ;
$stg = <STDIN>;
print("Number of times: ") ;
chomp($numb = <STDIN>);
print $stg x $numb;
```

15.6 (i) Use $x in the assignment. (ii) Use ** instead of ^ for exponentiation.

15.7

```perl
#!/usr/bin/perl
$x="A" ;
while (<>) {
    print $x++ . ". " . $_ ;
}
```

After Z., the program prefixes an A and prints AA., AB., AC., etc.

15.8 `perl -e '$x=A ; print $x++ while $y++ < 26'`

15.9

```perl
#!/usr/bin/perl
print("Enter a number: ") ;
$number = <STDIN> ;
if ($number > 0) {
    for ($x = 1 ; $x <= $number ; $x++) {
        print("$x\n") ;
    }
} else {
    print("Not a positive number\n") ;
}
```

15.10 (ii)

15.11

```perl
#!/usr/bin/perl
print("Enter a number: ") ;
$number = <STDIN> ;
if ( $number > 255 || $number < 0) {
    print("Not a valid number\n") ;
} elsif ($number > 223) {
    print("C\n") ;
```

```perl
} elsif ($number > 126) {
    print("B\n") ;
} else {
    print("A\n") ;
}
```

15.12

```perl
#!/usr/bin/perl
$number = 1 ;
while ($number != 0) {
    print("Enter a number: ") ;
    $number = <STDIN> ;
    chop ($number) ;
    $total+= $number if $number != 0 ;
}
print "The total is $total\n" ;
```

15.13

```perl
#!/usr/bin/perl
die("Two arguments required\n") if $#ARGV != 1 ;
open (INFILE, "$ARGV[1]") ;
while (<INFILE>) {
    if (/$ARGV[0]/) {
        print ; exit ;
    }
}
```

15.14

```perl
#!/usr/bin/perl
# Note that you can assign a null string with qw
@month = qw/'' Jan Feb Mar Apr May Jun Jul Aug Sep Oct Nov Dec/ ;
$i = 1 ;
while ($i <= 12) {
    print $i . ". " . $month[$i] . "\n" ;
    $i++ ;
}
```

15.15   An array element is accessed with the $ prefix; use **print $arr{N}.**

15.16

```perl
#!/usr/bin/perl
$file = $ARGV[0] ;
if (-e $file) {
    if (-B $file) {
        print("$file is a binary file\n") ;
```

```
    } else {
        print("$file is not a binary file\n") ;
    }
} else {
    print("$file does not exist\n") ;
}
```

15.17 `perl -ne 's/(\w+)/\u$1/g ; print' foo`

15.18

```
#!/usr/bin/perl
open(INFILE, "/etc/passwd");
while <INFILE>) {
    split(/:/);
    print if ($_[2] == 1);
}
```

Chapter 16

16.1   Compiling, assembling, and linking.

16.2   **as** and **ld**.

16.3   Yes.

16.4   **cc** assumes a library name to have the `lib` prefix and `.a` suffix. The library files are in `/lib` and `/usr/lib` and the include files in `/usr/include`.

16.5   **make** will report an error if `cc` is not preceded by a tab.

16.6   The compiler automatically includes object files in this library without an explicit instruction.

16.7   (i) Smaller executables since the library code is not included in the executable. (ii) Easier maintenance since a modification made to a library doesn't require modification of the programs using the library.

16.8   (i) `admin -i foo s.foo` (ii) `get -e s.foo` (iii) `delta s.foo`

16.9   Use **sccsdiff** **-r**_sid1_ **-r**_sid2_ **s.foo**, where `s.foo` is the SCCS file containing the deltas _sid1_ and _sid2_.

16.10 Because they are displayed by the **prs** command.

16.11 When you make a change to a delta that is not the latest one. A branch delta uses a set of four numbers, so 1.2.1 is not a valid SID.

Chapter 17

17.1   System calls are built into the kernel, but library functions are built on top of them. When a system call is invoked, the processor switches to the kernel mode and returns to the user mode when the call returns.

17.2   Because the value of `errno` can change later with subsequent system calls even if they return success.

17.3   A file descriptor is an integer allocated to a file on opening. It is used by all system calls that perform some operation on the file—like **read, write, close, lseek**.

17.4   They all return a file descriptor.
17.5   This program terminates when the file descriptor table overflows:

```
#include <fcntl.h>

int main(void) {
    int fd;                    /* File descriptors for read and write */
    while (1) {
        if ((fd = open("/etc/passwd", O_RDONLY)) == -1) {
          perror("open");
          exit (1);
        }
        printf("File des: %d\n", fd);
    }
    exit(0);
}
```

17.6   (i) fd = open("foo", O_WRONLY | O_TRUNC);
        (ii) fd = open("foo", O_WRONLY | O_APPEND);
17.7   (i), (iv), and (vii) are opening mode flags; the rest are status flags. A file can be
        opened in one of the modes, but each mode can be associated with one or more
        status flags. O_SYNC ensures that **write** doesn't return until the physical write to
        disk has been completed.
17.8

```
#include <fcntl.h>
#include <unistd.h>

int main(int argc, char **argv) {
    int fd, n;
    char u;
    fd = open(argv[1], O_RDONLY);
    while ((n = read(fd, &u, 1)) > 0) {
        if (u >=97 && u <= 122)        /* Test for lowercase letter */
        u -= 32;                       /* and change it to uppercase */
        write(STDOUT_FILENO, &u, 1);
    }
    close(fd);
    exit(0);
}
```

17.9

```
#include <fcntl.h>
#include <sys/stat.h>
int main(void) {
    int fd;
```

```
    mode_t old_mode;
    old_mode = umask(0);                        /* No mask */
    fd = open("foo", O_WRONLY | O_CREAT, S_IRUSR | S_IWUSR | S_IRGRP |
                    S_IWGRP | S_IROTH | S_IWOTH);
    mkdir("bar", S_IRWXU | S_IRWXG | S_IRWXO);
    close(fd);              /* File needs to be closed before deletion */
    system("ls -ld foo bar");   /* system is discussed in Chapter 18 */
    unlink("foo");
    rmdir("bar");
    umask(old_mode);             /* Revert to previous mask */
    system("ls -ld foo bar");
    exit(0);
}
```

17.10

```
#include <sys/stat.h>
#include <unistd.h>

int main(int argc, char **argv) {
    struct stat statbuf;
    int exists = 1;
    if ((access(argv[1], F_OK) == 0)) {
        lstat(argv[1], &statbuf);
        if (S_ISREG(statbuf.st_mode)) {    /* If ordinary file exists */
            unlink(argv[1]);                /* then remove it */
            exists = 0;
        }
    } else
        exists = 0;
    if (exists == 0)
        mkdir(argv[1], S_IRWXU | S_IRGRP | S_IXGRP | S_IROTH | S_IXOTH);
    exit(0);
}
```

17.11

```
#include <stdio.h>
#define PATH_LENGTH 200
int main(int argc, char **argv) {
    char newdir[PATH_LENGTH + 1];
    if (chdir(argv[1]) == -1) {
        fprintf(stderr, "Can't change directory\n");
        exit(1);
    }
    getcwd(newdir, PATH_LENGTH);                  /* Getting new directory */
    printf("pwd: %s\n", newdir);
```

```
      exit(0);
   }
```

The change is not permanent as it took place in a separate process.

17.12

```
#include <sys/types.h>
#include <sys/stat.h>
#include <stdio.h>
#include <dirent.h>

int main(void) {
   DIR *dir; off_t size;
   struct dirent *direntry;  struct stat statbuf;

   if ((dir = opendir(".")) != NULL)
      while ((direntry = readdir(dir)) != NULL)
         if (lstat(direntry->d_name, &statbuf) == 0)
            if (S_ISREG(statbuf.st_mode))
               if ((size = statbuf.st_size) > 100000)
                  printf("%s: %d\n", direntry->d_name, size);
               else if (size == 0)
                  unlink(direntry->d_name);
   exit(0);
}
```

17.13

```
#include <fcntl.h>
#include <sys/stat.h>

int main(void) {
   int fd;
   mode_t old_mode;
   old_mode = umask(0);                        /* No mask */
   fd = open("foo", O_WRONLY | O_CREAT, S_IRUSR | S_IWUSR |
                                        S_IRGRP | S_IROTH);
   chmod("foo", S_IRWXU | S_IRGRP | S_IWGRP | S_IROTH);
   system("ls -l foo");
   fchmod(fd, S_IRUSR | S_IRGRP);     /* Can use fchmod also */
   system("ls -l foo");
   umask(old_mode);                   /* Revert to previous mask */
   exit(0);
}
```

Chapter 18

18.1 Because the addresses specified in the executable don't point to actual memory locations. The text segment is loaded directly from the disk file.

18.2 When a process makes a system call that keeps the CPU idle.

18.3 **fork** returns the PID in the parent and zero in the child. This makes it possible for the parent to control the child.

18.4 dup, dup2, fcntl, pipe.

18.5

```
#include <sys/types.h>
#include <stdio.h>

int main(void) {
   if (fork() > 0)
      fork();
   printf("PID: %d PPID: %d\n", getpid(), getppid());
}
```

18.6 (i)

```
#include <stdio.h>
int main(void) {
    execl("/bin/wc", "wc", "-l", "-c", "/etc/passwd", (char *) 0);
    printf("execl error\n");
}
```

(ii)

```
#include <stdio.h>
int main(int argc, char **argv) {
    char *cmdargs[] = { "wc", "-l", "-c", "/etc/passwd", NULL };
    execv("/bin/wc", cmdargs);
    printf("execv error\n");
}
```

When using **execlp** and **execvp**, change the first argument to "wc".

18.7 A parent *should* wait to pick up the exit status of the child from the process table. If it doesn't, the child turns into a zombie and retains its process table entry.

18.8

```
#include <stdio.h>
#include <sys/wait.h>

int main (int argc, chr **argv) {
     int a, b, c, status;
```

```
switch(fork()) {
    case 0:
        a = atoi(argv[1]); b = atoi(argv[2]);
        c = a + b ;
        exit(c);
     default:
        wait(&status);
        printf("The sum of the two numbers is %d\n", WEXITSTATUS(status));
        exit(20);
    }
}
```

18.9   The exit status is actually 8 bits long, and the value set inside the shell script is a large value. $? stores only the last 8 bits.

18.10 False.

18.11

```
#include <unistd.h>

int main (void) {
    dup2(STDOUT_FILENO, STDERR_FILENO);
    write(STDERR_FILENO, "hello dolly\n", 12);
    exit(0);
}
```

18.12 A background process has no controlling terminal, so it can't be sent a signal from the keyboard.

18.13 The output of this program will always show two lines for the SIGKILL and SIGSTOP signals:

```
#include <stdio.h>
#include <signal.h>

int main (void) {
    struct sigaction act;
    act.sa_handler = SIG_IGN;                /* Disposition set to ignore */
    int i;
    for (i = 1; i <= 32; i++)
        if (sigaction (i, &act, NULL) == -1)
            printf("Signal %d can't be ignored\n", i);
}
```

18.14 Because both processes need to use the descriptors of the pipe, which is possible only if one process inherits the descriptors from the other.

Chapter 19

19.1   In /sbin and /usr/sbin. The PATH for a superuser doesn't include the current directory.

19.2   It doesn't ask for the old password.

19.3   SHELL and HOME.

19.4   `usermod -s /bin/bash romeo`

19.5   The password encryption was world-readable in `/etc/passwd` of older systems. This made it vulnerable to attack by hackers. However, `/etc/shadow` is not world-readable.

19.6   The user is running a restricted shell.

19.7   s and t signify the SUID and sticky bits respectively.

19.8   `ls` obtains the numeric UID and GID from the inode and then looks up `/etc/passwd` for the name representation of UID and `/etc/group` for the name representation of GID.

19.9   `find /bin /usr/bin -perm -4000 -print`

19.10 Signifies the state the system is in and is displayed by **who -r**.

19.11 `/etc/inittab` is the control file used by `init`. **telinit q** activates the changes.

19.12 Printing, network services, and user logins.

19.13 Use **shutdown -y -g0**. Linux allows the use of *[Ctrl][Alt][Del]*.

19.14 The boot file system contains the UNIX kernel. The swap file system stores the process images when they can't be held in memory.

19.15 The root file system because it contains the essential utilities that keep the system running.

19.16 To check the file system for consistency.

19.17 `-perm 1000` matches a file having exactly those permissions, but `-perm -1000` matches only 1 (the sticky bit) and ignores the other three octal digits.

19.18 By using this crontab entry: 00 09-22 * * 1,2,3,4,5 df -t.

19.19 `du -s .`

19.20 (i) `doscp *.htm *.html /dev/fd0` (ii) `mcopy *.htm *.html a:`

19.21 (i) On this system **tar** looks for `.c` files in the current directory and there are none. (ii) A file `foo.c` exists in diskette in the form `./foo.c`.

Index